Criminal Litigation

Criminal Litigation

Martin Iller

LLB (Nottingham), Solicitor (Hons)
John Mackrell and John Marshall Prizeman
Senior Lecturer, The College of Law, Lancaster Gate

George Goodwin

LLB (Southampton), Solicitor
Senior Lecturer, The College of Law, Guildford

London
Butterworths
1985

United Kingdom Butterworth & Co (Publishers) Ltd, 88 Kingsway, London wc2b 6ab and 61A North Castle Street, Edinburgh eh2 3lj

Australia   Butterworths Pty Ltd, Sydney, Melbourne, Brisbane, Adelaide, Perth, Canberra and Hobart

Canada   Butterworth & Co (Canada) Ltd, Toronto and Vancouver

New Zealand   Butterworths of New Zealand Ltd, Wellington and Auckland

Singapore   Butterworth & Co (Asia) Pte Ltd, Singapore

South Africa   Butterworth Publishers (Pty) Ltd, Durban and Pretoria

USA   Butterworth Legal Publishers, St Paul, Minnesota, Seattle, Washington, Boston, Massachusetts, Austin, Texas, and D & S Publishers, Clearwater, Florida

British Library Cataloguing in Publication Data
Iller, M. S.
   Criminal litigation.
   1. Criminal procedure——England
   I. Title   II. Goodwin G. A.
   344.205′5   KD8276

   ISBN Hardcover 0 406 25813 9
        Softcover 0 406 50000 2

Made and printed in Great Britain by
Butler & Tanner Ltd, Frome and London

To Diana, Tricia, Emma and Wendy

Preface

The objects of this book are twofold. First, to provide a working text for those studying for the Law Society's Final Examination and secondly, to assist trainee solicitors and those in their first years of admission in developing their litigation skills. In order to secure the latter objective, it has been necessary both to include material that is not in the Finals syllabus (in particular the chapter relating to juveniles) and to set out in the footnotes references which, although necessary for the assiduous practitioner, go far beyond the requirements of the Finals student. Notwithstanding the above objectives it is also hoped that this book will provide a useful starting point for those with a wider interest in the criminal justice system.

Until recently, one would have been able to assert with a degree of confidence that the law was as stated at a specified date. Unfortunately this has proved to be a forlorn hope, but, so far as possible the law is stated as at 1st May 1985, subject to two important qualifications. First, the work has been written on the basis that the Police and Criminal Evidence Act 1984 is fully in force and that the Fifth Draft of the Codes of Practice (May 1985) represents the form in which they will be laid before Parliament. Readers are, however, advised to consult the published Codes carefully as and when they become available since there may well be alterations. It is understood that the 1984 Act and the Codes of Practice will be implemented early in 1986.

Secondly, we have taken the opportunity to incorporate into the text the provisions of the Magistrates' Courts (Advance Information) Rules 1985 which came into force on 20 May last. These make important procedural changes with regard to the pre-trial disclosure of prosecution evidence in the case of either way offences. The exigencies of publishing have meant that we have had to incorporate the provisions so as to cause minimum disruption to the text. We hope, however, that the changes will not be too hard to follow.

Finally, we should like to extend our gratitude to our wives, Diana Iller and Dr Tricia Goodwin who, at no small disruption to their own careers, transcribed the entirety of the text (quite simply, we could not have written this book without them), and acknowledge the valuable contribution made by Peter Johnson a solicitor in private practice and former colleague of one of the writers who gave us unlimited access to his considerable professional expertise. We should also like to thank our colleagues Penny Black and Lorraine Redman for reading and checking much of the draft text and Godfrey Gypps for the open ended loan of his playback machine without which transcription would have been impossible, or at any rate far more expensive. Last, but by no means least, we are greatly indebted to the staff of Messrs Butterworths for their assistance and encouragement in bringing this project to fruition.

Ealing, 2 August 1985 M. S. Iller
G. A. Goodwin

Contents

Table of statutes

List of cases

CHAPTER 1

Introduction—Getting the feel of criminal procedure

Over the last ten years criminal procedure has been a growth area in two senses. First, Parliament has set so fast a legislative pace that even the most diligent and quick-minded have found it difficult to keep up. Second, an increase in crime has led to more prosecutions. One of the effects of this has been to involve more practising solicitors in handling criminal litigation, usually on behalf of legally aided defendants. It seems that this trend of wider professional involvement will continue as a result of the setting up of the statutory Duty Solicitor scheme under s 1 of the Legal Aid Act 1982. Notwithstanding the major changes that have been and still are taking place, the basic structure of criminal procedure is relatively straightforward. Put broadly, the major factors are:

(1) the two methods of trial;
(2) the age of the accused;
(3) whether the offence charged is triable summarily or on indictment;
(4) whether or not the accused has been or is likely to be arrested; and
(5) the nature of his plea.

These factors profoundly influence the course of criminal proceedings: major issues of strategy are thus readily identifiable.

1 FIVE MAJOR FACTORS

(1) Two methods of trial

Offences may be tried either, (a) *summarily* in a magistrates' court, or (b) *on indictment* before a judge and jury. The method of trial will depend upon the *category* of the offence and whether the accused is an *adult* (17 or over) or a *juvenile* (under 17).

(a) Summary trial. This takes place in a magistrates' court. The vast majority of offences (approximately 98%) are dealt with in this way. Although there are a few magistrates who are legally qualified (known as *stipendiaries*), the vast majority (often referred to as *lay magistrates*) are not. For those practising in the large Inner London courts, such as Marylebone or Bow Street, appearances before stipendiaries will be relatively common. Outside London, however, the typical summary trial will take place before a 'bench' composed of three lay magistrates. Although they may seek the advice of their legally qualified clerk (known as the Clerk to the Justices) on matters of law, evidence and procedure, magistrates are judges of both law and fact. Summary trial is much more informal than trial on indictment. Both solicitors and counsel have rights of audience, and neither the members of the court, nor the advocates appearing before it are robed. Many argue, that this informality goes too far, in particular because the accused and his representative will often have very little idea of the allegations that he is required to meet, apart from the brief statement of the offence in the summons or on the charge sheet. This is because, notwithstanding recent changes, there is no unified system of pre-trial disclosure of prosecution evidence in summary trials. On the other hand, a magistrates' court is often much more attractive to those pleading guilty because its powers of sentencing are limited in comparison with the Crown Court.

(b) Trial on indictment. This takes place before a judge (either a High Court judge, Circuit judge or Recorder) and a jury of lay people summonsed from a cross-section of the community. The jury decide questions of *fact*, in particular the guilt or innocence of the accused, but all points of *law*, evidence and procedure are decided by the judge. The course of a trial on indictment is thus significantly different from that of a summary trial because whenever such points arise the jury will be sent out whilst the ruling of the judge is sought.

The prosecution of an indictable offence will nevertheless usually *start* in a magistrates' court because, as a preliminary to trial on indictment, the accused will normally be brought before the magistrates to ascertain whether or not there is sufficient evidence to justify a trial on indictment. If there is, the accused will be *committed* to stand trial at the Crown Court. This 'filter process' (known as *committal proceedings*) is, however, largely a formality, because most committals (with the agreement of the defence) now take place without any consideration of the evidence at all. It is only when there is any dispute as to the existence of a prima facie case that the magistrates will exercise a judicial function. Whatever form the proceedings take, however, the prosecution must disclose to the defence prior to the committal most, if not all, of the evidence that they propose to adduce at the trial. From the point of view of the defence, this represents a major advantage over the procedure on summary trial.[1]

(2) Category of offender

Offenders are broadly divided into *adults* (17 or over) and *juveniles* (under 17). Juveniles are a special category of offenders who are subject to their own specialised sentencing regime, and can generally only be tried *summarily* in a *juvenile court* whatever the offence with which they are charged. The only exceptions are when they are charged with homicide, offences carrying a maximum of 14 years' imprisonment or more, or when a juvenile is charged jointly with an adult. There are other important age related sub-divisions, for example, adults under 21 cannot be imprisoned, but the division of offenders into 'adults' and 'juveniles' is by far the most important.

(3) Category of offence

If the accused is an *adult* the category of offence with which he is charged will determine whether or not he is to be tried summarily or on indictment. All criminal offences are now[2] triable either:

1 Where an *indictable* offence is tried summarily the prosecution is now required to disclose prescribed information as to the evidence they propose to adduce. See further p 279, post.
2 Interpretation Act 1978, Sch 1: attempts and incitement adopt the category of the relevant substantive offence.

(a) on indictment only; or
(b) summarily only; or
(c) summarily or on indictment (known as 'either way' offences).

There is, arguably, a fourth category comprising offences (other than arson) under the Criminal Damage Act 1971, s 1. These will be triable either way or summarily only, depending on whether the value of the property destroyed or of the damage done exceeds £400. In practice, however, they should be regarded as a special category of either way offence.

Next to the age of the offender, the category of the offence is the most important factor. In practice, you will soon become adept at classifying the more common offences; for example, it will not take long to remember that careless driving may only be tried summarily and that theft is triable either way, but in cases of doubt you should always consult one of the major standard reference works such as *Stone's Justices' Manual* or *Archbold's Criminal Pleading and Practice*.

The three categories in outline

(a) Offences triable only on indictment. Not surprisingly, this category comprises all the more serious offences. It embraces all *common law* offences, for example, murder, manslaughter, riot, affray, unlawful assembly and conspiracy to defraud, and *statutory* offences in which the statute creating the offence only specifies a penalty following conviction on indictment.[3] Examples of the latter include causing grievous bodily harm etc with intent (Offences Against the Person Act 1861, s 18), rape (Sexual Offences Act 1956, s 1), robbery (Theft Act 1968, s 8), conspiracy (other than to defraud) (Criminal Law Act 1977, s 1) and causing death by reckless driving (Road Traffic Act 1972, s 1).

(b) Offences only triable summarily. All such offences are statutory and may be identified from the fact that the statute creating them only provides for a penalty on summary conviction. There are an almost infinite number of such offences. In particular the vast majority of road traffic offences are 'summary only' (including drink/drive offences), the only major exceptions are causing death by reckless driving (indictable only), and reckless driving, driving whilst disqualified and vehicle-related Theft Act offences (all triable 'either way').

This category also includes a number of serious offences relating to the police and matters of public order,[4] in particular, behaviour with intent to provoke a breach of the peace (Public Order Act 1936, s 5) and assaulting or obstructing a constable in the execution of his duty (Police Act 1964, s 51(1) and (3)). The present lack of rules as to obligatory pre-trial disclosure of prosecution evidence in respect of summary offences gives rise to particular difficulty in such cases.

(c) Offences triable either summarily or on indictment. This important group comprises all the more common serious offences, including most offences under the Theft Acts 1968 and 1978, the Misuse of Drugs Act 1971 and the Criminal Damage Act 1971. Either way offences fall into two cate-

---

3 And which are not made specifically triable 'either way' by Magistrates' Courts Act 1980, Sch 1.
4 The vast majority of public order offences arising out of major public disturbances, eg the 'riots' in the summer of 1981 are prosecuted as 'summary only' offences.

gories. First, those that are made triable either way by the *statute creating them*, for example, possession of an offensive weapon in a public place (Prevention of Crime Act 1953, s 1) and reckless driving (Road Traffic Act 1972, s 2 and Sch 4). Second, those offences which, although on the face of them 'indictable only' are expressly *made* triable either way by the Magistrates' Courts Act 1980, s 17.

If the offence is triable either way the magistrates must hold *mode of trial proceedings* to decide whether to try the case themselves or committing it for trial to the Crown Court. The mode of trial is determined in two stages, the first of which involves the magistrates deciding, after hearing representations from the parties and considering (inter alia) the seriousness of the offence, which of the two methods of trial is more appropriate. If they decide trial on indictment is more appropriate they will go on to hold committal proceedings. If, however, they opt for summary trial, the accused *must* consent as well. An adult charged with an either way offence thus has a right to *insist* upon being tried on indictment. In contrast, juveniles have no such right.

Three further points call for brief mention. First, as already stated, certain minor offences of criminal damage are sometimes only triable summarily. These offences have their own special mode of trial procedure which will be considered more fully in chapter 8. Second, magistrates' sentencing powers in respect of either way offences are much more limited than those available to the Crown Court after trial on indictment. For example, if a person were convicted of burglary by a magistrates' court, the maximum sentence it could impose would be six months' imprisonment and/or a £2000 fine, whereas after conviction in the Crown Court he could receive a term of up to 14 years imprisonment and/or an unlimited fine for the same offence, (although this would be unlikely). In order to give magistrates greater flexibility they accordingly have power to commit an adult whom they have convicted of an either way offence to the Crown Court for *sentence* if, having heard about his 'character and antecedents' they consider their own powers are inadequate. The Crown Court may then deal with the offender as if he had been convicted on indictment.[5] Third, whenever the term 'indictable offence' appears in a statute it shall be taken to include both 'indictable only' and 'either way' offences.[6] This extended definition is important in certain areas especially in relation to costs. Accordingly, whenever the phrase 'indictable offence' appears in this book, the extended meaning is implied, unless otherwise stated.

(4) Arrest and summons: the investigation and commencement of proceedings

Most offences that come to court will have initially been investigated by the police, who will also collect evidence, take the decision whether or not to prosecute,[7] prepare the case and (in certain counties) actually conduct their

---

5 Magistrates' Courts Act 1980, s 38.
6 Interpretation Act 1978, Sch 1.
7 In many counties both adults and juveniles are not prosecuted but *cautioned*. Guidelines for cautioning and prosecuting have been issued by the Attorney-General (H/O circular 26/1983) and see [1985] Crim LR 4. For cautioning of juveniles see p 313, post.

own advocacy,[8] at any rate in the magistrates' court.[9] A significant number of prosecutions are also undertaken by other agencies and private individuals.

Irrespective of the category of offender or offence or who prosecutes, formal proceedings will commence in one of the following two ways:

(a) by *charge* after *arrest without warrant*; or

(b) by the laying of an *information* followed by the issue of a *summons* or *warrant for arrest*.

(a) Charge after arrest without warrant. Not surprisingly, the police have much wider powers of arrest than other individuals or bodies. These powers are now largely contained in the Police and Criminal Evidence Act 1984. Most prosecutions for indictable offences will begin with the police arresting a suspect *without* a warrant, taking him to a police station, interrogating him and, finally, if there is sufficient evidence to justify a prosecution, charging him with an offence or offences. He will then either be released on bail to appear before a magistrates' court on a fixed date or brought before a magistrates' court in custody, usually the next day. The charge will have been written down on a *charge sheet*, a copy of which will be given to the accused and the original will be presented to the clerk to the justices. The charge sheet thus becomes an 'information' and gives the magistrates their jurisdiction to try the case or to hold committal proceedings depending on the category of the offence charged.

(b) Laying of an information followed by a warrant for arrest or summons. If an accused is not brought before a court under procedure **(a)** above, the prosecution will commence by the 'laying of an information' before a magistrate or a clerk to the justices either orally or in writing. Contrary to popular belief, commencement of a prosecution by application for a warrant for arrest is unusual. Not only are magistrates' powers to issue warrants circumscribed but, perhaps more importantly, the police have such wide powers to arrest without warrant that applying for a warrant will usually be unnecessary. It is far more likely that the laying of an information before a magistrate will be followed by the issue of a summons by the court which will set out the particulars of the alleged offence and require the accused to appear before a magistrates' court on a fixed date (sometimes referred to as the 'return date'). The vast majority of prosecutions for minor offences, in particular most motoring offences, will commence in this way.

The initial impact of the proceedings on the accused will differ significantly depending upon which of the above methods is used. First, if he is arrested without warrant he will undoubtedly be detained for some time at a police station before being charged, whereas if he is proceeded against by way of summons, he will frequently not see the inside of a police station at any stage. Second, if he has been arrested he will make his first appearance before the magistrates either *in custody* or *on bail* and will either remain in custody pending disposal of his case or, in the meantime be released on bail. The significance of release on bail is that it places him under a statutory duty to appear at court on the date fixed. If he fails to appear without reasonable cause a warrant for his arrest will probably be issued and he will be liable to

---

8 The conduct of most prosecutions will be transferred to an independent prosecuting service headed by the Director of Public Prosecutions when the Prosecution of Offences Act 1985 comes into force.

9 Trials on indictment must be prosecuted by counsel (*R v George Maxwell (Developments) Ltd* [1980] 2 All ER 99 (first instance)).

be prosecuted for the offence of absconding. However, if the accused is summonsed, he is, generally speaking under no obligation to attend. Magistrates do have power in certain circumstances to compel his attendance by issuing a warrant for his arrest, but, in general, an accused may be tried and convicted in his absence and even, in certain circumstances, be given the option of pleading guilty by post.[10]

(5) The plea

Although the law caters for more esoteric eventualities, the accused will generally plead 'guilty' or 'not guilty'. Whatever the category of offence, the likelihood of there being a 'fight' will govern the preparation of the case and the course of the trial. A plea of 'not guilty' will require the prosecution to prove every element of its case beyond reasonable doubt by adducing admissible evidence which will be subject to cross-examination; the defence will need to prepare their client's case accordingly. On the other hand, when the accused pleads 'guilty', the prosecution will normally only be required to acquaint the court with the brief facts of the case; the efforts of the defence will be directed towards mitigating on their client's behalf.

2 FOUR TYPICAL CASES

Section 1 is deliberately simplified, but the detail can come later. This section introduces you to four fictitious characters, all of whom will be re-appearing from time to time in later chapters. It will, however, be possible to see immediately how the factors outlined in the preceding section 1 operate to influence events.

CASE 1

DEFENDANT   Duncan McCARTHY, 19 years, born 9.6.6–
                      11 Inkerman Terrace, Weyford

OFFENCE   Burglary   PLEA   Not Guilty

EMPLOYMENT STATUS   Hospital Porter

Weyford General Hospital has a social club which stays open until 10.30 pm on weekdays. At 11.30 pm on the evening of 5 August 198– the club steward left the premises after locking the bar and securing all exits and windows. At 1.00 am the following day a night security officer was alerted by a member of the night nursing staff who said that she had seen a man looking through the window in her office. As soon as he had realised she was there he had made off. The security officer went to patrol the grounds and almost immediately noticed that the alarm system in the social club was ringing. He alerted the main gate and telephoned the police. Within five minutes two uniformed officers, Sgt Trinder and PC Vaughan arrived in a patrol car.

Sgt Trinder went with the security officer to make a search of the social club. They found that entry had been effected through an insecure fire-door. The

---

10 Magistrates' Courts Act 1980, s 12: see p 449, post. When the 'fixed penalty' system for designated motoring offences such as speeding, contained in Transport Act 1982 comes into force, the offender may be given the opportunity to pay a fixed fine thus obviating the need for a formal prosecution at all.

THE CRIMINAL COURTS—PATHS TO TRIAL

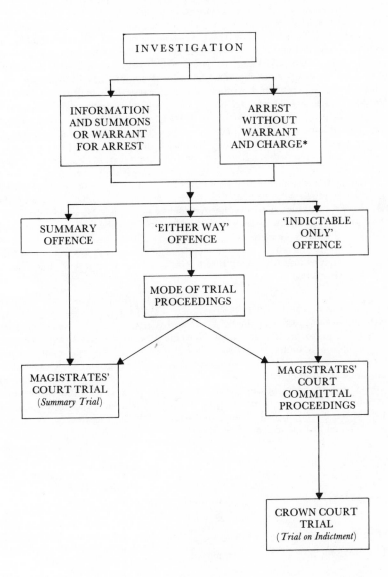

* Juveniles will usually be released and proceeded against by summons.

padlock to the bar area had been forced and the cash register opened. Inquiries with the steward subsequently revealed that a total of £50 in cash had been stolen. No fingerprints were found to help the police.

In the meantime PC Vaughan had interviewed the night nurse who said that she did not know whether it was important or not, but she had seen a group of about three or four young men hanging around and behaving noisily outside the club shortly before closing time as she was coming on duty. She said that she had recognised one of them as being a porter employed at the hospital, his name was Duncan McCARTHY. PC Vaughan reported this to Sgt Trinder. Sgt Trinder knew of McCARTHY as a person with convictions for theft and a known associate of local criminals. He reported back to the station, as a result of which two CID officers Det Sgt Forsyth and Det Con Tarbuck were dispatched to interview McCARTHY, who was known to live at 11 Inkerman Terrace, with his wife Tina. What happens next will become a subject of dispute between the prosecution and defence, but suffice it to say for the time being, that McCARTHY is arrested on suspicion of burglary and cautioned and searched. Before being taken back to Weyford police station, his premises are also searched and £40 in cash is found in the bedroom. On arrival at the police station at 3.00 am a record is made of his belongings by the custody officer who decides that there is insufficient evidence to charge him but that his continued detention for questioning is justified. He hands him over to the two CID officers for interviewing. McCARTHY refuses to make a written statement, is ultimately charged with burglary at 6.30 am, and brought before the Weyford magistrates in custody the same morning. The charge sheet is handed to the court (this technically constitutes the 'laying of the information') and read out to McCARTHY when he appears.

Comment

McCARTHY is an 'adult' and the offence charged is triable 'either way'. It is easy enough therefore to predict the course that the proceedings will follow. The most important factor is that *even if the magistrates consider summary trial more appropriate* McCARTHY has a right to insist on trial before a judge and jury at the Crown Court. Whatever course is adopted it is clear that the case cannot be disposed of at the first hearing. It will therefore be adjourned without the mode of trial procedure having taken place or McCARTHY being required to plead. The issue of bail thus becomes of immediate importance because when the magistrates adjourn McCARTHY must be remanded either on bail or in custody.

CASE 2

DEFENDANT	Anthony JONES, 51 years, born 21.1.3– 23 Raglan House, Weyford
OFFENCE	Theft PLEA Guilty
EMPLOYMENT STATUS	Unemployed

The complainant in this case is Softsell Supermarket PLC of Weyford. At 2.00 pm on 10 September 198-, Anthony JONES is seen by a store detective carrying a wire basket supplied by the store in his right hand, a shopping bag in his left. The store detective sees him place three items of goods in his shopping bag, and two tins in the wire basket. The detective then sees him go to the check-out and only pay for the articles in the wire basket. The detective follows him outside and stops him on the pavement and asks him to accompany her to the manager's office. She tells him what she has seen and cautions him. He says 'It was stupid of me, I'm sorry to have caused you all this trouble.'

The police are informed and arrive a few moments later and arrest JONES and take him to Weyford Police station where the custody officer deals with him in a similar way to McCarthy. He elects to make a written statement under caution which he himself writes out, amounting to a full admission of the offence. He also admits to three other offences committed on previous occasions. He is then taken back before the custody officer who decides that there is sufficient evidence to charge him and, having cautioned him, charges him with the one offence of theft committed on 10 September. Enquiries have revealed that although unemployed he has a fixed address. Accordingly the custody officer takes the view that he should be released on bail. He is accordingly bailed to appear before the Weyford magistrates on 2 October and given a copy of the charge sheet which will contain the details of the terms of his bail.

Comment

Once again, the accused is an 'adult' charged with an 'either way' offence, but since he proposes to plead 'guilty' the proceedings are likely to take a very different course. Assuming the magistrates decide summary trial is appropriate (which they almost certainly will) Jones will not wish to be tried on indictment. As a result the case will in all probability be disposed of on the first hearing (although there may be an adjournment to obtain further information eg a probation officer's report) before sentencing.

CASE 3

DEFENDANT	Mary Adams, 31 years, born 25.8.5–
	45 Alma Road, Weyford

OFFENCE	Careless driving	PLEA	Unknown
EMPLOYMENT STATUS	Senior lecturer, Weyford Polytechnic		

On 21 November 198– Mary Adams was driving home from work at about 6.00 pm. In order to reach her home she must make a right hand turn off the main road. This involves crossing the oncoming flow of traffic at the bottom of a steep hill which bends off to the right about 120 yards from the junction. On the evening in question she had entered the junction and begun to turn right when she realised that a car was coming down the hill at speed. She braked suddenly but the oncoming car was unable to stop in time and collided with the rear near side wing of her car. Fortunately, neither she nor the driver of the other vehicle was injured but both cars were extensively damaged. A nearby resident called the police and shortly afterwards two police officers arrived by car. They interviewed both drivers and took down their particulars. Both were cautioned and invited to go to the police station to make a statement. The driver of the other car agreed to do so but Adams declined. Arrangements were made for both cars to be towed away. Adams was still badly shaken and one of the police officers ran her home.

A decision is taken to prosecute her for careless driving. Accordingly the police apply in writing to the Weyford magistrates (the 'laying of the information') for the issue of a summons requiring her to attend court to answer to the information. The summons which requires her to attend on 16 February 198– is duly issued and served by post.

Comment

As can readily be seen, Mary Adams is an 'adult' charged with a 'summary only' offence. Since she has been summonsed the issue of bail will be unlikely to arise at any stage. Strictly speaking she is not *obliged* to attend on 16 February (she may be given the opportunity to plead guilty by post) although she must send her driving licence to the court. Much will depend upon her plea. If she decides to plead 'not guilty' an adjournment is likely, but unlike McCarthy she will not need to be remanded in custody or on bail.

CASE 4

DEFENDANT	John Tyrell, 16 years, born 7.11.6– 15 Palmerston Court, Weyford		
OFFENCE	Unauthorised taking of a motor vehicle	PLEA	Guilty
EMPLOYMENT STATUS	Unemployed		

John Tyrell lives at home with his parents. He left school at the end of last term but has not yet got a job. He is now claiming supplementary benefit. On 10 October 198– he went to the neighbouring town of Camborough to meet some friends in a pub. By the time he was ready to go home it was after midnight and the last bus had gone. It was cold and beginning to rain. Having tried unsuccessfully to hitch a lift, he saw an old Morris 1100 parked by the road-side and decided to take it. He had a set of various old car keys which he had been collecting for the past year or so, and was thus able to get in the car and start it. He drove into Weyford city centre where he parked in a side road before walking home. He is about half a mile from home when a police patrol car pulls up next to him and two officers get out. Tyrell had been in trouble with the police before and had been cautioned on two previous occasions. One of the officers recognises him, and asks him where he has been and what he has been doing. The officer is not satisfied with his answers and the two policemen search him. One of them finds the set of car keys and asks him what they are for. He is unable to give a satisfactory explanation and is arrested and cautioned.

Tyrell is taken to the police station. Because he is a juvenile, however, his parents are contacted and his father comes to the police station. In the meantime the custody officer has decided that as yet there is not enough evidence to charge him but that his continued detention for questioning is justified. No interview takes place, however, until Mr Tyrell arrives at the police station. In the meantime the Morris 1100 has been reported stolen and the police are anxious to ask Tyrell questions about this as well. When his father arrives at the police station a CID officer, to whom the case has been referred, explains his son's rights to him and indicates that he is entitled to have legal advice. He has already given Tyrell a copy of the written form advising him of these rights and his father is referred to this. The CID officer informs Tyrell, in his father's presence, that a Morris 1100 has been reported stolen and asks him whether he had anything to do with it. Tyrell asks if he can have a word with his father. Mr Tyrell tells the police officer that his son is prepared to make a statement and Tyrell asks if he may dictate this to the police officer. Tyrell then makes a statement admitting the taking of the Morris 1100 and states where he left it. He then signs this; it is also signed by Mr Tyrell.

Because the local policy is to refer a case to their 'Juvenile Bureau' before the decision to prosecute is taken, Tyrell is told that he may be prosecuted for the offence. He is then released unconditionally. In due course a decision is taken by the Juvenile Bureau to prosecute and a summons is issued requiring him to attend before the juvenile court on 20 January 198–.

Comment

Tyrell is a 'juvenile'; accordingly his case can only be tried summarily before magistrates in a juvenile court even though he is charged with an either way offence. Although he has been arrested he has subsequently been released unconditionally and proceeded against by way of summons. This is the normal procedure for juveniles in many areas of the country unless the offence is very grave.

3 THE PROBLEM AREAS OF CRIMINAL LITIGATION

On the face of it, therefore, conducting criminal litigation is relatively straightforward compared, say, to the many twists and turns involved in running even a simple civil claim in the Queen's Bench Division of the High Court. Having said that, however, you may need to consult detailed statutory provisions and regulations or wrestle with complicated case law even though the offence is a relatively trifling and based on simple facts. For example, in order to protect the interests of an accused who is being invited to go on an identification parade or is being detained at a police station without charge you will need to be fully acquainted with the relevant Codes of Practice implemented under the Police and Criminal Evidence Act 1984. Similarly, when applying for bail or mitigating on behalf of a client who has pleaded guilty, you will need a detailed grasp of the Bail Act 1976 and the sentencing statutes. Last, and by no means least, you will often need to be able to find your way through the labyrynthine complexities and over the administrative hurdles of the legal aid system if you want to get paid. These and many other problems will be considered in the following chapters.

CHAPTER 2

An outline of the criminal litigation system

This chapter examines in greater detail the structure of the criminal courts and the roles played by the prosecution and defence in conducting criminal proceedings.

1 PARTIES TO PROCEEDINGS

(1) The prosecutor

The police

Although, in general, any individual may prosecute, most prosecutions are brought by the police. In magistrates' courts cases may be listed as '*Police v Adams*', or in the name of the chief constable or the arresting or case officer. In the Crown Court, however, prosecutions are conducted in the Queen's name, for example, '*R (or Regina) v McCarthy*'.[1]

Most police forces have prosecuting solicitors' departments.[2] These consist of solicitors or barristers who are employed by the police authority to present summary cases, prepare cases for, and brief counsel on, trial on indictment, and advise police officers when requested on points of procedure or evidence. The size of the department varies from force to force, as does its precise functions and responsibilities. If a police force does not have a prosecuting solicitors' department, the work of conducting prosecutions will be shouldered by police officers, with firms of solicitors employed to conduct and advise on weightier prosecutions.

The Director of Public Prosecutions and the Attorney General

The Director of Public Prosecutions is a qualified lawyer appointed by the Crown and the nearest this country has to a State prosecuting service. He may take over any prosecution, whether brought by the police or otherwise.[3] In addition he must be notified of most types of serious crime, such as murder, manslaughter, and armed robbery, and usually of offences involving police officers, so that he may institute or take over the prosecution of those offences if he considers it appropriate.[4]

The Attorney General is a member of the government and therefore a political appointment. He advises government departments on legal matters, but may also take over the prosecution of difficult or notorious cases. He

1 Even if the prosecution is brought in the officer's name, he is regarded as an agent of his police force, and thus the proceedings do not terminate with his death. *Hawkins v Bepey* [1980] 1 All ER 797.
2 These will shortly be replaced by the Crown Prosecuting service to be set up under the Prosecution of Offences Act 1985. For a summary see p 478, post.
3 This includes the power to take over proceedings so as to offer no evidence and thus abort the case. *Raymond v A-G* [1982] QB 839.
4 Prosecution of Offenders Act 1979 and regulations made thereunder.

sometimes appears for the Crown in prosecutions of importance or sensitivity. He is also responsible for supervising the work of the DPP.

The Attorney General has another function. He may refer a case which has been tried on indictment and resulted in acquittal to the Court of Appeal for it to express its opinion on a point of law. This is an important provision because the prosecution has no right of appeal against an acquittal. It thus enables the Court of Appeal to give guidance or directions where the interpretation of the law is required. The decision of the trial court is not impugned in any way by this procedure, however, and the acquittal will stand whatever the result. These cases in which the defendant is entitled to anonymity are reported as, for example, 'Attorney General's reference (No 1) of 1984'.

Consent to prosecution

As a general rule everyone, including the police, has a right to prosecute. Occasionally however leave is required. This must be obtained from the Attorney General or the DPP, depending on the relevant offence. The consent of the Attorney General is generally required in offences of a political complexion, such as prosecutions for wearing political uniforms (Public Order Act 1936), or involving national security (Official Secrets Act 1911). The DPP's consent is more usually required when the offence is likely to be sensitive on a personal rather than a political basis. Thus his consent is needed for a person to be prosecuted for theft from his spouse,[5] or on a charge of incest,[6] as well as for more recondite offences such as removing surface soil from agricultural land with a view to sale and without planning consent.[7] Any arrest will still be lawful, even if consent to bring the prosecution has not been received.

Prosecutions by other agencies or individuals

Approximately one quarter of all prosecutions are not brought by the police, but by other bodies or by private citizens. Prosecutions for certain types of offence are commonly brought by government departments. For example, HM Customs and Excise prosecute for infringement of regulations concerning Value Added Tax and major drug offences, the Department of Health and Social Security prosecutes for failure to declare sources of income whilst claiming supplementary benefit, and the Department of Transport prosecutes the owners and drivers of overloaded lorries. These departments have their own staff of 'in house' lawyers to advise and bring prosecutions. However, they commonly instruct outside firms of solicitors to act for them as well, although the practice of different departments varies.

Local Authorities also bring prosecutions in many different situations. For example, they institute proceedings under the Food Hygiene Regulations, relating to dirty food shops or businesses, and under the various Acts and Regulations concerned with trading standards. They also use magistrates' courts to pursue rent or rates defaulters. Although they have their own solicitors' departments, the preliminary work on the prosecution will usually be done by the administrative department itself. In some cases that depart-

5 Theft Act 1968, s 30(4).
6 Sexual Offences Act 1956, Sch 2.
7 Agricultural Land (Removal of Surface Soil) Act 1953, ss 1 and 3.

ment may conduct the entire proceedings without using the solicitors' department at all. Practice does, however, vary from authority to authority.

Many private agencies bring prosecutions. The most active of these is the RSPCA which prosecutes in approximately 1000 cases of illegal cruelty to animals each year.[8] Prosecutions are also brought by such bodies as diverse as the Civil Aviation Authority and the Hereford and District Angling Association.[9] It is common for the larger retail stores to prosecute in shoplifting cases. The prosecutor's name will be that of the store, as for example, '*Softsell Supermarkets PLC v Jones*' (case 2). It appears from the Royal Commission on Criminal Procedure that many stores assume this burden not through choice, but because the police decline to prosecute, particularly in London.[10] Even in these cases, however, the Commission found that the police are still closely involved in the initial steps. They attend the store as requested and take the suspect and the store's detective to the police station. The police will interview the suspect and take a statement from him if he will provide one. They may then leave it to the store to issue a summons, or they may charge the suspect and bail him. The store will normally have to provide a solicitor to prosecute the defendant in court.[11]

Finally, private citizens sometimes bring prosecutions, most commonly for assault or criminal damage, often arising out of neighbour disputes over such problems as shared drives, boundaries, or the activities of children or pets. In such cases the parties often commence prosecutions against each other. Although they may instruct solicitors to act for them in the prosecution, they will have to be prepared to pay for their solicitors' services since legal aid although available to defendants *cannot* be granted for prosecutions.

(2) The defendant

The accused will be named in the proceedings, unless he is charged with a 'rape offence',[12] when he is entitled to anonymity unless and until he is found guilty.[13] If, however, the accused is a *juvenile* there are rules prohibiting the press from publishing any details or particulars which could lead to his identity being established whatever the offence.[14]

There is no general statutory requirement for an accused to be legally represented although legal aid may be available. If the accused is a juvenile he may be represented by his parents or guardian if there is no lawyer acting for him. Once convicted, however, an accused cannot receive a custodial sentence for the *first time* unless he is either legally represented, or has applied for legal aid but been refused on the grounds that his income and capital are too high, or has had the opportunity of applying for legal aid but has failed to do so.[15] The position is the same.

Corporations (limited companies and other unincorporated bodies) are subject to special rules. In magistrates' courts, a properly appointed representative of a corporation may enter a plea, make representations as to mode

8 Royal Commission on Criminal Procedure, Research Study 10, p 88, HMSO.
9 Research Study 10, op cit, p 87.
10 Research Study 10, op cit, p 104 et seq.
11 Research Study 10, op cit.
12 As defined in Sexual Offences (Amendment) Act 1976, s 7.
13 Ibid, ss 4 and 6.
14 Children and Young Persons Act 1933, ss 39 and 49.
15 Powers of Criminal Courts Act 1973, s 21; Criminal Justice Act 1982, s 3.

of trial and elect trial on indictment. He may also acknowledge service of a summons. Otherwise, a corporation must be represented in proceedings by a solicitor or barrister.[16]

Duty solicitor schemes

For some years busy magistrates' courts have, in conjunction with local law societies, arranged for solicitors to give advice to unrepresented defendants and appear to make bail or legal aid applications for the accused, or make a short speech in mitigation. These schemes were voluntary but are now regulated by statute.[17] They will be considered further in chapter 6.

(3) **Rights of audience**

(a) *The magistrates' court*

Both solicitors and barristers have full rights of audience in magistrates' courts. In addition, police officers frequently conduct prosecutions although pratice varies throughout the country. The prosecution may be conducted by a 'court inspector', or even the officer in charge of the case. Where there is no prosecuting solicitors' department, the proportion of cases prosecuted by police officers tends to be higher.[18]

Certain statutes give specific authority to persons other than solicitors or barristers to conduct prosecutions. For example, under the Local Government Act 1972 an officer, duly authorised by his Local Authority may conduct prosecutions on behalf of the authority. Thus, an officer from the rates department might conduct proceedings for non payment of rates. Similar provisions apply for example, to officers of the Department of Health and Social Security and Customs and Excise.[19]

It should be noted finally that an unrepresented prosecutor or defendant is entitled to have assistance from a friend, whether a lawyer or not, who is permitted to take notes at the proceedings and give advice if necessary.[20]

(b) *The Crown Court*

In the Crown Court barristers have full rights of audience. A solicitor may always appear in *chambers* applications, for example on a bail application, but may only appear in *open court* for an accused in the following situations:

(i) If the accused has been convicted by a magistrates' court and *appeals* against conviction or sentence, provided he, a partner, or an employee of his, conducted the proceedings in the magistrates' court.

(ii) If the accused has been committed by a magistrates' court for *sentence*.

16 Magistrates' Courts Act 1980, s 46 and Sch 3.
17 Legal Aid Act 1982, s 2 and regulations made thereunder.
18 Royal Commission on Criminal Procedure Research Study 11, pp 12 and 13.
19 Social Security Act 1975, s 147; Customs and Excise Management Act 1979, s 155.
20 *McKenzie v McKenzie* [1971] P 33. The friend is known as a 'McKenzie person'—for obvious reasons.

Again, the solicitor or his partner or employee must have appeared before the magistrates' court.

(iii) In *Class 4*[1] trials before certain specified locations of the Crown Court for which the Lord Chancellor has directed that solicitors may appear for the defence (generally because there are insufficient local barristers in the area).

Solicitors and barristers must always appear robed and with wing collars and 'tabs' in open court but not in chambers. Barristers must wear horsehair wigs in open court; solicitors must not do so. The prosecution must always be represented by counsel in a trial on indictment.[2] The accused need not be represented but almost invariably is.

Finally, it should be noted that only barristers have rights of audience in open court in the higher courts although solicitors may appear in chambers applications.

2 THE STRUCTURE OF THE COURTS

(1) The magistrates' court

Since the magistrates' court is so important in the prosecution of offenders, a short description is in order. In the court room itself the magistrates, sit on a raised podium—'the bench'. Their clerk sits in front of and below them. Facing them will be benches for solicitors and counsel, the press and members of the public. The 'witness box' from which evidence will be given will be near the front of the court, and the 'dock', where the accused will sit when not giving evidence on the other side of the room. The layout may vary; the architectural style may be anything from 'Victorian Nonconformist Chapel' to 'Glass and Concrete 1984'. It may be a small building or a multi-court complex. Behind the scenes, there is a hive of activity; summonses must be issued, applications for legal aid considered and processed, hearing dates fixed and fines collected. This bureaucracy is presided over by the clerk.

(a) Magistrates

As already indicated, there are two types of magistrate. *Lay magistrates* (also known as 'Justices of the Peace') are unpaid (although they claim expenses) and sit in court as and when their other commitments permit. They do not need to be legally qualified, and usually are not. They are appointed by the Crown to sit for a *commission area*, usually as a result of recommendations by local advisory committees. The commission area is the non-metropolitan administrative county, except in Greater London where the Inner London boroughs together comprise a commission area, and are ringed by four outer commission areas.[3] Most commission areas are divided into *petty sessions* areas. There will be at least one court house for each area and each magistrate is assigned to a petty sessions area, although appointed for the entire commission area.

A lay magistrate must live either in or within 15 miles of his commission area. This is the only mandatory prerequisite for appointment. However, in

1 For classification of offences see p 3, ante.
2 *R v George Maxwell Developments Ltd* [1980] 2 All ER 99.
3 Justices of the Peace Act 1979, ss 1 and 2.

A TYPICAL MAGISTRATES' COURT

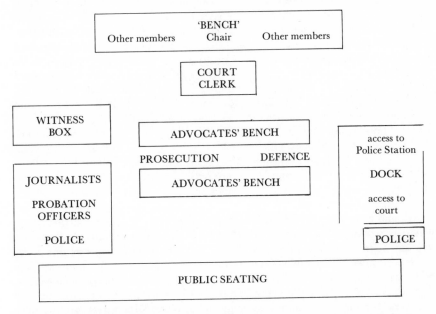

A typical magistrates' court might look like this. There are many variations, both in layout and in ancillary facilities.

addition, persons convicted of treason,[4] corrupt election practices[5] and un-discharged bankrupts are disqualified.[6] Furthermore, on occasions a magistrate may be temporarily disqualifed from sitting. For example a solicitor who is also a justice must not sit in a case which a partner or employee is conducting.[7] Thus a magistrate must always consider before hearing any case whether there is a possibility that he is disqualified due to bias.[8]

Each commission area has an elected committee of justices, known as the Magistrates' Court Committee. This is responsible for the administration of the courts within the area. In addition, it organises training courses for new justices to attend after appointment but before they sit in court for the first time. The committees also organise updating and refresher courses for all their magistrates, covering, for example, changes in the law and particular problem areas.

A magistrate may be removed from office by the Lord Chancellor or may be placed on the 'supplemental list'.[9] In the former case he ceases to be a magistrate, but in the latter case he formally retains the status of a Justice of the Peace. A magistrate will only be removed for serious misconduct, but

4 Forfeiture Act 1870, s 2.
5 Representation of the People Act 1893, s 161.
6 Bankruptcy Act 1883, s 32 and 1890, s 9.
7 Solicitors Act 1974, s 38.
8 *R v Altrincham Justices, ex p Pennington* [1975] QB 549—and see *Stone's Justices' Manual* (1985) para 1.6.
9 Effectively, a reserve list of magistrates.

may be placed on the supplemental list if, for example, he fails to sit sufficiently frequently. In any event, lay justices will be placed on the supplemental list when they reach the age of 70 years.[10]

The other type of magistrate is a 'stipendiary'. He or she is a full-time
professional magistrate and is appointed by the Queen from solicitors or
barristers of at least seven years' standing. A stipendiary magistrate is
appointed to a particular court, but is also ex officio a justice of the peace
for the commission area within which the court is situated. Stipendiary
magistrates have been appointed for Inner London and the larger cities
although because of the volume of cases lay justices still handle much of the
work. Those appointed for London are known as Metropolitan Stipendiary
Magistrates. They are ex officio justices for all of the London commission
areas and also for Essex, Hertfordshire, Kent and Surrey.[11] The Lord Chancellor may appoint stipendiaries temporarily to any court if it is necessary in
the interests of justice to do so.[12] Stipendiary magistrates usually retire at the
age of 70.

Stipendiaries have wider powers in that they may try a case sitting alone
whereas whenever lay justices are *trying* an offence there must be between
two and *seven* of them on the bench. The usual number is three as this is the
lowest number that enables them to decide a case by simple majority. This
is because any power which can be exercised by two lay justices can be
exercised by a stipendiary sitting alone.[13] Otherwise their respective powers
are very similar. For example a single magistrate, stipendiary or lay, may
grant bail, issue warrants for arrest or hear committal proceedings.

Magistrates must generally sit in open court so as to give access to both
the press and public. The major exception to this rule is proceedings in
juvenile courts, where the public, but not the press, are excluded. In addition, the magistrates must sit in a court-house, which is normally that appropriate to the petty sessions area to which they are assigned.[14] Magistrates can
nevertheless exercise certain powers outside the court-house, such as the
issuing of summonses compelling witnesses to attend court.

(b) Justices' clerks

The magistrates' committee for each commission area is responsible for the
appointment of clerks to its courts. Justices' clerks must generally be solicitors
or barristers of at least five years' standing.[15] The quieter parts of a county
may have one clerk to two or three courts. A large town may have a magistrates' court building with several individual courts sitting every weekday.
It may, therefore, also appoint deputy clerks; these may or may not be
legally qualified.

The clerk for each court has two important tasks. He must advise the
magistrates upon matters of law and procedure upon which they seek his
guidance, and he must superintend the work of the court staff, for example,
in issuing summonses, keeping records of paid fines, and arranging lists of

10 Justices of the Peace Act 1979, ss 6–19.
11 Justices of the Peace Act 1979, s 31.
12 Ibid, s 15. This was done at Newbury Magistrates' Court in 1984 to clear up a backlog of
   cases arising out of disturbances at RAF Greenham Common.
13 Justices of the Peace Act 1979, s 33.
14 Magistrates' Courts Act 1980, ss 147 and 150. Other premises can be used as an occasional
   court house.
15 Justices of the Peace Act 1979, s 26.

cases for hearing. Although a court with stipendiary magistrates will have a justices clerk, it is less necessary for a stipendiary to seek guidance about matters of law or procedure. The clerk obviously cannot be in two places at once. Accordingly, a court may sit without the justices' clerk present provided that his role is filled by a deputy, who need not be legally qualified but who must be of the appropriate administrative grade.

Surprisingly, the clerk's function during the proceedings is not set out in statute but in a *Practice Direction*.[16] This provides, for example, that the clerk may or may not take notes of the evidence, although the bench may request that he do so. In practice, he is likely to take some notes as he is responsible for refreshing the justices' memories on matters of evidence. He is also required to advise the justices on any points of law, including sentencing options.

During the trial the clerk should not act as an advocate but can assist an unrepresented defendant to present his case.[17] On other occasions he will adopt a more active role. For example he is responsible for bringing proceedings to enforce fines, and in such a case his name will appear as a party, and he will examine the defaulter on oath in the presence of the magistrates.

Most lay benches retire into a private room in order to decide any matter of difficulty or substance. The clerk is not supposed to retire with the justices, but they may send for him and consult him on any matter of law. It is, however, for the justices to decide both questions of law and fact, and although the clerk has the duty to advise them on the law, they are not obliged to follow his advice.[18] Nevertheless, a clerk can have a considerable influence on the course of proceedings. Notwithstanding their training and experience, lay justices may well rely heavily upon their clerk's, for example, advice on a point of evidence. The clerk may also have influence behind the scenes. For example, most applications for Legal Aid for summary offences are considered initially by the clerk, and will only be referred to a magistrate if the application is refused. The justice then has the delicate task of overturning the decision of his clerk.[19]

(2) Jurisdictions and powers of magistrates' courts

(a) Summary trial of adults

The jurisdiction of a magistrates' court to try an adult for a summary offence is primarily governed by territorial considerations. A magistrates' court may try an adult for any summary offence committed within the *commission* area,[20] (not the petty sessions area). In practice, this is not of great importance as most common offences are committed locally.

This relatively narrow jurisdiction could cause problems, particularly with motoring offences, if an offence is alleged to have been committed on, or just over, the border. Accordingly there are specific provisions to avoid this. Offences committed on, along or within 500 yards of a commission area boundary can be tried in either commission area, as may offences 'begun' in one area and finished in another.[1]

16 [1981] 2 All ER 831.
17 *Simms v Moore* [1970] 2 QB 327.
18 *R v Orpin* [1975] QB 283; *Jones v Nicks* [1977] RTR 72.
19 Where the clerk refuses legal aid in respect of an *indictable* offence, appeal now lies to a Criminal Legal Aid Committee under Legal Aid Act 1972, s 6. See p 215, post.
20 Magistrates' Courts Act 1980, s 2.
 1 Magistrates' Courts Act 1980, s 3.

EXAMPLE: A motorist is followed by police, during which time he crosses from Surrey into Hampshire, where he is stopped by the Surrey police who prosecute him for driving whilst uninsured (a summary offence). He can be prosecuted in any magistrates' court in either Surrey or Hampshire, as the offence was begun in the former county but finished in the latter.

Neither of the last two provisions would have been applicable if instead the motorist had committed two separate offences of driving whilst uninsured on two different dates in different counties. It would, however, be inconvenient and expensive to proceed in two courts. Accordingly, a magistrates' court which tries a person for an offence may also try any other summary offence even if committed in another area.[2] Further, if there are proceedings already pending against an accused and it is expedient to try another person with or at the same time as him, the court may try the second accused even if it would not otherwise have had jurisdiction.[3]

In contrast, a magistrates' court may try any *either way* offence, such as reckless driving, provided that it was committed in England or Wales,[4] and the accused has consented to summary trial.[5]

(b) Summary trial of juveniles

Juveniles must normally be tried and sentenced by the juvenile court, although there are exceptions to this rule. Subject thereto, the rules as to whether a juvenile court has territorial jurisdiction to try a juvenile accused of an offence are the same as for adults.[6]

(c) Magistrates sitting as examining justices

As already noted, magistrates' courts are theoretically supposed to 'screen' all indictable offences to ascertain whether there is a prima facie case against the accused to justify trial on indictment.

Magistrates have jurisdiction to sit as examining justices for offences committed anywhere in England and Wales.[7] In practice, offences are mainly local and the magistrates' court at which committal proceedings will be brought will normally be the one for the petty sessions area where the crime was committed. Committal proceedings may be heard by one justice, stipendiary or otherwise,[8] although lay justices will usually sit as a bench of two or three.

(d) Ancillary powers available to magistrates

Magistrates' courts have an important part to play in procedure before trial or committal. A magistrate may be asked to issue a summons or a warrant.

2 Magistrates' Courts Act 1980, s 2(6).
3 Ibid, ss 1(2)(b) and 2(2).
4 Ibid, ss 2(4).
5 Note that in addition certain statutes extend the jurisdiction of English courts, including magistrates' courts, to offences committed outside the jurisdiction, eg Civil Aviation Act 1982; Territorial Waters Jurisdiction Act 1878; Merchant Shipping Act 1894.
6 As to trial of juveniles generally, see chapter 10.
7 Magistrates' Courts Act 1980, s 2(3). Save as above, offences committed outside the jurisdiction are outside the scope of this work.
8 Ibid, s 4(1).

Once proceedings have started, there will be applications for adjournments, remands and bail to deal with.

> EXAMPLE: *Police v McCARTHY (case 1)*. In this case proceedings were commenced when McCARTHY was charged by the police. The magistrates' court was not directly involved in the initiation of the proceedings. He was brought before the justices the same morning, when the case was *adjourned* because the prosecution were not ready to proceed. McCARTHY will want to apply for *bail*, and if he wants a solicitor to represent him, he will undoubtedly need *legal aid*. The powers to adjourn proceedings, grant or refuse bail and grant legal aid are examples of the magistrates' ancilliary functions.

We shall now outline the six most important of these.

(i) Summonses. A summons notifies the accused that proceedings are being taken against him and requires him to attend to answer them. It may be used as an originating process, as in MARY ADAMS' case, or for some other purpose, for example, to bring to court a defendant who has failed to pay a fine, or to require a witness to give evidence at a trial. The power to issue a summons is exercisable by a single magistrate.[9] The mechanism for obtaining a summons to *commence proceedings* is considered later in this chapter; other types of summons will be considered where appropriate in subsequent chapters.

The territorial jurisdiction of a magistrates' court to issue summonses commencing proceedings is set out in s 1(2) of the Magistrates' Courts Act 1980. The power exists if:

(a) the offence was *committed* or is *suspected to have been committed* within the commission area, or

(b) it appears to the magistrate that it is *necessary or expedient*, with a view to the better administration of justice, that the person charged should be tried *jointly* with, or in the same place as, some other person who is charged with an offence and who is in custody, or is being, or is to be, proceeded against, within the area, or

(c) the person charged *resides*, or is *believed to reside* or be, within the area, or

(d) any other enactment gives a magistrates' court for the area jurisdiction to try the offence, or

(e) the offence was committed outside England and Wales and, where it is an offence exclusively punishable on summary conviction, if a magistrates' court for the area would have jurisdiction to try the offence if the offender were before it.

The power to issue these summonses thus primarily depends on the offence being committed in the commission area. Clause (c) is not as wide as it appears, as a summons cannot be issued on this basis unless the offence is indictable[10]. Clause (d) enables a summons to be issued for example against the motorist who commits two different offences in different commission areas on different occasions.

(ii) Warrants for arrest. Warrants for arrest also compel the accused to attend court. However, whereas a summons requires the accused to attend court, a warrant is an order directed to the police to arrest him.

There are two different types of warrant for arrest: the warrant which

9 Magistrates' Courts Act 1980, s 1(7).
10 Ibid, s 1(5).

commences *proceedings*, and the warrant which compels attendance after proceedings have been commenced. The latter is often called a 'bench warrant'. In either case, they can be issued by a single justice.[11]

As already noted, warrants to commence proceedings are rare in practice.

The same jurisdictional qualifications as for issuing summonses apply. In addition, if the offender is at least 17 years of age the offence must be indictable or punishable by imprisonment, or the accused's address must not be sufficiently established for a summons to be served.[12] When a magistrate issues an originating warrant, he may direct that it is endorsed (or 'backed') for bail. The warrant will be executed by the police, who will release the accused on bail if the warrant is 'backed'. If the warrant is not backed for bail the police have the same powers and duties as they do in relation to someone they have arrested without warrant. The justice issuing the warrant will specify if it is backed for bail.

'Bench warrants', may be issued in a variety of circumstances of which the following are common examples:

(a) when an accused has been bailed to appear before the court, either by the police or by the court itself, but fails to appear on the appointed day;

(b) when the court wishes to impose a sentence of imprisonment or disqualification on an accused who is absent;

(c) when a witness who has been summonsed to attend to give evidence fails to appear at the trial.

As with originating warrants the police must release the arrested person on bail if the warrant is 'backed', otherwise they must bring the arrested person before the court as soon as practicable.

EXAMPLE: *Police v Mary ADAMS (case 3)*. The proceedings cannot be started by warrant for arrest because her address is clearly well-established and the offence with which she is charged is summary only, and not imprisonable.[13] If she does not turn up at court on the return day, the court can proceed to try her in her absence. If it does so, and finds her guilty, it can issue a *bench warrant* if it is considering disqualifying her from driving.[14]

(iii) Bind over. A magistrates' court may order persons appearing before it to keep the peace and be of good behaviour. This power, which is thought to derive from the Justices of the Peace Act 1361, requires the person to enter into a recognizance to that effect. A recognizance is a promise to keep to the terms of the order in a specified sum of money.[15] If the promise is broken, a court can order the person to pay up ('forfeit') all or part of the promised sum. The period of the bind over will be fixed by the court. It will not usually exceed 12 months, although there is no statutory maximum. Refusal to enter into the recognizance when required to do so can be punished by committal to prison for up to six months.[16]

The power to bind over can arise in two different ways. The court can

---

11 See eg Magistrates' Courts Act 1980, s 1(7), s 10(1) and s 13.

12 Ibid, s 1(4). It would appear that if the accused is under 17 the power to issue a warrant is unfettered. In practice it is used even less frequently than for adults.

13 S 1(7), ante.

14 Magistrates' Courts Act 1980, s 13.

15 The amount may be nominal or substantive but if the latter, the person's means should be investigated: *R v Central Criminal Court, ex p Boulding* [1984] QB 813.

16 Magistrates' Courts Act 1980, s 115(3).

exercise the power of its own motion (in other words, without a specific application) if it seems appropriate to do so. This is often used against disorderly parties or witnesses.[17] Alternatively, the court can be asked to exercise the power by an aggrieved person who has laid a *complaint*. This leads to the issue of a summons requiring the respondent to attend court to show cause why he should not be bound over.

(iv) Adjournments and remands. It will often be impossible to dispose of the case on the accused's first appearance. Whenever it is impractical or impossible to proceed, it will be necessary to *adjourn* the proceedings until another day.

Powers of adjournment. Magistrates' courts have wide powers of adjournment at all stages of the proceedings. They may adjourn either before or during committal proceedings,[18] before or during summary trial[19] or before or during mode of trial proceedings.[20] Furthermore, the court may adjourn *after* conviction for 'inquiries or a report'[1] or on the more restricted ground of requiring a medical report on the defendant's mental or physical condition.[2] The following are the most common reasons for adjourning.

(a) The first hearing date is often fixed on the assumption that the accused will plead guilty. This is particularly likely in cases commenced by summons; the summons may well be accompanied by a note asking the accused to write back to the court, indicating in advance what his plea will be, and stating that if he intends to plead not guilty then the case will be adjourned on the return date. There are two reasons why this is necessary. First, the prosecutor will not get his witnesses to court for the first hearing on the off-chance that the accused pleads 'not guilty'. Second, even if the accused has already told the court or the prosecutor that he intends to plead 'not guilty' the court may not have time both to hear a contested trial and also to deal with the rest of the business allocated to that day. Interestingly, approximately 93% of all adjournments are applied for by the prosecution.[3]

EXAMPLE: *Police v Mary ADAMS (case 3).* As will be shown later, if Mary ADAMS were to plead 'guilty' she might not appear before a court at any stage, but if she were to decide to plead 'not guilty' it is most unlikely that the court would have time to deal with a contested case on the date mentioned in the summons. In such a case, proceedings would probably be adjourned generally ('sine die') by agreement, without either party needing to attend. Both sides would subsequently have to find out when their witnesses could be available, and then arrange a *trial date* convenient to the court and each other.

(b) If the offence is to be tried on indictment the prosecutor must prepare for committal proceedings. This may be a lengthy process, as the evidence which the prosecutor intends to use at committal will usually have to be put into the form of written statements[4] and served on the defence. Additionally, if the offence is triable either way, 'mode of trial' proceedings will first have to be held.

17 Justices of the Peace Act 1361.
18 Magistrates' Court Act 1980, s 5.
19 Ibid, s 18.
20 Ibid, s 10.
1 Ibid, s 10(3).
2 Ibid, s 30.
3 House of Commons Select Committee on Home Affairs 1984, HMSO.
4 Magistrates' Courts Act 1980, s 102.

EXAMPLE: *Police v Duncan McCARTHY (case 1)*. On the morning that McCARTHY first appears before the magistrates in custody, it soon becomes apparent that although he intends to plead 'not guilty', neither he nor the duty solicitor have had time to consider mode of trial. In any event, the prosecution will not be in a position to bring committal proceedings for two or three weeks, and will not prepare for committal until they have an indication as to whether he wants to be tried on indictment. It will therefore be necessary to adjourn at least once.

(c) After conviction, the court may consider that it has insufficient information about the defendant on which to sentence him. In such a case an adjournment would be necessary for more information to be obtained, usually from the probation service.

EXAMPLE: *Softsell Supermarkets v Anthony JONES (case 2)*. When JONES goes to court for the first time, he is seen by the duty solicitor who advises him to agree to summary trial and to plead 'guilty'. The magistrates decide that before sentencing him they require further information about him, and therefore adjourn the proceedings. At the same time they ask the probation service to prepare a 'social inquiry report' on his home life and family background.

Adjournments 'sine die'. A court may either *adjourn* to a date which it will specify on adjourning, or subject as below adjourn generally. The latter is called an adjournment sine die, and the revised date will be arranged in the court office and notified by the court to the parties. This is used particularly when the trial date cannot be fixed on the adjournment because the availability of witnesses are not known. When a magistrates' court also *remands* an accused, however, it must fix a date; it cannot adjourn and remand sine die.

Power to remand. At the same time that a magistrates' court adjourns proceedings it may (and sometimes must) remand the accused. Thus an *adjournment* defers the proceedings, whereas a *remand* secures the accused's reappearance at the next hearing. The accused can either be released *on bail*, which puts him under a statutory duty to return on the appointed day, or remanded in *custody*, in which case he will usually be detained in a prison pending the next hearing. The governor of the prison is responsible for ensuring that he is produced back in court on the date to which he has been remanded.[5] The statutory provisions relating to remands are very complex and are considered in detail in chapter 7. The following rules should however be borne in mind.

If the court remands *in custody* prior to conviction it can generally only do so for a maximum of *eight clear days* at a time.[6]

If it remands *on bail* prior to conviction there is *no time limit*, provided the accused consents, but the court must remand to *a fixed date*.

If the accused is *committed* to the Crown Court for trial or sentence he will be committed on bail or in custody. Committal, unlike remands, will not be to a fixed date, irrespective of whether he is committed on bail or in custody.

After conviction the defendant can be remanded *in custody* for up to *three weeks*, or *on bail* for up to *four weeks* at a time if the magistrates adjourn for reports.[7]

5 Subject to *R v Governor of Brixton Prison, ex p Walsh* [1985] AC 154.
6 Magistrates' Courts Act 1980, s 128(6).
7 Ibid, s 10(3).

(v) Legal aid. Many people who appear before criminal courts charged with offences of any substance apply for legal aid. Magistrates and their clerks are empowered to receive and consider applications for legal aid orders for proceedings in the magistrates' court. They also deal with the majority of applications for legal aid for proceedings in the Crown Court, including appeals. The granting of legal aid is subject to financial and other criteria and will be considered further in chapter 6.

(vi) Warrants of further detention. The Police and Criminal Evidence Act 1984, s 43 empowers a magistrates' court to issue a warrant on the application of the police, authorising the continued detention without charge of a suspect beyond the basic *24 hours'* period allowed by the Act for up to a further *72 hours*. Unlike other types of warrant, warrants of detention can only be authorised by at least two lay justices (or a stipendiary).

(3) The Crown Court

There is only one Crown Court. It is a superior court of record and part of the Supreme Court, equivalent in status to, but not part of, the High Court.[8] It tries offences on indictment, hears appeals against conviction or sentence from magistrates' courts, and deals with persons committed for sentence.

In practice the Crown Court sits in various locations throughout England and Wales, officially styled, for example, 'The Crown Court at Croydon', but generally known as 'Croydon Crown Court'. The Crown Court in London is called the 'Central Criminal Court',[9] or, more colloquially, 'the Old Bailey'. The Crown Court is organised into three 'tiers'. The *first tier* has judges of the High Court in attendance. These courts deal with the entire range of indictable offences and also High Court civil work. The *second tier* has High Court judges sitting regularly to hear criminal cases but does not handle civil work. The *third tier* has no High Court judges and handles no civil work. It tries less serious indictable offences which form the bulk of Crown Court work. Third tier courts also hear all appeals from magistrates' courts and deal with defendants who have been committed for sentence.

All of the locations of the Crown Court are grouped into 'Circuits' over which a High Court judge presides. He will give administrative directions to the courts in the circuit, with particular reference to the classes of offence which each may take.[10]

(a) *Jurisdiction of the Crown Court as a court of trial*

Jurisdiction. The Crown Court may try any matter over which English courts have jurisdiction, other than summary offences. The jurisdiction of the Crown Court is limited to offences committed in England and Wales, although, as with the magistrates' courts, there are exceptions. Subject to this, branches are not limited to trying offences committed within their own catchment area. Indictable offences are divided into four classes:[11]

Class 1: offences of the utmost gravity such as murder
Class 2: other extremely grave offences, including rape and manslaughter.

8 Supreme Court Act 1981, s 1.
9 Ibid, s 8(3).
10 See infra.
11 Practice Note [1971] 3 All ER 829, CA, (1972) 56 Cr App Rep 52.

Class 3: all indictable offences not specifically allocated to classes 1, 2 or 4.

Class 4: the bulk of offences triable on indictment. It includes offences as serious as robbery and causing grievous bodily harm with intent, and all *either way* offences.

Allocation. When a case is committed for trial at the Crown Court, the magistrates specify the particular court to which it is committed. This will be the appropriate *third tier* Crown Court for that petty sessions area, unless the case is in Classes 1 to 3, when they must commit to the most convenient branch of the Crown Court where a High Court judge sits.

(b) Jurisdiction of the Crown Court on appeals and committals for sentence

Appeals. A defendant has a right of appeal to the Crown Court from a magistrates' court in certain circumstances. He may appeal against conviction and sentence if he pleaded not guilty. If he pleaded guilty at summary trial he may only appeal against sentence.[12] Appeals are considered further in chapter 14.

Committals for sentence. As mentioned in chapter 1, magistrates' courts' sentencing powers are limited. They cannot generally impose a punishment of more than six months' imprisonment or a fine of £2000 or both, even in respect of the most serious types of offence with which they are empowered to deal. To compensate for this there are provisions enabling a magistrates' court to commit a defendant to the Crown Court for sentence. The three most important apply when:

(i) an *adult* is convicted of an *either way* offence and greater punishment than that available to the magistrates seems appropriate because of his antecedents;[13]

(ii) a *juvenile* aged *15 or 16* is found guilty of an imprisonable offence and it appears that the maximum sentence of youth custody available to the magistrates should be exceeded;[14]

(iii) an offender who is still subject to a suspended sentence of imprisonment, a probation order or a conditional discharge imposed by the Crown Court on a previous occasion, is convicted of an offence which infringes the earlier sentence or order.[15]

These and other powers[16] to commit offenders for sentence are considered further in chapter 13.

(c) Personnel

Trials. There is no office of 'Crown Court Judge' as such. The judges who sit in the Crown Court come into three categories.

High Court judges. They sit in *first* and *second* tier courts and try all Class 1 and Class 2 offences, unless the presiding judge permits a specific Class 2 case to be tried by a circuit judge or recorder. Class 3 offences are also listed

12 Magistrates' Courts Act 1980, s 108.
13 Ibid, s 38.
14 Ibid, s 37.
15 Powers of Criminal Courts Act 1973, ss 6(4), 8(6) and 24(2).
16 For example, under Criminal Justice Act 1967, s 56.

for hearing before a High Court judge unless they appear suitable for a circuit judge or recorder.

Circuit judges are full-time judges. They are appointed from barristers of *ten years'* standing or recorders of *three years'* standing. Most of them also sit in the county court for part of the year. They hear all Class 4 cases unless it appears to the Crown Court listing officer that a particular case is sufficiently serious to warrant it being tried by a High Court judge. If necessary deputy circuit judges may also be appointed.

Recorders are appointed from barristers or solicitors, in either case of *ten years'* standing. They are part time judges who may continue to practice when not required in a judicial capacity. They also normally hear Class 4 cases only. Deputy recorders can be appointed if necessary from among the same persons who would qualify as recorders.

Lay justices may also sit in trials with a judge or recorder in the Crown Court.[17] They are entitled to participate in and vote on matters of law but play no part in the summing up to the jury.

Whatever the category of offence the judge or recorder will sit with a jury. The judge must decide matters of law and guide the jury by summing up to them before they retire to consider their verdict. The jury are thus the sole arbiters of guilt or innocence.

Appeals and committals for sentence. These will be heard by a circuit judge or a recorder. The judge will normally sit with at least two and no more than four lay justices.[18] The lay justices must not include those who were concerned in the hearing in the court below. In contrast with trials on indictment, the judge retains the sole right to decide matters of law, but questions of fact are decided by a majority—if necessary the judge has a casting vote.

(d) Ancillary powers and duties of the Crown Court

Apart from holding trials on indictment, and hearing appeals from and sentencing persons committed by magistrates, the Crown Court has other ancillary functions.

Adjournments. As with magistrates' courts, the Crown Court can adjourn whenever necessary. An adjournment may be ordered by a judge, either before or during a trial, although pre-trial adjournments may sometimes be granted by the listing officer. Because the accused is not committed to appear on a particular date, there is no need for him to be brought to court for this purpose.

Power to grant bail and commit to custody. The Crown Court has a general power to grant bail to anyone who is to appear before it. This includes a defendant who has been convicted by the magistrates' court and who is appealing or has been committed for sentence. The Crown Court may also grant bail to an accused whose case is *still pending* in the magistrates' court, provided that the magistrates have remanded *in custody* and certified that they have heard a fully argued bail application.[19] If bail is applied for during the trial, for example, at the end of a day's sitting, or at the end of

17 Supreme Court Act 1981, s 73(3).
18 Ibid, s 74.
19 Ibid, s 81 (as amended).

the trial, application is made in open court to the judge hearing the case. All other applications are heard in chambers.

Legal aid. The Crown Court can grant legal aid[20] to the accused in any case of which it is seised, even if the magistrates refused to grant it. In fact, statistics indicate that about 95% of persons appearing before the Crown Court have the benefit of legal aid orders, and that most of these are granted by magistrates under the provisions already considered.

(4) The higher courts

(a) *The Queens Bench Divisional Court*

The Queens Bench Divisional Court has two separate functions in criminal proceedings.

(i) *Appeals by way of case stated*

After the *conclusion* of summary trial or committal proceedings, either the prosecution or the defence may ask the magistrates to state the particulars of the case and the reasons for their decision in writing, for consideration by the Divisional Court,[1] who can confirm, amend or reverse the decision appealed against. Appeals by way of case stated can only be made on points of law and the Divisional Court hears only argument. If the defendant decides to appeal by way of case stated he loses the right of appeal on both law and fact to the Crown Court. This procedure is the only right of appeal that the prosecutor has from the decision of a magistrates' court.

The Divisional Court also hears appeals by way of case stated from decisions of the Crown Court but only when the latter was sitting as an *appellate* court.[2]

(ii) *Judicial review*

The Divisional Court hears applications for judicial review of decisions of, or proceedings in, magistrates' courts. It may quash the decision or proceedings appealed against (certiorari) or alternatively, issue an order that the inferior court carries out its duty in a particular way (mandamus and prohibition). Both prosecution and defence can apply for judicial review. Applications lie on matters of law rather than on the factual merits of the case. Judicial review is also available to challenge decisions of the Crown Court, again only when sitting as an *appellate* court.[3]

Civil legal aid is available for both sets of proceedings. Application is made to the relevant legal aid Area Secretary.

(b) *The Court of Appeal*

The Criminal Division of the Court of Appeal hears appeals against conviction or sentence from the Crown Court sitting as a court of trial. It also hears appeals against sentence in respect of offenders committed to the Crown Court for sentence. Unless the appeal is based solely on a point of law, leave to appeal is required from the Court of Appeal. This is usually

---

20 Legal Aid Act 1974, s 29(5) to (7).
1 Supreme Court Act 1981, s 28.
2 Ibid, s 28.
3 Ibid, s 29.

considered by a single judge of the Court of Appeal. If leave is granted the appeal itself is heard by either three judges, in the case of appeals against conviction, or two judges, in appeals against sentence. The court may consist of Lord Justices of Appeal or puisne judges, or a mixture of the two. The appeal normally consists of argument by counsel, although the Court may receive additional evidence.

A legal aid order granted for the Crown Court includes the cost of counsel advising on appeal. It also includes the preparation by counsel of written grounds of appeal, upon which the single judge will decide whether or not to grant leave. Legal aid for the appeal itself is granted by the Registrar of Criminal Appeals or the Court itself, and will frequently cover counsel only. The Court can also grant bail prior to the hearing of the appeal. The application for bail is normally made to the single judge of the Court of Appeal and considered at the same time as he considers the application for leave.

(c) The House of Lords

The Appellate Committee of the House of Lords hears appeals in criminal cases from the Divisional Court and the Court of Appeal. In order for an appeal to proceed, the court against whose decision the appeal is made *must* certify that a point of law of sufficient importance is raised in the case. It must also give leave to appeal to the House. If it does not give leave, the aggrieved party must apply by way of petition to the House of Lords for leave to appeal. The petition for leave is considered by an appeal committee of the House, which can hold an oral hearing. If leave is granted, the appeal itself will usually be heard by five Lords of Appeal in Ordinary at a later date.

The Court of Appeal can grant bail, pending appeal, but the House of Lords has no power to do so. Legal aid for appeal to the House of Lords cannot be granted by the House itself. In appeals from the Court of Appeal it is granted by that Court. When the appeal is from the Divisional Court application must be made to the relevant legal aid Area Secretary for a legal aid certificate, because the proceedings are civil.

3 COMMENCING A PROSECUTION

(1) The decision to prosecute

As we have seen, all manner of bodies or individuals may bring a prosecution for all manner of different reasons. For example individuals may be motivated by personal grievance, and stores may have a standard policy in shoplifting cases.

The police, however, have to consider many factors.

In many cases the decision to take matters further rests with the individual constable on the beat. Particularly in the case of minor offences it is primarily his decision whether to arrest, report, or simply to administer a verbal warning. Even if a suspect is arrested or told he may be prosecuted, it does not mean that proceedings will necessarily follow.[4]

The decision to proceed will be taken by the police, possibly after consultation with a prosecuting solicitor or, in serious cases, with the Attorney General or Director of Public Prosecutions. The decision may reflect the

---

4 See eg *Holgate-Mohammed v Duke* [1984] AC 437, HL.

THE CRIMINAL COURTS

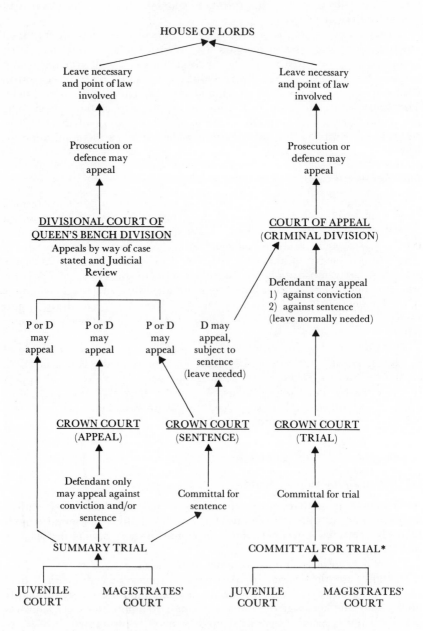

* Committal proceedings can also be challenged by Judicial Review.

policy of a particular force, for which the Chief Constable is operationally responsible. The following matters must be considered.

(i) Does the evidence justify bringing a prosecution at all?[5]
(ii) What type of charge should be preferred? For example, if there is a minor incident, should the charge be common assault (summary only) or assault occasioning actual bodily harm (triable either way)?
(iii) If a prosecution could be brought, would it be better formally to *caution*[6] the suspect rather than prosecute him?
(iv) How should the proceedings be commenced? For example, should an arrested person or someone who has gone voluntarily to the police station, be charged immediately or released on bail to return for possible charge at a later date?[6] Should a summons be issued instead?

(2) Bringing the accused before the court

In theory all criminal proceedings are started by the laying of an 'information' which is the step whereby a magistrate is 'informed' of an alleged offence,[7] and asked to issue either a summons or a warrant. As we have already seen, however, proceedings are often commenced by arrest without warrant followed by charge. These three alternatives will now be examined in turn.

Information leading to the issue of a summons

Stage one—laying the information. The prosecutor either takes or posts a written form to the appropriate magistrates' court office, or attends in person to lay the information orally,[8] although this is unusual. The Police tend to use their own standard forms, based on the precedents in works such as *Stone's Justices' Manual*. Private prosecutors can either buy standard forms from Law Stationers, or their local court may be able to supply a form. The information must contain enough facts to enable a summons to be issued. It must thus contain the name and address of the offender and details of the alleged offence. The offence must be described in ordinary language, even if this does not include all the constituent elements of the offence. It should also give sufficient facts to show the nature of the offence, and if, as will usually be the case, the offence is a statutory one, it should contain a reference to the relevant provision.[9] The information must only contain one offence. If the prosecutor wishes to charge two offences, he must lay separate informations, otherwise the validity of the information is open to challenge on the grounds of duplicity. If an information does charge more than one offence the magistrates must not try the information.[10] If they do, any conviction will be quashed by the Divisional Court.

5 I e is there a reasonable prospect of conviction rather than a mere prima facie case (the '51% rule'). Guidance is given in the Attorney General's 'Criteria for Prosecution' issued in 1983. See also Sanders, 'Prosecution Decisions and the Attorney General's Guidelines' [1985] Crim LR 4.
6 A formal warning, given by a senior officer to a person who admits the offence, of the consequences of offending again.
7 After a person is committed for trial to the Crown Court, he will, in essence, be cited for an offence again, this time in the indictment. This and other refinements on the basic system are considered in chapter 11.
8 Magistrates' Courts Act 1980, s 1(3); Magistrates' Courts rules 1981, r 4(2).
9 Magistrates' Courts Rules 1981, r 100.
10 Ibid, r 12.

Duplicity is easier to define than to spot. An obvious example of duplicity would be if an information alleged that an accused had driven 'without due care and attention *or* without reasonable consideration for other road users'[11] as it has been held that these are two offences. If a prosecutor wished to allege both, he would need to lay two informations each containing one offence (it would be sufficient if they were set out in separate paragraphs in the same document). Judicial interpretation of statutes has, however, led to some fine distinctions. An information which alleges that the accused drove 'whilst unfit to do so through drink or drugs'[12] has been held not to be duplicitous. Other offences *only* have the *appearance* of duplicity. Thus, 'continuing' offence, such as obstructing a highway, charged in an information on the basis that the offence was committed 'on and after' a particular date is not duplicitous.[13]

An information may be duplicitous because it is laid out incorrectly. However, in *DPP v Shah*[14] the House of Lords held that a written information which contained details of the accused's name, address and occupation and a general statement of the relevant statutory provisions and regulations at the top, followed by a list of five specific offences, was *not* duplicitous. The moral is that you should always read the summons and the statutes creating the offences carefully, and consult the reference books to see if the matter has previously been decided.

Can anything be done about an information which is duplicitous? It is clear that if the court proceeds to try it, the whole proceedings will be void and the conviction and information must be quashed. As will be seen later, this can be important as most summary offences are subject to a time limit of six months within which an information must be laid. If, therefore, an information is quashed outside that period, it is too late to start again. If a duplicitous information is spotted before the proceedings start, the prosecutor can always apply to withdraw the summons, and lay a fresh information if he is still in time. There is, however, no authority as to whether the court has power to amend duplicitous informations.[15] The learned editors of *Stone's Justices' Manual* take the view that duplicity cannot be cured by amendment, on the authority of *Griffiths v Freeman*.[16] However, that case was not concerned with duplicity, and remarks contained in the judgments are, strictly speaking, *obiter*. Others have suggested that duplicity could be cured by deleting all but one offence.[17]

Stage two — issuing the summons. Once the information is delivered to the court, it must at some stage be considered either by a magistrate or by a clerk to the justices, to decide whether or not proceedings ought to be commenced.[18] Obviously the information says very little about the alleged offence and thus this function is to ensure that there is no obvious error, such as a charge under a repealed statute.

---

11 Road Traffic Act 1972, s 3.
12 *Thomas v Knights* [1947] KB 336. See also *Horrix v Malam* [1984] RTR 112.
13 *Hodgetts v Chiltern District Council* [1983] 2 AC 120, HL.
14 [1984] 1 WLR 886, HL, overruling the Divisional Court.
15 Magistrates' Courts Act 1980, s 123.
16 *Griffiths v Freeman* [1970] 1 All ER 1117.
17 See Brian Harris, *Criminal jurisdiction of Magistrates*, 9th edn p 198; also Phillip K Dodd — Clerk to the Justices for the City of Manchester in *Motoring Offences* 1982, College of Law at p 94.
18 This is a judicial act, which cannot be delegated; *R v Manchester Stipendiary Magistrate, ex p Hill* [1983] 1 AC 328.

SUMMONS/INFORMATION M.C. Act 1980 S1; M.C. Rules 1981 r.98

Weyford.......Magistrates' Court   (Court Code.9999.........)

> Ms Mary ADAMS
> 45 Almas Road
> Weyford
>
>   Private/Nominated address

You are hereby summoned to appear on 15 Feb 198—before the

Magistrates' Court at ...Court House Weyford.............................

to answer to the following information laid today ....

that you ....Mary Adams...

on ....21st November 198—.....................................
Steephill Road
at Weyford..... did drive a motor vehicle on a road without
due care and attention contrary to s 3 and Sch 4, Road
(Alleged offence)   Traffic Act 1972

Informant Inspector Harold Keppel
Address The Police Station, Letsby Avenue, Weyford
Date 15 January 198—   **H. Smith**   *(signature)*
~~Metropolitan Stipendiary Magistrate~~/Justices' Clerk/~~Justice of the Peace~~.

STATEMENT OF FACTS (Magistrates' Courts Act, 1980, Section 12(1)(b).)
IF YOU INFORM THE CLERK of the Court that you wish to plead guilty to the offence set out in the summons served herewith, without appearing before the Court, and the Court proceeds to hear and dispose of the case in your absence under Section 12 of the Magistrates' Courts Act 1980, the following Statement of Facts will be read out in open Court before the Court decides whether to accept your plea. If your plea of guilty is accepted the Court will not, unless it adjourns the case after convicting you and before sentencing you, permit any other statement to be made by or on behalf of the prosecutor with respect to any facts relating to the offence.
On 21st November 198— at about 6.00 pm you were driving a Vauxhall Astra motor car registration number ABC 123 on Steephill Road, Weyford, travelling south. You started to turn right into Downdale Road across the path of a motor car travelling north down Steephill Road. The oncoming vehicle swerved and braked but was unable to avoid a collision, causing damage to both vehicles. Police officers attended the scene and when they told you that you would be reported you made no reply.

M Keppel

Signed on behalf of the prosecutor

The summons will be prepared from the information by clerical staff, and although it may be signed personally by the clerk or a magistrate, it will usually be authenticated by a facsimile rubber stamp.[19]

If a summons alleges more than one offence, these must be set out in separate paragraphs. Many courts nowadays find it more convenient to issue separate summonses for each offence, particularly as the larger courts may have pro forma summonses printed up for all the more common summary offences. When a person is accused of an offence for which he is liable to have his driving licence endorsed if he is convicted, the summons will bear a notice reminding the accused that his driving licence must either be produced at the hearing, or sent beforehand.[20]

Information leading to a warrant for arrest

An information can be laid asking for a warrant for arrest to be issued rather than a summons provided that additional procedural requirements are satisfied. The information must be in *writing*, must be 'substantiated' *on oath*, and must be issued by a magistrate. Furthermore, the power to issue a warrant only exists:[1]

(i) if the offence is triable on indictment; or
(ii) if the offence is punishable by imprisonment; or
(iii) if the address of the accused is not sufficiently established to enable a summons to be served on him; or
(iv) if the accused is a juvenile.

If issued, the warrant will be addressed to the police force of the area in which the accused is suspected to be.[2], and will authorize detention on the same basis as if the person had been arrested without warrant, or will be 'backed for bail'. It must state which of the foregoing grounds for issuing a warrant applies.

As already noted, this method of instituting proceedings is little used.[3]

Arrest without warrant followed by charge

In these cases the accused will have been arrested, searched and interrogated before the decision to charge him is taken. When the accused is charged, the details of the alleged offence will be set out in a 'charge sheet'. This will specify not only the offence or offences charged, but also whether the accused is in custody or on bail, and in the latter case the date and time he must appear before the court. The police will then send a copy of the charge sheet to the appropriate court. Technically, the information is 'laid' when the charge is read out to the court on the accused's first appearance.

(3) Time limits

There is no general time limit within which proceedings for an *indictable* offence must be commenced, but proceedings for a *summary* offence must usually be taken within six months from the date of the offence. This means

---

19 *R v Brentford Justices' ex p Catlin* [1975] 2 QB 455, approved in *Ex p Hill*, op cit.
20 Road Traffic Act 1972, s 101.
 1 Magistrates' Courts Act 1980, s 1(4) op cit.
 2 Magistrates' Courts Rules 1981, r 96.
 3 See Royal Commission on Criminal Procedure *The Law and Procedure*; Cmnd 8092-1 (1981), para 179.

BLANKSHIRE POLICE

COPY FOR ACCUSED PERSON

Full name of person charged...ANTHONY JONES............................
Address....23, Raglan House, Weyford..................................
Date of birth....21/1/3-.......Occupation....Unemployed................

You are charged with the following offence(s):-

that on the 10th day of September 198- at Softsell supermarket, High
Street, Weyford, you did steal certain goods that were the property
of Softsell Limited, to wit one packet of biscuits, one tin of soup
and one jar of coffee, to the value of £3.50 contrary to Section 1(1)
Theft Act 1968.

Do you wish to say anything? You are not obliged to say anything unless
you wish to do so but whatever you say will be taken down in writing
and may be given in evidence.   **No reply**

Time and date charged 15-00 hrs; 10th September 198-

Signature of person charging *Jane Smith*   (Store detective)

Signature of officer taking charge **Arthur Brown** Custody Officer **Sgt. 3112**

COURT (First appearance) Weyford
ON day/date   10.30 am 2nd October 198-
Released/Not Released   BAIL
Date/time: 10/9/8- 15.00 hrs
Officer releasing: **Arthur Brown**   Custody Officer **Sgt 3112**

that no *information* can be laid after that date. Provided one has been laid in time any summons based upon it can be issued outside the limitation.[4] Note that the starting point is the *commission* of the offence, and not the acquisition of knowledge by the prosecutor. Thus for most summary offences, such as careless driving, the period is certain. Where the offence is continuous, such as in public nuisance, the six month period runs from the *last* incident on which the offence is based.

(4) Service of summonses

The summons must be served on the accused after issue but before the day specified on the summons for the accused to attend court. A summons can be served on an accused other than a corporation in one of the following ways:

(i)   personal service on the accused: or
(ii) leaving it with someone at his last known or usual residence; or
(iii) by sending it through the post in an envelope addressed to him at his last known or usual residence.[5]

Postal service will be effected by the court; personal service will normally be attempted by the police, for which purpose the court office will send the summons to the police station.

Irrespective of the method of service used, the court may not proceed unless it is satisfied that the summons has come to the notice of the accused. If the summons is served personally, the officer serving will complete a certificate to that effect, and return this to the court. If the summons is served by any other method, then the fact that it came to the accused's attention must be proved. A letter from the accused is sufficient, and most courts attach to summonses a form for him to use to acknowledge receipt of the summons and at the same time to give an indication of his intended plea. Alternatively, if the offence is summary only and the summons is sent by recorded delivery or registered letter post, service may be proved by completion of the delivery receipt.[6]

(5) Abuse of the process of the court

It is obviously desirable not only that proceedings should be commenced as soon as possible, but also that there should be as few delays as possible between commencement and trial. Where delay has occurred it may be possible to apply for the proceedings to be dismissed if to proceed with them would be an abuse of the court.

In *R v Brentford Justices, ex p Wong*[7] the police laid an information against the accused alleging careless driving two days before the expiry of the six months' time limit. They had not at that stage decided whether or not to prosecute, and only did so approximately *3 months* later. A further delay produced the result that the accused was served with the summons itself more than *10 months* after the alleged offence and the case did not finally

4 Magistrates' Courts Act 1980, s 127; unless statute provides a later date, see eg Supplementary Benefits Act 1976, s 26(3)(b). An information is 'laid' for limitation purposes when it is received at the clerk's office by a member of staff expressly or implicitly authorised to receive it, *Ex p Hill*, op cit.
5 Magistrates' Courts Rules 1981, r 99(1); service can always be made on a corporation's registered office or if none on its main place of business: r 99(3).
6 Magistrates' Courts Rules 1981, r 99(2).
7 [1981] QB 445, DC.

come on for hearing until *15 months* after the incident. The Divisional Court held that magistrates have jurisdiction to dismiss informations in cases where they feel it would be an abuse for them to be continued. The Court expressed the view that the facts of this case came into that category as there were clear indications that the prosecution had laid the information simply to preserve their position, rather than as the first stage in a bona fide prosecution.

A similar result occurred in *R v Watford Justices, ex p Outrim*.[8] An information was laid within *6 weeks* of an alleged offence of driving with excess alcohol, but the summons was not served by the police until *22 months* after it had been issued to them, through no fault of the accused. The Divisional Court stated that magistrates should consider exercising their discretion to dismiss when the delay had been unconscienable or such as to produce substantial prejudice to the accused. *22 months* was too long a delay and there was an obvious inference that the accused would be substantially prejudiced by the proceedings continuing.

Both these cases were concerned with *summary* offences, to which a time limit applies. There is no time limit for commencing most indictable offences but there is the remote possibility that delay may constitute an abuse of process. In *R v Grays Justices, ex p Graham*[9] the Divisional Court refused to intervene to prevent magistrates hearing committal proceedings in *February 1982* in respect of reissued summonses relating to indictable offences alleged to have been committed in *January 1980*. This was so even though earlier summonses in respect of the same offences, issued in *June 1981* had been dismissed at earlier committal proceedings in *August 1981*, because the prosecution offered no evidence on that occasion. The court held that despite the period of time that had elapsed, the delays that had occurred were inherent in the investigation and prosecution of a complicated set of facts, and that in the absence of bad faith or improper use of the court procedures[10] there was, on the facts, no basis to interfere. The court did, however, agree that in appropriate cases mere delay by itself could amount to an abuse.

It is therefore always worth considering asking magistrates to dismiss a summons or charge when there has been a long delay, especially if there have been numerous prosecution applications for adjournment. If any delay has arisen from the conduct of the accused, however, this must seriously affect the chances of success.

(6) Notices of intended prosecution

Section 179 of the Road Traffic Act 1972 imposes an additional limitation period in respect of the following offences:

  (i) reckless driving (s 2), careless and inconsiderate driving (s 3) and cycling (ss 17 and 18);
  (ii) all speeding offences;
  (iii) certain offences in relation to traffic and police signs (ss 22 and 22A);
  (iv) leaving a vehicle in a dangerous position (s 24).

---

8 [1983] RTR 26.
9 [1982] QB 1239.
10 Such as the prosecutor seeking committal on fresh charges which were based on the same facts as previous charges which had been dismissed on the merits see *R v Horsham Justices, ex p Reeves* (1982) 75 Cr App Rep 236n.

In order for the prosecution to be valid the prosecutor must:

(i) *have warned the accused 'at the time of the offence' that he might be prosecuted.* Ideally this warning should be given as soon as possible whilst the parties are still at the scene. However, there has been much litigation on the meaning of 'at the time of the offence' and what constitutes a proper warning;[11] or

(ii) *serve the accused with a summons within 14 days of the offence.* It is seldom possible to do this. It has not been decided whether or not a charge sheet is a 'summons' for these purposes; or

(iii) *serve the accused with a notice that he may be prosecuted for one of the offences within 14 days of commission of the offence.* The notice should specify the offence. As might be expected, there has been considerable litigation on the subject of when the notice has to be posted in order for it to be properly served. In general it must be posted *within* the 14-day period in the normal course of post. If, therefore, the notice is sent in good time but is delayed by the postal authorities, it may still be good even if received late.[12]

It should be noted that compliance with s 179 is presumed unless raised by the defence and that the burden of proving that the section was not complied with lies on the accused, who must prove the issues on the balance of probability.[13]

Section 179 does not apply when an 'accident' occurred at the same time as, or immediately after, the offence owing to the presence on the road of the vehicle in which the offence was committed.[14] This important proviso[15] was inserted into the Road Traffic Act because in the case of multiple motorway crashes the complex task of sorting out whom should be prosecuted and for what was impossible to achieve within the 14-day period. The question of whether the accident occurred at the time of the offence is one of fact.[16]

11 See *Wilkinson's Road Traffic Offences* (11th edn) at p 143 et seq.
12 Ibid, p 146.
13 This is the civil standard of proof—and see *Offen v Ranson* [1980] RTR 484, DC.
14 Provided that the driver was aware that an accident had occurred. If he was unaware, then a notice must be served. *Bentley v Dickinson* (1983) 147 JP 526, CA.
15 Road Traffic Act 1972, s 179(3A).
16 An accident has been defined as 'an unfortunate error or mishap', see *Chief Constable of Staffordshire v Lees* [1981] RTR 506, DC. See also *Wilkinson*, op cit, pp 25, 182 and 183.

CHAPTER 3

The police

1 INTRODUCTION

(1) The role of the solicitor

Solicitors specialising in criminal law will experience regular contact with police officers when, for example, visiting a police station to see a client in custody, attending court to apply for bail or liaising with an investigating officer to obtain information about a case. It is therefore helpful to have at least an outline knowledge of the operating methods of the police, in order to develop some kind of working relationship. Furthermore, there are a number of key situations in which a detailed knowledge of what the police can and cannot do will be needed in order to protect a client's interests.

(a) The client in custody. You may be required to argue your entitlement to access or to advise a client as to whether or not he should answer questions or make a statement.

(b) The client on an identification parade. You may be required to attend as an observer to ensure that the client's interests are protected and procedures are observed.

(c) The client who alleges that the police have acted unlawfully or unfairly. Leaving aside civil[1] and disciplinary[2] proceedings, police conduct may have an important bearing on the outcome of a criminal prosecution in the following circumstances.

(*i*) *When it is relevant to the offence charged.* In the case of some offences, for example assaulting or obstructing a police officer in the execution of his duty,[3] or breathalyser offences,[4] the prosecution may be required to prove that the police were acting lawfully in order to establish the essential ingredients of the offence charged.

(*ii*) *When it is relevant to the admissibility of prosecution evidence.* Although there is no *general* discretion to exclude evidence solely on the ground that it has

---

1 For a useful summary of the position vis-a-vis civil proceedings see Gifford 'Civil Claims Against the Police' LAG Bulletin July 1983, p 84.
2 Under Part IX of the Police and Criminal Evidence Act 1984.
3 Police Act 1964, s 51(1) and (3). Many of the leading cases on police powers have been prosecutions under s 51(1): see eg *Lindley v Rutter* [1981] QB 128 (legality of personal search); *McLorie v Oxford* [1982] QB 1290 (power to enter and search premises) and *Lavin v Albert* [1982] AC 546 (power of arrest): or s 51(3) see eg *Moss v McLachlan* (1985) 149 JP 167 (powers to prevent anticipated breach of the peace).
4 Police conduct is now less likely to be of relevance to charges under s 6(1) of the Road Traffic Act 1972 (driving etc with excess alcohol) but may still be relevant to a charge under s 7(4) ibid (refusing without reasonable excuse to provide a specimen) where it is alleged that the police officer is trespassing at the time of the request: see in particular *Fox v Chief Constable of Gwent* [1985] 1 All ER 230.

been illegally or unfairly obtained, the court is *obliged* to exclude the written or oral confession of an accused person if it was obtained by oppression or as a result of conduct likely to render unreliable any confession that he might have made.[5] The court also has a *limited* discretion to exclude prosecution evidence if its admission would have an adverse effect on the fairness of the proceedings.[6] In exercising this discretion the court must look at all the circumstances, 'including the circumstances in which the evidence was obtained'.[7]

(*iii*) *When it is relevant to the credibility of police witnesses.* On occasions there may be a dispute between police witnesses and an accused especially as to what was said in reply to police questioning (such replies are often colloquially referred to as 'verbals'). If it can be shown that the police have broken the law or the Codes of Practice,[8] especially if they have lied about it and been found out, this may have the effect of casting doubt on the remainder of their testimony. It is not suggested that the police act improperly as a matter of course, but you must always do your utmost to protect a client, subject to your remaining within the law and complying with the ethical rules of the legal profession.[9]

(2) Structure of police forces in outline

Many people, lawyers included, know surprisingly little about the structure of the police force and its working methods. There are approximately 120,000 regular police officers in England and Wales, 27,000 of whom are in the Metropolitan Police Force. England and Wales is divided into 43 areas (approximating more or less to the counties) each of which has a regular police force maintained by a Police Authority which, with the exception of Greater London, comprises a committee of local councillors and magistrates. Operational control of each police force is under the direction of a Chief Constable who is appointed by the authority, the main exception being the Metropolitan Police Area, in which the police authority is the Home Secretary and operational control is vested in the Commissioner of Police for the Metropolis.[10] Police authorities also employ traffic wardens and other civilian staff who carry out certain investigative tasks such as fingerprinting and scenes of crime work. Most forces also make use of special constables who perform unpaid voluntary police duties in their spare time.

Broadly, each police force is divided into three branches:

uniformed;
criminal investigation ('CID'); and
road traffic.

The role of the uniformed police is primarily that of crime prevention and maintaining law and order (most arrests of suspects are carried out by the

5 Police and Criminal Evidence Act 1984, s 76(2). The burden of proving lack of oppression etc if called upon to do so lies on the prosecution. See further p 146, et seq.
6 Ibid, s 78(1).
7 Ibid. The section will be highly relevant in certain areas, in particular, identification parades. It is discussed more fully at p 150, post.
8 These regulate conduct of detention and interrogation, identification parades, and searches of persons and premises. They are issued by the Home Secretary under Part VI of the Police and Criminal Evidence Act 1984 and are discussed further at p 43, post.
9 See further p 170, et seq.
10 For further background information see Royal Commission on Criminal Procedure Investigation and Prosecution of Criminal Offences in England and Wales: The Law and Procedure, (Cmnd 8092/1) pp 1–5.

uniformed branch) whereas the CID (whose officers are plain-clothed and known as 'detectives'), investigate crime and, generally, interrogate suspects. The road traffic department is responsible for maintaining road safety and for the prosecution of road traffic offenders. Many police forces have other specialist departments: for example, the Metropolitan Police has a number of specialist CID departments, such as the serious crime squad (C1), the company fraud squad (C6), the flying squad (C8) and the anti-terrorist squad (C13). The assistance of the expertise of the Metropolitan Police Force departments is also available to any force in England and Wales which requests their help in carrying out an investigation. The Metropolitan Police also have responsibility for certain national policing duties, such as the protection of Royalty and visiting dignatories (the Royal and Diplomatic Protection Squad) and security (the Special Branch).[11] Some police forces also maintain uniformed 'task forces' for availability in emergencies, for example, the Instant Response Units in the Metropolitan Police Area.

The ranks in the police force are as follows:

Metropolitan	*Others*
Commissioner	Chief constable
Deputy commissioner	Deputy chief constable
Assistant commissioner	Assistant chief constable
Deputy assistant commissioner	
Commander	
Chief superintendent	
Superintendent	
Chief inspector	
Inspector	
Sergeant	
Constable	

CID and uniformed ranks coincide up to Commander level in the Metropolitan Police and Chief Superintendent level in other forces.

On a day-to-day level solicitors' contact with the police will rarely be at a level above that of inspector. Most police stations are run by a uniformed inspector (although there may be upward or downward variation depending on size). Routine CID work is carried out by detective constables and detective sergeants under the supervision of higher ranks thus the officer in operational charge of the case is unlikely to be a detective inspector or above unless the offence is serious.[12]

(3) Powers to investigate versus individual rights

Each individual police officer holds his or her commission from the Queen. He is not, in theory, an agent of the police force to which he is attached or of central government. He has no greater powers than any other citizen save in so far as he is given powers either at common law or by statute. In reality, however, he is invested with a wide range of powers to assist him in crime prevention and detection. Broadly, these are:

11 For further information see Criminal Justice in Britain, HMSO. 'Policing London' published quarterly by the GLC also provides much valuable background information concerning the organisation of the Metropolitan Police Force. It should be noted that some local forces also maintain a Special Branch.

12 For further information as to the administrative divisions within the Metropolitan Police see Policing London (1982) September, p 7 and (1983) October/November, p 8.

- to *stop and search* persons on reasonable suspicion;[13]
- to *arrest* persons either under a warrant or (on reasonable suspicion) without warrant and search them;
- to *enter and search* premises for persons, the proceeds of crime or evidence thereof, and to *seize* things found there either without warrant or under a search warrant;
- to *detain* arrested persons for questioning;
- to *take fingerprints*, and other body specimens and photographs;
- to use *reasonable force* in the exercise of such powers.[14]

In the course of an investigation, police officers may also invite an accused person to attend on an identification parade and may, in limited circumstances, apply to the Home Secretary for permission to intercept telephone calls.[15] Police officers also have at their disposal an increasingly sophisticated array of technological hardware for long-range surveillance and data storage and retrieval.[16] Nevertheless, the powers to arrest, search and interrogate suspects are still those most relied upon in investigating crime.

The suspect, on the face of it, lacks the same impressive backup to assist him in asserting his innocence. He does, however, possess four important 'rights'. The first of these is what has come to be known as the 'right of silence'. Under this not only is the suspect entitled to refuse to answer questions at every stage in a criminal investigation, but (with the exception of alibi evidence) he can also keep back any fact which would exculpate him until his trial. Indeed he is perfectly entitled to refuse to give evidence at his trial at all.[17] He may say,

'Ask me no question. I shall answer none. Prove your case.'

If he exercises this 'right' at any stage the court or jury may not infer that such silence is in itself evidence of guilt.[18] Secondly, various provisions of the Police and Criminal Evidence Act 1984 and the Codes of Pratice are designed to ensure that not only is the 'right of silence' protected, but that a suspect should be properly treated whilst in detention and (save in exceptional circumstances) be entitled to legal advice.

The final two 'rights' belong more properly to the law of evidence but are

---

13 The concept of 'reasonable suspicion' is a recurrent theme. See further Bevan and Lidstone *A Guide to the Police and Criminal Evidence Act 1984*. Butterworths (1985) p 5 et seq.

14 Criminal Law Act 1967, s 3 (which has not been repealed by the Police and Criminal Evidence Act 1984) provides that, 'a *person* may use such force as is reasonable in the circumstances in the prevention of crime, or in effecting or assisting in the lawful arrest of offenders or suspected offenders or of persons unlawfully at large'. S 117 of the Police and Criminal Evidence Act 1984 provides that, 'a *police officer* may use reasonable force, *if necessary*, in the exercise of any power conferred by the Act unless the exercise of that power requires the consent of some person other than a police officer'. See further Bevan and Lidstone (op cit) p 167 et seq.

15 The Interception of Communications Bill (1985) deals with 'telephone tapping' and allied matters. For the background to the Bill see 'The Interception of Communications in the United Kingdom' (1985) Cmnd 9438 HMSO: see also *Malone v United Kingdom* (1985) 7 EHRR 17.

16 For an interesting background article on the use of computers within the Metropolitan Police see Policing London (1983) April/May, p 8. Under s 28 of the Data Protection Act 1984 a subject may be refused access to his data if this would prejudice 'prevention or detection of crime or the prosecution or apprehension of offenders'.

17 Note however that if he does give evidence he may be asked any question in cross-examination notwithstanding that it would tend to criminate as to the offence charged: Criminal Evidence Act 1898, s 1(e), see generally p 150, post.

18 For a further discussion of inferences that may be drawn from an accused's silence under questioning or failure to give evidence see p 141, post. The underlying rationale of the rule is the maxim 'nemo renetur se ipsum prodere', ie 'no one can be required to be his own betrayer'. See *R v Sang* [1980] AC 402 at p 455 per Lord Scarman.

nevertheless so central to the investigation and prosecution process that it is necessary to be aware of them from the outset. One is the 'presumption of innocence' whereby the prosecution must prove every element of their case beyond reasonable doubt and the other is the protection afforded by the judicial control over the admission of confessions and other unfairly obtained evidence.

2 POLICE POWERS AND THE POLICE AND CRIMINAL EVIDENCE ACT 1984

Police powers have been radically altered by the 1984 Act. It is important to realise however that this Act is not a fully comprehensive code. In some respects it adds to pre-existing powers (for example 'stop and search') in others it replaces the earlier law entirely (for example powers of arrest). The most revolutionary changes are contained in Parts IV to VI which set out detailed new provisions governing police powers to detain, interrogate and search arrested persons. Their powers are further regulated by four Codes of Practice issued by the Home Secretary under s 66 of the 1984 Act governing:

  (i) Detention, Treatment and Questioning of Persons by the Police (the 'Detention Code');
 (ii) Identification of Persons Suspected of Crime (the 'Identification Code');
(iii) Searching of Premises and Seizure of Property (the 'Search of Premises Code'); and
 (iv) Stop and Search (the 'Stop and Search Code').

The Detention and Identification Codes are perhaps the most important. They replace and extend the Judges Rules and Administrative Directions[18] and the Home Office Circular on Identification Parades.[19] All the Codes are admissible in evidence and any provision thereof must be taken into account in determining any question arising in criminal or civil proceedings if it appears to the court to be relevant.[20] Furthermore, failure to observe any provision of these codes prima facie renders a police officer 'liable to disciplinary proceedings'.[1] Ostensibly, they have greater force than their predecessors, although only time will tell the extent to which they will change the pattern of criminal investigation.

3 DETENTION WITHOUT ARREST: 'STOP AND SEARCH'

The police have no general power to question, stop or search members of the public without their consent:[2] the exercise of such powers is generally dependent upon the person having first been *lawfully arrested*. There are,

18 As annexed to Home Office Circular No 89/1978.
19 As annexed to Home Office Circular No 109/1978.
20 Police and Criminal Evidence Act 1984, s 67(11). The codes are supplemented by 'Notes for Guidance' which although not provisions of the codes provide guidance as to their application and interpretation.
 1 Ibid, s 67(8). A breach of the provisions of any code shall not of itself render a police officer liable to any criminal or civil proceedings: ibid, s 67(10). See further Bevan and Lidstone (op cit) p 311 et seq.
 2 See eg *Rice v Connolly* [1966] 2 QB 414 and *Kenlin v Gardiner* [1967] 2 QB 510 and *Collins v Wilcock* [1984] 3 All ER 374. Note 1B to the Detention Code recognises that the 'duty' of citizens to help the police is civic rather than legal.

however, a number of important statutory provisions entitling the police to 'stop and search' members of the public even where there are no independent grounds for arrest.[3]

(1) Statutory powers of stop and search

Part I of the 1984 Act has done two things. Firstly, it has extended police powers of stop and search whilst leaving existing powers more or less unchanged. Secondly, it has made the exercise of *any* such power subject to statutory safeguards, and to the 'Stop and Search Code'.

(a) Stop and search under the 1984 Act: s 1

A police officer[4] may search any person or vehicle[5] (including an unattended vehicle) found in a public place,[6] for 'stolen or prohibited articles' and detain the person or vehicle for a reasonable period for such purpose subject to the essential precondition that he has reasonable grounds for suspecting that he will find such articles. Reasonable force may be used 'if necessary'.

A 'prohibited article'[7] is defined as:

   (i) an offensive weapon;[8] or
   (ii) an article made or adapted for use in the course of or in connection with burglary, theft, an offence under s 12 (taking a conveyance without authority) or s 15 (obtaining property by deception) of the Theft Act 1968.[9]

For the first time the police therefore have power to stop and search persons on their way to football matches or public demonstrations for offensive weapons *provided* that they reasonably suspect that they will find such articles.[9a]

3 There is considerable controversy over the effectiveness of these powers as an aid in crime prevention especially in view of the damaging effect that their injudicious exercise may have in community relations. The notes for guidance to para 1 of the Stop and Search Code have advised that such powers should be used 'responsibly and sparingly'. The arrest rate from such stops appears to be low. See Royal Commission on Criminal Procedure: Investigation and Prosecution of Criminal Offences in England and Wales (Cmnd 8092/1) Appendices 2 and 3; Steer, Uncovering Crime, The Police Role, Royal Commission on Criminal Procedure Research Study No 6 HMSO 1980 and McConville, 'Search of Persons and Premises: New Data from London' [1983] Crim LR 605. For a contrary view see 'The use, effectiveness and impact of police stop and search powers'. Willis (1983) Home Office.
4 Either in uniform or plain clothes: if he is not in uniform he must produce documentary evidence that he is a police officer: Police and Criminal Evidence Act 1984, s 2(2).
5 A police officer has no power to stop a vehicle unless he is in uniform: 1984 Act, s 2(9)(b).
6 Or any other place, other than a dwelling, to which people have ready access at the time when he proposes to exercise the power: 1984 Act, s 1(1). A police officer may not search a person found in a garden, yard or other land occupied with the dwelling unless he reasonably believes that he does not reside there or have the occupier's permission to be there: ibid, s 1(4). Similar rules apply to vehicles: ibid, s 1(5).
7 Ibid, s 1(7). See further Bevan and Lidstone (op cit) chapter 3 and Hargeaves and Levinson *A practitioner's guide to the Police and Criminal Evidence Act* 1984 (1985) Legal Action Group, chapter 2
8 Any article made or adapted for use for causing injury to persons or intended by the person having it with him for such use by him or by some other persons: ibid, s 1(9).
9 Ibid, s 1(8).
9a Persons entering sports grounds may be searched, with their consent, as a condition of entry. Nothing in the 1984 Act or the Stop and Search Code affects this: see Stop and Search Code, para 4, note 4A.

(b) *Other statutory powers*

Some fourteen other independent powers still exist.[10] The most important of these are the powers to stop and search for controlled drugs,[11] firearms[12] and evidence of terrorist offences.[13]

(2) Statutory safeguards: 1984 Act, ss 2 and 3

Whenever a 'stop' under any of the foregoing powers[14] leads to a 'search'[15] the following procedures must be observed.

(a) *Before* the search is commenced the officer must take reasonable steps to:
   (i) provide *documentary evidence* that he is a police officer (if not in uniform); and
   (ii) give his *name* and the *police station* to which he is attached to the person to be searched, *explain* to him the *object* and grounds of the search, and *inform him* of his right to receive a copy of the written search record.[16]
(b) The person or vehicle to be searched may only be detained for such time as is reasonably required for the search to be carried out.[17]
(c) The search must be carried out either at the place of the 'stop' or nearby.[18]
(d) Persons searched may not be required to remove any of their clothing in public other than their outer coat, jacket or gloves;[19]
(e) Whenever a search has been carried out[20] the officer *must*, if practicable, make a *written record* of the search on its completion; otherwise it must be made as soon afterwards as is practicable. This record must contain certain prescribed information.[1]
(f) The person or owner of the vehicle searched is entitled to a *copy* of the record if he requests it within *12 months* of the date of the search.[2]

Where an unattended vehicle has been searched similar provisions apply.[3] Some of these safeguards are, however, rather less substantial than they

---

10 See the Investigation and Prosecution of Criminal Offences in England and Wales: the Law and Procedure (op cit.) Appendix 1, and Police and Criminal Evidence Act 1984, Sch 7, Part I.
11 Misuse of Drugs Act 1971, s 23.
12 Firearms Act 1968, s 47.
13 Prevention of Terrorism (Temporary Provisions) Act 1984, s 12 and Sch 3. See further Hargreaves and Levinson (op cit) chapter 8.
14 With the exception of searches under Police and Criminal Evidence Act 1984, s 6 (searches of *vehicles* in goods areas by police employed by statutory undertakers) and Aviation Security Act 1982, s 27(2) (searches of *vehicles* leaving airport security areas), and presumably, searches that take place with the person's consent.
15 A police officer need not proceed from a 'stop' to 'search' if it appears to him either that no such search is required or that it is impracticable: 1984 Act, s 2(2).
16 1984 Act, s 2(2) and (3). The person to be searched need not be informed of his rights to receive a copy of the search record if it is not practicable to make one: ibid, ss 2(4) and 3(1).
17 Ibid, s 2(8).
18 Ibid.
19 Ibid, s 2(9)(a).
20 Police are therefore under no duty to record 'stops' which do not lead to 'searches'.
 1 1984 Act, s 3(6). The record must contain the object, grounds, date, time and place of the search, whether anything, and if so what, was found, details of any personal injury and damage to property resulting therefrom and the name of the officer compiling it.
 2 Ibid, s 3(8) and (9).
 3 Ibid, ss 2(6), 3(8) and (9).

initially appear. For example, para (d) does not prevent the police requiring a person to remove further clothing in a police van or at a police station provided that it is 'nearby'. Similarly, the searching officer is only required to make a written record under para (e) 'if practicable'. This effectively absolves him from making a record in searches involving a number of persons, for example, at pop festivals, public demonstrations or football matches.[3a]

(3) Powers to stop vehicles: 1984 Act, s 4

Although s 1 of the 1984 Act does not specifically give a police officer power to 'stop' a vehicle but only to 'detain' it, a uniformed police officer has a general power to stop vehicles[4] provided that he is acting in the execution of his duty.[5] There is, however, no doubt that the police have, on occasions, carried out more widespread and random stops of vehicles[6] the legal basis for which has been disconcertingly vague. Section 4 gives the police power in restricted circumstances to carry out road checks[7] in order to ascertain whether a vehicle is carrying persons who have committed or are intending to commit a serious arrestable offence,[8] are witnesses to such an offence or are unlawfully at large (for example, an escaped prisoner). A road check may generally only be carried out on the written authority of a superintendent,[9] and, in the first instance they may only be authorised for up to *seven days*.[10] It must be restricted to a particular locality.[11] It may, however, be renewed *ad infinitum* for successive periods of up to seven days on the appropriate authority provided that the primary grounds still exist.[12] In cases of urgency an officer of lower rank may authorise a road check[13] but must refer his decision to a superintendent or above as soon as practicable.[14] It should be noted that a road check may only be authorised if there are reasonable grounds' for believing that, for example, a serious arrestable offence has been committed and that the person who committed it is or is about to be in the locality to which the road check relates.[15] Finally, it must be stressed that *section 4* only gives the police power to *stop* vehicles. If

3a See Stop and Search Code, para 4:1.

4 Road Traffic Act 1972, s 159. A person who fails to do so is guilty of an offence under that section.

5 See *R v Waterfield* [1964] 1 QB 164, CCA and *Beard v Wood* [1980] RTR 454. *Steel v Goacher* [1983] RTR 98.

6 See Royal Commission on Criminal Procedure: Report, Cmnd 8092, para 3.31.

7 For definition see 1984 Act, s 4(2). In common parlance a 'roadblock.'

8 Other than a road traffic offence or vehicle excise offence: 1984 Act, s 4(1). For definition of 'serious arrestable offence' see ibid s 116 and Sch 5 and see generally p 49, post. It appears that the police will thus have power to impose road checks where, for example serious public disorder such as mass picketing is likely, see ibid, s 116(6)(a).

9 1984 Act, s 4(3). These powers may in certain circumstances be delegated to a chief inspector: ibid, s 107 and see p 60, post.

10 Ibid, s 4(11).

11 Ibid, s 4(10).

12 Ibid, s 4(12).

13 Ibid, s 4(5).

14 Ibid, s 4(6)–(9). The senior officer to whom this is referred may either confirm or reverse the junior officer's decision.

15 See ibid, s 4(4). Note that where the road check is to search for witnesses to a serious arrestable offence there is no need for there to be reasonable grounds for believing that such persons are in the locality therefore, in theory, if a police force were looking for witnesses to a murder, forces could authorise roadblocks nationwide. Usually the public have been prepared to co-operate voluntarily.

they then wish to search the vehicle or persons in it they require independent grounds.[15a]

(4) The 'Stop and Search Code'

The Code applies to *all* statutory powers of stop and search (other than road checks under s 4). In particular it emphasises the following:

(a) The powers referred to are only exercisable on reasonable suspicion, and should be used responsibly and fairly, so as to avoid creating mistrust in the community (*Para 1:5 and Notes for guidance*).

(b) Persons must be treated courteously and considerately (ibid).

(c) There is no power to detain a person merely in order to find grounds for a search (*Para 2:1*).

(d) Suspicion may be confirmed or eliminated as a result of questioning but cannot be provided by a refusal to answer questions (*Para 2:3*).

(e) Every reasonable effort should be made to reduce embarrassment to a minimum (*Para 3:5*).

(f) Force should only be used as a last resort (*Para 3:1*).

(g) A person should only be detained for so long as it takes to carry out the search; this should usually take no more than a minute or so (*Para 3:2*).

(h) There is no power to detain a person if he is unwilling to give his name and address (*Para 4:.4*).

(i) A record is required for each person searched.[15b] If a person and his vehicle are searched a record must be made in respect of both (*Para 4:6*).

(j) 'Reasonable suspicion' should be based on objective criteria; a 'hunch' is not enough. It requires the same level of suspicion as for arrest without warrant (*Annex B*).

4 ARREST WITHOUT WARRANT AND ANCILLARY POWERS

'Arrest' is a concept of major constitutional importance, since it entails depriving a person of the freedom to go as he pleases. In the context of policing it means much more than that. Once a person is arrested he comes under the physical and psychological control of the arresting officer. After arrest he may, and probably will, be searched and thereafter taken to a police station—each step increasing his awareness of being a captive.[16] Arrest thus marks the commencement of what may be (subject to statutory limitations

15a Eg under ibid s 1 (stop and search), s 17 (power to enter premises), 18 (entry and search after arrest) or s 32 (search upon arrest). Note that a vehicle is 'premises' for the purpose of the 1984 Act: ibid, s 23. For the power to detain a vehicle after it has been stopped under RTA 1972, s 159 see further *Lodwick v Sanders* [1985] 1 All ER 577 and the commentary thereon [1985] Crim LR 210.

15b This must not include a racial description: Stop and Search Code, para 4:5(ii).

16 See generally the Royal Commission on Criminal Procedure Research Study No 1: Irving: Police Interrogation, the Psychological Approach and No 2: Irving: 'A Case Study of Current Practice' (HMSO).

in Part IV of the 1984 Act) a period of detention[17] and interrogation[18] at a police station, leading to the arrested person being charged with an offence or released without charge.

It will be recalled[19] that the prosecution of an offence will normally begin either by summons, or charge preceded by an arrest. Arrest (almost invariably without warrant) tends to be reserved for more serious offences as the statistics contained in the Royal Commission Report on Criminal Procedure shows:[20]

	Summons	*Arrest and Charge*
Indictable	24%	76%
Non-indictable	87%	13%

Police powers of arrest without warrant are now almost exclusively contained in Part III of the 1984 Act. Although the power varies depending upon the category of offence, one of the main effects of Part III has been to create a power of arrest for *every* offence in appropriate cases.

(1) Key definitions

There are three categories of offence:

(a) arrestable offences;
(b) serious arrestable offences; and
(c) other offences.

These distinctions are important because both the power of arrest itself and ancillary powers, such as those to enter and search premises, are wider in the case of arrestable offences. Furthermore, persons arrested on suspicion of having committed a '*serious* arrestable offence' may, in certain circumstances, be detained for questioning, held incommunicado and denied access to a solicitor for longer periods than in the case of the other two categories. Categories (a) and (b) are both defined in the 1984 Act.

(a) Arrestable offence: 1984 Act, s 24(1)

This is defined as:

(i) an offence for which the sentence is fixed by law (for example murder); or
(ii) an offence for which a person aged 21 years or over (not previously

17 Research suggests that most suspects are detained for relatively short periods. See Softley, 'The Police Interrogation Code: An Observational Study in Four Police Stations'; Royal Commission on Criminal Procedure Research Study No 4 Table 2:2 (HMSO). Out of a sample of 218 suspects, 175 (80%) had been charged or released in 9 hours, 215 (98·6%) within 24 hours. A survey carried out by the Metropolitan Police in 1979 showed a similar proportion (95%: n = 48,343)
18 Most interviews are relatively short: see Softley op cit table 5:1. 60% of the sample made a full confession or other damaging admission. It is undoubtedly the case that arrest used more as an aid to police investigation than as a method of securing the accused's attendance at court. This was implicitly recognised in *Holgate-Mohammed v Duke* [1984] AC 437.
19 See pp 4 and 31, ante.
20 Op cit, Appendix. This gives a somewhat misleading picture because the vast proportion of non-indictable offences are motoring offences. By way of contrast the offence of assault on a constable, although summary only, almost invariably involves arrest (87%).

convicted) may be sentenced to five or more years'[1] imprisonment (for example theft, burglary or criminal damage); or

(iii) any offence referred to in s 24(2) of the 1984 Act (for example offences under ss 12 and 25 of the Theft Act 1968).

All three categories extend to conspiring or attempting to commit any of the above offences or inciting, aiding, abetting, counselling or procuring any such offences.[2]

(b) *Serious arrestable offence: 1984 Act, s 116*

Certain arrestable offences will always be 'serious', others *may* be if they satisfy certain prescribed criteria.

(i) Arrestable offences that are always serious. These include murder, manslaughter, rape, serious sexual offences against children and young persons and serious firearms offences.[3]

(ii) Arrestable offences that may be serious. Other arrestable offences are only serious if their commission has led, or is intended or likely to lead to:[4]

– *serious* harm to the security of the state or to public order; or
– *serious* interference with the administration of justice or the investigation of offences or of a particular offence; or
– the death of, or *serious* injury[5] to any person; or
– *substantial* financial gain or *serious* financial loss[6] to any person.

Although a considerable improvement on the definition in the original Bill one can still see problems arising. An offence involving possession of a controlled drug could, for example, be construed as 'serious' even though the only person likely to be seriously injured by it is the person arrested. The greatest area of dispute, however, is likely to be as to the interpretation of 'substantial financial gain' and 'serious financial loss' in the case of offences of dishonesty. Nevertheless it is submitted, that many 'standard' offences of dishonesty will not come within the definition. For example, the fictitious defendants McCARTHY (*Case 1*), JONES (*Case 2*) and TYRRELL (*Case 4*) were arrested for arrestable offences, but it is hard to envisage any of those offences being treated as a 'serious arrestable offence' in the circumstances.

(2) **Powers of arrest without warrant**

These are now wholly contained in Part III of the 1984 Act. The primary powers are those set out in s 24 (arrestable offences) and s 25 (other offences).

---

1 This part of the definition is wider than that contained in s 2(1) of the Criminal Law Act 1967 in that it is not confined to statutory offences. Thus, for example, manslaughter, affray and conspiracy to defraud are now for the first time, arrestable offences. The definition also embraces offences of criminal damage where the value involved does not exceed £400: see p 281 post.
2 1984 Act, s 24(3).
3 1984 Act, Sch 5, Parts I and II.
4 An arrestable offence which consists of making a threat is serious if carrying out the threat would be likely to lead to any of the consequences set out in the 1984 Act, s 116(4).
5 Injury includes any disease, an impairment of the person's physical or mental condition: ibid, s 116(8).
6 'Loss' is to be judged subjectively, ie is it 'serious for the person who suffers it': ibid, s 116(7). If therefore in the course of a burglary a person steals £100 which represents the victim's life savings the offence will come within the s 116 definition.

There are, however, a number of miscellaneous powers which also require brief mention.

(a) Arrestable offences: 1984 Act, s 24

This provides (inter alia) that a police officer[7] may arrest anyone:

(i) *about to*, or whom he has reasonable grounds for suspecting to be about to, commit an arrestable offence;

(ii) *in the act of*, or whom he has reasonable grounds for suspecting to be in the act of, committing such an offence;

(iii) *guilty of*, or whom he has reasonable grounds for suspecting to be guilty of, such an offence, *provided* that he has reasonable grounds for suspecting that such an offence has been committed.

Section 24 thus effectively empowers a police officer to arrest a suspect before, during or after the commission of a suspected arrestable offence. The phrase 'reasonable grounds for suspecting, is a recurrent theme and means something less than prima facie proof.[8] Thus, even if Duncan McCARTHY (*case 1*) were to be subsequently released because it was decided that there was insufficient evidence to charge him, this of itself would not render his original arrest unlawful. Finally, it should be noted that these powers extend to persons *under* 21 even though they may not be sentenced to imprisonment. Thus, John TYRELL (*Case 4*) may be arrested without warrant under s 24.

(b) General power of arrest 1984 Act, s 25

The Act provides the police with a general power of arrest without warrant for non-arrestable (ie *all* other) offences provided that certain conditions are made out.

(i) The power of arrest. A police officer having reasonable grounds for suspecting that any offence other than an arrestable offence *is being* or *has been* attempted or committed may arrest anyone:

– whom he has reasonable grounds to suspect is *in the course* of committing or attempting to commit such an offence; or

– whom he has reasonable grounds to suspect *has* committed or attempted to commit such an offence;

provided that (in any case) it appears to him that *service of a summons* on that person is *impracticable* or *inappropriate* because one of the 'general arrest conditions' are satisfied.

(ii) The general arrest conditions: s 25(3). These are that either:

– the suspect's *name* is unknown to and cannot be ascertained by the officer or he has reasonable grounds for doubting whether a name furnished is that person's real name; or

---

7 Private individuals such as store detectives also have power to arrest for arrestable offences: 1984 Act s 24(4) and (5). The major difference between private individuals and the police is that individuals may only arrest a person whom they reasonably suspect to have committed an arrestable offence *if such an offence has actually been committed*. If it has not, they run the risk of an action in tort for false imprisonment. The effect of the decision in *Walters v WH Smith & Son Ltd*[1914] 1 KB 595 thus remains unchanged.

8 See *Hussien v Chong Fook Kam* [1970] AC 942 PC. See further Bevan and Lidstone (op cit) pp 5 et seq and 136 et seq.

- the suspect has failed to furnish a satisfactory *address for service*[9] or the officer has reasonable grounds for doubting whether an address furnished is a satisfactory address for service; or
- the officer has reasonable grounds for believing that arrest is *necessary* to prevent him from:
    - causing physical injury to himself or any other person;
    - suffering physical injury;
    - causing loss of or damage to property;
    - causing an offence against public decency;[10]
    - causing an unlawful obstruction of the highway; or
- the officer has reasonable grounds for believing that arrest is necessary to *protect* a child or other vulnerable person.

In order to arrest under section 25 two conditions must therefore be complied with. First, there must be reasonable grounds for suspecting that an offence has been committed or attempted eg. Secondly, it must appear that service of a summons is impracticable or inappropriate by reason of one or more of the 'general arrest conditions'. These conditions are extremely wide and will render certain groups, in particular those without a fixed address, liable to arrest for minor offences. They will also no doubt be invoked at public demonstrations in respect of offences such as obstruction of the highway. In addition, they appear to have the indirect effect of requiring citizens to carry some form of identification. Unfortunately, none of the four Codes of Practice give any further guidance as to the exercise of these powers. It would nevertheless be hard to envisage a police officer having grounds for arresting Mary ADAMS (*case 3*) at the scene of the accident, since even if she were to refuse to give her name and address, this could be readily ascertained through the Vehicle Registration Department.

(c) Miscellaneous powers of arrest without warrant

Prior to the coming into force of the 1984 Act there were no less than one hundred and nine separate powers of arrest without warrant.[11] These have all now been abolished[12] subject to certain important exceptions.[13] It must be stressed that when arresting under any of these retained provisions the 'general arrest conditions' in s 25 do not have to be met.

(i) Statutory powers preserved by 1984 Act, Sch 2. Powers of arrest under twenty-one different statutes have been preserved, the most important being:

Public Order Act 1936, s 7(3): persons reasonably suspected to be committing offences under the 1936 Act;

---

9 An address is satisfactory if it appears that the person will be at it for a sufficiently long period for it to be possible to serve him with a summons, or some other nominated person will accept service or a summons at it: 1984 Act, s 25(4).
10 Arrest is only authorised under this provision if members of the public going about their normal business cannot reasonably be expected to avoid the person: ibid, s 25(5). 'Public decency' is not defined. For a full discussion of the implications of s 25: see Bevan and Lidstone (op cit) p 139 et seq.
11 See in the Investigation and Prosecution of Criminal Offences in England and Wales (op cit) Appendix 9.
12 1984, s 26(1).
13 Ibid, s 26(2).

Road Traffic Act 1972, ss 5(5) and 7: blood/alcohol offences, and s 100: driving whilst disqualified;

Bail Act 1976, s 7: reasonable suspicion that person on bail is likely to abscond;

Criminal Law Act 1977, ss 6–10: offences of statutory trespass under the 1977 Act; and

Prevention of Terrorism (Temporary Provisions) Act 1984, ss 12 and 13.

(ii) Common law power of arrest for breach of the peace. Section 26 of the 1984 Act only abolishes *statutory* powers of arrest without warrant, the common law power relating to breaches of the peace has thus been preserved. Any person may arrest and detain a person who has committed a breach of the peace in his presence, or when there is a threat of a breach of the peace being renewed, or when the person effecting the arrest reasonably and honestly believes that a breach will otherwise be committed in the immediate future.[14] A 'breach of the peace' occurs whenever:

harm is done or likely to be done to a person, or, in his presence, to his property; or

a person is put in fear of being so harmed through an assault, affray, riot, unlawful assembly or other disturbance.[15]

This common law power is still likely, therefore, to be of considerable practical importance, for example at public demonstrations[16] if none of the 'general arrest conditions' can be satisfied.

(iii) Power to arrest for fingerprinting: 1984 Act, s 27. Where a person has been convicted of a 'recordable offence'[17] in respect of which his fingerprints have not been taken he may be arrested if he refuses to comply with a police officer's request to attend at a police station for fingerprinting provided that:

– he has not at any time been in police detention for the offence;

– the request is made within *one month* of conviction; and

– he has been given at least *seven days* within which to attend.

(3) Definition of arrest

The 1984 Act makes no attempt to define 'arrest' and accordingly the pre-Act cases on the topic are unaffected.[18] A person is 'arrested' either when he is seized or touched with a view to restraint or he has otherwise been deprived of his liberty to go where he pleases. Words may, therefore, be sufficient although there is no prescribed formula. An officer may use reasonable force, if necessary, in order to effect an arrest[19] and may enter and search premises to this end when the offence is arrestable or he is acting under a warrant.[20] Irving[1] describes commonplace arrest situations as follows:

14 See *R v Howell* [1982] QB 416 and *Albert v Lavin* [1982] AC 546.
15 Ibid.
16 For limitations on its use see *R v Chief Constable of Devon and Cornwall, ex p Central Electricity Generating Board* [1982] QB 458.
17 To be defined under regulations to be made by the Home Secretary under the 1984 Act, ss 27(4) and 118(1). It is likely to include all indictable only and either way offences and imprisonable summary only offences.
18 See for example *R v Inwood* [1973] 2 All ER 645, CA and *Spicer v Holt* [1977] AC 987, HL and *Hart v Chief Constable of Kent* [1983] RTR 484.
19 Criminal Law Act 1967, s 3 and Police and Criminal Evidence Act 1984, s 117.
20 1984 Act, s 17.
1 Op cit, p 100.

'The suspect may be arrested in a highly formal manner with a full caution or he may merely be told that he is "nicked". Those who have been questioned as suspects many times before do not appear to expect anything but the briefest explanation or formalities. However, suspects are apparently in no doubt about the fact that they are being arrested, about the details of the offence involved and the fact that they are under caution.'

(4) Duties and powers after arrest

A number of important powers and duties arise after a person has been arrested, in particular:

(a) the *duty* to caution him;
(b) the *duty* to inform him that he is under arrest and the grounds thereof;
(c) the *power* to search him;
(d) the *power* (in the case of arrestable offences) to search his premises; and
(e) (subject to a power of postponement) the *duty* to take him to a police station as soon as practicable after arrest.

(a) Duty to caution: Detention Code, para 10

This provides that as soon as a police officer has grounds to suspect a person of an offence, no questions (or further questions) must be put to him for the purpose of obtaining evidence relating to the offence until he has been cautioned in the following terms:

'You do not have to say anything unless you wish to do so, but what you say may be given in evidence.'

A person *must*, in any event be cautioned on arrest unless this is impracticable because of that person's condition or behaviour at that time or he is already under caution. The officer must also record the time when this was given in his pocket book. This is the first of several occasions upon which the *Paragraph 10* caution is required to be given. These will be dealt with later in the chapter. Minor verbal deviations will not invalidate the caution provided that its sense is preserved. The rationale behind the requirement is that it reminds the suspect of his 'right of silence'. The notes for guidance to *Paragraph 10* thus provide that where the suspect is unclear as to the significance of the caution, the officer administrating it should explain the 'right to silence' to him although the suspect should not be left with the false impression that failure to co-operate will not have any effect on his immediate treatment. The *Paragraph 10* caution is, however, somewhat of a 'paper tiger' in that failure to administrate it is not, of itself, likely to render in admissible any incriminating statements made by the accused in response to police questioning.[1a]

(b) Duty to inform person of arrest and grounds thereof: 1984 Act, s 28

Even though a police officer is acting within the powers of arrest conferred on him, *any* arrest will be *unlawful* unless as soon as practicable the person arrested is:

1a On the admittedly cynical prediction that the decision in *R v Prager* [1972] 1 All ER 1114 will be followed (failure to caution under Judges Rules, Rule II).

(i) informed that he is under arrest;[2] and

(ii) informed of the ground[3] for arrest (even if this is obvious).

The above information need not be supplied if it is not reasonably practicable to do so because the person arrested has escaped before it could be given.[4]

(c) *Search of arrested persons: 1984 Act, ss 32, 54 and 55*

Arrested persons may be liable to search at two stages. Firstly, after arrest otherwise than at a police station (s 32) and secondly, after arrival at a police station or arrest there (ss 54 and 55).

Upon arrest at a place other than at a police station s 32 provides that the person arrested may be searched by a police officer if there are reasonable grounds for believing that:

(i) he may present a danger to himself or others; or

(ii) he has on him any article which he might use to assist him in escape or which might be evidence relating to an offence.[5]

The power under s 32 differs from the 'stop and search' powers considered earlier in that it may only be exercised *after* the person has been arrested. Having said that, it effectively gives the police the power to search arrested persons more or less as a matter of routine. It would be difficult to argue, for example, that the police were acting illegally when they searched McCarthy (*case 1*) and Tyrell (*case 4*) after arrest. On the other hand any purported search of Mary Adams (*case 3*) under s 32 would have been unlawful because she was not arrested. The police have wide powers to seize and detain any articles they find which come within the above categories[6] but searches away from a police station tend to be cursory. Searches at a police station under s 54 or s 55 will be more thorough and are considered later in the chapter.

(d) *Power to enter and search premises: 1984 Act, ss 17, 18 and 32*

The police may need to enter and search premises for two purposes. Firstly, to search for the person whom they are seeking to arrest, and secondly in order to search for evidence or the proceeds of crime. Broadly, the 1984 Act gives them powers:

(i) prior to arrest, to enter and search premises for a *person* for the purpose of arresting him under a warrant for any offence or arresting him without warrant for an *arrestable* offence (s 17); and

(ii) after arrest for an *arrestable* offence, to enter and search premises

---

2 S 28(1) of the 1984 Act appears to require that the accused be specifically told that he is 'under arrest'.

3 Ibid s 28(3) the reasons given must be of sufficient detail so that he can understand the circumstances in which he is being arrested: *R v Telfer* [1976] Crim LR 562 (technical language need not be used). See also *Gelberg v Miller* [1961] 1 All ER 291. Where arrest is under s 25 ibid the suspect should thus be told which of the 'general arrest conditions' apply.

4 Ibid s 28(5).

5 Ibid, s 32(2).

6 Ibid, s 32(9) and see generally p 93, post. For searches of persons under the Prevention of Terrorism (Temporary Provisions) Act 1984 see ibid Sch 3, para 6.

occupied or controlled by the arrested person in order to search for *evidence* relating to *that* offence or *other arrestable offences* (s 18); and

(iii) after arrest for *any* offence, to enter and search premises on which the person arrested was found, to search for *evidence* relating to *that* offence (s 32).

As with personal searches the police have wide powers to seize and retain articles found in the course of such searches.[7]

(e) Duty to take arrested persons to a police station as soon as practicable: 1984 Act, s 30

The vast majority of arrests will take place away from a police station. After arrest a person must normally be taken to a 'designated police station', defined as a station to be used for the purpose of detaining arrested persons,[8] as soon as practicable.[8a] This step may only be postponed if the arrested person's presence elsewhere, 'is necessary in order to carry out such investigations as it is reasonable to carry out immediately'. The police might, for example, wish to search a suspect's home for evidence, or for the proceeds of a crime in order to forestall its disposal by others or try to find persons to confirm or refute an alibi.[9] Any delay and the reasons for it must be recorded when the person arrested first arrives at a police station.[10]

5 AFTER ARREST—DETENTION AT THE POLICE STATION

Once arrested a person will normally be taken back to a police station within 30 minutes.[11] A small proportion[12] of suspects may initially have attended voluntarily in the time honoured phrase, to 'help the police with their enquiries'. Since the police have no general power to detain a person for questioning,[13] s 29 of the 1984 Act provides that any person who attends voluntarily at a police station or accompanies a police officer to a station without having been arrested[14] shall:

---

7 1984 Act ss 19–22. For a more detailed consideration of powers of entry, search and seizure see p 84 et seq post.
8 Ibid s 35. Such stations are to be nominated by the Chief Officer of Police for the relevant area. An arrested person may be taken to a police station other than a 'designated police station in certain circumstances': ibid, s 32(3)–(5) and see p 58, post. If, however, he is to be detained for more than 6 hours after his arrival at the first police station he must be transferred to a 'designated station'.
8a Ibid, s 30(10).
9 An example given by Lord Denning MR in *Dallison v Caffery* [1965] 1 QB 348. See also *McCarrick v Oxford* [1983] RTR 117, CA.
10 1984 Act, s 30(11).
11 See Softley (op cit) p 60.
12 See Softley (op cit) p 60 and Irving (op cit) p 101.
13 The leading cases on detention for questioning without arrest are still therefore good authority: see eg *R v Lemsatef* [1977] 2 All ER 835, CA and *R v Houghton* (1978) 142 JP 402, CA. An arrest of a suspect *for the purpose of questioning* is however lawful provided that *grounds existed for the original arrest*: see *Holgate-Mohammed v Duke* [1984] AC 437, HL.
14 The Detention Code is however remarkably silent as to the treatment of such persons. They do not for example come within the jurisdiction of the custody officer at all prior to arrest and no written information is required to be kept concerning the time spent at the police station prior to arrest. See further p 84, post.

(i) be free to leave unless and until he is placed under arrest; and

(ii) be informed at once that he is under arrest if a decision is taken to prevent him leaving.

Whether under arrest or not, once a suspect is inside a police station, he is on police 'territory' in an environment which to many will be alien, threatening and disorientating.[15]

Whether these parts of the 1984 Act which deal with the detention and interviewing of suspects will bring about revolutionary changes will only become apparent once the Act and the Detention Code have been in operation for some time. A useful starting point is to consider the pre-1984 Act routine for the processing of arrested persons. This is well summarised by Softley:[16]

'What happens to a suspect when he is arrested and taken to a police station will to some extent depend on the facilities of the station, the practice of the force and the nature of the case; but every suspect will be booked in, searched and booked out. Typically, he will be taken to the charge room where his particulars will be taken and where he will be searched. All property on his person will be listed and retained by the police until he is released. He will be invited to sign the list as a true record and will be asked whether he wants anyone informed of his whereabouts. (The police will need to contact the parents of juveniles and will ask whether anyone is at home.) Usually the police will wish to interview the suspect. They may do this straightaway, but frequently there will be some delay before they are ready to proceed. During this period, juveniles may be detained in a detention room and adults in a cell. If the police charge the suspect, they will need to prepare a statement of his antecedents for the court, and may take fingerprints and photographs for their records before he is bailed or returned to the cells. The whole process can take as little as 30 minutes, but, in serious and exceptional cases, it may take longer than 24 hours.

'Before deciding whether to charge a suspect, or inform him that he may be prosecuted, the police may need to interview witnesses and get statements from them; they may need to arrange an identity parade, or to check the premises from which they believe property was stolen; they may need to ask the suspect to accompany them while, with his consent, they search his house or car. In one case, which was observed in a pilot study, the police needed two days to check the alibi of a suspect who was eventually charged with robbing a bank. Enquiries are sometimes delayed because a suspect refuses to give his name and address, or is too drunk to assist the police. In cases involving juveniles, problems sometimes arise in contacting parents or persuading an angry father to attend the police station.'

It remains to be seen whether this 'routine'[17] will fundamentally change. The major innovations will now be considered.

---

15 These and other situational factors are discussed by Irving (op cit) pp 27–43.

16 Softley (op cit) p 60. See also 'Policing London' (1984) November/December, p 8.

17 For further background information on processing of suspects, see Irving (op cit) pp 100–118.

(1) The ground rules for detention: the 1984 Act and the Detention Code

Section 34(1) of the 1984 Act provides that a person arrested for an offence shall not be kept in police detention except[18] in accordance with the provisions of Part IV (ss 33–52) of the Act. Part V (ss 53–65) contains detailed provisions as to the questioning and treatment of persons in police detention. Detention and interviewing is also regulated by the 'Detention Code'. The status of the Codes of Practice has already been discussed. The Detention Code is by far the longest and is intended to serve as a handbook for police officers, its express intention being:

> 'to provide strengthened safeguards for the suspect and clear and workable guidelines for the police.'

Copies of all the codes are to be freely available at police stations, not only to the police, but also to arrested persons, their friends and legal representatives.

(2) Key definitions

Part IV of the 1984 Act purports, in conjunction with the Detention Code, to set up a rigid administrative infrastructure for the processing of persons in detention, specifying time limits within which decisions must be taken, by whom those decisions are to be taken and the extent to which they must be recorded in writing. The major functionary of this new regime is the 'custody officer' and his primary recording medium is the 'custody record'. High level decisions must be referred to a 'superintendent' or, on occasions, an 'inspector'. 'Time limits' appear to play a major role at every stage. All these terms are dealt with in the 1984 Act and require further consideration.

'Custody officer': 1984 Act, s 36

Every 'designated police station'[19] must have at least one 'custody officer' whose major duties and powers are:

– to *ascertain* the *property* that an arrested person has with him and if necessary to search him for this purpose;[20]

– *to investigate* as soon as practicable whether or not there is *sufficient evidence to charge* an arrested person with the offence for which he was arrested;[1]

– *to authorise* the arrested person's *continued detention* under the 1984 Act either before or after he has been charged;[2]

---

18 Part IV does not apply to persons under 14 arrested without warrant otherwise than for homicide (ibid, s 52). See further p 311, post. Part IV also does not affect the powers referred to in s 51, in particular, powers of arrest and detention etc under the Prevention of Terrorism (Temporary Provisions) Act 1984 or the Immigration Act 1971. A person is not in 'police detention' until he either (i) arrives at a police station after arrest elsewhere or (ii) is arrested at a police station after having attended voluntarily: 1984 Act, s 118(2). The implications of this definition are fully discussed in Bevan and Lidstone (op cit) at p 178.
19 Designated by the Chief Officer of Police as one to be used for the purposes of detaining arrested persons.
20 1984 Act, s 54.
1 Ibid, s 37(1) and (10).
2 Ibid, ss 37(2) and 38(1).

- *to consider* the grant of *bail* where appropriate;[3]
- *to ensure* that all persons in police detention are treated in accordance with the provisions of the Act and the the Detention Code and that all required matters are recorded in a person's 'custody record'.[4]
- *to release* a person if at any time he becomes aware that a ground for his detention under Part IV of the 1984 Act no longer exists[4a]

The Act also provides that no person may be appointed custody officer unless he is at least a sergeant and that no officer may carry out the functions of the custody officer if he is involved in the investigation of the offence at the time that the function falls to be performed.[5]

The Act therefore appears to provide substantial protection for persons arrested in that their treatment at every stage is under the supervision of an independent and relatively senior police officer. His role, however, does not greatly differ from that of his predecessor, the station sergeant, whose functions were not dissimilar. Furthermore, unless the station is 'designated' it will not have a custody officer at all. An arrested person may only be taken in the first instance to a non-designated station in the limited circumstances set out in s 30 of the 1984 Act[6] and must be transferred to a designated station within six hours if not released. At non-designated stations, mainly those in rural areas, the duties of the custody officer must be carried out by an officer who is not involved in the investigation if such officer is 'readily available'.[7] Even at designated stations, however, an officer of *any rank* may perform the custody officer's functions if the latter is not 'readily available.[8]'

In addition, the custody officer's supervisory control over persons detained for questioning is likely to be limited. Although he is responsible for deciding whether or not there are grounds for detaining a suspect for questioning[9] and whether or not he should be delivered into the custody of the investigating officer for this purpose, once custody of the suspect is transferred, the duties to ensure that the provisions of the Act and Code are observed are transferred to the investigating officer. Although the latter is under a duty to report back to the custody officer, he will be in effective control of the suspect.[10] The Act anticipates that where the officer who made or authorised

---

3 1984 Act, ss 37(2) and 38(1).

4 Ibid, s 39 and Detention Code, para 2.3.

4a Ibid, s 34(2).

5 Ibid, s 36(3) and (5).

6 Broadly, either where there is no designated station in the locality and it does not appear necessary to keep the arrested person in detention for more than 6 hours or the arresting officer has no available assistance and he cannot take the arrested person to a designated police station without injury to any person (including the arrestee): 1984 Act, s 30(3)-(5).

7 Ibid, s 36(7). If no such officer is available the function shall be carried out by the officer who took him to the station or any other officer.

8 Ibid, s 36(4).

9 Ibid, s 37(2).

10 Ibid, s 39(2) provides that where a custody officer transfers a person to the custody of an investigating officer his duty to secure compliance with the Act and Codes of Practice (but not his duty to record prescribed information on a custody record) pass to the investigating officer who has a duty to report back if and when the suspect is returned to the custody of the custody officer: ibid, s 39(3). The decision as to whether to transfer custody is the responsibility of the custody officer: Detention Code, para 12.1.

the arrest is of a higher rank than the custody officer, disputes may arise as to the observance of the provisions of the Act and Codes. Where an officer of higher rank in any situation seeks to override the authority of the custody officer in relation to the arrested person's detention the custody officer must at once refer the matter to an officer of at least superintendent rank who is responsible for the police station.[11] The Act is silent as to what happens next, but it would seem that there is nothing to prevent the superintendent backing the senior officer provided that this does not infringe the provisions of the 1984 Act or any Code of Practice.

'Custody record'

The custody officer is required to open a separate custody record in respect of every person in police detention as soon as practicable[12] and is responsible for its accuracy and completeness.[13] This important document must (inter alia):

- *specify* the grounds for detaining a person either before or after charge;[14]

- *confirm* that a person whose detention has been authorised has received a written notice informing him (inter alia) of his right to legal advice before questioning;[15]

- *properly record* all property in the person's possession at the time of arrest;[16]

- *record* any request given for legal advice;[17]

- *record* prescribed details concerning intimate searches[18] and the taking of body samples;[19]

- *specify the reason* for holding him incommunicado or withholding access to legal advice (serious arrestable offences only);[20]

- *record details* of any request for legal advice';[1]

- *give details* of meals given during detention;[2]

- *record* any complaint about treatment since arrest;[3]

- *record* the time or times at which the person is not in the custody of the custody officer and the reason;[4]

---

11 1984 Act, s 39(6).
12 Detention Code, para 2.1. This includes a person who is arrested after attending voluntarily.
13 Ibid, para 2.3 and 1984 Act, s 39(1)(b).
14 1984 Act, ss 37(4) and 38(3), and Detention Code, para 3.10.
15 Detention Code, para 3.2. The written notice must inform the suspect of his rights: (i) to inform someone of his detention (s 56); (ii) to legal advice (s 58); (iii) to consult copies of the Codes of Practice; and (iv) receive a copy of his custody record.
16 1984 Act, s 54(2).
17 Ibid, s 58(2).
18 Ibid, s 55(10).
19 Ibid, ss 62(8) and 63(9).
20 Ibid, ss 56(6) and 58(9).
 1 Detention Code, para 6.11.
 2 Ibid, para 8.7.
 3 Ibid, para 9.3.
 4 Ibid, para 12.9

- *record* any complaint made during the course of an interview;[5]

- *record the reason* for interviewing a mentally ill or handicapped person in the absence of an adult or a juvenile in the absence of a parent or guardian;[6]

  record details concerning reviews of detention including the reason for any postponement;[7]

- *record the reasons* for detaining a person beyond 24 hours (serious arrestable offences only).[8]

It can be seen that this document may be of crucial importance during the course of a trial.[9] Accordingly the person detained or his legal representative is entitled to be supplied on request with a copy of the relevant record within 12 months of leaving police custody.[9a]

'Superintendent' and 'inspector': 1984 Act, s 107

There are a number of important powers that are exercisable only by an officer of at least one or other of the above ranks. For example, only a superintendent may authorise an intimate body search or the continued detention of a person accused of a serious arrestable offence beyond 24 hours after arrest. Section 107 provides that the powers of a superintendent or inspector may be exercised by a chief inspector or sergeant respectively if that officer has been so authorised by an officer of at least chief superintendent rank.

'Time limits': 1984 Act, s 45(2)

Part IV of the 1984 Act prescribes various time limits in which powers must be exercised or duties performed. Much of the apparent protection that this rigid time scale lays down is, however, diluted by s 45(2) which provides that:

'Any reference in Part IV of this Act to a period of time or time of day is to be treated as approximate only.'

It remains to be seen how much latitude the courts will give to the police on important matters such as infringement of detention periods.

(3) Reviews of detention: 1984 Act, s 40

A major change introduced by the Act is to make the detention of all persons arrested for an offence[10] subject to periodical review whether or not they

---

5 Detention Code, para 12.8.
6 Ibid, annex C.
7 Ibid, paras 16.3 and 16.5; 1984 Act, s 40(7).
8 1984 Act, s 42(5)(b).
9 All entries in custody and interview records must be timed and signed by the maker: Detention Code, para 2.5. For a discussion as to the extent to which such records will be admitted see chapter 5, p 187-8, post. The custody record is not wholly innovatory. Much of the information it will contain was previously recorded in the station Occurrence Book.
9a Detention Code, para 2.4. They should also be allowed, on reasonable notice, to inspect the original: ibid, Note for Guidance.
10 This includes persons arrested for breathalyser offences under Road Traffic Act 1972, s 7(5).

have been charged.[11] The duties under s 40 must be carried out by the 'review officer' who will be either:

- the 'custody officer' if the person has been charged; or
- an inspector or above not directly involved in the investigation if the person has not yet been charged.

The reviews must take place as following:

- first review: not later than *six hours* after the first authorisation of detention (*not* arrived at a police station);
- thereafter: at *nine hourly* intervals.

In carrying out the review the review officer must consider whether the grounds for detention[12] have ceased to apply, in which case the person *must* be released either with or without bail.[13] The person whose detention is subject to review or his solicitor[14] (if available) must be given the opportunity to make representations[15] either orally[16] or in writing about the detention unless the detained person is asleep and his solicitor is not available.

On the face of it, therefore, justification for the detention of all arrested persons is subject to continuing duties of review and recording. These safeguards are not, however, as potent as they might initially appear for two reasons. First, the time limits under the Act are only 'approximate'[17] and secondly, review may be postponed if:

(i) the person is being questioned and the review officer is satisfied that an interruption would prejudice the investigation; or
(ii) no review officer or custody officer is readily available; or
(iii) it is not practicable in the circumstances to carry out the review.[18]

If review is postponed, it must be carried out as soon as practicable[19] and the reason for the postponement recorded on the custody record.[20] Nevertheless the procedure affords no real protection to a person who is being held and interrogated without charge.

---

11 S 40 therefore applies to all persons detained under the Act including those accused of 'serious arrestable offences' whose detention without charge beyond 24 hours has been authorised by a superintendent or magistrates' court under ss 42 and 43 of the 1984 Act.
12 See pp 62 et seq, post.
13 1984 Act, ss 37(1) and 38(1) as applied by s 40(8) and (10) respectively.
14 Representations may be made by an 'appropriate adult' (for definition see p 83, post) in the case of juveniles or persons who are mentally ill or handicapped: Detention Code, para 16.1. Other persons having an interest in the person's welfare may make representations at the review officer's discretion: Detention Code, para 16.1.
15 Ibid, s 40(12).
16 The Review Officer may refuse to hear oral representations from the detained person if he considers that he is unfit to make them by reason of his condition or behaviour: ibid, s 40(14).
17 1984 Act, s 45(2).
18 Ibid, s 40(4).
19 Ibid, s 40(5).
20 Ibid, s 40(7).

6 DETENTION: WHAT FOR AND HOW LONG?

A person who has been arrested without warrant[1] and brought to a police station will ultimately be 'processed' in one or other of the following five ways:

(1) unconditional release (because there is insufficient evidence to proceed or he has been eliminated as a suspect);

(2) release with proceedings pending (the intention being to prosecute by way of summons);

(3) release on bail to attend at a specified police station (when enquiries cannot be completed forthwith);

(4) charge and release on bail (to appear before a magistrate's court);

(5) charge and retention in custody (until he can be brought before a magistrate's court).

Prior to the 1984 Act, the law governing what happened to an arrested person in the interim was disconcertingly vague.[2] One of the major objectives of Part IV of the Act is to lay down statutory criteria setting out the bases upon which persons may be detained before and after charge and the maximum duration of such detention with the notable exception of persons detained under the Prevention of Terrorism (Temporary Provisions) Act 1984 who may, broadly, be detained initially for *48 hours* following arrest and thereafter for up to a further five days on the authority of the Home Secretary. The rules differ significantly depending upon whether or not the person has been arrested for a 'serious arrestable offence'. These two possibilities will therefore be considered separately.

OFFENCES OTHER THAN SERIOUS ARRESTABLE OFFENCES

The primary duty of the custody officer is to determine whether there is sufficient evidence to charge an arrested person with the offence for which he has been arrested.[3] This must be carried out as soon as practicable after that person's arrival at the police station.[4] 'Sufficient evidence' is not statutorily defined but would appear to mean:

'sufficient evidence to prosecute a detained person'.[5]

---

1 Although arrests under a warrant for an offence are rare the law in this respect has been significantly changed. Where the warrant is backed for bail under s 117 of the Magistrates' Courts Act 1980, Part IV of the 1984 Act does *not apply at all*: the arrested person must be released (subject to the approval of any sureties) in accordance with the direction in the endorsement. Where, however, the warrant is *not* endorsed for bail the person arrested is to be treated *like any other person arrested without warrant*. He may therefore be detained and if necessary interrogated under the provisions of Part IV of the 1984 Act.

2 Magistrates' Courts Act 1980, s 43(4) required that a person arrested without warrant be brought before the court 'as soon as practicable'. For conflicting views as to its effect see *Re Sherman and Apps* (1980) 72 Cr App Rep 266 and *R v Malcherek* (1981) 73 Cr App Rep 173 at 187.

3 S 37(1).

4 Ibid, s 37(10).

5 See Detention Code, para 17.1. This paragraph applies to all persons in detention and imposes a general requirement that they should be charged as soon as this condition is satisfied.

1 When there is sufficient evidence to charge

(a) Charging procedure

The person will be charged or informed that he may be prosecuted. Having been charged or so informed he must once again be given the *Paragraph 10* caution[6] along with a copy of the charge sheet containing prescribed details.[7]

(b) Restriction on questioning after charge

Once a person has been charged or informed that he may be prosecuted, he must *not* be questioned further with regard to that offence except:

(i) where necessary for the purpose of *preventing or minimising harm or loss* to some other person or the public; or

(ii) in order to *clear up an ambiguity* in a previous answer or statement; or

(iii) where it is *in the interests of justice* that he should have put to him and have an opportunity to comment on information concerning the offence which has come to light since he was charged etc.

in which case he must again be cautioned.[8] Furthermore, after he has been charged or informed that he may be prosecuted he should not be referred to any written statement made by another person or the content of any interview with such person, without first being cautioned and then shown the statement or interview record without inviting any comment.[9]

The charging process therefore effectively guillotines any further questioning of the accused in respect of the offence charged and has until now been one of the major reasons why police officers may have been tempted to delay charging. Note, however, that it does not prevent further questioning in respect of other offences.[10]

(c) Processing after charge: 'Police Bail'

On being charged the accused must either be (i) released on bail or (ii) kept in custody. If he is released on bail this may be with sureties or security.[11] He will be required to surrender to bail or a magistrates' court on a date specified in the written bail record that he will receive (this will usually be on the reverse side of the charge sheet). The large majority of persons who are charged will be dealt with in this way, Anthony JONES (*Case 2*) being a typical example of this. In certain cases, however, the police may not wish to release an accused on bail. Unlike when he is brought before the magistrates, he does not enjoy the statutory 'right to bail'[12] but this distinction is

---

6 Detention Code, para 17.2. A person will be 'informed that he may be prosecuted' when it is proposed to release him unconditionally with a view to bringing him before the court by way of a summons.

7 Ibid, para 17.3.

8 Ibid, para 17.5.

9 Ibid, para 17.4.

10 The police may sometimes charge a person with a less serious offence (known as a 'holding charge') and apply to the magistrates for a remand back into police custody to continue their enquiries into other offences. For a fuller discussion see p 72, post.

11 Releases on 'police bail' are releases on bail in accordance with the Bail Act 1976: 1984 Act, s 47(1).

12 Bail Act 1976, s 4(1): often referred to as 'Court Bail'. See further pp 240 et seq, post.

academic since he may only be kept in police custody if one or more of the following criteria are satisfied:[13]

   (i) his *name or address* cannot be ascertained or the custody officer has reasonable grounds for doubting whether they are genuine; or

   (ii) there are reasonable grounds for believing that detention is *necessary for his own protection* or to prevent him from causing physical injury or loss of or damage to property; or

   (iii) the custody officer has reasonable grounds for believing that he will *fail to answer to bail* or that his detention is necessary to prevent him from *interfering with witnesses* or otherwise obstructing the course of justice, or

   (iv) (juveniles only) that the custody officer has reasonable grounds for believing that he ought to be detained *in his own interests.*

If necessary therefore a person may be detained after charge for a wide variety of reasons but, normally, this course will only be adopted in the case of more serious offences. Detention under the above provisions is only permitted whilst any one of them exists, otherwise the person must be released. The accused's ciontinued detention is also as always, subject to review under s 40. Subject to this, if the person is kept in custody he must be brought before a magistrates' court as soon as is practicable, and in any event, not later than the first sitting after which he is charged[14]—in practical terms on the day after he is charged. If there is not a court sitting on that day or the next day the custody officer is under a duty to inform the clerk to the justices who must convene a court for the day after the accused is charged,[15] unless that day is a Sunday or Bank Holiday in which case he must do so for the day after.[16]

> EXAMPLE 1. D is arrested by a uniformed officer at 11.00 pm on Wednesday whilst committing burglary. He is taken back to a designated station where the custody officer (who is readily available) gets round to his case at 1.05 am. After hearing the account of the arresting officer he determines that sufficient evidence exists to charge him. He is duly charged at 1.15 am on Thursday but the custody officer refuses bail because there is a suspicion that he might abscond. In the normal course of events D must come before the magistrates on Thursday morning. In some areas, however, magistrates do not sit every day of the week. If there were no court on Thursday or Friday the custody officer would be obliged to inform the clerk to the justices who would be required to convene a court for Friday at the latest.

> EXAMPLE 2. Same facts as EXAMPLE 1 except D is arrested at 11.00 pm on a Thursday, charged at 1.15 am on Friday and there is no court sitting on Friday or Saturday. The earliest date the clerk is obliged to convene a court is Monday next (assuming it is not a Bank Holiday). In the meantime D will remain in police custody, although he can try to persuade the review officer to change his mind each time he carries out the s 40 review, the first of which should be carried out at 7.15 am.

The police are not, of course, obliged to charge a suspect. They may merely

---

13 1984 Act, s 38(1). These are in some ways more liberal than the 'right to bail' where the offence is imprisonable.

14 Ibid, s 46(2). This only applies where he is to be brought before a magistrates' courts for the Petty Sessions area in which the police station at which he is charged is situated. If not, the position is covered by ibid, s 46(4).

15 Ibid, s 46(7).

16 Ibid, s 46(8).

**POLICE AND CRIMINAL EVIDENCE ACT 1984
SIMPLIFIED DIAGRAM OF PROCEDURE TO BE FOLLOWED
WHEN SUFFICIENT EVIDENCE TO CHARGE FROM OUTSET**

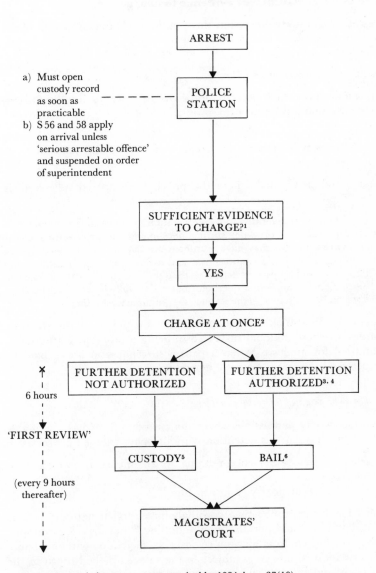

a) Must open
custody record
as soon as
practicable

b) S 56 and 58 apply
on arrival unless
'serious arrestable offence'
and suspended on order
of superintendent

6 hours

'FIRST REVIEW'

(every 9 hours
thereafter)

1 Must be carried out as soon as practicable: 1984 Act, s 37(10).
2 Detention Code Para 17: alternatively may inform that may be prosecuted.
3 *Must* release unless one of 4 conditions in s 38(1) ibid apply.
4 *Must* inform suspect of rights under s 56 and 58: Detention Code para 3.
5 *Must* be brought before magistrates as soon as practicable: s 46(2).
6 May alternatively release unconditionally or release without charge and issue summons.

inform him that he may be prosecuted and then release him with a view to proceeding by way of summons. This procedure is quite common with road traffic arrests and, in some areas, shoplifting offences.

(2) Where there is insufficient evidence to charge

In such a case the custody officer has three options. He may do either of the following.

(a) *Release the person unconditionally*[17]

He might adopt this course because, for example, there is insufficient evidence, or the decision is taken to administer a caution.

(b) *Release the person on bail to return to the police station on a specified future date*

This option is often adopted where the police have not completed their enquiries.

> EXAMPLE 3. D attends voluntarily at a police station to answer questions concerning the disappearance of his wife. During questioning the investigating officer forms the suspicion that he may have murdered her but has insufficient evidence on which to charge him. He cautions him and arrests him and then takes him before the custody officer who determines that there is insufficient evidence to charge. Since there are no further questions that can usefully be asked at this stage he is released on bail to return to the station (say) in three weeks' time.

A similar course will also often be adopted where the police are investigating fraud charges or where material suspected of being a prohibited drug needs to be submitted for analysis. When a person surrenders to police bail, he may be processed in the same way as if he had just been arrested.[18]

(c) *Order that he be detained for further enquiries*

Such detention is only permissible where the custody officer has reasonable grounds for believing that his detention without being charged is necessary:

   (i) to *secure* or *preserve* evidence relating to an offence for which he is under arrest; or
   (ii) to *obtain* such evidence by *questioning* him.[19]

The police for the first time now accordingly have explicit statutory powers not only to detain arrested persons for questioning,[20] but also, for example, in order to prevent them from alerting co-suspects. Detention without charge under this provision is, however, subject to the safeguards laid down in the Detention Code and the s 40 review procedure already discussed, as well as to the following time limits.

---

17   1984 Act, s 37(2).
18   Ibid, ss 37(1) and 47(5).
19   Ibid, s 37(2).
20   This power was recognised in *Holgate-Mohammed v Duke* supra as existing at common law in respect of persons lawfully arrested.

(3) Limits on detention without charge

The maximum period for which a person may be detained under the above provisions without being charged is *24 hours*[1] from 'the relevant time', which will generally be arrival at the police station to which he is taken after arrest.[2] Where, however, a person is arrested in a police area other than that in which his arrest is sought the 'relevant time' is calculated differently. If, for example, he is wanted in Newcastle and arrested in Swindon, the 24-hour period starts to run from:

– 24 hours after arrest; or
– on his arrival at the relevant police station, Newcastle

whichever is the earlier.[3] If the person attends voluntarily at a police station and is subsequently arrested, the 'relevant time' is the time of arrest.[4]

If further detention is authorised the suspect will normally be placed in a cell to await interview by the investigating officer. The Act does not, however, give the police an automatic right to detain the suspect for 24 hours. First, his continued detention is subject to s 40 review by the 'review officer'. Secondly, continued detention is only authorised so long as one of the grounds for detention without charge exists.[4a] Finally, as soon as the investigating officer believes that a prosecution should be brought and that there is sufficient evidence for it to succeed he must without delay cease questioning the suspect and bring him before the custody officer to be charged.[5] Once charged he will be processed in the same way as any other charged person and either bailed to appear before a magistrate or brought before the court in custody (provided that there are grounds for his continued detention).

EXAMPLE 4. D is arrested at 11.15 on Thursday night after having been involved in a disturbance during which a shopfront was damaged. Evidence against him is equivocal and the police suspect the involvement of several other persons. He arrives back at the station at 11.45 and the custody officer authorises his further detention at 1.15 am on Friday. This is reviewed at 7.15 am by the 'review officer' who authorises his continued detention. He is handed over to a CID officer for questioning at 7.30 am and by 9.00 am the officer has sufficient evidence to charge him. Questioning ceases and he is brought back before the custody officer, charged and cautioned at 9.15 am and released on bail without sureties to appear before Anytown magistrates on Monday week. (If he were refused bail and there were a court sitting that morning s 46 would apply and he would have to be brought before it in custody.)

(4) What happens at the end of the 24-hour period?

If the suspect is still being detained without charge at that time the custody officer must either:

(a) release him unconditionally; or
(b) release him on bail to attend at a police station: or
(c) charge him.[6]

---

1 S 41(1). Contrast the position in the case of 'serious arrestable offences' see further p 68, post.
2 Ibid, s 41(2)(d). An arrested person must, of course, normally be taken to a police station as soon as practicable (subject to postponement under s 30(10)) see p 55, ante.
3 Ibid, s 41(2)(a) and (3): provided he is not questioned as to the offence in Swindon area. For further more complicated possibilities see s 41(2), (5) and (6) and Bevan and Lidstone (op cit) p 197 et seq.
4 Ibid, s 41(2)(c).
4a Ibid, s 34(1).
5 Detention Code, para 17.1.　　　　　　　6 1984 Act, s 41(7).

**POLICE AND CRIMINAL EVIDENCE
ACT 1984
SIMPLIFIED DIAGRAM OF PROCEDURE ON DETENTION WITHOUT CHARGE**

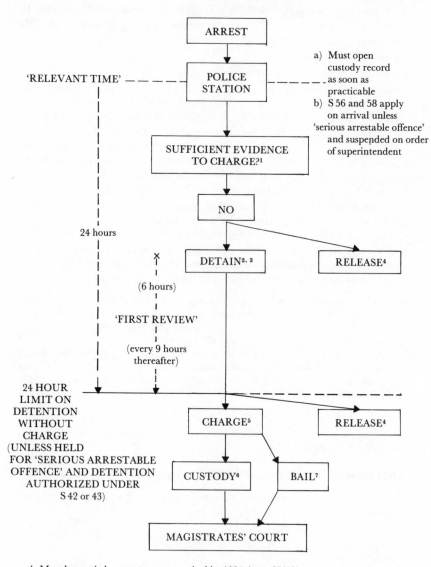

1 Must be carried out as soon as practicable: 1984 Act, s 37(10).
2 May only detain to secure or preserve evidence or obtain it by questioning: ibid, s 39(2).
3 Must inform suspect of rights under s 56 and 58: Detention Code para 3.
4 Unconditionally or on bail.
5 Must charge as soon as sufficient evidence: Stop questioning: Detention Code para 17.
6 Must be brought before magistrates as soon as practicable: 1984 Act, s 46(2).
7 May alternatively release unconditionally or release without charge and issue summons.

Options (a) and (b) have already been considered. If he is charged, the accused will be processed in the usual way and either released on bail or kept in custody and brought before a magistrates' court as soon as practicable. In the case of 'standard' offences, therefore, the 'new' provisions do not greatly differ from the pre-1984 Act practice.

SERIOUS ARRESTABLE OFFENCES

The initial duties of the custody officer are identical to those already considered in relation to other offences. He must first determine whether or not there is sufficient evidence to charge the person arrested.

(1) Where there is sufficient evidence to charge

The position is precisely the same as considered earlier in the case of other offences.

(2) Where there is insufficient evidence to charge

The position is initially the same as in the case of other offences. The custody officer must exercise one of the three options considered in the previous section. Further detention can, therefore only be justified on the basis of a need to secure or preserve evidence, or obtain such evidence by questioning the person arrested.

(3) Limits on detention without charge

As before, the arrested person's continued detention will be subject to review, and may only be continued so long as one of the statutory grounds exists. Similarly, the investigating officer is under an overriding duty to take him before the custody officer as soon as there is sufficient evidence to charge him. The only major difference concerns the permitted period of detention.

Stage 1—the first 24 hours: s 41

This is subject to the same rules as all other offences. Time runs from the 'relevant time' calculated as before. The three options of unconditional release, release on bail and charge are available at the end of the 24-hour period, but where appropriate, the police may also proceed to *Stages 2 or 3*.

Stage 2—detention for a further 12 hours on the authority of a superintendent: s 42

The suspect may be detained for a further period or periods not exceeding *12 hours* in aggregate on the authority of a superintendent or above *responsible for the police station* at which the person is detained. Such authority may only be given where that officer has reasonable grounds for believing that:

   (i) such further detention is necessary to secure or preserve evidence relating to a serious arrestable offence for which he is under arrest or to obtain such evidence by questioning him; and

  (ii) the investigation is being conducted diligently and expeditiously.[7]

The authority must be given before the initial 24-hour period has expired and cannot be given until the arrested person's detention has been reviewed under s 40 at least twice.[8] It is an essential prerequisite to the exercise of this authority that the person detained, or his solicitor, if available, should be given the opportunity to make oral or written[9] representations and, the officer authorising further detention is under a personal duty to inform the suspect of the grounds for his continued detention and record them on the custody record.[10]

The person detained must be informed of his rights under s 56 (right to have someone informed when arrested) and s 58 (right to legal advice) if these have not already been exercised. If the authorising officer decides to postpone these rights (which he is entitled to do for up to *36 hours* from arrest) the decision and the grounds thereof must also be recorded in the custody record.[11] At the end of *Stage 2* the custody officer must either:

  (a) release the detained person unconditionally, or

  (b) release him on bail; or

  (c) charge him; or

  (d) the police must apply to a magistrates' court for a *Warrant of Further Detention*.

Options (a) to (c) have already been discussed in the context of non-serious arrestable offences, option (d) is considered below.

Stage 3—detention on the authority of a magistrates' court: ss 43 and 44

Application[12] may be made to a magistrates' court sitting 'in camera'[13] for a 'Warrant of Further Detention'. The relevant law and procedure is extremely complicated—s 43 runs to no less than 19 subsections. Broadly, however, the police must satisfy the court[14] that:

   (i) further detention without charge is *necessary* to *secure* or *preserve evidence* relating to a serious arrestable offence for which the person is under arrest or to *obtain* such evidence by *questioning* him;

  (ii) the *investigation* is being conducted *diligently* and *expeditiously*.[15]

---

7 1984 Act, s 42(1).

8 Ibid, s 42(4). Because the 'detention clock' starts sooner (arrival at the police station) than the 'review clock' (first authorisation of detention) this may, in reality, only give the superintendent a few hours in which to make a decision.

9 Ibid, s 42(6)–(8). The superintendent may refuse to hear *oral* representations from the *suspect* if he considers that he is unfit to do so by reason of his condition or behaviour: ibid, s 42(8).

10 Ibid, s 42(5).

11 See further p 79 et seq, post.

12 Application under s 43 must be made on information supported by evidence on oath. The Act does not specify which officer should make the application.

13 1984 Act, s 45(1).

14 The court must comprise at least two lay justices or stipendiary magistrate.

15 Ibid, s 43(4). The decision as to whether these grounds exist eg whether the offence is a 'serious arrestable offence', unlike at *Stage 2*, is that of the *magistrates*. The information in support of the application requires certain prescribed information including the general nature of the evidence on which the person was arrested, what enquiries have been made and what further enquiries are proposed, and the reasons why further detention is necessary for this purpose: ibid, s 43(14).

The person in detention must be brought before the court and is entitled to a copy of the information[16] upon which the application is based and to legal representation.[17] The application must be made within 24 hours of the 'relevant time' (36 hours if the police have proceeded via *Stage 2*) although the Act does allow an extension of up to six hours in certain circumstances.[18] When hearing an application the magistrates' court may do one of the three following things.

(a) Refuse the application. The person must then be released (unconditionally or on bail) or charged, unless he has not yet been in detention for 24 hours (36 hours if the police have proceeded via *Stage 2*).[19] In the latter case detention may still continue up to the end of the 24 (or 36) hour period, as appropriate, if grounds still exist.[20]

(b) Adjourn the hearing. The court may do this either to give the person an opportunity to obtain legal advice or if it is not satisfied that there are reasonable grounds for believing that his further detention is justified. If it adjourns for the latter reason the person must be dealt with within 36 hours of the 'relevant time'.[1]

(c) Issue a Warrant of Further Detention. The warrant may be for such period as the court thinks fit, having regard to the evidence before it. The power to authorise a further period of detention is, however, limited in that the period ordered may not:

(i) be longer than *36 hours*; or
(ii) end later than *96 hours* after the 'relevant time'.[2]

Where, however, the court issues a warrant which expires less than 96 hours after the 'relevant time' further applications may be made to extend the period of detention for up to a further *36 hours*, subject again, to the overall *96 hour* limit.[3] These complicated provisions therefore enable a magistrates' court to authorise further detention in units of up to *36 hours* subject to the overall *96 hour* limit. Note that the police are not required to proceed to *Stage 3* via *Stage 2*. The officer in charge of the case may therefore, go before the magistrates and ask for a warrant prior to the expiry of *Stage 1* rather than first seek authority for further detention for up to 36 hours from a superintendent under *Stage 2*.

16 1984 Act, s 43(2).
17 Ibid, s 43(4). If he is not represented but wishes to be represented the court must adjourn to enable him to obtain representation. Legal aid is available subject to the usual criteria: Legal Aid Act 1974, s 28.
18 Ibid, s 43(5)(b), but if it appears that it would have been reasonable to make the application before the expiry of the 36-hour period the court must dismiss the application: ibid, s 43(7).
19 Ibid, s 44(15) and (16).
20 Ibid. It must be borne in mind that there will be no justification for further detention unless one of the grounds in s 37(2) continues to exist: ibid, s 34(1). Where the purported ground is the need to obtain further evidence by questioning him and the accused has exercised his 'right of silence' it is hard to see how such a ground can continue to exist.
1 Ibid, s 43(8)(b). If the accused intimates that he wishes to exercise his 'right of silence' it is likewise hard to see how a case for further detention for the purpose of *questioning* can be made out.
2 Ibid, ss 43(12) and 44(3)(b).
3 Ibid, s 44(3)(b).

(4) What happens at the end of the 36-hour period (or expiry of the warrant)?

The person in detention must be dealt with as at the end of *Stage 1*, in other words he must be released unconditionally or on bail, or charged. If he is charged he will then be processed in the usual way. It must be stressed that whilst in continued detention under s 42 or s 43 the s 40 review procedure must still be carried out. Furthermore, the suspect may still only be detained so long as one of the statutory grounds exists and he must be charged as soon as there is 'sufficient evidence'.

Holding charges: Magistrates' Courts Act 1980, s 128(7)

Under this provision a magistrates' court having power to remand a person in custody, may commit him to detention at a police station for up to *three clear days*. The 1984 Act adds a new subsection (8) to s 128 which provides that:

(a) detention shall only be ordered where necessary for inquiry into other offences;
(b) if so ordered the person must be brought back before the court as soon as the need ceases;
(c) such detention is subject to the duties imposed under s 39 (observance of and recording on custody record, and Codes of Practice) and s 40 (review procedure) of the 1984 Act.

The only prerequisite is that the person must, be brought before the court charged with an offence.[4] The provision thus enables police officers investigating a major offence initially to charge a relatively minor offence (the 'holding charge'), bring the accused before the court and ask for a three day remand back into police custody, and then continue their enquiries into the major offence. The prohibition against further questioning in *Paragraph 17.5* of the Detention Code does not apply because they are not questioning the suspect about the offence charged.

> EXAMPLE. D is arrested on suspicion of armed robbery. He puts up a struggle during which two police officers are assaulted. He is taken back to the station and arrives at 11 pm on a Wednesday night. Assuming that the robbery is classified as a 'serious arrestable offence' he may only be held under the 1984 Act (on the authority of a superintendent) until 11 am Friday (36 hours) before the expiry of which an application must be made for a Warrant of Further Detention. The magistrates could only authorise further detention for up to 36 hours in the first instance and the limit of authorised detention would be reached by 11 pm Sunday (96 hours).[5] If on the other hand he were charged with assaulting a police officer (the 'holding charge') he could be brought before the court on Thursday morning when the police could ask for a s 128(7) remand back into police custody in order to continue their enquiries into the armed robbery. Such remand could be until Monday morning thus constituting over 100 hours in detention.[6]

---

4 It is submitted that s 128(8)(a) does not permit use of s 128(7) where a person has not been charged with a 'holding charge'.
5 At which point he must be released or charged.
6 On the face of it there appears to be nothing to prevent the police asking for further remands back into police custody under s 128(7). It is not entirely clear whether they must *actually* remand the 'holding charge' in custody before s 128(7) may be used. The latter remand would be subject to the provisions of the Bail Act 1976: see p 240 et seq post.

This procedure would appear to be far easier for the police to operate and one can anticipate its use whenever feasible. Persons dealt with in this way are nevertheless given the protection of the 1984 Act. They must still be charged without delay under *Paragraph 17.1* of the Detention Code and are entitled to take advantage of the provisions of *s 56* (right not to be held incommunicado) and *s 58* (right to legal advice). Thus in the example given above, these rights could only be withheld until *11 pm Thursday* (24 hours), or *11.00 am Friday* (36 hours) on the authority of a superintendent[7].

RE-ARREST (ALL OFFENCES)

(1) Arrest for a further offence: 1984 Act, s 31. Where a person is at a police station in consequence of having been arrested for an offence and it appears that if he were released he would be liable to arrest for some other offence he must be arrested for that offence informed of the fact and given the grounds thereof. This does not, however, entitle the police to arrest the suspect for further offences as a means of prolonging his detention without charge. The 'relevant time' is calculated by reference to the offence for which he was originally arrested.[8]

(2) Re-arrest for the same offence. If a person is released without charge either unconditionally or on bail the power to re-arrest him will apparently depend upon the time of his release.

(a) If released before the expiry of 24 hours

The Act is silent. There is therefore no apparent restrictions on re-arresting him even though there is no further evidence available.

(b) If released at the expiry of 24 hours, 36 hours or a Warrant of Further Detention

The Act provides that in that event a person cannot be re-arrested without a warrant unless new evidence justifying a further arrest has come to light since his release.[9]

7 PERSONS IN DETENTION: POLICE POWERS AND DUTIES

Once detained, what happens to a person in detention?[10] After arrival at a police station suspects will probably be processed much as before in that he will probably[11] be:

- searched;
- told of the reason for his continued detention and informed of his 'rights';
- placed in a cell to await interrogation;

7 See generally p 79, post.
8 S 41(4). They may however apply for a remand back into police custody under Magistrates' Courts Act 1980, s 128(7).
9 1984 Act, ss 41(9), 42(11) and 43(19).
10 Softley (op cit) and Irving (op cit) both provide useful background reading.
11 Although suspects can expect to be put through a standard set of procedures, suspect's experiences of arrest, detention and interview may vary considerably. See Irving, op cit, p 106.

- questioned;
- invited to make a written statement;
- fingerprinted; and
- charged or released.

The greatest tangible change is the new statutory right of access to legal advice,[12] backed by the proposed extention of the Duty Solicitor and 'Green Form' Schemes[13] to cover police stations. Even more profound changes will take place if and when the tape recording of interviews becomes standard practice. Although this is unlikely until after 1987, field trials have already started in six police areas[14] and will continue for two years.[15] The criminal lawyer will therefore need to move with the times.

(1) Searches of detained persons

(a)   *General Powers to search: 1984 Act, s 54: Detention Code, Paragraph 4*

The custody officer is under a duty to ascertain everything that an arrested person has with him on arrival and record details on the custody record. He is empowered to carry out a personal search if he considers it necessary to effect this purpose but may only search to the extent that he considers it necessary. Search is thus, in practice, a matter of routine. Any property, other than that which is subject to legal privilege[16] may be retained, save that clothes and personal effects may only be retained if the custody officer believes they may be used by the person arrested:

- to cause *physical injury* to himself or any other person;
- to *damage* property;
- to *interfere* with evidence;
- to assist him in *escape* from police detention; or
- he has reasonable grounds for believing that they may be *evidence* relating to an offence.[17]

The person arrested must be given reasons for the seizure of any property (although, suprisingly, not the reason for the original search) unless he is violent or likely to become violent, or incapable of understanding what is said to him.[18] Anything seized may be retained as long as it is necessary in

12 1984 Act, s 58 see p 80, post.
13 S 59 of the 1984 Act amends Legal Aid Act 1982, s 1 to provide for an extension of the Duty Solicitor scheme to cover persons 'helping police with their inquiries' and exercising their rights under s 58 of the 1984 Act. The final draft of the scheme has not as yet been approved. It was orirginally anticipated that all persons in detention would be entitled to the services of the Duty Solicitor or to 'Green Form' Advice and Assistance (irrespective of means). It is now unclear as to what the ultimate scope of free legal advice will be.
14 Trials began in late 1983 in 5 Police areas: Metropolitan Police, (Holborn and Croydon), Merseyside (Wirral), Leicestershire (Leicester Central), Hampshire (Winchester) and Northumbria (South Tyneside) under a Steering Committee set up by the then Home Secretary Mr Whitelaw. See the Tape Recording of Police Interviews with suspects: Procedural guidance, Home Office, October 1983.
15 For a progress report see: 'Tape Recording the Questioning of Suspects: the Field Trial guidelines David Roberts' [1984] Crim LR 537. So far the experiments have met with police approval: see Home Office Research Study No 82 (HMSO).
16 As defined in s 10 of the 1984 Act: see p 86, post.
17 Ibid, s 54(4). As to reasonableness see *Lindley v Rutter* (supra).
18 Ibid, s 54(5). It is argued by Hargreaves and Levinson (op cit) that the suspect may still be entitled to the reason for the search at common law, see *Brazil v Chief Constable of Surrey* [1983] 3 All ER 537.

all the circumstances but will normally be returned when the person is released.[19] Where, however, articles have been seized as potential evidence, or because they are reasonably believed to be the fruits of crime they may be retained for use as evidence or forensic examination or in order to establish the lawful owner.[20]

The purpose in carrying out a search may range from the need to make an inventory so as to rebut allegations that property has been planted or stolen, to the need to search for articles which may be of evidential value. Indeed the concept of personal 'search' also takes in the possibility of examining a person's body to search for evidence in the form of concealed articles or other materials. There are seven possible degrees of search:[1]

   (i) the order to the suspect to turn out his pockets;
  (ii) the 'frisk', ie feeling about the body for hard objects concealed in or under clothing;
 (iii) the search of the suspect's pockets;
 (iv) the removal of top clothing;
  (v) the 'strip search' involving removal of the whole or most of his clothing;
 (vi) the 'intimate search' of a person's bodily orifices;
(vii) the 'internal search' by means of X-ray or body scan.

In addition a person may be 'searched' by the removal of body samples or the taking of fingerprints.

The effect of s 54 is to give to custody officers and those to whom their duties may be delegated a virtually unfettered discretion in every case to search an arrested person up to stage (iv), whether or not he is eventually charged. Reasonable force may be used if 'necessary'.[2]

(b) 'Strip searches' and 'intimate searches': 1984 Act, s 55: Detention Code, Annex A

'Strip searches' are not referred to in the 1984 Act, but the Detention Code provides that such searches may only take place if the custody officer considers it 'necessary' to remove an article which the detained person would not be allowed to keep.[3] An 'intimate search'[4] can only be carried out on the authority[5] of a superintendent or above who has reasonable grounds for believing that the arrested person may have concealed on him an article which could be used to cause physical injury to himself or others and which might be so used whilst he is in police detention or that, he may have a Class A drug concealed on him.[6] The police thus have no general power to conduct

---

19 1984 Act, s 22(3) and see Detention Code, para 4.
20 See ibid, s 22(2).
 1 On search generally see Wolchover [1983] LSG 1054.
 2 1984 Act, s 117. Detention Code, para 4.1 provides that a search may only be carried out by an officer of the same sex. Reasonable force may be used if necessary to secure compliance with reasonable instructions or to prevent escape, injury, damage to property or the destruction of evidence (ibid, para 8.9).
 3 Ibid, Annex A, para 5.
 4 A search which consists of the physical examination of a person's body orifices: 1984 Act, s 118.
 5 An officer may only authorise such a search if he has reasonable grounds for believing that an article cannot be found without such search: ibid, s 55(2). The authorisation may be given orally or in writing but if given orally must be confirmed in writing as soon as practicable: ibid, s 55(3).
 6 Provided that he was in the possession of it with the appropriate criminal intent before arrest, namely, to commit an offence under s 5(3) of the Misuse of Drugs Act 1971 (possession with intent to supply).

intimate body searches for the purpose of finding evidence.

Nevertheless, their powers to seize and retain anything they find are as wide as those in respect of ordinary searches this point is largely academic.[7] Intimate searches other than those for drugs[8] must take place at a police station, hospital, doctor's surgery or other place used for medical purposes[9] and may only be carried out by a doctor or registered nurse unless a superintendent or above considers this is not practicable.[10] If so, it must be carried out by a police officer of the same sex.[11] Searches by X-ray or body scan are not dealt with at all in the Act although their use is clearly contemplated.[12]

(c) *Body samples: 1984 Act, ss 62 and 63: Identification Code, Paragraph 5*

The police may wish to 'search' a person's body not for the purpose of finding objects but in order to remove body samples. The Act divides samples into 'intimate'[13] and 'non intimate'[14] respectively.

(i) 'Intimate samples'. These may only be taken with the written consent of the person to be examined,[15] *and* the authorisation of an officer of at least superintendent rank.[16] Such authorisation may only be given if he reasonably suspects the person's involvement in a *serious arrestable offence* and believes that the sample will tend to confirm or disprove this.[17] Samples, other than of urine or saliva, must be taken by a doctor[18] and detailed particulars, including the basis upon which authorisation was given must be recorded on the custody record.[19] Ostensibly, therefore, a suspect may never be forced to give an intimate sample against his will. This 'right' to withhold consent is, however, rendered virtually meaningless by virtue of s 62(10) of the 1984 Act which provides that where a suspect refuses consent 'without good cause' the court[20] or jury[1] may draw such inference from the refusal as appears proper and may treat such inference as, or as capable of amounting to, corroboration of any evidence against the person in relation to which the refusal is

---

7 The custody officer may seize and retain the same categories of things found as in the case of ordinary searches: ibid, s 55(12). See p 74, ante.

8 Drug searches must not be at a police station: (ibid, s 55(9)) but otherwise s 55(8) applies.

9 Ibid, s 55(8).

10 Ibid, s 55(5). Drug searches may only be carried out by a doctor or registered nurse: ibid, s 55(4).

11 Ibid, s 55(7).

12 See generally Walton, 'Some Recent Advantages in Police Technology,' Med Sci Law, (1982) Vol 22, No 1 p. 2 et seq.

13 Blood, semen, or any other tissue fluid, urine, saliva or pubic hair, or a swab taken from a person's body orifice: ibid, s 65.

14 Hair (other than pubic), a sample from a nail or from under a nail, or a swab (other than from a body orifice) and a footprint or other body impression other than part of a hand: ibid.

15 Ibid, s 62(1)(b) and (4). The consent must be that of the person himself unless he is under 17 as to which see ibid, s 65.

16 Ibid, s 62(1)(a). The authorisation may be given orally or in writing but if given orally shall be confirmed in writing as soon as practicable.

17 Ibid, s 62(2).

18 Ibid, s 62(9). Note that s 62 does not apply to requests to give samples of blood or urine made under Sch 8 to the Road Traffic Act 1972, ibid, s 62(11).

19 Ibid, ss 62(7) and (8).

20 Magistrates may draw this inference in determining (i) whether to commit a person for trial, (ii) whether there is a case to answer or (iii) whether he is guilty. In trials on indictment the judge may take it into account in deciding whether there is a case to answer.

1 The jury may draw such inference in determining guilt.

material.[2] It is hard to envisage circumstances in which an accused will have good cause[3] for refusing once a superintendent has authorised the taking of an intimate sample, but in any event, the pressure upon the suspect to agree, or on his lawyer to advise him to agree, will be very great.

(ii) 'Non intimate'. These samples may be taken from a person whatever the offence under investigation provided he consents in writing.[4] Refusal may however be overridden on the authority of a superintendent or above if he has reasonable grounds for suspecting the person's involvement in a *serious arrestable offence* and believes that the taking of the sample will tend to confirm or disprove this.[5] There is no requirement that the sample should be taken by a doctor but, once again, the reasons for the taking of the sample must be recorded on the person's custody record along with details of any authorisation for it to be taken without his consent.[6]

(d) Fingerprints: 1984 Act, s61: Identification Code, Paragraph 3

This is the final aspect of 'search'. Fingerprints may not be taken from a person unless:

  (i) he consents;[7] or
 (ii) he is detained at a police station and a superintendent or above authorises them to be taken because he has reasonable grounds for suspecting the person's involvement in *any* offence and for believing that his fingerprints will tend to confirm or disprove this;[8] or
(iii) he is detained at a police station and he has been charged or informed that he will be reported for a 'recordable offence' and has not yet had his fingerprints taken in the course of the investigation;[9] or
 (iv) he has been convicted of a 'recordable offence'.[10]

The taking of fingerprints of any person over the age of ten years without consent can therefore be authorised either before or after charge more or less as a matter of routine. Whenever they are taken without consent the person

2 S 62(10) will be of particular significance in relation to sexual offences where corroboration is required either as a matter of law or practice, see further p 163, post.
3 Cause would clearly exist if there were no reasonable grounds for suspecting the person's involvement in a 'serious arrestable offence' but it nevertheless represents a serious inroad into the 'right of silence'. Para 5.2 and Note 5A of the Identification Code require that before a sample is taken an accused must be warned in the following terms: 'You do not have to [provide this sample] [allow this swab to be taken], but I must warn you that if you do not do so, a court may treat such a refusal as supporting any relevant evidence against you.'
4 1984 Act, s 63(1) and (2). See generally Identification Code, para 5.
5 Ibid, s 63(4). The authority if given orally must be confirmed in writing as soon as practicable, and communicated to the person to be served: ibid, ss 63(6) and (7).
6 Ibid, s 63(5). Unlike in the case of intimate searches no inference may be drawn from a person's refusal to consent to a non-intimate search, presumably it is thought that this is unnecessary since the suspect's refusal may be overridden on the appropriate authority. Reasonable force may be used: 1984 Act, s 118 and Identification Code, para 5.6.
7 The consent must be in writing if the person is at a police station ibid, s 61(1) and (2), otherwise oral consent is sufficient,
8 1984 Act, s 61(3) (a) and (4).
9 1984 Act, s 61(3)(b).
10 Ibid, s 61(6). For the probable definition of 'recordable offence' see p 52 ante.

must be told the reason, which must be recorded on his custody record as soon as practicable.[11]

(e) Destruction of fingerprints and samples: 1984 Act, s 64

Where fingerprints or samples are taken from a person and he is subsequently cleared of that offence,[12] or not prosecuted for it[13] any fingerprints or samples taken must be destroyed as soon as practicable after the conclusion of the proceedings or the decision not to prosecute is taken. If any fingerprints or samples have been taken from a person who is not suspected of having committed the offence under investigation they must be destroyed as soon as they have fulfilled the purpose for which they were taken.[14] A person may witness the destruction of his fingerprints on request.[15]

(f) Photographs: Identification Code, Paragraph 4

Photographs of suspects will often be taken. The 1984 Act does not deal with this aspect at all but detailed rules are contained in the Identification Code. The basic rule is that the police may only photograph a person in police custody with his written consent unless:

(i) he is arrested at the same time as a number of other persons and it is considered necessary to establish who was arrested at what time and what place; or

(ii) he has been charged with or reported for a 'recordable offence' and not yet been released or brought before a court; or

(iii) he has been convicted of a recordable offence and his photograph is not yet on record as a result of (i) or (ii).

However, force must *never* be used and the reasons for taking photographs without consent must be recorded. In practical terms, the exceptions are so wide as more or less to endorse routine photographing of persons after mass arrest or once they have been charged.

(2) Right to inform others of arrest and to legal advice: 1984 Act, ss 56 and 58

These provisions arguably represent the most important change introduced by the 1984 Act. Their effectiveness will, however, depend largely upon the willingness of the legal profession to respond to the opportunity that they have now been given, to have virtually unrestricted access to persons in detention other than those charged with 'serious arrestable offences'. The proposed extension of the Duty Solicitor and Green Form Schemes to cover advice and assistance at police stations potentially adds a new dimension to the defence solicitor's role in criminal litigation.[16]

11 1984 Act, s 61(7) and (8). None of the above restrictions apply to persons who are suspected illegal immigrants or who are arrested or detained under the terrorism provisions: ibid, s 61(10).
12 Ibid, s 64(1).
13 Provided that he has not admitted the offence and been dealt with by way of caution: ibid, s 64(2).
14 Ibid, s 64(3). For example, where the public is voluntarily finger printed during a murder inquiry.
15 Ibid, s 64(6). Provided this is made within *one month* of being cleared etc: Identification Code, para 3.4.
16 For further discussions see pp 98 et seq, post. It is understood that the '24 hour' scheme has already been introduced 'unofficially' in some areas, eg London and Nottingham.

(*a*) *Duties of custody officer: Detention Code, Paragraph 3*

When an arrested person is brought to a police station, or a person who has attended voluntarily is subsequently arrested, the custody officer must open a custody record and inform him of his rights:

  (i)   to inform someone of his detention;
  (ii) to legal advice; and
  (iii) to consult the Codes of Practice.[17]

He must also be given a *written notice* which sets out these rights and contains the *Paragraph 10* caution.[18] He will then be invited to sign the custody record acknowledging receipt.[19] The first two of these 'rights' must now be considered in detail.

(*b*) *The right to have someone informed of arrest: 1984 Act, s 56; Detention Code, Paragraph 5*

The Act in effect provides that as soon as person arrives at a police station[20] he shall be entitled on request to have 'one friend or relative or other person who is known to him or who is likely to take an interest in his welfare',[1] told that he has been arrested and that he is being held there. This right is further exercisable when he is transferred to another station.[2] The right may only be postponed on the authority of a superintendent or above in a case of a person who is in detention for a 'serious arrestable offence'.[3] The grounds for such postponement are that there are reasonable grounds for believing that telling the named person:

  (i)   will lead to *interference* with or harm to *evidence* connected with a serious arrestable offence, or interference with or physical injury to other *persons;* or
  (ii) will *alert* other persons suspected of such an offence; or
  (iii) will *hinder* the recovery of any *property* obtained as a result of such an offence.[4]

The reason for any such delay must be communicated to the arrested person[5] and noted on his custody record.[6] In any event the s 56 right may only be postponed until:

17 See Detention Code, para 3.1.
18 Ibid, para 3.2.
19 Ibid.
20 1984 Act, s 56(1). The right accrues to any person who has been arrested and is being held in custody in a police station or other premises.
 1 The definition is clearly wide enough to include interested parties such as a probation officer or Member of Parliament. The definition of 'reasonably named person' is considered in Home Office Circular 74/1978, para 5 (reproduced in part in The Investigation and Prosecution of Criminal Offences in England and Wales: The Law and Procedure, op cit, p 166 et seq.) If the named person cannot be contacted the detainee may choose up to two alternatives but thereafter further attempts are within the custody officer's discretion (Detention Code, para 5.1). Communication will normally be by letter or telephone, this will not be confidential unless the communication is with a solicitor or solictor's clerk. Before communicating with someone other than a solicitor or solicitor's clerk a person should be informed that what he says or writes may be read or listened to and given in evidence: ibid para 5.8.
 2 1984 Act, s 56(8).
 3 Ibid, s 56(2).
 4 Ibid, s 56(5).
 5 Ibid, s 56(6)(a).
 6 Ibid, s 56 (6)(b).

(i) the reason for authorising delay ceases to subsist; or

(ii) the expiry of *36 hours*[7] after the 'relevant time';[8]

whichever is the earlier.[9]

This section is a considerable improvement on its predecessor, s 62 of the Criminal Law Act 1977.[10] Even so, when a suspect is detained after arrest for a 'serious arrestable offence' coming within the above criteria the police are in effect not even required to confirm or deny whether they are holding him during the first 36 hours of detention.

Paragraph 5 of the Detention Code gives detailed guidelines as to how the section should be operated. In particular the Code reminds police officers of the detained person's rights on transfer to another police station. It will thus not be permissible to 'hide' a person's whereabouts by switching him between stations (unless he is detained for a 'serious arrestable offence' in which the right to communicate has been postponed in which case there seems to be nothing to prevent this). If an enquiry as to a person's whereabouts is made by a friend, relative or other 'interested party', the prescribed information, subject as above, should be supplied.

(c) Right to legal advice: 1984 Act, s 58; Detention Code, Paragraph 6

A person who has been arrested is entitled, if he so requests, to consult a solicitor privately at any time after arrival at the police station.[11] The request and the time at which it was made must be recorded on his custody record[12] and he must be permitted to consult a solicitor[13] as soon as practicable[14] unless he is in detention for a *serious arrestable offence* and a superintendent or above authorises delay on the same grounds as those relating to s 56.[15] The reason for any such postponement must be communicated to the detainee and noted on his custody record.[16] A request for legal advice may only be postponed until the reason for authorising delay ceases to subsist or the expiry of *36 hours* from the 'relevant time' whichever is the earlier.[17] Once again, this section is a considerable improvement upon the vaguely formulated 'rights' contained in the Judge's Rules and Administrative Direction and combined with the availability of Duty Solicitors is likely to render the attendance of solicitors at interviews far more commonplace than hitherto.

---

7 Where a person has been arrested or detained under ss 12 and 13 of the Prevention of Terrorism (Temporary Provisions) Act 1984 he may be held incommunicado on the authority of a superintendent or above for up to 48 hours after arrest or the commencement of detention in certain circumstances. For further details see 1984 Act, s 56(11).

8 For definition see p 67, ante. Postponement up to 36 hours is not, apparently, dependent upon detention without charge on the authority of a superintendent under s 42, but it is likely that such detention will also be authorised: see p 69 ante.

9 See s 56(3) in conjunction with s 56(9).

10 Research suggests that this right was very rarely exercised see Softley (op cit) Table 3, Column 1, p 66.

11 Ibid, s 58(2)

12 Unless he makes it whilst at court after being charged with an offence: ibid, s 58(3).

13 Although the Act uses the word 'solicitor' para 6.9 of the Detention Code provides that a clerk or legal executive shall be admitted to the police station for the purpose of giving advice unless an inspector or above directs otherwise on the grounds that such a visit will hinder the investigation of crime.

14 1984 Act, s 58(4).

15 Ibid, s 58(6)–(11).

16 Ibid, s 58(9).

17 Ibid, s 58(5) and (11). Where a person is detained under the Prevention of Terrorism (Temporary Provisions) Act 1984 access may again be postponed for up to 48 hours under s 58(13).

Paragraph 6 and *Annex B* to the Detention Code contains additional guidelines. These are of great importance and require careful study. The Code in particular provides that:

 (i) a person who requests legal advice but does not name a solicitor shall be informed of the availability of the Duty Solicitor (where such a scheme is in operation) and given a list of other solicitors who have indicated that they are available;

 (ii) access may not be delayed or denied on the ground that the solicitor may advise the person not to answer any questions;

 (iii) the person concerned is entitled to consult and communicate *privately*, either in person, in writing or by telephone;[18]

 (iv) access may not be delayed or denied on the ground that the solicitor was initially asked to attend by *someone else*, provided that the person himself then wishes to see the solicitor;

 (v) where legal advice has been requested the police should not interview the person further until advice has been given, without his written consent being obtained or on the authority of a superintendent on the ground of *immediate* risk to persons or property or *unreasonable* delay to the investigation;

 (vi) the solicitor, if consulted and available, must be permitted to attend the interview and may only be required to leave if his conduct is such that the investigating officer cannot properly put questions to the suspect, but such 'misconduct' must clearly go beyond challenge to an improper or badly-put question or a request for adjournment for the purpose of legal advice.

 (vii) if a solicitor is excluded the suspect should be given the opportunity to consult another solicitor before the interview continues;

These new provisions will require solicitors to be able to develop a whole new range of skills when advising clients in detention and sitting in on interviews.[19]

(3) Police interviewing

Notwithstanding conflicting research data[20] the interrogation of a person suspected of crime is still one of the primary means of securing evidence to support a conviction. A full admission of guilt or an adverse admission falling short of this may arise, at any stage up to the suspect being charged, in the form of either:

 (i) *oral* statements made to the arresting officer on apprehension[1] prior to arrival at the police station;

---

18 Note that in the case of terrorist offences a commander or assistant chief constable may in specified circumstances require that a detained person can consult a solicitor in the sight and hearing of a uniformed inspector or above not connected with the case: 1984 Act, 58(14)–(18).

19 The practical implications of this are considered further at p 103, post.

20 See Baldwin and McConville, 'Confessions in Crown Court Trials' Research Study 5, Royal Commission on Criminal Procedure (HMSO) pp 28–29 and Mitchell, 'Confessions and Police Interrogations' [1983] Crim LR 596. Irving (op cit) p 118, found that interrogation was regarded by all C.I.D. officers interviewed as of central importance to criminal investigation.

 1 The overwhelming majority of suspects appear to be arrested by the uniformed branch. Irving (op cit) p 100 found that suspects are not normally questioned at length before entering the station. Baldwin and McConville (op cit) pp 20–21 found that only a minute proportion (barely 0·3% of a sample of 3,000) made damaging admissions on the way to the police station. A larger proportion (approximately 11%) made damaging admissions when first apprehended.

(ii) *oral* replies to formal interrogation (usually by a C.I.D. officer) at the police station; and/or

(iii) a *written statement* under caution (usually made at the conclusion of interrogation) signed by the accused.

Oral admissions are often colloquially referred to as 'verbals' especially if the accused alleges fabrication. As a matter of law, all such admissions, whether full or partial, written or oral, are classified as 'confessions'[2] and any future reference is to be construed accordingly. The questioning of suspects is regulated primarily by the Detention Code. (Tape recorded interviews will have their own Code of Practice when generally introduced.[3]) As has already been noted, these Codes do not have statutory force and breaches of the Detention Code will not of themselves render a confession automatically inadmissible. It is nevertheless of great importance to be conversant with its provisions, in particular, the following:

Para 8: deals with the conditions of detention for all persons whether charged or not in particular accommodation, clothing and meals.

Para 10: requires a person to be *cautioned* not only on arrest but also when he is interviewed and for the caution to be repeated in certain circumstances.

Para 11: requires an *accurate record*, including times, breaks and persons present to be kept of every interview whether or not it takes place at a police station. This must be made during the interview, unless this would be impracticable or interfere with its conduct in which case it must be made as soon as practicable thereafter. It also *forbids* torture, inhuman or degrading treatment, use of or threat of violence to the suspect, family or other connected persons. It also *forbids* unsolicited indications by the interviewing officer of what action will be taken if a person answers questions, makes a statement or refuses to do so.

Para 12: deals with the conduct of interviews and in particular requires:

- at least eight hours *rest* within 24, preferably at night;
- adequately heated, lit and ventilated *interview rooms*;
- interviews to be conducted with *suspect seated*;
- *meals* in accordance with *para 8* and refreshment *breaks* at two hourly intervals if practicable;
- recording of *complaints*;
- the recording of *reasons* for delaying a break in the interview;
- the giving of an *opportunity* to the suspect to read, sign or correct the record if he is at the police station at the time the written record is made;
- that where the person is a child, young person or is suffering from mental illness or handicap a third party present at the interview should be given an opportunity of signing the record of an interview.
- that the purpose of any interview is to be to obtain any explanation of the facts and not necessarily to obtain an admission (*Notes for Guidance*).

2 Confession is defined in s 82 of the 1984 Act as any statement wholly or partly adverse to the person who made it, whether made to a person in authority or not and whether made in words or otherwise. For a fuller discussion see p 140, post.

3 S 60 of the 1984 Act, when in operation, will impose certain duties on the Home Secretary to issue a Code of Practice to specify those offences which are to be the subject of tape recorded interviews.

Para 13: deals with arrested juveniles, the mentally ill and mentally handicapped and requires that such persons must not be interviewed in the absence of 'an appropriate adult'[4] unless a superintendent or above believes that the delay in contacting such a person will involve an immediate risk of harm to persons or serious loss of or damage to property.

Para 14: deals with the use of interpreters when interviewing persons who cannot understand English or who are deaf.

Annex D deals with the making of written statements and in particular requires that:

- Where a person wants to make a written statement he must be given the opportunity to write this himself on the prescribed form without any prompting;[5]
- Where the police officer writes the statement it must record the exact words spoken and must not edit or paraphrase a statement;

Annex E summarises and collates all the provisions in The Detention Code dealing with the mentally ill and mentally handicapped; in particular it reiterates *Para 1:4* which provides that if an officer has *any* suspicion, or is told in good faith, that a person of any age, *whether or not he is in detention*, may be mentally ill or mentally handicapped, or mentally *incapable of understanding the significance of questions put to him or his replies*, then he shall be *treated* as a mentally ill or mentally handicapped person for the purposes of this and the other Codes.

The object of these rules is primarily to ensure that persons in detention and undergoing interrogation are treated fairly and without oppression. Irving has, however, shown that many interrogation techniques are manipulative[6] and that situational factors inherent in arrest, detention and questioning may be highly stressful for some suspects. Although a detailed study of interrogation techniques is outside the scope of this book, it is a subject with which conscientious criminal practitioners should at least be acquainted.[7]

Suspects will normally be interviewed by one or more CID officers, usually in an interview room containing no more than a table and chairs. In between times the suspect will be kept in one of the detention cells. The length and number of interviews will depend upon a number of factors including the seriousness or complexity of the offence and the response of the suspect. Verbatim notes will not usually be taken[8] unless the offence is a serious one, or involves complicated facts, in which case, a detailed questionnaire, sometimes pre-prepared,[9] may be used. The suspect will not normally be invited to make a statement until the termination of interrogation. He may write

4 In the case of a juvenile this will be his parent or guardian or a social worker (if he is in care) or some other responsible adult (not a police officer or employed by the police). In the case of the mentally ill or the mentally handicapped it will be the nearest available relative or some other person who is responsible for his care or custody or another responsible adult (not a police officer or employed by the police) preferably who have experience of dealing with mentally ill or mentally handicapped people. Detention Code, para 1.7.

5 Irving (op cit) p 129 found that statements were rarely written down by the suspect despite formal invitations to do so.

6 See Irving (op cit) Research Study 1. A useful summary of techniques observed is contained in Irving (op cit) Research Study 2 pp 138–151.

7 See further p 103, post.

8 Irving op cit p 128 did not observe a single interview conducted at normal speed with the note taker making an accurate verbatim note in longhand. The Detention Code (para 11.3) now appears to lay down far more stringent requirements for the recording of interviews.

9 This has long been the practice in large fraud cases. Full interview records initialled by the suspect have been more or less standard in some police areas, eg Metropolitan Police, for several years.

this himself[10] or the officer may take it down for him.[11] If he has confessed, he will then normally be charged. Disputes on matters arising in interviews tend to be of two kinds. Either the suspect will subsequently maintain that a written confession was obtained by oppresion or as a result of other unfair pressure, or he will assert that adverse verbal statements attributed to him are either untrue or have been inaccurately recorded. Although such disputes are not as common as is often supposed,[12] they represent those cases where the powers and duties of the police often require the closest scrutiny.[13]

8 PERSONS ATTENDING AT A POLICE STATION VOLUNTARILY

As already noted, such persons are free to leave unless and until arrested.[14] The 1984 Act and the Detention Code is nevertheless relevant in the following respects.

(1) Questioning during voluntary attendance

Such persons have an *absolute* right to inform persons of their whereabouts and obtain legal advice at any time. Note 1A to the Detention Code reminds officers of this and requires that such persons should be treated with no less consideration than arrested suspects. They must be cautioned in the usual way as soon as there are grounds to believe that they have committed an offence. Records of interviews should be kept in the same way as with persons under arrest.[15]

(2) Arrest and subsequent detention

This is subject to the same rules as in the case of any other arrested person. Note in particular that the 'relevant time' for the purpose of computing the maximum period of lawful detention without charge is the moment of arrest. Thus, when a person is merely 'helping the police with enquiries' the custody officer has no duties towards him at all, nor are there any requirements for any review or written records to be kept during this 'voluntary' period.

9 POWERS OF ENTRY, SEARCH AND SEIZURE[15a]

So far we have been largely concerned with the individual suspect and the powers that the police have to arrest and detain him. The police also have

---

10 In which case it will begin: 'I make this statement of my own free will. I understand that I need not say anything unless I wish to do so and that whatever I say may be given in evidence', Detention Code, Annex D, para 2.

11 In which it will begin: 'I [name] wish to make a statement. I want someone to write down what I say. I understand that I need not say anything unless I wish to do so and what I say may be given in evidence', ibid, para 4.

12 See Vennard, 'Disputes Within Trials Over the Admissibility and Accuracy of Incriminating Statements: Some Research Evidence' [1984] Crim LR 15.

13 See further p 187, post.

14 P 55, ante.

15 Para 11.3 of the Detention Code requires that an accurate record be kept of each interview with a person suspected of crime.

15a For a fuller consideration of these powers see the excellent review in chapter 4 of Bevan and Lidstone, op cit.

wide powers to enter and search premises and seize things found there. In certain circumstances these powers extend beyond the premises and property of persons suspected of crime. The need for such powers is broadly to enable the police:

- to search for and arrest persons suspected of crime;
- to search for evidence relating to offences; and
- to recover stolen property or other proceeds of crime.

Research evidence suggests that searches of premises are most common in cases of theft, handling and burglary, and offences involving drugs. In nearly 40% of the searches surveyed, the police found evidence connecting the suspect with the offence under investigation, another 10% revealed material evidence relating to other offences.[16]

The police have no general right to enter and search premises and may never search for or seize 'items subject to legal privilege'. They nevertheless have numerous specific powers, exercisable either:

1. Without warrant (or with the consent of the owner); or
2. Under the warrant of a magistrate;
3. Under the warrant of a circuit judge where the articles sought are 'excluded' or 'special procedure' material.

They also have wide powers to seize and detain what they find but these are entirely dependent upon their having authority to search in the first instance. All searches of premises are now governed by the 'Search of Premises Code' some of the more important provisions of which are as follows.

Para 4: An occupier's consent to the search of his premises must be given in writing.
Para 5:
- Search must be made at a *reasonable hour* unless this might frustrate the purpose of the search.
- The occupier must be told the *purpose* and *grounds* of the search and the *authority* under which it is made.
- *Reasonable force* may only be used if (inter alia) the occupier refuses entry, or is absent, or if necessary to avoid alerting the occupier, frustrating the object of the search or endangering police officers.
- Searches must be conducted with *due consideration* for property and privacy. Reasonable force may only be used in cases of non co-operation.
- A friend or neighbour must not be discouraged or prevented from witnessing the search unless it would thereby be seriously hindered.
- Premises should not be searched at a time when the occupier is likely to be asleep unless this is unavoidable (*Notes for Guidance*).
Para 7: A written record of every search carried out must be made or caused to be made by the officer in charge on arrival at the police station giving details, inter alia, of the articles seized, and whether and if so why force was used or damage caused.
Para 8: Details of all searches are to be entered up in a 'Search Register' maintained at each sub-divisional police station.

16 Taken from a four week survey conducted in September 1979. See 'The Investigation and Prosecution of Criminal Offences in England and Wales: the Law and Procedure' op cit appendix 7, p 126 et seq.

These provisions will hopefully ensure that all searches are carried out with the minimum of disruption, but breaches will not prima facie affect the admissibility of any relevant evidence found.[17] There is, in addition one important category of material that is immune from search and seizure.

'Items subject to legal privilege': 1984 Act, s 10

These are defined as:

(1)(a) communications between a professional legal adviser[18] and his client or any person representing his client made in connection with the giving of legal advice to the client;

(b) communications between a professional legal adviser and his client or any person representing his client or between such an adviser or his client or any such representative and any other person made in connection with or in contemplation of legal proceedings and for the purposes of such proceedings; and

(c) items enclosed with or referred to in such communications and made:

(i) in connection with the giving of legal advice; or

(ii) in connection with or in contemplation of legal proceedings and for the purposes of such proceedings,

when they are in the possession of a person who is entitled to possession of them.

(2) Items held with the intention of furthering a criminal purpose are not items subject to legal privilege.

The police may never search persons or premises for such items, nor may they seize anything which they reasonably believe to be such an item. Four further matters require consideration. First, 'legal privilege' in this context is solely concerned with immunity from search and seizure but is closely related to the issue of admissibility of such items in evidence.[19] Secondly, the definition will cover most items in a solicitor's file (unless there is an intention to further a criminal purpose such as perverting the course of justice). For example, solicitor/client correspondence, instructions to counsel, proofs of evidence, and correspondence with enquiry agents or expert witnesses but not necessarily enclosures[20] will be covered. Problems may arise, however, where a client deposits material with a solicitor that may be of evidential value, for example, company accounts and documents. Such items will not normally come within s 10(1)(c)[1] but they will almost certainly[2] constitute 'excluded material' or 'special procedure material'[3] to which access may only be obtained by an application to a circuit judge. Thirdly, items remain

---

17 *R v Sang*, supra, subject to the discretion in s 78(1) of the 1984 Act to exclude prosecution evidence, the admission of which would have an adverse effect on the fairness of the proceedings. See p 150, post.

18 The term 'professional legal adviser' is clearly wide enough to include non-admitted persons such as law centre staff provided that they are employed at least in part to give legal advice.

19 The topic of legal privilege generally is discussed further at p 149, post.

20 1984 Act s 10(1)(c). Such enclosures will only come within the definition if they were made in connection with the giving of legal advice or in connection with or in contemplation of legal proceedings and for the purpose of such proceedings. The subsection would therefore, for example, cover a handwriting sample taken for the purpose of the proceedings but would not cover a pre-existing sample of the client's handwriting although the latter specimen would be 'special procedure material' see p 90 post and see *R v King* [1983] 1 All ER 929, CA, as to admissibility.

1 Because they will not have been made in connection with the giving of legal advice or in connection with or in contemplation of the legal proceedings and for the purposes of such proceedings. See s 10(1)(c) supra.

2 See further Bevan and Lidstone (op cit) p 95 et seq. and Hargreaves and Levinson (op cit) Ch. 3.

3 Defined at p 90, post.

'subject to legal privilege' so long as they are in the possession of a person who is entitled to such possession. Items will thus continue to be protected so long as they are in the possession of authorised third parties such as enquiry agents and experts.[4] Finally, if such items are wrongfully seized or examined by the police there is, in theory, no rule prohibiting their admission in evidence although the court may exercise its discretion to exclude such evidence under s 78(1) of the 1984 Act if its admission would have an adverse effect on the fairness of the proceedings.[4a]

(1) Powers of entry and search without a warrant

(a) Entry and search by permission

A police officer may enter with the consent of the occupier, but must comply with the 'Search of Premises Code'[5] and any permission must be given in writing in order to be valid.[6] If the officer does not have a warrant or other power of entry, the occupier can refuse. Even if entry is permitted, consent may be withdrawn at any time.[7] Once inside, a police officer may only search the premises with the occupier's permission but, again, such permission may be refused or withdrawn if the officer has no independent right of search. If, however, the occupier does give the police permission to search his premises, their powers of seizure are as wide as when searching under a warrant or other power.[8]

(b) Entry to restrain a breach of the peace

The 1984 Act[9] specifically abolishes all common law powers of entry apart from that to deal with or prevent a breach of the peace.[10] It appears uncertain whether this right confers any additional powers of search and seizure.[11]

(c) Entry to effect an arrest etc: 1984 Act, s 17

Section 17(1) gives the police extensive powers to enter and search without a warrant. A police officer may enter and search any premises[12] in order (inter alia):

4 It will also therefore include a copy of a client's proof of evidence which is sent to a co-accused's solicitor. See further p 149, post.

4a See further p 150 post. See also *R v Heston-Francois* [1984] QB 278, CA (power of judge to stay proceedings).

5 See p 85, ante.

6 See Search of Premises Code, para 4. If at the time a person is not suspected of an offence the officer must tell him so when stating the purpose of the search. In the case of a lodging house or similar accommodation a search should not be made solely on the basis of the landlord's consent unless the tenant is unavailable and the matter is urgent: ibid note 4A.

7 See *Robson v Hallett* [1967] 2 QB 939: officers should be given a reasonable opportunity to leave after which they become trespassers.

8 See 1984 Act, s 19(1).

9 Ibid, s 17(5).

10 Ibid, s 17(6).

11 *Thomas v Sawkins* [1935] 2 KB 249.

12 'Premises' includes any place in particular, any vehicle, vessel, aircraft or hovercraft, offshore installation and tent or moveable structure, 1984 Act, s 23.

    (i) to execute a warrant of arrest issued in connection with criminal proceedings;

    (ii) to arrest without warrant a person for an arrestable offence;

    (iii) to arrest without warrant a person for certain offences under the Public Order Act 1936 and Criminal Law Act 1977; or

    (iv) to save life or limb or prevent serious damage to property.

These powers may only be exercised if the police officer has reasonable grounds for believing that the person whom he is seeking is on the premises (unless he is entering under power (iv)), and any search must be limited to such extent as is 'reasonably required for the purpose for which the power of entry is exercised'.[13] Reasonable force may only be used if it is 'necessary'.[14]

The section in theory only confers powers to enter and search for people as opposed to evidence or the proceeds of crime. Nevertheless, if in the course of such search the police happen to find anything which appears to be evidence or the proceeds of any offence (other than items subject to legal privilege) they have wide powers of seizure and retention.[15]

(d) Entry and search after arrest

There are two powers: one entitles the police to search premises 'occupied or controlled' by a suspect after he has been arrested elsewhere for an *arrestable* offence and the other entitles them to search the premises on which a suspect has been found after arrest for any offence.

(i) Search after arrest (arrestable offences only): 1984 Act, s 18. After arrest the police may enter and search premises 'occupied or controlled'[16] by him if there are reasonable grounds for suspecting that there is *evidence*[17] on those premises relating to the offence for which he has been arrested or some 'other arrestable offence' which is 'connected with or similar' to that offence.[18] The powers under this section may be exercised before taking the suspect to a police station if this is 'necessary for the effective investigation of the offence', otherwise the written authority of an inspector or above must first be obtained.[19] Apparently there is no time limit following arrest within which the power must be exercised.

The police may only search to the extent that is reasonably required for the purpose of discovering evidence relating to the offence for which the person has been arrested or some other connected or similar arrestable offence, but, in practice, this is not a serious restriction, because the police may seize anything which they find other than items which they have reasonable grounds for suspecting to be subject to legal privilege. Whenever a search is

13 1984 Act, s 17(4). For the restriction on searching premises which consist of two or more separate dwellings see s 17(2)(b).

14 Ibid, s 117. See generally Search of Premises Code, paras 5.8–5.10: a police officer should normally ask for permission of the occupier to enter before using force. For a discussion of what constitutes 'force' see *Swales v Cox* [1981] QB 489.

15 1984 Act, s 19. See further p 93, post.

16 For definition of 'premises' see note 12 p 87, ante. 'Occupied or controlled' is not statutorily defined.

17 Other than items subject to legal privilege ibid s 18(1). There appears therefore to be no restriction on searching for evidence which is 'excluded material' or 'special procedure material' under this section. See further p 000, post.

18 Ibid, s 18(1). This effectively reverses the decision in *McLoric v Oxford* [1982] QB 1290.

19 Ibid, s18(5). Any search conducted without prior authority must be reported to an inspector or above as soon as practicable after the search.

carried out under this section details of the grounds for the search, and the nature of any evidence sought, must be recorded on the arrested person's custody record.[20]

(ii) Search of premises on which the person was when arrested (all offences): 1984 Act, s 32. This section empowers the police to enter and search any premises[1] on which a person was when arrested or immediately prior to arrest. In one sense this power is wider than s 18 in that it is not limited to arrestable offences or to premises occupied or controlled by the person arrested, but in another it is narrower in that:

- the police may only search for evidence relating to the offence for which he was arrested;[2]
- search is only permitted if there are reasonable grounds for believing that there is evidence on the premises relating to the offence for which he has been arrested;[3] and
- the power of search is limited to the extent that it is reasonably required for the purposes of discovering any such evidence.[4]

Provided, therefore, that the police have reasonable grounds for believing that there is evidence relating to the offence on the premises they may, for example, search premises on which a burglar has been caught 'red-handed' for abandoned housebreaking implements even if the occupier does not consent (although he normally would).

(2) Powers of entry and search under a magistrates' warrant

Search warrants other than for 'excluded' or 'special procedure' material may be applied for either under existing statutory powers or under s 8 of the 1984 Act. In either case, the new safeguards in ss 15 and 16 of the 1984 Act[5] will apply.

(a) *Existing statutory powers*

There are more than fifty statutory provisions[6] authorising a magistrate to issue search warrants for stolen goods, drugs, firearms and other prohibited articles.[7] Most of these powers are unchanged by the provisions of the 1984 Act save for a number of minor consequential repeals.[8] A magistrate may, for example, issue a search warrant under the Firearms Act 1968, Forgery Act 1913, Misuse of Drugs Act 1971 or Obscene Publications Act 1959. Any

---

20 Ibid, s 18(7) and (8). Searches must be conducted with due consideration for the property and privacy of the occupier and with no more disturbance than necessary: Search of Premises Code, para 5.9.
1 As defined by s 23 see note 17, p 87, ante.
2 S 32(2)(b): contrast the wider powers of personal search under s 32(2)(a) p 54, ante.
3 Ibid, s 32(6).
4 Ibid, s 32(3), but the police officer has much wider powers to seize anything that he finds: see p 93, post.
5 See p 92, post.
6 See 'Investigation and Prosecution of Criminal Offences in England and Wales: the Law and Procedure', op cit, Appendix 5. This is no longer up to date e.g. the Data Protection Act 1984 creates new powers to issue warrants.
7 Power to search may also be given on occasions by written authority of the police officer, for example, under the Official Secrets Act 1911 and see ibid, appendix 5, Table 5.2.
8 1984 Act, Sch 7, Part I.

officer executing a warrant now has the same wide powers of seizure as when searching without a warrant.[9]

(b) Serious arrestable offences: 1984 Act, s 8

The 1984 Act creates a new general power to apply for a warrant to search for evidence of a serious arrestable offence. In order for a warrant to be issued a magistrate must be satisfied that there are reasonable grounds for believing that:

 (i) a serious arrestable offence has been committed; and
 (ii) there is material on the premises specified in the application which is likely to be of substantial value to its investigation; and
 (iii) such material is likely to be relevant evidence (and does not consist of items subject to legal privilege, excluded material or special procedure material); and
 (iv) one or more of the following conditions apply:

 – it is not practicable to communicate with any person entitled to grant entry to the premises; or
 – it is practicable to communicate with such a person but not with any person entitled to grant access to the evidence; or
 – entry will not be granted unless a warrant is produced or;
 – the purposes of the search might be frustrated or seriously prejudiced unless a constable arriving at the premises can secure immediate entry to them.

Although the section is confined to *serious arrestable* offences it should be noted that the officer does not have to establish that the premises are occupied by a person suspected of such an offence. On the face of it, s 8 requires stringent criteria to be satisfied before such a warrant can be issued but, in reality, the magistrate will have little to go on apart from the information given, albeit on oath, by the officer concerned.[10] Nevertheless, the police are now able, for the first time, to apply for a search warrant when investigating numerous serious offences, for example, murder and rape, where no explicit power previously existed.

(c) 'Excluded' and 'Special Procedure' material: 1984, ss 9–14 and Sch 1[10a]

As has already been shown, items subject to legal privilege are wholly exempt from search and seizure. Furthermore, the police may only obtain access by 'Production Order' or warrant to material coming within either of the above two categories by applying to a *circuit judge*.

'*Excluded material*' is defined[11] as either:

9 1984 Act, s 19.
10 Disquiet has been expressed on previous occasions at the ease with which magistrates have granted search warrants on the basis of minimal and often uncorroborated facts presented by the police. See eg Police Complaints Board Triennial Review Report 1983: (HMSO) Cmnd 8853 para 4.9.
10a See further Bevan and Lidstone (op cit) for an invaluable summary of these opaque provisions at p 95 et seq.
11 1984 Act, s 11.

(i) *personal records*[12] which a person has acquired or created in the course of any trade, business, profession or other occupation or for the purposes of any paid or unpaid office and which he holds in confidence;[13]

(ii) *human tissue* or tissue fluid which has been taken for the purposes of diagnosis or medical treatment and which a person holds in confidence: or

(iii) *journalistic material*[14] which a person holds in confidence[15] and which consists of documents or records other than documents.[16]

'Special Procedure material' is defined[17] as material other than items subject to legal professional privilege and excluded material which is either:

(i) journalistic material which is not excluded material, ie not held in confidence; or

(ii) material other than items subject to legal privilege and excluded material in the possession of a person who acquired or created it in the course of any trade, business, profession or other occupation or office (paid or unpaid) and holds it in confidence.[18]

The procedural rules are extremely complicated but, broadly, the police may apply to a circuit judge either for an order to be given access to such material within seven days (a 'Production Order') or (in more restricted circumstances) a search warrant.

A Production Order is applied for *inter partes* and requires the police to satisfy the appropriate 'access conditions' set out in Schedule 1 to the Act. Very broadly, if access is sought to 'special procedure material' the police must show that either:

(i) it is admissable evidence likely to be of substantial value in the investigation of a *'serious arrestable offence'* of which production should be ordered on the balance of public interest; or

---

12 Defined in 1984 Act s 12 as documentary and other records concerning an individual who can be identified from them relating to:
  (a) his physical or mental health;
  (b) his spiritual counselling or assistance given or to be given to him;
  (c) counselling or assistance given or to be given to him, for the purposes of his personal welfare, by any voluntary organisation or by any individual who:
    (i) by reason of his office or occupation has responsibilities for his personal welfare; or
    (ii) by reason of an order of the court has responsibilities for his supervision.
This definition effectively restricts this category to records held by the 'caring professions' and will not normally therefore extend to records kept by accountants, bankers or employers (although personnel records may qualify where there is a counselling element).
13 Ie subject to an express or implied undertaking to so hold it or to a restriction on disclosure or obligation of secrecy contained in any enactment: ibid, s 11(2).
14 Defined by s 13 as material acquired or created for the purposes of journalism and in the possession of a person who acquired or created it for that purpose. A person who receives material from someone who intends that the recipient shall use it for the purposes of journalism is to be taken to have acquired it for such purpose.
15 Ibid, s 11(3), ie held subject to an express or implied undertaking to so hold it or restriction or obligation of secrecy contained in any enactment provided that it has been continuously held by one or more persons subject to such an undertaking etc since it was first acquired or created for the purposes of journalism.
16 Ibid, s 11(1)(c).
17 Ibid, s 14.
18 As defined in s 11(2) supra. For the position where material is passed onto or created by an employee see s 14(3) and (4).

(ii) (but for the restrictions imposed by s 9(2) of the 1984 Act) a magistrate would have power to issue a search warrant under any other enactment eg under s 16 of the Forgery Act 1913.

On the other hand, if access is sought to 'excluded material' the only ground available is (ii) above. Thus, the police may not obtain an order in respect of 'excluded material' on the basis that it constitutes evidence of a serious arrestable offence; they must show instead that it is also material in respect of which a magistrates' warrant could otherwise issue, for example, because the 'excluded material' contains evidence of an offence under the Official Secrets Act 1911.

Failure to comply with a Production Order may be dealt with as if it were a contempt of court[19] or, if ground (ii) above can be established, may be followed up by an application for a search warrant. As an alternative, the police may initially apply ex parte for a search warrant if they can show that a Production Order could be made *and* that, *inter alia*, it is not practicable to communicate with the person entitled to grant entry or that an application for a Production Order may seriously prejudice the investigation.[20] These rules are so full of technicalities that one seriously wonders how often the police will seek to make use of them particularly since both sets of 'access conditions' require the police to make out reasonable grounds for believing that there is 'excluded' or 'special procedure material' on the relevant premises. The police will thus not be able to ask a judge to authorise a 'fishing expedition', they will have to specify the relevant material with some degree of particularity.[1]

(d) Restrictions on search warrants: 1984 Act, ss 15 and 16 and Search of Premises Code

The 1984 Act lays down detailed rules applicable to all search warrants whether granted by a magistrate or a judge. Whenever a search warrant is applied for and executed the requirements of ss 15 and 16 *must* be complied with, otherwise the entry on or search of the premises will be unlawful. Section 15 sets out detailed formal requirements which in particular stipulate prescribed information[2] that must be supplied by an officer when applying for a warrant. Section 16 requires that (inter alia):

(a) all warrants must be executed within one month of the date of issue; and
(b) all warrants must be executed at a 'reasonable hour' unless it appears that there are reasonable grounds for suspecting that the purpose of the search may be frustrated on entry at a reasonable hour; and
(c) any articles seized must be listed on the warrant.
(d) a warrant may only authorise entry on one occasion and must be returned to the court which issued it and kept there for 12 months during which period the occupier will be entitled to inspect it.

19 1984 Act, Sch 1, para 15.
20 Ibid, para 14.
 1 There is apparently nothing to prevent the police searching for excluded material or special procedure material in the course of a search without warrant under s 17, s 18 or s 32 of the 1984 Act. Furthermore the police may seize such material if they find it in the course of any lawful search of premises. Additionally, there is nothing to prevent them seeking access by consent to information stored on a computer (see Data Protection Act 1984, s 28(1)). For a further discussion of these provisions see Bevan and Lidstone (op cit) chapter 4 and Hargreaves and Levinson (op cit) Chapter 3.
 2 See 1984 Act, s 15(2).

Paragraph 1 of the Search of Premises Code deals specifically with applications for search warrants and provides (inter alia) that:

   (i) information received shall be checked and anonymous sources corroborated;

  (ii) the nature of the articles concerned and their location shall be ascertained as specifically as is possible;

 (iii) an application for a search warrant requires the authority of an *inspector* or above (or the chief officer available, in an emergency);

 (iv) applications for access to 'excluded' or 'special procedure material' require the authority of a *superintendent* or above.

  (v) in cases involving community issues the police community liaison officer must be consulted before a warrant is executed.

(3) Seizure and retention

(a) *The general power: 1984 Act, s 19*

Once the police are lawfully inside premises either with the consent of the occupier or under any of the statutory powers considered above they may seize anything other than items subject to legal privilege (including, it seems, 'excluded' and special procedure material), if they have reasonable grounds for believing either that it is evidence in relation to any other offence, or that it has been obtained in consequence of the commission of any offence, and in either case that it is necessary to seize it in order to prevent it being concealed, lost, damaged, altered or destroyed.

Section 19 thus confers very wide powers of seizure. The occupier of the premises searched may not himself be under suspicion; nevertheless, if he allows the police to search his premises or they have power to search under a warrant they may take any material coming within the above categories even if he objects. Furthermore, the power of seizure is not limited to articles that may be evidence or proceeds of the offence under investigation but extends to those that are evidence or proceeds of any offence. The only partial safeguards are that the occupier of the premises on which articles were seized is entitled to a record of what has been taken within a reasonable time from the making of the request[3] and the need for 'reasonable' belief.[3a]

(b) *How long may a seized article be retained? 1984 Act, s 21*

Any article seized under these provisions may be retained so long as is necessary in all the circumstances. In particular:

   – for use as evidence at a trial; or
   – for forensic examination; or
   – to establish its lawful owner (subject to there being reasonable grounds for believing that it has been obtained in consequence of the commission of an offence).[4]

An article may not be retained for any of the above purposes, however, if a photograph or copy would be sufficient.

---

3 See generally 1984 Act, s 21.
3a See *Reynolds v Metropolitan Police Comr* [1984] 3 All ER 649.
4 Ibid, s 22(3).

(4) Bank accounts

The police may, on occasions, seek access to a suspect's bank account in order to find evidence relating to an offence or to freeze the moneys found in it with a view to their being made the subject of a forfeiture order.[5]

> EXAMPLE. D is arrested and charged with robbery at X Bank on 10 July. The police have reason to believe that a substantial sum of cash was paid into an account in D's name at Y Bank on 15 July. Confirmation of this would provide strong circumstantial evidence of D's involvement if he has no other visible means of support. Additionally, the police (and X Bank) will be anxious to ensure that he cannot draw on the account in the meantime.

The police have two available remedies. First, they may apply to a court[6] for an order permitting them to inspect and take copies of a bank account under Bankers' Books Evidence Act 1879, s 7 provided that proceedings have been commenced.[7] Secondly, they may apply for an injunction under the Supreme Court Act 1981, s 37 restraining the accused from operating the account until further order if they can establish that there are reasonable grounds for believing that it contains moneys that have been obtained from another by theft or deception. Their public duty to seek out and recover stolen property with a view to restoring it to the rightful owner gives them sufficient locus standi.[8] Nevertheless, this does not entitle them to apply for an injunction freezing all an accused's assets with a view to providing a fund to satisfy any future restitution, compensation or forfeiture order or order for costs.[9]

10 OTHER INVESTIGATIVE POWERS

The police now have at their disposal a number of sophisticated technical aids for fighting and detecting crime, including high grade surveillance equipment, X-ray equipment for examining hand baggage or parcels and increasingly rapid and sophisticated computer based retrieval systems. Notwithstanding this, the majority of offences are detected and evidence assembled as a result of the interrogation and search of suspects and premises. Two other important aspects of investigation nevertheless require further attention: (1) identification evidence; and (2) surveillance and eavesdropping.

(1) Identification evidence

(a) Identification parades and photographs

The police will sometimes wish to ascertain whether eye-witnesses can identify a suspect. In order for such evidence to have any cogency it must take place in sufficiently controlled circumstances to allow the minimum margin for error. The holding of an identification parade in which a witness is taken along a line of people of similar appearance to the suspect, in order to see

---

5 For the limitations on such orders see *R v Cuthbertson* [1981] AC 470.
6 A magistrates' court or judge: 1984 Act, s 7.
7 Ibid, s 7. This probably requires the subject to have at least been arrested and charged.
8 *West Mercia Constabulary v Wagener* [1981] 3 All ER 378.
9 *Chief Constable of Kent v V* [1983] QB 34. See further C.P. Walker 'Police Powers and Bank Accounts' [1983] Crim LR 723.

whether the witness can pick him out, is the traditional albeit somewhat illogical way of establishing identity or eliminating a suspect. Identity may also be established by means of photographs but great care needs to be taken lest this procedure in any way 'points' to the suspect, for example, if it is clearly a photograph taken whilst in custody.

The police have no power to compel a suspect to take part in a parade nor can they force members of the public to assist in the holding of one. Although discussion of the rules relating to the admissibility of identification evidence belong to the law of evidence it is nevertheless necessary at this point to outline the procedures that need to be adopted. The 1984 Act makes no mention of identification evidence save to provide for the issue of a Code of Practice (the Identification Code).

(b) Organisation of identification parades

Parades will take place in a police station or, more rarely, in a prison. The parade may take place either in a normal room or in one equipped with a 'screen' permitting witnesses to see members of the parade without themselves being seen. The parade must be set up and conducted by a uniformed officer of at least inspector rank who is not involved in the investigation (the 'identification officer'). No officer who is involved in the investigation may take any part in setting up the parade. Parades must be conducted in accordance with Annex A of the Code.

(c) Rights of the suspect

Whenever identity is in dispute a suspect is entitled to ask to be put on a parade. If this is practicable, one must be held. Conversely he is not obliged to take part in a parade if the police request it; if he refuses, however, he runs certain risks. Before agreeing to take part in a parade a suspect must be informed of his right to refuse to go on such a parade, but will be warned that if he refuses he may be confronted by a witness. He must further be warned that his refusal may be given in evidence in any subsequent trial, at which a witness may be given an opportunity of identifying him in court. This warning must be given along with other prescribed information before any parade takes place and the suspect must also be given a written 'Notice to Suspect' confirming this.[10]

If a suspect refuses to go on a parade the police must first of all try to make arrangements for him to be seen in a group of people (for example, he may be introduced into a shopping area or, on occasions, even placed on an escalator).[11] If the suspect again refuses to take part or it is impracticable to arrange a group identification, the police may as a last resort proceed to a direct confrontation.

Whichever course is adopted, the suspect must at least be given a reasonable opportunity to have a solicitor or friend present[12] (a 'screen' parade can *never* take place unless such a person is present).[12a] When a parade[13] takes

10 See Identification Code, paras 2.7 and 2.8. The suspect will be asked to sign a second copy indicating whether or not he consents to a parade. This must be retained by the identification officer.
11 This tactic has, for example, been employed in Brixton because of difficulties in persuading black members of the public to take part in identification parades.
12 Identification Code Annex A para 1. The suspect is not therefore entitled to have a solicitor present. This must be regarded as one of the most serious defects in the Code.
12a Unless the parade is recorded on video: ibid, Annex A, para 2.
13 Or group identification.

place without a solicitor or friend present a colour photograph of the parade must be taken unless any of the parade members object.[14]

(d) *The conduct of the parade*

It is important that defence solicitors should become familiar with what happens on an identification parade and the prescribed procedure that should be followed. The following points, in particular, should be noted.

(i) Preliminary procedure. Before the parade starts the parade officer (who must be an uniformed officer of at least inspector rank not involved in the investigation)[15] must explain the procedures governing the conduct of the parade and must ensure that all unauthorised persons are strictly excluded from the place where the parade is to be held. Details of the parade or group identification must be recorded by writing on the prescribed form.[15a]

(ii) Segregation of witnesses. It is the responsibility of the parade officer to ensure that the witnesses do not:

- *communicate* with each other or overhear a witness who has already seen the parade;
- *see* any member of the parade;
- *be prompted* by any photograph or description of the suspect or given any other clue as to his identity; or
- *see* the suspect in any circumstances before or after the parade.

In addition, the police officer conducting the witness to the parade must not discuss its composition with him or disclose whether any previous witness has made any identification.

(e) *The parade itself*

The parade will normally[16] consist of *at least eight* persons other than the suspect who are, as far as possible, similar in age, height, general appearance and position in life. Before the parade takes place, the suspect must be asked whether he has any objection to the arrangements of any of the participants. Where practicable, steps must be taken to remove the objection. If not practicable, the identification officer must explain why. The suspect is free to select his own position in the line and to change his position on each occasion, should there be more than one witness attending the parade. Each position in the line must be clearly numbered, whether by means of a numeral laid on the floor in front of each parade member or by other means.

(f) *Witnesses*

Witnesses must be brought in one by one. Immediately before each witness inspects the parade he must be told that the person he saw may or may not

---

14 Identification Code, Annex A, para 20. A copy shall be supplied on request within a reasonable time.

15 Identification Code, para 2.2.

15a Annex A, paras 12 and 13.

16 Ibid, Unless there are two suspects of roughly similar appearance in which case they may be paraded together with at least 12 other persons, ibid. In no circumstances should more than two suspects be included in one parade, ibid. If all members of a similar group are possible suspects separate parades should be held for each member of the group. Where police officers in uniform for the parade, numerals or other identifying badges shall be concealed. Ibid Annex A para 9.

be on it, and that if he cannot make a positive identification he should say so. He will be asked to walk carefully along the parade at least twice taking as much care and time as he wishes, and then asked whether the person he saw in person on an earlier relevant occasion[17] is on the parade. He will then normally be requested to make an identification by saying the number concerned.[18] If the witness makes an identification after the parade has ended the suspect, and if present his solicitor, shall be informed, and consideration should be given as to whether there should be a fresh parade.[19]. Great care needs to be taken if the witness wishes to hear the suspect speak, adopt any specified posture or move. The Code requires the parade officer to remind the witness that the parade has been selected on the basis of physical appearance and must specifically ask him whether he is capable of identifying any person on that basis. The parade may nevertheless be asked to comply with such a request.[20]

IDENTIFICATION PARADES

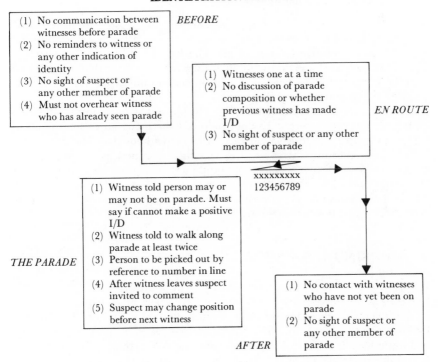

(g) *Use of photographs for identification*[21]

The Identification Code also sets out detailed rules concerning the use of photographs or identikit pictures and in particular, provides the following safeguards:

17 See identification Code, Annex A, para 14.
18 Ibid, para 15.
19 Ibid, para 16.
20 Ibid, para 17.
21 Ibid, Annex C.

(i) Such pictures should not be shown where *there is a suspect already available*. An identification parade should be held. Only one witness may be shown photographs at any one time.

(ii) The witness must be shown *at least 12* photographs at a time, all as far as possible of similar type. If they include a *suspect* the other photographs must have *as close a resemblance to the suspect as possible*.

(iii) If the witness makes a *positive identification* other witnesses must not be shown photographs and an identification parade should be held.

(iv) Where a *witness attending an identification* parade has previously been shown photographs or photofit pictures the suspect and his legal representative *must* be informed on this fact before committal proceedings or summary trial.

On the face of it the Code provides stringent safeguards; as will become apparent,[22] any solicitor present needs to be supremely vigilant.

(2) Surveillance and eavesdropping

The use of long range photographic equipment and closed circuit television is likely to become increasingly commonplace. The 1984 Act does not deal with this aspect of investigation at all. The Royal Commission on Criminal Procedure took the view that such operations were no more than an intensive form of observation which, since not in themselves unlawful, did not require any additional powers.

Similarly, evidence obtained by eavesdropping has been admitted in evidence, at any rate where it has not involved the police in trespassing. Any attempt to enter and 'bug' a person's premises without their consent would, prima facie, constitute trespass, and evidence obtained as a result thereof might not be admitted.[23] Telephone tapping is not prima facie illegal,[24] but the permission of the Home Secretary is required as a matter of practice. It will become subject to the provisions of the Interception of Communications Bill (1985) when this becomes law.

11 ADVISING THE CLIENT

At present, most clients are not seen by their solicitors until *after they have been charged*. The first contact will usually have taken place either at court or at the solicitor's office. Under 1984 Act the position is likely to be radically different for three reasons. First, the police can never deny a suspect access to legal advice if requested unless postponement is authorized in the case of a 'serious arrestable offence'.[1] Secondly, he must be reminded of the above right both orally and in writing as soon as practicable.[2] Thirdly, when in operation, the extended Duty Solicitor scheme will provide a back-up service for those clients who do not have a solicitor or whose solicitor is unavailable.[3]

22 P 104, post.
23 See s 78(1) of the 1984 Act, p 150 post.
24 *Malone v Metropolitan Police Comr* [1979] Ch 344. But see p 42 ante.
 1 See p 80, ante.
 2 See p 79, ante. Earlier research has suggested very few suspects actually ask to see a solicitor while in custody. See Softley, op cit, p 68 and sources quoted in the Royal Commission Report on Criminal Procedure, op cit, para 4.83.
 3 The person in custody shall be asked to sign on the custody record to signify whether or not he wants legal advice at this point: Detention Code, para 3.4.

It can, therefore, be predicted with some certainty that defence solicitors may now be involved in the early stages of a criminal investigation on a quite unprecedented scale. It is vital from the outset to appreciate where the solicitor's duty lies. If a solicitor is asked, either as Duty Solicitor or in a private capacity, to advise and represent a client who has not been charged, the overriding duty is to that client. The solicitor is there, of course, to ensure in particular that the innocent do not confess to crimes that they did not commit and are not falsely picked out of incorrectly conducted identification parades. The solicitor's duties, however, go far beyond that. Every client must be advised as to his rights, in particular, his right to refuse to answer any questions at all or make a written statement, even if he admits his guilt or it appears that the police evidence against him is overwhelming.[4] Every suspect has the 'right of silence', the right to refuse to give intimate body samples and the right to refuse an identity parade. Although the waiver of these rights must ultimately rest with the client, your task is to advise him as to his rights and to help him to the appropriate decision.

To carry out these duties effectively you will need to have a detailed grasp of the relevant provisions of the 1984 Act and Codes of Practice, a sound knowledge of criminal law and evidence and a working knowledge of police organisational structures and working methods, plus considerable stamina and strength of character. Although much attention has been given to the psychological pressures on the suspect whilst in a police station,[5] little attention has been paid to the psychological pressures on third parties, *particularly solicitors*. The police station may be far more of an alien territory to you as it is to the client. Attendances will often be outside office hours when fatigue, the pressure of other work and worry as to likelihood of payment[6] may cloud your judgment. When instructed by a relative, there may even be uncertainty as to whether the client actually wants to see you. Quite apart from this, you may already know officers at the police station: the exigencies of establishing a working relationship can prove to be inhibiting.

Pressures such as these are likely to be even greater for the Duty Solicitor, who must recognise at all times his or her duty is to maintain an independent role. Independence is vital because the Duty Solicitor's presence will usually render it more or less impossible to raise any allegations of police impropriety at the trial. By all means maintain a high standard of courtesy and professional conduct in relations with the police. You should never be rude about individual officers, or about the police in general, but treat them with the respect which the vast majority deserve. However, you must also make it plain why you are there. Contrary to the well-publicised utterances of certain senior police officers[7] most criminal practitioners and police officers have a very successful working relationship and respect and trust each other as fellow professionals. It is all too easy therefore for police and defence solicitors to see themselves as separate parts of the machinery of criminal justice in which the suspect is the 'outsider'. It should be remembered at all times that you are there for one purpose, and one purpose only: to represent the client's interests.

---

4 For the ethical position of continuing to act in such circumstances see p 171, post.
5 See Irving, op cit, pp 11–41 and 100–150 which should be compulsory reading for every solicitor before he/she ventures near a police station.
6 For remuneration under the Green Form scheme for attending at a police station, see p 228, post.
7 See for example 'In the Office of Constable', Sir Robert Mark (Fontana 1979), p 163.

Three aspects of the defence solicitor's role now require closer examination. These are:

(1) gaining access to the client in custody;
(2) advising the client in custody;
(3) identification parades.

The practical consequences of disputing police evidence will be considered in later chapters.[8]

(1) **Gaining access**

As already indicated, gaining access is likely to cause fewer problems than it has in the past. Nevertheless, difficulties may still arise, particularly where the client is arrested for a 'serious arrestable offence'. If the first contact is from a friend or relative it is vital that as much background information as possible is obtained as to the station to which the client has been taken and the status of the person who is instructing you. It has now been established that a third party may instruct a solicitor on behalf of a client in custody,[9] but it is advisable for you to see the relative in person if possible, and to ask him to accompany you to the police station when a visit is contemplated. On receiving instructions in such a case the first thing you should do is to contact the station and ask to speak to the investigating officer. Any replies should be carefully noted, particularly if information or access is refused under s 58 of the 1984 Act. If access is not being denied under this section then, although strictly speaking a solicitor cannot demand to speak to the client on the telephone, the request should be made and any replies if necessary noted in writing. The officer should be reminded that the s 58 right includes a right to consult a solicitor at any time either in person or on the telephone. You should also be sure to enquire whether or not the suspect has been arrested or is at the police station voluntarily. If no further information is forthcoming it may be worth asking whether there is a Duty Solicitor available and, if so, discussing the case with him or her. This may give forth further information and, in the long run, save an unnecessary journey to the police station.

If the replies received are unsatisfactory it is clearly not sufficient to leave it there. You should follow up with a visit to the police station.[10] If a follow up visit is intended you should inform the police of your impending arrival and request that no further questioning takes place until you arrive.[11] If the client contacts you in person or you are given an opportunity to speak to him on the telephone you should always advise him not to answer any, or any further, questions until you arrive and ensure that this request is conveyed to a police officer. You should also make a contemporaneous note of any conversation.

8 See especially p 157 et seq, post.
9 *R v Jones* (1984) 128 Sol Jo 171, CA. See now Detention Code: Annex B: para 2
10 Remuneration may be claimed under the Green Form scheme. This is, however, limited in the first instance to £50, ie less than 2 hours' work. If therefore a long visit is anticipated authority for an extension should be sought from the Area Secretary over the telephone. The Green Form may be completed on the suspect's behalf by a third party, provided that they have sufficient details concerning this financial eligibility: Legal Advice and Assistance (No 2) Regulations 1980. The Scheme will be extended to £75 in due course when the 1984 Act is fully operational. It is intended, however, that the scheme should not be means tested
11 See p 81 ante, as to the limited circumstances in which interrogation can take place after a request for a solicitor has been made.

(2) Advising the client and attending on interviews

If your presence is required at a police station to advise a client it is vital that you go there well prepared. You must have with you copies of the Codes of Practice, a client questionnaire form, legal aid forms, your business card or (if you are unadmitted) a letter of introduction on the firm's notepaper. Last but not least you will need a hard surface, preferably a clip board, on which to make contemporaneous notes.[12]

Once there, there are three separate aspects to the role of the solicitor:

(a) obtaining access;
(b) advising the client privately; and
(c) attending at the interview (if any).

(a) Obtaining access

It must be stressed that if the client is being detained in respect of a 'serious arrestable offence' the police are not even obliged to confirm or deny that they are holding him. If difficulties are anticipated first contact should always be made with whoever is carrying out the duties of custody officer. If no co-operation is forthcoming you should make a careful note of any replies and ask to see the superintendent responsible for the police station.

If the police admit that they are holding a suspect but are refusing access under s 58 it is important that you insist on speaking to the superintendent who has given authority. If you are told that no one is available you should remind the officer that the withholding of access to legal advice can only take place as long as one of the prescribed reasons for authorising delay exists, for example, likelihood of interference with or harm to evidence connected with a 'serious arrestable offence'. It is particularly important that the case for withholding access under s 58 is made out. Every attempt should therefore be made to seek justification for it. In such cases, you must always find out how long the suspect has been at the station, when the next review of detention is proposed, and the reasons for continued detention without charge.

(b) Advising the client

Once access has been granted you are entitled to consult with the client *privately* unless he is charged with a terrorist offence. Before you can advise him adequately you must, however, obtain information from an officer acquainted with the case as to the nature of the offences under investigation and the evidence thereon. The client must then be reminded that he does not *have* to say anything but that the final decision must be his. This is a very difficult decision for the client to take and, if he is in any doubt at all, you should advise him to say nothing. Before doing this, however, you must obtain some instructions from the client as to what his version of the story is and also find out whether or not he has as yet made any verbal admissions to the police or made any written statement. If the client vehemently protests

12 See Nash, 'Called to a police station', LAG Bulletin March 1968, p 64. Although dealing with pre-1984 practice this article still contains much helpful information.

his innocence it may, on the face of it, be advisable for him to agree to an interview or to make a statement. The problem is, however, that once begun, interviews are very difficult to bring to an end. If, many months later, police officers give evidence of questioning which was brought to an end on the solicitor's advice when 'the going got rough' this may have a more damning effect than if no interview had taken place. The client may be confused about dates, places and events and the evidence that he gives at the trial may be different from that which he gave under interrogation. Additionally, it has to be remembered that even if he does give answers or makes a statement that is *wholly favourable* this will not be admissible at the trial to prove the truth of the facts stated but merely to show consistency.[13] On the other hand, if he does not make a statement or agree to answer questions, the 'right to silence', in theory, precludes the drawing of an inference of guilt.[14] In practice, however, a jury or magistrates' court may regard this as the reaction of a guilty man. In cases of doubt, the best compromise is to advise the client to make a written statement rather than agree to an interview since the client then has greater control over events.

If, on the other hand, the client wishes to admit his guilt he should never be actively discouraged from doing so although he must still be advised that he is entitled to put the prosecution to the proof of their case. It may be that the client has failed to appreciate that the evidence against him is not as strong as it appears, for example, he will probably be unaware that evidence of a co-suspect is not normally admissible against him. In such cases, however, it is if anything even more important that he is advised by his solicitor of his right to silence. The new statutory definition of 'confession'[15] clearly contemplates the possible exclusion of confessions as a result of oppression or things said or done by persons *other than those investigating the case*. This creates particular dangers for those acting as Duty Solicitors. There is always the possibility that an accused will subsequently seek to retract a confession alleging undue pressure from his then solicitor. On the other hand, if the desire to confess is clearly genuine and provided that the client realises that he does not have to admit to the offence then, clearly, much is to be gained by his agreeing to make a statement. It gives the opportunity not only to put forward mitigating factors at a very early stage but also to minimise the possibility of loss to the victim, for example, by assisting in the recovery of stolen property. Great care should, however, be taken if anything resembling a 'deal' is being offered, on the basis, for example, that if the suspect makes a statement he will be charged with less serious offences or that if he implicates other persons some form of immunity from prosecution may be arranged. Such cases need to be handled with the greatest of care by persons of authority and experience. Although there may be exceptional cases when such an arrangement is in the client's interests the general advice should be to avoid any form of premature 'plea bargaining'. If you feel that you are not sufficiently experienced to make a decision on the matter, you should refer it at once to someone of seniority in your firm.

In some cases, especially complicated frauds, the police may wish to interview the client from a prepared questionnaire. Although this may have considerable advantages to both parties in complicated cases you must make

---

13 See further post.
14 For a definition of the 'right of silence' see p 42, ante. For the inferences that may be drawn see p 141, post.
15 See p 146, post.

sure before agreeing to do so that you read the questionnaire carefully. It has not been unknown for a lengthy prepared questionnaire already to contain at the end the sentence, 'I therefore charge you with ...'! Any documents to be referred to should also be carefully studied before the interview begins. The police are not under any obligation to restrict the questions to those in the questionnaire and, as has been noted, once an interview begins it is difficult to terminate it prematurely, without incurring prejudice.

It has been assumed until now that the client seeking advice will automatically be in detention but this may not be the case necessarily. On occasions, he may have been 'invited' to the station to 'help the police with their inquiries'. You may thus be afforded the advance opportunity in deciding whether or not to attend with the client. In any event the tactical considerations discussed above will be of equal application but additional points require mention. First, you can impose any conditions you wish since the interview is entirely voluntary. It may well be advisable therefore to arrange for the interview to take place away from the police station thus freeing the client (and you) from any of the psychological pressures entailed in a police station interview. It goes without saying, of course, that you can insist on being present throughout the interview and should at all times do so, rather than abandon your client. Secondly, you may sometimes find that the police attempt to pressurise you or your client by saying that if you do not agree to come to the station they will arrest the client. The temptation is to reply, 'Do your worst' since he normally cannot be detained for longer than 24 hours nor can he be denied access to legal advice. However, there is always the risk, for example in a large fraud, that access may be denied under s 58 of the 1984 Act on the ground that it is a 'serious arrestable offence' because it was intended to lead to substantial financial gain.[16]

(c) *The interview*

As already indicated[17] the possible introduction of tape recorded interviews in the not too distant future will revolutionise the defence solicitor's role. At present, however, it is likely that the interview will take one of three forms:

    (i) interviewer or other police officer present taking rough notes only;[18]

    (ii) verbatim account recorded in question and answer form as the interview progresses with the suspect signing the bottom of each page and initialling each answer; or

    (iii) interview on the basis of a prepared questionnaire with similar signing and initialling.

Great care should always be taken to ensure that everything is recorded accurately because it will be well nigh impossible to take issue with any errors or ambiguities at a later date. You must remember that you are there to protect your client and that you should, therefore, always interrupt if any question or answer is ambiguous or is such that you do not think that your client should answer it. If the client wishes to take advice before answering a question you are entitled to seek an adjournment and consult with him

16 See p 49, ante.
17 See p 74, ante.
18 Such interviews are likely to be extremely rare in view of the requirements of para 11.3 of the Detention Code. See p 82, ante.

privately, although once begun interruptions in questioning may appear prejudicial at the trial. It is also important that you ensure that there are breaks in the questioning if the client is getting tired or needs refreshment (or within reason if you do: you need to be more alert than anyone).

(3) **Identification parades**

Nowhere is the presence of a solicitor more required than at an identification parade. It is therefore regrettable that the Identification Code does not give the suspect a right to this unless the parade is behind a 'screen'. Attending on a parade on behalf of a client is one of the most pressurized situations that you will face in practice. It will often take place outside office hours in a highly-charged atmosphere, conducted by a relatively senior police officer who will often, understandably, be anxious to get the whole thing over because of the disruption that parades cause to police stations and members of the public. It is very easy therefore for a solicitor to be made to feel that he or she is being 'unreasonable' by insisting that some point or other is observed before the parade takes place. You must not be afraid of this as it is your responsibility to ensure that the identification parade is correctly carried out. The consequences of mistaken identification are catastrophic. Identification evidence appears to be accorded far greater weight than its cogency often justifies. Experiments have also shown that potential jurors have difficulty in evaluating the credibility of such testimony.[19] You must, therefore, be alert at all times to obvious breaches of the rules and also other less obvious factors that may affect the fairness of the parade. The following points in particular need to be borne in mind.

(a) *Is a parade compulsory?*

No suspect is obliged to attend on a parade[20] but if he does not there is always the attendant risk of his being identified in less favourable circumstances, such as on a group identification or, even worse, a confrontation. Conversely, the client may ask to be put on a parade provided that it is 'practicable to hold one'.[1] If such a request is refused you should ask for the reason. Before any decision can be taken it is, however, essential that you are possessed of sufficient information to be able to evaluate whether or not any useful purpose would be served by a parade. The first thing that you must do, therefore, is to insist on being given details of the initial description given by the identifying witnesses. Until this information is available you should advise the client to refuse to attend on a parade and make sure that the reason for refusing is recorded. If the description that is given does not remotely resemble the client it is utterly pointless agreeing to a parade since it can clearly have no evidential value. If you were to agree to a parade in such circumstances and the client were picked out, differences between the initial description and your client's actual appearance may not be afforded the weight they deserve at the trial. Paradoxically, the more the client's description tallies with that given by the witness, the more point there is in

19 See Lloyd-Bostock and Clifford, *Evaluating Witness Evidence* (1983) John Willey & Sons, especially Chapter 4 and Loftus, *Eye Witness Testimony* (1979) Harvard University Press.
20 See p 95, ante.
 1 Identification Code para 2.1. It should be noted from ibid, para 2.4 that a group identification may also be arranged where the officer *in charge of the investigation* considers, either because of fear on the part of the witness, or some other reason, that in the circumstances it is more 'satisfactory' than a parade.

having a parade provided that the other eight members look as similar to the client as possible (thus revealing the inherent illogicality of identification parades).

(b) Before the parade

Always have the Identification Code with you as a checklist. In an ideal world a suspect should have four persons representing his interests. One in the room in which the witnesses are to wait, one accompanying the witnesses from the waiting room to the parade: one in the parade area and another to escort the witness from the parade area to the room in which the witness will wait after the parade. In practice, of course, this is impossible and all that can be done is to rely upon fair play. It is vital, however, that you inspect the waiting room and all areas of the route, in particular to ensure that there are no circumstances in which the witness or witnesses could have an opportunity to see the suspect in circumstances which identify him as such. Care also needs to be taken if the client is not in custody to ensure that he arrives at a separate entrance, preferably unaccompanied. Ideally he should be infiltrated into the parade without even the other members being aware that he is the suspect. Where there is more than one witness every effort should be made to ensure that they do not speak to each other at any stage, either before or after the parade. Since you cannot be in four places at one time you will have to rely on the efficiency and fairness of the police. The writers' experiences of parades has been that they have always been conducted with scrupulous fairness, but, at the risk of repetition, a solicitor's duty is to protect his or her client.

(c) The composition of the parade

The other persons on the parade (at least *eight*) must resemble the suspect in age, height, general appearance and position in life. You must ensure that this is complied with within reason, even at the risk of appearing 'unreasonable'. If your objections are overruled you should make sure that they are recorded and make a note of them. It used to be thought that a suspect was entitled to form the parade from persons of his own choosing but it has been held that this is not the case. The composition of the parade is entirely in the discretion of the parade officer subject to any discrepancies being liable to adverse comment at the trial.[2] Conversely, if it is not possible to get a parade of eight people together who resemble the client sufficiently it may be better to hold a small parade than no parade at all, bearing in mind the possible damaging affect of a group identification or confrontation.

(d) Before the parade starts

Once the composition of the parade is to your satisfaction it is important for you to examine the other members in detail to ensure that there are no other discrepancies that might make your client stand out. For example, if he has been in police detention, ensure that he has a change of clothing and an opportunity to wash and shave etc. so that he does not stand out by virtue of his haggard and dishevelled appearance. Within reason, you can ask the other members of the parade to do what you like, for example, to remove

2 See *R v Thorne* [1981] Crim LR 702, CA.

items of clothing, footwear, or watches and rings. If the suspect has a distinguishing scar or birth mark that makes him stand out this should be covered with sticking plaster and a piece placed in a similar position on the face of each of the other members in the line up. The suspect may stand where he likes and change position where there is more than one witness.

(e)   *The parade itself*

You *must* keep a careful record of *everything* that happens and a note of all the positions on the parade. Photographing of parades is, unfortunately, not automatic and the Identification Code is curiously silent as to the provision of the names and addresses of the other members of the line up. Nevertheless there is no harm in your seeking permission to take a photograph or asking the officer, or the other members of the line up themselves, whether they are willing to furnish their names and addresses. The parade itself will often take place in a highly-charged atmosphere. It is important therefore to tell the suspect to try to be as relaxed as possible and to try and avoid all eye movement (in particular he should not look at his solicitor). There may be occasions in which the witness asks the suspect to speak. As part of your initial request for information you should therefore always ask whether there is any possibility of the suspect being identified by voice: if so, the remainder of the line up has to be composed accordingly, for example, all with Glaswegian accents.

(f)   *The end of the parade*

At the end of the parade the identification officer will ask whether the suspect wishes to make any comments on the conduct of the parade. If there are any it is important that the protests are made in the leaving of the parade and recorded. It will be too late to do anything about it later on.

CHAPTER 4

Criminal evidence in outline

INTRODUCTION

The law of evidence is seen by many as a subject so shrouded in mystery that close contact should be avoided at all costs. The basic principles are, in fact, relatively straightforward, but the subject often seems more complicated than it really is. There are two main reasons for this. First, many come to the subject having little or no idea as to the order in which a trial is conducted. Confusion is therefore inevitable. Secondly, there are so many reported cases. These help to foster the illusion of complexity; but you will find that many are no more than factual illustrations of basic principles. Each case is bound to be different because there are so many variables, for example, the offence charged, the way in which it was committed and the available evidence. The primary object of the law of evidence is simple. It is to ensure that the accused receives a fair trial. It is therefore a pragmatic subject; the problem is, that pragmatism does not always make for coherent legal principles. That being said, there are only five major rules of evidence.

(1) Trial takes place on the 'facts in issue'

Every offence may be broken down into a number of constituent elements, for example, on a charge under s 12 Theft Act 1968 the prosecution must prove that:

(i) the accused
(ii) took
(iii) a conveyance
(iv) for his own use etc.

These elements of the offence charged usually constitute the sole *'facts in issue'* on which the trial will take place, but other facts in issue, such as self defence to a charge of assault, may arise during the course of a trial.

(2) The prosecution must almost always make the running

On a plea of 'not guilty' the prosecution normally has to prove *every* 'fact in issue' *beyond reasonable doubt* in order to secure a conviction. This burden extends not only to proving the constituent elements of the offence charged but also in general to negativing special defences raised by the accused.[1] Furthermore, if a dispute arises as to the admissibility of any item of prosecution evidence the prosecution also has the burden of establishing its admissibility beyond reasonable doubt. Conversely, the defence very rarely has the burden of proving a 'fact in issue': if it does[2] the standard of proof is on the balance of probabilities only.

1 For example, self defence and duress. See p 115, post.
2 The most well known being when the defence of insanity is raised see p 115 post.

(3) 'Facts in issue' must normally be proved by adducing evidence

The proof or non-proof of a 'fact in issue' is normally achieved by the prosecution and/or defence 'adducing' evidence by either:

(a) calling witnesses (*oral evidence*); and/or
(b) producing documents (*documentary evidence*); and/or
(c) producing things (*real evidence*).

On occasions, however, 'facts in issue' are capable of being established or refuted without adducing evidence, for example, by the prosecutor or the accused formally admitting in the proceedings that a particular fact exists.

(4) Evidence is always subjected to 'quality control'

The law of evidence provides five 'quality control' tests. These are the most important aspect of the subject.

Test 1:   Evidence must be factually (and legally) relevant

In order to be admissible, evidence must be *relevant* to a 'fact in issue'. Relevancy is largely a matter of common sense. There are, however, certain kinds of evidence which, although *factually* relevant, are normally excluded *as a matter of law* because of the disproportionately prejudicial effect they might have (ie they are not '*legally* relevant'). For example, the prosecution cannot normally adduce evidence of an accused's bad character or misbehaviour on other occasions solely for the purpose of proving that he is *ipso facto* more likely to have committed the offence with which he is now charged.[3] Likewise, opinion evidence (unless it is that of an expert) is excluded. The rationale behind exclusion is that a juror might regard such evidence as highly 'relevant' (perhaps *too* 'relevant'), and that this could result in unfairness to the accused.

Test 2:   Relevant evidence must also be legally admissible

Even if evidence passes the 'relevance' test it may still be inadmissible because it infringes one or more of the following four exclusionary rules.

(i) The rule against hearsay. Perhaps the major distinguishing feature of the English criminal trial is that issues are normally decided on the basis of witnesses giving oral evidence *on oath* of what *they* themselves saw, heard or felt, such evidence being tested by *cross-examination*. Any attempt to adduce evidence of what a witness saw, heard or felt other than by calling him is termed 'hearsay' and is prima facie inadmissible. The 'hearsay rule' may therefore more accurately be described as the 'perceiver rule' or even (less accurately but more memorably) the 'eye witness rule'. There are, however, numerous important common law and statutory exceptions which have as much if not more significance than the rule itself.[4]

(ii) Confessions. Any adverse *oral* or *written* statement made by an *accused*

---

3 Although anomalously an accused may adduce evidence of his own general good character to show that he is *not* the sort of person who is likely to have committed the offence charged: see p 131, post.
4 There are so many exceptions that they have almost come to appear more important than the main rule. They are discussed further at p 138, post.

is termed 'a confession' and is admissible against the maker (but not against any other person). Confessions thus constitute an important exception to the hearsay rule.

EXAMPLE: A and B are accused of murdering X. A makes a written statement in which he admits carrying out the murder. The prosecution may prima facie produce A's confession in order to prove A murdered X without calling the 'eye witness' (A himself). The prosecution are, therefore, in theory, adducing hearsay evidence. This is borne out by the fact that if A's confession were to also implicate B it would *not* generally be admissible in evidence against B.[5]

Confessions are also subject to their own special exclusionary rules. Broadly, a confession can only be admitted if the court is satisfied beyond reasonable doubt that it was not obtained by oppression or as a result of anything said or done that was likely in the circumstances to render unreliable *any confession that the accused might have made*. This exclusionary rule which has its origins in the eighteenth century[6] is now contained, albeit in a significantly amended form,[7] in s 76 of the Police and Criminal Evidence Act 1984. Breaches of one or more of the Codes of Practice may well be relevant in this context although, as will be shown, such breaches will not automatically lead to exclusion.[8]

(iii) Public policy and private privilege. Provided that evidence is relevant and admissible it will normally be admitted. If, therefore, a witness is capable of giving oral evidence or producing a document or thing which satisfies both these criteria he may generally be compelled by either party to attend court to do so under pain of imprisonment should he fail to attend. There are, however, certain occasions when dictates of public policy require that this general rule be overridden, for example, when disclosure would be detrimental to national security. In addition, certain rights of personal privacy are protected by what is known as 'private privilege'. By far the most important instances of this are communications between a client and his legal advisers (*'legal professional privilege'*) and the right of a witness to refuse to answer a question or produce a document on the ground that to do so might tend to incriminate him (*'privilege against self incrimination'*).

(iv) Judicial discretion to exclude evidence on the ground of unfairness: Police and Criminal Evidence Act 1984, s 78(1). Although confessions obtained in breach of s 76 *must* be excluded, the court is not otherwise required to exclude evidence solely on the ground that it has been obtained by unfair or improper means.[9] The court does, however, have a limited *discretion* to exclude prosecution evidence under s 78(1) if, having regard to all the circumstances, *including the circumstances in which it was obtained*, its admission would have such an adverse effect on the *fairness of the proceedings*

5 Although if A and B are tried together the jury will usually see the whole unedited confession and be directed, by the judge, somewhat artificially, to disregard it in determining the issue of B's guilt; see further p 141, post.
6 See eg *DPP v Pin Ling* [1976] AC 574 at 599, HL per Lord Hailsham.
7 The common law exclusionary rule required that the prosecution proved that the confession was 'voluntary' ie that it had not been obtained 'by fear of prejudice or hope of advantage [excited] or held out by a person in authority' or by oppression.
8 See p 146, post.
9 *R v Sang* [1980] AC 402, HL. It is submitted that the basic rationale behind *R v Sang* ie that it is not the function of the courts to discipline the police for improper behaviour has not been affected by s 78(1) of the 1984 Act. All that s 78(1) has done is to give the court power to examine the circumstances in which evidence was obtained when deciding whether or not its admission would have an unfair effect *on the proceedings*.

that it ought to be excluded. The exercise of this discretion is most likely to be sought by the defence in two situations. First, where the evidence, although technically admissible, is disproportionately prejudicial,[10] and secondly, where it is 'tainted' because it has been illegally or unfairly obtained. Only time will tell to what extent the courts will be prepared to exercise this discretion in the defence's favour.

Test 3:   All oral evidence is subject to cross-examination

Establishing that a witness's evidence is relevant and admissible and getting him to court is often less than half the battle. Oral evidence will almost invariably be given on oath or affirmation (the only exception being where the witness is a child of 'tender years'). From then on the witness is on his own. It is up to the person calling him to take him through his story (*'examination-in-chief'*), he cannot be prompted (no *'leading questions'* may be asked) and he cannot refer to any previous statement that he has made, (unless it was made or verified by him *contemporaneously* with the events to which he is testifying and the court grants him leave to *'refresh his memory'* from it). Once examination-in-chief is completed, advocates for the other parties (including the co-accused) are entitled to *'cross-examine'*. Cross-examination is often seen as the jewel in the crown of the adversarial system and the only truly effective way of testing evidence.[11] A cross-examiner's lines of attack are various. He may try to suggest that the witness is mistaken, biased, a liar or the sort of person who is such a bad lot that nothing he says should be believed. Witnesses are thus to a large extent fair game to the cross-examiner: his only constraints are the ethics of his profession and certain rules which prohibit the creation of a mutiplicity of side issues. Cross-examiners can therefore, up to a point, throw as much 'mud' at their opponent's witnesses as they think fit or prudent.

The only witness exempt from this relatively *laissez-faire* scheme of things is the accused himself. An accused is never *obliged* to give evidence in his own defence,[12] but if he does, he may be asked questions in cross-examination notwithstanding that they tend to incriminate him as to the offences charged:[13] he thus often becomes the strongest prosecution witness! He is, however, protected from the general 'mudslinging' to which other witnesses are prone in that he cannot be cross-examined as to his *previous* bad character and convictions unless he loses this protection because he comes within one of the three 'provisos' to *s1(f)* of the Criminal Evidence Act 1898. If, for example, he untruthfully sets himself up as being of good character or goes into the witness box and 'slings mud' at the prosecution witnesses (or to a limited extent at his co-accused) he is liable to get some thrown back at him. When this happens he is said to have 'thrown away his shield'.

10 Where, for example, a person makes a confession whilst under the influence of drugs in circumstances where the confession does not infringe s 76(2) of the 1984 Act. See further p 148, post. S 83(2) of the 1984 Act also apparently preserves any common law discretionary power to exclude evidence whether by the putting of questions or otherwise. It is, however, hard to see in practical terms what this adds to s 78(1). See generally *Cross on Evidence* 6th edn p 170 et seq.
11 Psychological research into the ability of jurors to distinguish between correct and incorrect evidence suggest however that it may not as effective method as has been commonly supposed. The major experiments are summarised in chapter 3 of Evaluating Witness Evidence, ed. Lloyd-Bostock and Clifford: John Wiley & Sons 1983.
12 Criminal Evidence Act 1898, s 1(a).
13 Ibid, s 1(e).

Test 4: Sometimes one prosecution witness may not be enough

The general rule is that a conviction may be secured on the evidence of a single witness, provided that his testimony is capable of proving all the relevant 'facts in issue'.[14] As a matter of common sense, however, the more witnesses one can muster and the better they stand up to cross-examination, the stronger one's case becomes; or the greater the 'cogency' of the evidence. There are, however, certain circumstances in which a person *cannot* be convicted[15] without corroboration, and other occasions when, although conviction without *corroboration* is possible, a *warning* must first be given as to the dangers of convicting on uncorroborated evidence.[16] Finally, there are certain kinds of evidence (in particular disputed evidence of identification) which although not requiring corroboration or a corroboration warning may require a *direction* that they should only be acted upon with caution.

Test 5: The judge controls the jury

Obviously enough, this test only applies to trials on indictment. The judge has power to rule that certain kinds of evidence should not go before the jury at all (this will, sensibly enough, be determined in their absence). Furthermore he may, in appropriate circumstances direct a jury to acquit.[17] Finally, if the trial 'goes the distance' he always has the last word. After all the evidence has been called and prosecution and defence counsel have made their closing speeches to the jury the judge will *sum up*. In his summing up he will summarise the evidence, explain the relevant substantive law, and direct the jury on evidential issues such as the burden of proof. The way in which he discharges this duty will therefore have a strong influence on the jury since the judge's words will be the last thing they hear before retiring.

(5) The law of evidence primarily regulates what happens during the trial

The preceding four principles govern what must be proved, by whom and to what standard. They also govern how it is to be proved and the quality of evidence that must be produced in order to prove it. There is, however, no guarantee that evidential issues will arise in such a comfortable sequence during the course of a trial. An outline understanding of what takes place during a trial is therefore essential before the rules of evidence can be put into context. It is therefore suggested that if you have never seen a trial at first hand you should take the opportunity of visiting your local Crown Court or magistrates' court and hear a case being tried. It may also prove helpful to read the sections on trials on indictment[18] and summary trial[19] in this work.

A familiarity with the order of proceedings at a criminal trial will make many of the problems that this subject causes disappear, or at least become more manageable.

14 A person may thus be convicted where the sole evidence against him is fingerprint evidence or his own confession.
15 Eg where the only prosecution evidence is the unsworn evidence of a child. As to corroboration generally, see p 163, et seq, post.
16 Eg where the prosecution witness himself took part in the offence charged (known as an 'accomplice').
17 As a result of the defence successfully submitting to the judge at the end of the prosecution case that there is no case to answer.
18 See p 296, et seq, post.
19 See p 374, et seq, post.

A FICTITIOUS CASE: POLICE (LATER REGINA) v DONOGHUE AND STEPHENSON

Unfortunately, the four scenarios in chapter 1 are all far too straightforward to be of great use in a chapter on evidence. You must therefore be introduced to two further defendants whose case is rather more complicated. It is most unlikely that you would ever encounter all these problems in one case, but in criminal litigation nothing is impossible.

The Defendants

Norbert DONOGHUE (1)
Previous convictions:

> Taking conveyance without consent (× 2);
> Assaulting police officer in the execution of his duty;
> Criminal damage.

William STEPHENSON (2)
Previous convictions:

> Burglary

The Prosecution Case

On Friday, 6 July at 9.30 pm a green Jaguar registration ABC 123J belonging to Tony ATKIN was taken from outside his home without his permission. The incident was seen from an upstairs bedroom window in a house opposite by Andrea BOURHILL who went across to Tony ATKIN's house and alerted him. He immediately called the police. At 10.00 pm PC Peter MACMILLAN arrived at ATKIN's house and radioed details of the stolen car back to the police station. He then:

> (i) took a statement from Tony ATKIN confirming that he owned the car and that he parked it outside his house at 8.30 pm on 6 July from whence it was taken without his permission;
> (ii) took a statement from Andrea BOURHILL the two most important extracts from which are:
>
> > 'I recognised one of the boys, it was Nobby DONOGHUE, I knew it was him because I used to go out with him' and
> > 'I did not recognise the other boy who got into the passenger seat but I would describe him as 5'9" tall, of medium build with dark brown curly shoulder length hair and a straggly beard. I think I would recognise him if I saw him again.'

At 11.30 am on Saturday, 7 July PC Alan ANDREWS and WPC Jane HOPKINSON were on mobile patrol when they spotted the missing Jaguar parked in a side road approximately 100 yards from the 'House of Lords' public house. Having inspected the car they took up position outside the 'House of Lords' and at approximately midday saw DONOGHUE and STEPHENSON leave the public bar and walk towards the parked Jaguar. DONOGHUE looked up and on noticing the police car was seen to say something to STEPHENSON, at which they both turned round and began walking in the opposite direction. At this point the two police officers got out of their car and went up to the two suspects and asked them what they were doing.

DONOGHUE replied, 'None of your bloody business', at which STEPHENSON was heard to say, 'Come off it Nobby you know it's about the motor, the game's up.'

DONOGHUE then tried to run away but was restrained by PC ANDREWS whilst WPC HOPKINSON radioed for assistance. Both suspects were then arrested and cautioned and taken back to the police station where they arrived at 12.15 pm. They were taken before the custody officer who authorised their further detention for questioning. They were put in separate cells.

DONOGHUE was interviewed on two occasions by DS YOUNG between 8.00 pm and 10.00 pm on 7 July and again from 6.00 am to 7.00 am on 8 July. At the end of the second interview DONOGHUE made a statement under caution, the most significant extract from which is:

'On Friday night I took Tony ATKIN's green Jaguar to go to a disco. I was with Bill STEPHENSON and he told me it was OK to take it because he had got Tony's permission but couldn't drive it because he wasn't insured. It was a stupid thing to do and I am very sorry. I would never have done it if Billy hadn't have said it was OK.'

In the meantime PC ANDREWS and WPC HOPKINSON were sent by DS YOUNG to search STEPHENSON's flat without first obtaining the authority of an inspector. They entered forcibly and there found a number of housebreaking implements which they seized and brought back to the police station.

STEPHENSON was interviewed by DS YOUNG at 3.00 pm on 7 July and asked if he was prepared to go on an identity parade. He consented and the parade took place at 5.30 pm. He was picked out by the witness Andrea BOURHILL. He was then returned to his cell and interviewed once more by DS YOUNG at 7.00 pm. He still refused to answer any questions or make a statement. He was not interviewed further.

Both defendants were formally charged at 7.30 pm on 7 July with taking a conveyance without the consent of the lawful owner Tony ATKIN contrary to s 12(1) Theft Act 1968. Both were then released on bail and went to see solicitors.

The Defence Case

Both now vehemently deny the charge. DONOGHUE instructs his solicitor that he spent the whole of Friday evening at home with his wife Monica DONOGHUE. He also puts a completely different complexion on Andrea BOURHILL's evidence saying that the night before (5 July) there had been a big row between BOURHILL (an ex-girlfriend) and himself because he had decided he was going to stay with Monica. They split up, and he alleges that BOURHILL said, 'I'll make you sorry for this'. He also says that she has two previous convictions for shoplifting.

DONOGHUE further says that he was kept in a cold cell and not given refreshment of any kind during his detention. He further alleges that during the course of the first interview DS YOUNG indicated to him that:

(a) if he confessed he could go home;
(b) if he didn't confess he could 'stay there and rot' so far as DS YOUNG was concerned;
(c) he could not see his solicitor, or notify his wife of his arrest, because this was inconvenient;
(d) his wife must have known about the car as well and if he did not co-operate 'She'd get her collar felt, too'.
(e) Andrea BOURHILL had made a statement saying that she'd seen him taking the car.

During the second interview DONOGHUE further alleged that DS YOUNG said that:

(a) he was getting very bored and wanted to go off duty and that if he didn't 'give him what he wanted' then DONOGHUE was going to get hurt; and
(b) (untruthfully) STEPHENSON had already made a statement saying it was all DONOGHUE's idea.

DONOGHUE now says that he had nothing to do with the taking of the car and only made the statement because of the pressure that had been put on him.

STEPHENSON also denies any involvement in the offence. He complains that his request to have a solicitor present at the identification parade was refused because 'there was not enough time'. He also says that the eight other persons on the parade were all clean shaven. The parade took place in the yard at the rear of the police station and he is convinced that he saw BOURHILL looking out of the windows over-looking the courtyard before the parade took place. He also complains that a lot of pressure was put on him similar to that exerted against DONOGHUE but that he did not sign anything and did not make any admissions. He also maintains that when he got home his flat had been ransacked and left in a shambles. He maintains that what the police alleged to be 'housebreaking implements' are old tyre levers and other implements for doing spare time motor repairs.

The remainder of this chapter expands the basic principles set out in section I, referring to DONOGHUE and STEPHENSON wherever possible. It is assumed that they are both being tried on indictment.

PRINCIPLE I: TRIAL TAKES PLACE ON THE 'FACTS IN ISSUE'

In order to secure a conviction the prosecution must prove that:

    (a) DONOGHUE and STEPHENSON;
    (b) took a conveyance;
    (c) for their own use;
    (d) without having the consent of the owner Tony ATKIN or other lawful authority.

These four essential elements, constitute the 'facts in issue'. Failure, in the first instance, to adduce some evidence tending to prove each of them, and, ultimately, to prove each of them beyond reasonable doubt would be fatal to the prosecution case. The relevant facts in issue can normally be deter-mined from the summons, chargesheet or indictment but there are two com-mon instances in which you will need to look further.

(a) **Special defences**

On occasions an accused may raise a defence which goes beyond mere denial, ('it wasn't me') and seeks to introduce some new element ('I did it but ...'). A common example is, self defence to a charge of assault. This new element will constitute a further fact in issue, the burden of disproving which will almost invariably lie with the prosecution.

(b) **Secondary facts in issue**

An issue may arise during the course of a trial, as to the admissibility of an item of evidence. In such a case the burden of proof will lie upon the party arguing for its admission.

> EXAMPLE: If at the trial DONOGHUE's counsel were to submit to the judge that his client's written statement under caution should not be admitted because it was obtained by oppression it would be necessary to hold a 'trial within a trial' in the absence of the jury at which the *prosecution* would have to prove *beyond reasonable doubt* that the confession was *not* obtained by oppression.

PRINCIPLE II: THE PROSECUTION MUST ALMOST ALWAYS MAKE THE RUNNING

When an accused pleads 'not guilty' the prosecution must normally prove every fact in issue beyond reasonable doubt.[20] This burden manifests itself at two stages. Firstly, the prosecution is required to adduce evidence which is *capable* of proving all the facts in issue (this is often referred to as making out a *prima facie case*). If it does not, the defence advocate is entitled to submit that there is no case to answer. Secondly, if the trial runs its full course the jury or magistrates must be satisfied beyond reasonable doubt that *on the evidence as a whole* the accused is guilty. As a general rule, therefore, the prosecution must make the running at every stage.[1] On occasions, however, the *defence* has the burden of either *proving* a fact in issue or adducing *some* evidence of support of it before it can become a fact in issue.

(1) Facts in issue which the defence must prove

There are *three* situations in which this burden may lie on the defence. In each case, the standard of proof is on the balance of probabilities.[2]

(a) Insanity

Every man is presumed to be same until the contrary is proved.[3] Thus it is for the defence, by means of expert medical evidence or otherwise to prove that at the time of the commission of the offence the accused was insane within the *McNaghten* definition.[4]

(b) Burdens imposed by statute

Certain statutes expressly provide that the burden of proving a specific fact in issue lies with the accused. Examples include the defences of diminished responsibility to a charge of murder,[5] 'lawful authority or reasonable excuse' to a charge of carrying an offensive weapon in a public place,[6] and absence of corruption in respect of money received by civil servants or local government officers.[7]

A further burden has been placed on an accused as a result of s 74 of the Police and Criminal Evidence Act 1984. This complex section broadly provides that in criminal proceedings proof of the fact that the accused[8] or a person other than the accused[9] has been convicted of an offence by any court

---

20 *Woolmington v DPP* [1935] AC 462, HL.
1 It is accepted that this does present a simplistic view. There will inevitably be occasions when the case against the accused is so overwhelming that conviction is inevitable unless he calls evidence to refute it. See generally *Cross* (op cit) p 107 et seq.
2 *R v Carr-Briant* [1943] KB 607, CCA.
3 *McNaghten's case* (1843) 10 Cl & Fin 200.
4 Contrast the position where the defence is one of automatism when the accused only bears an *evidential* burden: *Bratty v A-G for Northern Ireland* [1963] AC 386, HL.
5 Homicide Act 1957, s 2(2). Other important examples may be found in Road Traffic Act 1972, s 6(2) (being in charge of a motor vehicle with an alcohol concentration above the prescribed limit. The defendant must prove that there was no likelihood of his driving whilst over the limit) and s 10 ibid (alcohol consumed after ceasing to drive motor vehicle—the 'hip flask' defence).
6 Prevention of Crime Act 1953, s 1(1).
7 Prevention of Corruption Act 1916, s 2.
8 1984 Act, s 74(3).
9 Ibid, s 74(1) and (2).

in the United Kingdom creates a presumption that he committed that offence unless the contrary is proved. The limited occasions upon which an accused's previous convictions may be admitted in evidence on his trial for a subsequent offence will be considered in due course.[10] Convictions of persons other than the accused may be relevant when, for example, a receiver is tried separately from the thief.[11]

> EXAMPLE: T is convicted of theft. At the subsequent trial of the receiver (R) the prosecution may now[12] adduce T's conviction as evidence that the goods which form the subject of the receiving charge were in fact stolen. Once T's conviction has been proved in the required manner[13] R would have to prove, on the balance of probabilities, that T's conviction was wrong if he wished to dispute its correctness.

(c) *Offences subject to exceptions: Magistrates' Courts Act 1980, s 101 and R v Edwards*[14]

Section 101 of the 1980 Act provides that:

> 'Where the defendant to an information relies for his defence on any *exception, exemption, proviso, excuse or qualification,* whether or not it accompanies the description of the offence ... in the enactment creating the offence ... the burden of proving the exception, exemption, proviso, excuse or qualification shall be on him and this notwithstanding that the information or complaint contains an allegation negativing the exemption, exception, proviso, excuse or qualification'.

This tortuously worded section applies to numerous summary offences prohibiting the carrying out of activities without the appropriate authorisation such as driving a motor vehicle on a road, using or installing a television or radio or parking a hopper on a public highway. In such cases it will be for the accused to prove that he holds the necessary licence or authority. *R v Edwards*[15] has established that there is a similar rule at common law for indictable offences:

> 'arising under enactments which prohibit the doing of an act, save in specified circumstances or by persons of specified classes or with specified qualifications or with the licence or permission of specified authorities'.[16]

The major problem is deciding whether, as a matter of construction, the offence charged comes within s 101 or the rule in *R v Edwards*.[17] The existence of words such as *'unless'*, *'other than'*, or *'provided always'* will usually indicate that one or other of the rules applies, but each offence will need to be considered individually.[18] The rule is based primarily on expediency the theory being that it ought to be much easier for an accused to prove that he had the relevant authority than for the prosecution to prove that he did not. It is arguable, however, that the rationale behind the rule has to a large extent disappeared because access to such information is often computerised

---

10 Pp 157 et seq, post.
11 Another example would be offences under Criminal Law Act 1967, ss 4 and 5.
12 Prior to the coming into force of this section the prosecution would have been required to prove the theft all over again.
13 See p 145, post.
14 [1975] QB 27, CA.
15 Supra.
16 Ibid at pp 39–40.
17 Supra.
18 Contrast, for example, *R v Putland and Sorrell* [1946] 1 All ER 85, CCA and *R v Oliver* [1944] KB 68, CCA. See generally *Cross* (op cit) p 123 et seq.

and therefore far more readily available to the prosecution than used to be the case.

Limited nature of the accused's burden

Whenever any of the above three exceptions apply, the accused only has the burden on *that specific issue*; he is not required to prove his innocence. Thus, for example, on a charge of carrying an offensive weapon in a public place without lawful authority the prosecution must still establish the accused's identity, and prove the carrying of an offensive weapon in a public place. It is only then that the accused is required to prove lawful authority or other excuse.

(2) **Issues upon which the defence must adduce some evidence before they can become facts in issue**

Once the prosecution establishes a prima facie case the defence runs a substantial risk by staying silent, even though the ultimate burden of proof still remains with the prosecution. There are however certain defences which will *not become facts in issue at all* unless and until the defence adduces *some* evidence in support of them.

> EXAMPLE: D is charged with assaulting X. If defence counsel adduces no evidence alleging that D was acting in self defence, he may not raise it in his closing speech, nor is the judge required in his summing up to hypothesise as to possible defences that have not been raised. However, once the defence adduces evidence of self defence, this becomes a fact in issue which the *prosecution must disprove.*

All that the defence are required to do is to introduce *some* evidence; they are not, for example, required to prove self defence.[19] This is sometimes therefore called an 'evidential burden'. Other examples of where the accused has been held to have this 'evidential burden' are where the defence is one of non-insane automatism,[20] provocation,[1] drunkenness,[2] duress[3] and mechanical defect.[4] There is some uncertainty as to the exact status of the defence of alibi[5] but in practical terms no alibi is going to get very far if the accused does not call evidence in support of it.

PRINCIPLE III: FACTS IN ISSUE MUST BE PROVED BY ADDUCING EVIDENCE

It has already been shown how facts in issue are primarily proved or disproved by adducing evidence but that other methods of proof may on occasions be utilised. The relevant rules must now be examined more closely.

---

19 *R v Lobell* [1957] 1 QB 547; see also *R v Hamand* [1985] LS Gaz R 1561, CA.
20 *Bratty v A-G for Northern Ireland* [1963] AC 386, HL; *Moses v Winder* [1981] RTR 37.
 1 *Mancini v DPP* [1942] AC 1.
 2 *DPP v Majewski* [1977] AC 443, HL.
 3 *R v Gill* [1963] 2 All ER 688, CCA.
 4 *R v Spurge* [1961] 2 QB 205, CCA.
 5 See *Cross* (op cit) p 111.

(1) Oral evidence (testimony)

Oral evidence can only generally be received if it is sworn.[6] The one exception to this is when the witness is a child of 'tender years'. Such children may be permitted to give unsworn evidence if they satisfy certain criteria. This apart, all witnesses are generally *'competent'* to give evidence and may be *compelled* to do so by the party who wishes to call them. Four categories of witness are however subject to special rules.

(a) Children of tender years

The law has always regarded the evidence of children with caution especially when it has related to sexual offences. Whenever a child of 'tender years'[7] is called to give evidence, therefore, the court will take the initiative and enquire into his competence to take the oath. The test laid down in *R v Hayes*[8] requires not a belief in divine sanction but that:

> 'the child has a sufficient appreciation of the solemnity of the occasion and the added responsibility to tell the truth which is involved in taking an oath, over and above the duty to tell the truth which is an ordinary duty of normal social conduct.'

In order to ascertain this he must be questioned by the judge in the presence of the jury or by the magistrates in open court. If the court forms the view that he does not understand the nature of the oath, he may nevertheless be permitted to give *unsworn* evidence under s 38(1) of the Children and Young Persons Act 1933 if, in the opinion of the court:

> 'he is possessed of sufficient intelligence to justify the reception of the evidence, and understands the duty of speaking the truth.'

As can be seen, the distinction between the *Hayes* test and that imposed under s 38(1) is marginal. It is nevertheless a crucial distinction when a child is called as a prosecution witness, because s 38(1) further provides that an accused:

> 'shall not be liable to be convicted of the offence unless [the unsworn evidence] is corroborated by some other material evidence in support thereof implicating him.'

Thus, where a child gives unsworn evidence the prosecutor is faced with one of those rare occasions when, as a matter of law, he must fail *unless* he adduces *corroborative evidence*.[9] Quite apart from issues of competence, the evidence of children gives rise to serious practical difficulties. Child witnesses most frequently give evidence in prosecutions for sexual offences. Although, in theory, a child witness may be cross-examined as freely as any other witness, cross-examination must be conducted discreetly to avoid losing the magistrates' or the jury's sympathy.

6 The present law is contained in the Oaths Act 1978. Any person objecting to being sworn is entitled to affirm: ibid, s 5.

7 There is no hard and fast rule as to age. Each case must be taken on its own facts. See eg *R v Khan* (1981) 73 Cr App Rep 190, CA and *R v Campbell* (1983) 147 JP 392, CA.

8 [1977] 2 All ER 288, CA. If the judge exercises his discretion wrongly or fails to enquire when he should this may provide grounds for a successful appeal (as in *R v Kahn*, supra) but the appellate court will only interfere in exceptional circumstances.

9 For a discussion of corroboration generally see p 163, et seq, post. Note that one 'unsworn' child cannot corroborate another 'unsworn' child but a 'sworn' child can corroborate an 'unsworn' child and vice versa: *DPP v Hester* [1973] AC 296.

(b) The accused

An accused's competence and compellability as a witness in his own trial is subject to quite complicated rules which are best analysed from three aspects:

- (i) as a witness for the prosecution;
- (ii) as a witness on his own behalf; and
- (iii) as a witness for a co-accused.

(i) As a witness for the prosecution. Not surprisingly, the prosecution cannot call an accused to give evidence against himself. If, however, he elects to give evidence in his defence the Criminal Evidence Act 1898, s 1(e) entitles the prosecution to cross-examine him as to the offence(s) charged with a view to securing damaging admissions or exposing contradictions in his testimony.

> EXAMPLE: The prosecution cannot call DONOGHUE to give evidence against himself. If, however, DONOGHUE gives evidence on his own behalf (which he is more or less obliged to do, since he is raising an alibi) prosecuting counsel can still do him a lot of damage in cross-examination by asking him, for example, why it was that he changed direction when he saw the police car and tried to run away after STEPHENSON's outburst. If his replies are evasive or unsatisfactory this will be evidence in the case against him.

What, however, of a person accused who wishes to 'turn Queen's evidence' and testify against his *co-accused?* The basic rule is that whilst proceedings are still pending against a person, the prosecution may not call him to give evidence against his co-accused.[10] As a general rule therefore an accused will only become competent for the prosecution once he has been acquitted or pleaded guilty.[11] Sometimes a person will plead guilty and offer to turn 'Queen's evidence' in the hope of receiving a more lenient sentence. It is entirely for the magistrates or the judge to decide whether to sentence him before he gives evidence or to wait until the conclusion of the case.[12]

> EXAMPLE: It will be recalled that DONOGHUE made a confession in which he implicated STEPHENSON. If they were both to plead 'not guilty' the confession, if admitted, would only be evidence against DONOGHUE. Furthermore, so long as proceedings were pending against DONOGHUE the prosecution could not call him as a witness to give evidence against STEPHENSON. If, however, DONOGHUE were to plead guilty he would be compelled to give evidence against STEPHENSON.

If a co-accused indicates that he is prepared to testify on behalf of the prosecution against his co-accused prosecuting counsel will normally ask for a short adjournment after pleas had been taken and indicate his intention to call the person who has just pleaded guilty as a prosecution witness. It is then for the judge or magistrates to decide whether or not to sentence him before he gives evidence. If he is called he must be treated as an 'accomplice'. The appropriate corroboration warning will thus be necessary.[12a]

---

10 This is so whether they are to be tried jointly or separately *R v Pipe* (1966) 51 Cr App Rep 17, CA.

11 Or the prosecution has agreed not to proceed against him. 'Deals' of this kind in 'supergrass' cases have attracted a deal of public controversy and some judicial disquiet see eg *R v Turner* (1975) 61 Cr App Rep 67, CA (Bertie Smalls) and *R v Lowe* (1977) 66 Cr App Rep 122, CA (Charles Lowe). For an interesting article on 'Supergrasses' see Seymour, 'What good have supergrasses done for anyone but themselves?' LAG Bulletin December 1982, 7.

12 See *R v Weekes* (1980) 74 Cr App Rep 161, CA. It is, apparently, better sentencing practice to sentence all parties and accomplices together. This represents a remarkable change in approach from *R v Payne* [1950] 1 All ER 102 (desirable to sentence accomplice *before* he gives evidence).

12a See p 163, post.

Note, however, that where an accused gives evidence *on his own behalf* there is nothing to prevent prosecuting counsel cross-examining him with a view to making him implicate a co-accused.[13] Thus, if DONOGHUE and STEPHENSON were both to plead 'not guilty' and each give evidence on his own behalf, prosecuting counsel would be entitled to cross-examine them in such a way as to try and make them incriminate each other.[14]

(ii) As a witness for himself. Section 1(a) of the Criminal Evidence Act 1898 provides that an accused may, but does not have to, give evidence on his own behalf '*at any stage in the proceedings*'.[15] In practice, it is never easy to decide whether or not to call your client. An accused is never *obliged* to go into the witness box to give evidence, but as a matter of common sense, if he declines to do so his chances of acquittal are often slim. If he does elect not to give evidence, the prosecution must not comment on this failure in any way[16] although counsel for a co-accused may do so. Conversely, the judge *is* entitled to comment in his summing up but only to a very limited extent.[17] In particular, he must always emphasise to the jury that in not giving evidence the accused is doing no more than exercising his 'right of silence' and that his failure to testify must never be treated as evidence of guilt.

The other side of the coin is that if he *does* give evidence, he is liable to be cross-examined extensively by prosecuting counsel as to the offence charged[18] as well as by counsel for any co-accused who will be trying to pick up any scraps that favour his client. Although he will have his 'shield' to protect him from questions concerning his previous character and convictions (unless he has thrown it away), the case against him may often look much blacker after he has stepped out of the box than it did before he stepped into it.

(iii) As a witness for a co-accused. On a true construction of s 1(a) of the Criminal Evidence Act 1898 an accused who, having pleaded 'not guilty', elects not to give evidence on his own behalf is competent (but *not* compellable) to give evidence for his co-accused, although such an outcome would be unlikely. If an accused has *already* pleaded 'guilty'[19] he is fully *competent* and *compellable* to give evidence on behalf of a former co-accused. This occurs when, for example, an accused who has pleaded not guilty wishes to call a co-accused who has already pleaded guilty to give evidence exonerating him.

(c) Spouse of accused: Police and Criminal Evidence Act 1984, s 80

(i) As a witness for the prosecution. An accused's spouse is normally

---

13 This would in many ways be more advantageous than calling a co-accused as a prosecution witness because in the latter case he could not be cross-examined or asked leading questions. For an example of how far this rule goes see *R v Paul* [1920] 2 KB 183, CCA.

14 A witness who gives evidence in his own defence may equally implicate his co-accused in chief. If he does, this is admissible in evidence against that co-accused: *R v Rudd* (1948) 64 TLR 240, CCA.

15 He is therefore entitled to give evidence on a 'trial within a trial' *R v Cowell* [1940] 2 KB 49.

16 Criminal Evidence Act 1898, s 1(b).

17 See *R v Bathurst* [1968] 2 QB 99, CA. The suggested direction to the jury in that case was 'the accused is not bound to give evidence ... he can sit back and see if the prosecution have proved their case, and ... while the jury have been deprived of the opportunity of hearing his story tested in cross-examination, the one thing they must not do is to assume that he is guilty because he has not gone into the witness box'. Note that the direction may be in stronger terms where the accused is under some legal or evidential burden. See also *R v Sparrow* [1973] 2 All ER 129, CA.

18 P 119, ante.

19 *R v Boal* [1965] 1 QB 402, CCA or been acquitted *R v Conti* (1973) 58 Cr App Rep 387, CA or is being tried separately *R v Richardson* (1967) 51 Cr App Rep 381.

competent to give evidence for the prosecution whatever the offence charged[20] but will only be *compellable*,[1] broadly, where the charge either involves *violence* to that spouse or to any person who was *under 16* at the time of the offence, or consists of a sexual offence[2] against a person *under 16* at that time.

> EXAMPLE: Suppose that the police were to interview DONOGHUE's wife Monica and she were to say that far from being at home all Friday night her husband had come home at 1.00 am in the morning and said:
>   'There's going to be a bit of trouble, because I've nicked Tony ATKIN's motor'.[3]
>   The police could call her as a witness if, *and only if*, she were willing to testify. If, however, DONOGHUE had been charged with an offence of assault occasioning *her* actual bodily harm, the prosecution could compel her to attend court to give evidence on their behalf.

A non-compellable spouse should think carefully before agreeing to give evidence for the prosecution because if she does, she cannot then refuse to answer questions. She should therefore be warned of this fact before she is sworn and told that she must not give evidence if she does not want to.[4]

(ii) As a witness for the defence. A spouse will always be *competent* and *compellable* as a witness on behalf of her own spouse unless she is jointly charged with him.[5] She will always be *competent* (but not *compellable* unless she would be compellable for the prosecution) to give evidence on behalf of her spouse's co-accused.

> EXAMPLE: DONOGHUE could compel his wife to give evidence in support of his alibi (although tactically this might be unwise if she were unwilling to do so). STEPHENSON could ask her to give evidence on his behalf if, for example, he were to claim that he spent the Friday evening at the DONOGHUE's house, but if she were to refuse, he could not compel her to come to court.[6]

Calling a spouse as a defence witness always involves risks. On the one hand, there may be the veiled suggestion that a husband or wife is giving evidence out of misguided loyalty,[7] on the other hand failure to call a spouse who could have given material evidence may create a bad impression. Note, however, that if a spouse is not called by the defence the prosecution may not comment on it in any way[8] although the judge *may* do so.[9]

> EXAMPLE: If DONOGHUE were to give evidence in support of his alibi and did *not* call his wife, as a matter of common sense the jury would probably draw an adverse conclusion. The fact that the prosecution would be precluded from making

---

20 1984 Act, s 80(1)(a). See further *Cross on Evidence* (op cit) p 197 et seq.
1 Ibid, s 80(3).
2 Defined in s 80(7) is an offence under the Sexual Offences Act 1956, the Indecency with Children Act 1960, the Sexual Offences Act 1967, Criminal Law Act 1977, s 54 and Protection of Children Act 1978.
3 Mrs Donoghue could of course give evidence of this as an exception to the hearsay rule because it comes within the definition of a confession.
4 *R v Pitt* [1983] QB 25, CA.
5 1984 Act, s 80(4). The Act is silent on the position where H and W are jointly *tried* but on different charges.
6 If however she were to give evidence on behalf of DONOGHUE, STEPHENSON's counsel could endeavour to elicit this information from her in cross-examination.
7 For an example of an improper summing up along these lines see *R v Turnbull* [1977] QB 224, CA.
8 1984 Act, s 80(8).
9 Although the judge should comment with great circumspection *R v Naudeer* [1984] 3 All ER 1036, CA.

any reference to this failure in their closing speech, would not therefore have a very great effect on them.[10]

(iii) Husband and wife jointly charged. In such a case spouses are in a similar position to other co-accused. So long as a jointly charged spouse is still 'liable to be convicted of that offence at the trial', she cannot give evidence on behalf of the other spouse.[11] Once he or she has pleaded guilty or for any other reason is no longer 'liable to conviction' the ordinary spouse rules considered earlier will apply. Jointly charged spouses are, however, still *competent* (but *not* compellable) to give evidence on behalf of a co-accused.[12]

Interpretation. The relevant date for determining whether a witness is married to the accused is the date upon which he or she gives evidence. Thus, if the witness were to marry the accused between the commission of the offence and the date of the trial, s 80 would apply.[13] Conversely, if a witness has been but is no longer married to the accused by the date upon which he or she gives evidence, that witness is treated as never having been married.[14]

> EXAMPLE: If between 6 July and the date of the trial Mr and Mrs DONOGHUE were to divorce, the prosecutor could compel her to attend and give evidence whatever the offence charged.

Furthermore, the above rules do *not* apply to co-habitees, who have no special immunity nor protection.

(d) Mental incapacity

There may be occasions, albeit rare, when it will be necessary to determine whether or not a person whose intellectual capacity is impaired either due to illness, congenital disability or some temporary cause such as drunkenness is capable of understanding the nature of the proceedings. There is very little guidance on the subject but if the issue arises, the magistrates, or the judge in the presence of the jury will enquire into competence and may receive evidence on a *voir dire* if necessary. If the witness is adjudged competent he is then in the same position as any other witness save that where he testifies for the prosecution the judge may sometimes be required to warn the jury of the special need for caution before relying on his evidence.[15]

---

10 If prosecution counsel *did* comment, defence counsel may ask for a re-trial. If defence counsel raises no objection the trial judge is under a duty to point out prosecution counsel's error when summing up: *R v Naudeer*, supra.
11 S 80(4). This subsection does not therefore apply when the spouses are being tried separately. The Act is also silent as to the position when they are tried together on different charges.
12 S 80(1)(b).
13 Such a witness would thus remain competent for the prosecution but would only be compellable where a spouse were charged with an offence within s 80(3) of the 1984 Act. The decision in *Hoskyn v Metropolitan Police Comr* [1979] AC 474, HL is to this limited extent thus preserved. It is interesting to speculate whether, on its specific facts, *Hoskyn* would be decided differently under the new Act. In that case, the defendant, who was charged with causing grievous bodily harm to X married X before his trial. Under the law as it then was X was held to be competent but not compellable to give evidence for the prosecution. It is submitted that the decision would still be the same because X would not have been the defendant's wife at the time the offence was committed: see s 80(3)(a) of the 1984 Act.
14 S 80(5). This section will apply whether the parties have been divorced or the marriage has been held to be voidable. If the marriage were held to be void s 80 would not apply in any event.
15 *R v Bagshaw* [1984] 1 All ER 971, CA, and *R v Spencer* [1985] 1 All ER 673, CA.

(2) Documentary evidence

Documents do not play so large a part in criminal as in civil cases with the notable exception of offences involving fraud.[16] Before being received in evidence a document[17] must satisfy two criteria. First, must be proved[18] to be *authentic*. Secondly it must be *admissible*. Authenticity must normally be established by a witness producing the original and formally identifying it.[19] Secondary evidence, for example a photocopy or oral testimony as to what the document contained, is only generally admissible if it can be proved that the original has been lost or destroyed and proper search has been made for it.[20] In the case of public and judicial documents, however, the stringent requirements of the 'originality' rule are considerably relaxed. Thus, for example, convictions and acquittals on indictment may be proved by certificate and those on summary trial by production of a copy of the record of the conviction, signed by the justices' clerk.[1] The rule has also been considerably relaxed in relation to wider categories of 'documents' such as video recordings where it has been held that 'subject to proof of authenticity' copies are generally admissible.[2] Establishing that the contents of the document are admissible in evidence may cause greater problems. Quite apart from the special rules relating to confessions, the contents of documents are often inadmissible because they infringe the hearsay rule.

> EXAMPLE: If the prosecution wish to adduce DONOGHUE's statement under caution in evidence they must first prove its authenticity and secondly prove that it is admissible ie that it was not obtained by oppression etc. The statement is prima facie hearsay but, because it is a confession it is admissible against DONOGHUE (but not STEPHENSON) as an exception to the rule.

In any event, documents usually require witnesses to 'bring them to life'. Oral testimony will normally be needed not merely to establish their authenticity but to explain the circumstances in which they came into being before their true significance can be appreciated.

(3) Real evidence

Real evidence broadly comprises those items of evidence which the tribunal of fact can see and weigh up for itself rather than second hand through the

---

16 The main significance of documents in such cases is that they will often be put to the suspect for his comments whilst under interrogation with a view to securing damaging admissions on them. Similarly, when admitted in evidence at the trial their main use will be as a vehicle for cross-examining the accused if he gives evidence.

17 The definition embraces not merely written or printed material but also things such as tape recordings: see eg *R v Senat* (1968) 52 Cr App Rep 282, CA; films: see *Senior v Holdworth, ex p Independent Television News Ltd* [1976] QB 23, CA and video recordings: see eg *Kajala v Noble* (1982) 75 Cr App Rep 149, DC. For the purposes of the Police and Criminal Evidence Act 1984 the term 'document' includes all documents in writing, maps, plans, photographs, discs, tapes, films, microfilm: ibid, s 118.

18 The burden of proving authenticity appears to be only on the balance of probabilities even where the document is being put forward by the prosecution: *R v Robson* [1972] 2 All ER 699.

19 And, for example, confirming the handwriting of the maker. For detailed discussion for proof of handwriting see *Cross* (op cit) p 603 et seq.

20 The circumstances in which the original need not be produced include where opponent has failed to produce document after being given notice requiring him to do so and where the production of the original is impossible. See further *Cross* (op cit) p 598 et seq.

1 Police and Criminal Evidence Act 1984, s 73.

2 See *Kajala v Noble*, supra.

medium of oral testimony. The most obvious example is the way in which the court 'weighs up' a witness's evidence.[3]

> EXAMPLE: When DONOGHUE gives evidence in support of his alibi (which in reality he must) the way in which he gives his evidence (for example whether he contradicts himself under cross-examination) and its inherent plausibility will be material factors in influencing the jury as to whether or not they believe him.

A court may also look at photographs, video films, listen to tape recordings or view objects such as a bald tyre, or a weapon and draw such conclusions as may be justified. Once again, however, such evidence frequently depends upon oral testimony to 'bring it to life'. For example, when seeking to adduce a film or tape recording in evidence witnesses will have to be called to give direct evidence as to where and when the film or recording was made and who the voices on the recording are.[4] Similarly, a forensic expert may need to be called to confirm that marks on a weapon are in fact blood stains and that they in some way link the accused with the crime. In the latter example the prosecution might also need to call other witnesses to prove, for example, that a weapon was found in the possession of the accused and that it was the same weapon that is now produced in court. You must always therefore be sure that when acting on behalf of a party against whom such evidence[5] is tendered you examine the 'chain' of possession very carefully and ask yourself, if necessary with expert help,[6] what the item actually proves.

(4) Methods of proof without evidence

There are four situations in which facts may be proved other than by one of the three methods considered above. In such cases proof can often be effected merely by the advocate addressing the court to direct its attention to the relevant rule.

(a) Judicial notice

This simple method of proving facts is underused largely because its potential scope is not appreciated. The court may accept the existence or non-existence of certain facts *without* requiring proof by evidence on the ground that they are common knowledge or emanate from proper sources. Examples of facts within the former category include matters arising in the ordinary course of nature, the fact that cats are normally kept for domestic circumstances and that criminals lead unhappy lives. Examples of facts judicially noted after consulting the proper sources include the existence and contents of statutes, rules of court governing procedure, and the meaning of words in common use. In practical terms, however, judicial notice of everyday facts is taken in

---

3 Although courts may well be less adept at this than is commonly supposed: see Wells and Lindsey, 'How do people infer the accuracy of eye witness memory? Studies of Performance and Better Memory Analysis,' Evaluating Witness Evidence (op cit) p 41 et seq.

4 There is some confusion of terminology here. Broadly it can be stated that on the issue of authenticity items such as films and tape recordings are treated as documentary evidence but that when their contents are played back the court is perceiving them with their own unaided senses, therefore they become real evidence. The distinction is arguably academic.

5 'Real evidence' in the sense of 'forensic evidence' is used far less frequently than is commonly supposed (*Irving*, op cit, received evidence that it resulted in about two charges per detective per year). Real evidence is far more likely to be of significance when the accused is arrested in the possession of property which is intrinsically incriminating eg weapons, tools, car keys, credit cards, or goods taken from a supermarket.

6 See p 191, post.

our courts on countless occasions without anyone realising it. As *Cross*[7] rightly says:

> 'The tacit applications of the doctrine of judicial notice are more numerous and more important than the express ones. A great deal is taken for granted when any question of relevance is considered or assumed. For example, evidence is constantly given that persons accused of burglary were found in possession of jemmies or skeleton keys, that powder puffs and pots of vaseline were found on the premises of those charged with homosexuality,[8] and that the accused became confused when charged; these facts are only relevant provided there is a common practice to use such things in the commission of the crime, or provided that guilty people tend more than innocent ones to become confused when charged, but no one ever thinks of calling evidence on such a subject.'

Use of local knowledge or personal experience by lay magistrates.
Because lay magistrates come from such diverse backgrounds and often have strong connections with the locality in which they sit, it is inevitable that they may consciously or unconsciously utilise their familiarity with local conditions[9] or tap the expertise of one of their number, for example a doctor,[10] who possesses specialised knowledge. Such a course is permissible provided that such knowledge is used as an aid in interpreting the evidence rather than in substitution for it.

(b) Presumptions

A detailed discussion of this topic is outside the scope of this work.[11] The word 'presumption' is used in a number of different contexts. For example, it is *conclusively* presumed that a child under ten cannot commit a crime,[12] that a boy under 14 cannot commit rape or have unlawful sexual intercourse,[13] and, with increasing absurdity, that everyone knows what the law is. It is also presumed *until the contrary is proved* that:

a person is sane;
a child between 10–14 lacks criminal intent; and
a person accused of a criminal offence is innocent, until proved guilty.

The word presumption further is also applied to a number of recognised situations in which on proof of Fact A, Fact B is presumed to exist without the need to call further evidence. The burden of rebutting Fact B then lies with the other party.[14] The four major examples in this context are the presumptions of death, legitimacy, marriage and regularity. The presumption of regularity is the one most commonly encountered in criminal cases.[15] It most commonly arises in those instances when conviction depends upon the correct working of some mechanical device such as traffic lights or a

---

7 Op cit, p 72 et seq.
8 This example is surely open to question: see p 128, post.
9 See eg *Ingram v Percival* [1969] 1 QB 548 (local knowledge of tidal waters); *Borthwick v Vickers* [1973] RTR 390 (lay-out of roads in Hartlepool) and *Kajala v Noble*, supra, (date of public disturbances in Southall).
10 *Wetheral v Harrison* [1976] QB 773.
11 For a general discussion see *Cross* (op cit) Chapter III.
12 Children and Young Persons Act 1933, s 50 (as amended).
13 *R v Waite* [1892] 2 QB 600.
14 These are sometimes referred to as 'rebuttable presumptions of law' or 'evidential presumptions'.
15 For an interesting example of where the presumption of marriage affected the competence of a prosecution witness to testify see *R v Yacoob* (1981) 72 Cr App Rep 313, CA.

police speedometer. In such cases, provided that the prosecution can prove that the machine was in proper working order when examined (Fact A) it will be presumed that it was functioning correctly at the time of the alleged offence (Fact B) in the absence of evidence to the contrary.

(c) Inferences of fact

There are certain well recognised situations in which on proof of Fact A, magistrates or a jury are *entitled* (but not *obliged*) to infer Fact B. The most well known of these is the 'doctrine of recent possession' whereby any person charged with theft or handling who has been found in possession of goods shortly after their having been missed and fails to give an adequate explanation of how he came by them (Fact A) may be presumed to have handled or stolen them as the case may be (Fact B). This so-called 'doctrine' is merely an example of one of many stock situations[16] in which a court or a jury is entitled to infer proof of a fact in issue from circumstantial evidence. It does not in any way affect the burden of proof. As a matter of common sense, however, it is the kind of evidence that is often so damning, that unless the accused can produce a plausible explanation conviction will almost inevitably follow.

(d) Formal admissions: Criminal Justice Act 1967, s 10

This section provides that:

(1) Subject to the provisions of this section, any fact of which oral evidence may be given in any criminal proceedings may be admitted for the purpose of those proceedings by or on behalf of the prosecutor or defendant, and the admission by any party of any such fact under this section shall as against that party be conclusive evidence in those proceedings of the fact admitted.

(2) An admission under this section:

(a) may be made before or at the proceedings;

(b) if made otherwise than in court, shall be in writing;

(c) if made in writing by an individual, shall purport to be signed by the person making it . . .;

(d) If made on behalf of a defendant who is an individual, shall be made by his counsel or solicitor;

(e) if made at any stage before the trial by a defendant who is an individual, must be approved by his counsel or solicitor (whether at the time it was made or subsequently) before or at the proceedings in question.

(3) An admission under this section for the purpose of proceedings relating to any matter shall be treated as an admission for the purpose of any subsequent criminal proceedings relating to that matter (including any appeal or retrial).

(4) An admission under this section may with the leave of the court be withdrawn in the proceedings for the purpose of which it is made or any subsequent criminal proceedings relating to the same matter.

It thus enables facts, including facts in issue, to be admitted before the trial begins. If this is done there is no need for any evidence to be tendered: the admitted fact is presumed to be conclusively proved.

---

16 The whole topic of circumstantial evidence is discussed exhaustively in *Cross* (op cit) chapter 1. Magistrates can and frequently do, for example, infer careless driving from the circumstances in which an accident took place or that the person proved to be the owner of a vehicle was in fact driving it at the relevant time. See eg *Elliott v Loake* [1983] Crim LR 36. For inferences that may be drawn from a person's voluntary presence in a football crowd see *Allen v Ireland* [1984] 1 WLR 903; *Parrish v Garfitt* [1984] 1 WLR 911n.

EXAMPLE: DONOGHUE and STEPHENSON's legal representatives could, if they wished, formally admit under s 10 that ATKIN's car was taken without his permission thus obviating the needs for any evidence to be given on this issue. This would not be prejudicial because the sole issue in this case is whether or not it was DONOGHUE and STEPHENSON who took it.

Unfortunately, however, s 10 is not made anywhere near enough use of, especially in fraud trials where the sole issued is often that of dishonesty.[17] As a result valuable court time is often taken up in calling evidence to prove facts which cannot seriously be disputed.

PRINCIPLE IV: EVIDENCE IS ALWAYS SUBJECTED TO 'QUALITY CONTROL'

As already stated, the bulk of the law of evidence is concerned with ensuring that only evidence of a sufficiently high quality goes before the court. The five tests must now be considered in greater detail.

Test 1: In order to be admissible evidence must be factually (and legally) relevant

Whether or not evidence is relevant is largely a matter of common sense and experience. The classic definition of relevance is that of Stephen who defined the word 'relevant' as meaning:

'Any two facts ... [that] are so related to each other that according to the common course of events, one either taken by itself or in connection with other facts proves or renders probable the past, present, or future, existence or non existence of the other.'[18]

Evidence may be either 'direct' (for example 'I saw D shoot X') or 'circumstantial' (for example, D is found in possession of the gun which shot X, or the gun is found in a dustbin nearby with D's fingerprints on it).[19] Additionally, when a witness gives evidence he will usually be permitted to 'set the scene' by recounting facts which although not strictly relevant put events into context.

EXAMPLE: Andrea BOURHILL will probably be allowed to start her evidence by saying 'I was watching television on the evening of 6 July when I heard a noise outside'.

The way in which Andrea BOURHILL organises her leisure activities is in no way relevant to any of the facts in issue in *R v* DONOGHUE *and* STEPHENSON but it puts the events of Friday, 6 July into context.[20] Such statements are said to form part of the 'res gestae'. The res gestae principle is important because it may sometimes let in evidence which would otherwise

---

17 The topic is discussed further at p 175, post.
18 *Digest of the Law of Evidence* (12th edn), Art 1.
19 The prosecution will have to adduce expert evidence that the fingerprints of the accused or those found on the relevant object have at least 16 matching ridge characteristics. The person may be convicted where there is no other evidence of identity *R v Castleton* (1909) 3 Cr App Rep 74, CCA. For an interesting discussion on the work of fingerprint experts see Campbell: 'Fingerprints: A review' [1985] Crim LR 195.
20 For an extreme example of this see *O'Leary v R* (1946) 73 CLR 566, High Court of Australia (serious acts of violence during drunken orgy leading up to a murder held to be admissible under the principle).

be inadmissible because it is, for example, hearsay, or opinion evidence. These implications will be considered in due course.[1]

Legal relevance

Provided that evidence is *factually* relevant it will normally be admitted.

> EXAMPLE: The case against DONOGHUE, on the face of it, appears strong. He has been seen by a witness who says she has seen him driving the car away ('direct evidence'). He has also been observed by PC ANDREWS behaving in a guilty way and has made a statement under caution admitting his presence ('circumstantial evidence').

But what of the case against STEPHENSON, especially the alleged find of housebreaking implements at his home? Is this relevant to a charge of taking a vehicle without consent?[2] It is clear that somewhere along the line evidence crosses the frontier from relevance to irrelevance and a lawyer would probably accept that the frontier had been crossed in relation to this item of evidence. But would a lay person see it the same way? There is always a danger that he would not and that he would 'hang the dog with a bad name'. The law of evidence thus empowers a judge or magistrates to rule against the admission of certain kinds of evidence on the ground that they are not relevant as a matter of law. As *Cross* states:

> '... one of the objects of the law of evidence is to prevent common sense from having a free rein because there are cases in which to permit it might lead to an unjust result.'[3]

There are three kinds of evidence that are normally excluded on the ground that they are not 'legally relevant' namely:

(a) evidence of *character* and *previous misconduct* (the rule against 'similar fact' evidence);
(b) *opinion* evidence;
(c) *self serving* statements made out of court (the rule against 'self-corroboration').

The basic rules are relatively simple, but, as is so often the case with evidence, these are complicated by a number of important exceptions.

(a) Evidence of character and previous misconduct (the 'similar fact' rule)

It is much easier to start with what the prosecution cannot do. The prosecution can never adduce evidence of a person's general bad character or misconduct on other occasions with the object of proving that he is *ipso facto* more likely to have committed the offence with which he is now charged. For example, the prosecution cannot adduce evidence of DONOGHUE or STEPHENSON's previous convictions and the circumstances in which those offences were committed to prove that they are both such thoroughly bad characters that they are just the sort of people likely to have driven off in someone else's car without permission. Similarly, the housebreaking implements found at STEPHENSON's home (if proved to be such) could not be ad-

---

1 Pp 134 and 145, post.
2 In any event it would be liable to exclusion under s 78(1) of the Police and Criminal Evidence Act 1984 discussed at p 150, post.
3 Op cit, p 349.

mitted in evidence because their possession shows no more than a general pro-
pensity for wrongdoing.[4] Likewise, any oblique references to the accused's previous misconduct, for example, during interrogation would be inadmissible.

> EXAMPLE: If the evidence of DS YOUNG's interrogation of DONOGHUE (which the
> defence would see prior to committal) were to contain dialogue such as:
> I said (DS YOUNG) 'Been up to your old tricks again Nobby, this looks like one
> of yours'.
> He said (DONOGHUE) 'I want my brief'.
> I said 'He hasn't been much use to you in the past'.

objection could be taken to DS YOUNG recounting this in oral evidence.[5]

> EXAMPLE: Supposing that whoever had taken ATKIN's car had placed a card
> through his door with the words upon it:
> 'Help control pollution, support your local car thieves'
> and that on the two previous occasions that DONOGHUE had been convicted of s 12
> offences, the prosecution could prove that similar cards had been delivered through
> the victim's doors. Suppose also that a large collection of ignition keys or speci-
> alised car breaking implements had been found at STEPHENSON's flat.[6]

One's 'gut reaction' would surely be that such evidence points to something
far more specific than general disposition and that it ought to be admitted.[7]
The major difficulty concerns how to create a legal principle from a 'gut
reaction'. Formulating a satisfactory test for the admission of evidence of this
kind has caused much judicial agonizing. In the leading case of *DPP v
Boardman*[8] Lord Wilberforce stated that:

> 'The basic principle must be that the admission of similar fact evidence ... is
> exceptional and requires a strong degree of probative force. This probative force
> is derived, if at all, from the circumstances that the facts testified to by the several
> witnesses bear to each other such a striking similarity that they must, when judged
> by experience and common sense, either all be true or have arisen from a cause
> common to the witnesses or from pure coincidence.'

In order to be admissible therefore such evidence must in effect be 'super
relevant'; it must do more than raise or strengthen a suspicion, it must point
strongly to guilt. If it does, it will be admitted *notwithstanding* that it reveals
details of the accused's bad behaviour[9] on other occasions. The categories of
'similar fact' evidence are never closed, but examples of where such evidence
may be admitted include, for the purpose of showing system[10] (especially in

---

4 *Makin v A-G for New South Wales* [1894] AC 57, PC.
5 The judge, of course, has the discretionary power to control the fairness of the proceedings
   under s 78(1) of the 1984 Act but, it is submitted, such evidence is not a matter for the
   discretion of the judge: he is obliged to exclude it, but see *Turner v Underwood* [1948] 2 KB
   284, DC.
6 See for example *R v Reading* [1966] 1 All ER 521n, CCA.
7 For an excellent introduction to the whole bedevilled topic of similar fact evidence see
   Elliott, Young Persons Guide to Similar Fact Evidence, [1983] Crim LR 284 and 352. See
   also *Cross on Evidence* (op cit) p 310 et seq.
8 [1975] AC 421, HL at 444.
9 It is often (wrongly) assumed that in order to be admissible behaviour on other occasions
   must constitute commission of a 'strikingly similar' criminal offence. This is not so: see *R v
   Barrington* [1981] 1 All ER 1132, CA (employment of a particular method of seduction in an
   indecent assault case) and *R v Lewis* (1982) 147 JP 493, CA, (indecent assault, defence of
   innocent association: defendant member of paedophile information group) and *R v Seaman*
   (1978) 67 Cr App Rep 234, CA (suspicious behaviour in supermarket on two previous
   occasions: permissible to use this rebut defence of accident on charge of theft of bacon from
   same supermarket).
10 See eg *R v Ollis* [1900] 2 QB 758.

fraud cases), in order to rebut a defence of mistake,[11] accident[12] or innocent association[13] or where the defence is one of mistaken identification.[14] Prior to the decision in *DPP v Boardman*[15] it was thought that sexual offences, especially those involving homosexual practices formed a special category but in *Boardman* the House of Lords emphatically rejected such a notion. That being said, disputes as to the admissibility of 'similar fact' evidence tend to arise most frequently in such cases and continue to cause problems.[16]

Fortunately, cases involving 'similar fact' evidence are rarely encountered in practice. They tend to arise most frequently in two situations, usually, but not exclusively, in prosecutions for sexual offences:

(1) when the accused is to be tried on several charges *at the same time* and the prosecution argue that the evidence on one charge is admissible as evidence on another and vice versa.[17]

(2) when the accused admits that he behaved in the way alleged but maintains that he was acting innocently.[18]

Although the presumption will always be against the admission of 'similar fact' evidence, the defence must always prepare its arguments meticulously. Once such evidence is admitted, the prejudice to the accused is bound to be substantial, especially since he is liable to be cross-examined as to the other incidents if he gives evidence.[19] Whenever the topic rears its ugly head there is no choice but to consult the leading cases in detail and prepare your ground accordingly.

Right of defence to adduce 'similar fact' evidence. Conversely, there is nothing to prevent an accused adducing evidence of his own or a co-accused's general disposition in an endeavour to prove that he was *less* likely to have committed the offence than his co-accused[20] provided that such evidence is relevant to an issue in the case. Thus, for example, an accused charged with arson of a hostel and manslaughter was not permitted to adduce evidence that his co-accused had started fires on previous occasions,[1] because his defence was that he was asleep elsewhere when the offence was committed. As he was maintaining that he was not involved at all, the propensities of his co-accused had no bearing on his defence.

---

11 *R v Mortimer* (1936) 25 Cr App Rep 150, CCA.
12 *R v Smith* (1915) 84 LJKB 2153 (the 'brides in the bath' case) and *R v Seaman*, supra.
13 See eg *R v Lewis*, supra.
14 See eg *R v Reading*, supra, and *R v Mustafa* (1976) 65 Cr App Rep 26 (suspicious behaviour by defendant on previous occasion at store).
15 [1975] AC 421, HL.
16 The major post-Boardman 'similar fact', sex cases are discussed in *Cross* (op cit) p 314 et seq.
17 It is often not appreciated that an accused may well be tried for several offences of the same or similar character at the same time even though they do not come within an exception to the 'similar fact' rule. If this happens, in the normal course of events the judge will direct the jury or, the magistrates must direct themselves to consider each offence separately and not treat evidence on *offence 1* as admissible in respect of *offence 2* and vice versa. If however the offences come within the similar fact rule evidence on *offence 1* will be admissible to prove *offence 2* etc., as, for example, in *Boardman v DPP*, supra: see generally *R v Scarrott* [1978] QB 1016, CA.
18 As for example in *R v Seaman* and *R v Lewis*, supra.
19 See further p 158, post.
20 *Lowery v R* [1974] AC 85, PC.
 1 *R v Neale* (1977) 65 Cr App Rep 304, CA.

Statutory exceptions. Certain specific offences, for example, driving whilst disqualified, and possession of a firearm, having previously been sentenced to imprisonment for a term of three years or more inevitably involve the limited disclosure of an accused's previous convictions. This is because in such cases the commission of the earlier offence is one of the facts in issue. Furthermore, s 27(3) Theft Act 1968 provides that on a charge of handling stolen goods, evidence showing that the accused had in his possession stolen goods from any theft taking place within *12 months* preceding the offence charged or has been convicted of theft or handling within the preceding *five years* is admissible on the issue of whether or not he knew or believed goods to be stolen.[2] Such provisions are not part of the 'similar fact' rule at all but instances, albeit rare, when statute provides for the admission of a previous conviction notwithstanding that this may incidentally create prejudice, because its existence constitutes or is deemed to be relevant to a fact in issue in the case.

Evidence of the accused's good character. The accused may give evidence of his own *good character* by seeking to elicit this from prosecution witnesses in cross-examination, by giving evidence himself to this effect, or by calling character witnesses. Such evidence is admissible not merely on credibility but on the general issue of guilt.[3] In other words the accused can assert that his previous character shows him to be the sort of person who would *not* commit such an offence. By virtue of a 19th century case[4] which is still good authority,[5] he may not, however, adduce evidence of specific instances of good behaviour,[6] only of his general good reputation. Nevertheless, a good deal of latitude is, in practice, accorded to the accused.[7] Woe betide him if he is not telling the truth. If he gives evidence he will have 'thrown away his shield'[8] and be liable to cross-examination on his previous convictions, and even if he does not do so the prosecution may at common law call evidence in rebuttal to prove his convictions and bad character.[9]

(b) Opinion evidence

Witnesses may generally only give evidence of what they saw, heard or otherwise perceived. It is for the magistrates or the jury to draw inferences from those facts. The only major exception to this rule is where the court receives expert evidence.[10] Before this can be done, however, two criteria must be satisfied. First, the expert evidence to be tendered must relate to a

---

2 For the limited scope of this provision see *R v Bradley* (1979) 70 Cr App Rep 200.

3 *R v Bryant* [1979] QB 108, CA.

4 *R v Rowton* (1865) Le & Ca 520, CCR.

5 *R v Redgrave* (1981) 74 Cr App Rep 10, CA.

6 Accordingly, in *R v Redgrave*, supra, on charges involving allegations of homosexuality the defendant was not allowed to put in evidence letters from girlfriends purporting to show previous heterosexual relationships. The Court of Appeal appeared to overlook the point that the letters were in any event hearsay.

7 Thus, for example, the accused is usually permitted to put forward his lack of previous convictions although in theory this goes to disposition rather than reputation. This latitude seems however not to be based on any definable legal principles: see *R v Redgrave*, supra. Where the accused has convictions that are spent it is in the judge's discretion as to whether he should allow him to be put forward as a man of good character: see *R v Nye* (1982) 75 Cr App Rep 247, CA.

8 Under the first limb of *s 1(f)(ii)* of the Criminal Evidence Act 1898 see p 159, post.

9 *R v Butterwasser* [1948] 1 KB 4, CCA.

10 Not all expert evidence is necessarily opinion evidence: part may consist of findings of fact based on observation (fact) and part on the inference to the drawn from them (opinion). In

specialized matter which is not within the competence of the court or jury to determine.[11] Secondly the witness must qualify as an 'expert'. Although certain kinds of experts, such as forensic scientists are readily accepted as such, competence to give expert evidence may sometimes have to be determined as a preliminary issue by the magistrates or the judge in the presence of the jury. In such cases this will largely be a question of fact but it must be stressed that lack of formal qualifications is not fatal.[12] Quite apart from issues relating to expert evidence it is not always easy to distinguish between 'fact' and 'opinion' in the case of lay witnesses.

> EXAMPLE: Consider the following extract from Andrea BOURHILL's testimony. 'I saw DONOGHUE try the off-side door of the car. He was looking up and down the road in a suspicious manner. It was obvious he was up to something.'

The first sentence is clearly as statement of fact, the third a statement of opinion, but what of the second? Is 'in a suspicious manner' a statement of fact or opinion? Witnesses are granted some latitude in conveying their perceptions and thus statements such as 'the accused appeared drunk', 'the accused was behaving objectionably', 'the accused was looking about furtively' are frequently admitted, presumably on the basis that such language is more descriptive than evaluative. In addition, and somewhat anomolously, opinion as to the speed of a vehicle *is* admissible.

(c) *Self serving statements: 'The rule against self corroboration'*

As a general rule, evidence of what a witness said out of court cannot be admitted for the purpose of bolstering up what he says in court. Thus if, for example, Andrea BOURHILL were to tell her tale to fifteen people the prosecution would not be permitted call them all as witnesses, to corroborate Andrea's testimony, because they add nothing. As a further illustration of the rule, Andrea BOURHILL's written statement to the police is not admissible to augment the evidence that she gives on oath.[13] There are, however, *five* circumstances in which previous consistent statements may be admitted for certain limited purposes.

(i) Evidence of past identification.

> EXAMPLE: When Andrea BOURHILL gives evidence against STEPHENSON she will not be asked 'Do you see that person here in court today?' but will be asked whether she attended on an identification parade and whether on that occasion she picked a person out.

Strictly speaking, this offends against the main rule because what is in reality being adduced in evidence is her out of court statement made on a previous

---

coming to his opinion an expert is entitled to draw upon facts directly observed by him. He may also refer to journals and the corpus of knowledge appertaining to his field without this needing to be strictly proved *R v Abadom* [1983] 1 All ER 364, CA.

11 Contrast *R v Turner* [1975] QB 834, CA (psychiatric evidence not admissible on issue of provocation) and *R v Smith* [1979] 3 All ER 605, CA (defence of automatism).

12 See eg *R v Silverlock* [1894] 2 QB 766 (amateur handwriting expert) and *R v Oakley* [1979] RTR 417 (police officer entitled to give expert evidence as to causation of accidents): contrast *R v MacKenney* (1981) 76 Cr App Rep 271, CA (psychologist incompetent to give expert evidence on matters within province of a psychiatrist).

13 She could however continue looking at it up until the moment she goes into court. She could also 'refresh her memory' from it subject to certain conditions. See p 153, post. The document itself could not however be evidence in the case because it would prima facie be hearsay, but see p 142, post.

occasion.[14] It would nevertheless be intolerable if the only admissible evidence of identification were to be a 'dock identification' many months after the event.[15] Out of court identification is thus admissible for the purpose of proving identity.

(ii) Evidence to negative recent fabrication.

EXAMPLE: Supposing that Mrs DONOGHUE had contacted a solicitor on the afternoon of Saturday, 7 July whilst DONOGHUE was still in the police station and had told her that DONOGHUE had been with her the whole of Friday evening, 6 July.

If she were to give evidence in support of DONOGHUE's alibi at the trial and prosecuting counsel were to suggest that she had made up this story in collusion with her husband after the event, the solicitor could give evidence that Mrs DONOGHUE had made a consistent statement before she had had an opportunity to see her husband. Furthermore, if the solicitor had had sufficient presence of mind (which she should have done) to ask Mrs DONOGHUE to make a written statement, this document, on proof of authenticity, would also be admissible. Somewhat artificially, such a statement is generally[16] only admissible to *rebut* recent fabrication; it is not as such admissible evidence, as in this case, to support DONOGHUE's alibi. In practical terms, however, the absence of an opportunity for fabrication will materially strengthen the weight of a witness's testimony.

(iii) Self serving statements by an accused.
As has already been shown, when an accused is arrested, interrogated and charged by the police, evidence will almost invariably be given at the trial of what was said by him under interrogation and any written statement under caution made by him will also be produced. Sometimes, what was said or written by the accused will contain no incriminating admissions or be partly favourable and partly adverse. The adverse parts are, of course, admissible under the confessions rule provided they are not excluded under s 76 of the Police and Criminal Evidence Act 1984, but what of the favourable parts? When the statement is partly adverse and partly favourable, the favourable parts must not be 'edited' out:[17] the whole record of the interrogation or the complete written statement must usually[18] be put in evidence so that the magistrates or jury can weigh up the adverse part in the overall context of what the accused said or wrote. Where the interrogation record or written statement is 'mixed' in this way, the favourable parts, although strictly speaking self serving statements[19] are nevertheless admissible on the issue of guilt although they are

---

14 But it nevertheless appears to be admissible on the basis of dicta in *R v Christie* [1914] AC 545.

15 If a witness cannot remember whom he picked out on the parade or *whether he picked out anyone at all* the evidence of persons at the parade as to which person the witness picked out is admissible as evidence of identification: *R v Osbourne and Virtue* [1973] QB 678, CA. See also Libbling, 'Evidence of past identification' [1977] Crim LR 268.

16 Reduced into document form such a statement may in certain circumstances be admissible with leave of the court under s 68 of the Police and Criminal Evidence Act 1984, for example if the witness has died see p 142, post.

17 See eg *R v Penfold and Penfold* (1979) 71 Cr App Rep 4; *R v Pearce* (1979) 69 Cr App Rep 365, CA.

18 Admissions will not normally be edited out merely because they are prejudicial to a co-accused: *R v Gunewardene* [1951] 2 KB 600, CCA. This statement must however be considered in the light of s 78(1) of the Police and Criminal Evidence Act 1984 see p 150, post. For the correct procedure on editing statements see *R v Weaver* [1968] 1 QB 353, CA.

19 And hearsay.

not to be given the same weight as the adverse parts.[20] Where, however, the accused makes no damaging admissions but, for example, persists in denying the charge and gives an account of himself which is entirely consistent with the defence he advances at the trial, his out of court statement is at best[1] only admissible as evidence of his reaction when accused of the offence. Whether any juror (or lawyer) can realistically make such fine distinctions is open to serious doubt, but, in practical terms, consistency may well be a potent factor in assessing the credibility of an accused's evidence.[2]

(iv) Facts forming part of the res gestae. The concept of 'res gestae' is a classic example of that well known legal maxim, 'If in doubt, use Latin'. In its wider sense, the doctrine of res gestae enables a witness to give evidence which although not strictly relevant 'sets the scene'. In its narrower sense, however, it includes statements:

> 'made in such conditions (always being those of approximate but not exact con-temporaneity) of involvement or pressure as to exclude the possibility of concoction or distortion to the advantage of the maker or the disadvantage of the accused'.[3]

On occasions, it thus permits the admission of a statement which would otherwise be excluded as self serving.[4]

> EXAMPLE: Supposing that Andrea BOURHILL, having witnessed ATKIN's car being driven off had rushed into Tony ATKIN's house shouting :
> 'Tony, Tony, Nobby has just driven off your Jag',
> Tony ATKIN when giving evidence might be allowed[5] to recount Andrea's out-burst. Under the 'res gestae' principle this would be admissible to support Andrea's evidence that DONOGHUE took the car.

(v) Evidence of recent complaint in a sexual case. The male or female victim and any person to whom the complaint is communicated may give evidence to the court of a complaint made after the event provided that it was made at the earliest reasonable opportunity and was not made in re-sponse to an inducement or leading question. Recent complaints are, how-ever, only admissible to show consistency or to rebut a defence of consent and thus cannot constitute corroboration of the victim's evidence. When, however, the victim has been independently observed in a distressed condi-tion, such evidence *may* be capable of constituting corroboration if the obser-vation took place in circumstances where the victim did not realise he or she was being observed.[6]

---

20 *R v Duncan* (1981) 73 Cr App Rep 359, CA. Approved in *R v Kurshid* [1984] Crim LR 288.
 1 *R v Storey* (1968) 52 Cr App Rep 334, CA. Where however the statement is a prepared one made with a view to its being included as part of the prosecution case it may be excluded altogether: *R v Pearce* (1979) 69 Cr App Rep 365. See also *R v Kurshid*, supra.
 2 The prosecutor will often invite a court to infer guilt from the accused's inconsistencies. For the potency of such evidence see further Vennard, 'Trials in the Magistrates Court' (1982) Home Office Research Study No 71 (HMSO).
 3 *Ratten v R* [1972] AC 378, PC, per Lord Wilberforce at 391.
 4 Or hearsay.
 5 The court has an overriding discretion to exclude it on the grounds of unfairness under s 78(1) of the 1984 Act. See post, p 150
 6 For two recent examples see *R v Chauhan* (1981) 73 Cr App Rep 232 and *R v Dowley* [1983] Crim LR 168. Discussed in Oughton, 'The Distressing Nature of Corroboration' [1984] Crim LR.

Test 2. Evidence that is factually (and legally) relevant may still be excluded if it is inadmissible

Even if evidence can satisfy the relevance test by being logically probative (and not being mere evidence of disposition, opinion evidence or a self serving statement) it may nevertheless be liable to exclusion because:

(a) It is hearsay; or
(b) It is an inadmissible confession; or
(c) It is subject to dictates of public policy or private privilege; or
(d) The court in its discretion excludes it on the ground of unfairness.

In other words, the fact that evidence is *relevant* does not necessarily mean that it will *ipso facto* be *admissible*.

(a) The rule against hearsay

This rule more than any other has bewildered generations of students (and lawyers).[7] The basic rule is that:

'A statement other than one made by a person while giving oral evidence in the proceedings is inadmissible if it is tendered to prove the truth of any fact stated in it'.

The rationale behind the rule is simple enough. When relevant evidence consists of the perceptions (usually, but not necessarily, visual) of a witness, the only way in which those perceptions may be proved is by calling that witness to give *oral* evidence, which may then be tested by cross-examination. The court is thereby given the opportunity of evaluating the perceiver's reliability at first hand.

EXAMPLE: The only way to prove Andrea BOURHILL's assertion that she saw DONOGHUE driving off in Tony ATKIN's car is by calling her to give oral evidence of her perception of that fact. The prosecution cannot (subject to certain exceptions):
(1) Call DC MACMILLAN to recount what Andrea BOURHILL told him; or
(2) Tender Andrea BOURHILL's written statement in which she recounts what she saw.

To do either of these things would infringe the rule against hearsay, because the court would not have had the opportunity of hearing her evidence tested at first hand. Thus far the rule is perfectly straightforward: if a party wishes to tender relevant 'eye witness'[8] evidence he must bring his 'eye witness' to court and put her in the witness box.

Confusion arises largely as a result of two misconceptions. First it is often assumed that no witness can *ever* give evidence on oath of *what somebody else said*. This is not necessarily so: the purpose for which the reported speech is being tendered in evidence must first be identified.

EXAMPLE: Supposing that you, an innocent bystander were to hear Andrea BOURHILL shouting to Norbert DONOGHUE 'I saw you take that car. You are nothing but a rotten thief; come here if you dare and I will scratch your eyes out'.

If BOURHILL were to be prosecuted for an offence under s 5 of the Public Order Act 1936 (using insulting and threatening words with an intent to provoke a breach of the peace) the prosecution could quite clearly call you

---

7 And judges. In *Myers v DPP* [1965] AC 1001, the House of Lords in holding that certain microfilm records were inadmissible hearsay overruled the Court of Appeal which had unanimously been of the opposite persuasion!
8 Or 'ear witness', 'touch witness' or 'smell witness'.

to give evidence of the words that she spoke. The use of 'insulting and threatening words' is one of the facts in issue in the case, therefore your evidence is admissible to prove that fact. You could not, however, be asked to give evidence against DONOGHUE if he were prosecuted under s 12 of the Theft Act because the facts in issue would now be whether or not he took a conveyance without the owner's consent. You could not normally give evidence of this fact, because you were not an 'eye witness' to it.[9] The 'eye witness' to the talking (assuming that she is telling the truth) is Andrea BOURHILL. It can be seen, therefore, that evidence by a witness of what another person said will not be hearsay, if *what* he said (rather than the *truth* of what he said) is relevant to a fact in issue.[10]

The second misconception is to assume that reported speech is the *only* kind of evidence which infringes the hearsay rule. Evidence contained in a document is just as likely (if not much more likely) to constitute hearsay. For example, it will not, *prima facie*, be possible to adduce Andrea BOURHILL's evidence of having seen DONOGHUE take the car by tendering her written statement: she must be called to give oral evidence.[11]

Is it hearsay?

The major problem therefore is spotting those cases where the rule has been infringed. The examples given so far have been relatively straightforward but on occasions the operations of the rule are less obvious.

EXAMPLE: Suppose that, instead of having the testimony of Andrea BOURHILL to rely upon, the only available evidence was that of a bystander (Mr X) who saw two men answering DONOGHUE and STEPHENSON's description driving a green Jaguar registration ABC 123J on Friday 6th July at 10 pm. The following chapter of disasters then took place:—

(1) Mr X shortly afterwards dictated the registration number to DC MACMILLAN who recorded it in his notebook, but neglected to ask Mr X to sign the note or read it back to Mr X.

(2) At the trial Mr X cannot now remember the car number.

In the above example the prosecution would be stuck. The amnesiac Mr X could not 'refresh his memory' from DC MACMILLAN's note because it was not 'made or verified' by him.[12] Furthermore, DC MACMILLAN could not give evidence of the registration number because to do so would be hearsay.[13] By doing so the prosecution would be endeavouring to prove that the 'eyewitness' Mr X saw a green Jaguar ABC 123J on Friday 6th July at 10 pm. The rule can therefore produce apparently absurd results. In the above example disaster could have been avoided by DC MACMILLAN either asking Mr X to sign the note of the car number or by reading it back to him for confirmation. If he had done either of these things Mr X (subject to the leave of the court) could then have 'refreshed his memory' from the note.[14]

On occasions, the rule can produce even more extraordinary results.

---

9 You might be able to give evidence of DONOGHUE's *reaction* to the accusation in certain circumstances: see p 141 et seq, post.

10 *Subramaniam v Public Prosecutor* [1956] 1 WLR 965, PC. Accordingly W may give evidence as to what X has told him concerning his state of mind or bodily condition. See eg *Ratten v R*, supra.

11 Even if she were to be called the statement could still not be admitted since it would still be hearsay. It would also of course be self serving. See ante p 132

12 See p 153, post.

13 For an example of where precisely this difficulty arose see *Jones v Metcalf* [1967] 3 All ER 205, DC.

14 This course was upheld in *R v Kelsey* (1981) 74 Cr App Rep 213, CA. It would however be

EXAMPLE: Suppose that DONOGHUE, having taken ATKIN's car had acquired a wrecked *dark blue* Jaguar of similar make, registration ABC 345K and, having resprayed ATKIN's Jaguar dark blue, had fitted it up with the wrecked Jaguar's number plates and then sold it on with the wrecked car's log book. Suppose further that when questioned by the police he said:

'What green Jaguar, I've sold a blue one, no, I don't know anything about a green one. It's all above board, here's the Notification of Change. I'm just sending it off to Swansea.'

At the trial, the prosecution, in an endeavour to prove that the 'blue' Jaguar sold by DONOGHUE was in fact the 'green' car taken from ATKIN, seek to adduce in evidence the microfilmed work sheets from the factory which show, from the engine number indelibly imprinted on the cylinder block, that the 'blue' Jaguar must in fact be ATKIN's 'green' one.[15]

Hopefully, it will immediately have been realised that the microfilm records are *prima facie* hearsay, because they are being tendered to prove the truth of a fact (the engraving of the number), other than by calling an 'eye witness' to it (for example, the person who actually engraved it). Because such a result would make it virtually impossible to prove the contents of business and other records[16] this kind of evidence is now normally admissible under a statutory exception to the rule.[17] Breaches of the rule may also occur when a police officer puts allegations of witnesses to a suspect who either denies or does not comment upon them.[18]

EXAMPLE: Suppose that during the course of interviewing STEPHENSON, DS YOUNG were to put the substance of Andrea BOURHILL's evidence to him in the form of a series of questions, each of which he in turn denies or refuses to answer:

DS YOUNG: I've got a witness who says she saw you.
STEPHENSON: Rubbish, I don't believe you.
DS YOUNG: She was looking out of her window when you and DONOGHUE took the car.
STEPHENSON: No reply.
[etc, etc.]

To prove the truth of BOURHILL's allegation the prosecution must call her. There is a real danger that a jury could misinterpret the questioning of DS YOUNG as being evidence of identification in its own right and for this reason such evidence should be excluded.[19]

As a general rule, hearsay objections tend to be taken to prosecution evidence but the rule applies equally to defence evidence. This has also been known to produce remarkable results.

---

necessary to call the police officer to produce the original note and to give evidence to identify it as the one that he made at the time.

15 *Myers v DPP*, supra, was based on similar facts to these.

16 The court may however be invited to draw inferences of fact where a transaction which should have been recorded has not been recorded. See eg *R v Patel* [1981] 3 All ER 94, CA (absence of defendant from Home Office immigration records prima facie infers that he entered the country illegally although, on the facts, the record was held to have been incorrectly proved) see also *R v Shone* (1982) 76 Cr App Rep 72, CA (absence of article from stock record may support inference that it had not been sold) and *R v Muir* (1983) 79 Cr App Rep 153, CA.

17 The effect of *Myers*, supra, was largely neutralised by Criminal Evidence Act 1965 now re-enacted in an extended form in ss 68 and 69 of the Police and Criminal Evidence Act 1984: see p 142 et seq, post.

18 *R v Christie*, supra. For a recent example see *R v Martin* (1983) Times, 1 July.

19 The position would of course be different if STEPHENSON's replies had amounted to a confession.

EXAMPLE:

(1) *Sparks v R*[1]

A white man was tried and convicted of indecently assaulting a three-year-old girl who did not give evidence. The ruling of the trial judge that her mother could not give evidence to the effect that the child had described her attacker as coloured because to do so would infringe the rule against hearsay was upheld by the Privy Council.[2]

(2) *R v Turner*[3]

A third party confessed to committing a crime for which the accused was on trial. The Court of Appeal upheld the judge's ruling that in order to prove that fact it was necessary to call the third party to give evidence.[4]

Conclusion

As a good working rule, when examining an item of evidence, look for the 'perceiver' or 'eye witness' at the beginning of the chain. The only way that the evidence may be adduced is by calling that person to give oral evidence on oath. Nothing else will do, unless one of the various exceptions considered below can be invoked.

EXCEPTIONS TO THE HEARSAY RULE

The exceptions are so numerous that they are as important as the rule itself. Clearly, no more than a summary can be made of them in this book. The order in which they are set out differs somewhat from that in other textbooks and is based primarily upon the frequency with which they are met in practice.

(i) Admission of non-contentious evidence by written statement. The rule against hearsay would cause extreme inconvenience if applied inflexibly because it would require the parties to call every witness to give oral evidence even in those instances where their opponent was prepared to accept it as true. Various statutes thus provide for the admission of a witness's written statement without his being called, *provided* that the prescribed procedural criteria are satisfied and (generally) that the party on whom the statement is served consents.

Admission of written statements at trials (summary and on indictment): Criminal Justice Act 1967, s 9. A witness's written statement may be admissible in a criminal trial without the maker being called as a witness, provided that, (i) it is in the *proper form*, (ii) the party tendering the statement has *served* a copy on all other parties and (iii) no other party, has, within *seven days*, objected. To be in the proper form the statement must:

(a) purport to be *signed* by the person who made it; and
(b) contain a *declaration* that it is true to the best of the maker's knowledge and belief and it is made in the knowledge that if it is tendered in evidence he will be liable to prosecution if he has wilfully stated anything in it which is false or which he does not believe to be true.

1 [1964] AC 964, PC.
2 It is submitted that this case is inconsistent with *R v Osbourne*, supra. If out of court identification is admissible on behalf of the prosecution surely it must also be admissible on behalf of the defence. The appeal was allowed on other grounds.
3 (1975) 61 Cr App Rep 67, CA.
4 A statement taken from the third party by D's solicitor in these circumstances could now possibly be admitted under s 68 of the Police and Criminal Evidence Act 1984 if the third party has eg died or disappeared. See further p 142, post.

A statement complying with all the requirements of this section may be admitted at the trial as if it were oral evidence on oath by the person making it. Thus it may only contain *evidence that would be admissible if the maker were to give it on oath*. It must not therefore contain statements of hearsay, non-expert opinion or any other prejudicial material (for example, allusions to an accused's previous convictions).

Section 9 is frequently made use of by prosecutors, usually in summary proceedings, in an endeavour to dispense with the need to call non-contentious witnesses, for example, the 'loser' in a theft case.[5] It is nevertheless equally open to the defence to serve a witness's statement in s 9 form where it is appropriate[6]. Careful thought is required before agreeing to the use of a s 9 statement. It is always possible to insist on the maker being called and this should be done if it is wished to cross-examine him. However, to agree the admission of a s 9 statement does not amount to an acceptance of its contents. Evidence can still be called to contradict it, but in such circumstances the court may well require the case to be adjourned to enable the witness to be called to give oral evidence.[7] In practice therefore it is best only to agree a s 9 statement being tendered in evidence when it contains no contentious material.

Admission of written statements at committal proceedings: s 102 of the Magistrates' Courts Act 1980. This section lays down a similar procedure to that in s 9 of the 1967 Act for the admission of written statements at *committal proceedings*.[8] Written statements are admissible provided again that they are in the *proper form*, are *served* on the opposite party prior to the hearing and that party *consents* to their admission. In practice, the police will always take witness statements on prepared forms which comply with the formal requirements of both s 9 and s 102.[9]

Admission of evidence taken at committal proceedings in trials on indictment: Criminal Justice Act 1925, s 13. A written statement tendered at committal under s 102 of the 1980 Act (or a deposition taken from a witness who gives evidence on oath) may be admitted at the subsequent trial on indictment if the witness was made the subject of a 'conditional witness order' at the committal proceedings. If a 'full witness order' was made, the witness must normally attend to give evidence.[10]

> EXAMPLE: If DONOGHUE and STEPHENSON were to be tried on indictment, it is likely that all the prosecution evidence would be tendered in written form under s 102 at the committal proceedings before the magistrates, and that they would be committed for trial to the Crown Court without consideration of the evidence (under s 6(2) of the Magistrates' Courts Act 1980).

---

5 Where a person is tried on *indictment* the statement will often be admissible under Criminal Justice Act 1925, s 13, if it was tendered at committal. See infra.
6 Uses of s 9 statements are considered further at p 191, post.
7 See *Lister v Quaife* [1983] 2 All ER 29, DC.
8 For the use of such statements at committal proceedings generally see further p 326 et seq, post.
9 For examples see committal documents in *Police v McCARTHY*, post.
10 The only circumstances in which such a statement may be read are if it is proved that the witness is dead or insane, too ill to travel or has been kept out of the way at the procurement of the accused Criminal Justice Act 1925, s 13(3). The court nevertheless has an overriding general discretion to exclude such a statement if to admit it would be unfair to the accused: 1984 Act, s 78(1). For a pre-1984 Act example of when this was done see *R v Blithing* (1983) 77 Cr App Rep 86, CA. As to committals generally see further, post.

If defence counsel wished, for example, to cross-examine Andrea BOURHILL at the Crown Court trial (which in all probability he would) the defence must ask for a 'full witness order' at the committal proceedings. On the other hand it is unlikely that he would wish to cross-examine the loser ATKIN. If a 'conditional witness order' were made, his evidence could be read out at the trial under s 13 of the 1925 Act unless prior to the trial the defence were to notify the prosecution that his attendance was required.[11]

(ii) Miscellaneous provisions relating to written statements. There are a number of statutes which provide for the admission of a witness's evidence in the form of a written statement, in particular the depositions of persons dangerously ill,[12] the evidence of children or young persons in committal proceedings for sexual offences,[13] and details as to the registration particulars of vehicles and driving licence records.[14] Furthermore, the transcript of a witness's evidence given at a previous trial is admissible at common law, subject to the appropriate authentication, if he has since died, or is too ill to attend.[15]

(iii) Confessions. A confession is defined by s 82(1) of the Police and Criminal Evidence Act 1984 as:

> 'Any statement wholly or partly adverse to the person who made it, whether to a person in authority or not and whether made in words or otherwise.'

As well as being subject to its own special rules as to admissibility, a confession technically infringes the hearsay rule but is admissible because it would be unrealistic to expect the prosecution to call the accused to give evidence against himself. Disputes as to confessions tend to fall into two major categories. In the case of oral confessions ('verbals') the dispute will usually be as to whether the words alleged were ever spoken or whether they have been correctly recorded. Where, however, the confession is contained in a *written* record of the interrogation which has been signed and initialled by the accused[16] or in a *written statement* under *caution*, the dispute is more likely to be as to whether the accused's signature was obtained by oppression or whether it is reliable. The nature of the dispute will have a marked effect on the course of the trial. On a trial on indictment, if *admissibility* is in issue, a 'trial within a trial' will take place in the absence of the jury. If, however, *truth or accuracy* only is in issue, no such procedure will take place as it is for the jury to decide on the facts whether to accept the evidence or reject it.

It must again be emphasised however that an out of court confession whether oral or written is hearsay save insofar as it is tendered in evidence against the maker.[17] The Police and Criminal Evidence Act 1984 which in s 76(1) provides that:

---

11 See further p 190, post.
12 Magistrates' Courts Act 1980, s 105.
13 Ibid, s 103 and see further p 342, post.
14 See eg Road Traffic Act 1972, s 182(1) and Vehicles Excise Act 1971, s 31.
15 *R v Hall* [1973] QB 496; *R v Thompson* [1982] QB 647, CA.
16 *R v Fenlon* (1980) 71 Cr App Rep 307, CA. Such a record may not however be put before the jury if it is not signed or adopted by the defendant: *R v Dillon* (1983) Times, 21 October, CA.
17 For a recent example where such a confession was excluded, see *R v Spinks* [1982] 1 All ER 58], CA. The prosecution in that case could now rely upon s 74 of the Police and Criminal Evidence Act 1984: see p 116, ante.

'. . . a confession made by an *accused person* may be given in evidence against *him* in so far as it is relevant to any matter in issue in the proceedings. . .'

Accordingly, a confession will not be admissible in evidence against a co-accused unless he in some way adopts it as his own.

EXAMPLE: DONOGHUE's confession, if admitted, implicates not only him (because he admits taking the car), but also STEPHENSON: but it is *not* evidence against STEPHENSON, unless he adopts it. Thus, for example, if on being shown the statement STEPHENSON were to say:
'It looks as if he's told all there is to tell.'

DONOGHUE's confession would then be admissible against STEPHENSON as well. If he were to make no comment, the confession would not be so admissible.

An out of court confession implicating a co-accused may nevertheless still prejudice him because the magistrates or jury will in all probability see or hear it in its entirety. They will be warned (or warn themselves) to disregard those passages which implicate the co-accused, but in practical terms this may be an almost impossible exercise. The above situation should however be contrasted with those occasions when an accused implicates his co-accused *in the course of giving evidence* either in his own behalf or (rarely) for the prosecution. Such evidence will, of course, be admissible because it will not be hearsay.

A detailed examination of the law relating to confessions is outside the scope of this book, but there are a number of points which require mention. First, although the statement need not amount to a full confession of guilt, to be admissible it must, as a matter of construction, be at least partially adverse. If it is, then as has already been seen, the record of the interrogation or the written statement must, so far as possible, go before the court in its entirety so that remarks which on their own might appear damaging can be seen in context.[18] Secondly, although confessions will normally be spoken or written, a confession may be evidenced by conduct.[19] It must, however, be stressed that silence when in the face of an accusation cannot normally be admitted under the confessions rule.

EXAMPLE: Suppose that during STEPHENSON's interrogation by DS YOUNG a series of questions were put to him outlining the prosecution case but he made no reply to any of them. Not only is this not to be treated as a confession but, in addition, it can be argued that the *whole record* should be excluded on the grounds that it is hearsay and prejudicial.[20]

It will be recalled that an accused has a 'right to silence' and is thus not obliged to say anything in reply to police questioning, at any rate, after he has been cautioned.[1] Silence under interrogation may not therefore be treated as evidence of guilt although, it will be recalled, the judge may direct the jury to take into account the fact that an accused has only now revealed

---

18 See p 133, ante.
19 See eg *Parkes v R* [1976] 3 All ER 380, PC (when accused by murdered victim's mother, accused made no reply, later attacked her with a knife) and *Moriarty v London, Chatham and Dover Rly Co* (1870) LR 5 QB 314 (attempting to bribe witnesses) and *R v King* [1983] 1 All ER 929, CA (forging exhibits for use at trial).
20 See p 137, ante.
1 Although the Privy Council in *Hall v R* [1971] 1 All ER 322, PC and *Parkes v R*, supra, considered that the right of silence existed independently of the caution the Court of Appeal expressed some doubt as to the correctness of this in *R v Chandler* [1976] 3 All ER 105, CA. The point is probably now of less practical importance in view of the fact that under para 10 of the Detention Code the suspect must be cautioned at the latest on arrest.

his defence in assessing its weight.[2] Exceptionally, however, silence may be construed as a confession. For this to be so the accuser and the accused must have been on 'even terms'[3] and the accusation made in circumstances where a reply might reasonably have been expected.[4]

> EXAMPLE: It will be recalled that on STEPHENSON saying to DONOGHUE. 'The game's up', he made no reply and tried to run away. The prosecution may argue that PC ANDREW's evidence of this should be admissible under the confessions rule as evidence of guilt.

Thirdly, although a confession is only admissible if made by a party to the proceedings[5] a party may at common law still be bound by the admission of an agent such as his solicitor or counsel provided that the accused and his solicitor were acting in furtherance of a common purpose and the statement was made with the accused's authority.[6]

(iv) Documentary evidence: Police and Criminal Evidence Act 1984, s 68.

In order to get over the problems caused by *Myers v DPP*[7] the Criminal Evidence Act 1965 was enacted to enable certain trade or business records to be admissible in evidence. These provisions have now been updated and extended by the 1984 Act. The legislation is extremely complex but, broadly, a statement *contained in a document* is admissible in any proceedings as evidence of any fact stated in it of which direct oral evidence would be admissible provided that:

(a) the document is or forms part of a *record* compiled by a *person acting under a duty* from information supplied by a person (whether acting under a duty or not) who had, or may reasonably be supposed to have had, *personal knowledge* of the matters dealt with in that information; *and*

(b) the person who supplied the information is either:
  (i) dead, or by reason of his bodily or mental condition unfit to attend as a witness; or
  (ii) is outside the United Kingdom and it is not reasonably practicable to secure his attendance; or
  (iii) cannot reasonably be expected (having regard to the time which has elapsed since he supplied or acquired the information and to all the circumstances) to have any recollection of the matters dealt with in the information; or
  (iv) that all reasonable steps have been taken to identify him but that he cannot be identified; or
  (v) although his identity is known, all reasonable steps have been taken to find him and he cannot be found.[8]

Schedule 3 Part I to the 1984 Act provides that the section shall apply:

> where the information was supplied indirectly to the compiler through one or more intermediaries, provided that each intermediary was acting under a duty; or the person compiling the record *also* supplied the information.

---

2 See p 42, ante.

3 For example when the accuser is not a 'person in authority' (as in *Parkes v R*, supra) or possibly if the suspect has his solicitor present (*R v Chandler*, supra).

4 *R v Christie*, supra. In this context it is worth considering BOURHILL's hypothetical accusation against DONOGHUE on p 135.

5 See eg *R v Turner*, supra.

6 *R v Evans* (1981) Times, 6 May. Thus requiring supreme vigilance on the part of Duty Solicitors. Such admissions (sometimes called 'informal' admissions) should not be confused with formal admissions made under s 10 of the Criminal Justice Act 1967 see p 126, ante.

7 Supra.

8 1984 Act, s 68(2).

'Duty' is widely defined[9] as including reference to:

> 'a person acting in the course of any trade, business, profession or other occupation in which he is engaged or employed or for the purposes of any paid or unpaid office held by him'.

A number of important points need to be noted. In order to be admissible the statement must satisfy five primary criteria. First, it must be contained in a document.[10] Secondly, that document must be or form part of a record.[11] Thirdly, the compiler must have been 'acting under a duty'. Fourthly, the supplier must 'reasonably be supposed' to have had 'personal knowledge' of the information supplied and, finally, one or more of the required conditions in s 68(2) must be met, for example, that the supplier is dead.

A detailed discussion of this complicated but important section is outside the scope of this book. Nevertheless, whenever an opponent is seeking to tender such evidence it should be scrutinised carefully to ensure that all the provisions of the section are strictly complied with; they should never be taken for granted.

> EXAMPLE: In the example given earlier in which the prosecution were trying to prove that the '*blue*' Jaguar sold by DONOGHUE was, in reality, ATKIN's *green* Jaguar, it would be possible for the prosecution to tender the record from the factory on the basis either that the person who engraved the number could not be traced or that even if he were, he could not be expected to remember doing it. They will nevertheless be required to call direct evidence from the member of staff responsible for the compilation and keeping of the record to explain the method of recording and satisfy the court that their ground for admission is made out, by establishing, for example, that reasonable steps have been taken to trace the person who engraved the number.

Section 68 appears to be considerably wider in scope than its predecessor s 1 of the 1965 Act. For example, it now extends to records compiled by persons 'acting under a duty' not as previously, 'in the course of a trade or business'.

> EXAMPLE: Suppose that when DC MACMILLAN went to ATKIN's house a person came up to him outside the house and said:
> > 'It was DONOGHUE and STEPHENSON. I saw them. They got into that Jaguar and just drove off in it.'
> The witness refused to give his name and disappeared but DC MACMILLAN recorded the remark in his notebook.

On the face of it, the extract from the notebook will now be capable of admission under s 68.

> EXAMPLE: Suppose that Monica DONOGHUE were to make a statement to her husband's solicitors confirming his alibi, but disappeared before the trial and could not be traced.

Her written statement if proved to be authentic would be admissible under s 68 with the *leave* of the court.[12]

---

9 Ibid, Sch 3, Part I, para 6.
10 The definition is the same as that in s 10(1) of the Civil Evidence Act 1968 and includes map, plan, photograph, disc, tape, film or microfilm, 1984 Act, s 118(1). Presumably in the case of computer based information it would extend to material displayed on a Visual Display Unit.
11 This will be a question of fact and appears to comprise any information which is deliberately put in order so that it may subsequently be available to others. It may on occasions consist of a single document. See *R v Tirado* (1974) 59 Cr App Rep 80, CA and *R v Jones* [1978] 2 All ER 718; see also *H. v Schering Chemicals Ltd* [1983] 1 All ER 849.
12 Leave is *always* necessary in the case of statements prepared for pending or contemplated

The section, in theory, provides for the admission of hearsay evidence which is highly remote since evidence could be communicated from perceiver to compiler through any number of intermediaries provided that the latter were all acting under a duty.

There are three important provisions in Schedule 3 whose purpose is to ensure that 'quality control' is maintained. First, in deciding whether or not a statement is admissible the court may draw any reasonable inference from the circumstances in which the statement was made or came into being or any other circumstances including the form and contents of the document.[13] Secondly, in estimating the weight to be attached to any statement admissible in evidence the court must look at all the circumstances from which any inference can reasonably be drawn as to the accuracy or otherwise of the statement and in particular:

(a) to any question whether or not the person who supplied the information from which the record containing the statement was compiled did so *contemporaneously* with the occurrence or existence of the facts dealt with in that information; and

(b) to the question whether or not that person or any other person concerned with the compiling or keeping of the record containing the statement, had any incentive to *conceal or misrepresent* the facts.[14]

Finally, if a document is admitted under s 68 the credibility of the supplier of the information can be attacked in broadly the same way as if he had given evidence, for example, by showing that he has criminal convictions or has made a statement inconsistent with that recorded in the document admitted under s 68.[15]

(v) Computer records: 1984 Act, s 69. A number of recent cases have highlighted the difficulties that can arise when a computer print-out is produced. It may well be that such evidence is not hearsay at all if the computer is generating its own information. Thus, for example, if it is being used as a calculating machine the results of such calculations are admissible as original evidence; the computer is not being used to relay the perceptions of an 'eye witness'.[16] Alternatively, where the computer is being used to store supplied information, the print out will be just as likely to be hearsay as if it had been laboriously written up in longhand. Section 69 provides that a statement in a document produced by a computer shall not be admissible in evidence of any fact stated therein unless it is shown:

(a) 'That there are no reasonable grounds for believing that the statement is inaccurate because of improper use of the computer; or

(b) that at all material times the computer was operating properly, or if not, that any respect in which it was not operating properly or was out of operation was not such as to affect the production of the document or the accuracy of its contents.'

The net effect of s 69 therefore appears to be that *all* computer generated

---

proceedings: see 1984 Act Sch 3, Part I, para 2. Presumably, therefore, where a police officer writes up his own observations in his notebook (ie he is both compiler *and* supplier) leave will be required under this provision if it is sought to adduce the contents of the document under s 68.

13 1984 Act, Sch 3, Part III, para 14.

14 Ibid, Sch 3, Part I, para 7.

15 Ibid, para 3.

16 *R v Wood* (1983) 76 Cr App Rep 23, CA: *Castle v Cross* [1985] 1 All ER 87, DC.

documents, whether containing hearsay or not, must comply with the section, but that where it is sought to introduce such a document containing hearsay it is also subject to s 68. Rules of court are to be made prescribing the information that must in addition be given with regard to the statement.[17] Schedule 3 Part II provides for computer evidence to be given by certificate signed by a person in a responsible position in relation to the operation of the computer. The certificate shall be evidence of anything stated in it subject to the court's discretion to require oral evidence to be given on anything it contains (and to its general discretion to exclude evidence on the grounds of unfairness under s 78(1) of the 1984 Act).

(vi) Public documents and certificates. There are so many categories of public documents that they are almost beyond enumeration, for example, public registers, official certificates issued by public officers, and corporate records. Clearly, any attempt to adduce such a document to prove the truth of its contents will, prima facie, infringe the rule against hearsay. Nevertheless such documents are admissible at common law provided that:

(a) the document has been made and preserved for public use and contains facts of public interest;
(b) it is a record which is open to public inspection;
(c) the entry was made promptly after the events which it purports to record;
(d) the entry was made by a person who had a duty to enquire into the facts recorded by him and satisfy himself of their truth.[18]

The rule is of less practical importance that in previous times, however, because of the numerous statutory provisions[19] which enable facts to be proved by certificate. Note in particular that s 73 of the Police and Criminal Evidence Act 1984 provides that convictions may be proved by producing certificates authenticated by the appropriate officer of the court.

(vii) Res gestae. The basis of the rule has already been noted in relation to self serving statements. Thus, Andrea BOURHILL's hypothetical 'excited uttererance' to Tony ATKIN is capable of admission under the res gestae rule as an exception to the general rule against hearsay. This aspect of the res gestae 'doctrine' has always been of particular relevance when a hearsay remark has been uttered either by a victim or a bystander to a third party and the remark points directly or indirectly to the identity of an attacker. Under the 'doctrine' the third party may give evidence to prove identity. There are two dangers inherent in the admission of such evidence. One is inaccuracy: this can be adequately dealt with by cross-examining the third party as to what he heard. The other, is the age old fear which lies at the root of the hearsay rule of admitting concocted evidence. To counter this, hearsay evidence will only be admitted under this exception if the court is satisfied that the utterance was clearly made:[20]

17 These have yet to be made. Admission is also subject to rules set out in Sch 3 Pt II to the 1984 Act.
18 *Sturla v Freccia* (1880) 5 App Cas 623, HL, requirement has been considerably relaxed in modern times. See eg *R v Halpin* [1975] QB 907, CA (statements in annual returns admissible as prima facie proof of the truth of its contents where Registrar of Companies not enquired into the facts to satisfy himself as to their truth).
19 Eg Road Traffic Act 1960, s 242; Road Traffic Act 1972, s 10(3)(b); Police and Criminal Evidence Act 1984, Sch 3, Part I, para 5.
20 Per Lord Wilberforce in *Ratten v R*, supra.

'In circumstances of spontaneity or involvement in the event ... [when] the drama, leading up to the climax, has commenced and assumed such intensity and pressure[1] that the possibility of concoction can be disregarded.'[2]

(viii) Miscellaneous exceptions. There are several other minor exceptions to the rule, for example, dying declarations made by persons as to the cause of their injuries, statements by deceased persons as to their health, statements by deceased persons against their interests and statements made by such persons in the course of duty. These are outside the scope of this book and, save in the case of dying declarations,[3] of little practical significance.

(b) Inadmissible confessions

Even if what an accused said, wrote or did is *prima facie* admissible in evidence against him as an exception to the hearsay rule its admission is further subject to the special rules as to the admissibility of confession evidence.

(i) Obligatory exclusion under Police and Criminal Evidence Act 1984, s 76(2). The prosecution may, either on the representation of the defence or at the request of the court be required to prove beyond reasonable doubt that a confession was not obtained either:

(i) by *oppression* of the accused; or

(ii) in consequence of anything said or done which was likely in the circumstances existing at the time to have rendered unreliable *any* confession that he might have made.

If the prosecution fails to discharge this burden the court *must* exclude the confession (or such part of it in respect of which the burden is not discharged[4] even though it might be true).[5] Thus, in a trial on indictment, if a confession is excluded after a 'trial within a trial', the jury will never (with one exception noted below) get to hear of it. In a summary trial, the magistrates will know of the confession, but if they rule against its admission, they must disregard it in determining the issue of guilt.

The exclusion of a confession will not however affect the admissibility of any facts discovered as a result of the confession[6] although the fact that a confession led the police to discover these facts will remain 'behind the curtain' unless the accused himself or someone on his behalf gives evidence to this effect.

---

1 For an example of where a rather longer time lag was permitted see *R v Nye and Loan* (1977) 66 Cr App Rep 252, CA.

2 For a recent example see *R v Turnbull* [1984] Crim LR 620, CA.

3 Such evidence is only admissible on a homicide charge when made by a deceased who is in imminent danger of death and has abandoned all hope of recovery. For a recent example see *Nembhard v R* [1982] 1 All ER 183, PC. Such evidence requires neither corroboration nor a corroboration warning.

4 This follows the pre-1984 Act position eg *R v Smith* [1959] 2 QB 35, CMAC (first confession excluded, second confession made a day later admitted).

5 It would appear therefore that the decision in *Wong Kam-Ming v R* [1980] AC 247, PC, to the effect that an accused may not be cross-examined in the *voir dire* as to the truth of his confession is unaffected by s 76(2). It also follows therefore that an accused can only be cross-examined on the discrepancies between the evidence that he gives on the *voir dire* and later gives before the jury where the confession has been admitted. *Wong Kam Ming v R*, supra. See also *R v Brophy* [1982] AC 476, HL. As to the use to which an inadmissible confession may be put by a *co-accused*, see *R v Rowson* [1985] 2 All ER 539, CA.

6 1984 Act, s 76(4)(a) again following the pre-existing position.

EXAMPLE: In response to threats of violence from his interrogator D makes a written (and true) confession to murder in which he indicates that he buried the murder weapon in the middle of a wood. Forensic examination reveals D's fingerprints on it.

If the judge at the 'trial within a trial' believes D's evidence as to police threats, he must exclude the confession. The weapon and the fingerprint evidence would still be admissible in evidence although no evidence as to *how* it came to be found could be admitted unless adduced by D or his counsel.[7] It should further be noted that where an otherwise inadmissible confession is relevant to showing that the accused speaks, writes or expresses himself in a particular way, the confession may be admitted to the extent necessary to show that he does so.[8]

A detailed examination of s 76(2) is outside the scope of this book, but a number of general observations must be made. First, there is no longer any requirement that the oppression or other vitiating conduct should emanate from a 'person in authority'. In practice, this change is unlikely to prove significant but will require Duty Solicitors to exercise caution when advising clients.[9] Secondly 'oppression' is not specifically defined but under s 76(8) includes:

'torture, inhuman or degrading treatment, and the use or threat of violence (whether or not amounting to torture).'

For a fuller definition it is necessary to consult earlier cases[10] but, clearly, oppressive conduct will include lengthy questioning or intervals between questioning, sleep deprivation and lack of adequate refreshment. In sum, anything which having regard to the personal characteristics of the suspect tends to sap his free will. Clearly, proven breaches of the Codes of Practice will be highly germane to this issue. Finally, under the second limb, the court will no longer be concerned with 'voluntariness' but with 'reliability'. The test to be applied is whether *any* confession that the accused *might* have made could have been relied on. The court must first adjudicate on the facts, namely, what was said or done and what were the surrounding circumstances in which it was said or done. The judge (or magistrates) must then in the words of the Criminal Law Revision Committee in its Eleventh Report[11]

'imagine that he was present at the interrogation and heard the threat or inducement. In the light of all the evidence given he will consider whether, at the point when the threat was uttered or the inducement offered, any confession which the accused might make as a result of it would be likely to be unreliable'.

The above test is not entirely satisfactory, since s 76(2)(b) is not restricted to 'threats and inducements' but to anything said or done *whether during interrogation or otherwise*. Thus it is not essential that the offending deeds or words should take place contemporaneously with the confession.[12] What *is*

---

7 Ibid, s 76(5).
8 Ibid, s 76(4)(b). For example in *R v Voisin* [1918] 1 KB 531, CCA the accused's spelling of 'bloody Belgian' as 'Blady Belgiam' admissible in comparison with identical mispelling on a parcel containing victim's dismembered body.
9 See generally p 102, ante.
10 Eg *R v Prager* [1972] 1 All ER 114, CA; *R v Hudson* (1980) 72 Cr App Rep 163, CA; *R v Steel* [1981] 2 All ER 422, CA; *R v Gowan* [1982] Crim LR 821, CA.
11 Cmnd 4991 (HMSO), para 65.
12 'In the circumstances existing at the time' relates to what was said or done not to the time at which the confession was made. The possible implications of this are considered further by Peter Mirfield, 'The future law of Confessions' [1984] Crim LR 63 at 70.

clear, however, is that there must be a causal connection between the of-fending words or act and the urge to confess. As with the previous 'volun-tariness' test, each case will depend on its own facts but, in practice, securing the exclusion of confession evidence will be an uphill struggle.[13] All the surrounding circumstances will have to be investigated and corroboration of the accused's account sought whenever possible. Breaches of the Codes of Practice (if proved) will not, *of themselves*, result in exclusion but may be taken into account if they appear to the court to be relevant.[14] It is to be feared, however, that the 'reliability' criterion will result in less rather than more confessions being excluded.[15] That being said it is hard to imagine that the allegations made by DONOGHUE against the police, if substantiated, would not lead to the exclusion of his confession.[16] Note finally that any other persons who have a duty to investigate offences and charge offenders such as Customs and Excise officials and store detectives are required to 'have re-gard' to the provisions of the Code.[17]

(ii) Discretionary exclusion of confession evidence under Police and Criminal Evidence Act 1984, s 78.

It may be that there has been conduct, usually on the part of the police which, although improper, is not such as to lead to automatic exclusion under s 76(2). Examples might include breaches of s 41 (detention beyond *24 hours*) or s 58 (refusal of access to legal advice) of the 1984 Act. Alternatively, the police may not have 'said or done' any-thing which can be causally linked with the confession. The suspect may have volunteered a confession whilst drunk or under the influence of drugs or be suffering from illness or mentally defective. In such cases, unless there has been oppression, s 76(2) will not apply: the potential unreliability does not derive from anything 'said' or 'done' to the suspect. Section 78(1) gives the court a discretion to exclude prosecution evidence when in all the cir-cumstances, including those in which it was obtained, its admission would have such an adverse effect on the fairness of the proceedings that it ought to be excluded.[18] Occasions will no doubt arise, therefore, when exclusion will be sought under this subsection in addition to or in substitution for s 76(2). Only time will tell the extent to which the courts will exercise this exclusionary discretion. When there have been breaches of the Codes of Practice which do not result in exclusion under s 76(2) precedent suggests that it will be exercised sparingly.[19] However, if it can be established that the ac-cused was suffering from some permanent or temporary disability due to illness,

---

13 The difficulties are considered in depth by Fulford and Wood in 'Challenging a Confession Statement' LAG Bulletin September 1982, p 97, an article which is still of considerable practical use.

14 Police and Criminal Evidence Act 1984, s 67(11). If courts adopt the same approach as that adopted to breach of the Judges Rules in cases such as *R v Lemsatef* [1977] 2 All ER 835, CA, and *R v Houghton* (1978) 142 JP 402, CA, one cannot avoid feeling pessimistic. See infra.

15 It seems less likely that confessions would now be excluded in the circumstances existing, for example, in *R v Smith*, supra; *R v Cleary* (1963) 48 Cr App Rep 116, CCA; *R v Richards* [1967] 1 All ER 829, CA; *R v Northam* (1967) 52 Cr App Rep 97, CA or *R v Zaveckas* [1970] 1 All ER 413, CA.

16 The practical difficulty that you will now face in such circumstances however is the existence of the right to legal advice under s 58 of the 1984 Act (although this can be suspended in the case of 'serious arrestable offences'). It may well be much more difficult to allege oppression or other inducements. This may become even more difficult once the Duty Solicitor scheme is extended to police stations.

17 1984 Act, s 66(9).

18 Nothing in s 78(1) is to prejudice any other rule of law *requiring* a court to exclude evidence (1984 Act, s 78(2)) eg under s 76(2) or the 'similar fact' rule.

19 See eg *R v Prager* and *R v Lemsatef*, supra. But see also *R v Trickett* [1981] Crim LR 331.

drugs or mental deficiency such as to make it unfair to rely on the confession, discretion is perhaps more likely to be exercised in the accused's favour.[20]

(iii) Confessions by mentally handicapped persons: 1984 Act, s 77. As has been seen[1] the Detention Code provides that juveniles, the mentally ill and mentally handicapped are not generally to be interviewed in the absence of an appropriate adult. If a confession is obtained in breach of these requirements it may be attacked under ss 76(2) or 78(1). If the confession is nevertheless admitted, s 77 provides a further safeguard for the *mentally handicapped* (but not the other above two categories) where the case against him depends 'wholly or substantially' on a confession made by him in the absence of an independent person. In such cases, the judge must warn the jury in summing up (or the magistrates warn themselves) that there is a *special need for caution* before convicting in reliance on such a confession. It is to be hoped that this 'safeguard' does not deter a court from exercising its exclusionary powers under ss 76(2) and 78(1) where the circumstances justify it.

(c) Public policy and private privilege

Exclusion of evidence, that is otherwise relevant and admissible, on the grounds of public policy does not often arise in criminal proceedings. The most commonly met example is the rule that in public prosecutions[2] witnesses cannot be required to disclose their sources of information leading to the detection of crime, unless such evidence might establish a person's innocence. The other major instances where reasons of public policy may lead to the exclusion of evidence are outside the scope of this work.[3] On the other hand, there are two instances of private privilege which are of particular importance in criminal litigation namely:

    (i) legal professional privilege; and
    (ii) the privilege against self incrimination.

(i) Legal professional privilege. The protection afforded to the client[4] is two fold. First, communications between a client and his professional legal adviser are protected if the communication is made *in connection with the giving of legal advice*. The practical effect of this is that all communications between an accused and his solicitors and counsel comes within the first rule, unless the solicitor and the client are acting together for a criminal purpose. Thus if, for example, they enter into a conspiracy to manufacture false alibi evidence the communications would no longer be protected. Secondly, communications between a *third party* and the accused or his professional legal adviser are privileged provided that they were *made in contemplation of pending or anticipated ligitation and the purpose, or dominant purpose was to prepare for the litigation*.[5] Thus the vast majority of communications by a solicitor in the course of preparing a case, for example, in interviewing witnesses, corresponding with experts and relevant documents such as proofs of evidence and

---

20 For a pre-1984 Act example see *R v Powell* [1980] Crim LR 39 (diabetic suspect in suggestible state due to hypoglycaemia).
1 See p 83, ante. Annex E to the Detention Code sets out all the special procedures to observe when interviewing vulnerable suspects.
2 Not a private or police prosecution.
3 See generally *Cross* (op cit) chapter XII.
4 The privilege is that of the *client* and this cannot be waived by the solicitor without the client's authority.
5 *Waugh v British Railways Board* [1980] AC 521, HL.

instructions to counsel, will come within the second rule. Both rules are, however, subject to two important qualifications. First, the privilege only extends to communications, it does not cover enclosures. Thus, if a solicitor were to send pre-existing handwriting samples to an expert, the prosecution would be entitled to compel the expert to come to court and produce the samples.[6] The only material that would be privileged would be the oral or written communications passing between the solicitor and the expert. Secondly, the fact that a communication is privileged does not prevent another party or witness from adducing evidence of its contents. Thus, if a privileged communication were to be intercepted by a party there would be nothing to prevent its contents being adduced in evidence by him.[7]

(ii) Privilege against self incrimination. A witness can refuse to answer a question where, in the opinion of the judge or magistrates, the answer would tend to expose him or possibly his spouse to a criminal charge, penalty or forfeiture. This privilege is, however, limited in the case of an accused who gives evidence in that he may be asked any question in cross-examination relating to the *offence charged* notwithstanding that it would tend to incriminate him.[8] He is, however, protected from cross-examination as to *previous convictions and bad character* under s 1(f) of the Criminal Evidence Act 1898 unless he has 'thrown away his shield'.[9]

(d) Judicial discretion to exclude evidence: Police and Criminal Evidence Act 1984, s 78

The rule in *R v Sang*[10] to the effect that evidence that is relevant and not otherwise subject to exclusion is prima facie admissible even if it has been illegally or unfairly obtained remains. It must now, however, be read in conjunction with s 78(1) which provides that:

> 'In any proceedings the court may refuse to allow evidence on which the prosecution proposes to rely to be given if it appears to the court that, having regard to *all* the circumstances, including the circumstances in which the evidence was obtained, the admission of the evidence would have such an adverse effect on the fairness of the *proceedings* that the court ought not to admit it'.

The proviso clearly extends to all evidence and any attempt to categorise rigidly the circumstances in which it will be exercised must be avoided. It clearly embraces the pre-existing common law discretion, for example to exclude evidence whose prejudicial effect outweighed its probative value;[11] for example 'similar fact' evidence that was otherwise admissible but unduly

---

6 *R v King* [1983] 1 All ER 929, CA. For the extent to which documents may be searched for and seized prior to trial in the course of a criminal investigation see ante p 84 et seq.

7 See eg *Rumping v DPP* [1964] AC 814, HL. Communications between husband and wife are no longer prima facie privileged: see Police and Criminal Evidence Act 1984, s 80(9) abolishing Criminal Evidence Act 1898, s 1(d). The court does, however, have an overriding discretion to exclude evidence under s 78(1).

8 Criminal Evidence Act 1898, s 1(e).

9 See p 157 et seq, post.

10 Supra. Although it could be argued that since the sole question for determination in *R v Sang* was whether or not a judge's power to exclude evidence extended beyond confessions, the whole question should be considered afresh in the light of s 78(1).

11 The judge's power to control the fairness of the proceedings was recognised in *R v Sang*, supra. The extent to which this interrelates with s 82(3) of the 1984 Act retention of pre-existing powers to exclude evidence whether by preventing questions from being put or otherwise is unclear.

prejudicial,[12] identification evidence that is obtained in highly unsatisfactory circumstances,[13] or the cross-examination of an accused who had 'thrown away his shield'.[14] Instances of where the discretion might be exercised in confession cases have already been considered. This leaves open the question as to whether s 78(1) gives the court a much wider discretion than hitherto existed to exclude improperly obtained evidence discovered, for example, as a result of an illegal search or obtained by the activities of an agent provocateur,[15] especially since all the pre-existing common law discretion outlined above appears to have been preserved by s 82(3) of the 1984 Act. Clearly, s 78(1) now entitles the court to consider the circumstances in which evidence was obtained, but only in the context of whether the admission of that the evidence will affect the fairness of the *proceedings*. The court is not therefore required to consider wider issues such as the disciplining of police officers. It may well be, therefore, that the practical effect of s 78(1) in cases of alleged police misconduct will be minimal.[16, 17] For example, the 'find' of housebreaking implements in the illegal search of STEPHENSON's house will not be admissible because this evidence is simply not relevant to the facts in issue. If, however, forensic examination of the implements had linked them with a burglary, it is hard to envisage circumstances in which s 78(1) would be invoked to exclude such evidence if it clearly implicated STEPHENSON in the burglary. Accordingly, it has to be asked whether the effect of s 78(1) will be more than peripheral.

Test 3: Testing of evidence in court—examination and cross-examination

If a witness's evidence passes **Test 1** (it is relevant) and **Test 2** (it is not included under one of the four heads just considered) it will now be subjected to the full majesty of the adversary system. In order to appreciate this process fully it is necessary first to outline the order in which evidence is given in court. Witnesses are called in turn by the advocate for the party who wishes to adduce their testimony in evidence. He or she will first examine them 'in chief'. They will then be 'cross-examined' by the advocates for the other parties and finally may be 're-examined' by the advocate who called them. When there are two or more accused the order of examination will depend

---

12 The theoretical possibility of such a situation arising was acknowledged by Lord Du Parq in *Noor Mohamed v R* [1949] AC 182 at 191. Such instances are however likely to be extremely rare. See generally *Cross* (op cit) chapter X.

13 For a recent example of where identification evidence appears to have been excluded on these grounds see *R v Leckie and Ensley* [1983] Crim LR 543.

14 See eg *R v Watts* [1983] 3 All ER 101, CA. See generally p 137, post. The phrase 'evidence on which the prosecution proposes to rely' will presumably be taken to cover cross-examination of an accused on his character and convictions on the issue of credit. The accused's replies will be part of the evidence in the case. In any event s 82(3) clearly *would* cover such cross-examination since it specifically refers to the 'asking of questions'.

15 Although the substantive law does not recognise the defence of 'entrapment' it is arguable that s 78(1) gives the court an overriding discretion to exclude the evidence of the entrapper (that being the main issue in *R v Sang*).

16 Prior to *R v Sang* it was thought that discretion existed to exclude improperly obtained evidence where the misbehaviour of the police had been 'exceptional' see *dicta* of Lord Widgery CJ in *Jeffery v Black* [1978] QB 490 at 498, DC. This discretion had in theory been recognised by Lord Goddard CJ in *Kuruma Son of Kaniu v R* [1955] AC 197, PC. There appears, however, to have only been one reported decision in which it was exercised.

17 The possible application of s 78(1) to the taking of body samples has been effectively restricted by s 62(10). See p 76, ante.

upon the order in which the accused's names appear on the information or indictment.

> EXAMPLE: In *R v* DONOGHUE *and* STEPHENSON the order will be
> Prosecution witnesses:
>> Examined-in-chief by prosecution counsel
>> Cross-examined by counsel for DONOGHUE
>> Cross-examined by counsel for STEPHENSON
>> Re-examined by prosecution counsel
>
> DONOGHUE's witnesses:
>> Examined-in-chief by own counsel
>> Cross-examined by counsel for STEPHENSON
>> Cross-examined by prosecution counsel
>> Re-examined by own counsel
>
> STEPHENSON's witnesses:
>> Examined-in-chief by own counsel
>> Cross-examined by counsel for DONOGHUE
>> Cross-examined by prosecution counsel
>> Re-examined by own counsel.

Two points should be noted. First, when the defence calls its evidence the accused must normally give evidence first.[18] Secondly, when there is more than one accused the prosecution will always cross-examine last. This is important if you are to understand many of the rules which follow.

(a) Examination-in-chief

Having been duly sworn[19] a witness will first be examined by the advocate who calls him or her. The most important rule of examination-in-chief is that 'leading questions' must not generally be asked unless leave has been given to treat the witness as 'hostile'. The art of examination-in-chief is probably the most difficult skill for an advocate to acquire. The 'no leading questions' rule is designed to ensure that the witness tells his or her own story with the minimum of prompting.

> EXAMPLE: When giving her evidence Andrea BOURHILL could not be asked 'Were you looking out of your window on Friday 6 July at 9.00 pm when you saw DONOGHUE and STEPHENSON drive off Mr ATKIN's car'. The questioning would have to run as follows.
> Q. 'Can you remember where you were on the evening of Friday 6 July?'
> A. 'I was at home'.
> Q. 'Do you recall looking out of the window at any time?'
> A. 'Yes'.
> Q. 'At what time was this?'

and so on.[1] Only practice will tell you when a question infringes the rule. Some latitude is, however, allowed in relation to non-contentious matters so as to save court time. For example, a witness's address and occupation may normally be led. Similarly, an opposing advocate will often agree to a witness being led on those aspects of his evidence which are not in dispute.

As well as leading questions being prohibited, a witness may not normally refer to any previous statement as a prompt whilst giving evidence, unless

---

18 Police and Criminal Evidence Act 1984, s 79. The court has a discretion to change the order.
19 See p 118, ante.
 1 For further reading on advocacy skills see 'Advocacy at the Bar', Evans; Financial Training 1983.

the court gives him *leave to refresh his memory* in the circumstances outlined below. There is, however, no rule precluding him from reading through his written statement *before* he gives evidence. After some doubt, it has been held that this practice is not only necessary but desirable, although other parties should be informed when this has taken place.[2] Furthermore, when a witness has consulted his earlier statement *outside court* immediately before giving evidence the opposing advocate is not only entitled to see a copy but also to cross-examine the witness on it.[3]

Two important aspects of examination-in-chief must now be considered further.

(i) Refreshing memory. As an exception to the general rule set out above a witness may, with leave of the court, refresh his memory in the witness box from any document which was (a) *made or verified* by him, (b) *substantially contemporaneously* with the events to which he testifies. Police officers will frequently ask for leave to refresh their memories from notes made up in their pocket book,[4] for example, of an interview with a suspect, and such leave will almost always be granted. The rule is not, however, of exclusive application to police officers and any witness may ask for leave to refresh his memory provided the note satisfies the above two criteria.

> EXAMPLE: If Andrea BOURHILL were unable to recall the events of 6 July, prose-cution counsel could ask for leave for her to refresh her memory from her written statement provided that it had been made sufficiently contemporaneously (it was) and she herself had made or verified it (she did).[5]

Contemporaneity is a question of fact in each case, but it is necessary to show that the note was compiled at the earliest practicable opportunity while the facts were still fresh in the witness's mind. The term, 'refreshing memory' is, however, misleading because the witness may refer to a contemporaneous note even though he has no independent recall of the events to which it relates.[6] Cross-examination of police officers may thus be rendered parti-cularly difficult especially when (to the surprise of the uninitiated) two or more officers are given leave to refresh their memories from notebooks whose contents are identical.[7] The problem is particularly acute when the cross-examiner is endeavouring to attack disputed 'verbals'.[8]

Before cross-examining a witness who has refreshed his memory, the cross examiner is entitled to examine the note and may cross-examine on any part of it which has been referred to in chief without the whole note becoming an exhibit. However if, as is his right, he cross-examines on part of the note

---

2 *R v Richardson* [1971] 2 QB 484, CA. See also *Worley v Bentley* [1976] 2 All ER 449; and *R v Westwell* [1976] 2 All ER 812, CA.

3 *Owen v Edwards* (1983) 77 Cr App Rep 191, DC. In addition in any case where a witness's testimony is inconsistent with his out of court statement, the advocate calling him is under an ethical duty to draw this to his opponent's attention. See further p 170, post.

4 It has been held that a police officer who has taken brief jottings in the course of interviewing a suspect may refresh his memory from a full note made up in his note book a short time thereafter but that the original jottings should be retained and copies disclosed to the defence, *Attorney General's Reference (No 3 of 1979)* (1979) 69 Cr App Rep 411, CA.

5 For an unusual case in which a lay witness was refused leave to refresh her memory see *R v P and C* [1982] Crim LR 671, Oxford Crown Court.

6 For further discussion see *Cross* (op cit) p 248 et seq.

7 There is no objection to police officers refreshing their memory when notes represent a 'pool of recollection': *R v Bass* [1953] 1 QB 680, CCA.

8 For a helpful illustration of styles of cross-examination see: Chatelier: *Criminal Advocacy in the Magistrates' Court* (1981) Barry Rose p 29 et seq.

from which memory has not been refreshed in chief, the *whole note* will go before the jury or the magistrates as an exhibit. This may sometimes do more harm than good because it may contain prejudicial material. Although the note is not evidence as such, because it is both a self serving statement and *prima facie* hearsay,[9] its prejudicial potential in this context should never be overlooked.

(ii) Hostile witnesses. Every advocate who has been faced with a witness who does not 'come up to proof' knows how devastating this experience can be. The basic rule is that the advocate cannot lead or cross-examine his own witness merely because the witness gives evidence that is unfavourable. The best thing to do in the vast majority of cases is to ask as few questions as possible and call other witnesses in support of your case in an endeavour to repair the damage. The advocate may only *cross-examine* his own witness if leave of the court has been obtained to treat that witness as 'hostile', in other words that the witness is not merely unfavourable but shows no desire to give evidence fairly or to tell the truth. If leave is granted, the Criminal Procedure Act 1865, s 3 provides that a hostile witness may not be cross-examined as to his bad character but, subject to this, it seems that the court may sanction such cross-examination as it thinks fit.[10] A frequent basis of cross-examination is the fact that the witness has on a previous occasion made an oral or written statement which is inconsistent with the evidence that he has given on oath. In such circumstances, Criminal Procedure Act 1865, s 3 provides that the previous inconsistent statement may only be put to a hostile witness with *leave of the court.* Provided the court gives leave the witness must first be asked whether or not he has made such a statement and sufficient circumstances must be given to designate the occasion on which it was made. If he admits to making it he may then be cross-examined on it. If he denies making it the cross-examiner may then prove it by other evidence.[11] It must be stressed, however, that such a statement is hearsay and therefore not admissible to prove the truth of its contents. Its use is limited solely to destroying the credibility of the witness. At the end of the day, therefore, unless the witness can be persuaded to recant his testimony and adopt the earlier statement, it is of limited use.

> EXAMPLE: If when called, Andrea BOURHILL either refused to give evidence or departed substantially from the contents of her written statement, prosecuting counsel could either leave well alone and get on with the case by calling other evidence or apply for leave to treat her as hostile. Although he would be precluded from cross-examining her as to her previous shoplifting convictions he could apply for leave that the statement which she made to the police be put to her. If leave were given on both applications, counsel would be required to follow the procedure laid down in s 3. If BOURHILL were then to adopt her previous statement in the box her oral evidence would be admissible against the two accused. If, however, she were to repudiate her previous statement it would be only admissible on the issue of whether or not her oral testimony was to be believed. It would not be admissible identification evidence of the two accused because this would infringe the hearsay rule.[12]

---

9 See *R v Virgo* (1978) 67 Cr App Rep 323, CA.
10 The scope of cross-examination is governed primarily by common law; see *Cross* p 271.
11 Ie by calling someone to prove its authenticity if it is in writing or calling the person to whom it was uttered if it is oral.
12 It is also inadmissible because it would be a self serving statement. The judge must direct the jury carefully as to the limited purpose for which the statement may be used see *R v Askew* [1981] Crim LR 398, CA.

(*b*) *Cross-examination*

The objectives of cross-examination are:

(i)   to try and extract matters that are favourable to your case; and/or
(ii) to suggest that the witness, albeit honest, is mistaken or inconsistent or suffers from some disability (for example, short sightedness) that is likely to make his evidence unreliable; and/or
(iii) to suggest that he is biased or has some other improper motive for giving evidence; and/or
(iv) to suggest that he is of such bad character that he should not be believed.

Unlike examination-in-chief, there is no prohibition against leading questions, but as a matter of tactics, cross-examination by means of non-leading questions may be a more effective way of 'trapping' the witness into condemning himself out of his own mouth. Although the art of cross-examination is as much a matter of psychology and semantics as of law, there are a number of important legal rules which must be observed.

(i) Putting the client's case. The most important rule of cross-examination is that the cross-examiner must put all aspects of his client's case to the opponent's witnesses.[13] If he does not, he runs two dangers. First, failure to raise a matter may be taken as an admission that what a witness says is true. Secondly, if the accused later gives evidence which contradicts the evidence of a prosecution witness who was not challenged at the time it may be suggested that he has concocted his defence.

> EXAMPLE: If DONOGHUE were to continue with his assertion that Andrea BOUR-HILL's evidence has been manufactured out of spite this must be put to her in cross-examination. If defence counsel fails to do so and DONOGHUE whilst giving evidence alleges bias, he will be liable to be cross-examined as to why this was not raised before.[14]

(ii) The scope of cross-examination—witnesses other than the accused. The scope of cross-examination is virtually limitless provided that the questions go to the issues in the case. There are, however, three important restrictions. First, as a matter of professional ethics, questions attacking a witness's credit should not be asked unless there is some basis for them. It would thus not be open to DONOGHUE's counsel to cross-examine Andrea BOURHILL on her alleged relationship with DONOGHUE unless he has given instructions to do so and was satisfied that this line was necessary. Secondly, s 2(1) of the Sexual Offences (Amendment) Act 1976 provides that:

> 'If at a trial any person is for the time being charged with a rape offence[15] to which he pleads not guilty, then, except with the leave of the judge, no evidence and no question in cross-examination shall be adduced or asked at the trial, by or on behalf of any defendant at the trial, about any sexual experience of a complainant with a person other than the defendant'.

---

13 This includes cross-examination on behalf of a co-accused *R v Fenlon* (1980) 71 Cr App Rep 307, CA.
14 By alleging bias DONOGHUE would also be 'casting imputations' thus rendering him liable to cross-examination on his previous convictions under *s 1(f)(ii)* of the Criminal Evidence Act 1898 see p 159, post.
15 Ie rape, attempted rape, abetting, counselling and procuring rape or attempted rape, and incitement to rape: ibid, s 7(2).

This section does not preclude questioning the complainant about her relationship with the *accused* where consent is in issue, but otherwise, leave may only be given if it would be 'unfair' to the accused not to do so. Cross-examination will thus only generally be allowed where it is relevant to an issue in the case and is not merely directed to credit i.e. whether the witness is a person whose testimony is worthy of belief.[16] Thirdly, and most importantly, questions on credit are normally final. Thus, if, for example, counsel for DONOGHUE asked Andrea BOURHILL if she had had a row with DONOGHUE before they had split up and her answer was 'No', it would not normally be possible for DONOGHUE's counsel to continue further with his cross-examination on this aspect or to call evidence to rebut her denial. The reason for this is that otherwise the trial could end up being concerned more with the relationship between BOURHILL and DONOGHUE than it would about the facts in issue. There are, however, *four* exceptions when cross-examination or rebutting evidence may be permitted.

(*i*) *Where the cross-examination is directly relevant to a fact in issue.* It is not always easy to identify those occasions upon which an attack on the credit of a witness is relevant to a fact in issue. A commonly cited example is where a complainant in a rape case in which 'consent' is in issue is cross-examined as to her previous sexual experience with the accused. Such questioning goes to an issue in the case, namely consent, and is not merely being introduced as a side wind. Likewise, where there are suggestions that a prosecution witness has manufactured evidence or threatened witnesses this may be treated as being so fundamental to the issues in the case as to permit further cross-examination or rebutting evidence.[17]

(*ii*) *To show bias.* If a witness denies bias he may be cross-examined as to this and rebutting evidence may be called. This course is permitted where, for example, it is alleged that a witness has been seen outside court talking to persons who have already given evidence[18] or is related to one of the parties.[19] Thus, if Andrea BOURHILL were to deny bearing a grudge against DONOGHUE his counsel would probably be permitted to cross-examine her as to her relationship with him and call any witnesses who heard her utter threats to 'get even' with him.

(*iii*) *Where a witness has made a previous inconsistent oral or written statement.*[20] In the hands of a skilled advocate this is one of the most potent cross-examination weapons. The position is governed by ss 4 and 5 of the Criminal Procedure Act 1865. The basic framework of these complicated sections is as follows. Where a witness has made a previous oral or written statement which is inconsistent with the evidence he gives on oath he must first be asked whether he has made such previous statement and be given sufficient particulars to identify the occasion. If the answer is 'No', s 4 provides that the cross-examiner may prove it by other evidence. If the answer is 'Yes', s 5 provides that cross-examination shall fall into two stages. First, the witness may be cross-examined on the statement in general terms, for example when

---

16 See generally *R v Viola* [1982] 3 All ER 73, CA.

17 As in *R v Kelsey* (1981) 74 Cr App Rep 213, CA.

18 *R v Mendy* (1976) 64 Cr App Rep 4.

19 *Thomas v David* (1836) 7 C & P 350 (witness denied that she was the plaintiff's mistress; defendant entitled to call witnesses in rebuttal).

20 This includes a previous statement of an accused: possibly even a confession which has been ruled inadmissible. See *R v Rowson* (supra).

it was made and what was said without being shown the statement. Where however the statement is *in writing* and the cross-examiner wishes to confront the witness with any contradictions to his present testimony that it exhibits, the witness must first be shown those parts of the writing which are to be used to contradict him. If the witness goes back on what he has said on oath the cross-examiner's object has been achieved. If, however the witness sticks by his present testimony the advocate may then, if he wishes, cross-examine him on the written statement. This requires care because, if he does cross-examine on the written statement it will become an exhibit which, although not evidence of its contents, may display far more consistencies than inconsistencies and thus prove counter-productive.

As with cross-examination under s 3, however, the previous inconsistent statement can only be used for a destructive purpose it is not admissible to prove the truth of its contents and is thus not as such evidence on which the jury or magistrates can act.

> EXAMPLE: Suppose that DONOGHUE's wife Monica made a statement to the police saying that her husband had confessed to her that he had taken the car, but the prosecution decided not to call her. If she were to give evidence at the trial in support of his alibi, the prosecution could cross-examine her by confronting her with her previous statement. This could only be used to cast doubt on her evidence given on oath, but it would *not* be admissible to prove DONOGHUE's oral confession to her (unless, of course, she adopted it under cross-examination).

(iv) Previous convictions. It is open to a cross-examiner whether for prosecution or defence to put the previous convictions of an opponent's witness to him with a view to showing that he is not the sort of person who can be believed on oath. If he denies them, they may be proved by certificate.[21] The Rehabilitation of Offenders Act 1974 does not apply in criminal proceedings but a *Practice Note*[1] provides that questions on spent convictions should be avoided as far as possible.[2] It must be stressed, however, that it is dangerous for the defence to embark on such a line of cross-examination if the accused himself has previous convictions. Such a course may result in the accused 'throwing away his shield'.

> EXAMPLE: DONOGHUE's counsel can put Andrea BOURHILL's previous shoplifting convictions to her in cross-examination, and prove them by certificate if she denies them,[3] but this leaves his client open to cross-examination on credit as to his own previous convictions if he gives evidence.[4]

(iii) The scope of cross-examination: the accused

It will be recalled that an accused does not *have* to give evidence on his own behalf at all but that if he does he may be asked questions in cross-exami-

---

21 Cross-examination as to previous convictions is governed by Criminal Procedure Act 1865, s 6. Proof by certificate is now governed by Police and Criminal Evidence Act 1984, s 73.

1 *Practice Note* [1975] 2 All ER 1072.

2 Where there are previous convictions, including spent convictions, of prosecution witnesses they should nevertheless be revealed to the defence and it is then for the court to decide whether or not such questions should be put: see *R v Paraskeva* (1983) 76 Cr App Rep 162, CA (complainant sole prosecution witness, spent conviction for theft inadvertently not revealed by prosecution, conviction quashed).

3 If she is proved to have been convicted of the offence she is presumed to have committed it unless the contrary is proved Police and Criminal Evidence Act 1984, s 74(2).

4 If he has cast 'imputations' on a prosecution witness: Criminal Evidence Act 1898, s 1(*f*)(*ii*) considered post.

nation notwithstanding that they tend to incriminate him of the offence charged.[5] Thus, provided they relate to the offence charged, all questions are fair game. His inconsistencies can be exposed, if necessary by means of previous statements, as can the inherent improbabilities in his story. Unlike other witnesses, however, he may not otherwise be cross-examined as to his character or previous convictions unless he comes within the limited exceptions contained in Criminal Evidence Act 1898, s 1(f) which provides that:

'A person charged and called as a witness ... shall not be asked, and if asked, shall not be required to answer[6] any question tending to show[7] that he has committed or been convicted[8] of or been charged[9] with any offence other than that wherewith he is then charged, or is of bad character,[10] unless:
  (i) the proof that he has committed or been convicted of such other offences is admissible in evidence to show that he is guilty of the offence wherewith he is then charged; or
  (ii) he has personally, or by his advocate asked questions of the witnesses for the prosecution with a view to establishing his own good character, or has given evidence of his own good character, or the nature or conduct of the defence is such as to involve imputations on the character of the prosecutor or the witnesses for the prosecution; or
  (iii) he has given evidence against any other person charged in the same proceedings'.

These three provisoes will now briefly be considered in turn.[11]

Proviso 1(f)(i). This proviso will rarely need to be involved by the prosecution, since in cases where they are able to adduce 'similar fact' evidence as part of their case they will be freed from the constraints imposed by s 1(f) when cross-examining the accused as a result of the decision in *Jones v DPP*. It is only in rare instances where no previous reference has been made to the other offences that *s 1(f)(i)* will need to be involved.[12] In such unusual cases the cross-examiner is not restricted merely to putting the existence of the previous offences to the accused; he may cross-examine him in detail as to the circumstances in which they were committed. Cross-examination differs further from that under *s 1(f)(ii)* and *(iii)* in that it is not merely relevant to *credit* but to the *issue of guilt.*

---

5 Ibid, s 1(e), supra, subject to the restrictions considered at p 156, ante.
6 The section is by implication restricted to cross-examination. There is nothing therefore to prevent an accused from revealing his previous convictions in chief. See *Jones v DPP* [1962] AC 635.
7 Thus if the prosecution are permitted to adduce evidence as to other offences or convictions or the accused himself admits in chief to having previous convictions etc s 1(f) no longer applies: *Jones v DPP*, supra.
8 An offence committed *after* the offence charged comes within the section *R v Coltress* (1978) 68 Cr App Rep 193, CA.
9 This has been defined as meaning 'accused before the court' and not merely 'suspected or accused without prosecution': *Stirland v DPP* [1944] AC 315.
10 Character in s 1(f) does not mean 'general reputation' but may relate to specific events: *R v Dunkley* [1927] 1 KB 323, CCA.
11 For an exhaustive discussion on the topic see *Cross* (op cit) Chapter XI and Pattenden 'The purpose of cross-examination under s 1(f) of the Criminal Evidence Act 1898', [1982] Crim LR 707.
12 Although in theory cross-examination may thus be permissible under *s 1(f)(i)* even though the prosecution has not lead 'similar fact' evidence, but as a matter of practice the proper foundation should have been laid by the prosecution calling evidence. Per Lord Morris *Jones v DPP*, supra, in which case proviso *1 (f)(i)* becomes otiose.

EXAMPLE: Let us assume that the card:
   'Help control pollution, support your local car thieves'
referred to earlier[13] had been put through ATKIN's door, and that the prosecution had evidence that similar cards were put through another person's doors by DONOGHUE on the two previous occasions that he was convicted. It is possible (but never certain!) that they would be given leave to call evidence in support of this as part of their case as under to the 'similar fact' rule. If DONOGHUE were to give evidence he could be cross-examined without reference to s 1(f)(i) because such cross-examination would not 'tend to show' that he had committed the previous offences—the 'cat would already be out of the bag' as a result of the evidence adduced by the prosecution. Cross-examination would however be limited to the Theft Act, s 12 offences: no reference could be made to the assault or criminal damage charges.[14]

Proviso 1(f)(ii). This is by far the most commonly invoked proviso and requires the leave of the court before an accused may be cross-examined under it. It is divided into two separate 'limbs'.

The first deals with cases where the defence advocate has either cross-examined witnesses for the prosecution in an attempt to establish good character, or the accused has given evidence of or called witnesses with a view to establishing[15] his good character. Thus, if DONOGHUE were to assert in one or other of the above ways that he was a man of unblemished reputation,[16] the prosecution would be entitled, with leave, to cross-examine him as to his previous convictions and were to give evidence with a view to impugning his credit as a witness.[17] Problems may arise over interpretation. Each case will be a matter of fact and degree. Thus a mere denial of the offence charged will not infringe the rule but oblique assertions of good character, for example, that the accused is 'married with a family and in good employment' may.

The second limb concerns cases where the 'nature or conduct of the defence' is such as to involve 'imputations' on the character of the 'prosecutor or the witnesses for the prosecution'. Imputations may be cast either in the course of cross-examining prosecution witnesses or when the accused gives evidence. As a matter of procedure, whenever the conduct of the defence appears to be veering in this direction, the judge will normally warn the defence advocate to this effect, although this is not mandatory. The major difficulty is deciding when 'imputations on character' have been made. It is clear that a mere denial, however emphatic, does not of itself automatically throw away the shield but each case must be taken on its own facts. Note in particular that the defence of consent to a rape charge is not treated as an 'imputation',[18] but that otherwise the accused is not immune from cross-examination under $s\,1(f)(ii)$ merely because the nature of his defence is such that he has no choice but to cast 'imputations'.[19] DONOGHUE's allegations of

13 See p 129, ante.
14 This is because such cross-examination would 'tend to show' more than had already been revealed. Note that in those rare cases where proviso *1 (f)(i)* is invoked, cross-examination is limited to commission or conviction of other *relevant* offences: an accused may not therefore be cross-examined as to 'non relevant' offences, other *charges* or *bad character* under this proviso.
15 Thus the proviso does not come into operation where a witness makes an unsolicited reference to the accused's good character *R v Redd* [1923] 1 KB 104, CCA.
16 The extent to which an accused may adduce evidence of his own good character is discussed ante at p 131.
17 Cross-examination under this proviso is not however relevant to the issue of guilt.
18 *R v Turner* [1944] KB 463, CCA.
19 *Selvey v DPP* [1970] AC 304, HL.

bias against Andrea BOURHILL would obviously fall into this category. The definition of 'imputations' has been construed to include allegations that a prosecution witness[20] has committed a criminal offence, is of bad character,[1] or has fabricated evidence.[2] Allegations of the latter variety cause particular problems in cases where there is a substantial divergence between the accused's version of events and that given by the police. Defence counsel will frequently try to get round $s1(f)(ii)$ by suggesting emphatically that an officer is 'mistaken' rather than 'lying'. The Court of Appeal have recently held,[3] however, that each case must be taken on its own facts and that one must look at the substance rather than the form of the defence allegations. Thus, where the dispute relates to an event occupying a short time span, for example, a sentence or two of dialogue, allegations of 'mistake' do not inevitably raise the inference that the police witness is being accused of lying. Where, however, the divergence relates to matters taking place over a longer period of time, such an inference may be unavoidable.[4]

Before an accused can be cross-examined under either limb of this proviso the prosecution must obtain leave. It is thus within the judge's discretion to refuse leave if in all the circumstances to permit cross-examination of the accused would be prejudicial.[5]

EXAMPLE 1: Suppose that after a 'trial within a trial' DONOGHUE's confession is admitted. If, as he now must, his counsel were to cross-examine DS YOUNG by repeating the allegations of unfair pressure made in the 'trial within a trial' the judge will warn defence counsel of the possible consequences of this course. When DONOGHUE gives evidence (which in reality he must) prosecuting counsel will ask the judge in the absence of the jury for leave to put DONOGHUE's previous convictions to him.

EXAMPLE 2: DONOGHUE's predicament may usefully be contrasted with that of STEPHENSON. When cross-examining Andrea BOURHILL as to her purported identification of him there will be no need to cast imputations on her character, because his counsel will merely need to attack the accuracy of her evidence. The alleged irregularities in the conduct of the identification parade may similarly be put down to inefficiency rather than bad faith. Even STEPHENSON's denial of the remark attributed to him by PC ANDREWS can possibly be got round as a 'mistake', although if WPC HOPKINSON also gives similar evidence (as she probably will) counsel will be starting to 'sail close to the wind'.[6] There is, however, a strong possibility that STEPHENSON's burglary conviction will not be revealed unless he put himself forward as a person of good character.

Another major problem is that cross-examination under $s1(f)(ii)$ is only, in theory, relevant to the issue of *credit*. The prosecution in EXAMPLE 1 above will if granted leave put DONOGHUE's convictions to him one by one, asking whether he pleaded not guilty, and then with as much irony as can be mustered suggest that, he was not believed before, why should he be believed

---

20 Thus the proviso will not come into operation where, for example, imputations are made against a murder victim *R v Biggin* [1920] 1 KB 213, CCA.

1 See eg *R v Bishop* [1975] QB 274, CA (allegation of homosexual relationship with witness for the prosecution held to constitute an imputation justfying cross-examination of accused as to previous convictions).

2 Allegations that a witness is lying will not necessarily be construed as an imputation. Contrast *R v Rouse* [1904] 1 KB 184 and *R v Rappolt* (1911) 6 Cr App Rep 156, CCA.

3 *R v Britzman* [1983] 1 All ER 369, CA, but cf *R v St Louis* (1984) 79 Cr App Rep 53.

4 Per Lawton LJ in *Britzman*, supra.

5 The exercise of this discretion, has been preserved by s 82(3) of the Police and Criminal Act 1984. If not it will clearly come within s 78(1). See ante p 150.

6 See *R v Britzman*, supra.

now.[7] Although he cannot be cross-examined as to the circumstances in which the previous offences were committed[8] it is doubtful whether many jurors (or magistrates) can reasonably be expected to *disregard* an accused's previous convictions as *evidence of* guilt but take them into account in assessing the *credibility of his testimony*. Nevertheless, that is what s 1(f)(ii) requires them to do. It can be seen, however, that the more similar the previous offences are, the more difficult it becomes to make this distinction. In such a case, the defence may argue that leave to cross-examine should be refused on the ground of inevitable prejudice.[9] In any event, much of the force of such cross-examination may be lost if the accused pleaded guilty on previous occasions or if his convictions have already been revealed.

As a matter of tactics therefore it may be wiser to put the client's previous convictions to him in-chief if cross-examination under s 1(f)(ii) is inevitable so as to take the wind out of the prosecution's sails. The 'shield' is, in any event, a somewhat false protection. If there is no reference to the accused's character, good or bad, benches and juries will soon learn to realise he is hiding behind his 'shield'. Therefore, it is often better to get the accused's past out into the open rather than leave it to speculation. A different tactic may sometimes be employed in joint trials. If several co-accused wish to attack the same prosecution witness, it is sometimes possible for cross-examination to be conducted by counsel for the accused who is of good character (if there is one). This tactic will, however, require that the accused are separately represented and that there is close co-operation between their respective lawyers.

Proviso 1(f)(iii). This subsection will only ever apply when *two or more* accused who are being tried together (albeit not necessarily for identical offences) *plead 'not guilty'* and *at least one* of them gives evidence. In deciding whether or not one co-accused has given 'evidence against' another, motive is irrelevant.[10] The test is whether or not the evidence given supports the prosecution case or undermines the case of the co-accused in some material respect:[11] this will always be a question of fact. Section 1(f)(iii) differs from s 1(f)(ii) in that no leave is required from the court[12] but the judge may need to determine whether or not evidence has been 'given against a co-accused' as a preliminary point. On the other hand the two provisos are similar in that, once again, cross-examination is only relevant to the issue of credit.

EXAMPLE: If DONOGHUE and STEPHENSON give evidence to the effect that neither took part in the offence, ie 'alibi', there is no possibility of s 1(f)(iii) being invoked (although there is a serious risk of leave being granted to *prosecution* counsel to cross-examine DONOGHUE under s 1(f)(ii) if he attacks the prosecution witnesses). If, on the other hand, DONOGHUE were to give evidence along the same lines as

---

7 He is taken to have committed the previous offence unless the contrary is proved, s 74(3) of the 1984 Act.

8 *R v France and France* [1979] Crim LR 48. But cf *R v Duncalf* [1979] 2 All ER 1116, discussed by Pattenden (op cit).

9 At common law cross-examination under s 1(f)(ii) is disallowed if there was any risk of the jury being misled into thinking that it went to *guilt* and not 'merely' to credibility, *Maxwell v DPP* [1935] AC 309, HL, applied in *R v Watts* (1983) 77 Cr App Rep 126. For a trenchant criticism of *R v Watts* see *Archbold* (41st edn) Second Cumulative Supplement, para 365.

10 *Murdoch v Taylor* [1965] AC 574, HL.

11 *Murdoch v Taylor*, supra. The mere fact that the accused's evidence contradicts that of a co-accused will not *necessarily* bring it within the proviso *R v Bruce* [1975] 3 All ER 277, CA.

12 *Murdoch v Taylor*, supra.

that contained in his original statement under caution ie that STEPHENSON and he took the car, and that he drove it on the misapprehension that STEPHENSON had ATKIN's permission he would quite clearly be undermining STEPHENSON's alibi defence thus bringing $s\,1(f)(iii)$ into operation.

Sometimes both co-accused give 'evidence against' each other. Where there is a 'cut throat' defence of this kind, both accuseds' advocates may end up cross-examining their respective clients as to their previous convictions under $s\,1(f)(iii)$, while prosecuting counsel sits back and watches the fun. It is always important, therefore, to anticipate such problems, if necessary by liaising with the co-accused's solicitors before trial.

Interrelationship between $1(f)(ii)$ and $1(f)(iii)$

How do $1(f)(ii)$ and (iii) operate when an accused is liable to cross-examination under both? If the order of cross-examination is remembered, the problem is easier to solve.

> EXAMPLE: Suppose that DONOGHUE were to cast 'imputations' on the character of prosecution witnesses and to 'give evidence' against STEPHENSON (as in the previous example). After he had been examined-in-chief he would first be cross-examined by counsel for STEPHENSON who could put his previous convictions to him under $s\,1(f)(iii)$. He would then be cross-examined by prosecuting counsel who would have no need to apply for leave under $s\,1(f)(ii)$ because DONOGHUE's bad character would have been revealed. He would thus be freed from the constraints of $s\,1(f)$.[13]

If, on the other hand, there had been no 'cut throat' defence, prosecution counsel would have been able to seek leave under $s\,1(f)(ii)$ if either DONOGHUE or STEPHENSON attacked the character of the prosecution witnesses. It is theoretically possible that prosecuting counsel might wish to invoke $1(f)(iii)$ in circumstances where $s\,1(f)(ii)$ is not available to him, for example, where two accused both run 'cut throat' defences, but their respective counsel have agreed between themselves not to cross-examine under $s\,1(f)(iii)$. Prosecuting counsel could then, it seems, cross-examine under $s\,1(f)(iii)$ but would require leave before doing so.[14]

Relationship between 'similar fact' rule and $s\,1(f)$

This problem causes almost as much pain and suffering as the hearsay rule. The two provisions may be contrasted thus:

Similar fact evidence	*Cross-examination of an accused under the provisos to $s\,1(f)$:*
(1) Prosecution calls evidence as part of its case.	(1) Prosecution cross-examines the accused if and when he gives evidence.
(2) Admissible only if 'strikingly similar'.	(2) Cross-examination is allowed only if one of '*provisoes*' to $s\,1(f)$ applies.
(3) Relevant to *issue of guilt*.	(3) Such cross-examination is only relevant to the accused's *credit* as a witness (unless under $s\,1(f)(i)$).
(4) Witnesses may give evidence as to the detailed circumstances of the accused's misconduct.	(4) Details of the circumstances surrounding the offence may not be introduced (unless under $s\,1(f)(i)$).

---

13 *Jones v DPP*, supra.
14 Discussed by *Cross* (op cit) at p 375.

(c) Re-examination

Once a witness has been cross-examined, the person who called him may re-examine him on any new matters raised in cross-examination but as with examination-in-chief no leading questions may be asked. Re-examination is a much neglected art[15] since matters arising in cross-examination may give the re-examiner the opportunity to raise matters that he could not have introduced in chief.

> EXAMPLE: Once DS YOUNG has survived attempts at character assassination by DONOGHUE's counsel, prosecuting counsel may, if prepared, put to him his previous good service record, his fifteen commendations and the fact that he has been awarded the Queen's Police Medal for gallantry, none of which could have been put to him in chief, to repair any damage.

(d) Impeaching the credibility of a witness other than by cross-examination

Although a witness may not generally be cross-examined as to collateral issues,[16] somewhat anomalously a party (usually an accused) may call witnesses to testify as to the general reputation for truthfulness of an opponent's witness and such witnesses may also be asked whether or not in their opinion the previous witness is to be believed on oath.[17] Furthermore it is now well-established that medical evidence may be called with a view to proving that due to some mental or physical defect a witness's testimony cannot be relied upon.[18] On a more general level, if a prosecution witness gives unfavourable evidence the defence is free to call witnesses to give contradicting evidence. However, since the prosecution 'bats first' this could place them at a disadvantage if they are taken by surprise after closing their case. Although the general rule is that they may not call further evidence once their case is closed, they may be given leave to call rebutting evidence if the defence raises an issue which they could not reasonably have anticipated.[19]

Test 4: One witness will not always be enough

Assuming that evidence is relevant and admissible and stands up to cross-examination the general rule is that a person may be convicted on the evidence of *one witness alone*. There are, however, certain kinds of *prosecution* evidence for which corroboration is either *necessary* as a matter of law (for example, the unsworn evidence of a child), or a *warning* needs to be given as to the dangers of convicting without it (for example accomplice evidence). There are also other kinds of evidence which, although not requiring corroboration or a corroboration warning as such, nevertheless require a *direction to exercise caution* before convicting on the strength of them (for example disputed identification evidence). These are all matters which will usually arise at the end of the trial when the judge sums up to the jury or the magistrates direct themselves (or the clerk directs them) on matters of law.

---

15 See further Advocacy at the Bar (op cit) pp 167 et seq.
16 See p 156, ante.
17 *Toohey v Metropolitan Police Comr* [1965] AC 595, HL considered in *R v Richardson* [1969] 1 QB 299, CA; the witness may not however give evidence as to why he held that opinion.
18 *Toohey*, supra (medical evidence as to prosecution witness's tendency to hysteria wrongly excluded).
19 For recent example of where rebutting evidence was properly allowed see *R v Scott* (1984) 148 JP 731, CA. See also p 301, post.

Meaning of corroboration

In order for evidence to be *capable* of being corroborative it must confirm in some material particular, (a) that the crime was committed and (b) that the accused committed it. Subject to an appropriate direction it is then for the jury (or magistrates) to decide whether the evidence does in fact constitute corroboration. The corroborating evidence need not be identical provided it satisfies the above criteria. It may, therefore, include a confession or lies told out of court by the accused, or the evidence of other witnesses. Thus, for example, PC ANDREW's evidence of what STEPHENSON allegedly said when stopped is capable of corroborating Andrea BOURHILL's evidence of identification and vice versa. Note however that the lack of credibility of the accused *whilst giving evidence* on oath cannot generally be treated as corroboration. If, for example, the only prosecution witness were an accomplice and the only defence witness were the accused the mere fact that the magistrates or the jury believed the accomplice more than the accused could not be treated as corroboration; to do so would render the accomplice rule superfluous. Nevertheless, lies told by an accused in court *may* be capable of constituting corroboration if the court is satified that they are deliberate, relate to a material issue, are told out of realisation of guilt and are confirmed by independent evidence other than that of the witness to be corroborated.[20] Note finally that if the accused does not give evidence at all, this may never be treated as corroboration, because of the accused's 'right of silence'.

(a) Cases where there must be corroboration

There are certain occasions, albeit rare, when the prosecution will fail to make out a prima facie case unless they adduce corroborative evidence. The most notable of these are as follows.

(i) Where a child of tender years gives unsworn evidence for the prosecution. It will be recalled in such a case that no conviction is possible without corroboration by sworn evidence. It has been established that unsworn evidence of one child cannot be corroborated by the unsworn evidence of another, but a sworn child is capable of corroborating an unsworn child and vice versa.[1] Whenever the principal prosecution witness is a child of tender years who gives unsworn evidence the defence advocate must ensure that evidence that is prima facie corroborative has in fact been adduced. If it has not, the defence may make a successful submission of no case to answer.

(ii) Speeding offences. Statute provides[2] that no person may be convicted of such an offence on the opinion evidence of one witness alone. This rule does not, however, preclude a conviction where the sole evidence is that of a police officer who has followed the car for a specified distance in another vehicle and observed the speed by reference to his own speedometer. He will not then be giving opinion evidence, but evidence of fact. Similarly, if having stopped the driver and gone up to him the driver were to say when being taxed with the offence

> 'I'm terribly sorry I know I was going over 50, I just wasn't looking at what I was doing',

---

20 See *R v Lucas* [1981] QB 720; but see also *R v West* (1983) 79 Cr App Rep 45, CA.
1 *DPP v Kilbourne* [1973] AC 729, HL.
2 Road Traffic Regulations Act 1984, s 89.

this again would be sufficient to found a conviction since the accused's own confession, if admitted, would constitute corroboration.

(b) Cases where a corroboration warning must be given

There are three situations where although a conviction is *possible* without corroboration the judge must *warn* the jury of the danger of convicting on uncorroborated evidence. As we shall see, this constitutes a minefield for judges and is a fruitful source of appeals. As well as giving a warning the judge must also direct the jury as to the meaning of corroboration and direct them to what evidence is capable of amounting to corroboration.[3] In the magistrates' court the justices are placed in the unrealistic position of having to warn themselves.

(i) The evidence of the complainant in a sexual case. As a matter of tradition such allegations are regarded as easy to make but difficult to refute and accordingly a warning should always be given. Medical evidence may or may not amount to corroboration depending on the facts in issue.[4] As has already been noted, evidence of recent complaint or the complainant's distressed condition is admissible to show consistency but it cannot normally constitute corroboration.[5]

(ii) Sworn evidence of a child who testifies for the prosecution. Even where a child of tender years gives sworn evidence the judge should always give the corroboration warning and, where appropriate, advert the jury to the possibility of collusion. In such cases the unsworn evidence of another child is capable of constituting corroboration.[6]

(iii) Evidence of an accomplice. An accomplice is either any party to the crime charged, a receiver giving evidence against the thief or (extremely rarely) a party to a 'similar fact' crime. The first of these categories requires further consideration.[7] An accomplice warning may be needed in two situations. First, where the prosecution calls a co-accused who has pleaded guilty and 'turned Queen's evidence',[8] secondly, where a prosecution witness has never been charged but his complicity in the crime emerges during the course of his giving evidence. To be an accomplice the witness must be shown to be a party to the *crime actually charged*. Thus, for example, a prosecution witness on a murder charge who had taken part in the disturbance during which the murder was committed but had been unaware that the accused was carrying a knife was held not to come within the definition.[9]

---

3 This duty was recently re-emphasised by the Court of Appeal in *R v Cullinane* [1984] Crim LR 420, CA.
4 For a recent example of a case where medical evidence did not constitute corroboration see *R v Campbell* [1983] Crim LR 174, CA. As well as pointing to a commission of the offence it must also implicate the accused.
5 See p 134, ante, the complainant's distressed condition may on occasions constitute corroboration if the complainant did not realise he or she was being observed. See Oughton, 'The Distressing Nature of Corroboration', [1984] Crim LR 265.
6 *DPP v Kilbourne*, supra.
7 See further, Yates, 'Accomplice Evidence' [1984] Crim LR 213.
8 For the rules as to the competence and compellability of such witnesses see p 119, ante.
9 *Davies v DPP* [1954] AC 378.

(c) Evidence of disputed identity

As has already been noted, evidence of identity always causes problems and because of this a five-judge Court of Appeal in *R v Turnbull*[10] laid down guidelines to be followed in such cases. The case has given rise to much misunderstanding and should be read carefully by all criminal practitioners. In particular, it imposes no requirement as to corroboration or a corroboration warning. In summary the 'Turnbull guidelines' provide that:

(i) Whenever the prosecution case depends 'wholly or substantially' on *disputed* identification evidence the magistrates should warn themselves, or the judge should warn the jury of the *'special need for caution'* especially in relation to the possibility that witnesses may be mistaken even though convincing. No particular form of words is prescribed.

(ii) In every such case the magistrates must direct themselves, or the judge direct the jury to examine closely the *circumstances* in which the identification by each witness came to be made. For example 'how long, at what distance and in what light'.

(iii) The direction should *always* be given if there is any *material discrepancy* between the original description to the police and the accused's actual appearance.

(iv) Whenever the prosecution have reason to believe that there is such material discrepancy, they should supply the accused or his legal advisers with *details of the description* the police were first given.[11]

(v) If the quality of the evidence is *good* the case can be left to the jury even though there is *no other evidence* to support it *provided* an *adequate warning* has been given. If, on the other hand, the quality of the evidence is *poor*, for example where it is based solely on a fleeting glance or longer observation made in difficult situations, the judge should *withdraw the case from the jury and direct an acquittal* unless there is *other evidence* which goes to support the correctness of the identification.

As can be seen the purpose of the 'Turnbull guidelines' is to ensure that the magistrates' or the jury's minds are directed towards the *quality* of the evidence. Normally, it will be for the jury or the magistrates to evaluate the weight of the evidence having been appropriately warned. There may, however, be cases coming within guideline (v) where a submission of no case to answer may be made. In such instances however the jury (or magistrates) will have heard the evidence. Are there any circumstances where, by analogy with confessions, the defence can insist on a 'trial within a trial' in order to determine whether the evidence should be excluded altogether? The Court of Appeal has recently held that the holding of a 'trial within a trial' is inappropriate in identification cases.[12] It is submitted, however, that such a procedure may be necessary in those cases where, for example, there have been such flagrant breaches of the Identification Code that the court should exercise its discretion to exclude the evidence under s 78 (1) of the Police and Criminal Evidence Act 1984.[13]

10 [1977] QB 224, CA. For the correct direction in cases of disputed identity preceeded by identification by photographs, see *R v Dodson* [1984] 1 WLR 971.
11 Ideally a description should be sought before any identity parade is held see p 104, ante.
12 *R v Walshe* (1980) 74 Cr App Rep 85, CA.
13 See for example *R v Leckie and Ensley*, supra.

EXAMPLE: Andrea BOURHILL's identification of STEPHENSON is unsatisfactory in a number of respects. If there were no more than a discrepancy between her description and his actual appearance, the evidence would go before the jury duly warned[14] who would decide whether or not to accept it.

However, the alleged faults in the conduct of STEPHENSON's parade are a different matter. These may take the case outside *Turnbull* and involve the judge in deciding whether this evidence should be excluded altogether. In such a case, it is hard to see how this issue cannot be determined other than by means of a 'trial within a trial' in the absence of the jury.

(d) *Witnesses with a purpose of their own to serve*

There are two situations in which a warning as to the danger of accepting particular evidence is desirable but not essential. The first is when an accused gives evidence which implicates a co-accused,[15] the other is where a witness gives evidence from an improper motive, for example spite.[16] In such cases, the giving of a warning is entirely within the judges discretion, and even if a warning is given it need not amount to a full corroboration direction.

EXAMPLE: If in the course of BOURHILL's cross-examination on credit allegations were made by DONOGHUE that she was biased and had a purpose of her own to serve, the judge might feel it appropriate to give a warning to the jury to proceed with caution. Similarly, if DONOGHUE, instead of pleading alibi, had persisted with the story given in his statement under caution thus undermining STEPHENSON's defence, the judge would have a discretion to give the jury a warning to exercise caution,[17] in assessing the strength of DONOGHUE's evidence against STEPHENSON.

(e) *Persons suffering from mental illness or disability*

It has recently been held[18] that where a prosecution witness is suffering from mental disorder the judge may in appropriate circumstances need to warn the jury of the special need for caution. A full corroboration warning is not, however, required. Furthermore, when the case against a 'mentally handicapped' *accused* is based wholly or substantially on his confession the appropriate warning must be given under s 77 Police and Criminal Evidence Act 1984.[19]

Test 5: The judge's control of the jury.

This important judicial function has already been considered. The fact that there is no obvious counterpart in the magistrates' court is regrettable. To consider the relatively simple case of *R v DONOGHUE and STEPHENSON* and proceed on the assumption that they both plead alibi, DONOGHUE's confession is held admissible, and he 'throws away his shield', and the identification

---

14 The Court of Appeal have subsequently suggested that the full 'Turnbull warning' only need be given in 'fleeting glance' cases. See eg *R v Curry and Keeble* [1983] Crim LR 737, CA.
15 The matter was considered at length by the Court of Appeal in *R v Knowlden and Knowlden* (1983) 77 Cr App Rep 94. For the appropriate warning when the jury is shown identification evidence in the form of photographs or video films see *R v Dodson* [1984] 1 WLR 971.
16 *R v Beck* [1982] 1 All ER 807, CA.
17 DONOGHUE would of course have been liable to cross-examination by STEPHENSON's counsel under s 1(f)(iii).
18 *R v Spencer*, supra, overruling *R v Bagshaw*, supra.
19 See p 149, ante.

evidence against STEPHENSON is also admitted, the judge will still have much to do in summing up. He must (inter alia):

- outline the substantive law
- summarise the facts and the evidence
- direct the jury on the burden of proof
- direct the jury to consider the evidence against each accused separately

Re DONOGHUE

- direct that it is for them to determine whether they are sure that DONOGHUE's confession can be relied on;
- that in deciding whether or not to believe DONOGHUE's evidence they may take his convictions into account but must ignore them in determining guilt;
- and warn them to approach Andrea BOURHILL's evidence with caution (if he considers this appropriate);

Re STEPHENSON

- give the 'Turnbull' warning on Andrea's evidence;
- warn them that they must disregard anything in DONOGHUE's confession in so far as it implicates STEPHENSON.

Other matters may well arise during such a trial but the above summary hopefully ties together the main evidential points.

3 CONCLUSION

This chapter covers the basic elements of the law of criminal evidence but anyone hoping to become an advocate will need to study the subject in greater depth. One of the major disincentives to doing this is the fact that so many of the 'difficult' areas rarely give problems in practice. 'Similar fact' cases are few and far between, as are (surprisingly in view of the space they occupy) cases involving disputed confessions and illegally obtained evidence. However, hardly a contested trial will go by without the need to be aware of the basic rules against the admission of hearsay and opinion evidence arising, quite apart from all pervasive principles such as the burden of proof and legal professional privileges. Similarly, virtually every case will involve the admission of at least some evidence under one of the common exceptions to the hearsay rule, for example, under s 9 of the Criminal Justice Act 1967[20] or s 102 of the Magistrates' Courts Act 1980.[1] In the end, however, evidence is one of those subjects which can only be mastered by studying it in a practical context. Thus, the more trials you attend and the more problems you can examine and try to solve, the sooner you will come to terms with its apparent intricacies.

20 See p 138, ante.
 1 See p 139, ante.

CHAPTER 5

Preparing the case

This chapter considers preliminary strategy and the major tasks of preparation concentrating primarily on the client who intends to plead 'not guilty', reserving fuller discussion of the guilty client to the chapters on sentencing (Chapters 12 and 13). It must be stressed however, that every case, whatever the plea, should always be prepared meticulously. It is a popular misconception that criminal cases are 'won' by dazzling oratory, and that unless the advocate possesses such a gift he can never do his client's case justice. Unfortunately, clients are often much more impressed by the advocate whose performances are best suited to an amateur dramatic group than the one who presents the case firmly and clearly with minimum histrionics but maximum grasp of the facts and issues involved. The latter approach is, however, far more effective and is within everyone's reach; all that is required is hard work and application. As Sir David Napley says:

> The presentation of a client's case ... necessarily involves two distinct parts: the preparation and the presentation itself. It is, of course, impossible to express with precision the relative importance of these two aspects of advocacy and persuasion and yet it can be said with little fear of contradiction that while both parts are vital, the extent and quality of preparation is infinitely more important, significant and essential than the manner of presentation ... It can rarely if ever occur ... that the most skilled advocate can succeed where the work of preparation has been shoddy, incompetent or inadequate.[1]

Preparation is even more important when instructing counsel; a barrister can only ever be as good as the instructions he or she receives.

1 PROFESSIONAL ETHICS

The legal profession is rightly expected to uphold the highest standards of professional conduct and integrity. It is therefore necessary to summarise these at the outset.[2]

(1) The duties of the prosecution representative

Solicitor or counsel for the prosecution is not required to secure a conviction at all costs: his primary duty is to present the evidence to the court but not to seek to influence its decision in any way. For example, a prosecuting counsel or solicitor should never open a case with any facts that he cannot prove, neither may he address the court on sentence. Furthermore, he must make available to the defence any evidence in his possession which may be of assistance,[3] and inform the defence of any material inconsistency between

---

1 Sir David Napley, *The Technique of Persuasion* (3rd edn), p 9.
2 In cases of doubt consult the Law Society's Guide to Professional Conduct 1974.
3 See, for example, *R v Leyland Justices, ex p Hawthorn* [1979] QB 283. See also Law Society's Guide (op cit) Ch 3, paras 1 to 4.

the evidence given by a prosecution witness and any earlier statement made by him.

(2) The duties of the defence representative

The basic rule is that solicitor and counsel must do the best for their client subject to their overriding duty to the court. The following aspects are of particular importance in criminal cases.

(a) Confidentiality

As already noted the solicitor/client relationship is protected by privilege; the solicitor thus owes his or her client a duty to preserve confidentiality. The practical effect is that the solicitor is prohibited from divulging any details of his client's case or anything that has been told to him in confidence without the client's prior authority, subject to three exceptions. These are as follows.

Points of law. Any authorities to which a solicitor intends to refer should be disclosed to his opponent beforehand (this applies equally to the prosecution).

Alibi. In trials on indictment, details of an alibi defence must normally be disclosed at committal or within seven days thereafter.[4]

Expert evidence. In trials on indictment s 81 Police and Criminal Evidence Act 1984 provides for rules to be made governing the advance disclosure of expert evidence. As yet no rules have been made.

(b) Duty not to mislead the court

A solicitor's (and counsel's) duty to his or her client must always take second place to his or her duty to the court: if you lose the court's trust, you will have lost the most valuable asset that you possess. However small the deception, once you develop a reputation for untrustworthiness, your effectiveness as an advocate will be irreversibly diminished. In particular, you must be aware of the duty that you owe to the court in the following circumstances.

(i) *Arguing points of law.* It is not enough to produce to the court those authorities that are in your favour. You must also refer the courts to any authorities that are *against* you and endeavour to distinguish them.[5]

(ii) *Informing the court of errors.* If it is clear that the court has misdirected itself in some way, or there is some procedural defect (for example, an information is bad for duplicity) and neither the prosecution nor the court has taken the point, you must bring this irregularity to the court's attention, even though in doing so you are effectively throwing away your right of appeal. If you stay silent this may well go against you in the higher court.[6]

---

4 Criminal Justice Act 1967, s 11. See further pp 328 and 370, post.
5 See Law Society's Guide (op cit) ch 3, para 2.1.
6 See Law Society's Guide (op cit) ch 3, paras 1 and 2, note also *R v Edwards* (1983) 147 JP 316, CA (judge failed to direct jury on burden of proof in summing up—duty of defence counsel to draw this to court's attention); discussed more fully at [1983] Crim LR 703.

(iii) *Previous convictions.* So overriding is the solicitor's duty of confidentiality that he is under no obligation to disclose a client's previous convictions to the court even though he is aware of them. Problems may sometimes arise when mitigating for a client whose convictions have not been produced to the court by the prosecution. Although you are under no duty to disclose this omission, you cannot mitigate on the basis that the client is of previous good character; you must limit mitigation to the circumstances of the offence.

(c) Advising the client as to plea

A problem which frequently arises, at least in the mind of the public, is that of the client who protests his innocence when the evidence against him is overwhelming. A defence solicitor will often be asked 'How can you act for someone when you think he is guilty?' The answer is that it is not for the solicitor to be judge and jury: he must act in his client's interests so far as his duty to the court enables him to do so whatever his private feelings about the client's guilt or innocence may be. The solicitor has no right to pre-judge the issue and should leave no stone unturned in conducting his client's defence however hopeless a task it may appear.[7]

What, however, is to be done when you take the view that a plea of not guilty may, in the long run, only serve to make your client's position worse if and when he is subsequently convicted. Pressure should never be exerted on a client to plead guilty, however overwhelming the evidence and however implausible his defence. Nevertheless, the consequences of conviction must be explained to him. Such advice is particularly difficult in motoring cases where the client may perhaps justly feel aggrieved at being prosecuted for an offence such as careless driving of which he considers himself morally innocent. All that can be done is to explain the position fairly and frankly to the client in the light of the relevant law, the strengths and weaknesses of the respective parties' cases, and the likely cost, and leave the final decision to him. If, however, there is a fundamental disagreement with the client over the conduct of the case you should withdraw.[8]

You may sometimes be faced with the opposite situation; the client who has a defence but insists on pleading guilty in order to, 'get it all over with'. In such a case, every effort should be made to deter the client from this course but if he insists on pleading guilty he is entitled to do so. The client should, however, be asked to confirm in writing that he is pleading guilty against your advice; you should also give serious consideration as to whether you can continue to act in the circumstances.

What if the client admits his guilt to his solicitor but states that he intends to plead not guilty? A solicitor may continue to act, but only to a limited extent. This is because, technically, a plea of 'not guilty' does no more than to put the prosecution to proof of its case. Accordingly it is not unethical for a defence solicitor to continue to act if he or she is merely instructed to put the prosecution to proof or to instruct counsel to do so.[9]

EXAMPLE: *Police v Duncan McCARTHY (case 1)*
Suppose, that Duncan McCARTHY were to admit his guilt but ask his solicitor to continue to act? If he were to indicate that he still intended to plead not guilty it

---

7 See Law Society's Guide (op cit) Ch 1, para 1.1.
8 Ibid, Ch 3, para 4.2.
9 Ibid, para 1.2.

would be possible to represent him at committal proceedings, test the evidence by cross-examination and (if appropriate) make a submission of no case to answer. Similarly, if the case were committed for trial it would be permissible to cross-examine with a view to testing the reliability of the prosecution evidence or seek to have it ruled inadmissible. If appropriate, counsel could also submit that there was no case to answer at the close of the prosecution's case. It would not, however, be possible to cross-examine any of the prosecution witnesses in such a way as positively to suggest McCarthy's innocence. Furthermore, if McCarthy were to insist on giving perjured evidence or were to ask his solicitor to call perjured witnesses, for example in support of a false alibi, both his solicitor and counsel would be required to withdraw from the case, although they must not give the reason.

Technical defences: What if, on investigating the relevant law, a solicitor concludes that his client has a technical defence of which he is unaware but which constitutes a complete answer to the charge? The advent of the breath-alyser in particular has engendered all manner of technical but sustainable defences and its successor the Lion Intoximeter 3000 seems, if anything, to have inspired defence lawyers to even greater heights of ingenuity. There is nothing ethically wrong in probing complex legislation in order to ascertain whether or not the prosecution is in a position to prove all the constituent elements of the offence—it would be professionally negligent not to do so. In the same way, appeals may be highly technical and lack merit but if they constitute legitimate grounds they must be pursued. This principle does not, of course, give you carte blanche to 'invent' defences[10] by moulding the client's evidence to suit some nice point of law. If, therefore, on taking instructions you form a preliminary view that a technical defence may be available it is advisable in the first instance not to reveal this to the client. There cannot then be any suggestion that he has been led on by his solicitor.

(d)   *The client who changes instructions*

Clients will often give inconsistent instructions. This is not surprising. Their perception of events may often be blurred or distorted by the passage of time or stress and it is only by careful probing that the whole picture will emerge. It may often happen, that having taken a preliminary proof from a client who is to be tried on indictment, it becomes apparent on reading the committal papers that there are many other matters that need to be dealt with or explained. Up to a point, changes in the client's story are to be expected. On occasions, however, there may be such a fundamental divergence between the instructions originally given and those later tendered, that the only inference to be drawn is that he is trying to concoct a defence. In such circumstances you must question the client vigorously as to the reason for the change and only if entirely satisfied as to the explanation given should you continue to act.[11]

(e)   *Conflicts of interest*

In cases involving several accused a solicitor may find himself instructed by more than one client; co-accused may also be assigned by the court when it grants legal aid. Great care should be taken at the outset to discover whether there is any potential conflict that prevents you from acting for more than

10 Law Society Guide, para 4.8.
11 Ibid, para 4.11.

one of them. If such a conflict is revealed, for example, because two co-accused's defences undermine each other, you should not act for either. [12] Unfortunately, however, this rule is not always observed as punctiliously as it might be. Some solicitors still operate on a 'first come first served' basis, retain the original client, and send the co-accused elsewhere notwithstanding the fact that they have received confidential information from him. Such a course is to be deprecated.

(f) Interviewing prosecution witnesses

There is no property in a witness. A defence solicitor is therefore theoretically entitled to interview prosecution witnesses without any reference to the prosecution. It is not, however, a course to be recommended.[13] In the first place, it is likely to give rise to suspicion that an attempt has been made to pervert the course of justice; secondly, any attempt to use such evidence could well rebound when the circumstances in which it was obtained become apparent. If you wish to interview a prosecution witness the better course is for you to notify the prosecution beforehand of your intention to make an approach, and only then to contact the witness. Normally the prosecution will wish to be present at the interview in which case the nature of the defence may inevitably be revealed: you should, therefore, proceed with caution. When the case is to be tried on indictment it may be more appropriate to elicit further information by requiring the witness to attend to give oral evidence at the committal proceedings.

2 IDENTIFYING THE MAJOR ISSUES

It will be recalled that criminal prosecution tends to follow a more or less predictable course. It is now necessary to consider the most important features in a practical context.

(1) Venue: Crown Court, magistrates' court or juvenile court?

This is arguably the most important factor of all. Its influence can be seen in two ways. Firstly, as already noted, the defence solicitor can only be certain of seeing the prosecution evidence in advance, when the case is to be tried on indictment.[14] Secondly, the time lag between the accused's first appearance and his ultimate conviction or acquittal is likely to be far greater where there is to be a Crown Court trial. An awareness of the likely time scale is important; it gives you a better idea of how long you have to prepare the case, and what is feasible in the time available. Just because a trial date is on the distant horizon, however, does not mean that the file can be put away and forgotten about for six months. Preparatory work should always be done at the earliest possible opportunity—delay can be fatal: witnesses' memories will begin to fade and the case will lose any sense of urgency.

---

12 Ibid, Ch 1, para 2.1.
13 Ibid, Ch 3, para 10.4.
14 A limited form of pre-trial disclosure was introduced in May 1985 under s 48 of the Criminal Law Act 1977 in respect of *either way* offences tried summarily. See p 185 post.

Choice of venue

If the accused is charged with an either way offence, he has a *right* to decide where he is to be tried. The decision as to how this choice is to be exercised is thus of great strategic importance. This topic is considered more fully in chapter 8, but suffice it to say for the moment that where an accused intends to plead 'not guilty', there may be compelling reasons for electing for jury trial.

The intentions of a co-accused

If several accused are jointly charged with an either way offence and one of them elects trial on indictment, magistrates are usually most unwilling to commit some but deal with the others summarily. The situation may, there-fore, arise where a client, who wishes to plead guilty, is dragged up to the Crown Court due to the election of a co-accused.[15] A similar problem will arise when acting for a juvenile who is charged jointly with an adult and the adult elects jury trial. The magistrates will usually consider it to be in the 'interests of justice' to commit them both.[16] It is thus important to elicit a co-accused's intentions from his solicitor at as early a stage as possible: although the solicitor can refuse to answer on the grounds of privilege, such refusals are rare.

(2) How is the client pleading?

Clearly, it is important to know at as early a stage as possible how the client intends to plead. It is not, however, a matter which can be left entirely to him. It may sometimes be necessary for you to conduct detailed legal re-search in order to ascertain whether or not he is technically guilty as charged. It may not be possible finally to advise the client until a much later stage in the proceedings. It is often forgotten that the accused will not be asked to plead until the trial proper commences in the magistrates' court or until he is arraigned before the Crown Court. He thus has many months to reflect upon his position before he is finally called upon to decide.

When the client is charged with others, it is equally important to know their intended plea, especially if your client is pleading 'not guilty'.

> EXAMPLE: D is charged with burglary with X and Y. D's defence is one of alibi. If X and Y plead 'guilty' they will not be present in court during D's trial and can thus not do his case any damage (save in the very rare case of their being called as prosecution witnesses). Imagine, on the other hand, how much more perilous D's position could be if X and Y were both pleading 'not guilty'. Quite apart from the fact that the nature of the defences might be to undermine D's, (for example, that they were present with D but took no part), prosecution counsel may also be able to extract evidence from them in cross-examination which is damaging to D. Furthermore, if D has previous convictions, the ugly spectre of $s\,1(f)(iii)$ Criminal Evidence Act 1898 raises its head in the event of there being a 'cut throat' defence.

---

15 An extreme case with which one of the authors is familiar resulted in a female accused who wished to plead guilty to receiving a stolen cheque card before the magistrates being kept in custody for 14 months awaiting trial at the behest of her co-accused (both on bail) who elected for trial. Unfortunately an application for bail to a High Court judge failed: she was later put on probation for two years!

16 Magistrates' Courts Act 1980, s 29.

You should, therefore, always contact any co-accused's solicitors to try and find out how they are going to plead, although their solicitor can again refuse to answer on the ground of privilege. You yourself may receive a similar request, in which case, you must consider the position very carefully with your client. If he intends to plead guilty, nothing will normally be lost, but if he is pleading not guilty it is important to proceed with caution unless there is clearly no conflict between the co-accused.[17] At the end of the day, however, if co-accused's solicitors refuse to liaise they may only succeed in providing the prosecution with greater opportunity for exposing inconsistencies or taking advantage of a 'cut throat' defence.

(3) What does the prosecution have to prove and what is the defence?

You should always ask yourself the question, 'What must the prosecution prove in order to secure a conviction?' at as early a stage as possible in the proceedings. You should also always refer to one of the leading practitioners' books such as *Stone's Justices' Manual* or *Archbold* to remind yourself of the constituent elements of the offences charged even if it is one with which you think you are familiar. Such is the pace of progress that it is possible that recent case law or statutory amendment might have escaped your notice. Having done this, you should always write these elements down in tabular form so that as and when the prosecution's evidence becomes available, you can make a note as to what each prosecution witness is being tendered to prove. In *Police v McCarthy (case 1)* the charge sheet should be broken up as follows:

	Facts in issue?	*Evidence*
That on the 5th day of August 198–	No	
You Duncan McCARTHY	Yes	
Entered	No	
A building	No	
As a trespasser	No	
And stole £50 therein	No	

The right hand column can be completed on service of the committal statements. Such a breakdown is invaluable for two reasons:

- your mind is immediately directed to those matters (if any) which must be put to the prosecution witnesses in cross-examination; and
- it indicates at an early stage where the lines of battle are to be drawn.

This exercise is much more difficult to carry through when the client is to be tried summarily and there is no advance notice of the prosecution case. Much more must then be left to guesswork, but it is usually possible for you to anticipate where the main issues will lie, provided you obtain proper instructions. If Mary ADAMS *(case 3)*, for example, were to insist on pleading not guilty, a similar analysis of the offence of careless driving would readily reveal that the major issue would not be one of identity or whether she was

---

17 A copy of a client's statement so disclosed will still be an item subject to legal professional privilege within Police and Criminal Evidence Act 1984 s 11(1)(c) whilst in the hands of the accused's solicitor.

driving on a public road but whether in the circumstances her driving fell short of the objective standard required of the reasonable and prudent driver.

The other, equally important, side of the coin is to establish the nature of the client's defence. Although, in theory, the prosecution must generally prove all the 'facts in issue' beyond reasonable doubt in order to secure a conviction, in practice, however, the defence cannot just sit back and leave the prosecution to make the running. They must identify at as early a stage as possible the precise nature of their client's defence and having done so, direct their efforts towards obtaining evidence that will lend it credence. Notwithstanding the vast range of offences with which the criminal practitioner is required to deal, the client's defence[18] will usually fit into one of a few standard categories namely:

'I wasn't there' (*alibi*);
'I was there but I didn't do it' (*no actus reus*);
'I was there, I did it, but I didn't mean to steal it (or it was self defence etc)' (*no mens rea*).

Although certain offences, for example, those relating to drinking and driving, require special consideration, it is remarkable how many defences fall into one of the above three categories.[19] For example, even in fraud cases, the facts are often not in dispute, the sole issue is usually whether or not the accused acted dishonestly. This view is borne out by recent research conducted by the Home Office Research and Planning Unit[20] into contested trials in magistrates' courts. Out of a sample of contested charges which encompassed the more common either way and summary offences (other than motoring offences) they found as follows:

'Examination of the substance of the defendant's explanations disclosed that on the majority (56 per cent) of charges they denied the conduct which constituted the charges preferred. This category was divided into those who contended that they were absent from the scene and could not therefore have been responsible (26 charges); and those who denied having acted in the manner described by prosecution witnesses, albeit that their presence at the alleged incident was not in dispute (182 charges). Defendants contested the remaining (165) charges on the grounds that they had acted in the manner described by prosecution witnesses but had lacked the requisite intent. Defendants charged with offences against public order, criminal damage or being "suspected persons" typically denied the conduct ascribed to them, whereas the majority of charges of dishonesty were countered on the grounds of lack of intent.'[1]

(4) Is the client on bail?

If a client has been summoned, the issue of bail will rarely arise at any stage, but in cases begun by charge or arrest under a warrant it almost always will.

---

18 'Defence' in this context is not confined to those cases in which the prosecution having proved its case, the accused seeks to rely upon a general defence (for example, insanity) but extends to any circumstance in which the case advanced by the accused entitles him to an acquittal.

19 Certain offences require special treatment: see eg Fulford, 'Defending Homosexuals', LAG Bulletin, April 1982, 40; Wood and Gifford, 'Public Order Offences', LAG Bulletin, July 1982, 74 and February 1982, 23; Harrison, 'Supplementary Benefit Fraud', LAG Bulletin, January 1983, 9 and February 1983, 47; Bucknell, 'Notes on Some Controlled Drugs' [1985] Crim LR 260 contains much useful information.

20 Vennard, 'Contested Trials in the Magistrates' Courts' (1982) Home Office Research Study, No 71 (HMSO).

1 Ibid, p 13.

It cannot be emphasised too strongly how profound an effect the client being in custody will have on the conduct of the case. First, the efforts to secure bail often, rightly, assume paramount importance in the early stage. Secondly, instructions are much more difficult to obtain. Instead of being able to interview the client in the comfort and relative calm of his office, the solicitor will have to rely on snatched meetings in crowded cells as and when his client is brought up for remand, or make lengthy and often inconvenient journeys to a prison or remand centre where interviews are inevitably less easy to conduct. In Greater London during the past two years even interviews in prison have sometimes seemed a luxury due to many remand prisoners being kept in police cells. Thirdly, if applications for bail prove unsuccessful, time becomes of the essence, especially where the accused is to be tried on indictment. He may face many months in custody and, therefore, his solicitor's efforts must be geared towards being ready for trial as soon as possible and ensuring that the case is listed at an early date. Although there are possible advantages to the client in remaining in custody when he is guilty (time spent in custody will count towards any prison sentence he receives) there are none when he is innocent.

(5) Does the client have previous convictions?

There are three ways in which the existence of previous convictions may influence the proceedings.

Bail. If the client is in custody and the prosecution object to bail, his criminal record may well be put forward as a factor justifying his being kept in custody pending trial.

Trial. Whenever the client has previous convictions it will not be possible to put him forward as a man of good character or attack a prosecution witness or a co-accused without running the grave risk of falling foul of s $1(f)(ii)$ Criminal Evidence Act 1898. On the other hand if he is of good character not only may this be put forward as evidence of innocence, but cross-examination on credit is far more feasible

Sentence. Previous convictions may be relevant either where he is in breach of a suspended sentence or probation order or, in the case of motoring offences, where his previous endorsements render him liable to disqualification.

It is important therefore to ascertain whether or not his record poses problems. You should always, therefore, obtain a copy of his criminal record from the prosecution at as early a stage in the proceedings as possible.

(6) How is the client going to pay?

Many clients will be eligible for and receive legal aid to cover their representation. This may involve them in direct financial outlay in respect of their own legal fees (they may be required to make a contribution) and those of the prosecution (they may be ordered to pay the prosecution's costs wholly or in part if convicted). However, money (or rather lack of it) is nowhere near such a problem as when the accused is paying privately. Particular difficulties occur in those instances where, although the client protests his innocence, and is financially eligible, legal aid is refused because the offence is relatively minor. This is a common occurence where he is charged with a summary offence, especially a motoring offence. Difficult though it may be at times, all you can do is to advise the client as far as possible as to the likely cost.

3 TECHNIQUES OF PREPARATION

(1) The first interview with the client

As has already been shown, a defence solicitor may be involved in protecting the client's interests at the police station before he has even been charged. Characteristically, however, clients will have already been charged or have received a summons before a solicitor is consulted. The first meeting may take place in a variety of situations, not all of them conducive to taking adequate instructions. If the client is making his first appearance before the magistrates in police custody your first meeting will probably take place in a crowded cell beneath the court when all that can be done is to scribble down instructions for a bail application and fill in legal aid forms. If, on the other hand, the first appointment is at the office, a much more thorough interview can take place. Whatever the situation, your prime objectives should be as follows.

(a) **To obtain personal particulars.** Such matters as whether or not he has a fixed address, is employed or is married may be of particular importance if a bail application is to be made.

(b) **To obtain details of the charge.** It is remarkable how hazy clients often are about precisely what they have been charged with: phrases such as 'GBH', 'assault', 'drugs' and 'receiving' can cover a multitude of sins! If the initial interview is to be at the office the client should be told to bring the charge sheet/summons and any other relevant documents with him: it is surprising how often this is not done. If on the other hand he is in custody he should still have a copy of the charge sheet with him. It is also vital to know whether he is charged alone or with others and whether or not he faces other possible charges.

(c) **To recognise any potential conflict of interest.** The ethical position has already been outlined. It is important that when you are asked to act on behalf of more than one co-accused you seek out any potential conflict at as early a stage as possible.

(d) **To find out whether the client already has a solicitor or wishes to instruct someone else.** This is especially important for a Duty Solicitor since he is under a specific duty to make enquiries. In any event a solicitor should always avoid accusations of 'touting'.

(e) **To ascertain whether bail is an issue.** Often, this will speak for itself because the client will have already been released on police bail. If, however, sureties were required it is important that you confirm that they will be available to attend court when the client next appears. If, on the other hand, the client is in custody, much of your early effort will be towards securing his release on bail. Not surprisingly many clients will be more pre-occupied with getting bail than instructing a solicitor to prepare their defence. Your efforts to obtain bail will often be seen by the client as a crucial test of confidence.

(f) To obtain preliminary instructions. It may not be possible to advise a client fully as to plea or to take and prepare a full proof of evidence until much later in the proceedings. It is nevertheless important that you ask the client to outline his version of the events leading up to his being charged or summonsed, whether or not he has made a statement under caution or admitted guilt. Although final advice as to plea may well not be feasible, the sooner that you know in broad terms where your client stands the better.

(g) To consider legal aid. Legal aid should be applied for at the earliest possible moment. In addition, the client may be entitled to 'Green Form' Legal Advice and Assistance to cover the preliminary interview. The appropriate forms should always be completed without delay. A supply should always, therefore, be kept available.

(h) To find out whether he has any previous convictions. As has already been seen this may affect a number of important issues especially bail. Once again, clients are often very hazy about their 'form', especially if they have a long record. A copy of their record should therefore be sought without delay.

In view of the fact that the first meeting may be a hurried one it is advisable to have available a pro-forma instructions sheet. A suggested form appears at the end of this chapter as it would be completed by McCarthy's solicitor.

Relationship with the client

It is important from the very outset that the client gets the impression that you regard his case as being important—because it is (or should be) for both of you. In particular you should avoid being seen engaged in hearty banter with the police or court staff. After a short while in practice you will probably get to know the 'opposition' quite well and be on friendly terms with many of them. Nevertheless this can be most demoralising for the client who has spent a night in the cells. On the other hand, avoid identifying too closely with your client. Although being prosecuted is a stressful experience and may require the adoption of a supportive role on occasions, experienced criminal clients may try to exploit what they see as personal weakness.

Interviewing clients in prison

By the time you are instructed the client may already have appeared before the magistrates and been remanded in custody. It is important to follow the appropriate procedures when visiting a client in prison so as not to make matters more difficult than necessary. The prison authorities try so far as possible to give remand prisoners free access to their solicitor[2] but the need for security[3] and logistical problems of catering for so many prisoners and the multiplicity of requests for visits necessarily means that there are limits. You should always telephone in advance and arrange an appointment with

2 Prison Regulations 1964, reg 37(1) provides that the legal adviser (solicitor counsel or clerk) or a prisoner who is party to any legal proceedings shall be afforded reasonable facilities for interviewing him in connection with them, out of hearing, but in the sight of an officer. Furthermore an unconvicted prisoner may receive as many visits as he likes, subject to such limits as the Home Secretary Prescribed (ibid, reg 34(1)).

3 See *R v Secretary of State for the Home Department, ex p, McAvoy* [1984] 3 All ER 417.

the Prison Visits office. Normally, visits will be arranged between 9 am and 5 pm and will last for an hour. If, for any reason a longer period is required or a later time, because, for example, counsel will also be attending, the prison should be informed accordingly. When you attend you should always take a letter of introduction with you for production at the main gate otherwise you may be refused entry. Care should be taken not to infringe the provisions of the Prison Act 1952 or Prison Regulations 1964. In particular, you should never be party to the unauthorised smuggling in of tobacco or alcohol[4] or agree to bring in or take out a letter[5] (particularly dangerous since you may unwittingly become party to an attempt to pervert the course of justice). Any articles for the client should always be handed to the officer on duty. If the client wishes to give you written instructions or you have documents to give to him it is always wise to let the officer on duty know of this: you should also check the contents of anything given to you by the client before you leave. There is no restriction on solicitor/client correspondence, provided it relates to the proceedings in hand,[6] but the prison authorities may open it if they have reason to believe that it does not relate to the proceedings.[7]

(2) Preliminary tasks

Wherever the first interview has taken place you should now be in a position to ascertain what needs to be done next. There will usually be legal aid forms to submit and much time and effort may be directed towards applying for bail. You should not, however, lose sight of the fact that sooner or later your client will stand trial. You owe a duty to the court and to your client to prepare for trial as quickly as possible. Often the defence is not responsible for the delay; for example, the police will often not begin to interview witnesses until after they have charged the accused.[8] This is no excuse for sitting around doing nothing. At the very least you should contact the officer in charge of the case or the prosecuting solicitor and request the following information:

(a) a copy of the client's previous convictions (if any);
(b) a copy of any written records required to be kept under the Police and Criminal Evidence Act 1984 (for example custody record, stop and search record);
(c) a copy of any statement made under caution (or information regarding any tape recorded interviews);
(d) whether or not any further charges are likely;
(e) reasons for opposing bail (where the client is in custody); and
(f) details of the nature of the prosecution's case.

This should be sought at the earliest possible moment, in practice as soon as you are notified that legal aid has been granted or the client has put you in funds. You are entitled to receive items (a) to (c) and will usually obtain an answer on items (d) and (e) without any difficulty, but item (f) may pose problems (the prosecution's duties will be considered in detail in due course). Much will depend upon the attitude of the prosecutor. In many areas pro-

4 See Prison Act 1952, s 40 (punishable by up to 6 months' imprisonment and/or £400 fine).
5 See ibid, s 41 (punishable by fine of £400) and Prison Rules 1964, reg 85.
6 See ibid, reg 37A(1).
7 Ibid. Reference should also be made to the Prison Standing Orders. See LSG Digest (Jan-March 1985) p 4.
8 See 'Remands in Custody: Home Affairs Committee' (1983–4) HC 252-1, Vol I, para 25.

secution and defence have a sufficiently good working relationship that an outline of the case will readily be given. In others, early informal disclosure may not be forthcoming. In every case, however, it is up to the defence to seek it out.

(3) The client's proof of evidence

Experienced solicitors vary in their views as to the stage at which a detailed 'proof of evidence' should be taken from the client. A 'proof of evidence' is a written statement containing the relevant evidence and admissible that the client (or indeed, any other witness) will give. Some maintain that in cases where the prosecution evidence is to be disclosed in full prior to trial (which will always be the case in trial on indictment and may be so in certain summary trials) preparation of the proof should be left until this is available; others advise preparing the proof as soon as possible and amending it, where necessary, after the prosecution statements have been received. It is impossible to lay down any hard and fast rules. Where, for example, the charge is one of conspiracy to defraud, it may be impracticable to prepare a full proof until after the prosecution statements and exhibits have been received; on the other hand, in a summary case with no prior disclosure there may be no choice but to take a full proof straightaway. In the authors' view the sooner a solicitor can investigate his client's story the better: waiting for the prosecution to make the first move is timewasting and may result in important points being missed. The client needs to be interviewed in depth whilst his memory is still fresh although, if possible, the preliminary information referred to in the preceding section should be obtained first.

Everyone has their own style of obtaining proof from a client but the following points should always be borne in mind.

(a) **Allow sufficient time.** Even where the client is pleading guilty to a relatively minor offence, you will need to spend at least an hour taking down his explanation, his personal background and any other relevant matters to be put in mitigation. Where the client intends to plead 'not guilty' you must make doubly sure that you have sufficient time available to investigate the client's version of events. It is vital that you encourage your client to recall the events in question as accurately and vividly as possible. A rushed interview begets a badly prepared proof which in turn begets a badly prepared case.

(b) **Do not lead the client.** So far as possible you should elicit the client's version of events in the same way as if you were examining him in-chief. Where any documents are involved you should make sure that these are referred to and adequately explained. This approach is necessary for three reasons. First, circumstances will almost invariably require that the client elects to give evidence on his own behalf, in which case there will be no one to help him in the box. Secondly, his account must be entirely factual; one of the dangers of asking leading questions is that the questioner's own value judgments start to creep in. Thirdly, it is a solicitor's duty to remain entirely objective; there must never be any suggestion that you have, albeit unwittingly, put words into your client's mouth.

(c) **Do not allow anyone else to lead the client.** When representing certain clients, in particular juveniles, you may well have to cope with a well-meaning friend or parent. It may be very difficult (and in some cases undesirable) to persuade such a person that the client should be interviewed alone, but you must ensure that the account that you are given is not in any way influenced by third parties. Obtaining full instructions from young people may often prove difficult—they may see you as a symbol of authority and view you with suspicion—but you must ensure that you obtain *their* version of events unaided by outside influences.

(d) Probe the client's case for weaknesses or contradictions. Having obtained the client's 'story' you must not leave it there. One of the greatest shocks awaiting the inexperienced solicitor is seeing a client 'torn to pieces' in cross-examination due to a failure to anticipate the questions that would be put to him. Probing in this way requires tact as it is all too easy for the solicitor to give the impression that he has no confidence in his client's case but any contradiction or inconsistency, however innocent, may be pounced upon in cross-examination and produce a very bad impression. Many people have little idea of how great an ordeal exposure to cross-examination may be, and how a flustered appearance in the witness box can all too readily be misinterpreted as a sign of untruthfulness. Recent research[9] into trials in magistrates' courts suggests that a substantial proportion[10] of defendants will have their credibility attacked on the grounds that their evidence contains inconsistencies or is inherently improbable. Inconsistencies will need to be dealt with particularly carefully where the client has given a number of contradictory replies to the police or his story conflicts with that given in a written statement made by him. The improbability of the client's explanation will need careful probing where, for example, he maintains that he meant to pay for goods allegedly stolen but did not have sufficient money on him to pay for them. The effect of this exercise may, of course, be to so discredit your client's story that you are by no means convinced of his innocence. The ethical position in such circumstances has already been considered.

(e) Go carefully through any previous convictions. This has already been identified as one of the 'key issues'. If the client has previous convictions it is possible that these will be put to him in cross-examination with a view to undermining his credit if he 'throws away his shield' under $s1(f)(ii)$ or (iii) Criminal Evidence Act 1898. The details provided by the prosecution will not be sufficient. You must further ascertain whether or not he pleaded 'guilty' on previous occasions and whether or not he was represented: for example, if your client has always pleaded guilty before, this greatly limits the potential damage from 'throwing away his shield'.

(f) Look for good points. If a client has no previous convictions the opportunity to put him forward as a person of good character should not be wasted. Although as a strict matter of law the defence may only adduce evidence of his reputation rather than refer to any specific incidents, in practice, much latitude is allowed, so that details of the accused's career, background, family etc, can normally be allowed. Where the clients character is not spotless, but he has shown a willingness to reform over a number of years, serious thought should be given to putting the whole of his character in, good and bad: there is always a danger that sitting behind the 'shield' may do more harm than good because of the speculation it may create.

(g) Obtain further instructions on the prosecution statements. When a case is to be tried on indictment the defence will almost always

---

9 Home Office Research Study 71, supra, p 13 et seq.
10 53·7%.

receive copies of the prosecution witnesses' statements prior to committal. Within a few weeks of committal for trial they will also receive from the Crown Court written copies of all the prosecution witnesses' statements or depositions that were tendered at committal. Where the case is to be tried summarily the prosecution may be required to disclose its evidence in advance or do so voluntarily.[10a] In such cases you should go through the prosecution statements with the client very carefully noting his comments, taking particular care to deal with those areas in which there is a conflict with his original proof of evidence. The size of the case will largely influence the way in which these comments are set out. If the case is small, it may be possible to incorporate the client's comments into his existing proof and re-type it accordingly (a word processor makes this infinitely easier for all concerned). In larger cases involving substantial documentation the client's proof and his comments on the prosecution evidence may need to be drawn up in separate documents: it may well be advisable to obtain counsel's advice beforehand as to the format that he or she prefers. Having taken full instructions, the proof should be typed up in such a form as to leave adequate space for corrections and comments. A copy should then be sent to the client for his comments and alterations. Once it has been corrected he should be asked to sign and date it. This is important for two reasons. First to avoid any embarrassment should he subsequently change his instructions and second so that it may be admitted, if necessary, to rebut recent fabrication.

(4) Ensuring that the prosecution complies with its duties of disclosure

If the defence receives copies of the prosecution witnesses' statements in advance they will be able to:

1. evaluate the strengths and weaknesses of the case;
2. take detailed instructions from the client on areas of conflict;
3. prepare cross-examination in advance; and
4. consider other ways of refuting the prosecution case, for example, interviewing further witnesses, or drawing up plans.

As has already been seen, however, prior disclosure will only be automatic where an accused is to be tried on indictment or tried summarily for an indictable offence; in trials of summary offences much will depend on the nature of the case and the discretion of the prosecution authority. At present therefore there is no unified system of disclosure; the rules, such as they are, are based on a combination of statute, case law and rules of practice. They are best understood by breaking them down as follows:

(a) *information* the prosecution must disclose in every case;
(b) disclosure of the prosecution's *evidence* in summary trials;
(c) disclosure of the prosecution's *evidence* in trials on indictment;
(d) disclosure of *documents* and other exhibits.

(a) Information the prosecution must disclose in every case

Whether the trial is summary or on indictment the prosecution must always disclose:

(i) details of the accused's previous convictions;

10a This will depend upon whether the offence is indictable or summary only: see p 185, post.

   (ii) as a matter of practice, details of any co-accused's previous convictions if requested;

  (iii) details of any known convictions relating to a prosecution witness even where no request has been received from the defence;[11]

  (iv) previous inconsistent statements of prosecution witnesses;

   (v) details of witnesses whom the prosecution has interviewed but does not propose to call;

  (vi) details of any previous inconsistent description given by an identification witness.

Paragraph (iv), (v) and (vi) require further consideration. Under para. (iv), if the prosecution call a witness who gives evidence on a material issue that is inconsistent with an earlier statement in their possession, they must inform the defence of this inconsistency and give the defence a copy of that earlier inconsistent statement. Under para (v), whether the trial is summary[12] or on indictment the prosecution must supply particulars to the defence of any witness whom they do not propose to call but whom they know can give material evidence.[13] Until recently, however, it has not been entirely clear what particulars the defence are entitled to in the latter case. It was suggested by Lord Denning MR[14] that the duty of the prosecution went beyond supplying names and addresses and required them to supply the defence with a copy of any statement taken from the witness but, until recently, the extent of disclosure been left to the discretion of the prosecutor. Some would supply copies of unused witnesses' statements on request unless there were compelling reasons for not doing so, whereas others would only agree to disclosure, if at all, on a counsel to counsel basis. The position relating to trials on indictment has now been regularised by a Practice Note issued by the Attorney General[15] which provides, inter alia, that all 'unused material'[16] should normally be made available to the defence solicitor if it has a bearing on the offence charged and the surrounding circumstances of the case unless, broadly:

   (i) there are grounds for fearing that disclosure might lead to the witness being interfered with; or

  (ii) the statement may be needed by the prosecution for cross-examination should the witness be called by the defence; or

  (iii) the statement is to a greater or lesser extent 'sensitive' and it is not in the public interest to disclose it.

The Practice Note, which should be consulted in cases of doubt, gives numerous examples of situations falling within categories (ii) and (iii) above, for example, material may be 'sensitive' if it deals with national security, discloses the identity of an informant or it might leave the witness open to assault, or it contains details of private delicacy which might create a risk of domestic strife. The Note does, however, require any doubt to be resolved in

11 *R v Collister and Warhurst* (1955) 39 Cr App Rep 100, CCA.

12 *R v Leyland Justices ex p Hawthorn,* op cit.

13 *R v Bryant and Dickson* (1946) 110 JP 267, CCA.

14 *Dallison v Caffery* [1965] 1 QB 348, CA.

15 [1982] 1 All ER 734.

16 Defined as including '(i) all witness statements and documents which are not included in the committal bundle served on the defence; (ii) the statements of any witnesses who are to be called to give evidence at committal and (if not in the bundle) any documents referred to therein; (iii) the unedited version(s) of any edited statements or composite statement included in the committal bundle'.

favour of disclosure and suggests means whereby partial disclosure may be allowed where only part of the statement is 'sensitive'. Such disclosure as there is should normally take place before committal unless this would cause delay and is unlikely to influence the committal, in which case it should be done as soon as possible thereafter. The importance of this Practice Note cannot be over estimated and compliance with it should always be ensured by the writing of an appropriate letter (sometimes known as a '*Bryant letter*') to the prosecution requesting the appropriate material. There are no guide-lines for summary trials, but it is suggested that the same procedure should be followed where practicable.

Turning finally to para (vi), this is probably the most important aspect of the 'Turnbull guidelines' and yet is the one given the least prominence. If you were not at the identification parade this information should be sought at the earliest opportunity. The original description given by a witness will be bound to have been recorded somewhere, for example, in an officer's notebook thus appropriate enquiries may be of crucial importance.

(*b*) *Disclosure of the prosecution evidence in summary trials*

The crucial factor since 20 May 1985 is whether or not the offence is sum-mary or triable either way. In the case of either way offences the prosecutor must *on request* provide the accused or his representative with either (i) a copy of those parts of any written statement made by a witness on whose evidence the prosecutor proposes to rely, or (ii) a *summary* of all those facts which the prosecutor proposes to adduce in evidence.[17] Conversely, with summary only offences one is dependent upon the discretion of the prosecu-tor. In such cases the best that can be obtained is a brief outline of the prosecution case although certain magistrates' courts still hold 'pre-trial reviews' at which the nature of the prosecution case will be discussed infor-mally with the defence solicitor who will be given sight of the prosecution's witnesses' statements. Irrespective of the category of offence the prosecution may also serve a witness's statement under Criminal Justice Act 1967, s 9 with a view to it being read out at the trial. This procedure tends, however, to be reserved for non-controversial witnesses, for example, police officers in road traffic cases whose evidence is of a formal nature.

(*c*) *Disclosure of the prosecution evidence in trials on indictment*

The vast majority of committals take place without consideration of the evidence and accordingly the vast bulk if not all of the prosecution's evidence will be served on the defence prior to committal in the form of statements complying with s 102 of the Magistrates' Courts Act 1980. The only excep-tions will be those witnesses whom the prosecution intend to call to give oral evidence or those witnesses whose evidence is not tendered at committal. Where appropriate, however, the defence should request further information. It may be, for example, that the 'section 102' statement that is tendered at committal is not the first statement taken from the witness but an 'edited'

---

17 Magistrates' Courts (Advance Information) Rules 1985, r 4. Note in particular that (i) the accused must be given a written notice explaining r4 as soon after charge as practicable, (ii) the duty only exists so long as the mode of trial decision has not been taken, and (iii) the prosecutor may refuse to comply with such request if he considers it might lead to intimi-dation of a witness (r5).

version excluding inadmissible or prejudicial material.[18] It may be of crucial importance to see the unedited statement prior to committal or at any rate before trial.[19] Such prior statements are, of course, now within the category of 'unused material' and therefore can be sought under the provisions of the Attorney General's Practice Note.

Notices of Further Evidence. After committal, the defence will receive, copies of all the evidence tendered at committal including the written depositions of any witnesses who gave oral evidence. In addition, they will receive, where relevant, copies of 'unused material'. However, the prosecution is not restricted at the trial to calling only those witnesses whose evidence was tendered at committal. It may be, for example, that further witnesses come forward to give material evidence. Whenever this occurs the prosecution as a matter of practice[20] will serve a copy of the relevant witness's statement on the defence prior to the trial. Such a statement will usually be drawn up in 'section 9' form and will have annexed to it a Notice of Additional Evidence. To sum up, therefore, the defence will see in advance the statement of every witness that the prosecution proposes to call.

(d) Disclosure of documents and other exhibits

The prosecution may wish to rely on a variety of exhibits as part of its case. The most common will be statements under caution of the accused, photographs and plans. The potential variety of exhibits is nevertheless infinite; for example, in a major fraud case there may be many hundreds of pages containing extracts from books of accounts, correspondence and schedules prepared by the prosecution to simplify the issues or illustrate 'system'. Exhibits may also consist of a variety of items of 'real evidence' such as weapons, stolen goods and articles of clothing. Exhibits will normally remain in the custody of the prosecutor until the trial, although the court can impose such restrictions as it considers proper. If it does not do so, however, the prosecution may deal with the exhibits in such manner as appears best for the purposes of justice and is under no obligation to apply to the court for directions.[1]

(i) Summary trials. There appears to be a dearth of authority as to the duties of the prosecutor. The only situation in which a prosecutor will be obliged to disclose any exhibit upon which he intends to rely is when it is referred to in any statement tendered under s 9 of the Criminal Justice Act 1967:[2] the only other documents that the defence can ask for as of right is a copy of the client's (and as a matter of practice, any co-accuseds') statements under caution and records kept under the Police and Criminal Evidence Act 1984. In addition, they will be entitled to information relating to any tape-

---

18 A *Practice Note* [1969] 3 All ER 1033, CA requires the editing to normally be done by the legal representative of the prosecutor and not by a police officer.

19 For an example of a case where such prior statements were not disclosed although of crucial importance, see 'Report of Fisher Inquiry into the death of Maxwell Confait' HC HMSO 1977.

20 There appears to be no common law or statutory requirement obliging the prosecution to do this but it is a practice that is invariably followed.

1 *R v Lambeth Metropolitan Stipendiary Magistrate, ex P McComb* [1983] QB 551.

2 Criminal Justice Act 1967, s 9(3)(c) which requires a copy of any document referred to as an exhibit to be served along with the statement giving such information as may be necessary to enable the party on whom it is served to inspect that document or a copy thereof. Note that similar rules now apply to any document referred to in material disclosed under the Magistrates' Courts (Advance Information) Rules 1985: ibid, r 4(3).

recorded interview.[3] It is submitted, however, that you should ask the prosecution, where appropriate, whether there are any exhibits upon which they intend to rely, specifying their nature, and asking for facilities to inspect. This is particularly important in certain categories of case, for example, public order offences, if there is any likelihood that the prosecution will rely upon video recordings taken at the scene of the disturbance.[4] If facilities for inspection are refused in such a case the defence should apply for an adjournment. It may also be necessary on occasions to ask for facilities to inspect police equipment such as a Lion Intoximeter 3000 for possible malfunction. Facilities will usually be granted, but failing this the defence should consider applying for a witness summons. It has recently been held, however, that a witness summons should not be used as a means of obtaining general discovery, or of going on a 'fishing expedition' for material to be used in cross-examination.[5] It will be necessary, therefore, to be able to identify the material sought with some precision and show that it is, 'likely to be material evidence.'[5]

(ii) Trials on indictment. Copies of any documentary exhibits upon which the prosecution intends to rely will normally be served with the papers prior to committal.[6] In any event 'real' exhibits will usually be referred to in the body of the prosecution's witness statements and will be listed in a separate schedule served with the committal documents. After committal the exhibits will normally remain in the control of the prosecution until trial, as already noted. It is important to peruse the schedule of exhibits carefully and consider carefully the use to which the prosecution intends to put them, particularly where they are referred to in the statement of an expert witness.[7]

(iii) Other documents and things. What is the position where the prosecution have in their possession documents or things which they do not intend to tender in evidence? There appears to be little authority: documents and things do not come within the definition of 'unused material' in the Attorney General's Practice Note referred to above. Although it is not for a moment suggested that the defence should harass the prosecution at every turn, there may be cases where further information should be sought. A witness summons directed to the Chief Officer of Police could be considered as a last resort.[8] Particular problems may arise where an inquiry needs to be conducted into the observance of one of the Codes of Practice. As has already been seen the accused is entitled to copies of certain documents under the provisions of the Police and Criminal Evidence Act 1984, for example, copies

3 See Roberts, 'Tape Recordings, The Questioning of Suspects in the Field, Trial Guidelines' (1983) Law Society's Gazette, 26 October, p 2660.
4 See for example *Kajala v Noble* (1982) 75 Cr App Rep 149 (use of video recording of BBC News Programme used to identify accused). *R v Fowden and White* [1982] Crim LR 588 and *R v Grimer* (1982) 126 Sol Jo 641, CR (both cases concerned video recordings of shoplifting). See also *R v Dodson* [1984] 1 WLR 971 (photographs of robbery taken by automatic camera).
5 See *R v Crown Court at Manchester, ex p Williams* and *R v Skegness Magistrates' Court, ex p Cardy* [1985] RTR 49 and *R v Coventry Magistrates' Court, ex p Perks* [1985] RTR 74. Note however that in *Ex p Williams* (supra) Goff LJ suggested that where access was sought to the log and memory roll of a *specific* device, this should be disclosed voluntarily; see further p 190, ante.
6 Magistrates Courts Act 1980, s 102(3)(c) contains similar provisions to those in s 9 of the Criminal Justice Act 1967, supra.
7 The need to do so has been illustrated in a number of recent cases see eg *Preece v H M Advocate* [1981] Crim LR 783. For an interesting discussion as to the background of this see Expert Evidence in the light of *Preece v HM Advocate*: Brownlee, Med Sci Law (1982) Vol 22 No 4, p 237 et seq.
8 Once again, this is subject to the restrictions considered ante. See note 5, supra.

of any 'stop and search record' and extracts from his 'custody record'.[9] It may sometimes be necessary, however, to call for facilities to conduct a more wide ranging examination of the documentation contained at the relevant police station. In this context the dicta of Watkins LJ in *R v Hackney*[10] should be borne in mind:

> 'Records kept at police stations of the activities of persons in custody and of property obtained from them should, of course, be accurate ... Any enquiry into the completeness and accuracy of these records will often entail the questioning of many police officers in respect of one person in custody, with the result, no doubt, that in all but a very few cases, no dishonest conduct will be revealed and little, if any, neglect of duty ... The prosecution do not have to produce [these records] without some notice which allows them proper opportunity of proving and ex- plaining their contents by the evidence of officers who actually made the records ... When deciding what use, if any, should be made of such documents, the judge should take account of whether the defence before the trial began, could have given notice to the prosecution for the production of the documents so that proper steps could have been, at the outset of the trial, taken for production not only of the documents, but also to enable witnesses properly to inform the jury about the contents of them.'[11]

Conclusion

The rules as to disclosure are at present inconsistent and unnecessarily com- plicated. It is, however, of vital importance that the defence elicits as much information as it possibly can: on occasions persons have been wrongly con- victed because their solicitor failed to follow through this aspect of the case.

(5) Other defence tasks

There are a number of other matters to which the defence solicitor will need to give attention. Cases will vary in their seriousness or complexity but however large or small, some (or all) of the following matters need to be considered, at any rate on a not guilty plea.

(a) Other defence witnesses

Recent research suggests that in the majority of cases, the magistrates or the jury are left solely with the accused's word against the weight of the prose- cution evidence. Recent research[12] has found that:

> 'witnesses were called to corroborate the defendants' accounts in respect of only 27% (102) of charges on which the court found a case for the defence to answer. On the remainder of charges defendants relied on their own assertions of inno- cence. There were alibi witnesses in respect of half the charges which the defen- dants disputed on the grounds that they were absent from the scene but only a quarter of defendants who admitted having been present while denying the act or intent called witnesses to bear out their account of events.'

The availability of defence witnesses may therefore be crucial especially if they are independent and of good character.

---

9 For an interesting summary of police documentation pre 1984 Act, see 'Policing London' (GLC) No 15 (Nov/Dec) p8.
10 (1982) 74 Cr App Rep 194.
11 Ibid at 198.
12 'Contested Trials in the Magistrates' Courts' (op cit) at p 15.

Tracing witnesses. Always ask your client to provide names and addresses of possible witnesses. If he is unable to do so, do not leave it there. Appeals to the local newspaper may sometimes produce results. Also consider an enquiry agent. Good and reputable enquiry agents are worth their weight in gold. One cannot be expected to trace or interview every witness without assistance; a good enquiry agent, especially if he is an ex-police officer, will often be far more skilled at undertaking this task in any event.

Interviewing witnesses. Many people are frightened of going to court and are likely to be put off by a solicitor's letter inviting them to come to the office. Interviews should take place in surroundings convenient to the witness rather than the solicitor. Again, a good enquiry agent is invaluable since he or she will often be experienced at the preparation of proofs of evidence and will be able to undertake the task unsupervised, provided adequate instructions are given. Where the witness can give vital evidence, however, it is unwise to rely solely upon a statement taken by an enquiry agent. The witness should also be interviewed either by the solicitor himself or a competent member of his staff and be subjected as politely as possible to the same cross-examination process as his own client. Whoever interviews a witness, the following crucial points always need to be covered.

(*i*) *Check whether the witness has any previous convictions.* This requires tact but is an enquiry which must be made. The prosecution is entitled to cross-examine on credit, and the unexpected revelation of convictions may be very damaging.

(*ii*) *Confirm that the witness has not already given a statement to the police.* It may be, for one reason or another, that you have not yet been supplied with '*Bryant*' particulars. It is always dangerous to proceed further without following the safeguards considered earlier.

(*iii*) *Take care with friends and relatives.* Their evidence should be probed especially carefully since there is always the risk that they are coming forward to give evidence through misguided loyalty. You must be particularly on your guard if the account that they give conforms precisely with that given by the client.

(*iv*) *In no circumstances should the client be present at the interview.* When he is in custody you should endeavour where feasible to interview the witness before the witness has had an oportunity to visit the client in prison, to avoid suggestions of collusion.

(*v*) *Probe the evidence carefully.* A discredited defence witness is worse than no witness at all. It is quite acceptable and indeed consistent with truthfulness, that there will be discrepancies on small points of detail; nevertheless great care is required. For example, it is all too easy to get carried away because part of a witness's evidence favours a client and overlooks that another part of it damns him. Alibi witnesses can be particularly dangerous. Not only must they be tied, as tightly as possible, to the relevant time and place but in addition must be asked why it is, for example, that they are so certain that they were with the accused on *6th* and not 7th August. If this is not done there is always a danger that their evidence will be torn to shreds at the trial with potentially disastrous consequences.

(*vi*) *Always take a written proof and ask the witness to sign and date it.* This is important for three reasons. First, because if the witness departs from his proof in court it will be much easier to obtain leave to have him treated as 'hostile', secondly, the proof of evidence will be admissible to rebut any suggestion of recent fabrication, and thirdly, the statement may be admissible under s 68 of the Police and Criminal Evidence Act 1984 if, for example, the witness dies or disappears before the trial.

Getting witnesses to court. Many witnesses will not be particularly happy at the prospect of going to court. One of the defence solicitor's most important tasks is to put them at ease and explain to them just how important it is that they come to court to give evidence. What, however, if they remain unwilling? As a general rule it is possible (but not always advisable) to obtain an order compelling their attendance. The rules as to the issue of witness summonses in the magistrates' court and Crown Court differ and must now be considered separately.

(*i*) *Proceedings before a magistrates' court.* Application may be made to a magistrate or clerk to the justices for a witness summons on the ground that a person in England or Wales is likely to be able to give material evidence or produce any document or thing likely to be material evidence either at a summary trial or committal proceedings, *and* that he is unlikely to attend unless an order is made.[13] Practice varies from court to court but it is normal in the first instance to apply by letter. The most notable feature is the need to establish that the witness will not otherwise voluntarily attend. It is not therefore possible as in the Crown Court or in civil proceedings to apply for a witness summons or subpoena as of right. If it is issued, service of the summons will normally be effected by the police although you can ask to serve it yourself. The summons must be served on the witness either personally or by leaving it for him with some person at his last known or usual place of abode[14] along with a reasonable sum for his expenses in getting to court ('conduct money'). If the witness does not then attend, the court may issue a warrant for his arrest on being satisfied on oath:

- that he is likely to be able to give material evidence etc.;
- that he has been duly served with the summons and conduct money; and
- it appears to the court that there is no just excuse for his failure to attend.

'Swearing out' a warrant in these circumstances would be a last resort since if he gives evidence under duress the witness will probably be hostile. Although you may obtain leave to cross-examine him on his prior inconsistent statement, that statement is not evidence in the case and may only be used to attack his credibility.[15]

(*ii*) *Proceedings in the Crown Court.* Witnesses who give evidence or whose statements are tendered at committal proceedings will automatically be made the subject of either a full or conditional *witness order* (these terms are explained fully in chapter 11). It is most unlikely, however, that defence evidence of any kind will be tendered at committal proceedings, and, therefore, defence witnesses will need to be dealt with independently. Unlike a magistrates' court a witness summons may be issued requiring the attendance of a witness or the production of any document or thing without the need to

13 1980 Act, s 97(1). There is, therefore, no power to require production of a document purely for the purposes of cross-examination: it must be capable of being adduced in evidence of its own right; see *R v Cheltenham Justices, ex p Secretary of State for Trade* [1977] 1 All ER 460, DC.

14 Magistrates' Courts Rules 1981, r 99(1) and (6): service is thus not possible by post.

15 If the witness refuses to be sworn or give evidence he may be committed to custody for a period of up to one month and/or fined £1,000: 1980 Act, s 97(4).

satisfy any other requirement.[16] It is therefore a wise precaution to apply for the issue of witness summonses as a matter of course. Application is normally made by letter to the 'branch' of the Crown Court to which the accused has been committed to stand trial giving the full names and addresses of the persons in respect of whom witness summonses are required. The summonses will be issued and returned to the defence solicitor for service. They should be served on the witnesses personally. Conduct money is not normally served since the witness is entitled to recoup his daily travelling expenses from the Crown Court office. The Crown Court has power to issue a warrant if it is satisfied, on oath, that the witness is unlikely to comply with the summons or if it is satisfied that there are reasonable grounds for believing that he has failed to attend without just excuse.[17]

Use of Criminal Justice Act 1967, s 9. Persuading an unwilling witness to come to court requires tact and careful appreciation of the consequences of the potential disadvantages of compulsion. A way round this difficulty is to serve the witness's evidence in the form of a 'section 9' statement. Although this section is frequently used by the prosecution, it is equally available to the defence both in summary trials and trials on indictment. If the witness's evidence is likely to be non contentious this possibility should always be considered. Care must, however, be taken to ensure that the statement is in the correct form and that it does not contain any inadmissible or prejudicial material. It can, of course, only contain such testimony as would be admissible if the witness gave oral evidence.

(b) Expert witnesses

In the case of expert or technological evidence the prosecution has three major advantages. First, it has at its disposal a sophisticated range of technological hardware to aid it in crime detection[18] and the Metropolitan Police and Home Office Forensic Science Laboratories can provide expert evidence on matters such as pathology, handwriting, poisons, fingerprints, firearms, tyre marks, blood stains and contact traces. There is no similar general facility[18a] available to the defence who must make use of such limited private facilities as are available. Secondly, even if a defence expert can be found he or she will always be instructed at a relatively late stage and will thus be unable to visit the undisturbed scene of the crime or have an opportunity to be present, for example, at the original post mortem examination. Thirdly, very few solicitors possess the competence to analyse and evaluate prosecution forensic evidence. They will frequently therefore fail to appreciate the need for instructing their own expert let alone know where to look for one. In his article on *Preece v HM Advocate* Brownlee stated:

'Perhaps the most important lesson to be learned from the *Preece* case is that solicitors must diligently carry out their functions and grapple with scientific evidence. It is not enough to concentrate on the lay evidence and hope that the scientific evidence will go away. It is vital that solicitors are alert to both what is

---

16 Criminal Procedure (Attendance of Witnesses) Act 1965, s 2. The witness may however apply for a direction that the summons shall be of no effect if satisfied by the person to whom the summons was issued that he cannot give material evidence or produce the document required: ibid, s 2.
17 Ibid, s 4(1) and (2).
18 See HD Walton, 'Some Recent Advances in Police Technology', Med Sci Law (1982) Vol 22, No 1, p 2.
18a They may use the facilities of the Metropolitan Police and Home Office Laboratories but only on condition that the findings are made known to the prosecution.

said in evidence and what is not said. If solicitors fail to follow the import of the expert evidence and fail to have it thoroughly tested all sorts of injustices may follow for their clients, for the court and even for the expert. As the Ormrod Committee noted (Report of the Committee on Legal Education Cmnd 4595 (HMSO) 1971, para 96) there is much to be done in the area of improving the education of solicitors in the techniques of understanding and dealing with such technical evidence.'[19]

It is essential, therefore, that solicitors have some working knowledge of forensic science. The British Academy of Forensic Science and the Medico-Legal Society are two organisations which you should seriously consider joining. The British Academy's Journal 'Medicine, Science and the Law' frequently publishes articles of considerable general use to the criminal lawyer.

The need to consult an expert may arise in a variety of circumstances, for example, if acting in a murder case, you should always request a copy of the pathologist's report from the Coroner, and, if necessary, instruct your own expert to conduct an autopsy. Similarly, whenever there is medico-legal or technological evidence be it the read out from a Lion Intoximeter 3000, tape recorded evidence, or blood stains you should always consider the scientific aspect. If the client is legally aided you will be well advised, however, to obtain authority from the Criminal Legal Aid Committee before doing so.

Finding an expert is perhaps the most difficult task. Your colleagues or counsel may be able to help. Failing this the British Academy of Forensic Science, or your local Medico-Legal Association or the Contentious Business Department of the Law Society may be of assistance. You should always ensure, however, that you are satisfied that the witness is of sufficient status and experience (particularly in giving evidence before a court of law) and that his opinion, if it is of use, will stand up to cross-examination. It should always be borne in mind that an expert, although retained by the defence owes a higher duty to scientific objectivity; his or her evidence would be valueless otherwise. It is vital, therefore, that all the available material, favourable and unfavourable is placed before the expert and s/he is told very clearly the areas in which assistance is being sought. The areas of assistance on which expert advice may be sought are broadly threefold, namely:

(i) to point out weaknesses in the prosecution evidence and thus provide material for cross-examination;
(ii) to give expert testimony; and
(iii) to draw your attention to possible further avenues of enquiry.

In order to fulfil these requirements the expert must be instructed as fully as possible.

Another situation in which the possible need for expert evidence should not be overlooked is where it is suspected that the accused is suffering from some psychiatric disorder which may be relevant to his fitness to plead, to the issue of guilt, or to the likely sentence. Although such a need will arise

19 Brownlee: 'Expert Evidence in the Light of *Preece v H M Advocate*' Med Sci Law (1982) Vol 22 No 4, p 237 at p 243: 'Preece was convicted largely on forensic evidence that matched his blood group with bloodstains found on the victim's clothing. It only emerged after his conviction that both the accused and the victim had the same blood group (Group A) and that they were both probably secretors.

most obviously in murder cases, all kinds of offences may throw up a psychiatric element.

(c) Instructing counsel

Choice of the right counsel is crucial. If the client is to be tried on indictment counsel will have to be instructed for the trial and legal aid will cover this. Where the proceedings are before the magistrates' court, however (be it summary trial or committal proceedings) legal aid will rarely be extended to cover counsel, although there is nothing to prevent you from instructing one. Use of counsel in a magistrates' court should in any event be reserved for cases of exceptional complexity or gravity or where the client, who is paying privately, insists upon it. Where counsel is to be instructed it is of vital importance that the one selected is sufficiently experienced in the relevant type of work. Experience will soon tell you those counsel who can safely be used, but in cases of doubt the matter should be discussed with colleagues. It is particularly important that you should be satisfied as to the quality of other counsel in chambers since it is by no means uncommon for the counsel of your choice to be unavailable at the last moment because he or she is still engaged in another trial. If a set of chambers has been selected where there are several other members of equal standing it is much easier to agree to a substitute at the last moment rather than insisting on the return of the brief. In a substantial case it may be necessary to consider instructing leading counsel; if so, junior counsel's advice should always be sought. If the client is paying privately 'taking in a leader' will add massively to the cost and it is something which must be discussed with him very carefully. Where the client is legally aided there is no power to authorise leading counsel for proceedings before the magistrates. In the Crown Court authority must normally be sought by application to a judge after committal (magistrates may only authorise two counsel in charges of murder).

Unlike civil cases, it is not normal to instruct counsel so frequently on 'interlocutory' matters. At least one conference should nevertheless always be held prior to a trial on indictment and to this end counsel must be adequately instructed. In a complex or serious case it may be necessary to arrange a conference prior to committal and several conferences thereafter: in addition counsel's written advice on evidence may need to be sought.

(d) Preparing schedules

In complicated cases, for example major frauds, the prosecution may itself prepare detailed schedules setting out the individual frauds alleged in the conspiracy and the amounts involved with cross-references to the relevant exhibits. As far as the defence is concerned, however, such schedules are rarely prepared but can often prove invaluable. In all but the simplest of cases you should set out in chronological order the major events relating to the offences charged. This will give a much clearer picture of the time scale involved and is of particular use:

(i)   as an aid in cross-examination (it will be much easier to seize on any discrepancies in the prosecution evidence);
(ii) as a means of testing an alibi defence; and

   (iii) in cases where there is a disputed confession (it will be possible to note sequentially the events leading up to the accused's admission of guilt).

Where the case is to be tried on indictment, it will be possible to build up a schedule on the basis of the prosecution's evidence as disclosed at committal. Depending on the complexity of the case, this may be kept separate or incorporated into your existing schedule, in any event it will be of considerable assistance both to you and to counsel.

(e) *Visiting the scene and taking photographs*

Unfortunately, lack of time will often prevent you from visiting the scene as often as you would like, but it should always be considered, especially where the layout is material, for example in cases involving disputed identification. If there is time for nothing else, you should always try to visit the scene on the way to court when representing the client on a motoring offence arising out of an accident. Preparation of photographs and plans should also always be considered in cases of disputed identity or where there is a serious dispute between prosecution and defence as to the events that took place. Ideally you yourself should visit the scene and take any necessary photographs, time permitting, since it is you who will be conducting cross-examination or instructing counsel. Failing this, however, an enquiry agent may again be employed. Technically, if photographs are to be admitted in evidence, they must be proved by the person who took them coming to court, giving formal evidence on oath of the taking of the photographs, producing the unretouched negatives and identifying the prints. Generally, however, it should be possible to serve the photographer's statement, along with a set of prints under s 9 of the Criminal Justice Act 1967.

(f) *Material for mitigation*

Even if your client vehemently protests his innocence you should always bear in mind the unthinkable: he may be convicted. Preparing for a speech in mitigation is a skill all of its own which is considered in later chapters. Nevertheless, it should not be overlooked in the rush of enthusiasm to prepare the client's defence.

4 APPEARING IN COURT

Advocacy is a specialised skill which can only be acquired through practice and observation. It is also a skill with many parts each requiring a different approach. The solicitor's abilities as an advocate will need to be exercised in:

   – applying for bail;
   – representing accused in summary trials;
   – conducting committal proceedings; and
   – mitigating on behalf of guilty defendants.

In each case the objectives and therefore the emphasis is different, but thorough preparation is always the key to success. Each of the above aspects of advocacy will be considered in later chapters but the following general rules should always be observed.

(1) Always arrive on time

Obviously enough, a solicitor who arrives late and is flustered is less likely to do justice to his client's case and may incur the court's displeasure. Equally important, the client will be most unimpressed at his apparent lack of commitment. In addition, if the solicitor is not present, it is not unknown for the investigating officer to discuss the case 'informally' with the client. This may not always be in his interests.

(2) Be familiar with the court

You should get to know your local magistrates' court, who the magistrates are, their particular foibles and any idiosyncracies of practice adopted by the clerk. When appearing before a court for the first time you should always arrive early enough to be able to observe a few cases to see how the court operates.

(3) Familiarise the client with the court

You should make sure that if your client is on bail the need to arrive on time is impressed upon him. In addition, you should tell him what to do and where to go when he arrives and explain what is going to happen.

(4) Make sure that papers are in order

If the file is a mess, you are less likely to be able to put your client's case effectively. You may have to think very quickly on your feet; everything must therefore be at hand. If you propose to argue a point of law you should make sure that you have authorities available: if you wish to refer to case law, copies of the relevant reports should be available for the court and your opponent (and they should be thoroughly read beforehand).

(5) Dress smartly and be courteous at all times

This may sound pompous but it is nevertheless important. Like it or not, if the bench find *you* acceptable they are more likely to find your arguments acceptable. Slovenly dress or discourtesy may enhance your sense of 'street credibility' but it will not benefit your client in any way.

(6) Be ready to learn from others

If ever you can afford the time, you should try to observe experienced advocates in action and endeavour to analyse what it is that makes them effective. It may be that their style would not particularly suit you (so much of the art of advocacy is presenting yourself in a way that is agreeable to the court), but there will always be something useful that can be learned.

At the end of the day, however, the thing that is needed most is practice. Unfortunately, advocates are expected to learn by bitter experience, often at their client's expense, but if you follow the above rules you should at least minimise your mistakes.[20]

---

20 For further instruction see Chatelier, *Criminal Advocacy in the Magistrates' Court*: (Barry Rose) and McEvans, *Advocacy at the Bar* (Financial Training).

5 PRACTICAL EXAMPLES

(1) Police v Duncan McCarthy (case 1)

[As will be recalled from chapter 1, McCARTHY is arrested on *5 August*, and brought before the court next morning. He is seen by the court duty solicitor who unsuccessfully applies for bail on his behalf. He nevertheless asks her to continue to act for him and she applies for and is granted legal aid for this purpose. He is remanded in custody until *13 August* on which date (see chapter 7) his solicitor applies for bail which is granted. Proceedings are adjourned until *1 September* on which date mode of trial proceedings are held at which the accused refuses to consent to summary trial. On the same day he is committed to the Crown Court to stand trial (transcripts of the mode of trial and committal proceedings appear in chapters 8 and 11 respectively).]

McCARTHY's solicitor has taken the following preliminary steps.

(a) *At court* on *6 August*: she has completed a prelimary questionnaire as far as possible.

(b) *Between 6 and 13 August*: she has:

   (i) spoken to McCARTHY's sister to confirm that she will attend court to stand surety;

  (ii) contacted the officer in charge of the case to ascertain whether he intends to continue opposing bail and to try and find out the nature of the prosecution case;

 (iii) contacted McCARTHY's employers and obtained confirmation that he is to be suspended pending the outcome of the prosecution;

 (iv) (in a perfect world) visited McCARTHY in prison to obtain preliminary instructions, discuss mode of trial and possible witnesses to be followed up.

(c) *Between 13 August and 1 September*: she will make an appointment for McCARTHY to visit the office, a full preliminary proof of evidence will be obtained along the lines considered ante. During the same period she will consider most of the preparatory matters which appear from the previous section eg is it necessary to obtain a plan of the hospital grounds, to examine the scene of the break-in, contact possible witnesses? During the course of this period, the prosecution statements are served with a view to committal without consideration of the evidence. Ideally, she will arrange for a further short interview with him prior to committal at which the options are discussed and any further matters of importance arising from the committal statements will be covered.

(d) *1 September*: McCARTHY elects for trial on indictment and is committed for trial without consideration of the evidence under s 6(2) of the Magistrates' Courts' Act 1980. McCARTHY will again attend the office for interview at which a further amended proof of evidence will be taken incorporating his comments on the prosecution witness statements. (The final stages of preparation including briefing counsel are be dealt with in chapter 11.)

(2) Police v Mary ADAMS (case 3)

Having received the summons Mary ADAMS attends a solicitor's office taking the summons with her. Having considered the various options open to her she insists on pleading 'not guilty'. Although he does not hold out much chance of success her solicitor applies for legal aid which is refused. He informs her of this and she agrees to pay privately and pays him a sum on account. Her solicitor then writes to the court and the prosecuting police officer intimating that a plea of not guilty is intended and requests that the case be adjourned accordingly. (This will normally be done as a matter of course.) The new hearing date is fixed and she and her solicitor are informed of this by the court office. Her solicitor then makes a further appointment at which a detailed proof of evidence is obtained going carefully through, so far as possible, the circumstances of the accident having (ideally) visited the scene beforehand. At this stage the possibility and need for photographs will have to be considered along with the attendant extra expense.

(The course of Mary ADAMS trial and matters that may arise thereon are considered further in chapter 9.)

CLIENT RECORD SHEET

Fee earner's ref: AB/9690   Partner responsible: Alison Brown
First contact from: Duty Solicitor   Date: 6.8.8- Time: 9.45 a.m.
Instructions from Client/Other   Date: Time:

1. CLIENT'S PERSONAL PARTICULARS
   Surname: McCarthy   Full forenames: Duncan
   Date of birth: 9.6.6-   Place: Not known
   Present address: 11 Inkerman Terrace, Weyford
   Telephone: —   Work: not applicable
   How long living at address: approx 9 mths Owner/occupier; Tenant; Parents
   Any other address for contact: No
   Marital status: married Spouse name: Tina   Occupation: not working

2. CALLER'S DETAILS
   (i) Name: not applicable   (ii) Address
   (ii) Telephone no.:   (iv) Relationship to client:

3. PRESENT CHARGE(S):
   Indictable only/summary only/either way Mode of trial On indictment
   Probable plea: not guilty   Any other charges likely? No
   Any co-accused: No   Name of co-accused's
                               representative: N/A
   Officer in charge of case: D.S. Forsyth Telephone No: N/A
   Was statement made to police? No
   If yes: which police station? N/A
   Any convictions? Yes   Details: Date: Court: Penalty: Offence
   Prosecuting Solicitors: Blankshire Telephone No: Reference:
                           County

4. BAIL: Accused in custody/on bail   Bail details: N/A
   Where in custody Grisley Remand Centre Objections to bail: Abscond/further offences
   Possible sureties: Name   Address   Occupation Criminal
                                                            Record?
   1. Irene Johnstone   3 Cardigan Ave secretary No
                               Weyford
   2. N/A
   Relationship to accused: Surety 1   Surety 2
   Telephone no: Sister Wey. 2388 N/A
   Address of nearest police station: Weyford P.S

5. LEGAL AID: Green form Yes/No   Legal Aid applied for: Granted/Refused
   Private client – fee quoted £   Re-application: N/A Granted/Refused
                   fee paid £ N/A

6. EMPLOYMENT: Currently working Yes/No Employer: Name Weyford General Hospital
   Nature of Job? Hospital porter   Address:
   Time there: 10 months   Net Wages: £120 per week
   If unemployed: How long?   Previous jobs: None
   References available:

7. FINANCIAL POSITION: Current Income:
                       Current Liabilities: Mortgage £ N/A Rent £ 30 p.w.
   Lump sum to offer if fined £ N/A   Lodging £ N/A HP £ 15 p.w.
   Weekly offer to court if fined: to be Insurance £ N/A Outstanding fines £ None
                   advised

CHAPTER 6

Costs and legal aid

INTRODUCTION

Any client who instructs a solicitor in connection with a criminal case will have three principal questions concerning costs. These questions are:

'How much will my *own* legal costs be and can I get any help with them?'
'Will I have to pay the *other side*'s costs, and if so how much will they be?'
'Can I get any of *my* costs paid by the other side?'

The first of these questions is concerned with the costs incurred in the solicitor–client relationship (*'solicitor/client'* costs). The second and third questions concern costs ordered between the parties (*'inter partes'* costs).

This chapter attempts to provide the answers to these questions. Obviously they will normally be posed by an accused. Occasionally, however, a solicitor may be instructed to act for someone bringing a private prosecution, and they will be of equal interest to him.

Before looking at the detailed rules, it should be noted that the state has provided two separate funds which have an important impact on the answers to these questions. They both concern *solicitor and client* costs. The first of these funds is 'Legal Aid', which is the system by which the state pays solicitors and barristers for acting on behalf of persons charged with criminal offences. As shall be seen, an accused is not automatically entitled to legal aid. He has to show that he ought to receive legal aid because of both the nature of his case and his financial position. Legal aid is not available for bringing prosecutions.

The second of these funds is known as 'central funds'. A court trying any offence other than a summary offence, may order that a party's costs be paid out of central funds. Such orders can be made in favour of both the prosecution and the defence, subject to important qualifications and restrictions.

1 THE PROSECUTION'S COSTS

The prosecution will usually incur three different types of 'costs'.

Administrative costs. For example, a police authority will incur expenditure on extra officers or overtime due to the fact that on any given day a number of officers will not be available for duty because they are attending court. Similarly, if the authority employs solicitors, their salaries will be part of its administrative expenditure.

Legal costs. If a case reaches the Crown Court, counsel will have to be instructed. Similarly, the authority may engage local solicitors to conduct cases for it, or instruct counsel to appear in the magistrates' court.

Witnesses. Any party, including a prosecutor, who calls a witness is primarily responsible for payment of their expenses for attending court. This includes not only their travelling expenses but also any pay lost for time off work.

> EXAMPLE: Mary ADAMS (case 3). The following steps might typically have occurred as a direct part of the prosecution, assuming that the police have a prosecuting solicitors' department, and ADAMS pleads 'not guilty'.
>
>   (i) A senior officer looks at witness statements taken by and reports from the traffic division officers and decides that a prosecution is justified.
> (ii) An information is laid and a summons obtained and served.
> (iii) On receipt from the court of ADAMS' notification of a not guilty plea, the police and ADAMS' solicitor provisionally agree with the court on a date for trial, subject to the availability of witnesses.
> (iv) An officer checks with the prosecution witnesses that they can attend court on the agreed day.
>   (v) The court is notified that the date is convenient.
> (vi) The papers are passed to the prosecuting solicitor who will conduct the trial.
> (vii) Near the date of the trial an officer reminds the witnesses to attend.
> (viii) At trial the case is presented by the prosecuting solicitor. Two constables attended the scene, and they both give evidence orally, as do two non-police witnesses.

Similar considerations apply if a prosecution is brought by a local authority, a government department, a private agency, or even a private individual. The latter, however, does not usually have any form of financial backing and must prima facie fund it all out of his own pocket.

The prosecution therefore must be prepared to assume the burden of the entire cost of bringing the proceedings. They may seek to defray their expenditure in two ways. First, the accused may be ordered to pay towards the prosecution's costs, *but only if he is convicted*. Secondly, the prosecution's costs, *win or lose*, may be ordered out of *central funds*, but only if the offence charged is indictable. The position in relation to summary trials and to trials on indictment will now be considered in turn.

Orders for costs in summary trials

(a) Summary offences

When a magistrates' court tries an information charging a *summary* offence, it may order the accused to pay the prosecutors costs if *the accused is convicted*.[1] There are three restrictions:

   (i) if the court orders a monetary penalty (other than costs) in the sum of 25p or less, the court cannot order the accused to pay costs unless it is appropriate to do so;
  (ii) if the accused is a juvenile, the court can in effect only order him to pay costs personally up to the amount of any fine that they order him to pay personally. His parents can be ordered to pay costs if either the court does not fine the juvenile or orders any such fine to be paid by them;[2]
 (iii) the court must specify in any case where it makes an order the amount of costs, which must be such as are just and reasonable.[3]

---

1 Costs in Criminal Cases Act 1973, s 2.
2 Costs in Criminal Cases Act, s 2(2)(b); Children and Young Persons Act 1933, s 55.
3 Costs in Criminal Cases Act 1973, s 2(1) and (2).

The amount of costs must be specified by the court, not the clerk, although it can adjourn for him to make enquiries as to what an appropriate order would be.[4] In practice this means that prosecutors should usually prepare an advance estimate of the costs they have incurred.

The court can allow both legal costs and disbursements paid out and also other less direct forms of expenditure incurred by the party in whose favour the order is made. Thus an order can include not only the expenses of witnesses or the cost of instructing counsel to appear in the magistrates' court, but also the expense incurred by the police authority of having an officer at court.[5] This is an important principle since, as will be shown, a court's powers in respect of indictable offences are, curiously, more restricted.

Costs must not, however, be ordered as a hidden penalty; for example, a magistrates' court must not fine up to the maximum sum available to it[6] and then add on another £2,000 by way of costs unless these have actually been incurred. Neither must a court take a decision on policy not to award costs in certain circumstances: it must consider each case and each application on its own merits.[7] However, the magistrates always have a discretion whether to award costs inter partes, and provided they consider the matter judicially they cannot be compelled to do so.

Principles affecting orders for costs against defendants. The magistrates' court will take a number of factors into account in deciding whether to order costs against the defendant, and if so of what amount. The following are perhaps the most significant.

(*i*) *The defendant's means.* A court will normally consider the defendant's means before it fixes an amount for him to pay.[8] Impecuniousness is not by itself a reason not to order payment.

(*ii*) *Plea of guilty.* This is a matter which a court is entitled to take into account when fixing costs. However, such a plea does not mean that an order for costs is not appropriate at all. Much will depend on the nature of the case, and also whether the defendant pleaded guilty at the beginning of the case, or changed his plea to one of guilty later.[9]

(*iii*) *Custodial sentence imposed.* Orders for costs are not inappropriate merely because the defendant receives a custodial sentence. The nature of the case, the defendant's means and whether he made a profit out of the offence are likely to be crucial.

> EXAMPLE: *Police v Mary ADAMS* (case 3). The previous example outlined the administrative and other tasks performed by the prosecution. Assuming ADAMS were found guilty she might reasonably expect to suffer an order for her to pay the expenses of the civilian witnesses, plus a contribution towards the police officer's expenses plus some amount which would contribute towards the prosecution's general expenses.

(*b*) *Costs in indictable offences tried summarily*

If magistrates try an 'either way' offence they have exactly the same powers

---

4 *Bunston v Rawlings* [1982] 2 All ER 697.
5 *R v Burt, ex p Presburg* [1960] 1 QB 625.
6 Presently £2,000—Magistrates' Courts Act 1980, s 32.
7 *R v Highgate Justices, ex p Petrou* [1954] 1 All ER 406.
8 *R v Lytham Justices, ex p Carter* [1975] Crim LR 225.
9 *R v Lytham Justices, ex p Carter*, op cit.

to award costs inter partes as when trying summary offences. They are quantified in exactly the same way, and can only be awarded if the accused is *convicted*.

However, the court may also make an order for payment of the prosecution's costs out of central funds, *whether or not the accused is convicted*. One might expect that this provision would thus give a direct alternative to an order inter partes. The scope is, however, narrower, in that an order for costs against central funds can only cover such sums as are reasonably sufficient:

> to compensate the prosecutor for 'expenses properly incurred'; and
> to compensate any witness for the prosecution for expenses trouble or loss of time properly incurred in ... his attendance.'

'Expenses' of a *party* does not include an award for time or trouble.[10] Therefore, for example, a private prosecutor who conducts a case in person is not entitled to costs from central funds for anything other than legal costs and witness expenses. In contrast to an order for costs inter partes, there is no power to compensate for time and trouble for example wages lost in bringing the prosecution. However, witnesses may be compensated for the time and trouble caused by having to appear at court, providing that the claim is fair.[11]

When a court exercises its discretion to make an order out of central funds, it must not fix an arbitrary sum. Furthermore, the court cannot order a proportion of the costs to be paid out of central funds: it must order costs in full or nothing at all.[12] If the party in whose favour the order is made can satisfy the clerk there and then as to his expenses the order can be made immediately. This course is adopted by prosecutors, who supply details of their expenditure to the courts on the form, prescribed by regulations [Form D], at the end of the case.[13]

If a defendant is convicted, a court may award the prosecutor both his costs out of central funds *and* against the defendant. The effect of such an order is that the prosecutor will be paid out of central funds. As and when the defendant pays the costs ordered against him to the court, the Lord Chancellor's Department will be reimbursed for the payment it has made out of central funds.[14]

Orders for costs in trials on indictment

(a) Costs at the committal stage

The prosecution can never obtain an order for costs inter partes at committal proceedings, irrespective of the result. The court may however order the prosecution's costs to be paid out of central funds irrespective of the result of the committal proceedings.[15] This time the appropriate form is 'Form B'. The principles of assessment are the same as for central funds costs after summary trial.

10 *R v Stockport MC, ex p Cooper* (1984) 148 JP 261.
11 *R v Stockport MC, ex p Cooper*, op cit.
12 *R v Chertsey Justices, ex p Edwards & Co* [1974] 1 All ER 156.
13 Schedule to Costs in Criminal Cases Regulations 1908.
14 Costs in Criminal Cases Act 1973, s 16.
15 Ibid, s 1(1).

(b)   Costs in the Crown Court

The Crown Court may award costs *inter partes*, provided of course that the defendant has been *convicted*. The costs awarded may include a sum in respect of the costs of the committal proceeding before the magistrates. However, the court cannot order the defendant to pay more than can be awarded out of central funds.[16] This means that the indirect administrative costs of bringing proceedings, which in a large case can be massive, cannot be recovered.[17] The court may also order the prosecutor's costs out of central funds, whether or not the accused is convicted. As with orders in the magistrates' court, an order made by the Crown Court is limited to:

– legal costs incurred by the prosecution; and
– expenses, trouble and time lost by the witnesses.[18]

As in the magistrates' court, the judge may make an order for both inter partes and central funds costs. The principles for payment are broadly the same, save that costs are assessed after the case by the appropriate Crown Court Officer. Thus unlike the magistrates court, the judge does not have to specify a fixed sum but may leave this to be assessed.

The courts have frequently held that one of the consequences of electing trial in the Crown Court is that the case will inevitably cost more. If the Crown Court decides to order the defendant to pay costs, he may not complain that they are larger than they would have been in the magistrates' court.[19]

2   THE COSTS OF THE NON LEGALLY-AIDED ACCUSED

An accused who is not legally aided is prima facie liable to pay his own legal costs, irrespective of the outcome of the case. He may in some cases have an arrangement for these to be paid by his employer or by his insurance company or a motoring organisation. The accused may be able to obtain an order inter partes or against *central funds*. The former is available only if the accused is acquitted, and the latter only if the offence is indictable *and* he is acquitted.

Orders for costs in summary trial

(a)   Summary offences

The power to order payment by the prosecutor of the accused's costs is only available when the accused is acquitted.[20] The scope of the order is the same, and thus it can include not only legal costs and witness expenses, but also any lost earnings or profits he may have suffered. No costs can be ordered out of central funds.

---

16 *R v Maher* [1983] QB 784.
17 As in *Maher* itself, a case involving charges of murder and conspiracy to import dangerous drugs, where on appeal an order totalling £1,035,000 was reduced to £180,000 representing counsels fees, the *DPP's* expenses and witnesses' expenses.
18 1973 Act, ss 3(3)(b) and 1(1).
19 *R v Boyesen* (1980) 72 Cr App Rep 43.
20 Ibid, s 2.

(b) Indictable offences tried summarily

Again costs may be awarded inter partes or out of *central funds* if the accused is acquitted on the same basis as set out above.[1] Note that the principles of central funds orders are the same as already considered. Furthermore orders for payment of the defence witnesses' expenses out of central funds can be made even if the court does not order payment of the defendant's costs.[2]

(c) Principles upon which orders for costs in favour of the accused are made by magistrates' courts

The Court of Appeal has recently issued a practice note as to the awards of costs by magistrates' courts. Because of its importance it is set out in full.[3]

> LORD LANE CJ, at the sitting of the court, said:
> 1. I understand that there is a need for guidance to magistrates in exercising their powers to order costs in indictable offences.
> 2. Under section 1 of the Costs in Criminal Cases Act 1973 a magistrates' court dealing summarily with an indictable offence and dismissing the information, or inquiring into any offence as examining justices and determining not to commit the accused for trial, may order the payment out of central funds of the costs of the defence. A similar power exists under section 12(1) of the Act where an information is not proceeded with.
> 3. Whether to make such an award is a matter in the unfettered discretion of the court in the light of the circumstances of each particular case.
> 4. It should be accepted as normal practice that such an award be made unless there are positive reasons for making a different order. Examples of such reasons are:
> (a) Where the prosecution has acted spitefully or has instituted or continued proceedings without reasonable cause the defendant's costs should be paid by the prosecutor under section 2 of the Act. If there is any doubt whether payment will be forthcoming from the prosecutor the position of the defendant should be protected by making an order for costs from central funds in his favour as well.
> (b) Where the defendant's own conduct has brought suspicion on himself and has misled the prosecution into thinking that the case against him is stronger than it is the defendant can be left to pay his own costs.
> (c) Where there is ample evidence to support a conviction but the defendant is acquitted on a technicality which has no merit. Here again the defendant can be left to pay his own costs.
> (d) Where the defendant is acquitted on one charge but convicted on another. Here the court should make whatever order seems just having regard to the relative importance of the two charges and the conduct of the parties generally.

Although this practice note only applies to indictable offences, it is often taken as a statement of principle for courts to consider when faced with an application for costs in summary only cases as well. Thus, in the main, you are likely to succeed in an application for costs against the prosecutor only in those cases where the prosecution is clearly in the wrong, for example, by taking an unjustifiably long time to bring the proceedings to court, or has acted in bad faith.

---

1 Or if the prosecution fails to proceed with an information: 1973 Act, s 12.
2 This is available even if the defendant is convicted: ibid, s 1(4).
3 [1982] 1 WLR 1447.

Order for costs in trials on indictment

Inter partes costs can only be awarded on dismissal of committal proceedings if the court considers that the charge was not brought *in good faith*.[4] Orders for costs out of *central funds* can also be made on dismissal of committal proceedings but bad faith does not have to be shown.[5] In either case 'costs' have the same meaning as for the prosecutor. The principles are covered by the Practice Note considered earlier.

At a trial on indictment the court may order costs out of *central funds*[6] or inter partes.[7] These can include the costs incurred in the committal proceedings costs. However, the Court of Appeal has issued a separate Practice Direction dealing with trials on indictment:[8]

> 1. The principal power of the Crown Court to order the payment of the costs of an acquitted defendant either out of central funds under s 3 of the Costs in Criminal Cases Act 1973 or by the prosecutor under s 4 of that Act is limited to those cases in which the accused is acquitted on all counts in the indictment.
> 2. There is a subsidiary and unrestricted power under s 5 of the Indictments Act 1915 to order the prosecutor or the defendant to pay any costs incurred as a result of an amendment to or the severance of an indictment.
> 3. The exercise of those powers is in the unfettered discretion of the court in the light of the circumstances of each particular case.
> 4. It should be accepted as normal practice that an order should normally be made for the payment of the costs of an acquitted defendant out of central funds under s 3 of the 1973 Act unless there are positive reasons for making a different order. Examples of such reasons are: (a) where the prosecution has acted spitefully or has instituted or continued proceedings without reasonable cause, the defendant's costs should be paid by the prosecutor under s 4 of the 1973 Act; (b) where the defendant's own conduct has brought suspicion on himself and has misled the prosecution into thinking that the case against him is stronger than it is, the defendant can be left to pay his own costs; (c) where there is ample evidence to support a conviction but the defendant is acquitted on a technicality which has no merit, here again the defendant can be left to pay his own costs.
> 5. This Practice Direction is to take effect from 16th November 1981.

Note that for a central funds order to be made, the accused must be acquitted on all counts on the indictment. Inter partes orders are rare in any event, as most accused will be legally aided, but bad faith or unreasonable conduct on the part of the prosecutor would be necessary.

20 Ibid, s 2.

3 ENFORCEMENT OF ORDERS FOR COSTS INTER PARTES

A magistrates' court which makes an order for costs against the defendant will also enforce that order if necessary. If the Crown Court makes an order against him, it will specify in the order a magistrates' court which will be responsible for collection and enforcement.[9] In either case the costs will be paid through that magistrates' court (unless the Crown Court orders them

4   1973 Act, s 2(4).
5   Ibid, s 1(2).
6   Ibid. s 3(1)(b).
7   Ibid, s 4.
8   [1981] 3 All ER 703.
9   Administration of Justice Act 1970, s 41(1).

to be paid immediately). Orders for costs are enforceable in the same way as for a fine.[10]

4 LEGAL AID

The importance of legal aid in criminal litigation is almost impossible to exaggerate. The advantages to the solicitor and client can be expressed very simply: the solicitor (and counsel) has guaranteed payment for the work done and the client knows his liability for costs to *his own* solicitor cannot exceed the amount of any contribution he may have to pay. For this reason, if an accused instructs a solicitor who does not operate the legal aid scheme, the solicitor is still under a duty to consider whether the accused could benefit from legal aid, and advise him of its possible availability.[11]

There are in fact two schemes that a solicitor will encounter in criminal practice. The first, is the Legal Advice and Assistance Scheme(often called 'the Green Form' Scheme) and enables preliminary advice to be given, but does not in general permit a solicitor to appear in court for the client. To enable a solicitor to present the case itself, the accused must obtain a *Legal Aid Order*.

These two schemes are supplemented by a Duty Solicitor Scheme to assist unrepresented persons appearing before magistrates' courts, shortly to be extended to police stations.

Payment for the initial steps

(a) The Legal Advice and Assistance Scheme (the 'Green Form' Scheme)

This scheme is administered by the Law Society, through 15 *Legal Aid Areas*. Each area has an Area Committee of practising solicitors and barristers who are responsible for the implementation of the scheme and for assessing solicitors' bills. The day-to-day running of each Area is entrusted to a salaried solicitor, known as the Area Secretary, who is employed by the Law Society. He works with a secretariat which operates from the Area Office. The Area Secretary has a wide range of powers available to him, subject to the overall control of the committee.

Under the scheme[12] *any person* may receive oral or written advice from a solicitor on any matter of English law, including advice on whether and how to bring or defend any prosecutions. A person wanting advice under the Legal Advice and Assistance Scheme must sign a form (the 'Green Form'). This form is completed by his solicitor in the applicant's presence, and requires him to give details of capital and income. The capital and income sections are checked against a 'key card' which is supplied by the Area Office. This contains details of the current capital and income limits which are needed to establish whether the applicant is financially eligible and if so whether he has to pay a contribution. These are also set out on the key card and comprise fixed sums on a sliding scale depending on how much dispos-

---

10 See chapter 12, post. Note however that an order against the prosecutor is enforceable as a civil debt.
11 Notes for Guidance issued by the Council of the Law Society, Note 1, Legal Aid Handbook 1984, p 199.
12 Legal Aid Act 1974, ss 1–5; Legal Advice and Assistance Regulations (No 2) 1980, as amended.

able income the applicant has.[13] If the applicant is a child[14] he must be accompanied by his parent or guardian when the solicitor is consulted, unless the Area Committee give prior authority for the solicitor to be consulted by the child in their absence as when, for example, there is a conflict of interest between them, or he has been abandoned.[15] Sometimes an adult will be unable to attend a solicitor's office, but instead sends a relative or friend to obtain advice for them. The solicitor may give the advice, provided the agent has details of the client's means, so that financial eligibility can be established.[16] This may be useful where the client is unable to attend because of work or is in custody.

If the applicant is an adult, the relevant figures for capital and income are aggregated with those of his spouse, if any, unless they are separated or have conflicting interests. If a child is applying eligibility is based on the capitalised income of his parent or guardian.

There are two important limitations on the scope of the Green Form. Firstly, a solicitor cannot usually carry out work worth more than £50, including disbursements, but excluding Value Added Tax, unless he first applies to the Area Secretary for an extension of this limit. The Area Secretary may, however, be reluctant to grant this as he will expect the solicitor to apply for a legal aid order from the court.

Secondly, the scheme cannot usually be used for 'assistance by way of representation'. In other words the solicitor cannot either appear as an advocate or write to a court as the client's solicitor. He can, however, help a client with his own case, for example by drafting a speech for his client to read out, or a letter for him to sign and send to the court. There is one exception relevant to criminal procedure. A magistrates' court may direct that a solicitor 'within the precincts of the court' may represent an accused person under the Green Form scheme.[17] The main deficiency in this provision is that the court cannot extend the £50 limit on expenditure. In any event, its use will probably die out with the advent of statutory Duty Solicitor Schemes.

The effect of these restrictions is that the most significant use of the Green Form is to take initial instructions and prepare an application for a legal aid order.

Payment is claimed from the legal aid fund for work done under the Green Form scheme by completing the reverse of the form. This summarises the work that has been done, telephone calls made and letters written. The time spent is chargeable in accordance with rates which are uprated annually. The form itself, together with a consolidated claim form, must be is submitted to the Area Office which checks that the amount claimed does not exceed the authorised amount, and that the work has been charged at the correct rates. If everything is in order, in due course the solicitor's firm will receive from the Law Society a cheque for the amount claimed, less any contribution from the client. If the Area Secretary does not accept the claim this will usually be because he is not satisfied that the costs have been properly

13 No contribution is required out of capital. Persons receiving supplementary benefit or family income supplement automatically qualify *provided* their disposable capital is below the upper limit.
14 'Child' for these purposes means any person who has not attained the upper school leaving age, which is presently 16 years: 1980 Regs, regs 3 and 8.
15 See further chapter 10: Juveniles.
16 A specific form will be supplied 1980 Regs, reg 6.
17 1980 Regs, reg 19.

incurred. In this case the claim will be provisionally assessed and returned to the solicitor, who can either accept the assessment or appeal to the Council of the Law Society.

(b) The fixed-fee interview

Although this scheme is not part of the legal aid scheme as such, it is an alternative way in which a potential client can obtain preliminary advice. Notwithstanding the existence of the Green Form Scheme, many people are still reluctant to consult solicitors, probably out of fear of what it may cost. Accordingly, solicitors may if they wish operate a fixed fee interview scheme, whereby for £5 inclusive of VAT they will give advice to anyone on any matter for a period of up to half an hour. Unfortunately £4.35 plus VAT for half an hour is considerably below a commercial or even a Green Form rate for legal services, and so the scheme appears to be falling into disfavour.

(c) Legal aid orders

Legal aid is available for criminal proceedings before the magistrates' courts, the Crown Court and the higher courts. This chapter concentrates on the first two. Legal aid in the higher courts is dealt with in chapter 14. Legal aid in criminal cases is governed by the Legal Aid Acts 1974 and 1982, and regulations made thereunder. They are all set out in the Legal Aid Handbook prepared by the Law Society and published by HMSO.

Who gets legal aid?

Legal aid orders are granted by the court, and thus differ from the Green Form scheme. The Area Offices of the Law Society have important functions concerned with, for example, payment for legal aid work done in magistrates' courts. Each area has a Criminal Legal Aid Committee (CLAC) which hears appeals against the refusal of legal aid and applications to incur unusual expenditure.

Magistrates' courts

The powers of a magistrates' court to grant legal aid are set out in s 28 of the Legal Aid Act 1974. The most important powers arise as follows:

- when a person is brought before the court *charged*[18] with any offence;
- when a defendant *appeals* to the Crown Court against conviction or sentence.[19]
- when a defendant is *committed* to the Crown Court under any power for trial or sentence;
- when a person is brought before the court to be '*dealt with*'. This includes a person in breach of a probation order, or the requirements of a community service order, or who has committed an offence whilst on probation or under a conditional discharge, or who has committed an imprisonable offence whilst under a suspended or part suspended sentence.

18 Includes summonses.
19 In which case it can grant legal aid to either side. S 28(5) op cit.

The Crown Court

The court's powers are also set out in s 28 of the Act. It may grant a legal aid order:

- to a person appearing before it for trial or sentence or to be dealt with; and
- to either side when the defendant appeals to it against conviction or sentence

Both of these powers are enjoyed coextensively with magistrates' courts.

Who can do the work?

Proceedings before magistrates' courts

A legal aid order will state the name of the solicitor in whose favour it is made, together with the name of his firm. If an accused does not have a solicitor the court will appoint one from among the solicitors in the area who do criminal work. There is no panel system as such, save that certain solicitors (and counsel) can be specifically excluded from criminal legal aid work in the event of certain forms of misconduct.[20]

The order cannot cover the use of counsel except when the offence is indictable and the court considers it to be unusually grave or difficult so that representation by both solicitor and counsel are desirable.[1] Application should be made at the same time as the application for legal aid. If it is refused the solicitor may apply to the clerk for the order to be varied, either orally or in writing.[2] If the clerk refuses his application he must refer it to the court or to the CLAC. If the court refuses the application, it must be referred to the committee. If the CLAC then refuses it, the solicitor can reapply to the court, but if the court refuses again no further application may be made. In order to have the right of reference to the CLAC, the application for legal aid must be made not less than *14 days* before committal or summary trial, as the case may be. Even if counsel is authorised this will not extend to making an application to the magistrates for bail; the solicitor will have to do this himself. Leading counsel can never be authorised under a legal aid order in the magistrates' court, except on a charge of murder.

The above rules do not mean that a solicitor cannot instruct counsel to appear on behalf of his client in a magistrates' court. However, the maximum fee that can be paid is that which would be appropriate if a solicitor had conducted the case. Counsel's fees and the solicitor's fee will be apportioned as seems reasonable.[3]

The Crown Court

A legal aid order will normally cover representation by solicitor and counsel. As with such orders in the magistrates' court, this means that the solicitor

---

20 Legal Aid in Criminal Proceedings (General) Regulations 1968, reg 7.
1 Legal Aid Act 1974, s 30(2).
2 Legal Aid in Criminal Proceedings (General) Regulations 1968, reg 14A.
3 Legal Aid in Criminal Proceedings (Costs) Regulations 1982, reg 6(2) and 6(3). The solicitor will receive the balance, if any, after a reasonable fee for counsel has been assessed by the Area Committee.

will normally be appointed and named in the order. The solicitor has the responsibility of selecting counsel to appear on behalf of the client. The order cannot authorise leading counsel unless the case is one of murder or exceptional difficulty or importance. Application for variation should be made at the first instance in writing, to the judge. If he refuses, a further application may be made in Chambers.

In the limited circumstances where solicitors have rights of audience in the Crown Court the order may direct that representation be by solicitor only. It is also open to the Crown Court to limit a legal aid order to representation by counsel only. This power is exercisable only in cases of urgency when it appears to the court that there is insufficient time to instruct a solicitor.[4]

What work can be done?

The 1974 Act prescribes the scope of an order. A legal aid order consists 'of representation by a solicitor ... assigned by the court including advice on the preparation ... for those proceedings'.[5] This does not tell you very much about what he can do. Some guidance is given in the Legal Aid in Criminal Proceedings (Costs) Regulations 1982, which permit payment for, inter alia:

- preparation;
- attendance at court with counsel if counsel is assigned;
- preparing for advocacy;
- advocacy;
- travelling;
- waiting time and dealing with routine letters;
- 'ascertaining the prosecution case';
- instructing expert witnesses, consultations and views.

Because of the very general nature of a legal aid order, you may have to justify any expenditure you have incurred, particularly in the Crown Court, where cases are more expensive to conduct. You can apply to the CLAC for prior approval to incur expenditure.[6] This is particularly useful if you wish to call an expert or take other steps which may prove expensive, since if prior approval is granted the cost cannot be disallowed on 'taxation' (vetting by the court), unless in between obtaining approval and incurring the expenditure it becomes apparent that the step is unnecessary.[7]

However, certain specific matters are dealt with in the 1974 Act. A legal aid order, both for magistrates' courts and the Crown Court, includes authority to advise on whether an appeal should be entered, and if so instructed by the defendant to assist him in giving notice of intention to appeal or asking for a case to be stated. The order itself does not cover taking any further steps in the appeal proceedings for which a further legal aid order must be granted.[8] A legal aid order will cover applications for bail before the revelant court[9] but the following points shouild be noted. Firstly, in magistrates' courts counsel is not covered to make a bail application, even if he is otherwise authorised under the order. Secondly, an accused remanded

---

4 Legal Aid Act 1974, s 30(3).
5 Ibid., s 30(1).
6 Legal Aid in Criminal Proceedings (General) Regulations 1968, reg 14D. See further (1985)LSG 914
7 Legal Aid in Criminal Proceedings (Costs) Regulations 1982, reg 6(4).
8 Ibid., s 30(5) (6) and (7).
9 See chapter 7.

in custody by magistrates after hearing full argument may exercise his right to apply to the Crown Court for bail.[10] A legal aid order covers this application, but for solicitor only, unless the order authorised counsel. Thirdly, an application for bail to a judge of the High Court in chambers is not covered by a criminal legal aid order. If a client wishes to obtain legal aid he must apply for a *civil* legal aid certificate. Fourthly, if the Area Secretary thinks that the solicitor's attendance at court was unnecessary because, for example, he was not entitled to make a bail application,[11] he may run the risk that when his bill is assessed he will not receive the costs of that attendance. In order to avoid this he will have to show that there was some other reason for attending court, for example, because it was cheaper to take instructions there than to visit the accused in prison.

So far it has been assumed that a legal aid order will cover all the proceedings before the relevant court. There are, however, two important qualifications. Firstly, legal aid orders are not usually retrospective.[12] This means that they cannot cover work done before the date upon which they were made. Secondly, a court may refuse legal aid for the trial but grant it for the sentencing proceedings.[13] Additionally, in one limited situation a magistrates' court may limit a legal aid order to a bail application.[14]

'Through' legal aid orders

Generally, a legal aid order is specific to the court for which it is issued. This means that, save for giving advice on an appeal, a legal aid order for magistrates' court proceedings, cannot for example cover proceedings in the Crown Court. Thus, if an accused is committed to the Crown Court for trial or sentence, or wishes to appeal to the Crown Court, he must reapply for legal aid. There is, however, one exception, known as a 'through order'. This may be granted by a magistrates' court in respect of any indictable offence and covers proceedings in both the magistrates' court and the Crown Court.[15] Before such an order can be made, however, the court must be sitting as *examining justices*. This gives no difficulties so far as *indictable only* offences are concerned, since the magistrates sit as examining justices right from the outset. So far as *either way* offences are concerned, however, the court cannot sit as examining magistrates until *mode of trial* has been determined. Thus it appears that a through order can only be made *after* the mode of trial enquiry. This does not mean that legal aid cannot be granted before then since the court can convert the earlier order into a through order. It does mean, however, that the object of having only one legal aid order to cover the entire proceedings can only be fully realised in the most serious of cases. This can be important because unless a through order is made, no work can be done in preparation for the Crown Court trial until a legal aid order for trial is made at the *end* of committal proceedings.

10 Legal Aid Act 1974, s 30(1A) and (1B); For the right to apply in such circumstances, see p 239 post.

11 For example, because there has been no change in circumstances since the last full bail application: see p 250, post.

12 Other than unless granted by the Court of Appeal: ibid, s 30(9).

13 It may sometimes have to grant legal aid, subject to the defendant's means, if it wants to impose certain orders, such as youth custody: see chapter 12.

14 S 29(1)(c) and s 29 (1A).

15 Legal Aid Act 1982, s 2.

What are the criteria for granting legal aid?

There are two sets of criteria upon which a legal aid application will be assessed. Legal aid must be granted when it is (i) desirable to do so in the interests of justice and (ii) when it appears that the applicant's disposable income and disposable capital are such that he requires assistance in meeting the costs which he may incur in the proceedings.[16] These two issues will be dealt with in turn. However, it is important to remember that the two criteria are interdependent. In other words, a court cannot make a legal aid order even if it is in the interests of justice to do so if the applicant's financial position is such that he is able to pay for representation out of his own resources.

Criterion one—the interests of justice

The Legal Aid Act 1974, s 29(1) provides four situations in which the interests of justice are conclusively presumed:

(a) where a person is committed for trial on a charge of murder;
(b) if the prosecutor appeals from the Court of Appeal to the House of Lords;
(c) where a person charged with an offence before magistrates is brought before the court in pursuance of a remand in custody on an occasion where he may again be remanded or committed in custody and is not (but wishes to be) legally represented before the court when he was so remanded;[17]
(d) where a person who is to be sentenced or dealt with for an offence by a magistrates' court or the Crown Court is kept in custody to enable enquiries or reports to be made to assist the court in dealing with him for the offence.

Paragraph (c) appears to direct that, once a person has been remanded in custody, legal aid must be granted subject to means if he is to be further remanded. This provision must, however, be read in the light of s 29(1A), which enables a court to confine the legal aid order so granted to a bail application. The two provisions are hardly ever met since persons remanded in custody are usually granted full legal aid in any event.

In *any* situation other than the four outlined above it is for the court to decide the interests of justice issue. The question remains as to how that discretion is to be exercised. In 1964 a Home Office Departmental Committee on Legal Aid in Criminal Proceedings, chaired by Mr Justice Widgery, made recommendations as to the way in which discretion over granting legal aid in criminal cases should be exercised. These recommendations, colloquially known as the 'Widgery criteria' are still applied in determining whether the grant of legal aid is 'in the interests of justice'. There are five principal recommendations together with a series of suggestions as to when the discretion should be exercised in the applicant's favour.

The Widgery criteria are as follows:

(i) 'The charge is grave in the sense that the defendant is in real jeopardy of losing his liberty or livelihood or suffering serious damage to his reputation'.

---

16 Legal Aid Act 1974, s 29(1).
17 This ungrammatical sentence is quoted from the act: s 29(1)(c).

This recommendation includes both situations where the charge, if proved, would probably result automatically in a custodial sentence, as for example, armed robbery, and those where the same result might occur because of the applicant's record. For example, a person may be charged for the sixth time with taking a conveyance without consent. It would apply equally where the *fact* of conviction would in some way seriously affect the accused, as for example, a finding of dishonesty against a bank cashier.

(ii) 'The charge raises a substantial question of law'.

This is aimed at problems of interpretation over a new statute or recent case or where the offence charged is a difficult one.

(iii) 'The defendant has an inadequate knowledge of English or suffers from mental illness or physical disability'.

Persons within these categories might particularly need the assistance of a lawyer.

(iv) 'The defence will involve the tracing and interviewing of witnesses or the expert cross examination of a prosecution witness'.

The mere fact that the prosecution intends to call an expert will not, of itself, justify the grant of legal aid.

(v) 'Legal representation is desirable in the interests of someone other than the defendant'.

As the committee itself suggested, in a case of a sexual offence against a young child it is undesirable that the defendant should question the witness in person.

The committee also recommended that when magistrates were faced with committal proceedings in respect of an *indictable only* offence, legal aid should generally speaking always be granted subject to the applicant's means, without considering the Widgery criteria. In addition, once committal for trial or sentence had taken place, the committee recommended that legal aid should be granted automatically subject, again, to means.

In addition the higher courts have on occasions considered whether or not legal aid should be granted in certain situations and have indicated that it should be offered on the following occasions:

– where a deportation recommendation or a hospital order is being considered;
– on the accused being committed to the Crown Court for sentence; and
– where the defendant is normally resident abroad with no experience of English courts.

The Widgery criteria do not, and were never intended to provide a definition of the 'interests of justice'. Furthermore, the Legal Aid Act 1974 provides that if there is any doubt as to whether or not legal aid should be granted, doubt *must* be resolved in favour of the person applying for legal aid.[18] Notwithstanding this, there has been continual criticism of the way in which different magistrates' courts withhold or grant legal aid.[19] If legal aid is refused on this criterion, it may be possible to apply for the refusal to be reviewed by a CLAC[20] or for Judicial Review.[1]

18 Legal Aid Act 1974, s 29(6).
19 See eg 1982 Legal Action Group Bulletin June p 8.
20 Legal Aid Act 1982, s 5. See p 215, post.
 1 Under the provisions of the Supreme Court Act 1981, s 31 and Rules of the Supreme Court, Order 53. See p 468, post.

Criterion two—the defendant's financial position

The applicant's financial situation must always be such so as to warrant the grant of legal aid. This means that legal aid may always be refused on the basis that the applicant does not need assistance in paying for representation. This does not merely depend on the applicant's means, but also the likely cost of the case.[2] Clearly some offences are likely to incur greater expense than others. **Does the client have to pay a contribution?** Whenever a court grants legal aid it must normally make a legal aid contribution order, which requires an applicant to pay income or capital or both to the court.[3] However, a contribution order cannot be made when legal aid is granted in the following situations:

   (i) when the applicant's disposable income and disposable capital do not exceed the limits prescribed for each;

  (ii) when the applicant is in receipt of supplementary benefit;

 (iii) when the applicant is in receipt of family income supplement, provided that his disposable capital does not exceed the prescribed limit;

 (iv) if a legal aid contribution order has already been made in a lower court.

The applicant must submit a prescribed form, known as Form 5, giving full details of his financial position, at the same time as he applies for legal aid. If he fails to provide a statement of means, this does not, however, mean that legal aid cannot be granted. The applicant is then treated as if his disposable income and disposable capital both exceed the minimum, and the court can, in essence, guess what contribution to order him to pay.[4] This provision does not apply if the applicant failed to supply details of his means because of physical or mental disability. If the applicant is under 16, the court can require a statement of means from either the applicant himself, and, or instead, from an 'appropriate contributor'. This is either his mother or father or both as seems appropriate.[5]

A contribution is payable if the applicant has 'disposable income' or 'disposable capital' or both. This is calculated in accordance with complicated provisions contained in the Legal Aid in Criminal Proceedings (General) Regulations 1968.[6] Note that the principle of aggregation between spouses applies equally here as in the Green Form Scheme, and that so far as capital is concerned the value of the home, clothing and household effects is ignored.

A contribution of capital must be made if disposable capital exceeds £3,000.[7] The excess must be paid to the court. A contribution of income must be paid if the average disposable income exceeds £42 per week.[8]

Average weekly disposable income	*Weekly contribution*
Exceeding £42 but not exceeding £48	£1
Exceeding £46 but not exceeding £52	£2
Exceeding £52 but not exceeding £56	£3
Exceeding £56 but not exceeding £60	£4
Exceeding £60 but not exceeding £64	£5

2 Legal Aid Act 1982, ss 7–9 and Legal Aid in Criminal Proceedings (General) Regulations 1960, regs 18–26A.
3 Ibid.
4 1982 Act, s 7(5).
5 Legal Aid Act 1974, s 40: if the applicant is illegitimate then the man must have been adjudged to have been his father.
6 Second schedule to the 1968 Regulations.
7 At present the same as the maximum eligibility for Supplementary Benefit.
8 1968 Regs, reg 22. Although the payment is due weekly the court may agree to fortnightly or other periods.

and thereafter a further £1 for each £4 or part thereof by which the average weekly disposable income exceeds £64. The contribution is payable for six months from when the order was made, the first payment being due seven days later.[9]

The following additional points about contributions should be noted. Firstly, if the solicitor advised his client on the Green Form Scheme, any contribution that was paid to him by his client must be deducted from the contribution order by the court.[10] Secondly, there is in theory no maximum capital or income contribution. However, whenever the contribution becomes more than the likely cost of the case, the court has a choice: it can either collect the contribution or refuse legal aid altogether on the grounds that the defendant's means are such that he does not need legal aid at all. Thirdly, the regulations contain extremely complicated provisions concerned with re-assessment which are outside the scope of this work.

The effect of redetermination may be the amendment or revocation of a contribution order, although not of legal aid itself.[11] A legal aid order can be made *conditional* upon the payment of a contribution, if that contribution is required out of *capital*.[12] If the accused does not pay contributions under any order or falls into arrears there are, however, various consequences. If contributions are not paid a court may wait until the end of the case, when outstanding contributions may be enforced in the same way as a civil debt.[13] Alternatively, if the court is satisfied that the defendant both could and still can pay the outstanding amount, and that it would be just to do so, it may *revoke* the legal aid order. In such a case the court may still enforce the contributions, although it has the power to remit them. The solicitor will be entitled to be paid for the work he has done up to the date of revocation.[14]

How does the client obtain legal aid?

Legal aid may be applied for orally or in writing but, as has been shown, a written statement of means is almost invariably required.[15] Some courts have their own written applications prepared. However, the regulation provide a form ('form 1') which may be used for applications to the magistrates' courts. It requires you to include not only the client's personal details and information about the charges, but also includes a series of questions based on the Widgery criteria. Because this form may therefore reveal that the client has previous convictions, it contains an endorsement that it will not be shown to the court which tries the case, in the event of his pleading not guilty.

As already mentioned the statement of means form is 'form 5'. It should be completed and signed by the client but checked by the solicitor to make sure that no gaps have been left or questions unanswered. Whether the application is made orally or in writing, legal aid in the magistrates' court may be granted by a clerk to the justices or referred by him to a magistrate.

---

9 1968 Regs, regs 22(1) and 31(1).
10 Ibid, reg 18(2).
11 Ibid, reg 25A to C.
12 Legal Aid Act 1982, s 9(2).
13 Legal Aid Act 1974, s 35.
14 Legal Aid Act 1982, s 9(4) and 1968 Regs, reg 25D.
15 1968 Regs, regs 1 and 5; Unless the applicant is physically or mentally incapable of supplying such a statement: Legal Aid Act 1974, s 29(4).

The clerk may only refuse legal aid where the application is in relation to an indictable offence.[16]

Note that at committal for trial or sentence a solicitor should normally ask for legal aid to be 'extended' to cover proceedings in the Crown Court (unless the court has made a through order). Strictly speaking the application is not for an extension, but for a new legal aid order. Although a new legal aid *contribution* order cannot be made, the court can ask for the solicitor to confirm that his client's circumstances are unchanged; since the grant of a new legal aid order is subject to the 'interests of justice' and 'means' criteria as before.

Acting for more than one accused on legal aid

You may often be asked to act for more than one accused either by the accused themselves or by the court. As already noted, there is nothing objectionable in this, provided no conflict of interest arises. It will often be the case that all of the accused will be on legal aid and each legal aid order will name the same solicitor. If you do discover a conflict of interest, you must ask the court to amend the legal aid order to enable one (or sometimes all) of the accused to be represented by another solicitor.[17]

A further refinement arises in the Crown Court. When a solicitor is acting for more than one accused, he is entitled to brief separate counsel to appear for each accused; it has been held to be ultra vires for a Crown Court taxing officer to insist on the same counsel being briefed for each accused.[18] Separate representation is sometimes necessary when one accused has previous convictions and another does not.[19]

Appeals against the refusal of legal aid

There are three possible steps which can be taken if a client has been refused legal aid. Firstly, you can reapply. The regulations state that you can apply to the court 'at the trial or other proceedings'.[20] 'Other proceedings' is not defined, and theoretically could include adjournments or remands. In practice the provision tends only to be applied to major events such as committal.[1]

Secondly, when legal aid has been refused *for the first time* by a magistrates' court, magistrate or clerk to the justices the applicant may be able to apply to the CLAC for the refusal to be reviewed. The right of review is, however, only available if:

– the offence charged is indictable *and*
– refusal was on the grounds that legal aid is not required in the interests of justice *and*
– at the time that the application for legal aid was made, a date had already been fixed for committal or summary trial, that date being at least *21 days* after the application.[2]

16 Namely in those circumstances where an applicant may apply for review to the CLAC.
17 The new solicitor assigned by the court should be nominated by the defendant. *Baker v West Sussex Justices* (1984) 184 JP 129.
18 *R v O'Brien and Cliffe* (1984) Times, 24 December.
19 Because of the provisions of Criminal Evidence Act 1898, s 1(f)(ii): see p 159, ante.
20 1968 Regs, reg 5.
 1 See eg *R v Cambridge City Justices, ex p L (an infant)* (1979) 144 JP 149.
 2 1968 Regs, reg 6E.

IN THE WEYFORD MAGISTRATES' COURT
~~INNER LONDON COMMISSION AREA~~

APPLICATION FOR LEGAL AID

(Before completing this form read carefully the notes overleaf)

1. Name DUNCAN McCARTHY   Date of birth 9/6/6—

    Address 11 INKERMAN TERRACE
    WEYFORD

2. I apply for legal aid for the purpose of proceedings before the WEYFORD
    .... (Magistrates') (~~Juvenile~~) Court.
    AND THE CROWN COURT
    My case is due to be heard on 13th August at 10.00 a.m./~~p.m.~~

3. Name(s) of other persons charged with you in these proceedings
    NONE

4. The solicitor I wish to act for me is (state name and address) Alison Brown
    White & Co., Acol House
    Weyford

5. Describe shortly what it is you are accused of doing, e.g., 'stealing £50 from my
    employer', 'kicking a door causing £50 damage' Burglary —
    £60 cash from employer's social club.

    I understand that the court may order me to make a contribution to the costs of
    legal aid or to pay the whole costs if it considers that my means enable me to do
    so and if I am under 16, may make a similar order with respect to my parents.

    Signed D. McCarthy
    date: 6 August 198—

6. I am in real danger of a custodial sentence for the following reasons.... *I have previous convictions for dishonesty - last one was burglary - I got Detention Centre*

7. If you are convicted of the present charge will you be in breach of any court order, i.e., suspended sentence of imprisonment, conditional discharge, probation, community service, or are you subject to a deferred sentence? (Give brief details so far as you are able.)...... *No*

8. I am in real danger of losing my livelihood or suffering serious damage to my reputation because (give brief details).... *I have been suspended, but will be sacked if I am found guilty*

9. A substantial question of law is involved. (Give brief details.)........................

10. I shall be unable to follow the proceedings because

    (a) My knowledge of English is inadequate   YES/NO

    (b) I suffer from a disability, namely........

11. Witnesses have to be traced and interviewed on my behalf. (Give brief details.) *I have an alibi — I was in a pub with a friend I need help in tracing him*

12. The case involved expert cross examination of a prosecution witness. (Give brief details.)...... *Prosecution case not yet known*

13. The case is a very complex one, for example, mistaken identity (explain briefly).

14. Any other reason (please attach a piece of paper with full particulars).

APPLICATION FOR LEGAL AID

NOTES

A.   Questions 1 to 5 of the form overleaf MUST be completed before your application for legal aid can be considered.

B.   **Reasons for wanting legal aid** — Questions 6-14

When deciding whether to grant you legal aid, the court will need to know the reasons why it is in the interests of justice for you to be represented. You are therefore **requested** to complete questions 6-14 of the form to avoid the possibility of legal aid being refused because the court does not have sufficient information about the case. **If you need help in completing this form, and especially if you have previous convictions, you should see a solicitor.** He may be able to advise you free of charge or at a reduced fee. You will in any event need the help of a solicitor to answer question 9.

C.   If you plead "Not Guilty" the information contained on this form will **not** be made known to the Magistrates who try your case unless they convict you. If you are acquitted only the financial information contained in the Statement of Means will be given to them.

For official use only

Legal Aid 1

—————

Application
for
Legal Aid

Magistrates
Juvenile
Court

M.P.84(E)

STATEMENT OF MEANS BY APPLICANT OR APPROPRIATE CONTRIBUTOR FOR LEGAL AID PURPOSES
(TO BE ACCOMPANIED BY A COMPLETED APPLICATION FORM)

To apply for criminal legal aid you must complete this form. If you are not yet sixteen, then your mother or father may also be asked to complete one. If you have applied for legal aid for your child, and your child is sixteen years old or over, then you do not need to fill in this form. Your child should complete it, giving details of his or her own income.

This information is needed before legal aid can be granted, so to avoid any delay in your application being considered, please complete this form as fully and as carefully as possible.

SECTION 1—PERSONAL DETAILS

1. Full name (block letters please)..

2. Date of birth...

3. Home address...

    ....

4. Marital status (please tick one box)

    ☐ single   ☐ divorced

    ☐ married   ☐ widow(er)

    ☐ married but separated

5. Occupation (state 'unemployed' if appropriate)
    List here all your jobs, including any part-time work and your employer's name and address.
    (If you have more than one job, give the name and address of each employer: if self-employed state 'self-employed'.)

    ....

    ....

    ....

    ....

    ....

    ....

SECTION 2—PERSONAL DETAILS (DEPENDANT CHILD)

(To be completed only if application is in respect of a dependant child who has not attained the age of 16.)

If legal aid is being sought for a dependant child, and he or she is not yet sixteen, please answer the following questions about him or her.

1. Full name (block letters please)..

2. Date of birth...

3. Home address (if different from yours)...

    ....

4. Your relationship to him or her (e.g. father)..

LEGAL AID 5

————

Statement of
Means

HPL W8168

1.

NOTE. This form is not completed and is supplied as an illustration only.

SECTION 3—FINANCIAL DETAILS

Part A—Income

Please give below details of your net income (i.e. after the deduction of tax and national insurance) from all sources for the three months immediately before this form is completed. If you are married and living with your wife or husband, then you have to provide details of his or her income as well. The court may ask you to provide proof of the information you give in this form.

Your contribution, if any, will be assessed and collected on a weekly basis, so if you are paid monthly, please give weekly figures.

1. Do you receive Supplementary Benefit? (please tick one box)

    ☐ Yes—You do not need to complete the rest of this form, simply turn to the declaration on page five and sign it.

    ☐ No—Please go on to question two.

2. Do you receive Family Income Supplement? (please tick one box)

    ☐ Yes—There is no need to complete any more of Part A, so please turn to Part B—Capital and Savings.

    ☐ No—Please go on to question three.

3. Please give details of your INCOME in the table below.

Description of INCOME	Amount		Remarks	Please do not write in the spaces below
	Your income	Income of husband/wife		
(a) Weekly earnings or salary, including overtime, commission or bonuses. (please give net figures). Please attach with this form your last six wage slips and those of your spouse. If you do not have that many, please attach as many as you can.				
(b) If your earnings or those of your spouse change from week to week, give the amounts for the last 13 weeks. (If you do not have this information, please give the amounts for as many weeks as you can, and at least the last 6 weeks. You should if possible attach wage slips.)				
(c) Weekly income from any part-time job not included as (a) above. (Please give gross and net figures.)				
(d) Weekly income from state benefits—e.g. family allowance (please specify below)				
(e) Weekly gross income from sub-letting house, rooms, etc.				
(f) Any other income (please give details below)				
(g) If in a business of your own, please attach the most recent accounts available to support the above figures.				

IMPORTANT: If the information you have given in the table above is going to change soon, please give details of the changes in Section 5 of this form.

2.

Part B—Capital and Savings

Please give details of all your capital and savings. If you are married and living with your husband or wife, also give details of his or her capital and savings. You should give particulars of savings with the National Savings Bank or with other banks, National Savings Certificate, cash stocks and shares or any other investments. Please also give details of any property you own, such as houses or flats apart from the house or flat in which you live.

1. Please give details of your *CAPITAL* and *SAVINGS* in the table below.

| Description of CAPITAL and SAVINGS | Amount | | Remarks | Please do not write in the spaces below |
	You	Husband/Wife		
(a) Do you own house property (apart from your main or only dwelling)? *(Answer YES or NO)*	YES/NO	YES/NO		
(b) If YES state: (i) The value (*i.e. the approximate selling price*) (ii) The amount of any outstanding mortgage.				
(c) Give details of your savings. (state name of bank, building society etc. below)				
Give details of any articles of value that you own (*e.g. jewellery, furs, paintings*) with their approximate value.				

SECTION 4—ALLOWANCES AND DEDUCTIONS

In assessing your means for legal aid purposes, the court will make allowances for the cost of supporting your husband or wife, children and any other dependant relatives, and also for your accommodation costs and travelling expenses. If there are any other expenses which you think the court should make allowance for, please give details at question 5 below.

1. Please give the NUMBER of dependants who are *LIVING WITH YOU*.

Husband or wife	Children 18 and over	Children 16 and 17	Children 11 to 15	Children under 11	Other (*specify below*)	

3.

2.   If you pay maintenance to a dependant who does not live with you, please give details of the amounts you pay to support them.

Age of dependant	Your relationship to him or her	Amount you pay per week	Please do not write in the spaces below

3.   You may claim for the HOUSING EXPENSES of you and your wife or husband. Please give the amounts you pay each week. If you own more than one house, only give details connected with the house in which you live. If you are paying the housing expenses of (a) dependant(s) who do(es) not live with you, please give both amounts.

Description of payment	Amount per week	Amount per week for dependant(s)	
Rent			
Mortgage repayment			
Ground rent			
Service charge			
Rates			
Board and lodging			
Bed and breakfast			

3. (a)   Estimated weekly expenses in connection with sub-let property owned by you or your spouse.

Description of Payment	Amount per week	

4.   The TRAVELLING EXPENSES of you and your husband or wife may be taken into account. You may claim for the actual amounts that you and your husband or wife spend per week travelling to and from your place(s) of employment that will not be paid by your employer.

	You	Your husband or wife	
Amount spent			

4.

5. Please give details of any OTHER EXPENSES which you think the court should know about.

Description of expenditure	Amount spent per week

6. Allowance for contributions in respect of LEGAL ADVICE AND ASSISTANCE under the "green form" scheme in connection with this case.

    You may already have been given some advice and assistance by a solicitor under the "green form" scheme, and you may have paid, or been asked to pay, a contribution towards that advice. If this is the case, then the amount of your legal aid contribution will be reduced by the amount of "green form" contribution paid or due.

Name and address of the solicitor who gave the advice and assistance	Amount of contribution paid (or to be paid)

SECTION 5—FURTHER INFORMATION

This part of the form is set aside for you to give any financial information that you think the court should have when deciding upon your application for legal aid. You may also use this part of the form to tell the court of any future changes in circumstance that might alter your financial position.

SECTION 6—DECLARATION

Anyone who has knowingly or recklessly made a statement which is false in any way, or has knowingly withheld information is liable to be prosecuted and, if convicted, to either imprisonment for a term not exceeding four months, or to a fine or both. After your application has been considered by the court, you may be asked to give further information or to clarify information that you have already given. In particular you may be required to provide documentary proof of the information you have given (e.g. wage slips, rent books, etc.)

> I declare that to the best of my knowledge and belief, I have given a complete and correct statement of my income, savings and capital (and that of my husband or wife)* (and that of my child)**.
>
> Date.. Signed..
>
> * Delete if you are not living with your husband or wife, or if you are single.
> **Delete if legal aid is not sought for your child.

5.

It is unfortunate that the right of review is not extended to summary offences, as most criticism arises over discrepancies in relation to the granting of legal aid for these offences. Furthermore, it is possible that the right of review does not apply to juveniles.[3] If legal aid is refused by the court the defendant must be notified using a prescribed form, which gives directions for applying for review.[4] Even if it refuses legal aid the court must still work out what the applicant's contribution would have been, since if the review is successful the committee will make a contribution order. The committee will need a copy of the legal aid application as well as the notification.

The third possibility is an application to the Divisional Court of the Queen's Bench Division for Judicial Review. This is available against proceedings in magistrates' courts and also the Crown Court (provided that the latter is sitting as an appellate court). However, Judicial Review will only be available if a court has refused to consider an application at all, or taken into account the wrong considerations. It cannot be used to challenge a *bona fide* exercise of discretion with which the solicitor happens to disagree.

> EXAMPLE: Judicial Review would lie if a magistrates' court had a declared policy of never granting legal aid for persons charged with assault on the police. It would not lie if a court, having examined a wealthy applicant's means, decided he did not need legal aid to resist such a charge in the circumstances because of his financial position.

How is payment made?

When the case has been concluded[5] the solicitor is responsible for ensuring that a bill is submitted to the appropriate authority. For any magistrates' court proceedings, including committal, the appropriate authority is the Legal Aid Area Office; for any proceedings in the Crown Court it is the Taxing Office at the Crown Court. This means that when matters have been committed for trial to the Crown Court or have been tried in the magistrates' court and subsequently appealed, two bills must be submitted, even, at present, in the case of through orders.

When the magistrates' court proceedings have finished the solicitor must complete and return a form of bill known as LA/Rep/3B. A blank bill will be supplied with the legal aid order. He should at the same time send off the order and include on his bill any claim for expenses, for example, the cost of travelling to court. If he has received prior authorisation to incur expenditure, this should be sent as well. This must all be completed and sent off to the Area Office within three months of the conclusion of proceedings.[6]

The amount of costs to which a solicitor is entitled is determined by the Legal Aid in Criminal Proceedings (Costs) Regulations 1982, as amended from time to time. Schedule 1 of the regulations specifies the fees a solicitor may claim for work done by a 'fee earner'[7] in the magistrates' court (and the Crown Court). Schedule 2 provides for fees in respect of counsel, including his appearance in magistrates' courts where counsel was authorised.

Work in magistrates' courts is charged at three prescribed hourly rates, namely for preparation, for advocacy and for waiting, travelling and attend-

---

3 Compare Interpretation Act 1978, Sch 1 with 1968 Regs, reg 6F, reg 6G and reg 6H ('Parent or Guardian').
4 1968 Regs, reg 14A and reg 14B.
5 The passing of sentence unless sentence is deferred.
6 1968 Costs Regs, reg 4.
7 Someone for whom the firm can make a direct charge for services to a client.

ing counsel at court. In addition, a fixed fee is allowed for each routine letter written and each routine telephone call made or received.

On receipt of the solicitor's bill, the area office will check it and the Area Secretary will either approve the claim for payment or make a provisional assessment. If the claim is approved, or the solicitor accepts the provisional assessment, then in due course he will receive a cheque from the Law Society's computer in London. If he wishes to object to the provisional assessment, then he can ask for it to be reviewed. If still dissatisfied, he is entitled to make written representations to the Council of the Law Society, who have power to vary the assessment.

It is important for a solicitor to remember that he is not prevented from instructing counsel to appear in the magistrates' court merely because there is no authorisation under a legal aid order. In order to avoid any embarrassment over the apportionment of fees in such cases, a solicitor should approach counsel's clerk, explain the position on legal aid, and come to some arrangement over apportionment before counsel is instructed in the first place.

Claims for costs in the Crown Court are dealt with in a different way. As for magistrates' court work, a solicitor must submit a bill within three months of the conclusion of the proceedings. A failure to comply with the time limits could result in the bill being disallowed in whole or in part. A prescribed form of bill is supplied on request by the Crown Court and when completed it must be sent to the Crown Court, together with the legal aid order, counsel's brief, any expenditure authorisations, and all relevant papers. The solicitor's bill will be taxed by one of the Crown Court officers, often the court clerk. In order for taxation to take place the bill must be sufficiently detailed; for example, a solicitor is requested to give details of the fee earner who undertook each particular item of work. It is therefore very important that anyone involved with the file records the amount of time spent on the case.

Different rates are prescribed for:

  (i) preparation
  (ii) advocacy
  (iii) waiting, travelling and attending counsel at court
  (iv) writing routine letters and making or receiving routine phone calls.

However, for Crown Court work the rates for (i) and (iii) are further subdivided, depending on whether the work is carried out by:

  – a senior solicitor.
  – a solicitor, legal executive or equivalent.
  – an articled clerk or equivalent fee earner.

When a solicitor has carried out the advocacy then two rates are specified, namely 'senior solicitor' and 'solicitor'. Whereas in the magistrates' court system the idea of the 'fee earner' is not very important, as only one rate is provided, in the Crown Court it is important, because of the different rates.

Work will be paid for if it has been 'actually and reasonably done' at rates which are appropriate to 'such grades of fee earner as the appropriate authority considers reasonable'.[8] The Lord Chancellor's Department issued a circular[9] to guide taxing officers in the implementation of the regulations. The

8 1982 Costs Regs, reg 5.
9 Circular L62/84/12.

effect of this is that if the taxing officer considers that the work claimed for could and should have been done by a lower grade of fee earner, then the rate for the latter will be allowed.

> EXAMPLE: A partner serves a witness summons upon a witness. The taxing officer would probably think that this was not appropriate work for that person, and only allow the rate for an articled clerk.

If a fee earner attends court with counsel, the costs of his doing so should generally be allowed, although the taxing officer may well allow only the fee appropriate to a low grade fee earner, for example, an articled clerk, in a straightforward case.

When a bill is taxed the amount of costs is deemed to include an allowance for the overheads of the firm. It is for this reason that secretarial expenses, for example, are not allowed as a separate claimable item. However, Crown Court taxing officers must allow routine letters to be charged, and these do not comprise part of the overheads. The test is whether the letter written or telephone call made is one which a private client would normally be charged for. If there is any doubt this must be resolved in favour of the solicitor.[10]

If a solictor is dissatisfied with the taxation of a bill by the Crown Court, he may apply within 21 days for a redetermination, provided he gives reasons. He has a further right of appeal to the Chief Taxing Master of the High Court, within 21 days of the redetermination, provided he asks the determining officer to provide written reasons for the determination. The detailed provisions are set out in the Costs Regulations but further consideration is outside the scope of this work.[11]

5 COSTS AND THE LEGALLY AIDED ACCUSED

The first point to note is that the Costs in Criminal Cases Act 1973 and the Legal Aid Act 1982 exist quite independently of one another. This means that a court's powers under the Act of 1973 are exercisable irrespective of whether or not an accused has legal aid. However, 'expenses' for the purposes of ss 1–4 of the Act of 1973 include the costs under the Legal Aid Act incurred by the legal aid fund in paying for representation, and if a legally aided person obtains an order for costs either out of central funds or against the prosecution, these must be paid into the legal aid fund.

The second point of general application is that under the Legal Aid Scheme the accused can never be ordered to pay more than the actual cost of his case. Any contribution in excess of the actual sum must be returned to him, and any contribution still outstanding at the time his case is disposed of must be remitted in so far as it exceeds the cost of his being represented.[12] If the defendant receives an immediate custodial sentence, any contributions still due are automatically remitted.[13] Furthermore, the court finally dealing with the defendant has a wide discretion to remit contributions due or order repayment of any contribution made. That court will be the magistrates' court, unless the defendant was committed for trial or sentence in which case the power is exercised by the Crown Court.[14] The powers are to:

10　See Court of Appeal case no 830331, (1984) LSG 1496.
11　1982 Costs Regulations Reg, regs 10–11. Reg 12 provides a final appeal on a point of importance to a High Court Judge.
12　Legal Aid Act 1982, s 7(6).
13　1968 Regs, reg 25E(1)(b).
14　S 8 of the 1982 Act.

remit any sum which falls to be paid after the proceedings were completed;
remit or order repayment of any payment due from or made by an appropriate contributor;
remit or order repayment of any payment due from or made by a defendant who is acquitted.

Any appellate court may remit or order repayment of any payment due from or made by an appellant or an appropriate contributor if the appeal is against conviction and is successful.

Finally, there is no reason why a court cannot make an *inter partes* order for costs against a defendant merely because he is legally aided. The principles are the same as in any other case.

6 DUTY SOLICITORS

There will shortly be two different types of duty solicitor. One, which is already in existence, is concerned with providing assistance for unrepresented defendants at court. The other, which is not yet in existence, will be concerned with advising persons detained by the police.

The statutory duty solicitor scheme

The main object of duty solicitors schemes is to provide a service to accused persons appearing at court who are unrepresented but who want advice and help. They are mainly, but not exclusively, encountered in criminal courts. Most schemes were originally set up voluntarily in conjunction with the local Law Society and the local Magistrates' Court Committee. Solicitors attended on a rota basis, and gave their services free. The only method of paying the solicitor was either under the Green Form or for the court to grant legal aid immediately. The solicitor was thus not guaranteed payment. The voluntary schemes suffered from disadvantages. The remuneration system was not fair and amounted to 'pot luck'. Furthermore, they were dependant on the energy of the organiser and on whether local practitioners were prepared to co-operate in setting them up.

As a result of these and other problems a statutory duty solicitor scheme has been established.[15] The administrative structure of the scheme is that 24 regional committees have been established to oversee the working of the scheme. One of their functions is to establish whether a particular court needs a duty solicitor scheme; (a court can be compelled to have a scheme).[16] Each court with a scheme will have a local committee whose function is to organise rotas, issue instructions as to the operation of the scheme, and select duty solicitors.

Voluntary schemes were suspected of being used for young, inexperienced advocates to cut their teeth on. Under the statutory scheme any solicitor who wants to take part in it will have to satisfy the local committee of his competence and experience. In particular, he should have criminal advocacy experience, including conducting contested trials during the previous 18 months, and be able to provide proper advice and representation within the limited time available in a busy court. This in turn requires adequate know-

15 Legal Aid (Duty Solicitor) Scheme 1983.
16 Legal Aid Act 1982, s 1.

ledge of both magistrates' court procedure and the law relating to the more common offences coming before a magistrates' court. Furthermore, having been selected, a duty solicitor is subject to reselection every three years.

The solicitor must make sure that any person to whom he offers advice knows about the existing Green Form and legal aid schemes, and that he is entitled to consult or instruct any solicitor. The duty solicitor can only advise or act for a person if the latter does not have another solicitor whom he wants to instruct. If he has another solicitor who is unavailable, then the duty solicitor can act for him on that occasion only.

An accused can only use the solicitor acting in his capacity of duty solicitor once; if he wishes to be represented subsequently, he must instruct a solicitor, either privately or under a legal aid order. He can instruct the person whom he first saw as duty solicitor, provided that the latter told him of his right to approach any solicitor.

The scheme deals with the types of activity that can be undertaken. The duty solicitor must:

- give advice and representation to a defendant in custody who wishes to apply for bail;
- give advice and representation to a fine defaulter who is at risk of imprisonment;
- represent a defendant in custody who wants to plead guilty there and then;
- help a defendant apply for legal aid;
- give advice and representation to a defendant who is not in custody, provided the solicitor considers it necessary.

He is prohibited from representing a defendant at committal or on a *not guilty* plea, and cannot assist if the offence is not imprisonable, save in exceptional circumstances. In all bar the first category set out above, the solicitor should only take the appropriate steps if he does not consider that the case ought to be adjourned.[17]

Remuneration under the scheme is at the average of the advocacy and waiting/travelling rates for magistrates' court legal aid orders. This rate is payable for the time spent at court irrespective of whether the duty solicitor is actually doing anything. From the accused's point of view the big advantage is that the service is not means tested. Furthermore, there is no direct way at present to recover the cost of assistance from a person if he is found guilty.

24-Hour duty solicitor schemes

The second type of duty solicitor scheme has become necessary because of the various provisions in the Police and Criminal Evidence Act 1984, giving persons in custody the right of access to a solicitor. The scheme has yet to be set up, and has at the present time gone no further than a consultative paper issued by the Law Society.[18] The scheme will operate 24 hours per day, and ideally use solicitors qualified to operate the court scheme. It may prove impractical, however, to achieve this, particularly in London and the other large cities.

It seems likely that remuneration will be provided under the Green Form scheme, but with expenditure extended to £90 for those arrested for arrest-

17 The Scheme is ambiguous in places: see (1984) 103 LN 191.
18 (1984) LSG 1731.

able offences and £50 for those arrested for non-arrestable offences. Relatives will not be able to 'call out' the duty solicitor. There will be no means test.[19] As the scheme will operate on a 'call-out' basis, the remuneration system that applies to court Duty Solicitors is inappropriate. An interesting point is that if a suspect asks for his own solicitor rather than the Duty Solicitor, the former would be able to use the same modified 'Green Form' scheme. This could produce the anomaly of a client being entitled to up to £90 of advice (less the cost of travelling to and from the police station) which is not means tested if he is in custody, but only £50 of advice, assuming he qualifies at all, if he consults his solicitor after being released on bail.

Finally, it may be that solicitors find the prospect of court Duty Solicitors schemes more attractive than 24-hour schemes. Under s 1A of the Legal Aid Act 1982[20] a direction may be made by a local committee that participation in the 24-hour scheme is a prerequisite to participation in the court scheme.

7 A PRACTICAL EXAMPLE

This chapter concludes by examining a practical example of the effect of these rules.

> EXAMPLE: *R v Duncan McCARTHY (case 1)*. On his first appearance in court on 6 August McCARTHY saw the Duty Solicitor. She claimed the cost of giving advice on an hourly basis, and applied for legal aid, which was granted on 7 August. As he is working and has no dependents, McCARTHY had to pay a contribution. Under the order his solicitor applied for bail on 13 August, attended the mode of trial and committal proceedings on 1 September, and carried out all necessary interviews, examination of prosecution committal papers etc as well. Legal aid was granted for the Crown Court trial at the committal proceedings but McCARTHY did *not* have to pay another contribution. As the original order was not a 'through' order his solicitor submitted her bill on form LA/REP/3B to the Area Office for the work done prior to committal, and was paid by the Law Society Area Office. After committal the solicitor prepared the case for trial, briefed counsel and arranged a conference. At the conclusion of the Crown Court trial McCARTHY's solicitor then prepared her bill for taxation by the Crown Court and after taxation was paid by the Crown Court.

Note that irrespective of whether McCARTHY had been convicted or acquitted, and even if his legal aid contribution were ordered to be repaid, his solicitor would still have needed to have her Crown Court bill taxed, and would have been paid in exactly the same way. The return of contributions is not of direct concern to the solicitor, save that until taxation has taken place the court may be unable to work out the amount of any refund. The solicitor must therefore make sure that he or she submits his bill as soon as possible.

19 (1985) Guardian, 24 July.
20 Inserted by Police and Criminal Evidence Act 1984, s 59.

CHAPTER 7

Remands, adjournments and bail

As has already been noted, prosecutions once begun take time. The court may not be prepared to release the accused on bail pending trial and thus there is always the risk that he may spend many months in prison even though he is ultimately acquitted. This can often mean that the defence solicitor's initial efforts are more concerned with obtaining bail than with preparing the case for trial—the tail ends up wagging the dog. Understandable though this may be, particularly from the point of view of the accused and his relatives, there is a danger that hopeless bail applications can take up a disproportionate amount of your time at the expense of other, and ultimately more important, tasks.

This chapter has been divided into three sections, namely:

1. Adjournments and remands. The law relating to bail is so inextricably bound up with the court's powers in this context that it is now necessary to examine them in greater detail.

2. Bail: the substantive law and procedure. This section forms the bulk of the chapter. The law is now primarily governed by the Bail Act 1976—an Act which was ostensibly intended as a major liberalising reform, but whose major effect in the context of this work has been to make this section many times longer than it would have been before 1 May 1978[1] without any obvious benefit to the accused.

3. Bail in practice. So complicated has the substantive law become that it is difficult to integrate it with its practical operation. It will be shown that, despite the major statutory upheaval in May 1978, little of substance has changed at grass roots level.

1 ADJOURNMENTS AND REMANDS

(1) Magistrates' powers to adjourn and remand before conviction or committal for trial

A magistrates' court always has power to adjourn whether hearing committal proceedings,[2] mode of trial proceedings,[3] or summary trial.[4] At the same time it may (and sometimes *must*) remand the accused either in custody[5] or on bail. As has already been pointed out,[6] the adjournment defers the *proceedings*, whereas the remand is to *secure the attendance of the accused* at the

---

1 The date upon which the 1976 Act came into force.
2 Magistrates' Courts Act 1980, s 5(1).
3 Ibid, s 18(4).
4 Ibid, s 10(1).
5 In certain limited circumstances persons charged with an offence punishable with imprisonment may be remanded to a hospital for the purpose of obtaining a medical report: Mental Health Act 1983, s 35.
6 P 24, ante.

adjourned hearing. If remanded on bail, the accused commits an offence if he does not appear at the adjourned hearing, whereas if there is no remand, he is not obliged to appear at the adjourned hearing, although he runs the risk of being tried in his absence (or in certain limited circumstances having a warrant issued for his arrest) if he does not.[7]

Whether or not a magistrates' court is obliged to remand the accused when it adjourns will depend upon which of the three categories of offence it is dealing with.

(a) 'Indictable only' offences

From the first appearance onwards, the accused *must* be remanded because s 5(1) of the 1980 Act obliges magistrates to remand whenever they adjourn *committal proceedings*. In other words, if acting for an accused charged with, for example, rape, he will always have to be remanded in custody or on bail whenever the magistrates adjourn prior to committal for trial.

(b) 'Summary only' offences

Magistrates always have a *discretion* to remand[8] but will only normally do so if they consider the offence to be 'serious' (for example, because it is punishable by imprisonment or arises out of an incident of public disorder) or feel that it is necessary for some other reason to secure the accused's attendance. It is most unlikely that the court would ever feel the need to remand Mary ADAMS (*Case 3*), but the position might be different where, for example, an accused was known by the bench to have a very bad driving record and was likely to be disqualified if convicted.

(c) Offences triable 'either way'

Magistrates are usually obliged to remand an adult accused, whether or not the 'mode of trial' has been determined.[9] The position may be summarised as follows:

(i) If the accused is first brought before the court in custody or is surrendering to police bail the magistrates must *always* remand thereafter, whether or not the 'mode of trial' has been determined and whatever 'mode of trial' is ultimately adopted.

(ii) If the prosecution was begun by summons and the accused consents to summary trial he *may* be remanded at any stage. If he is remanded he *must* always be remanded thereafter on any subsequent adjournment.

(iii) If the prosecution was begun by summons and the accused is to be tried on indictment the position is the same as in (ii) above until mode of trial is determined, thereafter, if the magistrates adjourn, they *must* remand the accused because they will be adjourning committal proceedings.[10]

The occasions on which magistrates will not be obliged to remand an accused charged with an *either way* offence are therefore very restricted. He must have

7 P 286, post.
8 Magistrates' Courts Act 1980, s 10(4).
9 Ibid, ss 10(4) and 18(4).
10 Ibid, s 5(1).

initially appeared in answer to a summons, must have agreed to summary trial and must at no stage in the proceedings have been remanded. For example, if an accused were summonsed for reckless driving and agreed to summary trial, it is unlikely that the magistrates would exercise their discretion to remand him at any stage. If, however, having elected trial on indictment proceedings were adjourned because, for example, the prosecution were not ready for committal it would be necessary to apply for bail, because the magistrates, having determined 'mode of trial', would now be adjourning committal proceedings.

REMANDS IN THE MAGISTRATES' COURT

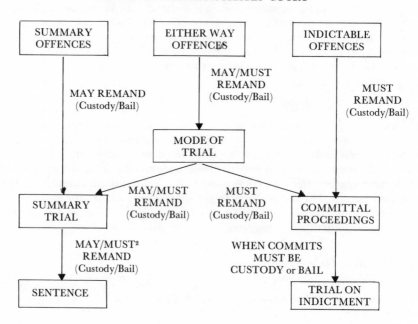

1 Only discretionary if D not previously in custody/on bail.
2 Obligatory when under MCA 1980 s 30: Obligatory to hospital when under MHA 1983 s 35.

Length of remands

One of the principal differences between adjournments and remands are the statutory limitations upon the period for which an accused may be remanded. The basic rule is contained in s 128(6) of the Magistrates' Courts Act 1980 which provides that *prior* to conviction or committal an accused may not normally[11] be remanded for more than *eight*[12] clear days at a time, save that if he is remanded on bail he may be remanded for a longer period if both he and the prosecution[13] consents. Remands on bail, therefore,

11 Note the exceptions contained in 1980 Act, s 128(6)(c), (improperly constituted court adjourning summary trial of an 'either way' offence); s 129(1) and (3) (miscellaneous powers to remand accused in his absence); s 131(1) (remand of a defendant already serving a custodial sentence); and s 35 of the Mental Health Act 1983 (remand to a hospital for psychiatric report).
12 'Eight clear days' means that up to 8 days may intervene between the remand date and the date of the accused's next appearance, inclusive of Saturdays, Sundays, Bank Holidays and religious festivals.
13 Ibid, s 128(1)(a).

present no problems in practice, because there is no limit as to the length of the remand, provided the accused and the prosecution consent (which they usually do). Thus where, for example, a court adjourns committal proceedings for six weeks, an accused who is granted bail can be remanded to the same date, but an accused who is remanded in custody will need to be brought back before the court at more or less weekly intervals until the date of the adjourned hearing.[14]

Until recently therefore a person charged with a serious offence such as armed robbery, for which bail was unlikely to be granted, might well be brought back before the court in custody many times over a period of months before the prosecution were ready to ask the magistrates to commit for trial. On each occasion that he was produced from prison, the court was obliged to hear a fully argued bail application, however hopeless its chances of success. Two recent changes in the law have, however, altered the position. First, as a result of the decision in *R v Nottingham Justices, ex p Davies*[15] a court's obligation to hear successive fully argued bail applications has been severely cut down so that in many cases a further remand in custody will be a formality unless there has been a change in circumstances: this decision is discussed more fully later in this chapter. Secondly, amendments to s 128 of the 1980 Act[16] now enable a magistrates' court, subject as below, to remand an adult accused in custody *in his absence* on up to *three* successive occasions, each for up to *eight clear days* at a time. It is uncertain how great a practical effect the latter provision has had as the accused has an absolute right to insist on being present at each remand and to withdraw his consent at any time. Many accused may therefore prefer a weekly excursion to court in order to get away from prison for the day. The procedural requirements[17] before an accused can be remanded in custody in his absence are complicated and fall into two stages.

Stage 1. The accused must be brought before the court. If the magistrates refuse bail, they can invite him to consent to being further remanded in custody in his absence but only if he is legally represented[18] and the court's powers under ss 128(3A) and (3B) of the 1980 Act are explained to him in ordinary language.[19] He must then be asked whether he consents:[20] he has an absolute right to refuse.

If he does consent, he will be remanded in custody for up to eight clear days.

Stage 2. On subsequent remands, provided that the court is satisfied that:-

(i) he has not withdrawn his consent;[1] and

---

14 Unless he consents to being remanded in his absence under 1980 Act, s 128(3A), see infra.
15 [1981] QB 38 DC.
16 See Criminal Justice Act 1982, Sch 9. S 128 in its consolidated form appears in *Stone's Justices' Manual* (1985) Vol 1, p 376.
17 See 1980 Act, ss 128(1A) and (3A): reference should also be made to Home Office Circular No 49/1983 published in (1983) 133 NLJ pp 395 et seq.
18 'Representation' requires the presence of solicitor or counsel in court (ibid, s 128(1B): it would therefore presumably include a duty solicitor.
19 There are no prescribed words for this purpose.
20 1980 Act, s 128(1C).
 1 1980 Act, s 128(3A)(d): Circular 49/1983 (supra) suggests that this may be done either through the accused's solicitor or by the accused writing to the court in person—the Governor should also be informed. The person consenting to a remand in his absence must be given a written form reminding him of his right to withdraw his consent.

(ii) he has a solicitor acting[2] for him; and

(iii) he has not been remanded in his absence on more than two occasions immediately preceding the present remand;[3]

it may[4] remand him in his absence for a further eight days.

Note, firstly that **Stage 1** may be dispensed with if the accused notifies the court in any other way prior to the next date on which he was due to be produced from custody that he does not wish to attend.[5] If, on the other hand, having given his consent, he subsequently withdraws it, the court must remand him in custody for as short a period as is necessary for him to be brought before the court.[6]

Put simply, these new provisions enable the court to remand an accused in custody without his being produced from custody for slightly over a month provided that he consents and subject to the safeguards indicated above.

> EXAMPLE. D appears before the court on *Monday 17 September 1984* charged with burglary. He is represented by the duty solicitor. Having followed the procedure as laid down, the court remands him in custody to *Wednesday 26 September*. On that day, provided he has not withdrawn his consent and also has a solicitor acting for him, for example, under a legal aid order, the court may further remand him to *Friday 5 October* on which occasion, if the criteria are again satisfied he can be remanded to *Friday 12 October*.[7] Since this is the third remand, the court can, subject as above, remand him in his absence once more to *Friday 19 October* but he must be brought back before the court on that date when, unless for example, he is granted bail or committed to the Crown Court for trial, the procedure can begin all over again. He will thus have been remanded in custody for a total of *31 clear days* without having to be brought before the court. If, say, on *3 October*, he or his solicitor had notified the court that consent was withdrawn, at the next hearing (*5 October*) the magistrates would have been obliged to remand him in custody to the earliest date (probably *Monday 8 October*) upon which date he would be brought to court.

Co-accused

Where there are several accused, some may be remanded on bail and others in custody. If, for example, a number of persons were to appear before a magistrates' court charged with offences arising out of a robbery but the prosecution were not ready to proceed with the committal for six weeks, there would be nothing to stop the court from adjourning the proceedings for six weeks and remanding those accused to whom it granted bail to the adjourned date. Only those who were remanded in custody would need to be produced every eight days pending the adjourned hearing (unless they consented to being remanded in their absence, in which case they would need to be produced at least once in the interim).

2 1980 Act, s 128(3B). There is no requirement that a solicitor representing an absent defendant should actually be present in court.

3 Ibid, s 128(3A)(b).

4 The court is not obliged to remand the accused in custody and should bear in mind the possibility of remanding him on bail (Circular 49/1983 (supra)). Fully argued bail applications will however be subject to the restriction in *R v Nottingham Justices, ex p Davies*, supra.

5 Ibid, s 128(3A)(a) which provides that consent may be given either in response to a question under s 128(1C) (supra) or otherwise. Circular 49/1983 (supra) para 6 envisages this consent being communicated to the court via the Prison Governor.

6 Circular 49/1983 (supra) suggests a period of one clear day.

7 It is assumed, for this example, that there will be no court sitting on a Saturday or a Sunday. Since weekends are included in computation of the 8 days' period, it is submitted that a remand to Monday 15 October would have been, ultra vires.

Further provisions as to remands

Remands in a magistrates' court, in practice, tend to follow a predictable pattern: the accused is either remanded on bail for such period as is appropriate or in custody for periods of up to eight clear days at a time unless and until he is either granted bail or dealt with. There are, however, four[8] further provisions contained in the Magistrates' Courts Act 1980 which require mention although they will not be met very often in practice.

(a) Power to further remand an accused who does not appear— s 129.

An accused who fails to surrender to bail without reasonable cause not only commits an offence under s 6(1) of the Bail Act 1976 but also runs the substantial risk of a warrant being issued for his arrest under s 7(1) of that Act. Section 129(1) of the 1980 Act does, however, enable a magistrates' court to further remand[9] an accused for such period as it thinks fit[10] if it is satisfied that he is

> 'unable by reason of illness or accident to appear or be brought before the court at the expiration of the period for which he was remanded'.

Thus, if you are notified that your client will be unable, due to accident or illness to answer to bail, an application can be made, if necessary prior to the expiration of the remand date, for him to be further remanded on bail.

Section 129(3) gives a magistrates' court a further general discretion to grant bail to an accused who has failed to surrender[11] even though he does not come within s 129(1). This is a useful 'last ditch' provision when faced with a situation where the client has failed to appear.[12]

(b) Remands in custody to an alternative magistrates' court—s 130.

Because of the long distances sometimes involved in ferrying an accused between the remand prison and the magistrates' court, especially where there might be numerous remands before committal for trial, the Criminal Law Act 1977 for the first time gave magistrates' courts power to remand in custody[13] to an alternative court nearer to the prison, until the 'home' court was ready to try the offence or commit it, at which stage the accused would be remanded back to the 'home' court.[14] In practice, however, the power is infrequently used and a Home Office circular of 10 July 1978 recommends that it should only be used where the prisoner is a high security risk ('Category A') or the journey is lengthy or inconvenient.

(c) Remands of prisoners already serving a custodial sentence— s 131.

Where the accused is already detained under a custodial sentence, he

---

8 Section 35 Mental Health Act 1983 is considered post at p 237.

9 This subsection thus empowers a court to remand either in custody or on bail.

10 Such remand is therefore not subject to the 8 clear day restriction generally imposed by s 128(6) of the 1980 Act.

11 S 129(3) only applies to an accused who has been on bail: there is no power to remand him in custody under this subsection.

12 One of the writers used this subsection to secure the further remand on bail for one day of an accused who rang up from Spain saying that he had made a mistake over the dates of his package holiday. The magistrates were not prepared to treat it as an 'accident' within s 129(1) but were persuaded to use s 129(3). Fortunately the client appeared in court the following day!

13 S 130(4A) enables applications for remands in custody in an accused's absence under s 128(3A) to be made in the 'alternative' court.

14 In the interim power to remand and grant legal aid is vested in the 'alternative' court (s 130(3)). If in the interim the accused is granted bail the jurisdiction automatically returns to the 'home' court (ibid, s 130(4)).

may be remanded in custody for up to *28 clear days:* the accused's consent is not required. This power was again introduced by the Criminal Law Act 1977 to avoid the need for magistrates to grant 'notional' bail to a person already serving a custodial sentence, this being the only way of circumventing the 'eight clear days' rule.[15] Note that the effect of this section is that he may be remanded in custody in his absence on up to three occasions for successive periods of 28 clear days provided that he consents and provided that the other criteria in s 128(1A) and (3A) of the 1980 Act are satisfied.[16]

(d) Remands into the custody of a constable—s 128(7).[17] A magistrates' court has power under s 128(7) whenever it has power to remand in custody,[18] instead to remand an adult to detention at a police station for up to *three clear days* at a time. Section 128(8) goes on to provide, however, that he can only be detained for so long as is necessary for the purpose of inquiry into other offences.[19] As soon as that need ceases he must be brought back before the court, and he is subject to the review provisions in s 40 of the Police and Criminal Evidence Act 1984.

(2) Adjournments and remands in the magistrates' court after conviction

The provisions as to remands *after* conviction differ substantially from those dealing with remands prior to conviction or committal for trial, in particular as to the periods for which a defendant may be remanded.

(a)   *General power to adjourn*

As has already been seen the court may not be in a position to deal with the defendant immediately after conviction: in some cases it may be virtually obliged to adjourn. Section 10(3) of the 1980 Act provides that a magistrates' court may adjourn for up to *four weeks at a time* to enable enquiries to be made before sentencing a defendant or otherwise dealing with him.[20] This power exists whether the offence is 'summary only' or 'either way' and may be combined with a remand on bail for a similar period. If, however, the magistrates remand in *custody* they cannot do so for more than *three weeks* at a time. In practical terms, therefore, a defendant who has hitherto been on bail will normally be granted bail after conviction when the court adjourns for enquiries, unless the magistrates now take a more serious view of the case because they know more about it. If a defendant for whom you are acting is remanded in custody, however, you would be advised to check as to how

---

15 If, however, it appears to the court that his sentence is due to expire during the 28-day period the 8 clear days rule' revives: 1980 Act, s 131(2).

16 It is submitted, however, s 128(3A) is implicitly subject to s 131(2), ie that there is no power to remand an accused in his absence for 28 clear days if his sentence is due to expire during that period.

17 As amended by Police and Criminal Evidence Act 1984, s 48. This subsection is used where the police charge him with a lesser offence (a 'holding charge') to enable them to continue their enquiries into more serious offences. See generally, p 72, ante.

18 There is, therefore, no power to remand under this subsection unless the accused is brought before the court charged with an offence.

19 This power should be contrasted with the power to detain remand prisoners in police cells because there is no room for them at a prison considered at p 238, post.

20 1980 Act, s 10(3). The purpose of this will usually be to ask the probation service to prepare a social inquiry report. There are certain circumstances in which they are virtually obliged to do so eg before passing a sentence of Youth Custody. See p 409, post.

long it will take to complete the further enquiries: a three-week remand in custody is the maximum and not the standard period of remand.

(*b*) *Adjournments for medical reports—1980 Act, s 30 and Mental Health Act 1983, s 35*

Under s 30 of the 1980 Act, whenever a defendant is tried for an imprisonable offence the court may remand him for successive periods of up to *four weeks* on bail or *three weeks* in custody in order to obtain a medical report on his mental or physical condition.[20a] Under s 35 of the 1983 Act the court may, in the same circumstances remand a defendant to a hospital for a report on his mental condition for up to *28 days* at a time (not exceeding *12 weeks* in all) provided that in addition:

(i) the court is satisfied on medical evidence that there is reason to suspect that he is suffering from mental illness, psychopathic disorder, severe mental impairment or mental impairment; and

(ii) it would be impracticable for a report to be made if he was remanded on bail; and

(iii) arrangements have been made for his admission to hospital.

MAGISTRATES' POWERS TO ADJOURN FOR REPORTS AFTER CONVICTION

	s 10(3) MCA 1980	s 30 MCA 1980	s 35 MHA 1983
1. When?	All cases	Imprisonable Offences	Imprisonable Offences *PLUS* Medical Evidence
2. Remand?	Discretionary	Obligatory (bail or custody)	Obligatory (to a hospital)
3. Period?	*4 weeks* at a time (*3 weeks* if remand in custody)	*4 weeks* at a time (bail) or *3 weeks* (in custody)	*28 days* at a time (*12 weeks* maximum)
4. Purpose?	Enquiries	Report into mental or physical condition	Report into mental condition

(3) What happens after committal to the Crown Court?

When an accused is committed for trial or sentence by a magistrates' court, the committal will always be on bail or in custody. The major difference between the two courts is that after an accused is committed to the Crown Court in custody he will no longer need to be produced from custody every eight days as in the magistrates' court, but will *remain in custody pending trial*

20a The power also exists where the court is satisfied that he did the act or made the omission charged.

unless in the interim he is granted bail.[1] As and when he appears before the Crown Court, that court may adjourn proceedings both before and after conviction. If so, he will either be granted bail or kept in custody. If the trial lasts several days, as it may well do, the question of bail will arise at the end of each day when it is adjourned part-heard.

(4) To where will the accused be remanded in custody?

If the accused is an adult aged *21 or over* he will normally be committed to prison. If he is aged *17–20* inclusive he will be committed to a remand centre, provided that one is available. If not he will be committed to prison[2] (even though the Criminal Justice Act 1982, s 1 provides that such a person can no longer be *sentenced* to imprisonment).

In practice, certain prisons are reserved almost entirely for the reception of remand prisoners, for example, Risley Remand Centre in the north of England and Wormwood Scrubs prison in the London area. In recent years, however, controversial use has been made of s 6 of the Imprisonment (Temporary Provisions) Act 1980 to detain remand prisoners in police cells to relieve overcrowding in prisons.[3]

This has resulted in[4] accused persons remanded by London courts being held in police stations as far apart as Southampton, Peterborough, Ipswich and Stroud.

2 BAIL—THE SUBSTANTIVE LAW AND PROCEDURE

(1) When can bail be granted?

Basically, an accused may be granted bail at any stage in the proceedings: like many areas of criminal procedure the jurisdiction of the various courts to grant bail is something which in practice one picks up as one goes along without realising it. Unfortunately, however, the different jurisdictions overlap. It is therefore necessary, before proceeding further, to list the principle provisions as to when bail may be granted and by which court or courts.

(a) *Bail before the first appearance*

An accused who has been arrested either under a warrant 'backed' for bail or without warrant, will usually have been bailed from the police station to appear at the first hearing before the magistrates. In neither case does the statutory 'right to bail' considered later in the chapter apply.[5] Where a person has been granted bail under the Police and Criminal Evidence Act

---

1 The Crown Court has power to remand a person to a hospital either for reports into or treatment of a mental condition either before or after trial under ss 35 and 36 of the Mental Health Act 1983 for up to 28 days at a time (12 weeks in all).

2 Criminal Justice Act 1948, s 27.

3 The section, inter alia, provides that a person on remand may be lawfully detained in custody of a constable if for any reason it is not practicable to secure his admission to prison or remand centre and until such time as he can be admitted or is required to appear before the court. Despite the citation of the Act, this section is of permanent duration.

4 See for example 'The Police Station as Prison' (1983) 133 NLJ 630.

5 As to 'police bail' see ante p 63. In fact, the provisions governing 'police bail' are now, if anything, more generous than those governing 'court bail', see p 240 post.

1984, to appear before a court, that court may appoint a later time for him to appear and enlarge the recognisances of any sureties accordingly.[6]

(b)   *The Magistrates' Court—the first appearance and beyond*

Magistrates' power to grant bail arises whenever:

(i)   they remand the accused (except where he is charged with treason);[7]
(ii)   they commit him for trial[8] or sentence;[9] or
(iii)   when the accused receives a custodial sentence and gives notice of appeal to the Crown Court[10] or asks the magistrates to state a case for the High Court.[11]

(c)   *The Crown Court*

The Crown Court's powers are contained in s 81 of the Supreme Court Act 1981 as amended by s 60 of the Criminal Justice Act 1982. The most notable occasions upon which bail may be granted are when an accused:

(i)   has been remanded in custody by a magistrates' court[12] who have issued a 'Full Argument Certificate' under s 5(6A) of the Bail Act 1976;[13]
(ii)   has been committed in custody by a magistrates' court for trial or sentence;[14]
(iii)   who is in custody pursuant to a sentence[15] imposed by a magistrates' court and has appealed to the Crown Court against conviction and/ or sentence.[16]

It should particularly be noted that an accused who has been remanded in custody by a magistrates' court may apply for bail to the Crown Court even though he is to be tried summarily, provided that the magistrates' court issues a 'Full Argument Certificate'. If he is to be tried on indictment he may apply either *before* or *after* committal proceedings have been held subject in the former case to the issue of a 'Full Argument Certificate'. The Crown Court may also grant bail when it adjourns proceedings either before or after conviction or, in limited circumstances, pending appeal to the Court of Appeal.

---

6   S 43(1) of the 1980 Act as inserted by s 47(8) Police and Criminal Evidence Act 1984. This provision is intended to cover those occasions when the date specified on the charge sheet for the accused's first appearance needs to be altered. As to sureties see pp 243 et seq, post.
7   Magistrates' Courts Act 1980, s 41: only a High Court judge or the Home Secretary may grant bail in these circumstances.
8   1980 Act, s 6(3).
9   Ibid, ss 37 and 38.
10   Ibid, s 113.
11   Ibid.
12   Supreme Court Act 1981, s 81(1)(9). There is thus no power to grant bail under this sub-section if the accused has been remanded on bail subject to conditions eg sureties which he finds unacceptable.
13   Ibid, s 81(1J).
14   Ibid, s 81(1)(a).
15   A juvenile is probably 'in custody' for the purposes of this section, where he has been made subject to a care order following conviction *R v P* (1979) 144 JP 39.
16   Ibid, s 81(1)(b). See further p 458, post.

(d)   The High Court

The High Court has power to grant bail or vary conditions whenever a magistrates' court has refused bail or imposed conditions.[17] As will be noted later this power is additional to the powers vested in the Crown Court. Thus, an accused who has been refused bail by the magistrates, in effect, has two options, either of which may be exercised without prejudice to the other. In practical terms, however, cost is the major inhibiting factor.

(e)   The Criminal Division of the Court of Appeal

The Criminal Division of the Court of Appeal may grant bail to a person appealing to it from the Crown Court against conviction or sentence or who is pursuing an appeal to the House of Lords[18] but this is rarely granted.[19]

(2) Principles upon which bail is granted: Bail Act 1976, s 4: 'The right to bail'

Prior to the coming into force of the Bail Act 1976 the grant of bail was governed almost entirely by common law. Criticism of the then existing system was substantial, in particular because of the lack of principle governing the grant or refusal of bail and the often vaguely formulated objections such as 'the seriousness of the offence', 'no fixed abode' and inquiries into further offences' frequently put forward by the police. The 1976 Act was passed therefore in an attempt to introduce principles into an area of the law in which there had hitherto been remarkably few. The purported major changes it introduced were:

(a) the creation of a statutory 'right to bail' in certain circumstances[20] subject to defined exceptions;[21]

(b) the abolition of the defendant's personal recognisance;[22]

(c) as a quid pro quo to (b) above, the creation of the offence of absconding;[1]

(d) the imposition of an obligation upon a magistrates' court or Crown Court to give reasons for refusing bail where the 'right to bail' applied.[2]

It seems, however, that the 1976 Act has had little impact on the number of defendants remanded or committed in custody.[3] Although, therefore, it may be argued that the 'right to bail' is little more than statutory window dressing it is nevertheless important to contrast the principles to be applied on those occasions where the 'right to bail' arises with those where it does not.

17 Criminal Justice Act 1967, s 22. Power also exists to grant bail on an application for judicial review: Criminal Justice Act 1948, s 37.
18 Criminal Appeal Act 1968, ss 19 and 36.
19 Since the appeal will be against the custodial sentence it should be noted that the grant of bail (by any court) in such circumstances will always stop a sentence running: see eg Magistrates' Courts Act 1980, s 114. See also *Archbold* (41st edn) 7/86.
20 Bail Act 1976, s 4.
21 Ibid, Sch 1, parts I and II.
22 Procedure whereby an accused granted bail could be required to enter into a recognisance for a specified sum of money: eg £500, which was liable to forfeiture if he absconded.
1 Ibid, ss 6(1) and (2).
2 Ibid, s 5.
3 See L. L. M. Cutts, 'Has the Bail Act made any difference?' (1982) 132 NLJ 1089 and East and Doherty, 'The practical operation of bail' Legal Action, March 1984, p 12.

(A) WHERE THE 'RIGHT TO BAIL' ARISES

Section 4 of the Bail Act 1976 provides that a person to whom the section applies 'shall be granted bail' except as provided in Sch 1 to the Act. The effect of the section is that an accused enjoys the statutory 'right to bail' from the moment of his first appearance before the court up to the moment of his conviction, whichever court is hearing his application. The right does not, however, exist *after* conviction unless:

(i) the court adjourns for inquiries or reports before sentencing him;[4] or
(ii) he appears or is brought before a magistrates' court to be dealt with for breach of a probation or community service order.[5]

What statute gives with one hand, however, it takes away with the other. The 'right to bail' in s 4 is expressly subject to the provisions of Sch 1 to the 1976 Act. Parts I and II of Sch 1, deal with '*imprisonable*' and '*non-imprisonable*' offences respectively and give *six* grounds for refusing bail in respect of the former and *four* in respect of the latter (three being common to both). In the vast majority of cases where bail is in issue, the accused will be charged with an imprisonable offence; Sch 1 thus considerably diminishes the practical significance of the 'right to bail'. Sch 1 is, however, exhaustive: it sets out the only grounds upon which a court may refuse bail.[6] The criminal advocate must therefore have its provisions at his or her fingertips.

Sch 1 Parts 1 and 2 provides that a defendant need not be granted bail if:

IMPRISONABLE OFFENCES ONLY

(1) The court is satisfied that there are substantial grounds for believing that if released on bail (whether subject to conditions or not) he would—
(a) fail to surrender to custody, or
(b) commit an offence whilst on bail, or
(c) interfere with witnesses or otherwise obstruct the course of justice whether in relation to himself or any other person.[7]

This is by far the most common ground invoked. The prime objective of bail should, of course, be to secure that the accused attends court. It is, however, interesting to note the extent to which the likelihood of committing further offences whilst on bail has assumed greater significance in the last thirty years, especially where the accused has a bad record.[8] The Home Office Working Party on bail suggested that there was some evidence to support this, especially where the accused was charged with robbery and burglary, and this has now so become part of judicial folklore that it is virtually accorded the status of a conclusive presumption. The risk of interference with witnesses is only likely to be raised where the offence is a very serious one, and should diminish in likelihood as the police complete their investigations—an important point to bear in mind when making subsequent applications, especially at committal. Because ground *(1)* is of such paramount

---

4 1976 Act, s 4(4).
5 Ibid, s 4(3).
6 Ibid, s 4(1).
7 Ibid, Sch 1, Part I, para 2.
8 See Vogler, 'The Changing Nature of Bail' LAG Bulletin February 1983, p 11. Use of the 'further offence' ground has also been most notable in serious public order disturbances (eg during the 1981 riots and the 1984 miners' strike) see *R v Mansfield Justices, ex p Sharkey* [1985] 1 All ER 193.

importance, Schedule 1 also requires the court in coming to its decision to
have regard to the following four 'considerations'[9] namely:

  (i)   the nature and seriousness of the offence or default (and the probable method
        of dealing with the defendant for it);
  (ii) the character, antecedents, associations and community ties of the defendant;
  (iii) the defendant's record as respects the fulfilment of his obligations under the
        previous grant of bail in criminal proceedings;
  (iv) except in the case of a defendant whose case is adjourned for inquiries or a
        report, the strength of the evidence of his having committed the offence or
        having defaulted,
        along with any other which appear relevant.

Their combined effect is to enable the pre-1976 Act grounds for refusal such
as 'no fixed abode', 'the seriousness of the offence'[10] etc to still be available,
but wrapped up in a new guise.

> EXAMPLE. D is brought before the court charged with taking a conveyance without
> consent, having been arrested without warrant. He has been living rough and is
> out of work. He also has two similar previous convictions and has served three
> months in a detention centre for one of these. Prior to the Bail Act 1976, the police
> would have merely put forward vague objections such as 'no fixed abode' or 'the
> accused's record' etc and he would have been remanded in custody. Now he will
> probably still be refused bail, ostensibly because, for example, the bench are
> 'satisfied' etc that he will 'fail to surrender to custody' having taken into account
> his 'character, antecedents, associations and community ties'. The only difference
> is that he will now be told why and get a piece of paper confirming this.

(2) *The court is satisfied that it has not been practicable to obtain sufficient information
     to take the decisions required by Schedule 1, Part I for want of time since the
     institution of the proceedings against him.*[11]
(3) *The court adjourns for inquiries or a report and it would be impracticable to
     complete these without keeping him in custody.*[12]

Grounds (2) and (3) may be contrasted in that the latter applies to inquiries
after conviction whereas the former will tend to be invoked prior to conviction. Ground (2) may, for example, be used as justification for refusing bail
on the first appearance to an accused who is 'living rough' even if the offence
is not particularly serious.

IMPRISONABLE AND NON-IMPRISONABLE OFFENCES

Although the following three grounds apply to both categories of offence, in
practical terms, they are only likely to be raised where the offence is imprisonable.

(4) *The court is satisfied that he should be kept in custody for his own protection or, if
     he is a child or young person, for his own welfare.*[13]

This tends to be put forward in cases involving adults, where the offence is
such that there is a real risk of 'revenge attacks', for example, a serious sex
offence or the supplying of a Class A drug which has ended in a fatality, or

---

9 1976 Act, Sch 1, Part I, para 9.
10 The relevant criminal statistics reveal that since 1979 approximately 5% of accused remanded on bail at magistrates' courts failed to appear. By far the highest non-appearance
   rates are for those bailed on motoring offences and drunkenness.
11 Ibid, para 5.
12 Ibid, para 7.
13 Ibid, Sch 1, Part I, para 3; and Part II, para 3.

because the accused's own health is such that he cannot safely be released, for example, because of drug addiction, such cases are likely to constitute the only occasions on which the accused's own solicitor asks for a remand in custody to protect his client.

(5) He is in custody in pursuance of the sentence of a court or under the Services Acts.[14]

Bail would often be futile. Note the power to remand in custody for up to 28 clear days under s 131 of the 1980 Act considered ante.

(6) Having been released on bail in the current proceedings he has been arrested under s 7 of the 1976 Act for absconding or breach of bail conditions.[15]

If arrested without warrant ground (6) will, only take effect if the grounds for arrest are made out. If they are not, the court is obliged to release the accused on the same terms as before.[16]

NON-IMPRISONABLE OFFENCES ONLY

(7) He has failed to surrender to bail granted in previous criminal proceedings and the court believes in view of that failure he would fail to surrender to custody if released on bail (whether subject to conditions or not).[17]

This ground will only be invoked in those cases where although the offence is a minor one the court still considers that there is a risk of the accused not attending, for example, where he is charged with careless driving or driving without insurance and there is a substantial likelihood of disqualification.

(B) WHERE THE 'RIGHT TO BAIL' DOES NOT APPLY

There are numerous occasions when bail may be granted but the 'right to bail' does not arise, for example, on committal for sentence or pending appeal after a custodial sentence. Where a court is considering bail in such cases, its discretion is unfettered by s 4 of the Bail Act 1976 or any of the matters contained in Sch 1, Parts I and II, nor is it obliged to give reasons for its refusal. If anything, it could be said that there is a presumption *against* the granting of bail in such cases and the courts have indicated on several occasions that bail should not normally be granted where, for example, magistrates commit for sentence under s 38 of the 1980 Act,[18] or pending an appeal against a custodial sentence.[19]

(3) 'Attaching strings': sureties, security and conditions: Bail Act 1976, s 3

Notwithstanding the wide powers that courts have to grant bail and the existence of the 'right to bail', if the offence is serious, an accused's chance of obtaining bail, even before conviction, may be very slim indeed in the face of sustained prosecution objections. Often his statutory duty to surrender to

14 1976 Act, Sch 1, Part I, para 5; and Part II, para 4.
15 Ibid, Sch 1, Part I, para 6; and Part II, para 5.
16 Ibid, s 7(5). For the consequences of absconding see further p 247, post.
17 Ibid, Sch 1, Part II, para 2.
18 See eg *R v Coe* [1969] 1 All ER 65 the reason being that they are committing to the Crown Court because they consider that the offence merits more than 6 months' imprisonment.
19 See eg *R v Walton* (1978) 68 Cr App Rep 293.

bail[20] and the powers of arrest will not, of themselves, be considered sufficient. In cases of doubt, the grant of bail may be made subject to one or more of the following three safeguards, namely:

(a) the taking of *sureties;*
(b) the deposit of a *security;* and
(c) the imposition of *conditions.*

None of these requirements can generally[1] be imposed, however, unless the offence is *imprisonable* and the court considers it *necessary*[2] in order to prevent the accused:

(i) failing to surrender to custody; and/or
(ii) committing an offence whilst on bail; and/or
(iii) interfering with witnesses or otherwise obstructing the course of justice.[3]

The ability to put forward constructive proposals as to sureties, and conditions (the offering of securities is of limited application) is vital. Where there are strong objections to bail they may make the difference between the success and failure of the application.

(a)   The power to take sureties (*1976 Act, s 3(3)*)

A surety is a person who undertakes to pay a specified sum of money should the person for whom he has stood surety fail to surrender to custody. The purpose of taking a surety is to provide someone other than the accused with an incentive to ensure that he surrenders to bail. Sureties may be taken whenever the power to grant bail arises (even in the case of 'police bail') but, save in the case of a parent or guardian consenting to be surety for a juvenile, a surety cannot be required to secure compliance with any conditions imposed under s 3(6). The 1976 Act empowers the court or a police officer who grants bail subject to sureties, when considering the suitability of a surety, to have regard to, amongst other things:

(i) the surety's financial *resources*;
(ii) his *character* and previous *convictions* (if any); and
(iii) his *proximity* (whether by place or kinship, residence or otherwise) to the accused.[4]

It is a common misconception that the surety must deposit the appropriate sum in court. This is not so. The money only becomes payable should the accused fail to surrender, and the court orders forfeiture of all or part of the sum. It is enforceable as if it were a fine.[5] The money or money's worth that

20 1976 Act, s 3(1).
1 The imposition of conditions that an accused makes himself available for medical examination are mandatory where he is granted bail on a murder charge (1976 Act, s 6A) and where the court remands on bail for a medical examination under s 30 of the Magistrates' Courts Act 1980 (ibid, s 30(2)).
2 It appears, however, that it is not an essential prerequisite for the court to have substantial grounds for believing that if granted bail any of these things are likely to happen, *ex p Sharkey* (supra). The risk must however be 'real not fanciful': ibid.
3 1976 Act, Sch 1, Part I, para 8. Where a court remands on bail after conviction the court may also impose a condition that the accused makes himself available for the purpose of enabling enquiries or a report to be made if they think that it is necessary in order to enquire into or report upon his physical or mental condition.
4 Ibid, s 8(2).
5 Magistrates' Courts Act 1980, s 120.

the surety 'puts up' must however be his or her own. It is an offence under s 9 of the 1976 Act punishable on indictment by up to *12 months'* imprisonment and/or a fine and summarily by up to *three months'* imprisonment and/or a £2000 fine, to agree to indemnify sureties.

(b) Security (1976 Act, s 3(5))

The power to require a security differs from sureties in three important respects. First, security can only be required if it appears that the accused is 'unlikely to remain in Great Britain' (ie England, Wales and Scotland). Secondly, the security must actually be deposited and thirdly it may be taken from the accused or given by a person 'on his behalf'. Home Office Circular 206/1977 gives guidance as to the form such a security might take, for example, cash, travellers cheques etc., but the court granting bail has a general discretion. Provisions exist[6] for forfeiture of the security should the accused fail to surrender to custody. Note, however, that in common with sureties security may be required whenever the power to grant bail arises, including 'police bail'.

(c) Imposition of conditions (1976 Act s 3(6))

The imposition of conditions is a relatively new feature in the history of bail.[7] Unlike taking sureties and requiring security, conditions can only be imposed by a court. The 1976 Act does not specify what conditions[8] may be imposed, but common conditions are that the accused:

   (i) reports daily or otherwise to the police station;
  (ii) keeps to a curfew;
 (iii) resides at a particular address;
 (iv) keeps away from certain people or places;
  (v) (far less frequently) surrenders his passport.[9]

Conditions should not be imposed unless they are capable of being complied with[10] although this does not always appear to have been taken to heart.[11] The attractiveness of s 3(6) conditions is that any reasonable suspicion of or apprehended breach of conditions entitles the police to arrest the defendant under s 7(3) of the 1976 Act. It can thus be argued that this draconian power will almost always substantially diminish the risk of the accused absconding or committing further offences whilst on bail. This topic is considered further in the third section of this chapter.

---

6 1976 Act, ss 5(7)–(9A).
7 For an interesting discussion of the background see Vogler (op cit). The power was first introduced by Criminal Justice Act 1967, s 21. East and Doherty (op cit) observed that 38% of those granted bail in their study had conditions imposed.
8 Note the special conditions which must be imposed in murder cases and remands for medical reports under s 30 of the 1980 Act noted supra at p 244, note 3.
9 This is the order of frequency revealed by the East and Doherty (op cit) study. In *ex p Sharkey* (supra) the Divisional Court upheld the decision of the Mansfield justices requiring that the accused did not visit any premises or place for the purpose of picketing or demonstrating in the then current miners' dispute other than to picket peacefully or demonstrate at their usual place of employment.
10 See Home Office Circular 206/1977.
11 See Vogler (op cit).

(4) Recording of information and giving of reasons: Bail Act 1976, s 5

Section 5 imposes certain obligations on the police and courts to record bail decisions and give reasons. These are quite unnecessarily complicated, but may be summarised as follows.

(a) A duty to make a record of the bail decision and give the accused a copy on request[12]

'This arises whenever (inter alia) bail is granted or conditions are imposed or varied. If bail is refused, however, the duty only arises where the right to bail' exists. Thus, for example, a custody officer granting 'police bail' would be under a s 5(1) duty; but would not be so if bail were refused. The resultant proliferation of paperwork is one of the most notable changes that the 1976 Act has brought about.

(b) A duty to give reasons for refusing bail[13]

This only arises in cases where the 'right to bail' exists and only applies in a magistrates' court and the Crown Court. It requires either court to announce its reasons when refusing bail or imposing or varying conditions and to include these in its s 5(1) record. The only exception to this is where an accused is before the Crown Court represented by solicitor or counsel and no request for reasons is made.

(c) A duty to advise an unrepresented accused of his right to apply to the Crown Court or a High Court Judge in Chambers[14]

This is a strangely drafted section. Its overall effect is that whenever a magistrates' court refuses bail to an unrepresented accused it must inform him of his right to apply for bail to a High Court judge (and to the Crown Court when it commits for trial or issues a 'Full Argument Certificate'). When, therefore, an unrepresented defendant is committed for sentence or gives notice of appeal against a custodial sentence he need only be informed of his right to apply to the High Court even though he can in fact also apply to the Crown Court.

(d) A duty to furnish an accused who has been refused bail after full argument with a certificate to that effect[15]

This is a most important document, the issue of which is an essential pre-requisite[16] to an application for bail to the Crown Court when a magistrates' court has remanded in custody prior to summary trial or committal. The significance of 'full' bail applications will be considered later on in this section.

---

12 1976 Act, s 5(1).
13 Ibid, s 5(3) and (4).
14 Ibid, s 5(6).
15 Ibid, s 5(6A).
16 And must therefore render the 'blanket' policy of refusing bail applications alleged to have taken place in some courts during the 1981 riots even more unlawful since it precludes the issue of a Full Argument Certificate thus denying the accused his right to apply to the Crown Court.

(5) **What happens if the accused fails to surrender or is in breach of conditions?**

Put simply, an accused who fails to answer to bail will have a warrant issued for his arrest and will be guilty of an offence, any surety will be liable to pay up the sum that he has stood for ('estreatment of his recognisance'), and any security will likewise be subject to forfeiture. There are, however, a number of points which require fuller consideration.

(a) *Preventative arrests: 1976 Act, s 7(3)*

A constable may arrest without warrant a person who has been released on bail 'in criminal proceedings' and is under a duty to surrender to a court[17] in any of the following three circumstances:

- (i) if he has reasonable grounds for believing that he is *not likely to surrender to custody*; or
- (ii) if he has reasonable grounds for believing that he *has broken or is likely to break* any of the *conditions* of his bail; or
- (iii) if any *surety* notifies a constable in writing that the accused is *unlikely to surrender* to custody and for that reason *wishes to be relieved* as a surety.

After arrest, the accused must be brought before a magistrate in the area in which he was arrested as soon as practicable and, in any event, within *24 hours*.[18] The only exception to this is where he was to have surrendered within the next 24 hours to the court granting bail, in which case he must be brought before that court.[19] If the magistrate is of the opinion that the accused is not likely to surrender to custody or has broken or is likely to break his conditions he has a discretion whether or not to grant bail.[20] If the magistrate is not so satisfied he must renew bail on the original terms.[21] Note that although the 'right to bail' still applies, arrest under s 7(3) is of itself a circumstance justifying the refusal of bail.[1] In no circumstance, however, will an accused arrested under this provision be guilty of the offence of absconding.

(b) *Failure to surrender*

Firstly, if the accused either fails to surrender to custody or having surrendered into custody leaves without permission before being dealt with, the court to which he was bailed to appear may (and usually will) issue a warrant for his arrest.[2] Although the warrant may be 'backed' for bail,[3] it is unlikely that it will be. When he is arrested and brought before the court under the warrant, the grant or refusal of bail will be governed by the same

---

17 S 7(3) of 1976 Act thus does not apply to a person who is to surrender at a police station.
18 1976 Act, s 7(4).
19 Ibid.
20 Ibid, s 7(5).
21 Ibid.
1 Ibid, Sch 1, Part I, para 6; Part II, para 5.
2 Ibid, s 7(1) and (2) 1; rarely, it may exercise its powers under s 129(1) or (3) Magistrates' Courts Act 1980, considered ante p 235.
3 Magistrates' Courts Act 1980, s 117; Supreme Court Act 1981, s 81(4) where the warrant is issued by a judge of the Crown Court.

principles as on remands:[4] once again, the fact of the accused's arrest is itself a ground for refusing bail in those cases where the 'right to bail' applies.[5]

Secondly, the accused will be guilty of an offence under s 6 of the 1976 Act either if he fails without reasonable cause to surrender at all,[6] or if, although having reasonable cause, he fails to surrender as soon as is reasonably practicable.[7] The burden of proving reasonable cause is on the accused[8] and the fact that he did not receive a written copy of the bail decision is not a reasonable cause.[9]

An accused charged with absconding may be dealt with in one of three ways.

(i) **Summarily before the magistrates.** This is possible whichever court the accused was bailed to and may be the most appropriate course where he has failed to surrender to the custody of, for example, the Crown Court but wishes to plead 'not guilty' to the Bail Act offence. On summary conviction, the offence is punishable by up to *three months' imprisonment* and/or a *£2,000 fine*.[10]

(ii) **On committal for sentence to the Crown Court.** If the accused is tried and convicted of absconding by a magistrates' court, it may commit him in custody or on bail to the Crown Court for sentence if the court thinks that the circumstances of the offence are such that greater punishment should be inflicted, or it is committing the accused for trial to the Crown Court for another offence and it would be appropriate for him to be dealt with for the absconding offence by the same court.[11] If so committed the accused is liable to a term not exceeding *12 months' imprisonment* and/or an *unlimited fine*.[12]

> EXAMPLE. D is on bail awaiting committal for trial to the Crown Court on a charge of burglary. On the date fixed for the committal proceedings, say, *25 April* he fails to attend. A warrant is accordingly issued for his arrest and he is arrested on *27 April*. He is held overnight and charged with an offence under s 6(1) of the 1976 Act. On the morning of *28 April* he is brought before the court when the magistrates remand him in custody on both the burglary and the absconding charge, to *3 May*. Before the committal proceedings on *3 May* the absconding charge will be put to him. If he pleads 'guilty' the magistrates may deal with him there and then, or alternatively commit the absconding charge along with the burglary. If, on the other hand, he disputes the charge and wishes to plead 'not guilty' it may be appropriate to commit the burglary and deal with the absconding charge separately. If he were to be subsequently convicted on the absconding charge the magistrates could still commit him to the Crown Court for sentence if they thought that their powers were insufficient.

(iii) **As a criminal contempt of court by the Crown Court, High Court or Court of Appeal.** If the accused fails to surrender to custody of any of the above courts (usually the Crown Court) a judge of the relevant

---

4 See p 240 et seq, ante, the s 4 'right to bail' will therefore usually apply. Unlike arrests under s 7(3) the court's discretion is not fettered in any way thus, it can, in theory, refuse to grant bail even where there is prima facie a good reason why the accused has not surrendered.
5 See note 1, p 247, supra.
6 1976 Act, s 6(1).
7 Ibid, s 6(2).
8 Ibid, s 6(3) and the standard of proof is on the balance of probabilities.
9 S 6(4).
10 Ibid, ss 6(5) and (7).
11 Ibid, s 6(6).
12 Ibid, s 6(7).

court may deal with the matter summarily without the formality of an indictment or empanelling a jury. The court's sentencing powers are the same as those in (**ii**) above. This is, however, an alternative to method (**i**) above and the Court of Appeal have stated in *R v Harbax Singh*[13] that, where an accused pleads 'not guilty' before the Crown Court to a charge of absconding, remittal for trial before the magistrates is more appropriate.

(c) Committing further offences whilst on bail

Commission of further offences is not, of itself, a breach of bail although it may incidentally involve a breach of condition. For example, an accused who commits several burglaries whilst on bail may also be in breach of his 'curfew'. Much will depend upon the nature of the further offences but if they are imprisonable, there will be strong grounds for the court dealing with the further offences to refuse bail. If the accused is remanded in custody for the further offences, his bail on the first offence is somewhat overtaken by events. He will still theoretically have to surrender to bail but in all probability it will not be renewed.[14]

(d) The position of the sureties

A surety's position is always precarious[15] and even though they are not your clients, you should always advise them in no uncertain terms as to what will happen if the accused absconds. Although the surety must be given an opportunity to show cause as to why the whole sum should not be forfeited[16] and although the court has a discretion to waive forfeiture or order it in part only[17] the burden of showing cause is prima facie upon the surety (as was confirmed in the recent case of *R v Uxbridge Justices, ex p Heward-Mills*[18]). The surety must show that he took all reasonable steps to secure the attendance of the person bailed or that there is some other compelling reason to excuse him, for example, that he was not told that the condition of bail had been varied.[19] Such reasons will, however, be closely scrutinised by the court. It was held by Forbes J in *R v Ipswich Crown Court, ex p Reddington*[20] that going to the police did not, of itself, relieve a surety. If done promptly before the accused's next appearance, however, this should amount to 'due diligence' since it empowers the police to arrest him under s 7(3) of the 1976 Act. Lack of means will not, of itself, be sufficient reason for not ordering forfeiture but

---

13 [1979] QB 319.
14 Presumably Sch 1, Part I, para 2 of the 1976 Act can be invoked even where the accused is in custody for other offences otherwise it is somewhat hard to see on what grounds refusal to raise bail for the original offences can be justified. S 131 of the 1980 Act (power to remand an accused already serving a custodial sentence) will not apply. Problems may sometimes arise over arranging his production before the court who granted bail. The prison governor will not be in contempt for failing to produce him and habeas corpus will not lie: *R v Governor of Brixton prison, ex p Walsh* [1985] AC 154, HL.
15 It is unclear whether the surety has a power of arrest at common law (1971) 136 JPN 400.
16 Magistrates' Courts' Act 1980, s 120(1).
17 Ibid, s 120(3).
18 [1983] 1 All ER 530 following *R v Southampton Justices, ex p Green* [1976] QB 11.
19 *R v Wells Street Justices, ex p Albanese* [1982] QB 333. See also *R v Salford Stipendiary Magistrate, ex p Monoghan* (1984) Times, 18 July (no duty to tell surety that accused likely to be charged with more serious offence).
20 [1981] Crim LR 618.

	Police Bail	Court Bail Before conviction	Court Bail After conviction/ before sentence where adjournments for reports etc.	Court Bail After conviction in other cases and after sentence
s 3(1) Duty to Surrender	✓	✓	✓	✓
(4) Sureties	✓	✓	✓	✓
(5) Security	✓	✓	✓	✓
(6) Conditions	—	✓	✓	✓
s 4 Right to Bail	—	✓	✓	—
s 5(1) Duty to record grant	✓	✓	✓	✓
Duty to record refusal	—	✓	✓	—
(3) Duty to give reasons for refusal/conditions	—	✓	✓	—
(Magistrates only)				
(6) Duty to inform unrepresented defendant of rights	—	✓	✓	—
(6A) Duty to issue "Full Argument Certificate"	—	✓	✓	—
s 6 Offence of absconding	✓	✓	✓	✓
s 7 Powers of arrest				
(1) With warrant	✓	✓	✓	✓
(2) Without warrant	✓	✓	✓	✓

the court is required to look into the surety's means before deciding whether to forfeit and, if so, how much.[1]

(6) What happens when bail is refused (or granted subject to conditions which cannot be fulfilled)?

There are three situations which require consideration, namely:

- (a) where bail is withheld prior to committal (or summary trial);
- (b) where the accused is committed to the Crown Court in custody; and
- (c) where a variation in conditions of bail is sought at any stage in the proceedings.

(a)   When bail is withheld prior to committal (or summary trial)

In this situation the accused now has three options open to him. It should be noted that these are not mutually exclusive in that he can, in theory, pursue any one or all of them in whichever order he chooses, subject as below. The alternatives are as follows.

(i) To re-apply for bail to the magistrates' court. Until 1980 the restriction upon the length of time for which magistrates could remand in custody meant that if bail was refused a further fully argued application

---

1 *R v Uxbridge Justices, ex p Heward-Mills*, supra. Note that judicial review will lie even against forfeiture by a Crown Court: *Smalley v Crown Court at Warwick* [1985] 1 All ER 769, HL.

could be made on each subsequent occasion upon which the accused was brought back before the court. In view of the fact that the composition of the bench would probably vary from application to application, it was not unheard of for an application which had failed before one bench to succeed before another even though framed in identical terms. However, as a result, of the decision of the Divisional Court in *R v Nottingham Justices, ex p Davies*[2] the right of the accused to make successive bail applications has now been seriously curtailed. The effect of the decision is as follows. Once an accused has made *two* unsuccessful applications for bail, a subsequent magistrates' court cannot go behind the earlier court's finding that one of the 'Schedule 1 grounds' for refusing bail exists, unless there has been either a *'change in circumstances'* or there are *'new considerations'* which were not before the court when the accused was last remanded in custody.[3] The rationale behind fixing the number of applications at two appears in the judgment of Donaldson LJ[4] (as he then was):

> 'the magic of a third application for bail requires a word of explanation. It appears that the first application is likely to be made by a duty solicitor who has no opportunity to take very full instructions from his client. The second application is likely to be made by a solicitor instructed privately or under legal aid who has had such an opportunity. In the case of the third and subsequent applications, it is thought that all material facts will already have emerged and that in the absence of 'new circumstances', full argument, if allowed, would in effect, involve an appeal against one or more previous decisions to remand in custody ... On the second application it is almost always possible for an applicant for bail or his advocate to submit correctly that there are matters to be considered by the court which were not considered on the first occasion. Where this is the experience of any particular bench of justices, the Nottingham practice is not only convenient, but right.'

Examples of 'changes in circumstances' might be, that the police have completed their inquiries and the likelihood of interference with witnesses has accordingly diminished, or that sureties and/or a fixed address are now available. It was further stated by Donaldson LJ in *R v Reading Crown Court, ex p Malik*[5] that the fact that the prosecution had completed its investigations and that the accused was about to be committed for trial would, as a general rule, constitute such a change, for example, because the court would now be much better able to assess 'the nature and seriousness of the offence'. A subsequent Divisional Court has, however, stated in *R v Slough Justices, ex p Duncan*[6] that the mere fact of committal and the consequences flowing therefrom will not, of itself, oblige the justices to hear a further full application. *Ex p Davies* has now received statutory recognition in the shape of the 'Full Argument Certificate' in the magistrates' court which must be issued on a remand in custody whenever 'full argument' (not statutorily defined) has taken place.[7]

Put simply, therefore, once a full application has been made you may be better advised to pursue an application before the Crown Court, because if you try to make a further full application before the magistrates without

---

2 Supra.
3 Note that where there are, the court must look not merely at the change or the new considerations but must consider *all* the circumstances de novo: *R v Barking Justices, ex p Shankshaft*, (1983) 147 JP 399.
4 *R v Nottingham Justices, ex p Davies*, supra at 42 et seq.
5 [1981] QB 451.
6 (1982) 75 Cr App Rep 384.
7 1976 Act, s 5(6A).

satisfying the *ex p Davies* test, you will not be given a hearing. It must, however, be stressed that local practice varies so that it is as well to ascertain the approach of the bench when appearing in an unfamiliar court. Some courts will, for example, allow the defence to 'save up' their full application until, say, their sureties are organised, whereas others will be less flexible. Since the issue of a 'Full Argument Certificate' is such a vital prerequisite to an application for bail to the Crown Court, it is to be hoped that courts will not invariably treat the first application by the Duty Solicitor as a 'full' argument. If they do, 'it will limit even further the accused's so called 'right to bail'.

(ii) To apply to the Crown Court. As has already been seen, application can be made to the Crown Court whenever the magistrates' court remands in custody provided that magistrates have given a 'Full Argument Certificate'. Note that if a legal aid order has been granted for the proceedings it will also cover the Crown Court application[8] but that unlike the case of applications after committal, legal aid will not extend to counsel, unless specifically authorised.[9]

The procedure for making such applications is governed by rr 19 and 20 of the Crown Court Rules 1982.[10] It involves applying on the prescribed form to the Crown Court to which the case will be or would have been committed for trial, or, where the offence is summary, to the Crown Court Centre which normally handles Class 4 work. It is vital that the Full Argument Certificate accompanies the application otherwise there will be delay in listing. Normally, the Crown Court will return a copy of the form with a hearing date, and a copy must then be served on the prosecution at least *24 hours* before the application is made. The hearing will normally be in chambers and the accused will not be entitled to be present without leave of the Crown Court. The court must also be notified whether prior application has been made to a High Court judge.

If bail is granted the accused will be bailed to appear before the relevant magistrates' court. If bail is refused there is nothing to prevent him from applying to a High Court judge in chambers. Otherwise, his only alternative prior to committal, is to re-apply to the magistrates on a subsequent remand, if there has been a 'change in circumstances' or 'new considerations' have arisen. If he is again unsuccessful he can re-apply to the Crown Court on the strength of the new 'Full Argument Certificate'.[11] In theory, this process could be repeated several times before summary trial or committal.

(iii) To apply to a High Court judge in chambers. A judge of the High Court has jurisdiction to grant bail whenever a magistrates' court refuses bail or imposes conditions.[12] The application is classified as civil proceedings and is governed by RSC, Ord 79. Where he is represented, application will be by way of summons in Form 97 with affidavit in support, copies of which must be served on the prosecution at least *24 hours* before the hearing. The summons will either need to be issued at the Crown Office at the Royal Courts of Justice or the nearest appropriate District Registry and a hearing

---

8 Legal Aid Act 1974, s 30(1A): there is, however, no power to grant legal aid for the bail application alone.
9 Ibid, s 30(1B). Counsel may be used even if not authorised but the sum allowed would only be that which would have been payable if a solicitor only had attended.
10 See also Practice Direction [1983] 2 All ER 261.
11 See Bail Act 1976, s 5(6A)(6B)(ii).
12 See p 240, ante.

date obtained. In cases of real emergency, the notice period can be dispensed with by agreement with the prosecution.[13] The hearing will be in chambers and solicitors therefore have rights of audience, although often counsel will be instructed. If bail is granted the accused will be bailed to appear at the magistrates' court at such time as they themselves could have directed.[14]

The major problem with obtaining representation has always been money. Unless an accused has the means to pay privately[15] an application for a civil legal aid certificate will have to be made to the relevant Area Committee. The generally held view had been that such applications were pointless because they would automatically be refused on the ground that the Official Solicitor procedure considered below was available. The Law Society have, however, recently reminded practitioners that legal aid *is* available for such applications and that there is no policy of automatically refusing them. The information required in support of such an application is, however, of such a nature as to suggest that very strong grounds are needed for an application for legal aid to succeed.[16]

Where the accused is refused legal aid, and cannot afford to pay privately, he may instead fill in a form, available at prisons, asking the Official Solicitor to apply on his behalf. 'Application' is however a misnomer because there will be no formal application as such and no affidavit will normally be placed before the judge. As a result such applications have little chance of success.[17]

If bail is refused by a High Court Judge no further application may be made to another High Court Judge or to the Divisional Court,[18] but this does not preclude re-applying to the Judge who refused bail if there is a 'change in circumstances', or going back before him/her to vary conditions. Indeed there is nothing to prevent the accused from later applying to the Crown Court where a 'Full Argument Certificate' has been issued, if this option has not yet been exercised. Furthermore, it may still be possible to re-apply to the magistrates on a subsequent remand or at the committal proceedings on the basis of a 'change in circumstances' or 'new considerations'.

(b) After committal or on appeal to the Crown Court

Where the magistrates commit for trial or sentence in custody or refuse bail pending an appeal, the accused has two options both of which may again be exercised without prejudice to the other.

(i) To apply to the Crown Court. If legal aid has been granted to cover the proceedings in the Crown Court this will automatically cover an application for bail.[19] Proceedings are governed by the same provisions of the Crown Court Rules 1982 as applications before committal except that no 'Full

---

13 For an example of how quickly bail can be obtained from the higher courts (in this case the Court of Appeal, Criminal Division) see Stephen Gold, 'Lessons to be Learned from Ballet Teacher' (1983) 133 NLJ 711.

14 Criminal Justice Act 1967, s 22(2).

15 A solicitor may still act privately for such an application even though he is representing the accused under a legal aid order. The application is separate proceedings and therefore not caught by reg 14(E) Legal Aid in Criminal Proceedings (General Regulations) 1968/1231 as amended by SI 1983/1863.

16 See Legal Aid Handbook 1984 HMSO p 249.

17 In 1980 the success rates were 9% and 69% for Official Solicitor and private applications respectively.

18 RSC Ord 79, r 9(12).

19 Unlike applications prior to committal, legal aid will cover the use of counsel where a solicitor has rights of audience, Legal Aid Act 1974, s 30(1).

**THREE ALTERNATIVES IF BAIL
REFUSED BY MAGISTRATES
PRIOR TO MODE OF TRIAL/SUMMARY TRIAL/COMMITTAL**

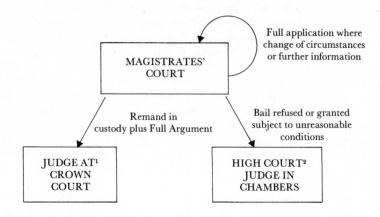

1   One application only per Full Argument Cert.
2   Can only re-apply to same judge.

Argument Certificate' is required. If a judge of the Crown Court refuses bail, it seems there is nothing to stop an accused making further applications to another judge of the Crown Court, although it will be necessary to show a 'change in circumstances' or 'new considerations' in the same way as with successive bail applications before the magistrates' court.[20] The application will usually be heard by a Circuit Judge or a Recorder in Chambers, though in more serious cases it may be dealt with by a High Court Judge.[21]

(ii) To apply to a High Court Judge in Chambers. This procedure is available after committal by or pending appeal from a magistrates' court on the same basis as prior to committal or summary trial subject to the same restrictions in RSC, Ord 79, r 9(12) if a High Court Judge has already refused bail.

(c)   Where variation in conditions of bail is sought at any stage in the proceedings: 1976 Act s 3(8)

On occasions a court may grant bail subject to conditions with which the accused is unable to comply, for example, imposing too high sureties; alternatively, conditions may have been imposed which now cause difficulties. An example of the latter might be where the accused is required to report to the police station at a specified hour and has subsequently obtained an offer of

20 Per Donaldson LJ in *ex p Malik*, supra.
21 See Practice Direction (1981) 73 Cr App Rep 370. At certain trial centres listing in front of a High Court judge may have the effect of rendering a separate application under RSC, Ord 79 virtually indistinguishable and thus pointless.

TWO ALTERNATIVES
WHEN BAIL REFUSED BY MAGISTRATES
ON COMMITTAL

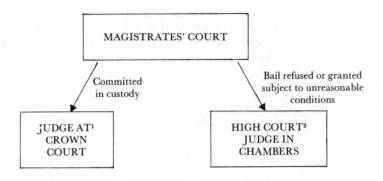

1 Can apply more than once subject to Ex p. Davis.
2 Can only re-apply to same judge.

employment that clashes with this. There are wide powers of variation which enable any court who has granted bail to vary or impose conditions on the application of the accused, the prosecutor or a police officer. The application for variation should normally be made to the court which granted bail or imposed conditions, save that where a person, having been granted bail by the magistrates, is committed to the Crown Court the application to vary may be made to the relevant magistrates' court or to the Crown Court.[1] The procedure varies but is usually very informal; a written (or oral) request to the relevant court to list the application for hearing coupled with notice to the prosecution usually being sufficient. A High Court Judge in Chambers may also vary conditions imposed by a magistrates' court so that, for example, if an accused could not comply with the require ments imposed as to sureties he could apply to a High Court Judge as an alternative to applying to the magistrates to vary the conditions under s 3(8) of the 1976 Act.[2] The same procedure as for an application to a High Court Judge for *bail* should be followed save that a modified summons form (Form 79A) should be used.

---

1 1976 Act, s 3(8).
2 Criminal Justice Act 1967, s 22. Note that prior to committal an accused who is granted bail subject to conditions with which he cannot comply cannot apply to the Crown Court since, having granted bail, the magistrates will not have issued a 'Full Argument Certificate'.

3 BAIL IN PRACTICE

(1) What happens on a bail application—a typical application in the magistrates' court

As has been seen bail can be granted by many courts and in many different circumstances but the application before a magistrates' court on behalf of a person accused of an 'imprisonable offence' is the one most frequently met in practice, and, notwithstanding the complicated substantive law involved, tends to follow a fairly predictable pattern. Subject to the usual caveat as to local variations, it may be split up into the following seven stages.

Stage (1): The appearance of the accused

Depending upon the circumstances, the accused will surrender to bail, be brought before the court in police custody having been arrested without warrant or will be produced from prison if he has been remanded in custody on a previous occasion. If he has been on bail he should report to the usher, warrant officer or gaoler (procedure varies) as soon as he arrives at court.

Stage (2): The court deals with the case (for example, trial, committal etc) or adjourns and remands

If the court adjourns, the question of bail will then need to be considered and the prosecution will be asked if they have any objections. If they indicate that they do not, it is unlikely that bail will be refused. In that case nothing more than a formal application for bail to be continued will be necessary. If, on the other hand, there are objections to bail the proceedings will normally proceed through *Stages (3)–(6)*. Much will depend upon whether or not the accused has been refused bail on a previous occasion. If he has, a further full application will, of course, not be possible unless there has been a 'change in circumstances'. The remaining stages proceed on the basis that a full application is to be made.

Stage (3): The prosecution will give their objections.

These may be put forward by the prosecution advocate; in some areas, however, especially in the Metropolitan Police Area, the police officer in charge of the case may go into the witness box to give objections. Although the court does not receive evidence on oath and the prosecution is not required to satisfy any 'standard of proof' in relation to the objections put forward it is important for the defence to ensure that such objections as are given come strictly within the Sch 1 exceptions to the Bail Act 1976. In *Re Moles*[3] a Divisional Court held that the strict rules of evidence were inherently inappropriate to an investigation into the existence or otherwise of substantial grounds for 'belief' as required by Sch 1 to the 1976 Act. Objections will often be based upon assertion which it is difficult to counter, and questioning of the objecting police officer is often not only difficult but counter-productive.

---

3 [1981] Crim LR 170. Justices are entitled to take into account their own knowledge of local events *ex p Sharkey* (supra) at 1338.

Stage (4): The accused or his representative will apply for bail

Hopefully the accused will be represented either by a duty solicitor[4] or solicitor or counsel acting under a legal aid order. He may ask questions of the investigating officer but is more likely to direct his energies to addressing the court. The contents of such an application will be considered later, but will consist in the main of attempts to counter prosecution objections either by denying their existence or more probably by putting forward factors in the accused's favour and offering sureties and appropriate conditions.

Stage (5): Sureties

If the surety or sureties to be tendered are present in court they will be called to give evidence on oath. As well as giving the prosecution an opportunity to object to the sureties put forward the court will need to be satisfied that a proposed surety has sufficient readily realisable resources to satisfy the amount of the recognizance in the event of forfeiture and fully understands the consequences of the accused failing to attend. The court will also have regard to the factors in s 8(2) of the 1976 Act. It must, however, be stressed that if the proposed sureties are not available the court may still fix one or more sureties with a view to their being taken later.

Stage (6): The court will then consider its decision

The bench may retire and may seek the assistance of persons other than the prosecution or the defence in appropriate cases; for example, it may make inquiries from the probation service as to the availability of a place in a bail hostel, if the accused has no fixed address.

Stage (7): The decision

If released on unconditional bail the accused is free to leave immediately and will be given a form notifying him of his release on bail and the date upon which he is required to surrender.[5] If, on the other hand, he is refused bail or granted bail subject to conditions he must be given reasons for the decision and a written note thereof.[6] If the sureties are available and can be taken there and then, they will also be required to sign an appropriate form.[7] Sureties may, however, have difficulty in getting to court. This may be compounded if the accused's case has to be remanded several times. His solicitor may ask the court for sureties to be made 'continuous' ie for each and every occasion that the accused's attendance is required; this may even be extended to cover the accused's initial attendance at the Crown Court.[8] Although this procedure is often convenient for the surety and the accused, the court is under no duty to inform the surety of any subsequent variation of the accused's conditions of bail; this could prejudice the surety where the accused absconds in circumstances where, if the surety had known of the variation, he would not have continued to stand.[9]

---

4 Such defendants possibly stand a better chance of obtaining bail than those who are unrepresented see LAG Bulletin June 1982, p 12 et seq.

5 1976 Act, s 5(1).

6 Ibid, ss 5(3) and (4).

7 Form in Stone's Justices' Manual (1985) Vol III p 7316.

8 Magistrates' Courts Act 1980, s 128(4)(c).

9 It is important, therefore, to ensure that the surety is made aware of any other conditions that have been imposed under s 3(6) of the 1976 Act (eg as to residence or deposit of a passport) if the sureties are made continuous: *R v Wells Street JJ, ex p Albanese*, supra.

If sureties are not available, the accused will be kept in custody until they are taken—this will mean that he will have to be returned to prison unless they are taken quickly. There are complicated provisions[10] which broadly enable sureties to be taken at a police station or prison to which the accused has been taken, subject to a right to apply (inter alia) to the court which fixed the recognisance if, for example, the surety is not acceptable to the police.[11] It is always advisable, therefore, particularly if the identity of the proposed sureties are known, to make arrangements with the Bench as to where they are to be taken. As already noted, it is possible for a court to grant bail subject to sureties even though none are as yet available.[12] In that case, the accused will be committed in custody unless and until suitable sureties are forthcoming. If they are not, he must be brought back before the court within eight clear days even though he has been remanded on bail, subject to sureties, for a longer period.[13]

(2) **Practical problems on contested bail applications**

Every contested bail application is different and will require individual attention. It is nevertheless possible to lay down certain broad guidelines as to the tactics to be adopted. Much of this section is written on the assumption that you will normally be applying for bail on behalf of an accused who has not yet been convicted and who will therefore be entitled to the s 4 'right to bail' subject to the provisos in Sch 1, Parts I and II. It is vital that you find out from the the prosecution at as early a stage as possible precisely what objections they intend to put forward. Just as with preparing for trial, bail applications are won on the work done out of court and should not be entirely dependent upon your powers of advocacy.

In practice virtually all contested bail applications will be in respect of imprisonable offences and the prosecution objections will almost always be based upon Sch 1, Part I, para 2 namely that there are substantial grounds for believing that if granted bail the accused would:

- fail to surrender to custody;
- commit further offences whilst on bail; or
- (much less frequently) that he would interfere with witnesses or otherwise obstruct the course of justice.

In order to support one or other of these contentions the prosecution will seek to rely upon one or more of the four factors contained in Sch 1, Part I, para 9 and, therefore, if you are to obtain bail for your client, your efforts will need to be directed primarily towards countering those '*Paragraph 9*' factors upon which the prosecution seek to rely, namely:

'*The nature and seriousness of the offence and the probable method of dealing with it*' The more serious the offence, the more strongly the prosecution will rely upon this factor and the more difficult it becomes to counter. This is especially the case if the accused is likely to receive a custodial sentence if convicted. Charges of burglary cause particular problems where an accused has previous convictions for the same offence. It may well be that the only effective method of countering objections will be by inviting the bench to

10 Bail Act 1976, s 8(4).
11 Ibid, s 8(5).
12 Ibid, s 8(3).
13 Magistrates' Courts Act 1980, s 128(2).

impose conditions such as a 'curfew'. Conversely, at a later stage in the proceedings, for example at committal, it may be possible to argue that the case disclosed by the committal papers is nowhere near as serious as was originally made out.

'Character, antecedents, associations and community ties' At the end of the day, the triumvirate of 'family, job and fixed address' are the most persuasive factors you can put forward in support of a bail application, particularly since they give the court so much more scope for imposing conditions. Often the objection that an accused is 'NFA' (of no fixed abode) will be very difficult to counter unless there are other compelling factors in the accused's favour. In such a case your efforts should be directed towards finding a fixed address for the accused with friends or relatives. Places in bail hostels are often hard to come by although you should always check with the probation service to see whether there is a vacancy. As a possible last resort, recourse could also be had to the local authority under the Housing (Homeless Persons) Act 1977. The prosecution will also often object to bail when the accused has previous convictions, especially where they are for the same or similar offences. This may to some extent be turned round to the accused's advantage where his record discloses that he has been granted bail on previous occasions and has not absconded. It should, however, be put forward with care. The argument that,

> 'my client has 15 previous convictions in the last ten years and has always answered to bail'

will not always be well received.

'The accused's previous bail record' Where the accused's record discloses a previous conviction for absconding you will clearly have difficulty in persuading the bench to grant bail. In such a case your efforts should be directed towards trying to contrast the circumstances in which your client absconded with his present situation. For example, if you can point to greater domestic stability it may be that this potentially fatal objection can be countered. Where, however, the present offence has been committed whilst your client has been on bail in respect of other charges, his chances of obtaining bail are very low indeed.

'The strength of the evidence of the accused having committed the offence' When the prosecution put this forward as an objection at an early stage in the proceedings it may be very difficult to counter since you will often not know the strengths and weaknesses of the prosecution case. It is very important, however, to take a careful note of the objections since it may well be that at a later stage, for example, at committal you can argue that the prosecution case is not as strong as was originally made out.

Having now made these general observations the following particular points should always be borne in mind.

(a) Bail applications in the magistrates' court

Although on occasions counsel may be instructed on a bail application, in the vast majority of cases the application will be made by the accused's solicitor. The ability to make a good bail application is one of the cornerstones of the solicitor advocate's art. Although every advocate develops his or her own style the following points should always be borne in mind.

(i) No contested bail application is easy. One of the principal effects of the Bail Act 1976 is to provide courts with a multiplicity of reasons for refusing bail. Thus, if the police or prosecution object to bail the court will find their reasons persuasive. The 'right to bail' notwithstanding, you must always therefore approach any such application upon the basis that you have an uphill task.

(ii) Keep the application short but individual. Nothing is more likely to irritate the court than a long rambling bail application. Although there may be cases where the issues are so complicated that a lengthy address is necessary, as a general rule of thumb a good bail application should not last for more than five minutes. This is particularly so when the application is in front of a stipendiary magistrate in a busy metropolitan court. Having said that, however, you should always try to find something special about the client's application so as to hold the court's interest. Magistrates are used to hearing the same standard bail application day in and day out to such an extent that one sometimes gets the impression that the whole court is running on 'automatic pilot'. It is particularly important to bear this in mind where a client is charged along with others since there is always a danger in such situations that the court will treat each case as a 'standard case'. One of your most important tasks as an advocate is to steer the court away from this approach.[14]

(iii) Approach the Bail Act 1976 with caution. Although, as has already been indicated, prosecution objections to bail must be brought within the framework of Schedule 1, Part I to the Act, at the end of the day, these give the magistrates such a wide discretion that lengthy reminders as to the law are not likely to be well received.

(iv) Make sure that sufficient information is obtained. At the risk of sounding obvious, no self respecting advocate should get up on his or her feet without adequate instructions or information as to the accused's personal background. There is no doubt, however, that if you have all the basic information at your fingertips you will always be more persuasive. This can be a problem where, for example, you are acting as Duty Solicitor or have only met the client at court that morning. In such a situation there will often be pressure for the case to be brought up before you have obtained adequate instructions. You should always resist this and, if necessary, be prepared to apply to the magistrates for the case to be stood out for an hour.

(v) Cross-examine police officers with caution. Practice varies from court to court, but in many areas objections to bail are given by a police officer. You must resist the temptation to ask too many questions since this may have the effect of steadily diminishing your prospects of success, especially where the officer in charge of the case is determined that the client should be remanded in custody. Each individual case must, however, be taken on its merits so that, for example, if the police officer making the objections is not familiar with the case a more searching approach may be adopted.

(vi) Make a careful note of the objections. This may prove invaluable on a future application to the magistrates or to the Crown Court or High

---

14 The practice in some courts of fixing standard bail conditions has been strongly criticised by the Divisional Court in *ex p Sharkey* (supra) as has been the practice of putting persons arrested on different occasions into the dock together.

Court. What has been made out as a 'serious offence with strong evidence' on the first hearing may appear in a very different light at committal when the prosecution statements are available. It may also provide you with advance information about the prosecution's case.

(vii) Make sure that you are familiar with ex parte Davies. In view of the severe restriction now placed upon the making of subsequent fully argued applications at the magistrates' court, it is important that where such leave is sought you are in a position to argue cogently that the case comes within the guidelines laid down by Donaldson LJ. It is particularly important that you bear this in mind when applying for bail at committal proceedings, since you are not entitled to make a further application as of right unless there has been a genuine 'change in circumstances'. It is as well to find out in advance how the court operates *ex parte Davies* because, as usual, there may be local variations.[15] This is particularly so where there is a Duty Solicitor scheme in operation. It is submitted that, whether represented by the Duty Solicitor or his own solicitor, the accused is entitled to two full applications, the first on his initial appearance in custody, the second on his next apearance. It is understood, however, that not all courts take this view.

(viii) Try to organise conditions of bail in advance. If sureties are likely to be required, it is always better to contact them beforehand and ensure that they come to court so that the accused may be released immediately if bail is granted. If the sureties cannot come to court, make arrangements for them to sign at the nearest convenient police station to where they live or work so that, if granted bail, the accused can be released forthwith. It will often be possible to liaise with the prosecution beforehand to find out whether they would be prepared to agree to bail if sureties were forthcoming. However, always bear in mind that the final decision as to bail rests with the court and any suggestion that the prosecution and defence have 'carved up' bail is likely to incur the magistrates' displeasure. That being said, it is always advisable to notify the prosecution in advance as to who the proposed sureties are so that there is no unnecessary delay whilst their suitability is investigated. Ideally proposed sureties should live in sufficient proximity to the accused to be able to maintain some regular contact but care should be taken before putting forward an accused's spouse as some courts will as a matter of principle not accept spouses as suitable sureties. It is also important to ensure that you have adequate details as to a surety's means, especially if he or she is to be called. You should also ask a proposed surety to bring to court documentary evidence of means wherever possible, for example a Building Society passbook.

(ix) Do not be caught by surprise. As has already been indicated, the grant of bail is a matter for the court and not one for agreement between the prosecution and defence. There may, therefore, be cases, albeit rare, where even though the prosecution do not object to bail the court takes the view that bail is not appropriate. This may sometimes happen at committal proceedings, even where these take place without consideration of the evidence. Some magistrates, especially stipendiaries, make a point of briefly perusing the committal papers before considering bail and the observation,

'It would appear that your client was caught red-handed and has made a full written confession to the police'

15 See also Hall, 'Nottingham Justices Revisited', Legal Action, July 1984, p 76.

may stop you in your tracks. Such problems should be anticipated wherever possible.

(b) Bail applications before the Crown Court[16]

As has already been seen, an accused who has been refused bail by a magistrates' court may now apply to the Crown Court for bail whenever he has been remanded or committed in custody, the only important difference being that in the former case, the magistrates must have issued a 'Full Argument Certificate'. In either case, proceedings will be in chambers and solicitors and barristers thus have equal rights of audience, but you will usually only be covered for legal aid for counsel if you are applying *after committal* to the Crown Court. Many applications fail because they are not properly prepared: either the solicitor conducting the application has not thought the application through adequately or counsel has not been properly briefed. Remember that the judge hearing the application will often know very little about the case apart from having seen a copy of the 'Full Argument Certificate' or committal documents. Indeed, where the case has already been committed, it may be advisable to postpone applying for bail until the papers have been sent to the Crown Court by the clerk to the justices (some Crown Courts refuse to list them until then in any event). It is important, therefore, whether applying in person or instructing counsel, to make sure that the judge has the following information:

(i)   details of the charges, the history of the proceedings and any previous bail decisions;

(ii) the likely plea;

(iii) full details of the accused's personal background dealing in particular with the answers that can be put forward to the prosecution objections;

(iv) any matters arising from the committal papers (where relevant) that support your application or require dealing with, for example, the relative weakness or strength of the evidence.

(v)   details of the accused's proposals as to sureties or other conditions.

Broadly, applications will fall into two categories: firstly, those where it is submitted that the magistrates refusal of bail was wrong in principle, and secondly, those where due to a change in circumstances it is now possible to deal with prosecution objections to bail adequately. In the latter case you may have the choice of re-applying to the magistrates' court on the basis of a 'change in circumstances'. It may be advisable to exhaust this avenue before applying to the Crown Court, especially where the case is ultimately to be committed for trial (some judges may be reluctant to grant bail until they have seen the committal papers). If sureties are being offered an attempt should be made before the hearing to agree their suitability with the prosecution. They should also be asked to attend at the Crown Court since, if bail is granted subject to sureties, their recognisances can be entered into before an officer of the Crown Court.[17] Alternatively, arrangements should be made via the prosecution for sureties to sign on at a nearby police station.

16 See also Hall, Bail: Appeals: Legal Action, December 1984, p 145.
17 See Crown Court Rules 1982, r 20(2).

(c) Applications in the High Court

As has been seen an application may be made to a High Court judge in chambers whenever a magistrates' court has refused bail and this can be made at any stage in the proceedings without prejudice to the accused's right to apply to the Crown Court. It is nevertheless generally regarded as being appropriate to reserve such an application as a last resort when all other avenues have proved unsuccessful. One of the major problems will be finance. An application for a civil legal aid certificate combined with an application for an emergency certificate may be made, where appropriate, but is only likely to be granted if the stringent conditions laid down in the Legal Aid Handbook can be complied with. It is still, however, possible for the solicitor to come to an arrangement with a legally-aided accused for him to pay privately because the application will be separate proceedings and thus will not be caught by the restrictions on 'topping up'.[18]

As has been seen, the procedure is in fact remarkably simple,[19] requiring only an originating application and an affidavit in support. The proceedings will be in chambers and thus solicitors have equal rights of audience. The most important document will be the affidavit which should either be sworn by the accused or his solicitor. It is vital that it deals fully with all aspects of the case, covering in particular all those matters referred to in the section on applications to the Crown Court. Because you will be in the High Court, it should be remembered that if the accused is granted bail you will have to draw up the order. It is also important to make arrangements as to where sureties are to enter into their recognisances since these will not be taken before the judge.

(3) Police v Duncan McCarthy (case 1): application for bail

Set out below is a scenario of Duncan McCarthy's case. It will be recalled from chapters 1 and 5 that he was charged with burglary at 6.30 am on *6 August 198-* and was brought before the Weyford magistrates, in custody, on the same day.

> The police are represented by a solicitor from the County Prosecuting Solicitors' Service who is instructed to oppose bail on the ground that there are substantial grounds for believing that if granted bail he would
> (a) fail to surrender to custody and
> (b) commit further offences whilst on bail. This being supported by the following two factors, namely,
> (i) the offence is serious in that it involves an offence against his employer and, if convicted he is likely to receive a custodial sentence, and
> (ii) McCarthy is of bad character having previous convictions for dishonesty. McCarthy consults the Duty Solicitor who makes an application for bail on his behalf arguing that he is a married man with a fixed address, in employment and is prepared to submit to a curfew and a condition of residence.
> The magistrates nevertheless refuse bail and adjourn the proceedings for one week to *12 August 198-* and remand McCarthy in custody to the same date: he refuses to consent to being further remanded in his absence. McCarthy indicates to the Duty Solicitor that he wishes her to continue acting for him and she accordingly files a written legal aid application with supporting statement of means

---

18 See p 253 note 15 ante.
19 For further detail see Bill Nash, 'Bail Applications to a Judge in Chambers', LAG, Bulletin May 1982, p 56 et seq.

NOTICE OF APPLICATION RELATING TO BAIL TO BE MADE
TO THE CROWN COURT

AT   EXCHESTER

CROWN COURT NO.

[OR]

SERIAL NO. AND

NAME AND LOCATION OF MAGISTRATES COURT   WEYFORD

Note: The appropriate office of the Crown Court should be consulted about the time and
place of the hearing before this notice is sent to the other party to the application.
A copy of this notice should be sent to the Crown Court.
In the case of an application for bail in the course of proceedings being held before
Magistrates the certificate prescribed by Section 5(6)A of the Bail Act 1976 (as
amended) should accompany this notice when it is lodged at the Crown Court
office.

TAKE NOTICE that an application relating to bail will be made to the
Crown Court

at **The Crown Court at Exchester**

on **18th August 198—**

at **10 a.m./p.m.**

on behalf of the defendant/appellant/prosecutor/respondent.

1. Defendant/appellant (block letters please) **9/6/6—**
   Surname **DUNCAN**   Date of birth **9/6/6—**
   Forename **MCCRIMMON**
   Home Address **11 INKERMAN TERRACE, WEYFORD, BLANKSHIRE**
   ....

2. Solicitor for the applicant
   Name **WHITE AND CO**
   Address **ACOL HOUSE, WEYFORD, BLANKSHIRE**
   ....

3. If defendant/appellant is in custody state:
   place of detention **EXCHESTER REMAND CENTRE**
   prison number (if applicable) **707567**
   length of time in custody **since 6th August 198—**
   date of last remand **13th August 198—**

4. State the particulars of proceedings during which the defendant/ap-
pellant was committed to custody or bailed or (un)conditionally including:

   (a) the stage reached in the proceedings as at the date of this
   application: **to be committed for trial on 1st September 198—**

   (b) the offences alleged: **Burglary**
   ....

   (c) (If the application relation relates to a case pending before
   Magistrates) Give details of next appearance:
   Place **Weyford Magistrates Court**
   Date **21st August 198—**   Time **10 a.m.**

5. Give details of any relevant previous applications for bail or variation
of conditions of bail:
Application made on 6th August 198— by duty solicitor.
Full application made 13th August 198— by present
solicitors.

6. Nature and grounds of application:
   (a) State fully the grounds relied on and list previous convictions
   (if any) **The accused is residing at a fixed address with his**
   wife. He denies the charge against him and is electing trial
   on indictment (it is understood that the evidence against him is
   by no means strong. His sister who lives nearby is in employ-
   ment and has no previous convictions is prepared to stand
   surety in the sum of £500 and the accused is required to comply
   with such conditions as the court may impose. He has three
   previous convictions for (1) theft (2) TDA and (3) burglary.

   (b) Give details of any proposed sureties and answer any objections raised previously.
   IRENE JOHNSON (address). There is no substantial risk that the
   accused will either abscond or commit further offences whilst
   on bail in view of (1) his denial of the charge and the weakness
   of the prosecution case: (2) his fixed address, the available
   surety and the availability of appropriate conditions.

on his behalf. She is notified the next day that legal aid has been granted with a contribution order.

During the intervening week she visits McCarthy in prison and obtains preliminary instructions in which he indicates that he wishes to be tried on indictment and intends to plead not guilty. He also informs her that his sister, Irene Johnstone, who is a married woman of 28 in part-time employment has visited him in prison and indicated that she is willing to stand surety in the sum of up to £500. McCarthy's solicitor telephones the Prosecuting Solicitors' Department prior to the hearing on the 12 August so that an opportunity may be taken to investigate Irene's suitability. The prosecution confirm that there is nothing known against her, but indicate that they will still be opposing bail. McCarthy's solicitor accordingly asks Irene Johnstone to be at court on *12 August* and to bring evidence of her means with her. She also contacts the Medical Superintendent of Weyford Hospital informing him of what has happened and indicating that McCarthy strongly denies the charge. The next day he rings back indicating that in the circumstances, a decision has been taken to suspend McCarthy on full pay pending the outcome of the proceedings and that if he is acquitted he will be able to resume normal duties.

There now follows a truncated resume of the proceedings on 12 August.

The case is called and McCarthy is brought up from the cells having been brought from the remand prison that morning. The court clerk asks him to confirm his name and address.

Prosecution: Sir, the prosecution is not yet ready to proceed. I have had an opportunity of discussing the case with my learned friend and she has indicated to me that the accused proposes to elect trial on indictment. I had intended to ask for this case to be tried summarily, but in view of the defence indication I propose to proceed on the basis that this case will now be committed for trial.

[Some courts would hold mode of trial proceedings forthwith, although practice varies. In this scenario it will be held on *1 September* immediately prior to committal: see Chapters 8 and 11].

I would accordingly ask for an adjournment for three weeks in order to prepare the case for committal and in the meantime ask that the defendant be remanded in custody for a further eight days. There are objections to bail in this case. These are ...'

[At this point the prosecution will repeat the objections to bail given on the first occasion and will produce a copy of McCarthy's criminal record to the court.]

Defence solicitor: Sir, I am instructed to apply for bail in this case. May I first deal with the two prosecution objections. As to the serious nature of the offence, I would say this. Whilst accepting that on the face of it this is a serious offence, although apparently not serious enough for the prosecution to be seeking trial on indictment, my client strenuously denies the charge. Sir, the evidence against him is tenuous in the extreme based, as I understand it, on a fleeting and unsatisfactory identification at night and other evidence which is either equivocal or circumstantial. With regard to the second objection I would submit that although he has previous convictions his record indicates that he has not re-offended for the past two years and that he is now a married man, with a fixed address and steady employment. In the intervening week I have ascertained from his employers that they are prepared to suspend him on full pay pending the outcome of these proceedings and I now produce a letter from the Medical Superintendent of the hospital confirming this. My client is prepared to submit to such conditions as you may see fit to impose including, if necessary, a curfew. Finally, my client's sister is present in court today and is willing to stand surety in the sum of £500. Sir, she is a married woman of 28, of good

WEYFORD MAGISTRATES' COURT

Accused... **Duncan McCarthy**...... Date of Birth **9/6/6-**

Offences...... **Burglary**......

DECISION OF THE COURT

DATE OF DECISION **13/8/198-**

- [✓] The accused is remanded to appear before the above named **Weyford** Magistrates' Court at **10**. am/~~pm~~ on **21/8/198-** between named Court on such day, time and place as may be notified to the accused by the appropriate officer of that Court

- [ ] The accused is committed to appear before the Crown Court on such day, time and place as may be notified to the accused by the appropriate officer of that Court

- [ ] The accused is granted unconditional bail

- [ ] The accused is granted bail subject to the conditions set out below

- [✓] The accused is refused bail and committed to custody

- [ ] The accused has consented to the hearing and determination in his absence of future applications for remands until .... and the notice overleaf applies.

N.B.　Failure to surrender to bail or comply with bail conditions can result in arrest. Failure to surrender to bail is an offence punishable by imprisonment and/or a fine

EXCEPTIONS TO RIGHT TO UNCONDITIONAL BAIL FOUND BY THE COURT. SCHEDULE 1

- [✓] Belief would fail to surrender Pt.1 p.2(a)
- [✓] Belief would commit offence on bail Pt.1 p.2(b)
- [ ] Belief would obstruct justice Pt.1 p.2(c)
- [ ] Custody for own protection/welfare Pts.1–11 pp.3
- [ ] Serving custodial sentence Pts.1–11 pp.4
- [ ] Insufficient information for bail decision Pt.1 p.5
- [ ] Arrested under S.7 Bail Act 1976 Pt.1 p.6 Pt.11 p.5
- [ ] Otherwise impracticable complete enquiries Pt.1 p.7
- [ ] Previous failure to surrender Pt.11 p.2

REASONS FOR FINDING EXCEPTIONS TO RIGHT TO UNCONDITIONAL BAIL

- [✓] Nature and gravity of the offence
- [✓] Accused's previous record
- [ ] Lack of community ties
- [ ] Failure to answer bail in the past
- [ ] Failure to comply with bail conditions in past
- [ ] Accused's demeanour in court[1]
- [ ] To secure preparation of reports

CONDITIONS TO BE COMPLIED WITH BEFORE/AND/OR AFTER RELEASE ON BAIL

- [ ] To provide .... sureties in the sum of £ .... each
- [ ] To live and sleep each night at
- [ ] To give prior notice to police of any change of address
- [ ] To observe a curfew between the hours of
- [ ] To report to .... Police Station each .... between
- [ ] Passport to be surrendered to/retained by police
- [ ] Not to contact directly or indirectly any person whose name is supplied to the accused by police in writing
- [ ] Not to come within .... of .... except to see Solicitor by prior written appointment
- [ ] To make himself available as and when required to enable inquiries or report to be made
- [ ] To provide a security in the sum of £ .... to be deposited with the court .... *to be deposited with the accused's Solicitors to be held unconditionally and irrevocably to the order of the Chief Clerk of the Magistrates' Court.*

CERTIFICATE AS TO HEARING OF FULL ARGUMENT ON APPLICATION FOR BAIL

(This certificate should accompany any application made for bail to the Crown Court under S.81(1)(g) Supreme Court Act 1981)

- [✓] It is hereby certified that today the court heard full argument on an application for bail made by or on behalf of the accused, before refusing the application and remanding the accused in custody.

- [✓] The court has not previously heard full argument on an application for bail by or on behalf of the accused in these proceedings.

- [ ] The court has previously heard full argument from the accused on an application for bail, but is satisfied (that there has been the following change in his circumstances:) *(That the following new considerations have been placed before it)*

....

J Smith *(signature)*

Clerk of the Court present during these proceedings

(1) This is *not* a reason contained in the Bail Act 1976 but is based on the decision in R v v Governor of Ashford Remond Centre ex p. Walsh [1984] Crim L.R. 618.

character, is a joint house owner, is in part-time employment as a secretary and has savings in the sum of £1500 in the Building Society. I understand that the prosecution have no objections as to her suitability as a surety and since the matter is entirely in your hands I now propose to call her.

[Irene Johnstone will now be called, briefly examined in chief and asked to produce her pass-book, and reminded as to the consequences and obligations of a surety. The prosecution ask no questions and the bench indicate their satisfaction.]

Chairman: The Bench will retire.

[The Bench return]

Chairman: We have decided to grant bail in this case subject to the following conditions, namely that the defendant's sister stand surety in the sum of £500; that the defendant continues to reside at 11 Inkerman Terrace, Weyford and informs the prosecution of any change of address and that he remains indoors between the hours of 9.30 pm and 7.30 am. The reason that we impose these conditions is because we consider it necessary for the purpose of preventing the defendant committing an offence whilst on bail. Proceedings will accordingly be adjourned to 1 September and you will be remanded on bail to that date. I must warn you that should you fail to attend on that date without reasonable cause you will commit an offence and a warrant will be issued for your arrest and it is most unlikely that you will be granted bail thereafter.

Defence Solicitor: Sir, I wonder whether, in the circumstances, you could consider making this surety continuous to secure my client's attendance at the Crown court. I understand that it is difficult to Mrs Johnstone to come to court, and there is no police station near to her work.

Chairman: (after consulting with clerk) No: in this court, we like to consider conditions afresh at committal, in which case, in the sureties' interests, we prefer them to be taken again. We are, however, prepared to make this surety continuous to the date of committal in case for any reason 1 September is not effective (pointedly) although we sincerely hope it will be.

Defence Solicitor: Thank you, Sir.

[McCARTHY will now be released from custody once his sister has signed the appropriate surety form and he will be provided with a copy of his bail record.] If the magistrates had refused bail they would have been required to issue a 'Full Argument Certificate' on the basis of which his solicitor could make an application for bail to the Crown Court, make a subsequent application to the magistrates if there were a 'change in circumstances' or, in theory, apply to a High Court judge in chambers.

CHAPTER 8

Offences triable either way

1 INTRODUCTION

'Either way' offences are those that *in the case of an adult* are triable either summarily or on indictment. It is a category which embraces a multitude of sins ranging from major thefts or burglaries by professional criminals to minor cases of shoplifting. With the exception of minor offences of criminal damage, which will be considered separately, they have a number of features in common. These are as follows.

(1) Mode of trial procedure

In every case, the magistrates *must* follow the prescribed 'mode of trial' procedure as a prelude either to summary trial or committal proceedings.

(2) The right of the accused to 'elect' trial on indictment

Summary trial can never take place without the consent of the accused. The right to 'elect trial' by jury is thus one of the few occasions during the course of a prosecution when the defence will have the initiative.[1]

(3) Magistrates' limited sentencing powers

Consent to summary trial has an obvious attraction for the guilty defendant. He faces much lower maximum penalties. This attraction may, however, be more apparent than real because of the power to commit him to the Crown Court for sentence under s 38 of the Magistrates' Courts Act 1980 should his 'character and antecedents' merit greater punishment than the magistrates can impose.

Consideration by the defence of the most appropriate venue is therefore a matter upon which the client needs very careful advice, especially where the charge is relatively minor, but the stakes are high, for example, if a local councillor is accused of shoplifting. The standard advice tends to be, 'Stay in the magistrates' court' if the plea is 'guilty' but 'elect for the Crown Court' if it is 'not guilty'. This may not always be good advice; each case must be considered individually.

2 THE 'MODE OF TRIAL' PROCEDURE

The procedure is set out in ss 19 to 22 of the 1980 Act and all the prescribed steps must be followed before the magistrates can proceed to summary trial[2]

---

1 Note, however, that where a prosecution is brought by the Attorney General or the Director of Public Prosecutions he may insist upon trial upon indictment irrespective of the wishes of the court or the accused, Magistrates' Courts Act 1980, s 19(4). Note that common assault either at common law or contrary to s 47 of the Offences Against the Person Act 1861 is *not* an either way offence: see *R v Harrow Justices, ex p Osaseri* (1985) Times, 13 July.
2 Mode of trial procedure may be conducted by a single lay justice: 1980 Act, s 18(5). He would not, however, be able to try the accused summarily although he could sit as an examining justice.

or hold committal proceedings: if they are not, the subsequent proceedings are a nullity. Thus, for example, when a magistrates' court proceeded to try an either way offence contrary to the Town and Country Planning Act 1971 without the necessary preliminaries the Divisional Court quashed the conviction.[3] The procedure looks extremely complicated on paper, but in practice, usually takes no more than a couple of minutes, as the extract from McCarthy (*case 1*) at the end of the chapter shows. It is important, however, to be aware of all the appropriate stages and the problems that can arise.

Stage 1. The case is called

The accused is normally required to be present.[4] He will usually be on bail, thus failure to attend will result in a warrant being issued for his arrest and the proceedings being adjourned. The court may, however, proceed in his absence if:

(a) by reason of his disorderly conduct *before the court* it is not practicable for the proceedings to be conducted in his presence;[5] or

(b) the court is satisfied that there is good reason for proceeding in his absence and he is *represented by counsel or solicitor* who indicates the accused's consent to this course.[6]

These two exceptions are rarely encountered. A solicitor representing an accused in either situation may only consent to summary trial on his behalf if instructed to do so, failing which the court has no power to try the accused and must hold committal proceedings.[7] You are far more likely to be faced with struggling (usually unsuccessfully) to convince the court not to issue a warrant for your client's arrest, because he has not appeared in answer to his bail. Indeed, even if he has not been on bail, the court may issue a warrant if they are not satisfied that there is good reason for proceeding in his absence.[8]

There are special rules where the accused is a *corporation*. It will be recalled that Sch 3 to the 1980 Act provides that a representative[9] of the corporation may attend on its behalf.[10] The representative may consent to summary trial or elect trial on indictment. If no representative attends, the magistrates may proceed to summary trial (if they consider it appropriate) without the corporation's consent.[11]

Stage 2. The charge is read to the accused

This speaks for itself. For example in the case of McCarthy (*case 1*) the clerk will tell him to stand up and then read out to him:

'Duncan McCarthy you are charged that on the 5th day of August 198– having

---

3 *R v Tottenham Justices, ex p Arthur's Transport Services* [1981] Crim LR 180. See also *R v Horseferry Road Justices, ex p Constable* [1981] Crim LR 504.
4 Magistrates' Courts Act 1980, s 18(2).
5 Ibid, s 18(3).
6 Ibid, s 23(1).
7 Ibid, s 23(4).
8 Ibid, s 26(2)(a).
9 A person duly appointed by the Corporation to represent it for that purpose: Criminal Justice Act 1925, s 33(6).
10 A Director or Company Secretary must appear for this purpose: Magistrates' Courts Act 1980, Sch 3, para 4. If counsel or solicitor attends he or she may be duly appointed as representative.
11 Ibid, Sch 3, para 5.

entered a building as a trespasser namely the Weyford General Hospital Social Club you therein stole £50 in cash contrary to section 9(1)(b) of the Theft Act 1968,'

and then tell him to sit down. McCARTHY's case is very straightforward but complications may sometimes arise even at this stage. Two important issues of principle have recently been the subject of much controversy, namely:

(a) Can the prosecution frustrate the right of the accused to elect trial on indictment by withdrawing the charge and preferring a lesser charge that is only triable summarily? and

(b) What is the relevant time for ascertaining whether the accused is an adult?

(a)   Can the prosecution frustrate the 'right to elect' by withdrawing the charges and preferring a charge is only triable summarily?[12]

In *R v Canterbury and St Augustine Justices, ex p Klisiak*[13] the High Court heard two applications for judicial review. The first applicant had been charged with criminal damage to the value of approximately £400, the second group of applicants with offences of assault occasioning actual bodily harm. Both these offences were triable 'either way'. In each case the prosecution, with the approval of the magistrates, offered no evidence on the original charges and re-charged the respective applicants with criminal damage to the value of £150 and assaulting a police office in the execution of his duty. Since the substituted offences were triable only summarily the applicants sought judicial review. The reason why they applied is clear enough—they did not want to be tried by magistrates, but by a judge and jury.[14] The Divisional Court refused the applications and held that although magistrates have an inherent jurisdiction to prevent abuses, in neither case could the prosecutor's conduct be said to have been oppressive, unjust or an abuse of process. Lord Lane CJ, who delivered the leading judgment, stated that there was no reason why prosecutors were obliged to charge the gravest possible offence on the facts, but did express the hope that in future, the lesser charges would be preferred at the outset. It is interesting, however, to note the James Report stated that:

> 'While it must remain a matter for the prosecution to decide which offences to charge, we would regard it as wrong for the prosecution to be influenced in its decision by considerations relating to the mode of trial ... Given the application of proper professional standards, however, we do not believe that there is any real danger of prosecutors attempting to manipulate the decisions on the mode of trial in this way.'[15]

Notwithstanding these observations it appears that the High Court will only be prepared to interfere if the offence itself is sufficiently serious to justify trial on indictment, so that a lesser charge will effectively amount to 'undercharging'. Perhaps therefore the position would be different if, for example, an offence of unlawful wounding were sought to be withdrawn and replaced with one of common assault.

---

12 A practice which it has been alleged is frequently adopted in public order cases see James Wood, 'Public Order Offences', LAG Bulletin February 1983, p 23.

13 [1982] QB 398, DC.

14 The House of Lords in *R v Islington North Juvenile Court, ex p Daley* [1983] 1 AC 347 apparently valued the right to trial by jury more highly than the court in *ex parte Klisiak*—see especially Lord Diplock at 364.

15 1975 Cmnd 6323, at para 94.

(b) What is the relevant time for ascertaining whether the accused is an adult?

As already noted, an accused only has a choice of court if he is an *adult*. The right to jury trial is seen by many to be so valuable that it has been avidly sought by those who have attained 17 before their case has been dealt with. There is an apparent inconsistency between s 18(1) and the 1980 Act which makes 'mode of trial' proceedings mandatory for all *adults* charged with 'either way' offences and s 24(1) of the same Act which makes summary trial obligatory for all *juveniles* charged with indictable offences (subject to certain exceptions). The House of Lords in *R v Islington North Juvenile Court, ex p Daley*[16] has held that the appropriate date for determining whether the accused has attained 17 is not necessarily the date of his first appearance before the court but *the occasion upon which the court makes its decision as to the mode of trial*.

> EXAMPLE: *Police v John* TYRELL *(case 4)*. Suppose that JOHN TYRELL had been born on *11 November 1967*. If the offence were to have been committed in *October 1983* at a time when he had not yet reached 16 there is little doubt that the proceedings would have been dealt with long before he approached his 17th birthday. What, however, if the offence were to have been committed in *October 1984?* If his first appearance were on or after *11 November 1984* he would clearly have to be remitted to an adult court who would be obliged to hold 'mode of trial' proceedings. If, however, he first appeared before the juvenile court on, say, *31 October 1984*, his right to elect would depend upon what happened on that occasion. If his case were merely adjourned to a later date without any decision being taken, by which time he would have attained 17, *ex p Daley* would apply and he would have to be remitted to an adult court for mode of trial proceedings. If, however, a plea were taken on 31 October 1984 he would have no right to elect and, if the proceedings were then adjourned, the juvenile court would have power to deal with him at the adjourned hearing as if he were still 16.[17]

Neither of the above problems will arise very frequently, but if they do you must anticipate them and be ready with appropriate authorities. If the magistrates are against you, you should consider asking for an immediate adjournment to enable you to apply to the High Court for judicial review. This is not, however, a course that should be undertaken unless it is clearly in the client's interests.

Stage 3. The prosecutor and the defendant make representations as to which mode of trial would be more suitable

'Representations' have been judicially defined in the following terms:

> 'It implies something less than evidence. It comprises submissions, coupled with assertions of fact and sometimes production of documents ... The nearest analogy is, perhaps, the speech in mitigation after a finding or plea of guilty in a criminal trial.'[18]

Generally it involves no more than the prosecution standing up and saying, for example:

> 'We are asking for summary trial in this case, your Worships. This is a minor case of shoplifting and the sum involved is small'

16 Supra.
17 Children and Young Persons Act 1963, s 29. The problem with the '*ex parte Daley* test' is, however, that there is no 'mode of trial' procedure as such for juveniles whatever offence they are charged with, therefore each case must be taken in its own facts. See *R v Lewes Juvenile Court ex p Turner* (1985) 149 JP 186. (D pleaded to charges before 17th birthday therefore no right to be remitted to adult court on attaining 17.)
18 *Ex p Klisiak* (supra) at 413.

or

> 'In this case the prosecution asks for trial on indictment. The charges are serious in that they involve a theft of several thousand pounds from the accused's employer. The accused was in a position of trust, your Worships, and the offences involved a calculated course of dishonesty.'

In most cases that is all the prosecutor will say. The defence advocate will often say even less. If the prosecution ask for summary trial and the accused is electing trial on indictment in any event, why should the defence make any representations at this stage at all? Failure to do so may not be in the client's interests even if he is legally aided because he may be penalised in costs. The Court of Appeal have indicated on several occasions, the most recent being in *R v Boyesen*,[19] that if an accused exercises his right to elect trial on indictment after the magistrates have determined that the case is suitable for summary trial he may be required to pay a contribution towards the prosecution's costs because of the extra expense which a jury trial necessarily involves. If, therefore, there is some compelling reason why the case is more suitable for trial on indictment, it should be put forward at this stage. For example, a relatively trivial theft may involve a difficult point of law or evidence which makes it more suitable for trial before a judge and jury, or (because of his position in the community) the accused may stand to lose a great deal if he is convicted. If, having persuaded the magistrates to opt for trial on indictment in such a case, the client is subsequently convicted, counsel may then at least point to the magistrates' decision when addressing the judge on costs.

Alternatively, you may wish to *oppose* the prosecution's request for trial on indictment, especially if your client intends to plead 'guilty'. In such a case it will almost always be in his interests to ask for summary trial in view of the limitations on magistrates' sentencing powers. Problems may arise where a client is charged with others, some or all of whom wish to elect for trial. It often seems to be assumed that if one co-accused who is jointly charged elects trial on indictment, the magistrates are obliged to commit his co-accused. Although there seems no authority on the point, it is submitted that this is wrong in principle since s 18(1) of the 1980 Act clearly requires the 'mode of trial' inquiry to be applied to each individual. If, therefore, the client proposes to plead 'guilty' (but his co-accused are electing trial on indictment) the magistrates should be urged to deal with his case separately if this is in his interests. This is especially so if it can be established that he played a minor part.

Stage 4. The magistrates' decision—Magistrates' Courts Act 1980, s 19(3)

It is most unlikely that the magistrates will retire unless there have been lengthy 'representations'. In the vast majority of cases the decision will be announced by the Chairman of the Bench, who will say, after brief consultation with his or her colleagues:

> 'We have decided the charge is suitable for summary trial'

or 'trial on indictment' as the case may be. The court is, however, required to give the matter serious consideration and magistrates have been criticised on occasions for assuming jurisdiction over cases which were more suitable

---

19 [1982] AC 768, HL.

for the Crown Court.[20] Section 19(3) of the 1980 Act[21] requires the court to have regard to the following matters when coming to its decision:

   (a) the *nature* of the case;
   (b) whether the circumstances make the offence one of *serious character*;
   (c) whether its *sentencing powers* in respect of the *instant offence* are adequate;
   (d) any other relevant circumstances.

These factors are largely self-explanatory but need to be borne in mind by the defence advocate who is, for example, arguing that trial on indictment is more appropriate. Note in particular that the court must *not*, at this stage take into account the *previous* character and convictions of the accused; these are irrelevant at the mode of trial stage[1] and therefore no reference should be made to them. If reference were made you could again apply for judicial review (but in practical terms this would only be necessary if the same bench proceeded to try your client notwithstanding your objections).

Whether the court will next proceed to **Stage 5A** or **Stage 5B** depends upon what decision the magistrates have come to as to the most appropriate method of trial.

Stage 5A. The court decides that trial on indictment is more appropriate—1980 Act, s 21[2]

The court will now be sitting as examining justices and must hold committal proceedings. In contrast to those cases where the magistrates decide on summary trial the accused will usually have *no further say in the matter*.[3] If the prosecution are not yet ready for committal, a further adjournment coupled with a remand of the accused will be necessary, but in most cases both sides will have anticipated the court's decision and committal proceedings will take place immediately. Most committals now take place under s 6(2) of the 1980 Act without any consideration of the evidence by the court so that in many cases the whole process from the start of the 'mode of trial' procedure to the conclusion of the committal will take no more than a few minutes. Note that s 25(3) and (4) of the 1980 Act enable the court to convert to summary trial and vice versa in certain circumstances; this will be discussed more fully later in the chapter.

Stage 5B. The court decides that summary trial is more appropriate—1980 Act, s 20

Unless the accused is not present, s 20(2) and (3) require the court, usually through their clerk, to take the following *three* steps:

   (a) To explain to the accused in *ordinary language* that the court considers summary trial more suitable but that it is up to the accused to decide where he wants to be tried;
   (b) To explain in *ordinary language* that if he is tried summarily and convicted the court may commit him to the Crown Court for sentence

20 See *R v Bodmin Justices, ex p McEwen* [1947] KB 321 per Lord Goddard CJ and *R v Kings Lynn Justices, ex p Carter* [1969] 1 QB 488 per Lord Parker CJ.
21 The magistrates are also required to consider whether the accused is aware of the prosecutor's duties of advance disclosure under the Magistrates' Courts (Advance Information) Rules 1985, r4: ibid, r6.
1 *R v Colchester Justices, ex p North East Essex Building Co Ltd* [1977] 3 All ER 567.
2 For an interesting recent example of where magistrates overrode the representations of both prosecution and defence and decided that trial on indictment was more appropriate, see *R v Horsham Justices, ex p Reeves* (1980) 75 Cr App Rep 236.
3 Unless it appears during the course of committal proceedings that the case was more suitable for summary trial after all: Magistrates' Courts Act 1980, s 25(3).

under s 38 of the 1980 Act if, on obtaining information about his character and antecedents they consider their sentencing powers inadequate;

(c) To ask him where he wants to be tried.

These three steps must be followed even where the accused intends to plead 'guilty' and even where either he or his advocate have agreed to summary trial at the 'representations' stage. Although the exact statutory wording does not have to be followed (the authors themselves have not done so in the example at the end of this chapter) it was held by the Divisional Court in *R v Horseferry Road Justices, ex p Constable*[4] that they should be adhered to if possible, especially where the accused is unrepresented. Even if he is represented his consent should be given in person rather than through his advocate, unless the magistrates are proceeding in his absence. The choice of venue is entirely in his hands. If he consents to summary trial, the charge will be put to him again. If he then pleads 'guilty' he will probably be dealt with there and then. If, on the other hand, he pleads 'not guilty', it may be necessary to adjourn to a mutually convenient trial date and remand him in custody or on bail. If, however, he elects trial on indictment, the magistrates will now hold committal proceedings as in **Stage 5A**.

MODE OF TRIAL PROCEDURE
OFFENCES OTHER THAN UNDER
S 1(1) CRIMINAL DAMAGE ACT 1971

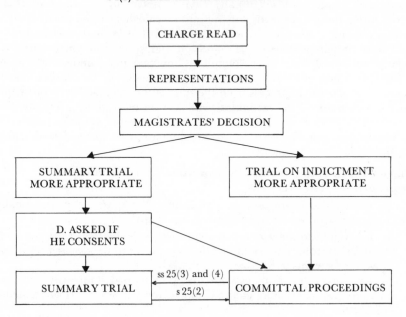

3 POWER TO CHANGE THE MODE OF TRIAL

Section 25 of the 1980 Act empowers the court either of its own motion or on the application of either party to change from summary trial to committal proceedings and vice versa. The power to switch from summary trial to committal proceedings may be exercised at any time before the prosecution

4 [1981] Crim LR 504.

has closed its case,[5] although it will usually be made before any evidence is called. The most common example is where the accused, having consented to summary trial on a previous occasion without the benefit of legal advice, now wishes to elect trial on indictment. He may also have pleaded 'guilty', so that an application for change of plea is also required. The discretion vested in the court under s 25(2) is a wide one and should be exercised according to the 'broad justice of the whole situation'.[6] The court should therefore look at all the circumstances including, in particular, whether or not the accused was represented, his age, whether he appreciated the significance of the choice he was making, and whether he realized that he had a good defence to the charge.[7] In deciding how to exercise their discretion the magistrates should *not*, however, take into account whether or not, in their view, the case is more suitable for summary trial.[7] If the accused has changed his mind more than once, it is, however, unlikely that the court will indulge him further, especially where there are co-accused,[8] but in an appropriate case the right to change election continues to exist even where a re-trial has been ordered.[9]

Conversely, the accused who has elected trial on indictment may wish to switch to summary trial. If it appears, having regard to the nature of the case, that the offence is after all more suitable for summary trial, the magistrates may change accordingly.[10] A change may also, in theory, be ordered on the application of the prosecutor or the court may do so of its own motion, subject in each case to the accused's consent. The circumstances in which an application by the accused to change to summary trial might be appropriate are summed up in the James Report:

'Cases may arise where the defendant, having elected trial by jury, changes his mind after committal proceedings have started, perhaps because he recognises the strength of the case against him and decides to admit the charge and plead guilty. There would be little point, in these circumstances, in insisting that the case should go to the Crown Court even though all the parties were content with summary trial.'[11]

Where, however, the only reason for the accused electing trial on indictment was in order to obtain the prosecution's witness statements so as to enable him to ascertain the strength of the case, it has been held that the magistrates are entitled to refuse to change over to summary trial even though the accused now wishes to plead guilty.[12] This seems a strange way to 'punish' the accused if, in all the circumstances, summary trial is more appropriate.[13]

---

5 Magistrates' Courts Act 1980, s 25(2).
6 Per Lord Widgery CJ in *R v Southampton City Justices, ex p Briggs* [1972] 1 All ER 573, DC.
7 See *R v Birmingham Justices, ex p Hodgson* [1985] 2 WLR 630 (D unrepresented, pleaded *guilty* and consented to summary trial because he thought he was guilty. Case remitted to fresh bench to consider change of plea and re-election) and *R v Highbury Corner Metropolitan Stipendiary Magistrate, ex p Weekes* [1985] 2 WLR 643. (D, aged 17, unrepresented. Consented to summary trial and pleaded *not guilty*. Unaware of significance of choice. Case remitted to fresh bench.)
8 See eg *R v West Bromwich Justices, ex p Pearson* [1981] Crim LR 709.
9 *R v Coventry City Justices, ex p Wilson* [1981] Crim LR 787.
10 Magistrates' Courts Act 1980, s 25(3) and (4).
11 Op cit, para 192.
12 *R v Warrington Justices, ex p McDonagh* [1981] Crim LR 629.
13 Electing trial on indictment so as to advise the accused as to plea and then seeking to withdraw the election if a guilty plea was appropriate was a fairly common defence ploy prior to *ex p McDonagh* (supra). It should no longer be necessary as a result of the Magistrates' Courts (Advance Information) Rules 1985.

SUMMARY OF SENTENCES BY COURT

Age Group	Non-custodial	Custodial	Other
		MAGISTRATES' COURTS	
10–16	Discharge Fine Bind Over of parents	–	Remit to juvenile court
17–20	Discharge Probation CSO Fine Attendance Centre	Detention Centre Youth Custody Hospital Order	Commit to Crown Court or another magistrates court for sentence
21+	as above, except Attendance Centre	Prison Hospital Order	As above
		JUVENILE COURTS	
10–13	Discharge Supervision Order Fine Bind Over of parents Attendance Centre	Care Order Hospital Order	Commit to Crown Court for trial (serious cases only)
14	as above	as above plus Detention Centre	as above
15–16	as above plus Community Service order if 16	as above plus Youth Custody	as above plus commit to Crown Court for sentence
		THE CROWN COURT	
10–16	as for juvenile court but no Fine limit	as for juvenile court but 12 months maximum Youth Custody	remit to juvenile court unless undesirable to do so
17–20	as for magistrates' court but no Fine limit	as for magistrates' court but no limit on Youth Custody	–
21+	as above	as for magistrates' court but no limit on term of Prison	–

4 MAGISTRATES' SENTENCING POWERS

Magistrates' powers are limited in comparison with the Crown Court. The guilty defendant is thus provided with a strong incentive to consent to summary trial, notwithstanding the magistrates' power to commit him to the Crown Court for sentence under s 38 of the 1980 Act. This topic is fully discussed in chapter 12, but a brief outline is necessary here.

(1) Schedule 1 offences

Offences listed in Sch 1 to the 1980 Act, carry up to *six months'* imprisonment and/or a £2,000 fine,[14] when dealt with by a magistrates' court.

(2) Other 'either way' offences

Where the offence is triable 'either way' by virtue of the statute creating it, for example under the Misuse of Drugs Act 1971 or Road Traffic Act 1972, magistrates' powers to imprison and/or fine, need to be considered separately.

(a) Imprisonment

The maximum term that can be imposed is six months or the maximum laid down by the statute creating the offence, whichever is *less*.[15] Thus, for example, although there are several 'either way' offences set out in Schedule 4 to the Misuse of Drugs Act 1971, for which a maximum of *twelve months'* imprisonment is provided on summary conviction, the maximum term that the magistrates can impose is *six months*. Conversely, the maximum term of imprisonment that a magistrates' court may impose for carrying an offensive weapon is that prescribed in the Prevention of Crime Act 1953, namely *three months*.

(b) Fines

The maximum fine which may be imposed is £2,000 or the sum prescribed in the relevant statute whichever is *greater*.[16] The only exceptions to this rule are certain offences under the Misuse of Drugs Act 1971 which prescribe maximum, fines of less than £2,000. In their case the *lesser* figure prevails.[17]

(3) Consecutive sentences of imprisonment and the power to commit to the Crown Court for sentence

Consideration of the characteristics of 'either way' offences would not be complete without a brief mention of these two important matters. First, s 133(2) of the 1980 Act provides that when magistrates sentence a defendant for two or more offences that are *all* triable 'either way', they may pass consecutive sentences not exceeding *12 months* in aggregate. Secondly, s 38 of the same Act provides that they may commit the defendant to the Crown Court to be sentenced if, on obtaining information about his 'character and antecedents', the court is of the opinion that their sentencing powers are inadequate. If they do so, the Crown Court has power to sentence him *as if*

14 Magistrates' Courts Act 1980, s 32(1).
15 Ibid, s 31.
16 Ibid, s 32(2).
17 Ibid, s 32(5).

he had just been convicted on indictment. Section 38 must be contrasted with the inquiry into suitability for summary trial that takes place at an earlier stage under s 19(3) of the 1980 Act. In the latter case the court is only concerned with whether the sentencing powers are adequate in regard to the *offence itself.* It may, however, be that after conviction and having found out more about the defendant, they form the view that, for example, a sentence of more than 6 months' imprisonment is appropriate.[18]

5 FACTORS IN DECIDING MODE OF TRIAL

If he is pleading 'guilty', he will usually be most anxious to ensure that the case is dealt with summarily, but if his record is so bad that committal for sentence is inevitable, he may still wish to elect trial on indictment. This is because he may wish to remain out on bail pending trial and 'arrange his affairs' before the inevitable custodial sentence commences. An accused may even elect trial on indictment where he knows that he will not be granted bail. The reason for this is that he will be treated as a prisoner on remand and thus, theoretically, be entitled to greater privileges than a prisoner serving a sentence, or committed for sentence under s 38.

If the accused proposes to plead 'not guilty', choice of venue is always of critical importance. It seems that, as a general rule, faced with the choice, solicitors tend to advise their clients to elect trial on indictment. A survey carried out by the Office of Population, Censuses and Surveys at the request of the James Committee[19] showed that out of 113 cases where solicitors made specific recommendations summary trial was recommended in only *three* cases. This has lead to allegations from certain quarters that solicitors recommend trial on indictment because it increases their legal fees.[20] Clearly such a motive is entirely improper and grossly irresponsible; it is also financially unsound as the level of remuneration and the delays in payment for work in the Crown Court compared with the quicker 'turnover' of magistrates' court work make Crown Court work financially less attractive. Nevertheless the accusation persists even though the James Report found it to be unsubstantiated.[1]

Another allegation sometimes heard is that inexperienced solicitors advise against summary trials because it is easier to leave the case to counsel. There is no doubt that the more experienced you become and the more familiar you are with the local bench, the more attractive the magistrates' court may become. The decison is never easy. Each case must be looked at on its own merits and much may depend on your own expertise as an advocate, your knowledge of the local bench and the co-operative attitude or otherwise of whoever is prosecuting. That having been said, the following factors are those most commonly taken into account.

(1) Factors in favour of electing trial on indictment

(a) Advance disclosure of the prosecution case

There is no doubt that until recently this was the strongest influencing factor since, prior to 20 May 1985 if the accused elected trial on indictment, the

18 The court only has power to commit under s 38 of the 1980 Act if they find out matters relating to the character and antecedents of the accused over and above those revealed during the mode of trial procedure: *R v Guildhall Justices, ex p Cooper* (1983) 147 JP 466.
19 See James Report (op cit) para 21 and appendix C.
20 Ibid, para 52.
 1 Ibid, para 50.

prosecution was required to tender most, if not all, of their evidence at the committal proceedings, whereas on summary trial the defence might have no idea of what evidence the prosecution proposed to call until the trial began. It was recognised that having to cross-examine witnesses 'blind' was a strong disincentive to agreeing to summary trial. In addition, being able to evaluate the strength of the prosecution case beforehand meant that the client could be advised more fully as to plea, especially where the evidence against him was overwhelming.

In certain areas, notably Birmingham, Coventry, Wolverhampton, Nottingham and Leeds, the prosecution evolved its own schemes with the co-operation of the magistrates' courts' clerks and defence solicitors. Broadly, these schemes involved the holding of a 'pre-trial review' at which not only did the prosecution outline its case and provide details of the nature of its evidence, but the defence was also expected to disclose information.[2] 'Pre-trial reviews' will no longer be necessary in the case of either way offences as a result of the recent changes outlined below. Nevertheless, such procedures will still have a place in the case of summary only offences.[3]

As already noted,[4] rule 4 of the Magistrates' Courts (Advance Information) Rules 1985 places the prosecutor under a *duty* to disclose his evidence, or a summary there of, *before* the mode of trial procedure takes place, *provided* that the accused or his representative requests it. It is hoped that this will have the effect of removing the need for an accused to elect trial on indictment *solely* for the purpose of obtaining advance disclosure of the prosecution case. Note, however, that the obligation only arises if the defence requests it *prior* to the mode of trial decision. Although the prosecution has an option to provide no more than a summary of its case it is understood that the Home Secretary has undertaken that 'full' disclosure will take place in all cases since the State Prosecuting Service becomes operational.

(b) The Crown Court is more suited to dealing with complicated issues of law and fact

Another reason sometimes put forward in favour of jury trial are the separate functions of the judge and jury. The major effect of this is that points of law, for example, as to the admissibility of evidence, are dealt with in the absence of the jury. However, magistrates, who may often not be legally qualified, are required to be arbiters of both law and fact: they may be required to consider the admissibility of an item of evidence as such, a confession, and then put it from their minds even if they have ruled against its admission.[5] It is also assumed that a judge, having a legally trained mind and lengthy professional experience, will be more receptive to the subtleties of the law of

2 For an interesting discussion of the various schemes see Barnett, 'Section 48: a viable alternative' (1983) 147 JPN 117; J. Baldwin 'Pre-Trial Disclosure in the Magistrates' Court' (1983) 147 JPN 499 and S. Hill 'Pre-Trial Reviews—a study in Coventry magistrates' court' (1984) 148 JPN 39. Other interesting articles are to be found at (1984) JPN 680, and (1985) JPN pp 179 and 185.
3 Law Society's Gazette (1983), 28 September, p 2330. In particular the Committee considered it to be unlikely that it would ever be in the best interests of the client or the solicitor to disclose any part of the defence before receiving *complete* disclosure of the prosecution case.
4 See p 185, ante.
5 Although such research as there is suggests that challenges to the admissibility of incriminating statements in summary trials are infrequent: J. Vennard, 'Contested Trials in magistrates' courts (1982)', Home Office Research Study No 71, HMSO.

evidence or to weighty matters of substantive criminal law than a bench of lay persons relying for guidance on their clerk. In addition, the jury will be subject to the judge's direction on matters of law and are bound to be influenced by his summing up on the facts. This may be an important factor where, for example, the case is one of disputed identity. If there is any error of law in the summing up this will be much easier to identify in a magistrates' court where the justices are not required to give any more than a bare verdict.

(c) Higher acquittal rate

There has been much argument as to whether the accused stands a better chance of acquittal before a jury than magistrates. On the one hand, magistrates are criticised as being 'case hardened' and too ready to believe the police, whereas it is suggested that juries are more sympathetic, even to the extent of returning a verdict of not guilty against the weight of the evidence in cases where they side with the accused. There is certainly no doubt that magistrates still attract criticism for their 'standard of justice'[6] but there is also no doubt that there are wide regional variations. Only practice and experience can tell you what to expect from your local magistrates' court and Crown Court centres.[7]

(2) Factors in favour of the magistrates' court

(a) Speed

It is often alleged that magistrates' courts provide a speedier trial and that this is a significant advantage, especially where a client has no previous convictions. For example, when a person is charged with a first offence of shoplifting the lengthy wait for the trial to come on at the Crown Court may impose an intolerable strain.[8] Again, however, much depends on the court and the likely length of the trial. In some magistrates' courts, especially in large cities, the summary trial of anything but the simplest 'not guilty' plea may involve a wait of many months. In addition, it may well be difficult to find a bench of lay magistrates that can sit on successive days. By the time a lengthy case has been adjourned part-heard by the magistrates, it may have been dealt with quicker if it had gone to the Crown Court.

(b) Less severe sentences

As already noted, magistrates have limited sentencing powers. This will only be an important consideration if you take the view that your client may receive a sentence of more than six months' imprisonment if he is convicted before the Crown Court, but that his record is not so bad that there is a risk that the magistrates will commit him for sentence. Again, much depends upon where you practice. Some benches and indeed some Circuit Judges have worse sentencing reputations than others. Only with experience and local knowledge will you be able to make an informed decision.

6 See eg M. King, 'Against Summary Trial' LAG Bulletin February 1982, p 14.
7 See S. Butler 'Acquittal Rates' (Home Office Research and Planning Unit Paper 16). Although Butler suggests that there is a significantly higher acquittal rate in contested cases in the Crown Court there are wide local variations.
8 Butler (op cit) Table 9 gives an *average* waiting time at the Crown Court of 15.7 weeks from committal to trial.

(c) Cost

The James Report[9] states that the average cost of trying an either way offence on indictment is three times greater than that of trying it summarily. Clearly this is an important factor if the client is paying privately but will still be relevant even if he is legally aided. Not only may he be required, subject to means, to make contribution to his legal aid but, in addition, he may be ordered to pay part of the prosecution costs. The latter are bound to be higher after a trial on indictment.

Conclusion

The above summary sets out the generally accepted arguments for and against electing trial on indictment. They should always be taken into account but a reasoned decision should be reached in each case. It is important not to 'elect for trial' merely because it is the usual practice; it may not necessarily be in the client's interest.

6 SPECIAL RULES AS TO CRIMINAL DAMAGE: 1980 ACT, s 22

(1) Effect on 'mode of trial' procedure

The following provisions only apply where the accused is charged with destroying or damaging property (other than by fire) contrary to Criminal Damage Act 1971, s 1(1).[10] As a preliminary the court must consider whether the 'value involved' (the cost of *replacement* if destroyed, or of *repair* if damaged), exceeds £400. The court may hear 'representations' from the prosecution and the defence as to value and has a discretion to receive evidence, but is not obliged to do so.[11]

If the 'value involved' *exceeds* £400 the procedure will be the same as for any other 'either way' offence. If it does not, the court must proceed as if the offence were triable only summarily. In that case the maximum punishment that can be imposed is *three months'* imprisonment and/or a £1,000 fine, and the defendant cannot be committed to the Crown Court for sentence under s 38 of the 1980 Act.[12]

If it is unclear whether the 'value involved' exceeds £400, the following steps must be taken:[13]

(a) the accused must be told in ordinary language that he can consent to summary trial and that if he does so, he will only be liable to the maximum punishments in s 33 of the 1980 Act (see above) and cannot be committed for sentence under s 38; and

(b) he must then be asked whether he consents to summary trial.

If he does the case proceeds to summary trial. If he does not, the 'mode of trial' procedure will then take place as with any other 'either way' offence.

9 Op cit.
10 Supra, see Magistrates' Courts Act 1980, Sch 2. These provisions also extend to attempts to commit such an offence, aiding, abetting, etc.
11 *R v Canterbury and St Augustine Justices, ex p Klisiak*, supra.
12 Magistrates' Courts Act 1980, s 33(1).
13 Ibid, s 22(4)–(6).

**MODE OF TRIAL PROCEDURE
OFFENCES UNDER
S 1(1) CRIMINAL DAMAGE ACT 1971**

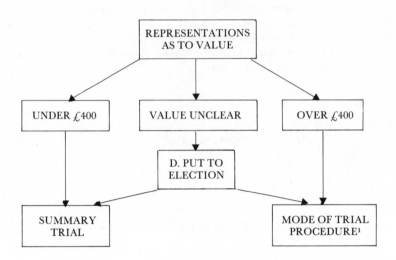

1 Same as for either way offences: see page 274.

(2) Offences forming part of a series: 1980 Act, s 22(7)

The above subsection provides that s 22 does not apply to a relevant offence of criminal damage where:

(a) it is one of two or more offences with which the accused is charged on the same occasion; and

(b) it appears to the court to constitute or form part of a series of two or more offences of the same or similar character.

The Divisional Court in *R v Hatfield Justices, ex p Castle*[14] has held that in order to come within the subsection the other offence or offences must be:

(i) triable either way; and

(ii) separated in time; and

(iii) of the same or similar character.

Thus s 22(7) will not apply when the accused is charged with criminal damage and assault whether arising out of the same incident (as in *ex p Castle*) or separated in time as in *R v Tottenham Justices, ex Tibble*.[15] Where, however, the criteria are satisfied, the value of property involved is immaterial. Thus in *R v St Helens Justices, ex p McClorie*[16] the accused was held to be entitled to elect trial on indictment where the values involved in two offences of criminal damage, namely damage to a padlock and to a police officer's watch, were £5 and £15 respectively. If, however, the accused had instead been charged

14 [1980] 3 All ER 509.
15 (1981) 73 Cr App Rep 55.
16 [1983] 1 WLR 1332.

with assaulting a police officer (which on the facts he could well have been), s 22(7) would not have applied.[17] Much will therefore depend upon the way in which the prosecutor formulates the charges.

7 TWO TYPICAL MODE OF TRIAL PROCEEDINGS

This section sets out the likely course that the 'mode of trial' procedure will take in the case of Duncan McCarthy and Anthony Jones.

(a) Police v Duncan McCarthy (case 1)[18]

McCarthy's solicitor, having discussed the case with him now that he is out on bail, advises trial on indictment, in view of the nature of the case and the fact that if convicted by the magistrates he is likely to be committed to the Crown Court for sentence. She thus contacts the prosecution who indicate that they are quite prepared for summary trial, but that if McCarthy is going to elect trial, they will be ready for committal at the adjourned hearing on *1 September*. Two days before the hearing, McCarthy's solicitor receives the committal documents. At the hearing the prosecution, who are represented by a solicitor, and McCarthy and his solicitor attend court.

Prosecution solicitor: In this case, Madam, the prosecution are asking for summary trial. Although the offence is one of burglary, the amount involved is small, there are no other persons involved and I would submit that your sentencing powers are more than adequate.

Defence solicitor: Madam, notwithstanding my client's right to elect trial, I submit that this case is not a trivial one and is more appropriate for trial before judge and jury.

I say this for three reasons. Firstly, there is to be a dispute as to the interpretation of certain statements which the prosecution say my client made to the police. There is a risk that in the course of cross-examination imputations may be cast on the character of police witnesses which may render my client liable to cross-examination as to his previous convictions. I would submit that this is an issue best dealt with by a Crown Court judge in the absence of the jury.

Chairman: Are you suggesting that we cannot distinguish law from fact?

Defence solicitor: No, not at all, Madam. This is a sensitive case involving as it does possible allegations against the police and one for which summary trial is not ideally suited. My second point is that this is not a trivial offence. It is an alleged burglary by an employee. You might feel therefore that your sentencing powers would not, in all the circumstances, be adequate. Thirdly, there is a dispute as to identification evidence combined with a defence of alibi which in my submission makes the case for trial on indictment even stronger.

Chairman: We are not entirely unfamiliar with cases of this kind, you know. [Turning to prosecutor] Do you have anything further to say?

Prosecutor: I am happy to leave the matter in your hands.

Chairman: The Bench will retire

[The court stands and the bench retire for five minutes at the end of which they return.]

Chairman: We have considered the matter carefully and we take the view that notwithstanding the matters of law involved in this case, it is nevertheless relatively simple and straightforward and is therefore more appropriate for summary trial.

Clerk: Will you stand up please, Mr McCarthy? This court has decided that your case is suitable to be tried here but it may only do so if you consent. You may,

---

17 Paradoxically, the two offences would, however, be of sufficiently 'similar character' to be tried together by the magistrates under the rule in *Re Clayton* [1983] 2 AC 473; see p 292, post.

18 It should be borne in mind that the procedure outlined below may be affected by the Magistrates' Courts (Advance Information) Rules 1985.

if you wish, be tried before a judge and jury at the Crown Court but I must warn you that if you consent to be tried by this court and you are convicted this court will have details of your previous character and convictions. If, having heard these, this court decides that a greater punishment should be inflicted than it has no power to impose, it may still commit you to the Crown Court to be sentenced there. Do you wish to be tried by this court or by a jury at the Crown Court?

McCarthy: [Looking at solicitor who is nodding pointedly] In the Crown Court.

The prosecution will then ask for the case to be committed under s 6(2) of the Magistrates' Courts Act 1980 and tender the original witness statements and exhibits to the court. This latter part of the proceedings will only take a further few moments and is set out in chapter 11.[19]

(b) Softsell Supermarkets v Anthony Jones (case 2)[20]

On the morning that he is due to appear Anthony JONES consults the Duty Solicitor who, having spoken to the solicitor instructed by the supermarket, and having seen a copy of JONES's statement under caution advises him to plead guilty. He is quite prepared to do so and also indicates that he wishes to be dealt with by the magistrates. The duty solicitor therefore advises JONES to consent to summary trial. After the warrant officer has called the case, the clerk ascertains that JONES is present and informs the bench as to who appears for the prosecution and for the defence respectively. The charge is then read to JONES after which the prosecutor addresses the bench on mode of trial.

Prosecuting solicitor: Sir, the prosecution are asking for summary trial in this case. As you can see from the charge, the offence is a relatively minor one, and all the goods have been recovered.

Duty solicitor: I agree, Sir; summary trial seems more appropriate in this case.

Bench: (after a few seconds' discussion) We are of the opinion that summary trial is appropriate.

The clerk now proceeds to ask JONES where he wants to be tried, using the same formula as was used for McCARTHY.

Jones: I want to be tried here, please.

Clerk: Do you plead guilty or not guilty?

Jones: Guilty, your Worships.

The court now proceeds to hear the brief facts of the case from the prosecution and then either sentences JONES, having heard a plea in mitigation, or alternatively adjourns and remands for reports. This is dealt with more fully in Chapter 13.[21]

19 See p 330, post.
20 See note 18, p 283, ante.
21 See note 18, p 283, ante.

CHAPTER 9

Trials in the magistrates' court

1 INTRODUCTION

This chapter concentrates on contested trials leaving consideration of the procedure on guilty pleas to chapter 13. Many contested summary trials are relatively straightforward, but some will require detailed research into the relevant law and practice. The accused may face charges that are very serious (for example, arising out of an incident of public disorder or an assault on the police) or highly technical (for example, drink/drive offences). Far too frequently, practitioners see the magistrates' court as a rough and ready forum in which anything goes. If you adopt such an attitude, you will never succeed as a criminal advocate.

2 PROCEDURE IN CONTESTED TRIALS

Contested trials in magistrates' courts present a number of problems, the most serious of which is that by the time the case comes to trial you may still know little or nothing about the case that your client has to meet.[1] You will often have little to go on other than the summons or charge sheet and what your client tells you. You will also need to adapt to local variations; for example, a very much terser style of advocacy should normally be adopted when appearing before a stipendiary as opposed to a lay bench. It is difficult to do more than generalise on many aspects of summary trial procedure, but, local variations notwithstanding, there is no substitute for thorough preparation. During the course of a trial you will need a silver tongue, a quick mind, and a lightning pen (often all three at the same time). You can only hope to develop these skills if you give each client's case, however small, the advance care it deserves. The main steps in the proceedings are:

Stage 1—The case is called
Stage 2—(rarely) The court gives directions on publicity
Stage 3—(rarely) The court hears argument on 'preliminary points'
Stage 4—The plea is taken (unless taken on an earlier adjournment).
Stage 5—The prosecution and defence call their evidence and make speeches
Stage 6—The bench gives its verdict

Each stage will now be considered in turn.

Stage 1. The case is called

Problems sometimes arise because either the prosecutor or the accused fails to answer.

---

1 The position has now been altered in the case of either way offences tried summarily as a result of the coming into force of the Magistrates' Courts (Advance Information) Rules 1985. See p 279, ante. Disclosure may also take place on a 'pre-trial review' in certain courts: see p 279, ante.

(a)   The prosecutor

If the accused is present but the prosecutor is not, s 15(1) of the Magistrates' Courts Act 1980 provides that the court may dismiss the information or, if evidence has been received on a previous occasion, proceed in the prosecutor's absence. Alternatively it may adjourn under s 10 of the 1980 Act. If acting for the accused, you should always apply for the information to be dismissed,[2] stressing that it is for the prosecution to be in a fit state to proceed, and that if they are not, the accused is entitled to be discharged. Courts' attitudes vary, some are hesitant to dismiss on the first occasion, and will adjourn to give the prosecutor one more chance.

Alternatively, the prosecutor may be legally represented although not present in person. In such a case, he is deemed to be present[3] through his representative. It may well be, however, that the prosecutor is himself a material witness. If this is the case, his representative may have no choice but to apply for an adjournment. This should be opposed. If an adjournment is refused the prosecution will have to proceed and may not be able to establish a prima facie case.

(b)   The accused

The accused may choose not to appear (reasons may vary from indolence and indifference, to wilful default), alternatively he may not know that he is supposed to be there, because he has never received a summons, or been notified on the new hearing date. The general rule is that a magistrates' court may either proceed to try the accused in his absence[4] (in which case a plea of 'not guilty' will be entered, if not already taken), or adjourn the proceedings. Where the proceedings were begun by summons, however, the court cannot try an accused in his absence unless they are first satisfied that the summons has been duly served within a 'reasonable time' before the hearing date or that the accused has appeared before the court on a previous occasion in answer to the information.[5] This general statement of the law is, however, misleading. The course that the court adopts will, in practical terms, be governed by whether or not the accused has been on bail.

(i) Accused not on bail. The accused has no statutory obligation to attend but may run the risk of being tried and convicted in his absence. Whether or not this is a real risk will depend on the circumstances. If, for example, an adjournment has been agreed between the parties beforehand there will be no need for the accused to attend. In the event of an adjournment in the accused's absence notice of the adjourned hearing date must be served on him. If he does not appear at the adjourned hearing the court must satisfy itself that such notice has been duly served before proceeding in his absence. Thus, for example, if Mary ADAMS (*case 3*) were to inform the court that she intended to plead 'not guilty' the proceedings would, in all probability be adjourned '*sine die*' without the need for her to attend. If she were not subsequently informed of the new hearing date, any conviction in her absence

---

2 Note that if the offence is 'summary only' it may be too late for the prosecution to lay a new information because they are by now outside the six-month time limit. According to official statistics a significant proportion of acquittals in the magistrates' court are due to the prosecution failing to appear or offering no evidence on the day. See Contested Trials in the Magistrates' Court: Royal Commission on Criminal Procedure: Research Study 6, p 15.

3 Magistrates' Courts Act 1980, s 122(2).

4 Ibid, s 11(1).

5 Ibid, s 11(2): the detailed rules as to the service of summonses are contained in Magistrates' Courts Rules 1981, r 99. See also p 36, ante.

would be void and the magistrates would have to fix a new date for her trial.[6]

Where, on the other hand, no such adjournment has been agreed or applied for the court may well proceed to try the accused in his absence, if they are satisfied as to service. The prosecution will still have to prove their case, so that it is theoretically possible for the court to acquit the accused in his absence, but in practice, conviction is more or less inevitable.

As with the prosecutor, an accused is not deemed to be absent when represented by solicitor or counsel[7] but this is of little practical use where he is pleading 'not guilty' since he is likely to be your only or main witness.

EXAMPLE: *Police v* Mary ADAMS *(case 3)*. If, on the day fixed for trial, she were not to attend, you should first ask for the case to be stood out, to enable you to try and find out where she was and play for time. If this proved unsuccessful, you should apply for an adjournment, trying to suggest that some unforeseen disaster must have befallen her. If this were refused you could still represent her, but the part that you could play would be necessarily limited to cross-examination of the prosecution witnesses, if any, and a submission at the end of the case that on all the evidence the charge had not been proved.

Even if the court does convict the accused in his absence, their powers to *sentence* him in his absence are restricted in two respects. They may not:

- imprison him, send him to detention centre or activate a suspended sentence of imprisonment;[8] or
- impose a disqualification[9] except on resumption of the hearing after an adjournment.

Thus if, for example, Mary ADAMS *(case 3)* were to be convicted in her absence and the court considered that a fine and endorsement were inadequate,[10] it would be necessary to adjourn to give her an opportunity to attend. If she did not do so, the court could proceed to disqualify her from driving if it thought fit provided that it was satisfied that she had received notification of the adjournment.

The final possibility, albeit rare, is for the court to adjourn and issue a warrant for the accused's arrest. They may do this, even though the accused has *not* hitherto been on bail but only if:

- the offence is punishable with *imprisonment*; and
- the information is substantiated on *oath*; and
- service of the summons can be proved or the accused has appeared on a previous occasion in answer to the information.[11]

(ii) Accused on bail. Although the court can, in theory, try an accused in his absence[12] it will, in all probability, issue a warrant for his arrest,[13] and adjourn the proceedings.

6 *R v Seisdon Justices, ex p Dougan* [1983] 1 All ER 6.
7 1980 Act, s 122(2).
8 Ibid, s 11(3): the court would have power to issue a warrant for his arrest under ibid, s 13.
9 Ibid, s 11(4): the court must send the accused adequate notice giving the reason for the adjournment (ibid, ss 10(2) and 11(4); the court may also issue a warrant for arrest but only where it proposes to disqualify. Note that 'disqualification' is not merely confined to 'disqualification from driving' (see eg Food and Drugs Act 1955, s 14).
10 The court would also probably need to adjourn if she had not sent her driving licence to the court.
11 1980 Act, s 13: for detailed rules as to service and proof thereof see Magistrates' Court Rules 1981, rr 67 and 99.
12 If the offence were triable either way this would presuppose that the court had previously held mode of trial proceedings in the accused's presence at which he had consented to summary trial.
13 This would be issued under s 7(1) of the Bail Act 1976.

Setting aside proceedings—Magistrates' Courts Act 1980, s 14

In proceedings begun by summons, it is possible that an accused is in total ignorance of its issue and purported service, because, for example, it has been sent to the wrong address, or left with a person at the accused's address who has not passed it on to him. Section 14 provides that if the accused did not know of the summons or the proceedings until a date after a magistrates' court has begun to try the information and makes a statutory declaration to that effect, the *summons* and subsequent proceedings are void, but *not* the *information* itself. The declaration must be served on the appropriate Clerk to the Justices within *21 days* of the accused coming to know of the proceedings, although the accused may apply to the court for an extension of time if it was otherwise unreasonable for the time limits to be complied with. Use of s 14 may only gain a Pyrrhic victory, however, because the prosecution will still be able to apply for a new summons to be issued based on the original information.

Stage 2. Applications relating to publicity

As a general rule proceedings should be held in open court and all evidence to the court should be communicated publicly. As Lord Diplock stated in *A-G v Leveller Magazines Ltd*:

> 'If the way that courts behave cannot be hidden from the public ear and eye this provides a safeguard against judicial arbitrariness or idiosyncrasy and maintains the public's confidence in the administration of justice.'[14]

Magistrates have a general common law power to hold proceedings *in camera* but only to the extent that they reasonably believe it to be necessary in the interests of justice. It is clear from two recent cases, however, that this power should only be exercised in wholly exceptional circumstances.[15]

Three important statutory provisions must also be noted. Firstly, where one or more of the accused is a juvenile charged jointly with an adult, the clerk is required to bring to the court's attention its powers under the Children and Young Persons Act 1933, s 39[16] to direct that nothing shall be published that is calculated to lead to the juvenile's identification. Secondly, where a child or young person is called as a witness in relation to an offence against decency or morality, the court may exclude the public but not the press from the court whilst he is giving evidence;[17] it may also prohibit publication of any material calculated to lead to his identification under s 39. Thirdly, a magistrates' court has power under the Contempt of Court Act 1981, s 4(2) to postpone the reporting of any part of the proceedings for such period as it thinks necessary where it appears to be necessary for avoiding a substantial risk of prejudice to the administration of justice. It also has power under s 11 of the 1981 Act to prohibit the publication of any name or other matter which it has ordered to be withheld from the public.

Stage 3. Preliminary applications

Either party may wish to apply for an adjournment because they are not ready to proceed. If the present date has been fixed well in advance, the

---

14 [1979] AC 440 at 449, HL.
15 *R v Ealing Justices, ex p Weafer* (1982) 74 Cr App Rep 204 and *R v Reigate Justices, ex p Argus Newspapers and Larcombe* (1983) 147 JP 385.
16 This section in fact extends to any child under 17 whether involved as a defendant or witness whatever the offence.
17 Children and Young Persons' Act 1933, s 37.

defence should resist a prosecution application whenever it considers it reasonable to do so, especially if they have been granted an adjournment on an earlier occasion. Conversely, should the defence be seeking a further adjournment in similar circumstances a good reason will be required, the magistrates will not adjourn as a matter of course.[18]

There are a number of other matters which may arise at this stage and which may result in an adjournment, or even in the dismissal of the information. The following are of particular importance:

    (a) challenges to the bench;
    (b) challenges as to jurisdiction;
    (c) defects in the information;
    (d) applications for separate trials.

These are complicated areas of the law which need to be mastered even though they do not often arise in practice.

(a) *Challenging the bench*

A client may sometimes complain that the composition of the bench is not to his liking and instruct you to apply for trial before a different bench. In trials on indictment the limited right of jury challenge allows him some control over who will try him, but there is no general right to challenge the composition of a bench of magistrates. There are, however, two special situations in which it may be challenged.

(i) On the ground of bias. A magistrate should not try a case if:

    – he is statutorily disqualified; or
    – he has some direct pecuniary interest however small; or
    – he has good reason to doubt his own ability to be completely impartial; or
    – if a fair and reasonably-minded person might have a reasonable suspicion in the circumstances that he was incapable of approaching the matter impartially.[19]

Magistrates will normally recognize potential conflict and withdraw voluntarily. If necessary, however, objections should be taken with the court before the trial begins. If a magistrate sits when disqualified under this rule, the proceedings may be challenged on an application for judicial review. Where a pecuniary interest, however small, can be established *certiorari* will lie whether or not the magistrate was influenced by it. Where a non pecuniary interest is alleged, the test to be applied is not whether any member of the bench is *actually* biased, but whether a reasonable and fair minded person sitting in court and knowing all the relevant facts would have a reasonable *suspicion* that a fair trial was not possible.[20]

(ii) On the ground that a magistrate has prior knowledge of the accused. The accused may complain to you on the ground that he will not receive a fair trial because he is one of the court 'regulars'. Section 42

---

18 Research conducted in 1982 (n = 259) showed that 93% of applications for adjournments were made by the Prosecution: see (1983) 147 JP 163. The Divisional Court will only rarely intervene to overturn a magistrates' decision as to adjournment. For three recent cases where a magistrates' refusal to allow an adjournment has been the subject of judicial review see *R v Macclesfield Justices, ex p Jones* [1983] RTR 143 (upheld): *Taylor v Baird* [1983] Crim LR 551 (upheld) and *R v Birmingham Justices, ex p Lamb* [1983] 3 All ER 23 (overturned).

19 This topic is more fully discussed in *Stone's Justices' Manual* 1985 p 9, et seq.

20 *R v Liverpool City Justices, ex p Topping* [1983] 1 All ER 490.

Magistrates' Courts' Act 1980 precludes a magistrate from trying the accused if it has been notified of his previous convictions during an earlier bail application *in the same proceedings*. Apart from this, however, there is no general rule debarring a magistrate from trying a case merely because he knows of the accused's previous history, but it is desirable that the court should not have an intimate knowledge of his previous criminal behaviour.[1] Each case will depend on its own facts. The problem has twice recently been considered by the Divisional Court.

(1) R v Sandwich Justices, ex p Berry[2]

B had the misfortune to attract prosecutions in respect of his driving on no less than six different occasions between August and October 1980. He was faced with six sets of charges, each set relating to offences committed on one day. His solicitor successfully applied for each set to be tried separately and further applied for each set to be tried by a new bench in order to obviate the risk of prejudice. The court granted the application for separate trials but refused to order that these be before separate benches and proceeded to try all six sets of charges in succession. A Divisional Court held that the matter was entirely within the discretion of the magistrates and that, in the circumstances, they had exercised this correctly, especially since they had reviewed the position after having heard each set of charges.[3]

(2) R v Liverpool City Justices, ex p Topping[4]

T appeared before the justices to be tried on a charge of criminal damage. As a matter of court policy, a computer printout of the court register was provided to the bench in all cases. This indicated that T was awaiting trial for seven other offences. T's solicitor objected to his client being tried by the bench on the ground of prejudice. His application was refused, on the basis that the clerk to the justices had decided that, *as a matter of policy*, accused persons would not be prejudiced by the bench seeing copies of the computerised court register indicating outstanding offences. D was tried and convicted. In quashing D's conviction the court stated that the Liverpool practice was most undesirable and wrong in law.

The position seems to be, therefore, that, provided there is no *appearance* of bias, magistrates have a discretion to try and accused notwithstanding that they are aware of outstanding charges.[5] *Ex p Berry* is distinguishable from *ex p Topping* in that in the former case the magistrates were held to be exercising their discretion correctly whereas in the latter they did not exercise it at all.

(b) Lack of jurisdiction

As already noted,[6] on rare occasions there may be no jurisdiction to try the information at all because, for example, it has not been laid in time, has not been considered by a justice or justices' clerk, or no Notice of Intended Prosecution has been given under s 179 of the Road Traffic Act 1972. You should ensure that you acquire the habit of always checking such points at an early stage in the proceedings; one day your client may have a pleasant surprise.

(c) Amendment to defects in the information

A magistrates' court is able to remedy most defects under s 123 of the Magistrates' Courts Act 1980 which provides that:

1 See eg *R v McElligot, ex p Gallagher* [1972] Crim LR 332.
2 (1982) 74 Cr App Rep 132.
3 Out of a total of 16 charges the magistrates in fact acquitted the accused of 7.
4 Supra.
5 *Ex p Berry*, supra, was distinguished and approved on its facts.
6 P 34, ante. Rarely, it may also be possible to argue for dismissal on the ground that the proceedings are an abuse of process. See p 36, ante; *R v Newcastle-upon-Tyne Justices, ex p Hindle* 1984 1 All ER 770.

'(1) No objection shall be allowed to any information or complaint, or to any summons or warrant to procure the presence of the defendant, for any defect in it in substance or in form, or for any variance between it and the evidence adduced on behalf of the prosecutor or complainant at the hearing of the information or complaint.

(2) If it appears to the magistrates' court that any variance between a summons or warrant and the evidence adduced on behalf of the prosecutor or complainant is such that the defendant has been misled by the variance, the court shall, on the application of the defendant, adjourn the hearing.'

On first reading, s 123 appears to enable the court to cure any defect, however substantial, even if it only emerges after the trial has commenced. It appears to prohibit objections both to defects in the substance or form of the information and to discrepancies between the information and the evidence adduced during the course of the trial. The only concession to the accused appears to be the right to an adjournment if he has been misled. The courts have, however, interpreted the scope of the section rather more restrictively. Lord Parker CJ in *Wright v Nicholson*[7] stated that s 100 of the Magistrates' Courts' Act 1952, (s 123's predecessor):

'cannot be read literally as meaning: there can be no attack on an information however fundamental the defect. It depends in every case whether, for instance, the variance between it and the evidence is such as to require an amendment: a misdescription of premises might not even require an amendment. '(If), unless the information is amended there might be grave injustice to the [accused], an amendment is called for. Once an amendment is called for and granted, then [s 123(2)] operates, which requires the court on the application of the defendant to adjourn.'

In Hutchinson (Cinemas) Ltd v Tyson[8] Lord Parker CJ also stated that :

'It seems to me that one might find an information which was so defective, so fundamentally bad, that it could not be cured at all and the only proper course would be for the justices to dismiss the information. At the other end of the scale there may be informations which are deficient in some minor particular, a misdescription of premises or data, where there could be no prejudice and where no amendment or further particulars are required at all. In between, there are informations, which are perfectly good as informations, albeit deficient, and can be cured not merely by a formal amendment, but by the delivery of particulars to supplement their contents.'

Unfortunately it is difficult to extract any firm principles from the many decided cases, perhaps because the defects that arise are so varied.[9] Take, for example, errors in setting out the accused's name or address. Mere spelling mistakes will probably not even require amendment,[10] but at the other end of the scale an information that names the *wrong person altogether* cannot even be cured by recourse to s 123, unless, possibly, the person summonsed appears and defends the case on the merits, thereby waiving the defect.[11]

A similar approach has been adopted to defects in the description of the offence. When, for example, the prosecution adduced evidence as to the

7 [1970] 1 All ER 12.
8 (1969) 134 JP 202: see also similar dicta of Lord Widgery CJ in *Garfield v Maddocks* [1974] QB 7.
9 A helpful list of the more important cases is provided in Harris, *Criminal Jurisdiction of Magistrates* (9th edition) at p 242.
10 See eg *Allan v Wiseman* [1975] RTR 217.
11 See *Marco (Croydon) Ltd (trading as AJ Bull Containers) v Metropolitan Police* [1984] RTR 24, but contrast *Tector v DHSS* (1983) Times, 29 June. The report of the *Marco* case suggests that in the case of a limited company appearance before the court will not waive the defect if the wrong company has been named.

defective condition of the rear *offside* tyre on the trial of an information
alleging an offence alleging a defective rear *nearside* tyre the magistrates
granted an application to amend the information. The Divisional Court, in
upholding the conviction stated that they would have done so even if the
information had not been amended.[12] On rare occasions, however, an information may be so defective as to be incapable of amendment because, for
example, it discloses no known offence or relates to an entirely different
factual situation.[13] Each case is a matter of degree. Where the accused's
defence is one of alibi, failure to amend, or to give the accused the opportunity of an adjournment, will normally result in the conviction being
quashed.[14] Conversely an amendment may be allowed even where the prosecution evidence has disclosed a completely different offence from the one
charged provided that the accused has not been prejudiced.[15]

> EXAMPLE: *Police v Mary* ADAMS *(case 3)*. If the offence had been described as having
> been committed at 'Almas Road' instead of 'Alma Road' or her car as a 'Ford
> Cortina' instead of a 'Ford Escort', no amendment would seem to be re-
> quired. Applying for an adjournment or insisting on amendment would be unlikely
> to endear her solicitor to the court. If, however, the information had stated that
> the offence had been committed on '*22 November*' instead of '*21*', the effect of this
> error would depend largely upon the significance, if any, of the date on which the
> alleged offence was committed. Since Mary ADAMS is not asserting that she was
> not involved in the relevant accident it is hard to see how a refusal by the court
> to amend the information or adjourn the proceedings would prejudice her.

Discussion of s 123 would not be complete without returning to the vexed
topic of the duplicitous information. It will be recalled[16] that if magistrates
proceed to try an information that charges more than one offence as opposed
to trying two or more informations together the proceedings are void. It is
important, therefore, that in cases of doubt the defence solicitor should ask
to see the information upon which the summons is based since. If it is
duplicitous the prosecution can only proceed if the court is prepared to allow
an amendment under s 123 deleting all but one of the offences charged.
Ironically, therefore, it would appear that an accused is in a better position
if the defect does not emerge until after the magistrates have begun the case.[17]

(d) Applications for separate trials

Problems may arise in one of two ways: (i) where the accused is charged
with more than one offence and (ii) where there are more than one accused
charged either jointly or separately with related offences. A magistrates'
court has always had jurisdiction to try persons *jointly* charged in one information,[18] but the House of Lords in *re Clayton*[19] has recently held that, contrary to earlier authority, magistrates also have a discretion to try two or

---

12 *R v Sandwell Justices, ex p West Midlands Passenger Transport Board* [1979] RTR 17.
13 See *Simpson v Roberts*, (1984) Times, 21 December.
14 As in *Wright v Nicholson*, supra.
15 See eg *R v Newcastle-upon-Tyne Justices, ex p John Bryce (Contractors) Ltd* [1976] 2 All ER 611
    (charge of permitting use of a vehicle with an unsecured loan amended to using a vehicle
    where offence based on same facts).
16 See p 32 ante.
17 See *Shah v Swallow* [1984] 2 All ER 528, HL. For an illuminating discussion of the decision
    in the Divisional Court see (1983) 147 JPN 819.
18 S 4(2) of the Criminal Attempts Act 1981 also permits joint trial of offences and attempts in
    certain circumstances.
19 [1983] 2 AC 473.

more informations together. In *re Clayton* the House held that where an accused is charged with two or more offences or two or more accused are charged on separate informations, the court may try the informations together even if the accused do not consent. This is so,[1] even if the accused are not present (as was the case in *re Clayton*). In such cases the magistrates should have regard to the views of the prosecution and the defence and, if necessary, of their clerk before deciding whether a joint trial in the absence of consent would be fair and just.

(i) Joint trial of offences. In *re Clayton*, the House of Lords suggested that when the facts are connected, offences can be tried together summarily in the same circumstances as on indictment; it gave as examples cases where the accused is charged with several motoring or shoplifting offences. Trials on indictment are governed by the Indictment Rules 1971, rule 9 of which provides that:

> 'Charges for any offences may be joined in the same indictment if those charges are founded on the same facts, or form part of a series of offences of the same or similar character.'

Rule 9 will be now therefore prayed in aid by prosecutors in summary trials. It is vital that the defence considers the implications of a prosecution request for joint trials most carefully. If an accused is charged with several offences *arising out of the same incident* the case for trying them together will be strong because there is no power in summary trials (unlike in trials on indictment) for the court to return a verdict (or accept a plea) of guilty to a lesser offence.[20] This difficulty can now be avoided by the prosecution laying two informations in the alternative.

> EXAMPLE: D is charged with assaulting a police officer in the execution of his duty. Prior to *re Clayton*, if the magistrates had been satisfied that there had been an assault but were not satisfied that the officer was acting in the execution of his duty, they would have had no alternative but to acquit.[1] They would not have been able to convict D of the lesser offences of common assault. Now the prosecution will be able to lay separate informations in the alternative and ask for them to be tried jointly.

It will be well nigh impossible to argue for separate trials, in such cases, although there may be occasions where such an application could be properly made.

> EXAMPLE: D is charged with careless driving and driving whilst disqualified. If the two charges were heard together D would be prejudiced because the bench would necessarily become aware of his previous bad driving record.

Where, on the other hand, the accused is charged with offences *arising out of separate incidents*, great caution should be exercised before agreeing to the informations being tried together. If they are, there is a real danger that the rule against the admission of 'similar fact' evidence[2] will be broken:

> EXAMPLE. D is charged with three offences of stealing groceries from three different supermarkets on different days. If tried on indictment, these three offences would undoubtedly be tried together but, unless they were 'strikingly similar', the judge would be required to direct the jury in strong terms that the evidence on each count must be considered separately and that evidence on one count is not admis-

---

20 *Lawrence v Same* [1968] 2 QB 93.
1 See eg *Lindley v Rutter* [1981] QB 128; *Bentley v Brudzinski* (1982) 75 Cr App Rep 217 and *Brazil v Chief Constable of Surrey* [1983] 3 All ER 537.
2 See p 128, ante.

sible to prove guilt on the others. If the offences were tried summarily, however, there will not be this separation of functions between judge and jury. It is open to doubt whether a lay bench will be adequately directed on the application or otherwise of the 'similar fact' rule.[3]

In practical terms, the decision in *re Clayton* may have fundamentally undermined the restrictions on admission of 'similar fact' evidence in summary trials. This is particularly unfortunate since the accused may have no idea of the evidence that the prosecution intends to call.

(ii) Joint trial of offenders. *Re Clayton* is also important in this context since the House of Lords implied that the practice relating to joinder of offenders in trials on indictment set out in *R v Assim*[4] should apply equally to summary trials. Prior to *re Clayton* magistrates had power to try two accused charged *jointly in the same information*, but *re Clayton* now empowers them to try two or more accused charged in separate informations and even though the offences are not the same (provided they are sufficiently related). The decision in *re Clayton* may therefore be used, for example,[5] to support a prosecution application for the joint trial of several accused on separate offences arising out of an incident of public disorder. You should, if the circumstances warrant,[6] argue that this is contrary to the interests of justice, especially if the prosecution have not disclosed their evidence beforehand. The court should, in particular, be referred to the *dicta* of Lord Roskill in *re Clayton* to the effect that the decision was not an invitation to magistrates' courts:

> 'to embark upon long and complicated summary trials with many charges being heard and many offenders being tried at the same time.'[7]

To sum up, there may be occasions where you will wish to apply for severance of offences or offenders. Such applications should, however, only be made sparingly especially since even if you do persuade the bench to try the informations separately, there is no guarantee they will be tried before differently constituted benches.[8]

Separate trial of cross-summonses

On occasions, two informants may apply for cross-summonses against each other, arising out of the same incident, usually an assault. The Divisional Court has recently held in *R v Epsom Justices, ex p Gibbons*[9] that magistrates have no jurisdiction to try cross-summonses together in any circumstances. The informations should be tried in the order in which they have been laid. It may still be necessary, however, to apply for the second information to be tried by a different bench if there is a risk that the magistrates will have difficulty in trying it in an impartial manner. This might arise, for example, where the accused in the first prosecution had cross-examined the informant on his previous convictions.

3 Another reason for electing trial on indictment. *Re Clayton* also appears to conflict with *R v Liverpool Justices, ex p Topping*, supra—if an accused is prejudiced by the bench *reading a computer print out* showing outstanding charges, surely he is even more prejudiced if the bench tries outstanding charges *at the same time*.
4 [1966] 2 QB 249, CCA.
5 Supra.
6 It may, of course, be the *defence* who wants a joint trial in such a case, eg in order to expose discrepancies better in the prosecution evidence.
7 *Re Clayton*, supra.
8 On the basis of the decision in *R v Sandwich Justices, ex p Berry*, supra.
9 [1984] QB 574.

Stage 4. The taking of the plea

When an accused appears before a magistrates' court he will normally be placed in the dock, but practice varies. Motoring offenders, for example, may be allowed to sit with their solicitors. The plea may have been taken on a previous occasion, but if not, the accused will be asked to stand up, the charge or charges will be read out, the plea will be taken, and he will then be invited to sit down. The accused will be asked to plead in person even where he is represented.

> EXAMPLE. *Police v Mary* ADAMS *(case 3)*. If ADAMS were to decide to plead 'not guilty', she would be asked to stand up and the clerk to the justices would address her thus:
> 'Mary ADAMS you are charged that on the 21st day of November 198– at the junction of Weyford High Street and Alma Road, you drove a motor vehicle without due care and attention contrary to section 3 of the Road Traffic Act 1972. How do you plead 'guilty' or 'not guilty'?'

The plea must be voluntary. If it is obtained by duress, for example, from a co-accused[10] or the court,[11] the Crown Court has jurisdiction to entertain an appeal against conviction. If the accused is not present and the magistrates decide to proceed to trial, a plea of 'not guilty' will be entered on his behalf. There is no authority as to whether the court has jurisdiction to accept a 'guilty' plea in the accused's absence, but, as a matter of practice, solicitors are often permitted to enter a plea to a motoring offence on behalf of their clients.

Two points require brief mention: (a) where the accused's plea is 'equivocal' and (b) where he wishes to change his plea.

(a) Equivocal pleas. A plea is 'equivocal' if the accused says or does anything which should lead the court to be uncertain as to whether he is pleading guilty or not guilty. Perhaps the most common example is where the accused pleads to an offence of theft in terms such as, 'guilty, but I did not mean to steal it'. When this occurs the court, should attempt to ascertain from the accused exactly what it is that he is saying. If any doubt remains, the court must enter a plea of 'not guilty'. Disputes concerning equivocal pleas tend to arise after the event, on appeals against conviction to the Crown Court. The topic is considered further in Chapter 14.

(b) Changes of plea. An accused may sometimes wish to change his plea from 'guilty' to 'not guilty' or vice versa. A change of plea is often sought where an accused has pleaded guilty on an earlier occasion without the benefit of representation. The court has a general discretion to permit a change of plea from 'guilty' to 'not guilty' at any stage prior to sentence,[12] but the discretion should be exercised sparingly and a change should only be permitted if the interests of justice require it.[13] If a change of plea is permitted the charge(s) will be put to the accused again.

---

10 See eg *R v Crown Court at Huntingdon, ex p Jordan* [1981] QB 857 (pressure on wife by husband to plead guilty held to amount to duress).

11 See eg *Tarlochan Gata Aura v R* [1982] Crim LR 49 (Bradford riots—plea of guilty induced by justices' policy of refusing to grant bail to those pleading not guilty).

12 *S (infant) v Manchester City Recorder* [1971] AC 481. Note that where the defendant is committed for sentence to the Crown Court, that court has the same power as the magistrates to allow a change of plea. Contrast the position where he appeals against conviction and/or sentence.

13 The need for a change of plea can sometimes arise as late as the solicitors' speech in mitigation. See eg *P Foster (Haulage) Ltd v Roberts* [1978] 2 All ER 751 (D's solicitor mistakenly thought that offences were absolute—refusal to allow change of plea upheld.)

Alternatively, the accused may wish to change his plea to 'guilty'. There is no direct authority on the point, but such changes are frequently permitted: the most commonly met instance being where an accused wishes to change his plea after obtaining legal advice.

> EXAMPLE. D appears before the court on bail charged with assault. Although he is unrepresented, the charge is put to him and he pleads 'not guilty'. He asks for an adjournment to obtain legal advice and accordingly the court grants his application and remands him on bail. On seeing a solicitor it becomes apparent that D has no defence but strong mitigation (for example, although intensely provoked he was not acting in self defence) and accordingly albeit reluctantly he accepts advice to plead 'guilty' at the adjourned hearing.

In the above example, the accused will be allowed to change his plea, but it would be wise to inform the court in advance so that other cases can be fitted in. In addition, the prosecutor should be informed, so that witnesses can be told that they need not come to court: if this is not done, the accused may be penalised in costs.

Stage 5. Prosecution and defence call their evidence

This part of the chapter sets out the normal sequence which will be adopted in a typical magistrates' court, but local practice may vary. An advocate appearing in an unfamiliar court would therefore be well advised to try and observe the court in action before his or her case is called. Trials in the magistrates' court present difficulties even for the most experienced advocates, particularly since, as already noted, you may have little or no advance knowledge of the prosecution case. It is vital, therefore, that you acquire a thorough grasp of the principles of the law of evidence. In particular, you should always be on your guard against a witness inadvertently giving hearsay evidence, or, as quite frequently happens in the magistrates' court, blurting out details of the accused's bad character. It is always important, therefore, to try to anticipate the problem before it arises; once inadmissible evidence has been given it may be difficult for the court to put it out of its mind.[14]

The other major practical difficulty is that you will not usually have anyone available to take a note. It is vital, therefore, that you devise a scheme for keeping an accurate note of the evidence-in-chief as it is presented, marking in some way those points on which you will have to cross-examine the witness. Every advocate develops his or her own way of taking notes. Some prefer the style which integrates question and answer into a single narrative, others prefer to note each question and answer separately. Whatever method one adopts the objective is to highlight the important points so that they may be picked out at a glance. You should allow yourself plenty of space, both in the margin and between each question and answer so that comments and points of emphasis can be subsequently added. Keeping a proper note is well nigh impossible when *cross-examining* a witness because it requires one to write the reply at the same time as formulating the next question. Although it may therefore be necessary to become selective in the replies that you note, you should never rush on to the next question but should always take the time to note down any important replies fully.

---

14 Whenever a magistrates' court hears inadmissible evidence it has a discretion to order a retrial before a fresh bench if it considers that it is no longer possible for the accused to receive a fair trial: *Elkington v Kelsey* [1948] 2KB 256.

(a) The order of speeches

Rule 13 of the Magistrates' Courts Rules 1981 lays down both the order in which the parties shall address the magistrates, and call their evidence. It provides that:

(1) On the summary trial of an information, where the accused does not plead guilty, the prosecutor shall call the evidence for the prosecution and before doing so may address the court.
(2) At the conclusion of the evidence for the prosecution, the accused may address the court, whether or not he afterwards ... calls evidence.
(3) At the conclusion of the evidence, if any, for the defence, the prosecutor may call evidence to rebut that evidence.
(4) At the conclusion of the evidence for the defence ... and the evidence, if any, in rebuttal, the accused may address the court if he has not already done so.
(5) Either party may, with the leave of the court, address the court a second time but where the court grants leave to one party it shall not refuse leave to the other.
(6) Where both parties address the court, the prosecutor shall address the court for the second time before the accused does so.

In a simple case the order of proceedings will therefore be:

- prosecutor's opening speech;
- prosecutor's evidence;
- defence evidence;
- defence closing speech;
- verdict.

In addition to the right to make 'speeches', parties may address the bench on points of law at any stage during the trial and the other party will have a right of reply.[15] One of the major difficulties facing defence advocates is that matters of law and fact are both decided by the magistrates. Particular difficulties can arise where the court is asked to rule on the admissibility of an item of evidence.

EXAMPLE. D wishes to argue that no reliance should be placed upon a written confession because it was obtained in breach of s 76(2) of the Police and Criminal Evidence Act 1984. Unlike a trial on indictment there will not be a 'trial within a trial'[16] and accordingly if the magistrates rule the confession to be admissible the evidence relating to it will not need to be repeated. On the other hand, if they exclude it the damage has already been done because having read it they may not be able to put it out of their minds.[17] The absence of a 'trial within a trial' also produces the anomalous result that even where the sole prosecution evidence consists of a confession it will hardly ever be possible to submit that there is no case to answer since the bench will almost certainly wish to hear evidence from the accused before ruling on inadmissibilty. This can only be given after the prosecution has closed its case.

Evidential problems will also arise when the prosecution seeks to adduce 'similar fact' evidence, or applies for leave to cross-examine the accused under Criminal Evidence Act 1898, *s 1(f)(ii)*.

(b) The prosecution case

(i) The opening speech. Although the prosecutor has a right to make an opening speech, it is a right that is often waived. If the case is straight-

---

15 This view is supported by the learned editors of *Stone's Justices' Manual* (1985) Vol 1, p 342 et seq.
16 *SJF (an infant) v Chief Constable of Kent, ex p Margate Juvenile Court* (1982) Times, 17 June.
17 Some courts get round this by having one bench give a preliminary ruling on admissibility and then adjourning for trial by a separate bench. The legality of this practice is open to doubt notwithstanding a magistrates' court's power to regulate its own procedure. See Magistrates' Courts Act 1980, s 121(6).

forward, the prosecutor will outline the 'brief facts' in a few sentences or even forego his right to an opening speech altogether. On the other hand, in cases where the facts are complex or there are numerous witnesses, the opening speech is of great tactical importance. It will be the first that the court have heard about the case and first impressions often die hard. It is therefore, vital that the defence advocate makes a very careful note of the opening speech so as to be able to point to any inconsistencies between it and the evidence which subsequently emerges.[18]

(ii) The prosecution evidence. The legal rules as to the admissibility of evidence and the examination of witnesses have already been considered. It is for the prosecutor to decide in what order he will present his evidence. In general, most evidence in summary trials will be given orally on oath, the major exception being those witnesses whose evidence has been served under s 9 of the Criminal Justice Act 1967 and not objected to. The latter will simply be read out.

> EXAMPLE. *Police v* Mary ADAMS (*case 3*). The prosecution is conducted by a solicitor from the County Prosecuting Solicitors' Department. There is only one issue on the evidence 'Did Mary ADAMS fall short of the standard required of the reasonably careful driver?'
>
> The prosecutor will briefly set the scene by recounting the date, time and place of the accident and then call her first witness, PC Smith. In giving evidence PC Smith will prove the sketch plan, and, having been given leave to refresh his memory from his notebook, give an eye witness account of the scene of the accident and give details of his interview with Mary ADAMS. Having been cross-examined and re-examined (if appropriate) he will be followed by two civilian witnesses Anthony HARBOTTLE, the driver of the other vehicle, and Jennifer JONES, the one passer-by who made a statement to the police. Each witness will be put through the same process.

Note that witnesses other than experts should not be present in court until called to give evidence, and having done so will usually be released. There is, therefore, the remote possibility that a witness may communicate with other witnesses outside the court. If this possibility is ever suspected you should try, if practicable, to have a member of staff outside the court as an observer to ensure fair play. Sometimes the prosecution is conducted by a police officer who also proposes to give evidence. If his evidence is not likely to be contentious the wisest course is, perhaps, not to raise the point at all. Otherwise the difficulty can usually be avoided by the officer giving his evidence first.[1]

The defence advocate will then be entitled to cross-examine each oral witness in turn. Cross-examination of prosecution witnesses is never easy especially in those cases where there has been no advance disclosure of the prosecution evidence. Frequently there is a marked divergence between the prosecution witnesses' evidence and the accused's instructions. The objects of cross-examination have already been considered,[2] but the following practical points should always be borne in mind. As well as noting what the witness

---

18 The prosecutor is of course under an ethical duty not to open with facts he cannot prove.

1 The professional Conduct Committee of the Bar has approved formal guidelines on the presence in court of police officers in charge of a case. See Law Society's Gazette (1982) 30 July, p 845. Such problems will hopefully not arise when the Prosecution of Offenders Act comes into force.

2 See p 154 ante.

has said in-chief, it is important to try and observe the way in which he or she gives evidence. Whereas a nervous and confused witness may sometimes be met head on, the self opinionated or dogmatic witness requires a more subtle approach. It will usually be futile coming into headlong conflict with police witnesses. Although the defence is required to 'put their client's case',[3] each aspect of the client's conflicting version which the defence 'puts' to the officer will often only serve to reinforce the evidence that he has already given.[4] The task should therefore be performed with as much brevity as intructions permit.

Cross-examination will be followed, where appropriate, by re-examination. You should ensure that the prosecutor does not try to raise matters which were not dealt with in the witnesses' evidence in-chief or cross-examination. If he does, you should draw this to the court's attention and, where appropriate, ask for leave to cross-examine on any new issues.

Finally, the court is entitled to question any witness although this should not normally be done until the conclusion of re-examintion. Questions from the bench may sometimes be devastating, especially where magistrates are relying upon 'local knowledge'. Within reason, magistrates are permitted to do this,[4] but they should bring this to the notice of the parties so that they have an opportunity of making representations. It is, in any event, especially important to take note of any questions that the bench may ask, since they may give an indication of the bench's views on the case.

Having presented all his evidence, the prosecutor will then formally close his case. It is vital to have previously noted the essential elements down, so as to be able to decide whether or not to make a submission of 'no case to answer'. As a general rule, once the prosecution has closed its case it can only call further evidence with leave of the court. Leave should only be granted in exceptional circumstances, for example when some purely technical matter requires formal proof, for example, that a stretch of highway has been formally designated as a motorway.[5] Subject to this, the prosecution case will stand or fall on the evidence that they have already tendered and they should not be permitted to call further evidence in order to counter what would otherwise be a successful submission of 'no case to answer'.[6]

(c) Submission of no case to answer

If the defence consider that the prosecution have failed to make out a prima facie case, they may submit that the information be dismissed on the ground that there is 'no case to answer'. The grounds on which such a submission may be made are set out in the following Practice Note:[7]

'... As a matter of practice justices should be guided by the following considerations. A submission that there is no case to answer may properly be made and upheld:
(a) where there has been no evidence to prove an essential element in the alleged offence;

---

3 See p 125 ante.
4 Various styles of cross-examination are usefully contrasted and dealt with in *Chatelier* (op cit) p 28 et seq.
5 *Royal v Prescott-Clarke* [1966] 2 All ER 366.
6 *R v Gainsborough Justices, ex p Green* (1983) 147 JP 434, but see *Wilkinson* (op cit) p 96 et seq and cases there cited.
7 [1962] 1 All ER 448. See also Royal Commission on Criminal Procedure: Research Study 6 p 16. Out of 394 sample charges analysed, 21 were dismissed at this stage. There is a helpful breakdown of the bases on which they were dismissed.

(b) when the evidence adduced by the prosecution has been so discredited as a result of cross-examination or is so manifestly unreliable that no reasonable tribunal could safely convict on it.'

Apart from these two situations a tribunal should not, in general, be called on to reach a decision as to conviction or acquittal until the whole of the evidence which either side wishes to tender has been placed before it. If, however, a submission is made that there is no case to answer the decision should depend not so much on whether the adjudicating tribunal (if compelled to do so) would at that stage convict or acquit, but on whether the evidence is such that a reasonable tribunal might convict. If a reasonable tribunal might convict on the evidence so far laid before it, there is a case to answer.'

As is apparent from the *Practice Note*, submissions of 'no case' fall into two broad categories. *Category (a)* embraces those situations where, on the evidence as it stands the prosecution has failed to prove an essential element of the offence charged, for example, where on a charge of taking a conveyance without the owner's consent, the prosecution fails to prove lack of consent.[8] Such a submission, if made out, is bound to succeed. If on the other hand the submission comes within *category (b)* magistrates are often unwilling to dismiss without hearing the accused give evidence. Such submissions should not therefore be made as a matter of routine but only where an essential item of prosecution evidence has been shown to be so inherently unreliable that the magistrates have no choice but to dismiss; otherwise you may do better saving up your ammunition for the final speech. For example, in a case involving disputed identification, reference to *R v Turnbull*[9] may have greater impact after all the evidence has been heard.

A submission of no case to answer is a matter of law or mixed law and fact upon whatever basis it is made. Accordingly the prosecutor has a right of reply but cannot normally call further evidence to cure a defect in his case. After the prosecutor has replied, the magistrates will normally retire. If the submission is upheld, the accused must be acquitted. If it is not upheld, or does not result in the dismissal of every charge upon which the accused is being tried, the trial will continue. The defence advocate may now be faced with a difficult choice. Either he can proceed to call his evidence and let the trial take its course, or may call no further evidence and merely make a closing speech.[10] The latter course may be more appropriate where it is proposed to ask the magistrates to state a case for the High Court if they convict. In theory, the magistrates having rejected a submission of 'no case' may still decide to acquit even though the defence calls no further evidence on the basis that the test they will now be applying will be, 'should we convict' and not 'might a reasonable tribunal convict'. In practice this is, however, unlikely.

Finally, whatever the basis of the defence submission you should always be sure that, if successful, it will stand up to the scrutiny of the Divisional Court. You will do your client no service by bamboozling a gullible bench and an inexperienced prosecutor into allowing a misconceived submission. The net result may well be an expensive and ultimately successful prosecution appeal by way of case stated.

8 Or some other element is lacking, see eg *Neal v Gribble* (1978) 68 Cr App Rep 9 (horse held not to be a conveyance).

9 [1977] 2 QB 224. See generally p 165, et seq, ante.

10 No appeal by way of case stated will lie unless the proceedings have terminated: similarly the Divisional Court will not interfere by way of judicial review to control the way in which a trial is being conducted: see eg *R v Wells Street Stipendiary Magistrate, ex p Seillon* [1978] 3 All ER 257 and *R v Rochford Justices, ex p Buck* (1978) 68 Cr App Rep 114, CA.

(d) The case for the defence

Subject to what has been said in *paragraph (c)* the defence will now present the accused's case. The defence may make an opening speech but should normally not do so unless the issues which they wish to raise are complex, or where, for example, the accused's case is so at odds with that presented by the prosecution, that the bench should be prepared for the shock.[11] If the defence do make an opening speech, they may not address the bench again at the end of their case *without leave*. If they are granted such leave, the prosecution will then have the right to make a closing speech immediately before the closing defence speech. Although the defence will still have the last word, it may be tactically unwise to give the prosecution the opportunity to address the court a second time.

The defence evidence, such as it is, will now be called, with the accused being called first, if he chooses to give evidence. Where there is more than one accused their evidence will be presented in the order that their names appear on the charge sheet or information.

EXAMPLE. *Police v* Mary ADAMS (*case 3*). The defence evidence will consist solely of the oral testimony of the client herself, because it has not been possible to trace other eye witnesses who could testify as to her lack of blameworthiness.

The accused and all other defence witnesses will in turn be examined in-chief, cross-examined, and re-examined if necessary, in exactly the same way as the prosecution witnesses. It is particularly important to remember that the accused may not be cross-examined as to his character and convictions unless he has 'thrown away his shield'.[12] One of the main duties of the defence advocate is therefore to protect him if he gives evidence.

Finally, it must be stressed that, irrespective of whether or not the prosecution case has been disclosed, the defence has no obligation to reveal any part of its case to the prosecution. If a defence of alibi is to be raised, there is no provision analogous to that in trials on indictment,[13] requiring the defence to provide particulars of the alibi in advance. Nevertheless, it is still advisable to do so because if this is not done, not only will the prosecution be granted an adjournment, but in addition, the magistrates may think that the conduct of the defence smacks of sharp practice. In the long run this may damage the client's case.

(e) Prosecution evidence in rebuttal

There are three situations in which the prosecutor will be allowed to call further evidence to rebut evidence adduced by the defence, although such leave is rarely sought in summary trials.

Firstly, it will be recalled that where the accused has sought to establish his own good character, the prosecution may not only apply for leave to cross-examine him under *s 1(f)(ii)* of the Criminal Evidence Act 1898 but may also at common law call rebutting evidence to show otherwise.

Secondly, it will also be further recalled that although answers given by witnesses under cross-examination relating to credit are normally final, there are certain circumstances in which rebutting evidence may be called, for example, to show bias or to prove previous convictions.

Thirdly, the prosecution may call rebutting evidence where matters have

11 If this opportunity is not given and the accused is convicted an application for judicial review will lie *R v Marylebone Justices, ex p Farrag* [1981] Crim LR 182.

12 Criminal Evidence Act 1898 s 1(f)(ii). See generally p 157, ante.

13 See Criminal Justice Act 1967, s 11 considered at p 328, post.

arisen during the defence case which the prosecutor could not possibly have foreseen. For example, when an accused gave evidence to the effect that he was in a public lavatory at the time of the offence, the prosecution was permitted to call rebutting evidence to prove that it was closed at the relevant time.[14] The defence are, of course, entitled to cross-examine in the usual way.

(f)   Closing speech for the defence

When all the defence evidence has been called, the defence will address the magistrates. Your task is to summarise the evidence that has been presented by the prosecution and the defence, dealing particularly with the strengths of the defence and any weaknesses in the prosecution evidence. If you consider it appropriate you should conclude with a tactful reminder to the magistrates that, save in certain circumstances, the burden of proving every issue beyond reasonable doubt lies with the prosecution. Bear in mind that, however, that if you include submissions on matters of law, the prosecution will be entitled to reply to them.

One of the major difficulties in many summary trials is that you will have little or no time beforehand to prepare your closing speech. It is entirely proper for you to ask the court for a few moments to marshall your material, but you must be sure that your notes of the evidence are organised in such a way that you can quickly pick up the important points. Certain categories of prosecution evidence will require a corroboration warning or need to be approached with caution.[15] In the magistrates' court, the clerk should advise the magistrates on such matters, but you should try to be aware in advance of those areas where a warning is needed so that you can draw them to the court's attention, as part of your closing speech, bearing in mind, however, that in doing so you may be giving the prosecution a right of reply.

Although a good closing speech can be of crucial importance, it should be kept as short and to the point as possible, so as to hold the court's interest. Speeches that ramble on or sound patronising are likely to have an adverse effect, particularly when addressed to a stipendiary.

> EXAMPLE. *Police v Mary* ADAMS (*case 3*). In this case, as with most motoring offences, the court has heard both parties' versions and will be unmoved by lengthy references to 'golden threads throughout the web of English Criminal Law'. It is more likely to be influenced by arguments directed to the layout of the road or prevailing conditions.

Stage 6. The verdict

Where the trial has taken place before a stipendiary magistrate he will normally announce his verdict without retiring, and will not normally give reasons unless a point of law is involved. Where the trial has been before a lay bench the verdict will be by simple majority, the chairman having no casting vote (it is for this reason that three justices usually sit for trials). If, however, an even numbered bench is equally divided they should either order a re-trial or acquit the defendant.[16]

Lay magistrates will usually retire to consider their verdict. They may request their clerk to retire with them but only in so far as necessary to advise them

---

14   *R v Blick* (1966) 50 Cr App Rep 280, CA.
15   See p 164 et seq ante.
16   *R v Bridgend Justices, ex p Randall* [1975] Crim LR 287.

on matters of law. He should only normally remain with them whilst he is still legitimately assisting them on matters within his function, otherwise he should return to the court. The exact scope of the clerk's functions are set out in a Practice Direction[17] of Lord Lane CJ. This provides (inter alia), that the clerk may:

   (i) advise the magistrate on questions of law, mixed law and fact, or practice and procedure;

   (ii) refresh their memory[18] as to any matters of evidence and draw attention to any issues involved in the matters before the court;

   (iii) assist the magistrates from his notes if they are in any doubt as to the evidence which has been given. The magistrates should ordinarily do this in open court to avoid any suspicion that the clerk has been involved in deciding issues of fact.

Although clerks now tend to hold less sway over their magistrates than sometimes used to be the case,[19] there may be occasions when it is necessary to draw these restrictions to the court's attention. This course should, however, be reserved for more flagrant cases, and be adapted with tact. Lay magistrates are not obliged to give reasons for their decision and very rarely do so, although a request for reasons may be appropriate when matters of law have been raised and you are considering asking the magistrates to state a case for the High Court. Finally it should be noted that magistrates, unlike juries, do not have power to find the accused not guilty of the offence charged but guilty of a lesser offence;[20] he must either be acquitted, or convicted.

When the accused is found not guilty he must be discharged although it may still be necessary to address the bench on the question of costs. The court has no power to award costs out of central funds unless the accused has been acquitted of an either way offence which has been tried summarily.[1] It can also award costs against the prosecution,[2] but should only do so if they have acted unreasonably or spitefully.[3] It follows therefore that the accused will often have to be advised that even if he is acquitted, he will still have to pay the costs of defending the charge: this is often a particularly bitter pill for the client charged with a road traffic offence. Thus even if Mary ADAMS (*case 3*) were acquitted her solicitor would need to advise her that she would still have to pay his fees for attending court to defend her unless malice on the part of the prosecution can be shown.

If the court finds the case proved and does not adjourn for reports it will proceed straight to sentence. The subsequent procedure is similar to that where the accused pleaded guilty at the outset, except that it will not be necessary to recount the facts of the case. Difficulties may arise in the defence speech in mitigation if it is clear that the magistrates have formed the impression that the accused was lying. It will be necessary therefore to tailor the mitigation accordingly. Even where the accused pleads 'not guilty', you should have prepared a speech in mitigation beforehand and, in the case of a motoring offence, considered the possibility of disqualification as well as reminding the client to bring his driving licence to court. You must also be prepared to advise on appeal and, if necessary, apply for bail where the

17 [1981] 2 All ER 831.

18 Magistrates must remain, and apparently appear to remain, awake throughout the trial, *R v Weston-super-Mare Justices, ex p Taylor* [1981] Crim LR 179.

19 But see eg *R v Guildford Justices, ex p Harding* (1981) 145 JP 174.

20 *Lawrence v Same*, supra. As already noted this difficulty can be got round by the prosecutor laying separate informations in the alternative.

1 Costs in Criminal Cases Act 1973, s 1(2).

2 Ibid, s 2(2).

3 See *Practice Note* [1982] 3 All ER 1152, CA.

client has received an immediate custodial sentence. Because of the strict time limits it is always advisable to give notice of appeal or apply for a case to be stated as soon as possible. Indeed, it is essential to do so when bail is to be applied for as the power to grant bail does not arise until the appeal or request to state a case has actually been lodged.[4] Appeals are considered further in Chapter 14.

4 Magistrates' Courts Act 1980, s 113(1).

CHAPTER 10

Juveniles

INTRODUCTION

A juvenile, for the purposes of *criminal* proceedings, is any person between the ages of *10* and *16* inclusive. No crime can be committed by a person under the age of *10 years*.[1] Juveniles are subdivided into 'children' (aged *10 to 13 years* inclusive) and 'young persons' (aged *14 to 16* years inclusive). This subdivision is important because a 'child' can only be convicted of a criminal offence if the prosecution can prove not only that he committed the offence with the requisite mens rea, but also that he did so with 'mischievous discretion', namely guilty knowledge that he was doing wrong.[2] However, a 'young person' is treated for the purposes of criminal responsibility in precisely the same way as an adult. The subdivisions also have importance in relation to the place the juvenile is tried, and the types of order that can be imposed on him if the case is proved against him.

Quite apart from this, however, a solicitor must always remember that a different approach is required when acting for juveniles rather than adults. A juvenile will usually be processed differently by the police and treated differently by the court as well. Difficulties will soon be encountered if this is not appreciated. This chapter will concentrate on those areas where the rules are different from those applying to adults.

1 PLACE OF TRIAL—THE JUVENILE COURT

As already stated in chapter 1, most juveniles will be tried in a juvenile court which must consist of magistrates drawn from the 'juvenile panel'.[3] These are elected from among their number by the magistrates for each petty sessional division and serve for three years.[4] The only exception is in Inner London, where the members of the Juvenile Panel are appointed from the magistracy by the Lord Chancellor.[5] A juvenile court must normally consist of not more than three justices, and must include a member of each sex, although in certain limited circumstances it may proceed even if this is not so;[6] thus trial by a 'single sex' bench or even by a stipendiary sitting alone, is possible but unlikely. Although the rules provide a basic framework for the setting up of juvenile panels, the way in which juvenile courts and their procedure have evolved will vary considerably from area to area.

---

1 Children and Young Persons' Act 1933, s 50, but note that there is no such restriction in the bringing of 'Care Proceedings' under Children and Young Persons Act 1969, s 1.
2 For a fuller discussion see Smith and Hogan, *Criminal Law* (5th edn) pp 161 et seq.
3 The rules as to the setting up of juvenile panels are contained in Children and Young Persons Act 1933, Sch 2.
4 The rules as to appointment and retirement of the juvenile panel are contained in the Juvenile Courts (Constitution) Rules 1954.
5 Stipendiary magistrates are ex officio members of the juvenile panel for their Petty Sessional Area: 1954 Rules (supra), r 2.
6 See ibid, r 12.

The buildings themselves vary considerably too. Some juvenile courts may use the adult magistrates' court,[7] but there is often a special juvenile court room. In the latter case the ordinary court furniture may be replaced by tables and chairs, although there will usually be a raised dais for the magistrates.[8] Remember the old adage 'get to know your court'; you will be much more comfortable when presenting your case if you are already familiar with the layout of the court in which you are appearing.

Although trial in the juvenile court is the norm, there are occasions when a juvenile will be tried or sentenced either by the Crown Court or the adult magistrates' court; these will be considered in detail in the next section.

2 THE FOUR CATEGORIES OF OFFENCE

The combined effect of legislation dating from 1933 to 1980 has resulted in there being *four* categories of offence relating to juveniles, as opposed to the *three* categories relating to adults. The effect of the provisions is that juveniles *must* be tried summarily before a juvenile court, unless they come within the first three categories set out below.[9] Furthermore, although the categories sometimes require a juvenile to be tried on indictment, a juvenile can *never* elect trial by jury. In addition, unless he is charged jointly with an adult his first appearance will be before a juvenile court, even if he is ultimately tried elsewhere. Provided these points are remembered, the following provisions, which are complicated in places, should not be too difficult to master. The categories are taken in order of seriousness of offence. Categories 3 and 4 are by far the most common.

Category 1. Juveniles charged with homicide

A juvenile charged with homicide *must* be tried on indictment.[10] Homicide is not statutorily defined in this context, but clearly embraces murder and manslaughter and may include causing death by reckless driving. Accordingly, although his first appearance will be before a juvenile court, the magistrates have no jurisdiction to try him and must hold committal proceedings, which will be subject to the same rules as those in the adult court.

Category 2. Juveniles liable to detention under Children and Young Persons Act 1933, s 53(2)

A juvenile may be committed for trial at the Crown Court if all three of the following qualifications are satisfied. First, the juvenile must be a 'young person'. Second, the offence with which he is charged must be punishable by imprisonment in the case of a person who has attained the age of 21 years for a term of *14 years* or more. Third, the magistrates must be of the opinion that if he were found guilty it would be necessary to impose a term of detention under Children and Young Persons Act 1933, s 53(2). This provision enables juveniles to be detained on the direction of the Home Secretary for a period not exceeding the maximum term of imprisonment available in

---

7 A juvenile court should not sit within 1 hour of an adult court in such circumstances; Children and Young Persons Act 1933, s 47(2) as amended.

8 'Social Workers and Solicitors in Child Care cases' See further, Linden Hilgendorff, HMSO 1981, p 89 et seq.

9 This is principally the combined effect of Children and Young Persons Act 1933, s 46 and Magistrates' Courts Act 1980, s 24(1).

10 Magistrates' Courts Act 1980, s 24(1).

respect of an adult. It follows therefore that there may be many occasions upon which a juvenile is charged with an offence which would have to be tried on indictment if he were an adult but which will still be tried summarily by a juvenile court because all three of the above criteria do not apply. Thus, if two school children of 15 held up another child on the way home from school and stole 50p, then strictly speaking a charge of robbery would lie. However, in the event of their being prosecuted it is most unlikely that the magistrates would consider it an appropriate case for committal to the Crown Court unless there were special aggravating features, because the long-term detention envisaged by this provision would not be necessary. In deciding whether or not the accused comes within this provision, the magistrates are not required to consider the evidence at this stage, but merely to look at the charge and hear representations from the prosecution and the defence.[11] If the court considers trial on indictment is appropriate, committal proceedings will then be held in the same way as in the case of an adult.[12]

Category 3. Juveniles charged with adults

The statutory provisions[13] dealing with juveniles and adults charged together appear horrendous but, as is so often the case, they give few difficulties in practice. They can be best understood by considering the following three points:

    (a) where will the juvenile first appear?
    (b) where will he be tried?
    (c) where will he be sentenced?

(a) Where will the juvenile first appear?

If he is charged jointly with an adult he must in the first instance be brought before an adult court, even if he is a 'child'.

> EXAMPLE: *Police v* John TYRELL. If, instead of taking the Morris 1100 on his own, John had taken it with another youth of 19, and they had been jointly charged with taking the vehicle without consent, both the 19 year old and John would have to be brought before the adult court in the first instance.

If, however, the juvenile and the adult are not jointly charged, but the adult is charged as a principal and the juvenile as an aider and abettor[14] or vice versa,[15] or the juvenile and the adult are charged with separate offences which arise out of the same or connected incidents, the juvenile may be brought before either court.

(b) Where will the juvenile be tried?

Even though he is brought before the adult court in the first instance, there is no guarantee that a juvenile will be tried and sentenced there.[16] The

---

11 *R v South Hackney Juvenile Court, ex p RB (a minor) and CB (a minor)* (1983) 77 Cr App Rep 294.
12 In deciding whether or not to hold committal proceedings the juvenile court is entitled to hear representations as to the accused's good character (*R v South Hackney Juvenile Court* supra). If it proceeds to hold committal proceedings the juvenile court may still revert to summary trial if, having considered the evidence, this appears appropriate: Magistrates' Courts' Act 1980 s 25(7).
13 Magistrates' Courts Act 1980, ss 24 and 29.
14 Children and Young Persons Act 1963, s 18.
15 Children and Young Persons Act 1933, s 46(1).
16 In whichever court the juvenile is tried the provisions of Children and Young Persons Act

statutory rules relating to juveniles jointly charged with adults[17] are contained mainly in ss 24 and 29 of the Magistrates' Courts Act 1980. In essence, the place where the juvenile is tried principally depends on whether the adult is to be committed to stand trial on indictment or is to be tried summarily.

(i) Adult committed for trial. If the offence charged is *indictable only* in the case of the adult, the adult must be committed for trial. If it is triable *either way* the adult's trial venue will be determined at the mode of trial proceedings. In either case, if the adult is to be committed for trial the magistrates *may* also commit the juvenile if they consider it 'necessary in the interests of justice'.[18] If they adopt this course they may at the same time commit the juvenile for any other indictable offence with which he is charged which arises out of the same or connected incidents.[19]

> EXAMPLE A (19) and J (16) commit a burglary together, using a stolen car driven by J. Whilst seeking to escape J commits the offence of reckless driving. They are jointly charged with (1) Burglary, and (2) Taking a vehicle without consent. J alone is charged with reckless driving. They are both brought before the adult court who decide that both charges against A are more suitable for trial on indictment. They also decide that in the 'interests of justice' J should be committed on the joint charges and therefore have power to also commit him on the reckless driving charge.

Whether it will be in the 'interests of justice' to commit a juvenile to the Crown Court will depend on a number of factors. On the one hand, juvenile courts are specifically designed to avoid the trauma of the adult court or the Crown Court and accordingly committing a juvenile to the Crown Court negatives this. On the other hand, if both the juvenile and the adult were to plead not guilty, it would normally be in the interests of justice that they be tried together, so that evidence would only be presented once, and their innocence or guilt determined by the same tribunal.

If the magistrates decide that it is not in the interests of justice to commit the juvenile to the Crown Court he *must* be tried summarily. If he pleads 'not guilty' the magistrates' court may (and normally will) remit him to the juvenile court for trial.[20] If he pleads 'guilty' the adult court will proceed to hear the brief facts in the usual way, but because their powers of sentence are very limited the juvenile will probably be remitted to the juvenile court for sentence.

To sum up, therefore, it is more likely than not that when a juvenile and adult are jointly charged, and the adult is committed for trial, the juvenile will be committed with him. A solicitor acting for a juvenile in these circumstances does not have much opportunity of influencing matters. Nevertheless the following practical points should be noted:

- if the juvenile is pleading 'not guilty' he is probably better off being tried on indictment;
- if he is pleading 'guilty' his solicitor should not be afraid to represent that it is in the 'interest of justice' for him to be dealt with summarily,

---

1933, s 34 (attendance of parents at court) and s 39 (power to prohibit publication in newspapers) will apply.
17 There are apparently no rules dealing with adults and juveniles charged as principal and aider and abettor etc, presumably therefore the juvenile can only be tried in the adult court.
18 Magistrates' Courts Act 1980, s 24(1)(b).
19 Ibid, s 24(2).
20 Ibid, s 29(2)(b).

especially if he is very young, or the offence is not particularly serious;
– the solicitor can still play as active a part in the committal proceedings as he could on behalf of an adult, since the prosecution must still make out a prima facie case.

(ii) Adult tried summarily. If the offence is triable only summarily, or the adult consents to summary trial of an either way offence, the juvenile *must* be tried with him in the adult court *unless* the adult (or each adult if more than one is charged) pleads 'guilty' *and* the juvenile pleads 'not guilty'. In the latter case, the adult court has a discretion to remit the juvenile to the juvenile court to be tried.[1]

EXAMPLES 1: J(15) is jointly charged with three adults with threatening behaviour. Two of the adults plead 'guilty' and one pleads 'not guilty'. Whatever J's intended plea, the adult court has no power to remit him for trial. If, however, he is convicted or pleads 'guilty' the adult court may still have to remit to the juvenile court for sentence because of their limited sentencing powers over juveniles.

2: A (19) and J (16) are jointly charged with theft from a supermarket. At the 'mode of trial' proceedings in respect of A the magistrates decide on summary trial and A consents. The charge is then put to both defendants. A pleads 'guilty', J pleads 'not guilty'. In these circumstances the bench might well consider it appropriate to remit J to the juvenile court. Having done so, they will proceed to hear the brief facts and sentence A.

(c) Sentencing jurisdiction over juveniles

Even if a juvenile is tried before the Crown Court or an adult magistrates' court, it by no means follows that if he is convicted he will be sentenced there. He may well be remitted to a juvenile court for sentencing, either on bail or in custody.

(i) The Crown Court which has committed a juvenile must remit him to a juvenile court to be sentenced unless the court is satisfied that it would be 'undesirable to do so'.[2] It would clearly be undesirable to remit if the offence merited punishment which a juvenile court had no power to impose, eg detention under s 53(2) of the Children and Young Persons Act 1933. However, the Court of Appeal has recently pointed out that as the sentencing powers of the Crown Court and juvenile court are now broadly speaking the same, remittal should seldom be necessary.[3]

(ii) An adult magistrates' court has very limited sentencing powers over juveniles. It must remit the juvenile to the juvenile court for sentence unless it is of the opinion that he can be dealt with by way of fine, discharge (absolute or conditional) or a recognisance from his parents,[4] although it does have its ancillary powers, for example to order compensation. Remittals to the juvenile court for sentence tend therefore to be the norm. When appearing on behalf of a convicted juvenile in the magistrates' court, you are therefore unlikely to be called upon to mitigate unless the bench is of the view (or you convince them) that the juvenile can be dealt with there and then.

1 Magistrates' Courts Act 1980, s 29(2). There is no right of appeal against such a decision: ibid s 29(4).
2 Children and Young Persons Act 1933, s 56(1).
3 *R v Lewis* (1984) 148 JP 329, CA.
4 Children and Young Persons Act 1933, s 56(1) and Children and Young Persons Act 1969, s 7(8).

Category 4. All other situations

The vast majority of juveniles are charged, either by themselves or with
other juveniles, with offences that do not come within categories 1 and 2.
Therefore whether the juvenile client is charged with an offence which for
an adult is triable summarily, either way or on indictment only, he will be
tried by a juvenile court. He will also be sentenced there unless he is aged 15
or 16, in which case the court may commit him to the Crown Court because
it considers that a term of youth custody of more than six months is appropriate.[5] In many cases, of course, the denial of a right to jury trial may be
seen as a positive disadvantage. It is for this reason that a solicitor must
always be vigilant as to whether his client has attained 17 before the court
commences to try him for an 'either way' offence, since if this is so, he must
be remitted to an adult court who must hold 'mode of trial' proceedings.[6]

3 THE INVESTIGATION AND COMMENCEMENT OF PROCEEDINGS

The prosecution of juveniles is broadly subject to the same rules as in the
case of adults, although with additional safeguards. Furthermore, the local
authority will frequently be involved, and although in a book on criminal
litigation one cannot spend too much time 'going backstage' an outline of
the administrative machinery of juvenile prosecutions is necessary. In addition, it is even more important than in the case of an adult to examine the
circumstances of arrest and detention, to ensure that the statutory requirements are complied with.

(1) Stop and search

Juveniles are liable to stop and search in precisely the same way as adults,
without any additional safeguards.

(2) Arrest

Juveniles can be arrested in precisely the same way as adults, but in addition
to the right to have someone informed of their arrest,[7] s 34 (2) of the Children
and Young Persons Act 1933[8] provides that:

> 'where a child or young person is detained at a police station or other premises
> after being arrested, his parent or guardian shall be informed of his detention as
> soon as practicable'.

When the juvenile is under a supervision order, the relevant social worker
must also be informed[9] but when he is in care the only requirement is to
inform the local authority.[10]

5 This power is only available if the offence is imprisonable in the case of someone of 21 or
   over: Magistrates' Courts Act 1980, s 37, see p 430 post.
6 The date for determining whether the accused is over 17 so as to be able to elect trial on
   indictment is that on which the court would, subject to his age, be able to proceed with
   'mode of trial' proceedings: *Re Daley* [1982] 2 All ER 974. Where, however, the offence is
   indictable only it is the date when the charge is put and the court is ready to proceed.
   R v Vale of Glamorgan Juvenile Justices, ex p Beattie (1985) 149 JP 120. See further chapter 8.
7 Police and Criminal Evidence Act 1984, s 56.
8 As amended by Police and Criminal Evidence Act 1984, s 57.
9 Children and Young Persons Act 1933, s 34(7).
10 Ibid, s 34(8).

(3) At the police station

A juvenile is subject to the provisions of the Police and Criminal Evidence Act 1984 and the relevant Codes of Practice in the same way as an adult, but there are additional procedures of which the defence solicitor should be aware.

(a) Search

The powers contained in the 1984 Act to search a person on arrest[11] and after arrival at a police station[12] apply without limitation. Intimate searches must, however, generally be done in the presence of a parent or some other adult of the same sex who is not a police officer.[13]

(b) Further detention

The relevant provisions are complicated but a distinction is drawn between 'children who have been arrested without warrant other than for homicide'[14] and 'arrested juveniles', which broadly means all young persons, and children if arrested for homicide, in either case arrested without warrant.[15] Arrested juveniles are subject to all the detention provisions in Part IV of the 1984 Act. The main differences between arrested juveniles and arrested children are as follows:

(i) Conditions of detention after charge. An arrested juvenile must be released either with or without bail unless the detention conditions in the Police and Criminal Evidence Act 1984 apply.[16] An arrested child is not subject to Part IV at all. Accordingly he is subject to the provisions in s 28 of the Children and Young Persons Act 1969 which provide that his case must be referred to the custody officer as soon as practicable. Having enquired into the case, the officer must release the child unless, because of the nature of the alleged offence, he considers that he ought to be detained in a place of safety.

(ii) Place of detention after charge. When an arrested juvenile is not released the custody officer must make arrangements for him to be taken into the care of a local authority unless either this is impracticable (or he is of 'so unruly a character' as to make it inappropriate to do so).[17] As indicated above an arrested child must either be released or taken to a place of safety.[18]

> EXAMPLE. *Police v* John TYRELL (case 4). It will be recalled that John TYRELL was in fact released without charge and subsequently summonsed—a common course, save in the most serious of cases. Supposing, however, he had not admitted the offence, the police would have had authority to detain him without charge, subject to precisely the same constraints as in the case of an adult. They would not, therefore, be entitled to hold him for more than 24 hours after his arrest since it is hard to imagine that taking a vehicle without consent can be said to constitute a 'serious arrestable offence'. If, however, he had been involved in a fatal accident,

---

11 Police and Criminal Evidence Act 1984, s 32.
12 Ibid, s 54.
13 Code of Practice, Annex A para 4.
14 Police and Criminal Evidence Act 1984, s 52 adopts the definition of 'child' contained in Children and Young Persons Act 1969—effectively those aged 11–13 inclusive.
15 1984 Act, s 37(15).
16 Ibid, s 38(1)(b).
17 Ibid, s 38(6); Detention Code paras 17.6, 17.9 and 17A.
18 As defined by Children and Young Persons Act 1933, s 107 as amended.

a superintendent could have authorised his further detention for questioning and an application could have been made for a warrant of further detention. If he were subsequently charged the custody officer would have been required to decide whether to release him or to bring him before a magistrates' court as soon as practicable, since it would appear to be impractical to place him in care, and he does not appear to be 'unruly'.

Once again, it cannot be emphasised strongly enough how important it is to be fully conversant with these provisions and that if you are called to a police station on behalf of a juvenile you must ensure that they are scrupulously observed. Note finally that whenever a child or young person is detained at a police station para 8.8 of the Code of Practice on Detention and Treatment provides that he:

> 'shall not be placed in a police cell unless no other secure accommodation is available and the custody officer considers it is not practicable to supervise him if he is not placed in a cell. He may not be placed in a cell with a detained adult'

(c) Interrogation

Once again the juvenile is entitled to all the safeguards contained in the Detention Code. There are, however, several important additional constraints which you must ensure are fully observed. Note in particular para 13 which when taken with s 34(2) of the Children and Young Persons Act 1933, as amended, obliges the police:

  (i) to notify the juvenile's parents, guardian or local authority (if in care) of his detention and whereabouts without delay;
 (ii) to inform the social services department when the persons in (i) cannot be contacted;
(iii) not to interview the juvenile in the absence of his parents or guardian, or if these are unavailable, some other responsible adult who is not a police officer (except in certain serious cases—see below);
(iv) to inform the relevant adult of the juvenile's right to legal advice before being interviewed.

These obligations must be fulfilled in every case before a juvenile is interviewed unless an officer of the rank of superintendant or above certifies and records in the custody record that there is an immediate risk of harm to person or persons or serious loss of or damage to property.[19]

(d) Identification parades, fingerprints and other matters

Once again, a juvenile is given the same safeguards in the Code of Practice as to Identification as an adult but it is important to note the following particular points:

(i) Presence of parent or guardian at parade. A juvenile cannot appear on an identification parade unless a parent, guardian, solicitor or other responsible person who is not a police officer is present.[20]

(ii) Parental consent to certain procedures. The Detention Code requires parental consent to those processes which require consent in the case of an adult suspect. The processes relevant are holding identification parades, fingerprinting, taking body impressions and body samples, and photograph-

19 'Annex C' to the Detention Code.
20 Similar provisions apply to the taking of fingerprints. Identification Code para 1.12.

ing.[21] Note that the provisions relating to 'children' differ significantly from those relating to 'young persons'. If the juvenile is a 'child' his parent or guardian may authorise any of the procedures but if he is a 'young person' his consent is required as well as that of the parent or guardian.

(4) Police policy in prosecuting juveniles

(a) Initial stages

In many cases the juvenile will not be arrested and taken to the police station at all, and of those that are, many are released to their parents without being charged (as in John TYRELL's case) pending the decision as to whether to prosecute. The remainder are usually charged and either released on police bail, or kept in custody pending court appearance.[22]

(b) The decision to prosecute

Many juveniles are not prosecuted at all. They are 'cautioned' instead. A caution is a formal warning in the presence of the juvenile's parents or guardian and can only be administered when the juvenile admits the offence under investigation. A caution does not count as a conviction but nevertheless forms part of the juvenile's 'record' if he re-offends. The decision as to whether to prosecute or caution is often only taken after consultation with other agencies eg social services or the education department. In many areas police forces have set up 'juvenile bureaux' in which the decision as to disposal is considered in conjunction with other agencies. There is wide regional variation as to the consultative machinery and the influence that such agencies have.[23] A solicitor will not often be involved in the cautioning process, but if he is, it is advisable for him to be sure that the police do in fact have sufficient evidence to secure a conviction before advising the juvenile and his parents to agree to a caution. Cautioning should not be taken lightly since even though it does not result in any punishment, it may represent the first rung of the ladder in the process of a juvenile's criminalisation. If the police decide to prosecute they must notify the local authority social services department. A solicitor is far more likely to be instructed after this step.

4 THE PRE-TRIAL STAGE. ADJOURNMENTS, BAIL AND LEGAL AID

Not only may there be a considerable time lag between the juvenile's first appearance and the final disposal of his case, but in addition the waiting period may be extended because of the need to refer the case to a juvenile bureau before he is prosecuted. A juvenile court's powers with regard to pre-trial matters such as adjournment and remand are normally governed by the same provisions as those relating to adults, but certain special features require brief mention.

21 See 1984 Act, Part V and Identification Code, para 1.10. The local authority must give consent if the juvenile is in care: para 1A.
22 See further: Royal Commission on Criminal Procedure. Research study 9, Cmnd 8092, table 3.
23 See Tutt and Giller, Police Cautioning and Juveniles: The Practice of Diversity; [1983] Crim LR 587; eg in 1981 the percentage of juveniles cautioned by reference to police areas varied from 64% (Lincolnshire) to 32% (South Wales).

(1) Adjournments and remands

It is unlikely that the prosecution or defence will often be in a position to proceed on the juvenile's first appearance, and accordingly an adjournment may be necessary.[24] Whether he appears before the juvenile court or the adult court, the court may always adjourn[1] and at the same time remand the juvenile. It is, however, only obliged to remand when it is adjourning committal proceedings; otherwise it is entirely within the court's discretion.[2]

> EXAMPLE. *Police v* John TYRELL (case 4). John is summoned to appear before the juvenile court on 20 January 1983. Since he intends to plead 'guilty' his plea will probably be taken there and then and the court will proceed to sentence if reports are available. If for any reason it is not possible to do so, his case may merely be adjourned without remanding him. If he had been jointly charged with an adult he would have appeared before the adult court. If an adjournment was necessary the court would almost certainly have been obliged to remand the adult and therefore might well have remanded John on bail as well.

The law relating to bail and remands is in essence the same as in the case of adults. There are, however, a number of important differences. If a juvenile is remanded in custody the remand must be to the care of a local authority, unless he is 14 or over, and the court certifies that it is not safe to do this because of his unruly character.[3] In the latter case, the juvenile must be committed to a remand centre although boys of 15 or over may be committed to prison if a remand centre is not available.[4] The power to order a 'certificate of unruliness' is severely prescribed by the Certificate of Unruly Character (Conditions) Order 1977[5] under which a certificate may only be issued on one of the following bases:

the juvenile is charged with an offence carrying *14 years'* imprisonment *or* an offence of violence, *or* he has a previous conviction for violence, *and either* a suitable place in a community home cannot be found *or* reports to his suitability are not available: or

he has persistently absconded from or disrupted a community home in the past.

Accordingly when applying for bail you will need to show that bail should be granted because none of the objections in Sch I, part 1 to the Bail Act 1976 have been made out. In addition, you must be able to oppose where appropriate the granting of a Certificate of Unruliness. This may not be easy if the local authority social services department raise strong objections to the accused being placed in a community home, which they may do if, for example, he is already in residential care and has been a disruptive influence.[6]

---

24 The advance disclosure rules apply to juveniles as well, prior to the taking of a plea (Magistrates' Courts (Advance Disclosure) Rules 1985, rr 4 and 5). There is a lacuna here. The rules only apply to either way offences, but, generally speaking, juveniles will always be tried summarily, even fo. indictable only offences, where there will be no advance disclosure by way of committal proceedings. See p 185, ante.

 1 Either under Magistrates' Courts Act 1980, s 10(1) (summary trial), s 5(1) (committal proceedings) or s 10(3) (adjournment after conviction for reports).

 2 Unlike adults charged with 'either way' offences, where the rule 'once a remand, always a remand' applies.

 3 Children and Young Persons Act 1969, s 23.

 4 Ibid, s 23(2) and (3).

 5 SI 1977/637.

 6 A juvenile remanded to the care of a local authority may not be placed in secure accommodation for more than 72 hours unless he is disruptive *and* this is authorised by a *Juvenile Court*; *R v Slough Juvenile Court, ex p Royal Berkshire County Council* [1984] 2 WLR 45. If he is before the latter court anyway this could be dealt with at the same time as the remand. Otherwise, the local authority must make a separate application to a juvenile court: Child Care Act 1980, s 21A.

The rules as to the period for which a juvenile may be remanded in custody are broadly the same as for adults.[7] He cannot therefore be remanded in custody for more than eight clear days at a time but, unlike an adult, he cannot be remanded in his absence,[8] or to an alternative court.[9]

(2) Legal advice and legal aid

Many juveniles are likely to be eligible for Legal Advice and Assistance under the Green Form Scheme or for legal aid in the same way as adults: similarly, they may take advantage of the duty solicitor scheme. Although the detailed principles relating to these topics is considered in chapter 6, it is as well to highlight some of the more important provisions relating to juveniles here.

(a) Legal advice and assistance

It is only when a juvenile is under 16 that he is treated any differently from an adult. In such cases, the application for advice and assistance should normally be made to the solicitor by the juvenile's parent or guardian or any other person in whose care he is, unless prior authority is obtained from the Area Office.[10] This might be necessary when, for example, the juvenile's parents are not prepared to come and see the solicitor. When assessing financial eligibility a juvenile aged 16 years will be assessed on his own resources in the same way as an adult, whereas if he is under 16 years the solicitor has a discretion to take into account the resources of his parents if 'having regard to all the circumstances, including the age and resources of the child and to any conflict of interest it appears just and equitable to do so'.[11]

> EXAMPLE. You receive a visit from a social worker accompanied by a juvenile who is already in care and has been charged with further offences. You would be able to accept instructions from the social worker (on the basis of de facto care) and disregard the resources of his parents if you consider it appropriate.

(b) Legal aid

Irrespective of which court they appear before, most juveniles will need representation and accordingly it will be necessary to apply for a legal aid order.[12] Eligibility is subject to the same criteria as in the case of an adult[13] and the procedure for applying is similar. There are, however, special rules relating to the determination of financial eligibility which although extremely complicated may be summarised as follows:

(i) any juvenile can apply for legal aid on his own behalf, or a parent or guardian can apply for him.

(ii) when a juvenile applies for legal aid and he is under the age of 16 his

---

7 See Magistrates' Courts Act 1980, ss 128–131.
8 Ibid, s 128(3A).
9 Ibid, s 130.
10 Legal Advice and Assistance Regs (No 2) 1980, reg 8.
11 Ibid, Sch 2, para 4.
12 Note there is no specific statutory provision enabling juveniles to receive legal aid for criminal proceedings unless 'magistrates' courts' is deemed to include 'juvenile court': Legal Aid Act 1974 s 28(2).
13 Namely 'desirable in the interests of justice': Legal Aid Act 1974, s 29(1); 'necessary on account of his disposable income and capital', ibid, s 29(2).

father or mother (known as an 'appropriate contributor') may also be required to provide a statement of means and may be required to make a contribution towards the cost of the juvenile's legal aid. Note that unlike the case of an adult, the submission of a statement of means is not a prerequisite to the granting of legal aid.[14] If, therefore, the juvenile's parents are uncooperative, or he is in care, the court may grant legal aid even though no statement of means has been completed.[15]

(iii) Once the juvenile has attained the age of 16 his mother and father can no longer be required to contribute, but in assessing his means any sums he receives from his parents may be taken into account as forming part of his disposable income.[16]

Irrespective of who applies for legal aid the order will be made in favour of the juvenile and thus it is from the juvenile that the solicitor will take his instructions, assisted by the parents unless there is a conflict of interest.

5 THE TRIAL

As has already been seen, the vast majority of juveniles will be tried in a juvenile court and this part of the chapter will, therefore, be concentrating on juvenile court procedure. Trial before a juvenile court is, of course, no more than a specialised form of summary trial and therefore much that takes place will follow the same course as in the adult court. There are, however, a few important differences in procedure and the solicitor must make sure that he is familiar with these, otherwise the juvenile bench will become irritated with him. In addition, the atmosphere tends to be much more informal than in the adult court. You must not allow yourself to be lulled into not taking the proceedings seriously enough. The juvenile court tries young people on criminal charges and the usual standard of proof is required.[17]

(1) Procedure in the juvenile court

Set out below are the major differences between juvenile and adult courts.

(a) Privacy

Juvenile courts are not open to the general public. Only the parties and their representatives, officers of the court and persons interested in the case, for example social workers, may be present along with the juvenile's parents and members of the press.[18] Although the court may authorise any other person to be present, it will not normally do so.

(b) Reporting restrictions

The media may not report the names of the juvenile or any details which would tend to lead to the juvenile being identified.[19] This rule may be waived

14 Legal Aid Act 1974, s 29(4) and (5).
15 The 'appropriate contributor's' contribution may be assessed at the full cost of the case if he does not furnish a statement.
16 The Legal Aid in Criminal Proceedings (General) (Amendment) Regulations 1983, SI 1983/1863, reg 19, Sch 2, para 1.
17 Higher in the case of 'children'. See further p 125, ante.
18 Children and Young Persons Act 1933, s 47.
19 Ibid, s 49. This also applies at the hearing of a juvenile's appeal to the Crown Court.

by the court on application or its own motion if the interests of justice to the juvenile appear to indicate otherwise. This rule also applies to any juvenile who gives evidence or who is otherwise involved in juvenile court proceedings. There are different rules when the juvenile appears before an adult court, which will be considered later in the chapter.

It may sometimes be necessary to take a decision as to whether or not the client should be identified. This might be necessary when, for example, there is a need to trace witnesses, in which case an application to lift restrictions will be necessary.

(c) *Presence of parent or guardian*

A juvenile court has power to require a parent or guardian to attend the proceedings and if necessary a summons or warrant may be issued[20] and may be included in the summons to the juvenile. The practice of most juvenile courts is to require both parents to attend in any case of significance. Make sure that if you are representing a juvenile you advise his parents of their need to attend, although most will attend automatically. If the juvenile is not represented by a solicitor the court may allow his parent or guardian to represent him.[21]

(d) *Conduct of proceedings*

Terminology is slightly different in the juvenile court. The juvenile is asked whether or not he 'admits' or 'denies' the offence, not whether he is 'guilty' or 'not guilty'. A slightly different form of oath is used. In the juvenile court all witnesses promise to tell the truth and do not swear that they will do so.[1] The different oath reflects that the juvenile court is itself run on less formal lines than the adult court. Juveniles are not placed in a dock but will normally be seated on a chair facing the magistrates, who will usually address the juvenile by his first name. If the charge is proved he will not be 'convicted' but 'a finding of guilt' will be recorded. This all requires the defence solicitor to tailor his advocacy style accordingly, but he must not be afraid to cross-examine strongly, or take points of law when necessary. Although acting from the best of motives, some juvenile court magistrates see their function as quasi-administrative ('what shall we do with this young person?') rather than judicial ('Are we sure that this person is guilty?').

Note finally that the court is under a duty to make enquiries as to the age of a juvenile but it would appear that any error due to mistake or misstatement will not render the proceedings invalid.[2] If a juvenile court finds out during the proceedings that the 'juvenile' before it is in fact an adult, it may nonetheless continue with the hearing, unless the offence is triable 'either way' and there has not yet been a mode of trial inquiry.[3] However, if it is known before the charge is put that the accused is not a juvenile, the juvenile court is not the appropriate forum and any proceedings there will be a nullity.[4]

---

20 Magistrates' Court (Children and Young Persons) Rules 1970, r 26.
21 Ibid, r 17(1).
1 Children and Young Persons Act 1963, s 28.
2 Children and Young Persons Act 1933, s 99.
3 Ibid, s 48(1).
4 *R v Chelsea Justices, ex p DPP* [1963] 3 All ER 657.

(2) **Procedure in the adult magistrates' court and the Crown Court**

When a juvenile is tried summarily in an adult magistrates' court or is committed to stand trial on indictment he is, broadly speaking, dealt with in the same way as an adult, although there are three major points of difference. Firstly, a parent or guardian may assist an unrepresented juvenile in an adult court.[5] In the Crown Court it is almost inconceivable that a juvenile would appear unrepresented.[6] Secondly, the adult court and the Crown Court may require the parent's attendance under s 34 of the Children and Young Persons Act 1933 in precisely the same way as in the juvenile court. Finally, it will be recalled that s 49 of the Children and Young Persons Act 1933 imposes restrictions on the reporting of proceedings before a juvenile court. In the adult court or the Crown Court the position is different, in that in order to preserve anonymity a direction is required from the court under s 39 of the 1933 Act. In practice, however, this direction will usually be given since chief officers of police are required to notify the clerk to the justices in advance in those cases where a direction may be necessary, and the clerk should also draw the court's attention to its power to make a direction before proceedings commence. Nevertheless, when acting for a juvenile appearing before an adult court, you should make sure that this is not overlooked. The committing magistrates' court should forward with the committal papers a statement indicating whether or not a direction was given under s 39 of the 1933 Act.[7]

6 SENTENCING

As already emphasised, the general policy is that wherever possible, sentencing should take place in a juvenile court, even if the juvenile is tried elsewhere. The detailed provisions as to the types of sentence available are contained in chapter 12 but a diagrammatic summary has been included at the end of this chapter as a ready reference. It is, however, essential to note an important point of principle relating to juveniles who attain the age of 17 years before proceedings are concluded. Such persons may be dealt with as if they were still under 17.[8] As we have already seen, the adult court is the appropriate forum if he has attained 17 before his first appearance, or in the case of either way offences, before inquiry into the mode of trial takes place, but if the juvenile court legitimately assumes jurisdiction it need not thereafter remit to the adult court. Obviously, if your client is convicted or has pleaded guilty and attains 17 before he is sentenced it will usually be in his interests to keep the case in the juvenile court.

7 APPEALS

Broadly, the appeal structure applies to juveniles in the same way as to adults. Consequent upon the rule that a juvenile must generally be tried summarily, most appeals will be to the Crown Court, which must usually sit with justices qualified for a juvenile panel. The Court of Appeal will only be concerned with appeals against conviction by the Crown Court when the

---

5 1970 Rules, r 5.

6 In the Crown Court only r 5 (parental assistance in conduct of defence) and r 8(2) (duty of court to assist unrepresented juvenile in cross-examination) apply.

7 Home Office Circular 14/65.

8 Children and Young Persons Act 1963, s 29.

juvenile has been committed to the latter for trial in the comparatively rare situations outlined earlier in the chapter, or where the juvenile has been committed for sentence, under s 37 of the Magistrates' Courts Act 1980. The Divisional Court has exactly the same functions as it does in respect of decisions of adult magistrates' courts.

A parent may appeal to the Crown Court against orders that he pay costs, compensation or a fine, but not against an order binding him over to take proper care and control of the juvenile; the latter does, of course, require consent anyway.

SENTENCING OPTIONS IN RESPECT OF JUVENILES

	Crown Court	*Magistrates' Court*	*Juvenile Court*
1. Detention during Her Majesty's pleasure for murder CYPA 1933, s 53(1)	✓ (indeterminate)	–	–
2. Detention for offences punishable with 14 years' imprisonment or more CYPA 1933, s 53(2)	✓ (up to maximum term of imprisonment)	–	–
3. Youth custody order: for imprisonable offences CJA 1982, s 6 *15/16 year olds only*	✓ (maximum 1 year)	–	✓ (maximum 6 months)
4. Detention centre order: for imprisonable offences CJA 1982, s 5 *14–16 year old males only*	✓ (maximum 4 months)	–	✓ (maximum 4 months)
5. Community service order: for imprisonable offences PCCA 1973, ss 14–17 *16 year olds only*	✓ (40–120 hours)	–	✓ (40–120 hours)
6. Attendance centre order: for imprisonable offences CJA 1982, ss 16–19	✓ (up to 24 hours — normally 12 hours)	–	✓ (up to 24 hours— normally 12 hours)
7. Fine: for any offence	✓ (no limit)	✓ (under 14 £100) (14–16 £400)	✓ (under 14 £100) (14–16 £400)
8. Absolute or conditional discharge: for any offence PCCA 1973, s 7	✓	✓	✓

SENTENCING OPTIONS IN RESPECT OF JUVENILES—*contd.*

	Crown Court	Magistrates' Court	Juvenile Court
9. Parental recognisance: for any offence CYPA 1969, s 7	✓ (£1,000)	✓ (£1,000)	✓ (£1,000)
10. Care orders: for imprisonable offence CYPA 1969, s 7	✓	–	✓
11. Supervision orders: for any offence CYPA 1969, s 7	✓	–	✓
12.(a) Hospital order: for imprisonable offence MHA 1983, s 37	✓	–	✓
(b) Restriction orders MHA 1983, s 43 *14–16 year olds only*	✓	–	(Commit to Crown Court)
13. Disqualification and endorsement (where appropriate) RTA 1972, Sch 4	✓	✓ (only where combined with 7–9 supra)	✓
14. Compensation order for any offence PCCA 1973, s 35 as amended by CJA 1982	✓ (no limit)	✓ (£2,000 per offence as an *alternative* to 7–9 supra)	✓ (£2,000 per offence)

The above table deals with the more important sentences and ancillary orders such as compensation. The most notable feature, already remarked upon is the extremely limited powers of an adult magistrates' court to deal with a juvenile convicted before it. It means that in most cases the magistrates will have to remit to the juvenile court whose powers of sentence are not significantly less than those of the Crown Court. It also means, however, that an adult court could not commit a 15 or 16 year old direct to the Crown Court under s 37 of the Magistrates' Courts Act 1980 where it considers a youth custody order of up to 12 months appropriate. It would have to remit to a juvenile court, who could then, if they considered it appropriate, commit the juvenile to the Crown Court. Whether the delay and cost that this occasions is justifiable is open to dispute.

CHAPTER 11

Trial on indictment

The lengthy time-lag that exists between the inception of a prosecution and its ultimate disposal at the Crown Court has already been noted. It is all too easy therefore to be lulled into a false sense of security and to leave preparation until the last minute. Early preparation is, however, essential. In the vast majority of cases, trial on indictment will be preceded by committal proceedings before a magistrates' court and it will not be possible adequately to consider the many tactical issues that can arise at the committal stage unless you have already done the necessary groundwork.

Trial on indictment without committal

Before looking at committals in detail, it should nevertheless be noted that there are three occasions when an accused may be tried on indictment *without* having first been committed for trial. These are rarely met in practice but require a brief mention.

(a) Voluntary Bills of Indictment. A prosecutor may ask a High Court judge to direct that a Voluntary Bill be 'preferred'. If this request is granted, an indictment charging the accused may be drawn up in accordance with the judge's direction. The application is made in writing by the prosecutor to the judge, with various supporting documents the most important of which are the prosecution's witness statements and a copy of the draft indictment. The judge will make his decision on the basis of the documents submitted and will rarely hear oral representations from the prosecutor. The accused has no *locus standi* and accordingly does not even have a right to make written representations.[1]

There are no restrictions on the use of the procedure, but it tends to be reserved for unusual cases, of which the following are examples.

EXAMPLES
(i) D is charged with murder. Committal proceedings are held at which the magistrates consider the evidence, hold that there is an insufficient prima facie case and discharge him. If the prosecutor felt that this decision was erroneous, he has no right of appeal as such, but can ask leave of a High Court judge to prefer a Voluntary Bill.
(ii) D is committed to stand trial charged with armed robbbery. Shortly before his trial his accomplice D2 is arrested. To save the time and trouble involved in holding separate committal proceedings for D2, the prosecutor can apply for a Voluntary Bill charging D1 and D2 together.
(iii) At committal proceedings, D disrupts them by unreasonably insisting that the prosecution calls all its witnesses, although there is a clear prima facie case. The prosecution may, in exceptional circumstances, abandon the committal proceedings and instead seek leave to prefer a Voluntary Bill.[2]

(b) Perjury. This offence may be prosecuted in the same way as any other, but there is a power, not often used, for a judge or chairman of a bench of

---

1 *R v Raymond* [1981] QB 910.
2 *R v Raymond*, supra.

magistrates to order the prosecution of any witness in the proceedings before him, in which case, he may also commit him for trial there and then if he considers this appropriate.[3]

(c) Order for retrial by the Court of Appeal. If a defendant appeals to the Court of Appeal, that court can, in certain circumstances, order a retrial, in which case it will direct that a new indictment be preferred without the need for further committal proceedings.[4]

1 COMMITTAL PROCEEDINGS

(1) Introduction

In the fullness of time, sometimes after numerous adjournments and frantic attempts by the defence to obtain their client's release on bail, the day fixed for the committal proceedings will finally arrive. Whether the offence charged is 'indictable only' or triable 'either way', the theoretical purpose of committal proceedings is the same, namely, for the magistrates to enquire into whether the evidence against him raises a sufficiently strong *prima facie* case to justify trial on indictment. In most committal proceedings, however, there is no dispute as to the existence of a *prima facie* case, and, accordingly magistrates have power to commit *without considering the evidence at all* where both sides agree to this course (which they usually do). What used to be a judicial inquiry has thus largely withered away to become no more than an administrative *imprimatur* which will often take up no more than five minutes of court time and will only require the defence advocate (if he is there at all) to be on his feet for a matter of seconds. In practice, by far the most important by-product of the committal stage has always been that the defence will receive advance notice of most, if not all, of the evidence that the prosecution intends to call at the trial.[4a]

(2) The two types of committal

Committals may be either (a) without consideration of the evidence; or (b) with consideration of the evidence. The vast majority will take place under method (a), but either the prosecution or the defence may opt for method (b) where appropriate. Appreciating the difference between (a) and (b) and when one or the other should be used is of vital importance, especially since the ultimate choice will lie with the defence. As with the right to refuse consent to the summary trial of an 'either way' offence, this power of selection' is one of the few occasions during the course of a prosecution when the accused has the initiative: it is an opportunity that should not be wasted.

(a) Committal without consideration of the evidence[5]*—(a 's 6(2) committal')*

If the accused is committed for trial under this provision, the court does not consider *any* evidence either written or oral. It is merely invited to commit the accused for trial on the basis of written statements in the prescribed form which must have been served by the prosecution on the defence, and to which the defence do not object. The whole procedure will take only a few

---

3 Perjury Act 1911, s 9; note however that this power will be abolished by s 28 of the Prosecution of Offences Act.

4 Criminal Appeal Act 1968, s 7.

4a In the case of 'either way' offences 'full' disclosure may have already taken place prior to the 'mode of trial' procedure: see p 279, ante.

5 Magistrates' Courts Act 1980, s 6(2).

moments from start to finish, and at *no* stage will the court be required to consider whether there is a case to answer.[6] This procedure can only take place, however, if the following requirements are *all* satisfied:

(i) all the evidence before the court consists of *written statements* in the prescribed form;

(ii) all the accused have solicitors *acting* for them (whether present in court or not);[7]

(iii) none of the accused wishes to submit that there is no case to answer, or call evidence.

(b) *Committal with consideration of the evidence*[8] — (a '*s 6(1) committal*')

The proceedings will differ in that the magistrates *will* be required to examine the evidence and decide whether the accused should be committed to stand trial. Evidence may be given orally (in which case it will be recorded in the form of a written 'deposition' which the witness will sign) or by means of written statements in the prescribed form, which will be read out to the court (where the other side do not object), or a combination of both. Obviously enough, proceedings will vary greatly in length depending upon the size of the case, and the areas in dispute, but whatever form they take, the court is required to consider whether or not a *prima facie* case has been made out on the evidence before it.

(3) Common procedural points

Although the two types of committal proceedings differ both in their purpose and form there are a number of procedural provisions that apply to *both*. These will now be considered in turn.

(a) Constitution and powers of the court

As with 'mode of trial' procedure a single lay magistrate may sit as an examining justice. Nevertheless, since committal proceedings are usually fitted into the court's ordinary schedule, the proceedings will usually be heard by a stipendiary or three lay magistrates sitting in open court, although s 4(2) Magistrates' Courts Act 1980 does give the court power to sit *in camera* in certain limited circumstances. The court has a general power to adjourn the proceedings[9] but if it does so it *must* remand the accused on bail or in custody. In theory, the court has the power to inquire into an offence as examining justices, even if it was committed outside their commission area,[10] but in practice, the proceedings will normally be held in the court for the area in which the offence was committed. The above provision is useful, however, where committal is sought in respect of a number of related offences, for example, a series of burglaries, not all of which have been committed locally.

(b) Representation and presence of the accused

There is no general requirement for an accused to be *represented* at committal proceedings although, as has been noted, he may not be committed under

6 Compare the wording of s 6(2) of the 1980 Act with s 6(1), post, where they are so required.
7 Ibid, s 6(2) as amended by Criminal Justice Act 1982, s 61.
8 Magistrates' Courts Act 1980, s 6(1).
9 Ibid, s 5.
10 Ibid, s 2(3).

s 6(2) of the 1980 Act unless he has a solicitor *acting* for him (whether present in court or not).

The *accused* must generally be present (he will, of course, be produced from custody or be answering to bail), although magistrates do have power to allow *evidence* to be given in his absence if either:

    (i) they consider that because of his disorderly conduct before them it is not practicable for the evidence to be given in his presence; or

   (ii) the accused cannot be present for reasons of health, but is represented by solicitor or counsel and has consented to evidence being given in his absence.[11]

In practice, however, a court will seldom proceed in his absence. The most likely reason for the accused's non-appearance will be that he has absconded, in which case, the magistrates will adjourn the proceedings and issue a warrant for his arrest.

(c) Joinder

The magistrates have jurisdiction to hear committal proceedings involving several offences or offenders in those circumstances where it would be proper for them all to be joined in the same indictment, that is to say, where they are founded on the same facts or form part of a series of offences of the same or similar character. This is so even if the accused are charged in separate informations and/or they object to this course being adopted.[12] As a result, committal proceedings may vary widely in size and complexity from a single accused charged with one offence of shoplifting to a large group charged with a series of armed robberies and related offences.[13]

(d) Press reports

As already noted the proceedings will normally take place in open court but there are restrictions as to what the press may report. The reason is obvious. If committal proceedings, and all matters ancillary thereto such as contested bail applications were fully reported this could prejudice the prospects of a fair trial, especially if the committal takes place under s 6(1). Section 8 of the Magistrates' Courts Act 1980 accordingly makes it unlawful to publish or broadcast any report of committal proceedings containing information other than that permitted by the section, broadly, the names of the accused and the offences charged,[14] unless an application has been made by the accused to lift reporting restrictions. In every case, Magistrates' Courts Rules 1981, rule 5 requires the clerk to explain the provisions of s 8 to the accused. Where there is only one accused the court *must* lift restrictions if this is requested. Where, however, there are two or more accused the court is only obliged to lift restrictions if *all of them* so request. If any accused objects the court may only lift restrictions if after hearing representations from them it considers it in the 'interests of justice'.[15] Thus the onus is on the accused who is applying to lift restrictions to satisfy the court that failure to do so will prejudice his chances of a fair trial.[16]

There are two classes of case in which you will need to discuss the lifting

11 Magistrates' Courts Act 1980, s 4(4).
12 The power of joinder is thus the same as on summary trial and trial on indictment.
13 See eg *R v Camberwell Green Justices ex p Christie* [1978] QB 602.
14 The press may also report the names of the witnesses and of the magistrates hearing the proceedings.
15 1980 Act, s 8 as amended by Criminal Justice (Amendment) Act 1981.
16 *R v Leeds Justices, ex p Sykes* [1983] 1 All ER 460.

of reporting restrictions with your client. Firstly, where publicity is necessary in order to encourage members of the public to come forward as witnesses and secondly, perhaps less obviously, where the alleged offence has achieved such local or national notoriety, that full reporting will *lessen* rather than fuel prejudice against the accused. The major problem is, of course, if the client's co-accused object. A possible way round this may be to suggest that the court should not only lift reporting restrictions under the 1980 Act, but also make an order under s 4 of the Contempt of Court Act 1981 confining the press to reporting only those matters (for example an appeal to alibi witnesses to come forward) that are necessary for the applicant's defence. Section 4 of the 1981 Act enables a court (including a magistrates' court) to postpone contemporaneous reporting of all or part of any legal proceedings where necessary to avoid 'a substantial risk of prejudice to the administration of justice'. Although it has been held[17] that this power to embargo details of committal proceedings should be used sparingly, it enables the court to give the applicant his publicity whilst, at the same time, not prejudicing his co-accused.

If you do succeed in having reporting restrictions lifted, you will be well advised to mention to the press the *reason* why you have done so, especially where the accused is appealing for witnesses to come forward. There is no guarantee that the appropriate aspect of the case will be publicised unless you explain your motives. Tact is necessary, because it must never be thought that the freedom of the press is being impinged upon, but most reporters will accede to any reasonable request.

Quite apart from the above rules, which are of general application, there are two special provisions relating to anonymity. Firstly, when acting for an accused charged with a rape offence, the committal proceedings will be subject to the provisions of the Sexual Offences (Amendment) Act 1976. Broadly, these provide that no material shall be published or broadcast that is likely to lead to the identification of either the complainant or the accused, unless the court otherwise directs.[18] In the case of the accused's name a magistrates' court[19] has power to make the appropriate direction but only a judge of the Crown Court may direct the publication of the complainant's name.[20]

> EXAMPLE. Bill Smith is charged with raping Mary Jones. His defence is one of alibi. His solicitor asks for reporting restrictions to be lifted at the committal proceedings in order to make an appeal for witnesses to come forward. If Bill Smith's name is also material, it will be necessary to ask for a direction under the 1976 Act (eg 'will anyone who saw Bill Smith in the Red Lion on the evening of Saturday—August 1984 please come forward'). In this example Mary Jones' identity is quite immaterial but this might not be the case if, for example, the defence was one of consent (eg 'Did anyone see Bill Smith with Mary Jones etc. on the— of August 1984').[1]

Secondly, it will be recalled that when one of the accused is a juvenile the court may prohibit publication of any particulars calculated to lead to his identification.[2]

---

17 *R v Horsham Justices, ex p Farquharson* [1982] QB 762—see also the comments of the Divisional Court in *ex p Farquharson* deprecating the overuse of s 11 of the Act of 1981 to give witnesses anonymity in *R v Central Criminal Court, ex p Crook* (1984) Times, 8 November.
18 1980 Act, ss 4 and 6.
19 Ibid, s 6(2).
20 Ibid, s 4(2).
 1 Because this would tend to identify her as the victim.
 2 Children and Young Persons Act 1933, s 39. Note a similar restriction applies in the juvenile court itself: ibid, s 49. See p 316 ante.

(e)   Use of written statements Magistrates' Courts Act 1980, s 102:

Whatever form the committal proceedings take, written witness statements are likely to be used. If the committal is under s 6(2) *all* the prosecution evidence will be tendered in the form of written statements but, even where there is to be a s 6(1) committal, there are bound to be at least some prosecution witnesses who will not need to give oral evidence. In either case, written statements must be in the form prescribed by s 102 Magistrates' Courts Act 1980 in order to be admissible. The formal requirements are that the statement must:

(i)   purport to be signed by the person who made it;
(ii) contain a declaration that it is true to the best of that person's knowledge and belief.

Its admission is, however, conditional upon a copy being served upon each of the other parties prior to its being tendered in evidence and upon none of them objecting to its use before it is so tendered. This provision is, therefore, very similar in form to s 9 of the Criminal Justice Act 1967 (which governs admission of written statements at *trials*) and standard police witness forms combine both. If the statement is admitted, any exhibit or object referred to in it shall be treated as if it has been produced and identified on oath by the maker.[3]

(4) Procedure on committal

The procedure to be followed at committals is contained in rules 5 to 11 of the Magistrates' Courts Rules 1981. The requirements laid down by these rules are mandatory so that if they are disregarded the committal and any subsequent conviction will be void.[4] There will, however, be substantial local variation in the precise order that proceedings will take and accordingly it is not possible to give more than a general picture.

(a)   Committal without consideration of the evidence

The procedure is very simple, so much so that even if it you are making your first appearance as an advocate it will be hard to go wrong. For the procedure to be used the prosecutor must first have served 'committal papers' on the defence solicitors. These will consist of statements of witnesses prepared to conform with s 102, along with copies of any exhibits referred to therein where practicable, together with a statement setting out the charge or charges, and a list of the statements and exhibits which are in the possession of the police. There is no prescribed time limit within which the s 102 statements must be served prior to the committal hearing. It is not uncommon for committal papers to be served on the defence at short notice, sometimes on the morning of the hearing itself.[5] This practice may sometimes put you in difficulties as it leaves insufficient time to check the statements to see if a s 6(2) committal is appropriate. If it is clear that you need time to peruse them, you should ask the prosecution if they will agree to an adjournment. If they refuse, you are entitled to refuse to consent to the statements

---

3   S 102(1) of the Act of 1980. The statement can thus only contain material that the witness could have given on oath.

4   *R v Phillips and Quayle* [1939] 1 KB 63, CCA.

5   This must be contrasted with Criminal Justice Act 1969, s 9 in that there is no requirement that the the party on whom the statement is served be given 7 days to consent to its admission. Note that advance disclosure under the Magistrates' Courts (Advance Information) Rules 1985 will not, of itself, constitute service for the purposes of s 102, although under the 1985 rules, at the very least, the substance of the prosecution case will be revealed at an early stage.

being admitted. An adjournment will then be inevitable because the prose-cution will not be in a position to proceed. This is, however, a course that should only be followed *in extremis*. Very few prosecutors will be so uncoop-erative and, in any event, a request to the magistrates to put the case back for an hour or so will usually be granted thus providing all the time that is necessary in a simple case. If you decide to stand on your rights, however, you must make sure that you notify the prosecution as soon as possible if, after due deliberation, you decide that a s 6(2) committal is appropriate. Failure to do so will only incur unnecessary costs. Similarly, you should notify the court if the proceedings are 'going short'. Since, however, the choice of form of committal usually rests with the defence, you should not be pressurised into agreeing to a s 6(2) committal on the basis of a five minute perusal of the papers in a crowded court waiting room. The decision as to the appropriate type of committal is never one to be taken lightly.

As a result of an amendment introduced by s 61 of the Criminal Justice Act 1982, the defence solicitor's presence in court is no longer strictly neces-sary; committal can take place under s 6(2) provided the accused has a solicitor *acting* for him. To what extent, therefore, is it still necessary to attend? Much will depend upon the nature of the case: for example there may be difficulties over bail, such as renewed police objections or the need for sureties to be retaken. Alternatively there may be some procedural aspect which requires the solicitor's attendance such as the need for the alibi warn-ing to be given. On the other hand there will be cases where the relationship with the prosecutor is such that all relevant matters such as confirmation that there will be no objections to the renewal of bail and agreement to the appropriate forms of witness order can be agreed over the telephone before-hand. If this is so, and the client is quite happy to attend on his own, your time can no doubt be more usefully spent.

Assuming, that the papers have been properly served and the defence is agreeable to a s 6(2) committal, the hearing will take the following form.

Stage 1. The accused will be placed in the dock and the charge read out to him, but he will not be asked to plead. If the offence is triable 'either way', the mode of trial enquiry may first have to take place unless this has been dealt with on an earlier adjournment.

Stage 2. The prosecutor will then hand to the clerk of the court the originals of the s 102 statements served on the accused, along with any exhibits[6] and invite the magistrates to commit the accused for trial under s 6(2).

Stage 3. The clerk will then ask the prosecutor if all the evidence to be presented at the committal is in the form of written statements and having ascertained whether or not the accused has a solicitor acting for him, will ask that solicitor (or the accused himself if the solicitor is not present in court) if the defence wish to:

(a) object to any of the statements;
(b) call any evidence;
(c) submit that there is no case to answer.

Stage 4. Assuming that the answer to all three is 'no', the court will then commit the accused to a specified Crown Court for trial. In deciding the

6 Alternatively, where the exhibit does not consist of documentary evidence but real evidence such as a knife, the police will usually ask that they retain it until trial: see *R v Lambeth Metropolitan Stipendiary Magistrate, ex p McComb* [1983] QB 551, CA.

location of the Crown Court to which the accused should be committed the magistrates are required to consider:

(a) the convenience of the defence, the prosecution and the witnesses;
(b) the expediting of the trial; and
(c) any direction given by the Lord Chief Justice under s 75 of the Supreme Court Act 1981.[7]

It will be recalled that the direction given under (c) above divides offences into Classes 1 to 4. The vast majority of offences come within Class 4, and thus, the accused will be committed to the nearest convenient location of the Crown Court as notified to the clerk by the presiding judge. It is only where the offence comes within Classes 1 to 3 or it is a Class 4 offence appropriate for trial by a High Court judge that the magistrates may need to consider committing it to anywhere other than the local third tier Crown Court.

Experience will soon tell you where your clients' cases will be committed, but if you are not sure, or are in an unfamiliar court it is as well to find out in advance—the client may ask and it does not look very impressive if you do not know. Sometimes, you may need to ask the magistrates to commit other than to the local Crown Court, because, for example the case has aroused strong local feeling, or because, although it is a Class 4 offence, it has some special feature, such as complicated financial transactions, that make it unsuitable for trial at the local third tier Crown Court. Although you may make representations as to venue at committal, these often fall on stony ground since magistrates tend to leave such decisions as to venue to the Crown Court. For this reason, many solicitors wait until after committal and then make an application to the Crown Court.

Stage 5. The proceedings are not yet concluded, since there are four other matters which may need to be dealt with.

(*i*) *The alibi warning.* The major advantage to the defence of committal proceedings is the advance warning that they receive as to the nature of the prosecution case. Conversely, the defence's duty of disclosure is limited to giving particulars of any defence of alibi upon which it proposes to rely.[8] Section 11 of the Criminal Justice Act 1967 provides that a defendant tried on indictment may not adduce evidence in support of an alibi without leave of the trial judge unless particulars are given either to the magistrates at the committal proceedings or in writing to the prosecution within *seven days* thereafter.[9] Rule 6(4) of the Magistrates' Court Rules 1981 requires the court to give an oral 'alibi warning' to the accused explaining the effect of s 11 and in addition to give him a written notice setting out the terms of the section. Defences of alibi are not in fact that common[9] and, therefore, the court may dispense with the above requirements if, having regard to the nature of the offence(s) charged, it is unnecessary to comply with them.[10]

The clerk will usually ask the defence advocate whether an alibi warning is appropriate. It is important, therefore, that you know exactly what constitutes 'evidence in support of an alibi'. It is defined as:

'evidence tending to show that by reason of the presence of the defendant at a particular place or in a particular area at a particular time he was not, or was

---

7 See p 25, ante.
8 See generally pp 176 et seq, ante.
9 S 11(8) of the Act of 1967.
10 1981 Rules, r 7(9).

unlikely to have been, at the place where the offence is alleged to have been committed *at the time of its alleged commission.*'[11]

'Alibi' thus has a restricted meaning as the following examples show.

EXAMPLES
(i) D is charged with living off the earnings of prostitution between 29 July and 21 August 1968 in Cardiff. The prosecution allege that on the 20 August 1968 he was seen fleeing from the flat of a prostitute. D wishes to adduce evidence that he was at his brother's house at the time. D is under no duty to give particulars to the prosecution: *R v Hassan.*[12]
(ii) D is charged with burglary of a factory. The prosecution allege that he was seen loitering suspiciously outside the factory the day before. D wishes to adduce evidence that he was elsewhere at the time. Again, he would be under no duty to give particulars under s 11 of the 1967 Act.

It is most important to have fully discussed the nature of the client's defence with him beforehand so as to be able to decide whether or not the warning needs to be put. In particular, it should be noted that the section applies even where the only evidence in support of the alibi is that of the accused himself.[13]

(*ii*) *Witness orders.* Unlike alibi warnings, which may be dispensed with, witness orders are mandatory in respect of each witness whose evidence is tendered at committal other than the accused and his character witnesses.[14] In practical terms, this means that in s 6(2) committals an order *must* be made in respect of each witness whose s 102 statement is handed to the clerk by the prosecution. There are two types of witness order and each witness will be served with a copy as soon as practicable after committal. A 'full' witness order requires the witness to attend the trial and give oral evidence,[15] although, albeit rarely, his s 102 statement may be tendered in evidence if the requirements of s 13(3) of the Criminal Justice Act 1925 are satisfied.[16] A 'conditional' witness order only requires the witness to attend the Crown Court trial if he is subsequently notified to do so. The accused thus has an absolute right to require the attendance of a conditionally bound witness at the trial, but if he does not do so, the prosecutor may adduce his evidence simply by tendering out his s 102 statement.[17]

In deciding whether to make a full or conditional order the magistrates should take into account any representations by the parties and in particular consider whether the witness's evidence is likely to be disputed.[18] In practice, the prosecution and defence will have agreed beforehand what order is to be requested in respect of each witness. As a general rule, you should only agree to a witness being conditionally bound if either his evidence is not likely to be contested at the trial (such as the 'loser' statement by the owner of a car allegedly stolen) or if you have clear instructions from your client that he intends to plead 'guilty' at the Crown Court. In practice magistrates will not refuse a request for a full order since a conditionally bound witness may always be notified subsequently that his attendance is required. If there is any uncertainty, it is probably better to ask for a full order, as it is always

11 S 11 of the Act of 1967.
12 [1970] 1 QB 423, CA.
13 *R v Jackson* [1973] Crim LR 356.
14 Criminal Procedure (Attendance of Witnesses) Act 1965, s 1.
15 Ibid, s 1.
16 See p 139 ante.
17 Criminal Justice Act 1925, s 13(2).
18 S 1(2) of the Act of 1965.

possible subsequently to notify the prosecution that the witness's attendance may be dispensed with.[19]

(*iii*) *Legal aid*. If the accused is legally aided, you should apply orally for an extension to cover proceedings in the Crown Court. Although magistrates do now have power to make a 'through order' for proceedings in both courts when they first grant legal aid,[20] local practice may vary, so it is as well to check the original order carefully and also to find out what procedure the court adopts.

(*iv*) *Bail*. On an accused being committed to the Crown Court for trial, he will be committed either on bail or in custody, and therefore an application will have to be made. Although this vexed topic has already been considered fully, the following particular points should be remembered.

- The 'right to bail' under the Bail Act still applies.
- If the client is still in custody you may be able to argue that the committal, of itself, constitutes a change in circumstances. Local practice may vary in this respect.
- If the client has been on bail subject to sureties, they will need to be present at court for renewal unless, unusually, the magistrates have made them 'continuous' to secure attendance of the accused at the Crown Court.
- If the client is committed in custody, he will stay in prison until he appears before the Crown Court unless in the meantime you obtain bail from the Crown Court (or a High Court judge in chambers).

The whole of the procedure outlined above will not take more than five minutes unless there is a contested bail application. An example of a typical[20] s 6(2) committal is shown below.

Police v Duncan McCarthy. In chapter 8 Duncan MCCARTHY elected trial at the Crown Court, the court having decided that the case was suitable for summary trial. Since the prosecution had anticipated this, they were ready to proceed with committal under s 6(2) and accordingly the dialogue is taken up again at that stage.

> *McCarthy:* I wish to be tried in the Crown Court
> *Clerk:* Very well, sit down please [to prosecution solicitor] Are you in a position to proceed with committal today?
> *Prosecution solicitor:* Yes, sir, the prosecution have served committal statements upon the defence. I shall be asking for committal under s 6(2) of the Magistrates' Courts Act 1980 and understand that my learned friend has no objection.
> *Defence solicitor:* That is so, sir.
> *Clerk:* Are you asking for reporting restrictions to be lifted?
> *Defence solicitor:* No sir.
> *Clerk:* Very well [turns to McCarthy] Stand up, please. You are charged that on on the Fifth of August 198–, having entered as a trespasser a building known as the Weyford General Hospital Social Club you stole £50 in money, contrary to s 9(1)(b) of the Theft Act 1968. Do you understand the charge?
> *McCarthy:* Yes sir.
> *Chairman:* Sit down.

---

19 Giving notice is not, however, equivalent to a full witness order: The judge at trial has a discretion to admit the statement rather than have the witness called—*R v Dadlani* (1970) 54 Cr App Rep 305, CA.

20 It is unlikely that the Magistrates' Courts (Advance Information) Rules 1985 will have any effect on this part of the proceedings.

STATEMENT OF WITNESS
C.J.Act s.9, M.C.Act s.102

Statement of ....FRANK PRICE...

Age of Witness (if under 21)...OVER 21..

Occupation of Witness........CLUB STEWARD.......................................

Address & Telephone Number....6, CHESTNUT WAY...................................

     ....WEYFORD, BLANKSHIRE...........................

     ....

This statement, consisting of 1 page each signed by me, is true to the best of
my knowledge and belief. I make it knowing that, if it is tendered in evidence,
I shall be liable to prosecution if I have wilfully stated in it anything
which I know to be false or do not believe to be true.

Dated the 6th of August 198-

    Signed ....**F. Price**..............................

    Signature witnessed by .*S.C. 345 Tarbuck*...........

I am the steward to Weyford General Hospital Social Club. The club stays
open until 10.30 p.m. each weekday. I am responsible for checking the bar
takings and leaving them secured in the cash till in the bar of the club.
My system is to compare the cash in the till with the till roll every night.
When the total amounts to £100 I bank £75 and keep the remaining £25 as a
float. I keep a full record of the club's takings, but as a check on the
float in the till I mark the total in the till on the till roll and sign it.

On the night of the 5th August the club had been quite busy. I remember that
Duncan McCARTHY has been here. I do not remember what time he left. I closed
the bar at 10.30 and balanced the till as described. I see from my mark on
the till roll that there was a total of £64-43p in the till. The vast majority
of this would have been in notes. I remember that there was a £20 note and
a Scottish £5 note. Both were taken that night by me at the bar. After
clearing up, I left the club at about 11-15 p.m. I had locked the till, secured
the bar area with a padlock, and checked all the windows, and the rear fire
door, which were secured. Finally, I locked the door and left.

At about 2-00 a.m. I was called to the club by the police. I was shown the
open till. It had £50.09p missing from it. There were no notes left.

I am the only person authorised to remove money from the till. I am the only
one with keys to both the padlock and the till. I now produce the till roll
(extract F.P.I.)

Signed ...**F. Price**...............................

Signature witnessed by ..*D.C. 345 Tarbuck*.........

STATEMENT OF WITNESS

C.J.Act s.9, M.C.Act s.102

Statement of ....ANN WALLACE...

Age of witness (if under 21)....OVER 21..

Occupation of Witness....3rd YEAR STUDENT NURSE...............................

Address & Telephone Number.....NURSES HOSTEL.................................

.....WEYFORD.......................................

....
This statement, consisting of 1 page each signed by me, is true to the best
of my knowledge and belief. I make it knowing that, if it is tendered in
evidence, I shall be liable to prosecution if I have wilfully stated in it
anything which I know to be false or do not believe to be true.

Dated the 6th of August   198-

Signed..A. Wallace.....................................

Signature witnessed by..D.C. 345 Tarbuck...........

I am a 3rd year student nurse and was in charge of ward 3 on the night of
6th August. I went on duty at 9.00 p.m. and on my way to the ward I noticed
a group of three or four young men outside the social club. I recognised
one as Duncan McCARTHY, a hospital porter. I heard him shout something like
'How about coming for a bit of night duty with me'. I ignored his remarks
and walked on. Although I do not know Duncan McCARTHY socially, I know him
by sight because he went to school with my younger sister. At about 12.55
a.m., I was on duty in ward 3 which is on the ground floor. I suddenly saw
a man's face pressed up against the window. As soon as he saw me turn round
he disappeared. I went over to the window and saw a man running away towards
the main gate. Immediately I alerted the hospital security at the main gate.
I only got a glimpse of the face at the window, but I am pretty sure it was
McCARTHY. In particular, I had a chance to notice that the person at the
window had short very fair hair, just like Duncan McCARTHY. I am willing
to attend court to give evidence.

Signed... A. Wallace ....

Signature witnessed by. D.C. 375 Tarbuck ....

STATEMENT OF WITNES

C.J.Act s.9, M.C.Act s.102

Statement of ....NORMAN STANLEY..

Age of Witness (if under 21) ....OVER 21.......................................

Occupation of Witness......SECURITY GUARD......................................

Address & Telephone Number ....39, SEYMOUR RD..................................

....WEYFORD..

....

This statement, consisting of 1 page each signed by me, is true to the best
of my knowledge and belief. I make it knowing that, if it is tendered in
evidence. I shall be liable to prosecution if I have wilfully stated in it
anything which I know to be false or do not believe to be true.

Dated the 6th of August   198–

Signed ....*N. Stanley*.................................

Signature witnessed by. *P.C. 345 Turbuck*..............

I am a security guard employed by the Weyford District Health Authority at
Weyford General Hospital. On the night of 5th August I was on duty at the
main gate of the hospital. At exactly 1.00 a.m. I received a telephone call
from a nurse who said that she had seen a man prowling adjacent to 'Lowe'
wing. I took a torch and went to look. I did not see anyone but on my way
back to the gate at about 1.20 a.m., I passed the Social Club Building. I
noticed that the rear fire door was open. I went inside and saw that the
entry to the bar counter had been forced. I went immediately to the main
gate and telephoned the Weyford Police Station. At about 1.30 a.m. I made
a note of my observations and the telephone call in the log book which the
duty officer keeps at the gatehouse, and which I now produce, marked NS1.
I remained at the gatehouse until the Police arrived about 5 minutes later.

Signed...... *N. Stanley*..........................
Signature witnesses by... *D. C. 345 Tarbuck*.........

STATEMENT OF WITNESS

€.J.Act s.9, M.C.Act s.102

Statement of....TERENCE MICHAEL TRINDER.......................................

Age of Witness (if under 21)....OVER 21.......................................

Occupation of Witness....POLICE SERGEANT 215..................................

Address & Telephone Number.....WEYFORD POLICE STATION.........................

....LETSBY AVENUE....................................

....
This statement, consisting of 1 page each signed by me, is true to the best
of my knowledge and belief. I make it knowing that, if it is tendered in
evidence. I shall be liable to prosecution if I have wilfully stated in it
anything which I know to be false or do not believe to be true.

Dated the 6th of August   198-

Signed...**P.S. 215 T.M. Trinder**...................

Signature witnessed by.............................

I am a police sergeant stationed at Weyford Police Station. On 5th August
at 1.25 a.m. I was on mobile patrol in a police vehicle with P.C. Arthur
VAUGHN when I received a radio message to go to Weyford General Hospital
in connection with a reported break in. On arrival at the main gate in Chancery
Road I was approached by a man in security uniform who introduced himself
as Norman STANLEY. As a result of what he told me I went to the Hospital
Social Club building where I saw that a fire door at the rear had been forced.
The grill covering the entrance to the bar area had been forced and the till
drawer levered open. I was then approached by P.C. VAUGHN, who had been
making enquiries in the hospital. As a result of what he told me I radioed
to Weyford Police Station with a request that C.I.D. officers interview
Duncan McCARTHY. P.C. VAUGHN and I then searched the grounds and found no
other signs of disturbance or intrusion.

Signed...**P.S 215 T.M. Trinder**......................

Signature witnessed by.............................

STATEMENT OF WITNESS

C.J.Act s.9, M.C.Act s.102

Statement of .... PETER FORSYTH ....

Age of Witness (if under 21) ......OVER 21 ....

Occupation of Witness ....DETECTIVE SERGEANT 820.................

Address & Telephone Number .....WEYFORD POLICE STATION.................

....

....

This statement, consisting of 2 page each signed by me, is true to the best
of my knowledge and belief. I make it knowing that, if it is tendered in
evidence, I shall be liable to prosecution if I have wilfully stated in it
anything which I know to be false or do not believe to be true.

Dated the 7th of August   198-

Signed ..*DS 820 Forsyth*.........

Signature witnessed by ....

At about 2-00 am, as a result of a radio message, I went to 11, Inkerman Terrace, Weyford, with D.C. TARBUCK. I knocked on the door, which was answered by a man who I now know to be Duncan McCARTHY. He did not seem surprised to see us. I said to him "Are you Duncan McCARTHY?', and he replied 'No, Muffin the Mule, you stupid copper'. I said 'There's no need to be offensive, may we come in?'. He said 'You might as well'.

I explained we were making enquiries in relation to an incident at the social club at Weyford Hospital. He said 'What Hospital Social CLub?' and I replied 'The one where you work. Would you mind telling me where you were this evening'. He said 'Yes', then 'I was out with me mates, drinking'. I said 'Where?'. He said 'Here and there'. I said 'Nowhere near the social club? - it was broken into tonight'. He made no reply. I asked him if I could search the premises and he said 'I suppose so, you won't find what you're looking for'. D.C. TARBUCK searched downstairs and I went upstairs. Halfway up I passed a young woman whom I now know to be Tina McCARTHY - she said 'What the hell do you want?'. I said 'You'd better speak to your husband - he's downstairs'. I then searched the bedroom and found under the mattress a wallet containing £40 in notes, including a £20 note and a Royal Bank of Scotland £5 note. I now produce the wallet (marked PF1) and the banknotes (marked PF2). I went back downstairs, showed the wallet to McCARTHY and said 'How do you explain this?' McCARTHY made no reply. I said 'I have reason to believe that the money I have just found is part of the proceeds of tonight's burglary'. McCARTHY replied 'Just my luck to get nicked over a Jock fiver'. I said 'I'm arresting you on suspicion of burglary' and cautioned him. He made no reply. D.C. TARBUCK and I conveyed him to Weyford Police Station where I handed him over to the Custody Officer. At 2.45 a.m. I formally requested permission from the Custody Officer to interview McCARTHY further. This permission was granted and at 3.00 a.m., in the company of D.C. TARBUCK I collected McCARTHY from the police cells and took him to an interview room. I cautioned him and reminded him that he could consult a solicitor if he wished. He declined to do so. I then interviewed McCARTHY and I produce the signed record of that interview marked PF3. At the conclusion of the interview, at 3,25 a.m., I returned McCARTHY to the Custody Officer. At 6,35 a.m. McCARTHY was charged in my presence by the Custody Officer with burglary. He was cautioned and made no reply.

Signed . *DS. 820. Forsyth* ....

Signature witnessed by ....

Prosecution solicitor: Sir, in this case the prosecution ask for committal for trial under s 6(2) of the Magistrates' Courts Act 1980. Copies of the statements, the originals of which I hand to your clerk, have been served on the defence.

[The prosecution solicitor then reads out a list of the names and addresses of the witnesses whose original s 102 statements he has handed to the clerk.]

Clerk: [To defence solicitor] I take it that you do not wish to object to any of the statements, make a submission or call evidence?

Defence solicitor: No sir.

Chairman: Very well. Stand up please McCarthy. You are committed to the Crown Court at Exchester to stand trial on this charge of burglary.

Clerk: [To defence solicitor] Is the alibi warning appropriate?

Defence solicitor: Yes sir, it should be put.

Clerk: I must warn you that at your trial you may not be permitted to give evidence of an alibi or call witnesses in support of an alibi, unless you have earlier given particulars of the alibi and of the witnesses. You may give those particulars now to this court, or at any time within the next seven days. No doubt your solicitor will explain the matter to you.

[The clerk hands a document explaining the effect of s 11 to the defence solicitor.]

Clerk: Have you both considered the question of witness orders?

[The solicitors will have agreed the orders to be made, in accordance with the matters we have already considered. These orders are now made and noted against the names on the list of witnesses. In the circumstances they are all fully bound.]

Defence solicitor: Sir, I apply for legal aid to be extended to cover the Crown Court trial. A legal aid contribution order has already been made. I have taken my client's instructions and can confirm that his means have not changed.

Chairman: [After briefly consulting with colleagues] Yes, we extend legal aid to cover the Crown Court trial. Do you wish to apply for bail?

Defence solicitor: Yes sir. The defendant was released on bail on 13 August and I would apply for this to continue, subject to the same conditions as were imposed on that occasion. It is proposed that his sister continues to stand surety for him in the sum of £500 and he is prepared to comply with the same conditions as to residence.[1] If you wish I shall call Mrs Johnstone so that you may hear evidence as to her suitability.

Prosecution solicitor: Sir, if it would assist the court, may I say that the prosecution have no objection to bail continuing in the same terms as before, and that this surety is quite acceptable.

Chairman: [Addressing defence solicitor] Thank you. In the circumstances it will not be necessary for us to hear you further.

Defence solicitor: Thank you, sir.

Chairman: Duncan McCarthy, you will be committed on bail with a surety in the sum of £500 and subject to the conditions that you continue to reside at 11 Inkermann Terrace, Weyford.

[The magistrates will then give a reason within Schedule 1 Part I Bail Act 1976 as to why these conditions are being imposed and may warn both McCarthy and his sister as to their respective fates should McCarthy abscond. McCarthy will be handed a copy of his bail record and his sister will sign the appropriate surety form.]

(b) *Committal with consideration of the evidence*

Section 6(1) committal proceedings may take one of several forms. In most cases, the prosecution will want a s 6(2) committal and the defence will be agreeable, because they are satisfied that the s 102 statements disclose a prima facie case. Most s 6(1) committals will, therefore, usually be at the request of the defence, although, rarely, the prosecution will, of their own initiative, invite the magistrates to consider the evidence. A s 6(1) committal may be relatively short and not even involve the prosecutor in calling wit-

---

1 See ante, p 266.

nesses to give oral evidence, in other instances, it may last for many weeks and involve the examination of numerous witnesses and voluminous exhibits.

EXAMPLES.
(i) The prosecutor serves a bundle of s 102 statements on D's solicitor and requests a s 6(2) committal. Having read them D's solicitor, although not wishing to cross-examine any of the prosecution's witnesses, nevertheless takes the view that the statements do not disclose a *prima facie* case. He will accordingly request a s 6(1) committal at which all the s 102 statements will be read out, with a view to making a submission of no case to answer.
(ii) Same as in (i) above except that D's solicitor wishes to cross-examine two of the prosecution witnesses. The committal proceedings will obviously take longer unless the prosecution takes the view that it can make out a *prima facie* case without calling the two witnesses that D's solicitor wishes to cross-examine.[2]
(iii) D is unrepresented and has no solicitor acting for him. The court *must* proceed to consider the evidence since a s 6(2) committal is not possible.

Choosing the appropriate form of committal will be considered further in the next section, but first the order of proceedings on a s 6(1) committal must be outlined since it differs from s 6(2) committals in a number of significant respects.

Stage 1. This will follow the same course as in s 6(2) committals: the accused will be placed in the dock, the charge(s) will be read (preceded by 'mode of trial' procedure where appropriate), and the issue of reporting restrictions will be raised.

Stage 2. The prosecutor will now present his case, usually after a short opening speech. He will then proceed either to call witnesses to give oral evidence or read out the s 102 statements of those witnesses whose attendance has not been required by the defence. Evidence given orally will be on oath (unless the court is receiving the unsworn evidence of a child). Examination in chief will be conducted in the usual way, although, as will be shown, cross-examination may well be more limited than at a trial. The clerk must take a verbatim note of oral evidence given by a witness whilst in the witness box. In most magistrates' courts this will be typed up in the form of a continuous narrative whilst the witness is giving evidence. When completed this will be read over to him aloud in open court and will then be signed by him. This written record of his evidence is known as a *deposition*.

The giving of oral evidence at committals thus proceeds at a much slower pace than at trials. This means that it is much more difficult to press home an advantage against a shaky or untruthful witness who has contradicted himself, because after each question and answer there will be a lull whilst it is typed out and read back to the witness. You should always refrain, therefore, from taking cross-examination too far, unless you are certain that you will thereby succeed in having the charges dismissed, because otherwise you may only succeed in rehearsing the witness for the trial. You should probe rather than confront, since unlike at a trial, you are under no obligation to put your client's case in cross-examination. Make sure, however, that you explain this to your client, who, being unaware of the purpose of committal proceedings may feel that you are letting him down by not doing so.

The deposition will form a continuous narrative and will thus differ from a trial transcript where each question and answer is recorded individually. The effect of this is that the full impact of a line of cross-examination will not always emerge satisfactorily. You should, therefore, always request that

2 The prosecution does not have to present at committal all the evidence it proposes to call at trial—see *R v Epping and Harlow Justices ex p Massaro* [1973] QB 433.

the question and answer is recorded in full if the clerk's adapted narrative does not convey the full sense of the passage.

It must also be stressed that your right to challenge the admissibility of prosecution evidence is less extensive than at a trial. Although the court must exclude evidence when the law requires them to do so, for example inadmissible hearsay, they have no *discretion* to exclude evidence under s 78(1) of the Police and Criminal Evidence Act 1978.

> EXAMPLE. B was charged, along with three others, with various offences of exporting firearms. At the committal proceedings the prosecution sought the permission of the examining justices for a 'dock identification' of B. B's application for an order of prohibition was refused on the ground that the discretion to allow or reject such evidence was entirely that of the trial judge (*R v Horsham Justices, ex p Bukhari*).[3]

Ex p Bukhari is also an illustration of the more general principle that the Divisional Court will not interfere with magistrates' conduct of committal proceedings unless it goes to jurisdiction. The fact that there is no effective right to challenge the decision of examining magistrates on a point of evidence[4] thus seriously curtails your scope for raising such matters.

In practice, it is unusual for the prosecution to adduce all of its evidence orally, and normally at least some, and occasionally all, of the witnesses' s 102 statements will be read out to the court. They need not be read out verbatim if the court so directs[5] and it is customary for the prosecutor to be allowed to summarise the substance of non-contentious statements so long as the defence do not object. The vast majority of written statements read out at a s 6(1) committal will be admissible by virtue of s 102 of the 1980 Act, but there are three other statutory provisions which allow for written evidence to be tendered although they are rarely met in practice. In summary they are:

	Statute reference	Nature of statement	Category of witness	Conditions for admission
(i)	MCA 1980, s 103	Written statement	Child (under 14) witness for prosecution re 'sexual offence' as defined by s 103	*Must* adduce evidence by written statement *unless* (inter alia) defence objects, or prosecution need to establish identity.
(ii)	MCA 1980, s 105	Deposition taken by magistrate	Witness who is medically certified as 'dangerously ill and unlikely to recover'.	Representative of party against whom tendered, must have been given opportunity to attend and cross-examine.
(iii)	CYPA 1933, s 42	Deposition taken by magistrate	Juvenile (under 17) victim of certain offences under Sexual Offences Act 1956 or any offence involving bodily injury where medically certified that attendance at court would involve 'serious danger to life or health'.	Notice and opportunity given to accused to attend and cross-examine

3 (1982) 74 Cr App Rep 291. Followed in *R v Highbury Corner Magistrates' Court, ex p Boyce* (1984) 79 Cr App Rep 132.
4 *R v Wells Street Stipendiary Magistrate, ex p Seillon* [1978] 3 All ER 257 and *ex p Bukhari,* supra.
5 S 102(5) of the Act of 1980.

Stage 3. After all the prosecution evidence has been presented, the defence may make a submission that there is no case to answer on the basis that the prosecution case is such that if the evidence were to remain uncontradicted at the trial no reasonably-minded jury, properly directed *could* convict on it. The submission can be made on the same grounds as those on summary trial, namely, that the prosecution have failed to prove an essential element of the offence, or, alternatively, that the prosecution evidence has been so discredited by cross-examination or is so manifestly unreliable that no reasonable tribunal could safely convict on it.[6]

A submission of 'no case to answer' will only rarely succeed since the burden on the prosecution is such a low one, namely to establish that there is sufficient evidence to put the accused on trial for *any* offence, not merely those originally charged.[7] The first question you must always ask yourself therefore is, 'If I succeed will my client walk out of a court a free man?' If so, a submission should be made if the evidence justifies it. If, on the other hand, the only result of the submission will be to reduce the number or severity of the charges you would be well advised to consider whether any benefit will accrue, particularly since, when the indictment is subsequently drafted any charge which you succeed in having dismissed at committal may be reinstated as a count in the indictment if the drafter feels that this course is justified on the evidence tendered at committal.[8]

> EXAMPLE. D is charged with theft of a motor vehicle and his defence is that he borrowed the car with the permission of the owner. If, on cross-examination of the owner, it becomes clear that this is in fact so, a submission, if successful, will result in D's discharge. If, however, all the defence succeeds in showing is that there is no evidence of an intent permanently to deprive, even though the theft charge, may be dismissed, the magistrates would still be entitled to commit D on a charge of taking a vehicle without consent.

If the charges are very serious, a partially successful submission may make sense if it results, for example, in the reduction of a charge of murder to one of manslaughter, since this would undoubtedly influence the drafter of the indictment in deciding whether to reinstate a murder count. In most cases, however, it is probably better to restrict yourself to those submissions that are likely to be wholly successful.

The prosecution have a right of reply, after which the magistrates will normally retire. On returning, they will either uphold the submission, in which case the accused will be discharged, or reject it, in which case the committal proceedings will continue. If the proceedings are dismissed, you should apply for an order for costs out of central funds, even if your client is legally aided, since this may result in the refund of any contribution that he has been required to make. It should be noted, however, that an application for costs from central funds is unlikely to succeed if the accused has been the agent of his own misfortune or has been discharged on a technicality.

Stage 4. If the submission is rejected, or no submission is made, the court will read over the charge to the accused. The charges will usually be the same as those originally put but, rarely, the court may add or substitute further charges, in which case they must be written down. If the accused is unrepresented, he will then be cautioned.[9]

---

6 *Practice Note* [1962] 1 All ER 448 considered at p 299, ante.
7 S 6(1) of the Act of 1980.
8 Administration of Justice (Miscellaneous Provisions) Act 1933, s 2(2).
9 Rules 7(6), 7(7) of the 1981 rules.

Stage 5. The alibi warning will now be given on the same principles as in s 6(2) committals, unless it appears unnecessary. Note that it arises at an earlier stage in the proceedings than in committals under s 6(2).[10]

Stage 6. The accused may now give evidence and call witnesses, or tender their s 102 statements if the prosecution consents. This right to call evidence exists even though an unsuccessful submission of no case to answer has already been made.[11] If any defence witness (including the accused) gives oral evidence this will be taken down in the form of a deposition in the same way as that of a prosecution witness. Similarly, any witness who gives oral evidence or has his s 102 statement tendered must be made the subject of a full or conditional witness order, the only exceptions being the accused and any witness who gives evidence solely as to character. In practice, it is most unusual for the accused to call *any* evidence at this stage. After the charge has been put and the alibi warning given, the accused's representative will in most cases stand up and say:

> 'My client does not propose to give evidence or call any witnesses, and reserves his defence until the trial'

or words to that effect. Most criminal lawyers advise against calling any evidence on behalf of the defence at the committal proceedings since all it does is to reveal their client's defence. Nevertheless, there may be rare cases where there is such overwhelming independent evidence that the accused could not conceivably have committed the offence, for example a cast-iron alibi or forensic evidence which completely demolishes the prosecution case, that the magistrates are bound to discharge him. Taking such a course may, however, be tactically unwise, since discharge at committal is not the equivalent of an acquittal.[12]

If the defence do adduce evidence they have the same option as in summary trials of making a speech either at the beginning or the close of their case. In practice, it will usually be wiser to opt for the latter. Note that if you submit that there is insufficient evidence to justify committal after having called evidence, the test that the magistrates will then be required to apply is whether on the whole of the evidence, any reasonably minded jury *would* convict.[13]

Stage 7. In the unlikely event of the defence calling witnesses, the magistrates will usually retire, and having applied the test outlined above will either discharge the accused or commit him for trial. Far more often, however, there will have been no defence evidence and accordingly the magistrates will proceed to commit the accused without further ado. The formal committal will be subject to the same principles as on s 6(2) committals as will the consideration of bail and legal aid, the only difference being that witness orders and the alibi warning will have already been dealt with.

(5) Which type of committal proceedings?

As already observed, the vast majority of committal proceedings take place under s 6(2) of the Magistrates' Courts Act 1980 without any consideration of the evidence. For this to happen, the prosecution must first offer a s 6(2) committal (which they usually do) and the defence must consent (which,

10 1981 Rules, r 7(9).
11 Ibid, r 7(10).
12 *R v Manchester City Stipendiary Magistrate, ex p Snelson* [1978] 2 All ER 62.
13 *Re Roberts* [1967] 1 WLR 474. Contrast this with test at p 343, ante.

again, they usually do). It is all too easy therefore to dismiss committal proceedings as no more than a tiresome administrative step which serves no ostensibly useful purpose. This is, however, a dangerously simplistic approach to adopt.

Usually, the initiative will be with the defence because the prosecution will offer a s 6(2) committal, but occasionally the prosecution will themselves ask the magistrates to consider the evidence. The two most common occasions on which they will do this are first, when the correctness of identification evidence is likely to be in dispute at the trial, and secondly, when they wish to assess the strength of their own case by tendering certain of their witnesses at committal. Guidelines issued by the Attorney General in May 1976,[14] required the prosecution to *always* offer a s 6(1) committal in disputed identity cases but problems arose in practice. The defence would often refrain from cross-examining identification witnesses at committal for tactical reasons, in busy courts lengthy delays arose, and unnecessary distress was sometimes caused to witnesses. Further guidance was thus issued in July 1979,[15] which sanctioned s 6(2) committals in disputed identification cases where both prosecution and defence and the magistrates considered it to be appropriate. Unless, therefore, the prosecution are concerned as to the reliability of their identification witnesses, or the defence feel that there is something positive to be gained from challenging or probing their evidence at committal, a s 6(2) committal in this type of case is now a common occurrence. As already noted, the other occasion upon which the prosecution may wish to present their evidence before the examining magistrates is where they themselves wish to see how their witnesses will 'stand up in court', for example, where their principal witness is an accomplice or an *agent provocateur*. If the prosecution do adopt this procedure they are under an obligation to serve the defence beforehand with copies of the written statements of those witnesses whom they propose to call (along with any previous 'unedited' statement) since such statements constitute 'unused material' within the *Attorney General's Guidelines*.[15a]

> EXAMPLE. D1 and D2 are charged with conspiracy to prevent the course of justice. The principal witnesses are W, a party to the conspiracy who has been given immunity and three police officers, who interviewed D1 and D2. The prosecutor decides to opt for a s 6(1) committal and proposes to call W to give oral evidence but not the three police officers, whose statements he proposes to tender under s 102 subject to defence agreement. The defence will thus receive copies of the three officers' statements under s 102 (and it will be up to them to decide whether or not they want them to be called) and that of W.

In reality, therefore, the decision as to type of committal will usually rest with the defence. It is unfortunately a decision to which too little consideration is usually given. In fact, one can go much further and say that there are many experienced practitioners, both solicitors and barristers who advise *never* to probe the prosecution case at committal because it always gives too much of the defence case away. One can see the force behind this, because, *failure to challenge the factual basis or admissibility of the evidence tendered by the prosecution at committal in no way prejudices the right of the defence to do so at the trial.*

14 See Hansard vol 912 No 115 of 27th May 1976.
15 In the form of a written answer in the House of Commons, reprinted in *Archbold* (41st edn) para 14.1.
15a The full text is set out in (1982) 74 Cr App Rep 302.

EXAMPLE. POLICE v DUNCAN McCARTHY. There are several places in which McCARTHY's instructions conflict with the witness statements tendered at committal, in particular as to the alleged verbal admissions made by him on arrest. As has already been shown, however, his solicitor agreed to a committal under s 6(2). This does not in any way estop defence counsel from cross-examining the prosecution witnesses or challenging the admissibility of their evidence at the trial.

There is no doubt that in many cases the defence solicitor, having perused the prosecution statements, will conclude that there is nothing to be gained from a s 6(1) committal since the evidence quite clearly disclose a prima facie case. This does not mean, however, that you should always agree to a s 6(2) committal as a matter of course. In every case, you should study the prosecution witnesses' statements carefully before deciding on the appropriate form of committal. The case of *R v Brooker*[16] stands as a cautionary tale.

> B was committed for trial on a charge of affray along with 12 other defendants *without* consideration of the evidence. Although he was represented, his solicitor failed to notice that the prosecution statements contained no reference to B at all. He was subsequently tried and convicted, and appealed on the ground that the trial was a nullity since the original committal was invalid.

His appeal was dismissed by the Court of Appeal on the basis that since committals under s 1 of the Criminal Justice Act 1967 (the predecessor of s 6(2)) did not require the magistrates to consider the evidence, the section had been complied with and the committal was valid. Scarman LJ (as he then was made) the following observations concerning the duties of defence solicitors:

> 'We do not know how it happened that the solicitor instructed for the appellant failed to note the obvious point that the written statements did not incriminate his client ... We would emphasise, however, that [s 6(2) of the 1980 Act] puts a duty upon legal advisers which is inescapable. It is not for them to agree with the prosecution that a committal may go forward, unless they have formed the opinion, upon a full consideration of the written statements, that there is a prima facie case against their client. It is not for them to attend proceedings without having carefully considered the material, the written statements, upon which the prosecution is relying for a committal. They have a duty to their client to consider the material and offer him independent advice measuring up to the standards required of a professional man and lawyer. Any failure to meet those standards, would, we think, certainly amount to professional negligence ... We would think that the Law Society should investigate what happened at those proceedings since public money has undoubtedly been spent in providing this appellant with legal aid which, in the event, was valueless.[17]

The defence solicitor thus has an onerous duty to discharge on behalf of his or her client.

At the end of the day, of course, you will usually conclude that a s 6(2) committal is appropriate. Nevertheless, it is important to be aware of the tactical considerations that need to be borne in mind before coming to this decision. In particular, the following questions always need to be asked.

(a) Do the statements contain any inadmissible material?

Always be on the lookout for any evidence that infringes the rule against hearsay, is a statement of opinion or contains any direct or indirect reference

16 (1977) 65 Cr App Rep 181.
17 Ibid, p 184.

to the client's previous convictions. In practice, such matters will normally have been 'edited out' beforehand, and the prosecution will serve a prepared statement based on the witnesses' original statement but excluding the inadmissible or prejudicial material.[18] If, however, it does contain any such material, you should draw it to the prosecutor's attention and make acceptance of the statement under s 102 conditional upon its being edited out. If the prosecution refuses, you can, of course, refuse to accept the statement, thus leaving it to the prosecution to decide whether to call the witness or agree to the deletion. This tactic should however only be adopted if the point at issue is so fundamental that the whole case turns upon it, if not, admissibility can still be challenged at the trial.[19]

(*b*) *Is there any chance of submitting that there is no case to answer?*

As already pointed out, a successful submission of 'no case to answer' will only usually serve any purpose if it can be made not only on the basis that the prosecution evidence does not disclose a prima facie case vis à vis the offence *charged* but also that it does not disclose *any other* indictable or either way[20] offence. On occasions, albeit rare, you may not wish to challenge any of the prosecution evidence, but argue that, *as it stands*, it discloses no case because, for example, there is no evidence to prove a constituent element of the offence or (as in *R v Brooker*,[21] there is no evidence identifying the accused). Alternatively, you may feel that, given the opportunity of cross-examining one or more of the prosecution witnesses, you will be able so to undermine their evidence that a successful submission will be possible. Such a course may be feasible where, for example, the prosecution case is based entirely on disputed evidence of identification. On the other hand, if you fail, bear in mind that by confronting a witness head on at committal you may have only served to make him even more convinced that he is right by the time he gives evidence at the Crown Court.

(*c*) *Even though there is a case to answer does the defence need to cross-examine any witnesses to find out more about the prosecution's case?*

Sir David Napley has always advocated making full use of committal proceedings to probe the strengths and weaknesses of the prosecution's case.[1] In particular he suggests that the defence should always consider the need to cross-examine certain prosecution witnesses first to test the truth of statements:

'There is a certain technique involved in the preparing of proofs of evidence ... as much available to the defence as to those concerned with the prosecution ... this technique ... is the ability by suggestion to implant into the mind of a witness or potential witness some belief as to the facts which he henceforward adopts as his own recollection ... [The preliminary hearing] ... enables the defence in the absence of the jury, to test the circumstances under which statements were taken; whether, for example, the witness was certain from the outset as to the time when he had actually seen X and, indeed as to the actual day when he saw him; and whether, moreover, it was necessarily X whom he saw.'[2]

---

18 The original statement will also be 'unused material' within the *Attorney General's Guidelines*: see p 345, n 15a, ante.

19 The statement should normally be left in its unvarnished form for the trial judge to deal with. *R v Weaver* [1968] 1 QB 353, CA.

20 Note that if an indictable only offence (eg aggravated burglary) is reduced to an either way offence, there is no jurisdiction to try the offence summarily, they *must* commit it for trial. *R v Cambridge Justices, ex p Fraser* [1985] 1 All ER 667.

21 Supra.

1 See Sir David Napley, *The Technique of Persuasion* (3rd edn) at pp 38 et seq.

2 Ibid, p 43.

and secondly to elicit further evidence which may be of assistance to the defence case.

> 'Thus emerges the second important aspect of cross-examination of witnesses in preliminary hearings, namely the probing for, and the eliciting of, data, facts and leads which may enable those preparing the defence to unearth facts or witnesses who would not otherwise be available ... Once the trial has commenced there is neither time nor opportunity, in most cases, to pursue further enquiries.'[3]

In both the examples given above, it can be seen that much may sometimes be gained from insistence on cross-examining certain prosecution witnesses. Inconsistencies may emerge which can later be put to the witness at the trial, or information may be revealed which sets the defence off on a new and profitable train of inquiry. The defence does, however, face two major difficulties. One is the lengthy delay that may be necessary in order to fit committal proceedings into a busy court schedule—a particularly acute problem if the client is in custody. The other is that, the prosecution do not have to call *all* their witnesses at committal, and thus, if you refuse to accept the statement of a witness because you wish to cross-examine him, the prosecution are perfectly at liberty to dispense with calling him if they consider that they can secure a committal without his evidence.

> EXAMPLE. M was charged with sexual assault on a young girl and wished through his legal representative to cross-examine her at the committal proceedings. Being so informed, the prosecution, who were unwilling to subject her to the experience of giving evidence at this stage, decided not to call her and to seek committal on other supporting evidence. M was committed for trial and sought to quash the committal order on the ground that he was deprived the opportunity of cross-examining the young girl. The application was refused on the basis that the only onus on the prosecution was to make out a *prima facie* case. They therefore had a discretion not to call even an important witness and failure to do so was not a breach of natural justice (*R v Epping and Harlow Justices, ex p Massaro*).[4]

Ex parte Massaro was followed by the Divisional Court in *R v Grays Justices, ex p Tetley*[5] in which the prosecutor, having agreed to the defence request to call four witnesses to give oral evidence, changed his mind on the day of the committal and successfully sought and obtained committal on the basis of those witnesses whose s 102 statements the defence had accepted.

The effect of the above two decisions is therefore that refusal to accept a witness's statement tendered under s 102 is no guarantee that defence will be able to cross-examine him. The prosecution will only be obliged to call him if their case stands or falls on his giving evidence; if not, they can quite properly proceed without him, thus considerably diminishing the defence's power to test the prosecution case.

(d) Any other reasons?

The three previous factors are the ones which will most commonly arise, but there may be other reasons for wanting a s 6(1) committal. For example, if the accused is being committed on a number of related offences for which an application for separate trials is to be sought from the Crown Court, it may be necessary to ask for a s 6(1) committal so that the potential prejudice of

---

3 *The Technique of Persuasion* (3rd Edn), p 45.
4 [1973] QB 433.
5 (1979) 70 Cr App Rep 11.

their being tried together may be more fully brought out.[6] Alternatively, where the accused is to be committed, for example, on serious fraud charges, it may be possible to submit that on the evidence, the charges should be reduced, and at the same time bring out mitigating factors in cross-examination with a view to a plea of guilty at the Crown Court. Tactics of this kind require very careful consideration and it may be advisable to seek the advice of experienced counsel, having first sought the appropriate legal aid extension where applicable.

(6) Challenging committal proceedings

Examining justices are subject to the control of the High Court by way of judicial review on the usual principles but apart from this there is no way of appealling against their decisions. Inevitably, however, there will be occasions upon which either the prosecution or the defence will feel aggrieved by a decision of the examining justices, and it is therefore necessary to consider briefly the most common circumstances in which this may arise, and what, if any, remedy is available.

(a) *Can the prosecution challenge the justices refusal to commit?*

Although there is no right of appeal as such, the prosecution may indirectly challenge the decision by either (i) applying to a High Court judge for a voluntary bill or; (ii) preferring fresh charges and seeking committal before a different bench. If the prosecution adopt option (i) the defence are virtually powerless to intervene, but if they seek to bring fresh charges before examining magistrates it may be possible to apply for judicial review for an order prohibiting the magistrates from holding fresh committal proceedings if it can be shown that these are vexatious or constitute an abuse of the process. Whether or not an order of prohibition will lie will depend on the facts as the following two cases show.

> S was charged with two offences under the Theft Act 1968. The prosecution, having already applied for an adjournment, were still unprepared at the resumed hearing. They were refused a further adjournment and, as they were not in a position to offer evidence, the defendant was discharged. Later, having prepared their case, they instituted fresh committal proceedings. S sought an order of prohibition which was refused on the ground that his earlier discharge did not entitle him to plead *autrefois acquit* or *estoppel per rem judicatem* and that accordingly the prosecution were perfectly entitled to bring fresh committal proceedings since they were not an abuse of the process (*R v Manchester City Stipendiary Magistrate, ex p Snelson*).[7]

> R was the subject of lengthy committal proceedings on 24 charges under the Theft Act during the course of which the prosecution called 14 witnesses and tendered 7 s 102 statements. At the end of their case the defence successfully submitted that there was no case to answer and R was discharged. Several months later the prosecution preferred 5 fresh charges which consisted of a condensed version of the original charges. The Divisional Court granted an order of prohibition on the ground that the prosecution's conduct in seeking committal on what were basically the same charges was vexatious and oppressive (*R v Horsham Justices, ex p Reeves*).[8]

---

6 The judge at the Crown Court will see the papers before the application is made and may be able to evaluate it more fully.

7 Supra.

8 (1980) 75 Cr App Rep 236.

(b)   Can the defence challenge the justices' finding that there is a case to answer?

If it is felt that the decision to commit was against the weight of the evidence there is no way of challenging it, but if the prosecution are unable to repair the defects in their case by the time of the trial the judge will direct the jury to to acquit: an occurrence which is by no means uncommon. Where, however, the committal itself is invalid, for example, because the provisions of rules 6 or 7 of the Magistrates' Courts Rules 1981 have not been complied with, an application by way of judicial review would lie to quash the committal, alternatively, an application could be made at the trial to quash the indictment. Furthermore, any conviction on indictment as a result of defective committal proceedings will be a nullity and will be quashed on appeal.[9] This is normally the equivalent of acquittal, thus precluding fresh proceedings on the principle against double jeopardy.[10] The Court of Appeal may, however, direct a retrial under the writ of *venire de novo*.

(c)   Can either party challenge the conduct of the proceedings before they are concluded?

It has already been observed that attempts to challenge examining magistrates' rulings on matters of evidence in the Divisional Court have met with no success. The Divisional Court will only intervene in committal proceedings where it can be shown that they are acting in excess of their jurisdiction. If, however, the defence feel that the magistrates have erred in admitting evidence or that it has been admitted in unsatisfactory circumstances as, for example, in the case of the 'dock identification' in *ex p Bukhari*,[11] it is important to refer counsel to the point when briefing him or her so that it may be raised at the trial.

2   THE PRE-TRIAL STAGE

As soon as possible after committal the clerk to the justices must send the depositions and/or s 102 statements tendered in evidence to the appropriate Crown Court with any exhibits that it has retained together with the covering documents required by rule 11 of the Magistrates' Courts' Rules 1981. In particular, one of the examining justices is required to sign the Certificate of Committal which (inter alia) confirms:

- The charges on which the accused has been committed;
- The type of committal proceedings;
- The depositions and written statements tendered in evidence, the names and addresses of the makers and the type of witness orders made;
- Whether or not the alibi warning was given.

The next step in the prosecution process will be for an officer at the Crown Court, or in a weighty case prosecution counsel, to draw up the indictment. This may well not take place for some time although, as will be noted later, the Indictment (Procedure) Rules 1971 purport to lay down stringent time limits. Similarly, although statute provides that the trial should take place not less than *two* and not more than *eight weeks* after committal this period

---

9   See eg *R v Phillips and Quayle* [1939] 1 KB 63.
10   However by analogy with the reasoning in *R v Dorking Justices, ex p Harrington* [1983] QB 1076 and *Weight v MacKay* [1984] 2 All ER 673, it is arguable that the rule against double jeopardy would not apply here anyway.
11   Supra.
12   A copy of Duncan McCarthy's certificate appears on p 00.

may (and almost invariably is) extended.[13] Nevertheless, counsel needs to be fully briefed well in advance, the evidence tendered by the prosecution at committal will need to be gone through carefully with the client, and the defence solicitor needs to guard against the risk of the Crown Court list collapsing in front of him and finding himself in the embarrassing position of being listed for hearing the next morning without counsel having been briefed. When acting for a client who is being tried on indictment the defence has two precious assets, knowledge of the case that they have to meet and time: they should not be wasted.

(1) Processing the accused

Before proceeding to consider the various steps that still need to be taken by the defence it is necessary to know in outline the steps that will be taken by the prosecution or by the Crown Court staff between committal and trial. All too often, breakdowns in communication arise because defence solicitors are unaware of how the system operates. This problem is partly due to the fact that, unlike in civil proceedings, there is no formal interlocutory stage so that very little communication takes place between the prosecution and the defence. This situation is likely to change in the near future as a result of the pilot schemes set up in late 1983 at six Crown Courts centres as a result of recommendations made to the Lord Chief Justice by Lord Justice Watkin's Working Party on Criminal Trials.

(a) Listing

Each Crown Court has a court administrator who has overall responsibility for the smooth running of the system. The mechanics of processing a case from committal to trial is largely the responsibility of the 'listing office' whose major task is to ensure that cases come on for trial and that judges are provided with a steady stream of casework. It is fair to say that relations between Crown Court listing offices and defence solicitors are not always the most cordial. This is perhaps inevitable in view of their competing interests, the latter under great pressure to clear backlogs and the former clamouring for more time for preparation. That being said, listing offices are not wholly insensitive to defence solicitors' problems; the advice must therefore always be to contact the court office and explain your problem to them—from the court's point of view there is nothing worse than a difficulty which they only become aware of on the morning of the case.

After a case has been committed and the papers have been sent to the Crown Court by the clerk to the justices, the listing office will enter particulars of the charges in their filing system and send out a copy of the evidence tendered at committal, the certificate of committal and a list of exhibits to each of the parties. Additional copies of the evidence may be supplied on the defence solicitor's request where, for example, he has authority to brief two counsel, but it is as well to ask for these rather than preparing copies yourself. Otherwise, you may well have your photo-copying fee disallowed on taxation. Normally, at the same time as receiving the documents from the court the defence will also receive a formal written request for information. This will ask you to indicate the length of trial, the name of counsel instructed, the nature of the plea and whether there is to be a 'trial within a trial'. You will be well advised to complete this form and indicate by covering letter, or

13 Supreme Court Act 1981, s 77; Crown Court Rules 1982, r 24. S 23 of the Prosecution of Offences Act 1985 will enable rules to be made imposing timetables on criminal proceedings.

telephone, any particular difficulties over listing, for example because you need extra time to trace witnesses. In those courts which are taking part in Lord Justice Watkin's Working Party's pilot scheme, rather fuller information will be required. Although a detailed discussion of the scheme is outside the scope of this work, it should be noted that it envisages a form (Form A) being given to the defence solicitor *at the conclusion of committal proceedings* requesting basic information concerning the case, including the likely plea. This will be followed up by a form (Form B) to be completed by counsel requiring a *firm indication* as to plea and any alternative pleas offered.

In particularly complicated cases a *pre-trial review*[14] may be necessary. This is most likely to arise where there are a large number of co-accused or where the facts are particularly involved. There is however no general system of pre-trial reviews, as is the case in civil litigation and if one is to be held the initiative is usually taken by the court rather than the parties. The tenor of the Watkin's Working Party report is that they are expensive and difficult to list but that there are cases where they may be beneficial. In a large fraud case, for example, where the sole issue is one of dishonesty, it may be that a substantial proportion of the prosecution evidence is not really in dispute so that a large proportion of exhibits and schedules can be agreed.[15]

It is always wise to check with the Crown Court centre as to what procedures they have, if any, for listing interlocutory matters so that you are not caught out. Certain centres, for example, give an early listing for cases involving several co-accused at an early stage for the judge to 'take pleas': those who wish to plead guilty will then be dealt with and the proceedings will be adjourned for the trial of the remaining accused who have pleaded 'not guilty'. Accordingly, the more you get to know about how your local Crown Court works the better.

Interlocutory matters aside, the average case will gradually work its way to the top of the list as earlier cases are disposed of. Approximately a fortnight before it is likely to come on for trial, it will appear in a 'Warned List', a copy of which will be sent to the defence. It is very important, therefore, that you keep your eyes open for any cases in which you are involved and that you contact the listing office *immediately* if any unforeseen problems arise. One advantage of briefing counsel early is that counsel's clerk will also be keeping his eyes open and should thus pick up any cases which happen to get overlooked. Local practice varies, but most Crown Court centres publish a weekly Warned List showing cases that are expected to be tried within the next two or three weeks. Some will subsequently issue a list showing cases fixed for hearing on specified days during the following week but other courts do not publish a fixed weekly list, instead they issue a Daily List each evening indicating those cases which are to be tried the following day. If this system is used the only warning that solicitors and counsel will receive is a telephone call from the listing office the preceding evening. You must, therefore, have a contact point, at which you can always get in touch with your client and witnesses. You should always check with the relevant Crown Court office as to the system operated so that you are not caught unawares. In some cases, the nature of the case renders a haphazard listing impracticable, for example, where the trial is likely to be lengthy or experts are to be called either for the prosecution or the defence. In obvious cases, the court may well take the

14 Procedure at the Central Criminal Court is governed by a series of practice rules which appear in *Archbold* (41st edn) at para 4.43.
15 The power to admit facts under s 10 of the Criminal Justice Act 1967 is not frequently used, partly because of the lack of opportunity at the pre-trial stage.

initiative and give a fixed date of its own motion but if it does not do so it is still possible to apply for a fixture. A hearing is seldom necessary, a written application to the listing office and notification to the prosecution will usually suffice. If this does not succeed, counsel should be instructed to make an application to the presiding judge.

(b) The indictment

At some stage during the pre-trial period the indictment must be drafted and served on the defence. As has already been noted, the Indictment (Procedure) Rules 1971[16] require a bill to be preferred within *28 days* of committal. Since, however, this period may be extended by further 28-day periods on the authority, in the first instance, of an officer of the Crown Court and subsequently on that of a judge, its effect on speeding up the process is minimal. This is particularly so in view of the fact that the accused may be validly tried and convicted on a bill of indictment preferred out of time.[17] This can often cause problems to the defence in that it by no means necessarily follows that the indictment when received, will contain the same charges, or 'counts' as they are known, as those upon which the accused was committed for trial. This is because, as already noted, an indictment may contain *any* counts founded on the facts disclosed by the evidence tendered at committal. Thus, for example, although in the case of Duncan McCarthy (*case 1*) it is unlikely that the drafter of the indictment would add any further counts. On the other hand, if an accused were to be committed for trial on a charge of unlawful taking of a conveyance, it would be quite permissible to add an alternative theft charge (or indeed to *substitute* a theft charge) if the evidence justified it. It can be seen, therefore, how important it is that you receive a copy of the indictment at as early a stage as possible, especially where there are several charges and/or several co-accused. If a copy is not forthcoming, you should make a formal written request in order to get things moving. When it is received it should be carefully compared with the charges in the Certificate of Committal for any additions, substitutions or deletions.

Each count charged in an indictment must contain a statement of the offence, a reference to any statute creating it and *particulars* which broadly set out:

- The full name of the accused;
- The date of the alleged offence (sometimes this will need to be expressed as a day unknown);
- The elements of the offence;
- The party injured.

The detailed discussion of the drafting and contents of indictments is outside the scope of this book but one point of particular importance needs to be noticed, namely that an accused may be charged with more than one offence in the same indictment and that more than one accused may be joined in the same indictment provided that the charges are either:

- founded on the *same* facts, or
- part of a series of offences of the *same character* or
- part of a series of offences of *similar character*.[18]

(i) The joinder of offences. The provisions of rule 9 are so wide that the circumstances in which offences may be joined as separate counts in an

16 Indictment (Procedure) Rules 1971, r 5.
17 *R v Sheerin* (1976) 64 Cr App Rep 68, CA and *R v Soffe* (1982) 75 Cr App Rep 133, CA.
18 Indictment Rules, r 9.

INDICTMENT   No.1357

THE CROWN COURT at EXCHESTER

The Queen v DUNCAN McCARTHY

charged as follows:
STATEMENT OF OFFENCE

Count 1
Burglary contrary to section 9(1)(b) of the Theft
Act 1968

PARTICULARS OF OFFENCE
DUNCAN McCARTHY, between the 5th and 6th days
of August 198-, having entered as a trespasser a
building known as the Social Club, Weyford General
Hospital, stole therefrom the sum of £50-09p in money.

INDICTMENT   No.   007

THE CROWN COURT at   EXCHESTER

The Queen v   JOHN SMITH and ARTHUR JONES
charged as follows:—

COUNT 1

Statement of Offence
Theft contrary to s1 of the Theft Act 1968
Particulars of Offence
JOHN SMITH on 1st February 1984 stole 5,000
cigar ettes belonging to Newgate Newsagents Ltd

COUNT 2

Statement of Offence
Theft contrary to s1 of the Theft Act 1968
Particulars of Offence
ARTHUR JONES on 1st February 1984 stole
5,000 cigarettes belonging to Newgate Newsagents Ltd

COUNT 3

Statement of Offence
Handling stolen goods contrary to s22(1), Theft Act 1968
Particulars of Offence
ARTHUR JONES on a day unknown between 31st January 1984
and 1st March 1984 dishonestly undertook or assisted in
the retention of certain stolen goods namely 5,000
cigarettes belonging to Newgate Newsagents Ltd knowing
or believing the same to be stolen.

indictment are virtually limitless. Provided one or other of the preceding three criteria is satisfied joinder is permissible. Several and the offences can thus be tried together provided the court is of the opinion that the accused will not be prejudiced or embarrassed.[19]

EXAMPLES

(i) V's car was taken without his consent. Two weeks later whilst driving it D is stopped by the police. On the evidence it is not clear whether D stole it, took it without the owner's consent, or was driving it knowing that the conveyance had been so taken by someone else. It is quite permissible for the indictment to contain three alternative counts of theft, taking, and driving respectively. No injustice is done to D and both the judge and the prosecution will explain to the jury that the counts are in the alternative.

(ii) D commits a robbery with the aid of a firearm using a stolen car. In the course of attempting to escape he shoots and seriously wounds a security guard and runs over and kills a pedestrian. Again, it is quite permissible, and indeed common sense, to join as counts in the same indictment charges of robbery, firearm offences, taking a vehicle without consent, wounding with intent and causing death by reckless driving.

In both the above examples the offences arise out of the same 'facts', although the facts constituting each offence are neither identical or contemporaneous.[20]

Greater potential injustice is likely to arise where joinder is sanctioned on the ground that the charges form part of a series of offences of 'same or similar character'.

EXAMPLES

(i) D is charged with sexual offences of similar nature in respect of three small boys. Not only may the three offences be joined as separate counts in the same indictment but in addition, provided that there is a sufficient nexus of 'striking similarity' the judge may direct the jury that evidence on count 1 is capable of corroborating the evidence on counts 2 and 3 etc.[1]

(ii) D is committed for trial on charges arising out of three armed robberies. Although there are no features of 'striking similarity' all three offences may still be joined as counts in the same indictment and thus be tried together. Prosecution counsel and the judge will, however, make it clear to the jury that each count must be considered separately in complete isolation from the other two.

As can be seen, the potential prejudice may in some ways be greater in EXAMPLE (ii) than EXAMPLE (i), nevertheless, the Court of Appeal has consistently upheld refusals by the trial judge to order separate trials even though the offences, albeit of the same or similar character, are not linked in any way. The leading case on the topic, *Ludlow v Metropolitan Police Commissioner*[2] illustrates just how tenuous the nexus can be for rule 9 to be satisfied. In that case the appellant was charged with, (i) attempted theft from a public house in Acton, and (ii) robbery from another public house in Acton some 16 days later in which he was alleged to have paid for a drink and snatched the money back. The House of Lords upheld joinder of these two counts on the basis that there was sufficient nexus both as to the facts, and the legal nature of the offences.

If, therefore, the accused faces an indictment charging several counts the *Ludlow* principle necessarily dictates that his chances of having them tried

19 Indictments Act 1915, s 5(3).
20 See *R v Barrell and Wilson* (1979) 69 Cr App Rep 250, CA.
 1 See eg *DPP v Boardman* [1975] AC 421, HL.
 2 [1971] AC 29, HL. See also *R v Kray* (1969) 53 Cr App Rep 569, CA.

separately are poor. There are two lines of attack, both of which will need to be discussed with counsel at an early stage, again thus emphasising the importance of obtaining a copy of the indictment as soon as possible. The first line is to argue that there is insufficient nexus even to satisfy the requirements of rule 9. For example, in two recent cases, convictions on counts alleging conspiracy to defraud and receiving the proceeds of a burglary,[3] and using a driving licence with intent to deceive and dangerous driving (the two offences being committed a month apart),[4] have been quashed on the ground of misjoinder. However, in another more recent case joinder was upheld where the indictment contained counts alleging handling a credit card stolen in a burglary, and the burglary itself.[5] The second line is to argue that notwithstanding technical compliance with rule 9, the court should be asked to exercise its discretion to order separate trials under Indictments Act 1915, s 5(3) on the ground that the joint trial of several counts would be prejudicial or embarrassing to the accused and that separate trials are required in the interest of justice. An example of the latter would be where one count is of a scandalous nature and likely to arouse hostile feelings in the minds of the jury.[6]

(ii) Joinder of offenders. It is equally permissible for two or more accused to be charged in the same indictment. They may be charged jointly in one count with committing the same offence. Alternatively, the indictment may contain several counts charging co-accused with separate offences provided that there is some linking factor, for example, two accused charged with offences of violence against separate victims both of which arise out of the same incident.[7]

Note also that s 27(1) of the Theft Act 1968 provides that where goods have been stolen, any number of persons who may have handled them at any time may be joined in the same indictment. The thief can also be joined in under the general rule considered above.

It can be seen, therefore, that perusal of the indictment is an important task which solicitors should not leave entirely to counsel. Although many, if not all, of the above points are strictly speaking within counsel's province, it is part of the solicitor's duty to instruct counsel properly and, if nothing else, press for an early sight of the indictment. In addition, clients will often be perplexed and dismayed at the possible prejudice caused by joint trials and you will therefore need to be able to explain these provisions adequately, however unsatisfactory they may seem to the client. Should an application for severance be necessary this can be made to the judge in open court on the day of the trial before the jury is empanelled, but normally counsel will advise that it be made to the presiding judge at as early a stage as possible. A hearing date should be obtained from the listing office and all other parties notified. Other applications relating to the indictment, for example, to amend one or more of the counts are usually dealt with at the start of the trial. This topic will be briefly considered later in the chapter.

(2) Final preparation

This part of the chapter outlines the final steps in preparing the defence case.

3 *R v Harward* (1981) 73 Cr App Rep 168, CA.
4 *R v Bogdal* [1982] RTR 395.
5 *R v McGlinchey* (1983) 78 Cr App Rep 282; see also *R v Bell* (1984) Cr App Rep 305.
6 See remarks of Lord Goddard CJ in *R v Sims* (1946) 31 Cr App Rep 158 at p 164.
7 *R v Assim* [1966] 2 QB 249.

In an ideal world this should involve little more than putting the finishing touches to the work done prior to committal.[8]

(a) Brief to counsel

Counsel must be briefed as early and as thoroughly as possible. As has already been shown, the system of listing cases for trial sometimes results in cases coming on for hearing quite suddenly when the counsel of your choice is involved in another case. Another member of chambers may have to present the case at very short notice, accordingly, a properly prepared brief is essential to enable him to find his way through the papers and present the case adequately.

Styles of drafting a brief differ, and no two solicitors, however competent, would prepare a brief on the same case in exactly the same way. There are, however, a number of standard features that a well-drawn brief should always contain. It will be headed with the relevant branch of the Crown Court, case number, the words '*Regina v* [*name of the defendant or defendants*], and be entitled 'Brief to counsel to appear on behalf of the defendant (name)'. Next should come a list of the enclosures that are being sent with the brief. This will include the committal documents received from the Crown Court, a copy of the indictment if it has yet been received, the client's proof of evidence and the proofs of any defence witnesses, and, finally, a copy of any legal aid order. All the enclosures must be clearly numbered so that they can be referred to in the body of the brief.

The main part of the brief comprises a description of the case for the prosecution and defence, summarizing the evidence to be presented, with cross references to the enclosures where appropriate. It should also include any points that you wish to raise with counsel on matters of law. The following order of presentation is suggested:

(i) Summarize the prosecution and defence cases;

(ii) Go through each of the prosecution witness's statements in turn commenting on their strengths and weaknesses and highlighting disputed issues and points of evidence;

(iii) Do likewise with the defence case.

It should conclude with information relevant to sentence so that in the event of the client being found guilty counsel can move to mitigation immediately.

Obviously the length of the brief will depend on the individual case. Practice will teach a solicitor to try and steer a middle course between a brief that consists of little more than a covering letter with the papers enclosed, and one that appears to be a potted version of *Archbold*.

Finally, you should include with the brief, but separate from it, a short set of instructions to counsel to advise on appeal. Although many solicitors do not do this, it is the required procedure, and has the advantage that in the event of conviction the process of appeal can be speeded up. It will, of course, be covered by the legal aid order.

When the brief is sent down to counsel you will have to discuss with the counsel's clerk the fee for the brief, unless the client is on legal aid. The back sheet should be marked with the fee or the words 'legal aid', as appropriate.

When should the brief be submitted? As already stated, the brief should be prepared as early as possible. If other documents, such as the indictment, materialise later these can be sent along together with a covering letter or a

8 If a solicitor has a 'through' legal aid order, he can start preparing for trial before committal, otherwise he will only be paid for the work relating to the committal.

BLANKSHIRE POLICE

Notice to defendant: proof by written statement

(C.J. Act 1967, s. 9; M.C. Act 1980, s. 102; M.C. Rules 1981, r. 70)

In the (county of Blankshire, Petty Sessional Division of Camborough).
To .McCarthy., of 11 Inkerman Terrace, Weyford, Blankshire

On the 1st day of Sept..., 19.8 the Magistrates' Court sitting at Weyford will hear evidence relating to the following charge(s) against you.
Burglary, s9(1)(b) Theft Act 1968

This offence (or these offences) may only be tried before a jury (or may be tried before a jury or by the Magistrates' Court) (or may be tried by the Magistrates' Court).

Written statements have been made by the witnesses named below and copies of their statements are enclosed. Each of these statements will be tendered in evidence before the magistrates unless you want the witness to give oral evidence. If you want any of these witnesses to give oral evidence you should inform me as soon as possible. (*If you do not do so within 7 days of receiving this notice and the offence(s) is/are tried by the Magistrates' Court you will lose your right to prevent the statement being tendered in evidence and will be able to require the attendance of the witness only with the leave of the Court. If the offence(s) is/are not tried by the Magistrates' Court this time limit will not apply but) if you have not informed me that you want the witness to attend he will not be present when you appear before the magistrates and delay and expense will be caused if he has then to be called.

(† A reply form (and prepaid envelope) is/are enclosed and it will help to save time and expense if you reply whether or not you wish any of these witnesses to give oral evidence.

If you intend to consult a solicitor about your case you should do so at once and hand this notice and the statements to him so that he may deal with them.)

Names of witnesses whose statements are enclosed: Frank Price, Ann Wallace, Norman Stanley, Sgt Trinder, DS Forsyth DC Tarbuck, Sgt Lander (custody)

Address any reply to: Mr Lloyd, Blankshire County Prosecuting Solicitor, Palace Road, Exchester

(signed) ....
(on behalf of the Prosecutor)

* Omit if offence cannot be tried by magistrates court.
† Omit if documents are sent to defendant's solicitor.

1 D. C. Tarbuck's statement is virtually identical to that of D. S. Forsyth and is omitted.
2 Custody officer—omitted.
3 This includes on Interrogation Record as on exhibit. Extract only supplied.

BLANKSHIRE POLICE

EXCHESTER
.... Division

WEYFORD
.... Station

DUNCAN McCARTHY
.... Name of Defendant

9999999/M
.... CRO No.

PREVIOUS CONVICTIONS

SENTENCE	COURT	DATE	OFFENCE	RELEASE DATE
2 Fine:£5	Weyford Juvenile Court		Theft	
2 Supervision disqualified for 1 year	Weyford Juvenile Court		Taking a conveyance No driving licence No insurance	
3 Detention Centre	Guildfleet Magistrates' Court		Burglary	

IN THE CROWN COURT AT EXCHESTER   LISTING NO. 1357

REGINA

V

DUNCAN McCARTHY

BRIEF TO COUNSEL FOR THE DEFENDANT

Counsel will find herewith:

1.   Copy Indictment

2.   Prosecution Statements tendered at committal under s.102 Magistrates'
     Courts Act 1980

3.   Defendant's Proof of Evidence

4.   Folder containing Proofs of Evidence of Defence Witnesses Tina McCarthy,
     Charles Hardy, Raymond Carter and statement of Jacqueline Stoddard
     served under S.9 Criminal Justice Act 1967

5.   Copy Custody Record

6.   Particulars of Alibi served on Prosecution in accordance with S.11
     Criminal Justice Act 1967

7.   Report of Inquiry Agent James Dawson with sketch plan and photographs
     of Ward 3, Weyford General Hospital attached

8.   Chronology of Events

9.   List of Defendant's previous convictions

10. Legal Aid Order

11. Instructions to Counsel to advise on appeal

Instructing solicitors act for the defendant Duncan McCarthy who was committed
on his own election by the Weyford Magistrates on 1st September 198–
to stand trial on a charge of burglary. Counsel is referred to the copy
indictment herewith (enclosure 1) which contains one count of burglary
to which the defendant intends to plead not guilty.

Counsel will see from the prosecution statements (<u>enclosure 2</u>) and the
chronology prepared by instructing solicitors (<u>Document 8</u>) that the facts of
the offence are very straightforward. The defendant is employed as a porter
by Weyford General Hospital whose clubhouse was burgled at approximately 1.20 a.m.
on **6** August 198 . There can be little dispute that the offence was actually
committed at the time alleged. The sole issue is whether or not it was committed
by the defendant.

The prosecution will no doubt argue that there are three items of evidence
which identify the defendant as the culprit. Firstly, the night nurse, Ann Wallace,
will say that she saw the defendant in the hospital grounds round about the
time the offence was committed. Secondly, the police found notes of a similar
type and denomination (in particular a Scottish £5 note) in the defendant's
wallet when they searched his premises (see evidence of Frank Price and D.S. Forsyth).
Thirdly, certain replies made by the defendant to D.S. Forsyth at Weyford
Police station are capable of being construed as a confession.

The defence is one of alibi and the counsel should note in this context that
particulars complying with S.11 Criminal Justice Act 1967 were served on the
prosecution within 7 days of committal (see <u>enclosure 6</u>). The defendant will
explain the presence of the £5 note by saying that this was acquired during
a holiday in Scotland in June of this year and that his somewhat belligerent
and unco-operative attitude whilst under interrogation stemmed from his previous
contact with the police. With regard to the latter point counsel is referred
to his record of previous convictions (<u>enclosure 10</u>) and is particularly requested
to consider whether or not, and if so at what stage, his character should
be revealed to the jury in view of the provisions of S.1(f) Criminal Evidence
Act 1898.

Turning now to the individual statements tendered at committal (<u>enclosure 2</u>) counsel
will note in general terms that although they contain certain potentially inadmissible
material and considerable scope for cross-examination, instructing solicitors
took the view that a section 6(2) committal was more appropriate in this case.

Statements have been left in their unvarnished form in accordance with the
direction in R v Weaver [1968] 1QB 353 . No doubt counsel will draw such matters
to prosecuting counsel's attention as he thinks fit. Counsel will note that
the prosecution have confirmed that none of the witnesses whose statements
have been tendered have previous convictions and that they are not in possession
of any "unused material" within the Attorny General's Practice Direction.
Counsel will further note that with the exception of Norman Stanley all prosecution
witnesses have been fully bound. Each witness will now be considered individually.

Ann Wallace.

She will say that she saw the defendant on two occasions, once at 9 p.m. and
later at 12.55 a.m. In instructing solicitors view her evidence as to the
incident at 9 p.m. is irrelevant. It can only be admissible, if at all, under
the res gestae principle (see for example O'Leary v R (1946) 73 C.LR 402.
Instructing solicitors took the view that as a matter of law it was not a
matter that could be raised on committal (R v Horsham JJ ex parte Bukhari
(1981) 74 Crim App R 291). Instructing solicitors nevertheless consider that
the 9 p.m. incident should go before the jury, since it may then be suggested
that the 12.55 a.m. "identification" was brought about by an association of
ideas through having seen the defendant earlier that evening.

So far as the second "identification" is concerned, subject to what counsel
has to say, instructing solicitors are of the opinion that a direction under
R v Turnbull [1977] QB 224 will be necessary having regard to the highly unsatisfactory circumstances in which it took place. In view of the fact that
this is such a crucial issue instructing solicitors arranged with the hospital
for our inquiry agent Mr. Dawson to attend to take photographs and prepare
a sketch plan of the relevant area to assist counsel in cross-examination
(see enclosure 9). Mr. Dawson will attend court in order to prove the sketch
plan and photographs unless counsel otherwise advises.

Frank Price

This witness will give evidence of the theft from the till and the amount
stolen. He will clearly be given leave by the judge to refresh his memory
from the till roll should this be necessary. But for the fact that he refers
to there being a Scottish £5 note in the "float" his evidence would not be
controversial. Counsel should note that he only refers to a "Scottish £5
note" and not a "Royal Bank of Scotland £5 note". Instructing solicitors
were tempted to ask for a S.6(1) committal in order to cross-examine Price
at the committal proceedings but finally took the view that any element of
surprise would be lost and that counsel would prefer to be left with a full
range of options for cross-examination at the trial.

Norman Stanley

Since this witness does little more than establish the time span within which
the burglary must have taken place instructing solicitors took the view that
there was nothing to be gained by this witness giving oral evidence and thus
agreed to his being conditionally bound. He would clearly have been entitled
to refresh his memory from the entry made in the security incident book if
he had given oral evidence and this may therefore be admitted as an exhibit
subject to the leave of the court.

Terence Michael Trinder (Sergeant)

This officer does no more than confirm the evidence of the previous witness
save that the references to the defendant in the closing sentences are clearly
inadmissible hearsay and in any event highly prejudicial. Instructing solicitors
have indicated to the prosecution that provided that a fresh statement is
prepared and served under section 9 of the Criminal Justice Act 1967 with
the offending sentences deleted instructing solicitors will be quite happy
to dispense with the attendance of this witness. It does however raise the
interesting speculation as to how the police "got on" to the the defendant
since he was clearly known to one or other of the officers.

<u>Detective Sergeant Peter Forsyth</u>
<u>and Detective Constable Bruce Tarbuck</u>

As is common, these two officers' statements are identical. The evidence
that they will give is prejudicial in three respects. Firstly, they will
give evidence of the wallet and money found in McCarthy's possession. The
explanation as to this has already been summarised and will be dealt with
in greater detail in due course. Counsel will note from the defendant's proof
of evidence that he denies giving permission for the search but little is
likely to be gained from pursuing this line. The prosecution would no doubt
argue that the two officers were entitled to be on the premises under S.17
(1) (b) of the Police and Criminal Evidence Act 1984 in that they had entered
to effect an arrest for an arrestable offence. It could however be argued
that, technically speaking, having located the defendant, their powers of
search under S.17 were exhausted. They should, in theory, have arrested him
first, and only then proceeded to search the premises under S.18 of the 1984
Act. Nevertheless, in instructing solicitors' view it is quite clear that
there is no possibility of successfully arguing that the evidence of what
was found should be excluded under S.78(1) of the 1984 Act.

The second prejudicial aspect is the defendant's reaction when arrested, in
particular the sentence "Just my luck to get nicked over a Jock fiver". Counsel
will note that the defendant denies ever having said this. Although the statement
is in any event equivocal counsel has no choice but to put the defendant's
denial to the two officers. There is, however the danger that if this is
done too vociferously the defendant will be liable to cross-examination as
to his previous character and convictions under S.1(f) (ii) Criminal Evidence
Act 1898 when he gives evidence. This aspect is considered further in the
next paragraph.

The third prejudicial aspect, albeit more oblique is the point that the defendant
at no time sought to reveal his defence to the two officers, and was generally
sullen and unco-operative. Although the Interrogation Record does not contain
any unequivocal confession of guilt it is nevertheless likely to create a
bad impression. Whilst instructing solicitors accept that the defendant was
merely exercising his "right of silence" the judge, as he is entitled to do,
is likely to make some oblique reference to this in his summing-up. Thus,
when the accused gives evidence, as he clearly must, the account that he will
give of his movements, although credible, will be twisted by his failure to
put it forward at the earliest possible moment. Instructing solicitors have
already pointed out that the defendant attributes his behaviour to his previous
contacts with the police. If he is to put this explanation forward this will

effectively result in his whole character being put in issue, thus freeing
the prosecution from the constraints imposed by S.1(f) Criminal Evidence Act
1898. In the circumstances counsel may well take the view that it is best
to bring out his previous convictions in chief, especially since the defendant
has always pleaded guilty on previous occasions and has shown positive signs
of settling down since his last conviction. So far as the defence case is concerned
the accused will give evidence on oath in accordance with his proof (enclosure
3) and will say that he left the hospital social club at 9.30 p.m. with the
intention of going straight home but bumped into a casual acquaintance known
only to him as "John" who took him to the "Robin Hood" public house where
he stayed until 10.45 p.m.. Counsel will note that he will say that a £20
note found in his wallet was acquired from "John" with whom he changed it
for four £5 notes, part of £30 in £5 notes that he had drawn out of the bank
that morning.

The defendant will further say that he arrived home at approximately 11.30 p.m.,
by this time extremely drunk, a fact which his wife (see enclosure 4) will
confirm.

So far as the evidence of D.S. Forsyth and D.C. Tarbuck is concerned, the
defendant will say that the two officers entered without consent and that
the interrogation at 11 Inkerman Terrace was considerably more hostile than
their statements would suggest, references being made to the defendant's previous
convictions. It may be significant that D.S. Forsyth and the defendant are
known to each other: counsel will note that the defendant says in his proof
that on a previous occasion D.S. Forsyth had falsely accused him of being
the ringleader of a gang of burglars but that no further action had been taken.
The defendant will say that it is against this background that he refused
to co-operate with the police and failed to put forward his alibi at an early
stage. Instructing solicitors have already drawn counsel's attention to the
implications of giving evidence along these lines. Apart from this however
some of the replies attributable to the defendant are unequivocally damaging
and counsel may well feel that cross-examination of the two police officers
should be handled as gently as possible.

Finally, the defendant will give evidence as to the circumstances in which
he came to be in possession of the Royal Bank of Scotland £5 note. As already
noted he will say that it is a left-over from his Scottish holiday earlier
this year and will further say that he did not cash it because it thought,
erroneously, that an English bank would not accept it without charging commission.

Counsel is now referred to the proofs of evidence of the other defence witnesses (see enclosure 4). Instructing solicitors have checked with prosecution who confirm that there are no convictions recorded against Tina McCarthy, but Hardy and Carter both have previous convictions, albeit several years ago, for minor offences of criminal damage and assault. Dealing first with Tina McCarthy counsel will note that she will confirm that the defendant arrived home at approximately 11.30 p.m. very drunk but not incoherent. She will further say that she went to bed and that after hearing him blundering about in the kitchen he finally came upstairs at 12.30 a.m. and came to bed. Further, whe will say that she was awoken at 2.30 a.m. having heard raised voices down-stairs. Thereafter, her evidence in part confirms that defendant's account of events, in particular with regard to the aggressive attitude of the police to the defendant's inebriated condition. It is crucial to appreciate that if her evidence is believed the defendant must be entitled to an acquattal since it seems clear that the burglary must have taken place at some time between 11.15 p.m. and 1.20 a.m. It would therefore have been impossible for the defendant to have committed the burglary and have been home by 11.30 p.m. even if an unknown accomplice had brought him home by car. For this reason instructing solicitors have questioned this witness most carefully as to how she can be sure of the time that the defendant arrived home. Counsel will note that her attention was drawn to the time because a late-night television programme had been about to finish and she did not wish to miss the end.

Turning now to the evidence of Charles Hardy and Raymond Carter, counsel will note that, unfortunately for the defence, they both parted company with the defendant shortly after leaving the social club and can therefore only give evidence to the fact that he had been drinking heavily. Accordingly, unless counsel otherwise advises, instructing solicitors do not propose to ask them to give evidence.

In order to render the defendant's explanation of the Scottish £5 note more plausible, instructing solicitors interviewed the manageress of the travel agency, Jacqueline Stoddard to confirm that the McCarthys booked a holiday during June of this year. A statement was served on the prosecution under S.9 Criminal Justice Act 1967 exhibiting an extract from the travel agency's books with a view to proving the booking under S.68 of the Police and Criminal Evidence Act 1984 but the prosecution have since written to instructing solicitors indicating that prosecuting counsel will formally admit the fact of the Scottish holiday under S.10 Criminal Justice Act 1967.

So far as the accused's possession of the £20 note is concerned, instructing
solicitors are obtaining a statement from the manager of the Weyford branch
of the Midland Provincial Bank exhibiting a computer-printed extract from
the defendant's bank account to prove the withdrawal of £30 on the morning
of 5th August. Unless otherwise advised by counsel instructing solicitors
propose to serve this on the prosecution under S.9 of the 1967 Act with a
certificate under S.69 of the 1984 Act. Instructing solicitors feel sure
that the prosecution will agree to the statement being read and the printout
being admitted under the Bankers Books Evidence Act 1879 in combination with
S.69 of the 1984 Act. Unfortunately however, instructing solicitors' endeavours
to trace the man referred to as "John" have proven unsuccessful. It was hoped
that he could confirm the defendant's movements up to 11 p.m. and the changing
of the £20 note. Reporting restrictions were not lifted at the committal
proceedings, and although a short advertisment appeared in the Weyford Echo
requesting "John" to come forward, he has not done so.

[The brief will next contain information enabling counsel to present mitigation
in the event of McCarthy being convicted. It will conclude as follows]

Instructing solicitors will arrange a conference with counsel's clerk as soon
as the case appears in the warned list. Instructing solicitors will be happy
to assist in any way if counsel wish further steps to be taken before them.
Counsel is accordingly requested to appear at the Crown Court at Exchester
to represent the defendant at his trial.

The following is an extract from the interview record Exhibit PF3 referred

to in D.S. FORSYTH'S statement.

McCARTHY has just been shown wallet and contents.

Q.   Do you admit that this is the wallet that was found under your mattress?

A.   Yes

Q.   How did you come by this Royal Bank of Scotland five pound note?

A.   Well I wouldn't have been given it by a Scotsman, would I?

Q.   Don't be facetious. Don't you realise you're in big trouble?

A.   If I told you the truth you wouldn't believe me.

Q.   I just might. Why don't you try?

A.   No, it's just a waste of time.

supplementary set of instructions. Some solicitors go so far as to send little more than a backsheet marked 'Brief to Counsel' down to chambers containing the barest details along with a copy of the legal aid order as soon as the case has been committed and deliver the main brief later. This will ensure that counsel's clerk is aware of the case and will watch out for it in the list. It also means that should the case be listed at very short notice *someone* from those chambers will be available to cover it.

Advice on evidence and conferences with counsel. Advice on evidence is not sought often enough in criminal cases, unlike in civil cases where it is sought as a matter of course. If the case is complicated in any way because, for example, there are several co-accused, it is based on complex facts, or there are difficult points of evidence involved, you should consider obtaining advice on evidence from counsel, in writing if necessary. If a detailed brief has not yet been delivered, you must prepare and send a separate set of instructions. These should contain as much detail as possible, and should be set out in exactly the same way as the brief, save that they will conclude, 'counsel is accordingly instructed to advise on evidence'. If, on the other hand, the brief has already been delivered all that is normally required is a short set of instructions.

Quite apart from seeking advice on evidence, the client ought to meet the person who is to represent him. Counsel will also want to meet the client and discuss the finer points of the case with him, particularly as he is likely to be the most important defence witness. It should be noted that the rules of the bar forbid counsel to meet any witness other than the client or an expert. If the client is on bail, then it is relatively easy to arrange for a conference with counsel at his chambers by telephoning counsel's clerk to make an appointment. If, however, he is in custody you will have to book an appointment with the relevant prison or remand centre. This normally has to be done in writing. Before doing so, you should check with counsel's clerk so as to fix a day when counsel will be able to attend. Conferences in prison need to be organised well in advance especially since they will often need to be held outside normal visiting hours.

Finally, whenever counsel advises orally take a careful note. Endeavours should be made to carry out his advice, and he should be contacted if it proves impossible to follow. It is particularly important for you to have kept a good note of oral advice if the counsel of your choice is not available for the trial and the brief has to be passed to another member of chambers. The new barrister will not necessarily know what his predecessor has advised.

(b) Alibi notice

It will be recalled that the accused is required to give particulars to the prosecution of any alibi upon which he intends to rely at trial within seven days of committal. He must also give the name and address of any witness that he proposes to call in support of the alibi.[9] There is no prescribed form, and it is normal practice simply to supply the information by letter. The duty is a continuing one, so that if, for example, further witnesses are traced, their details must be supplied. You should always ask the prosecutor to notify you if and when the police intend to interview the witness, so that you can be present.

9 For the meaning of 'alibi' see p 328 ante. Alibi witnesses should always be traced and interviewed and their bona fides established as soon as possible, since should particulars be given and the witness then fail to attend for interview by the police or not appear at the trial, the prosecution may be permitted to adduce the alibi notice as tending to disprove the alibi: see *R v Rossborough* (1985) Times, 1 April, CA, discussed and criticised by O'Connor in *Legal Action*, July 1985, p 93.

(c) Notices of further evidence

As a matter of practice, when the prosecution proposes to call a witness whose evidence was not tendered at committal they will serve a Notice of Further Evidence, accompanied by the witness's statement which will usually be tendered under s 9 of the Criminal Justice Act 1967. The procedure will be used, for example, in cases where the prosecution have deliberately decided not to present all of their evidence at committal, where more evidence has come to light as a result of forensic tests, where a co-accused has elected to turn 'Queen's Evidence' or where further investigations have shown an alibi witness to be unreliable. The steps that must be taken are the same as with any other s 9 statement received from the prosecution; you must take your client's instructions and consider whether the evidence is contested. If it is, you must reply within the seven-day period requesting that the witness be called. If the brief has been sent to counsel, you must send him the notice, together with the client's comments as soon as possible. In a situation where time is of the essence, counsel should be telephoned, especially when further witnesses may need to be interviewed in order to counter the new evidence.

(d) Getting the witnesses to court

After committal the defence must find out if there are any periods in the near future when the client or any of his witnesses cannot attend court for important reasons, such as pre-booked holidays or periods in hospital. You should notify the listing officer at the Crown Court of such dates as soon as possible.

If you think that any of your witnesses might be unreliable, or might find it difficult to attend court, you should obtain a witness summons and serve it on them.[10] You should not wait until the case arrives in the warned list to do this. Some solicitors summon all their witnesses as a matter of course and it may perhaps be that this 'safety first' approach is the best one.

Three other matters must also be attended to. First, if the client is on bail he must be kept informed of the case's progress. Although the police will probably notify him of the hearing date, it is his solicitor's job to tell him when he is required to surrender to bail. Secondly, if he is on bail with sureties, you must *ensure* that they attend court on the first day of the trial so that bail may be renewed for the duration of the proceedings without undue difficulty. Thirdly, you must not forget to notify the prosecution and the court if you require any of the prosecution witnesses who were conditionally bound to give oral evidence, or if the defence no longer requires the attendance of any fully bound witness.

3 THE TRIAL

(1) Introduction—the environment of the court

The constitution of the Crown Court is described in chapter 2.[10a] As with magistrates' courts, the Crown Court may vary from the magnificent opulence of Lewes, with its wooden benches and hammerbeam roofs to the 'cinema' style in concrete and glass of the Central Criminal Court and the Crown Court at Winchester, and the Hogarthian bustle of Inner London.

10 For the procedure for obtaining witness orders see p 190 et seq, ante.
10a See p 25, ante.

As much for your own confidence as for any other reason, you should take the opportunity of calling in at your local court and finding your way around before you are required to attend on a case of your own.

The court room itself will be laid out similarly to a magistrates' court, save that it will be bigger and grander. The judge will sit behind a bench on a raised daïs, facing the accused in the dock. Immediately in front of the judge, at a lower level, is a desk, at which the clerk will sit. In the well of the court will be two rows of benches for counsel, with a further row behind for solicitors, immediately beneath the dock. The jury box will be on one side of the court room and on the opposite side, near the bench, will be the witness box. On the same side will be benches for the press, police officers, the usher and probation officers. There will be seats for the public, usually in a gallery upstairs.

A TYPICAL CROWN COURT

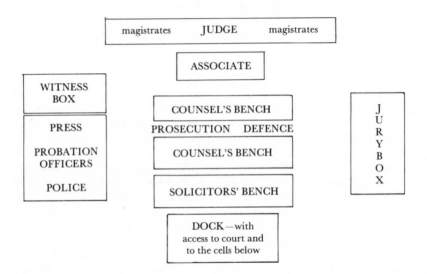

A typical Crown Court layout. There can be variations from this format. The public seating is usually in an upper gallery. In some class one Crown Courts the public gallery is arranged so that the jury is not visible to members of the public in the gallery.

(2) The solicitor's duties at the trial

Since the case will be presented by counsel the defence solicitor must be prepared to play the supporting role. That does not mean, however, that his day will be devoid of interest or occupation! It is unusual for admitted staff to attend with counsel, partly because it is not financially viable to do so. Solicitors' offices send all variety of persons to attend on counsel, from articled clerks and office juniors to aged relatives. Nevertheless, if the case requires the presence of a solicitor it is his duty to be there. The principal matters to which you must attend are set out below.

(a) **Counsel.** Identify yourself to counsel if you do not know him already. Counsel will usually want to have a final conference with the client before the case starts. You should be present at this. This is particularly important if there have been any discussions between counsel over compromising the proceedings. 'Holding counsel's hand' is often left to articled clerks and junior staff. If you are ever in any doubt as to a course that is being advocated you should always contact your principal or another senior member of staff.

(b) **The Client.** Assuming your client is not in custody, you should make sure that he reports to the usher and remains somewhere where he can be easily located. If he is in custody you should go to the cells beneath the court to find out if he has arrived from remand prison.

(c) **Witnesses.** You must keep a lookout for your witnesses and be prepared to telephone the office to put enquiries in hand if they do not appear at or shortly after the time arranged. Having located them, you must ensure that they remain somewhere where they can easily be found, and that they realise they must not 'wander off' (especially not to listen to the trial!).

(d) **Messages from the dock.** Make sure that your client has a supply of pencils and pieces of paper. He should be encouraged to pass notes down to you on matters that occur to him, but you should also impress upon him that it is for counsel to conduct the case. Messages should be passed to counsel as unobtrusively as possible. In particular, not a muscle should be moved whilst a witness is taking the oath.

(e) **Holding counsel's hand.** You must listen to the case and take a careful note of the evidence. Even the best counsel makes mistakes from time to time. In addition, the judge may ask a question to which counsel does not immediately know the answer. You should be prepared to supply counsel with information, papers or documents at short notice; in other words, you must work with counsel as part of a team.

(f) **Witness expenses.** When the defence witnesses have given evidence you should escort them to the appropriate office in the Crown Court building so that they can be paid their witness expenses; however, if the trial is very hectic, a friendly usher may do this for you.

(g) **Bail.** At each adjournment, you should ensure that counsel applies for bail, although bail will frequently be made continuous throughout the trial. If the client is halfway through his evidence, remember that since he is still on oath you must not discuss the case with him.

(h) **Attendance notes.** At the end of each day, you should complete an attendance note of the exact time spent at court and in travelling and briefly summarize what took place.

(i) **After the verdict.** At the end of the trial the solicitor will accompany counsel in congratulating the client on his acquittal, or in commiserating if he has been convicted. Sentencing procedure will be considered in the next chapter.

(j) **Substitutes.** Finally, it may be that you are unable to spend every day of a long trial at court. Whoever substitutes for you must be of sufficient competence to cope with all the above matters. They must know how and where to contact you or a senior member of the firm in the event of any difficulties arising.

(3) **The course of the trial**

The final section of this chapter explains the significance of the various stages in the trial, but since the part that the solicitor will play in its actual conduct is comparatively insignificant, these will only be considered in outline. Before proceeding further, however, the vexed matter of plea-bargaining must be considered.

Last minute conferences and 'plea bargaining'

There is a tendency and a temptation not to arrange a conference with counsel until the day of the trial. This is particularly so if the client has always intimated that he intends to plead guilty. Even so, it is important to set out material for mitigation in the brief and discuss it with counsel well before the day of the trial. If this is not done there is a danger that important mitigating factors will be overlooked or inadequately presented.

If the client intends to plead not guilty there is a further danger inherent in the last-minute conference. He will naturally be feeling nervous by this stage and will want to get it all over with. He may be amenable to changing his intended plea, particularly if the judge is prepared to give an 'indication' as to the way he is thinking with regard to sentence.

Plea bargaining, in the sense of the prosecution, defence and judge entering into a 'haggle' is not permissible. It is, however, permissible to ask the prosecution if they would 'accept' a plea of guilty to certain counts on the indictment, and not proceed with others. If prosecution counsel considers it to be in the public's interest he or she can indicate to defence counsel that certain pleas would be acceptable. If such a 'compromise' is reached the prosecution do not usually apply to withdraw counts but ask in open court for those counts to which the accused pleads 'not guilty' to 'lie on the file'. This means that they cannot be activated save with the leave of the Court of Appeal or the Crown Court. As an alternative the prosecution and defence may provisionally agree that the accused to plead guilty to a lesser offence. In either of these cases the judge must give his consent in open court.

One of the factors which may influence defence counsel in these negotiations is the question of possible sentence. The judge may be approached by counsel and be asked as to his views on sentence. The judge must not indicate what sentence he intends to pass nor may he specify the effect that a plea of guilty or not guilty would have. He may however indicate that he has a certain type of sentence in mind, irrespective of plea, and specify what that is. Both counsel may be present in these discussions, but it is not generally appreciated that the solicitor may be present too.[11] If counsel thinks that a discussion with the judge will serve some useful purpose, the solicitor should accompany him. If the client has maintained all along that he is innocent, you must not let him be talked into pleading guilty at the last minute, although it is permissible to advise him objectively as to his chances of success. It must, however, be impressed upon him that the final decision is his and his alone.

Stage 1. Commencement

The case will be called on by the usher. As has already been mentioned, part of the solicitor's job at the trial will involve finding out where in the building

---

11 *R v Turner* [1970] 2 QB 321, CA; the court must keep a record of these discussions: *R v Cullen* (1984) Times, 1 December.

the case will be tried, and approximately when. If the client is in custody or has been taken into custody on arrival at court, he will be taken into the dock by a prison officer. Otherwise he should go into court with his solicitor and he will be placed in the dock to sit with a prison officer.

Stage 2. Special pleas in bar

If appropriate, it is at this stage that special pleas are normally raised although they can be raised at any stage. They are rare in practice, but of considerable importance in a small number of cases. The special pleas in bar are as follows.

(*i*) *Autrefois acquit*. The accused has already been tried and acquitted of the offence.

(*ii*) *Autrefois convict*. The accused has already been convicted of the offence.

(*iii*) *Pardon*. The accused has been pardoned by the Queen for the offence.

(*iv*) *A plea to the jurisdiction*. The court has no jurisdiction to try the offence.

(*v*) *A demeurrer*. An objection to the wording of the indictment; this is now probably obsolete, and has been replaced by the procedure whereby defence counsel moves to quash the indictment.

All of these pleas are highly technical and the solicitor will be in counsel's hands if they occur. They are dealt with fully in *Archbold*.[12]

Stage 3. Arraignment

The accused will be asked by the associate to confirm his name and then the counts on the indictment will be 'put' to him in turn and he will be asked whether he pleads 'guilty' or 'not guilty' to each count.

If defence counsel moves to quash the indictment or to amend it, these motions will normally be heard before the plea is taken.

Motions to quash the indictment: The defence may move to quash an indictment or a count in an indictment before the plea is taken. The application is made in open court, and can only be granted on the ground that the indictment:

   (i) is unauthorised, or
  (ii) is fundamentally defective, or charges an offence which was neither committed for trial by the magistrates nor made out by the committal statements and depositions, or
 (iii) is duplicitous.

Motions to amend the indictment

The prosecution counsel may move to amend the indictment. The application must be granted unless, having regard to the merits of the case, the required amendment cannot be made without injustice. The normal time to apply for amendments is before the pleas are taken, although application can also be made at a later stage. Amendment is a convenient way of dealing with the following:[12a]

12 Op cit: paras 4.49 et seq.
12a Motions to quash and amend are dealt with in *Archbold*, op cit, at paras 1.110 and 1.63, respectively.

   (i) counts which are duplicitous;

  (ii) technical defects, such as the victim being incorrectly named; and

 (iii) the addition of a count which cites an offence not presently on the indictment, but in respect of which the prosecution are prepared to accept a plea.

The plea

The accused must enter a plea of guilty or not guilty. He may not enter a plea that is 'equivocal'. An equivocal plea is one that is ambiguous. The classical example involves an allegation of theft by shoplifting, in answer to which the defendant says 'guilty because I took the goods, although I didn't mean to steal'. The potential for ambiguity is twofold: the accused may be saying that he only formed an intention to steal at a later stage, or he may be denying dishonesty. Such an issue is resolved by the court entering a 'not guilty' plea on his behalf. Equivocal pleas are much less likely to arise in trials on indictment than in summary trials, because the accused will almost always be legally represented, and counsel will have carefully taken him through the counts before the trial. If the prosecution has agreed to accept a plea of 'guilty' to some counts and 'not guilty' to others, the defence solicitor must make sure that when his client answers, he tenders the appropriate pleas. There is no harm in turning round to the client, so as to assist him if necessary. The pleas must, however, be his not yours.

An accused may sometimes offer a plea of guilty to a lesser offence. As will shortly be seen, in a limited range of circumstances, specified in the Criminal Law Act 1967, the jury is able to return a verdict of not guilty to the principal offence, but guilty to a lesser one. The prosecutor is not obliged to accept such a plea and may elect to proceed on the original charges, unless a 'bargain' has been struck along the lines discussed earlier.

On rare occasions, the accused may say nothing when asked to plead. This may arise through lack of understanding, a deliberate decision, or some form of mental disturbance. The court must decide if the accused is 'mute of malice' or 'mute by visitation of God'. These quaint phrases seek to distinguish persons who are wilfully silent, from those who are silent for any other reason. A jury must be empanelled to try this issue, the burden being on the prosecution to show 'malice'. If the jury return a verdict of 'mute of malice' a 'not guilty' plea is entered, and the court proceeds to try the case in the usual way. If the jury find the accused 'mute by visitation of God', what happens next will depend on the reason, which must be specified by the jury. If the accused is deaf, or deaf and dumb, the court must adjourn in order to arrange for the attendance of an interpreter. If the cause appears to be insanity, the jury will normally be required to continue and decide if the accused is fit to plead at all. Evidence must be called on this issue by the defence if the accused is represented, but otherwise the prosecution has this duty. If he is found to be unfit to plead, he must be compulsorily detained in a mental hospital unless and until he improves.[13] Otherwise, a 'not guilty' plea is entered. Alternatively, the judge may postpone the issue of fitness to plead, and direct that the case proceeds on the basis of a 'not guilty' plea being entered. The advantage to the accused is that there is then still the possibility of acquittal, whereas if he is found unfit to plead, he must be detained compulsorily.

13 Criminal Procedure (Insanity) Act 1964, s 5.

Stage 4. The jury

After arraignment the jury who will try the case must be empanelled. Potential jurors are summoned by post and must attend the court for the period stated in the summons, usually two weeks. They must attend each day until discharged. This may be before the end of the period, but may be very much longer, if the juror has the misfortune to be allocated to a very long trial. Most jurors sit on three or four trials during their service, as in general trials last a comparatively short time.

Most registered electors, as shown on the electoral roll, are eligible but there are many categories of person who are ineligible or disqualified, for example solicitors and persons who have previously been sentenced to long terms of imprisonment. Furthermore, the court has a discretion to excuse any juror from all or part of his service.[14]

A jury is empanelled after arraignment so that the jurors are not aware of any matters on which the accused has pleaded guilty. Approximately twenty summoned jurors are brought into court from the waiting room set aside for their use (known as the 'jury in waiting'). There is a card for each juror and the associate pulls out twelve at random; these twelve enter the box in turn to take the jury oath, unless challenged by the defence or the prosecution. If a juror is challenged, he must leave the box, and will be replaced by another, selected at random.

Challenges and jury vetting. There are two general rights of challenge:

(i) each accused has the right to make three peremptory challenges (challenges for which no reason need be given);

(ii) each side may challenge individual jurors for 'cause', for example, on the ground that he is disqualified, ineligible or is or might be partial.

In addition, the prosecution may require that individual jurors should 'stand by'. This means that they are excluded from the body of prospective jurors from which the selection will be made unless it is impossible to select a jury without calling on them. Consequently, the prosecution may not have to resort to challenge under (ii) above.

'Jury vetting' arises when the police check whether a potential juror has criminal convictions because it is believed that an attempt is being made to introduce disqualified jurors or a previous trial has been aborted because of attempts to influence jurors. They will also check if it appears 'particularly important' to ensure that disqualified persons do not serve. The police are under no obligation to inform the defence that these checks have been carried out, and will not make any checks on behalf of the defence without the consent of the Director of Public Prosecutions.[15]

Jury vetting goes beyond checking for convictions in cases involving offences concerning national security, or in terrorist cases with a political element. It may only be carried out on the authority of the Attorney General.[16]

Discharge of juries. There are many important provisions which can result in an individual juror being discharged. Occasionally the entire jury may have to be discharged. If the former occurs, the trial may be able to continue. If the entire jury has to be discharged, however, the accused is not acquitted

14 See generally Juries Act 1974; Juries Disqualification Act 1984 and *Archbold,* op cit, paras 4.130 et seq.

15 Recommendations of Association of Chief Police Officers annexed to *Attorney General's Guidelines* (1981) 72 Cr App Rep 16.

16 *Attorney General's Guidelines* (1981) 72 Cr App Rep 14; see also *Archbold,* op cit, para 4.139.

but may, and usually will, be retried. The entire jury most commonly has to be discharged if it accidentally hears some significant inadmissible evidence prejudicial to the accused, or if it is 'hung' (fails to agree upon its verdict at the end of the trial).

Stage 5. The prosecution case

The trial will proceed in a similar order to that on summary trial, but with the added formality. Counsel for the prosecution will outline the case for the Crown by giving a summary of the facts and of the evidence to be presented in support of the charge. He will explain the burden of proof and how his evidence satisfies that burden. If the defence are prepared to make any formal admissions under s 10 of the Criminal Justice Act 1967 this is often a convenient time for this to be done. If, however, there is to be a 'trial within a trial' to determine the admissibility of a confession, prosecution counsel will make no reference to this evidence in his opening.

Each prosecution witness will then give evidence. They will be examined in chief, cross-examined, and re-examined in turn. The judge may ask questions, and the jury may request the judge to ask a question or questions for them. At whatever point it is most convenient to do so counsel will read out the statements tendered under s 102 of the Magistrates' Courts Act 1980, or depositions taken at committal in respect of those witnesses who were conditionally bound at committal and whose presence has not been required by the defence.[16a] He will also read out any statements served after committal under s 9 of the Criminal Justice Act 1967 to which the defence have not objected. Numerous evidential issues may arise during the course of the prosecution's case, for example, inquiry into the competence of a witness or objections to hearsay evidence. If the judge's ruling is sought on a major point he will hear argument from counsel in the absence of the jury. There may also be a 'trial within a trial' as to the admissibility of a disputed confession in the absence of the jury. When all the prosecution evidence has been presented, prosecution counsel will formally close the case. He will not be permitted to call further evidence save in exceptional circumstances, which will be considered later.

Stage 6. Defence submission of no case to answer

At the close of the prosecution case counsel for the defence may make a submission that there is no case to answer on all or any of the charges. This submission is a matter of law, and accordingly the judge must rule on it in the absence of the jury. Counsel for the prosecution is entitled to reply to the submission. If the submission is successful the judge will direct the jury to acquit the accused. The basis of the submission differs from that on summary trial. The test that the judge must apply was recently re-considered by the Court of Appeal in *R v Galbraith*.[17] The judge is only required to accept the submission and direct an acquittal if either:

(i) there is no evidence that the crime has been committed by the accused; or

(ii) the prosecution evidence, taken at its highest, is such that *no* jury, properly directed, could not convict on it.

16a Rarely, he may also tender the statement of a fully bound witness who has died or who otherwise comes within s 13 of the Criminal Justice Act 1925.
17 [1981] 2 All ER 1060, CA.

This differs from the test applicable on summary trial in a subtle but important way. The first limb is very similar in both courts in that it is primarily directed at the prosecution's failure to prove a constituent element of the offence. The second limb differs in that it recognises the separate functions of judge and jury. The test requires the judge to accept the submission only if the evidence is inherently weak, vague or inconsistent. Where, however, the issue revolves around the *reliability* of the evidence or other matters which are within the province of the jury the trial should proceed. Where the submission is based upon unsatisfactory identification evidence[18] the judge is presumably bound by *Galbraith*. Thus, the issue is not whether the evidence is credible, but whether it is so inherently weak that the jury should be denied the opportunity of believing it.

Stage 7. The defence case

The accused will almost invariably be represented but, if not, he must be informed that he is entitled to give evidence if he wants to, but is not obliged to do so. Counsel may make an opening speech, provided that he is calling factual witnessess other than the accused. In practice, however, it is rare for the defence to make an opening speech.

As with summary trials, the accused should normally be called to give evidence first,[19] if he is to do so at all. He will invariably be cross-examined by prosecution counsel. If the prosecution requires leave to cross-examine him as to his previous character and convictions because he has 'thrown away his shield' it will normally be necessary first to obtain leave from the judge in the absence of the jury. Any other defence witnesses will then be called in turn. Defence witnesses' evidence may sometimes be tendered under s 9 of the Criminal Justice Act 1967, although this is not made use of as often as it might be.

Where there is more than one accused the order in which their cases are presented is primarily determined by the order in which their names appear on the indictment.[20] If they are represented by one counsel, they are presumed to be running a joint defence.[1] When all the defence evidence has been presented, defence counsel will formally close his case.

Stage 8. Rebutting evidence

The prosecution may occasionally apply for leave to call such evidence on the same principles as in summary trials.[2]

18 See generally p 165 et seq, ante.
19 Police and Criminal Evidence Act 1984, s 79.
20 For the order of examination etc in the case of co-accused see p 151 et seq, ante.
 1 See p 161 as to when separate representation is needed because of s 1(f)(ii) of the 1984 Act.
 2 See p 301, ante. See also *R v Scott* (1984) 79 Cr App Rep 49.

Stage 9. Closing speeches and summing up

The final part of the trial commences with the advocates' closing speeches. Counsel for the prosecution will address the jury first, followed by counsel for the defence. They will both go through the evidence that has been presented and defence counsel will drawer on his or her powers of oratory in an endeavour to persuade the jury to acquit.

The judge will now sum up to the jury. He must:

   (i) explain thoroughly the ingredients of the charge;
  (ii) explain the burden and standard of proof;
 (iii) analyse the evidence presented for both sides and draw to their attention its strengths and weaknesses.[3]

When appropriate, the judge must give a corroboration warning, and deal with identification evidence. The judge will then send the jury out to consider their verdict. He will also tell them that they should try to reach a unanimous verdict, and that although he may, at an appropriate stage, be able to accept a majority verdict, it will be for him to say when that stage has been reached. Finally, he will ask them to choose a foreman to chair their discussions.

The judge will rise when the jury leaves to start its deliberations, and the accused will be taken down to the cells unless bail has been granted. As a general rule the jury must attempt to reach a unanimous verdict for at least two hours ten minutes. The period will be extended by the judge if he thinks that in view of the complexities of the case a longer period is necessary.[4] The jury may return to the court asking the judge for further directions at any stage. These directions must be given by the judge in open court with all the parties present. This also applies if the jury has been unable to reach a unanimous verdict and the judge considers that the time has come to accept a majority verdict, which in the usual jury of 12 may be 10:2 or 11:1. Although the judge may ultimately discharge a jury if they are unable to reach a verdict he must not, save as above, seek to influence them in any way, for example, by setting a time limit.[5]

Stage 10. The verdict

When the jury has reached a verdict it will return and deliver it to the court. The accused will be told to stand up and the clerk will read out each count on the indictment to which the accused pleaded not guilty. The foreman will deliver the verdict on each count. If the judge has given permission for a majority verdict to be reached the jury will be asked if they have reached a decision upon which at least ten are agreed. If the answer is yes, the foreman announces whether their verdict is guilty or not guilty. If the verdict is guilty he must then give the figures for the majority.

Alternative verdicts. When an accused faces more than one count, the jury must treat each separately,[6] and thus may convict him on one and acquit on others. However, a jury may sometimes be able to find a defendant not guilty of the offence charged, but guilty of a lesser offence. The relevant statutory provisions are set out in the Criminal Law Act 1967, ss4 and 6. The law is

3 See further p 167, ante.
4 Juries Act 1974, s 17.
5 See *R v Rose(Newton)* [1982] AC 822.
6 Although, rarely, evidence on one count is capable of corroborating that on another.

complicated, but broadly the lesser offence must also be indictable and in addition the allegations in the count must amount to or include expressly or by implication the lesser offence.[7]

It should finally be noted that an accused charged with causing death by reckless driving or of reckless driving may be acquitted on that charge but convicted of driving without due care and attention.[8]

Stage 11. Conclusion

If the accused is acquitted, the proceedings are concluded, subject to any question of costs, and he is discharged. If he is convicted, the judge will normally proceed immediately to sentence although he will often adjourn overnight to consider sentence if the offences are serious. If a social enquiry report is not available, the judge is unlikely to adjourn for one to be prepared; this is considered in the next two chapters. Finally, it must be stressed that counsel should already have been instructed to advise on appeal: appeals are considered in chapter 14.

Regina v Duncan McCarthy. This chapter concludes by taking up the story of Duncan McCARTHY from where it was left earlier in the chapter. The title of the action has changed because trials on Indictment will be brought in the name of the Queen.

By *7 September* McCARTHY's solicitor has served an alibi notice by letter on the prosecution, and at the same time asked for details of any convictions against any of the witnesses. She has also sent the committal papers with a backsheet, as a 'holding brief'.

By *30 September* she has seen McCARTHY and his wife, separately, and taken full proofs of evidence from them incorporating their comments on the prosecution statements tendered at committal, where relevant. In the light of this she has written to the hospital secretary asking for permission to inspect the view from the hospital ward, and to her inquiry agent asking him to report. She has also contacted McCARTHY's bank.

By *30 November* she has received the results of the above enquiries. In the light of these she prepares the s 9 statements referred to in the brief and serves them on the prosecution. She also takes full proofs from McCARTHY's companions at the club.

By *13 December* she has prepared and sent the brief to counsel. In a covering letter she asks counsel's clerk to contact her and arrange a conference. This is held on *20 December*, when McCARTHY and his solicitor attend counsel's chambers.

Having prepared the brief early, there is now little to do until the case appears in the list for hearing on *21 June*. She does, however, keep in contact with the court, Mr and Mrs McCARTHY, and her inquiry agent, to make sure that there are no dates approaching which should be avoided. She does not serve a witness summons on her agent as she knows him to be reliable.

At last, on *21 June* she attends the Crown Court with counsel as although the cost of a solicitor may not be allowed on taxation, she considers the case important enough to warrant her attention. The trial lasts nearly two days, and at about 3.45 pm on the second day the jury returns. The verdict is left to your imagination.

---

7 See generally *Metropolitan Police Comr v Wilson: R v Jenkins* [1984] AC 242.
8 Road Traffic Act 1972, Sch 4, Part IV.

CHAPTER 12

Sentencing principles and powers

INTRODUCTION

A solicitor, whether he is a young and inexperienced advocate, or has prac-
ticed for many years, will spend most of his time appearing for or advising
defendants who either intend to plead guilty or who have been found guilty.
You must be able to advise your client of the sentences available, and of the
likely possibilities. However, it may be helpful to see what happens when a
court sentences an offender. Detailed rules of procedure appear in the next
chapter.

> EXAMPLE: *Softsell Supermarkets v Anthony Jones* (case 2). JONES has pleaded guilty
> before Weyford magistrates' court to the shoplifting charge. The court decides that
> a report on the defendant's background would be useful. This report, called a
> 'social enquiry report' is prepared by the probation service, and will take about
> three weeks to compile. Accordingly, the case is adjourned and JONES is bailed to
> return in three weeks' time. Three weeks later he returns to court. The police
> present such details as they have of his past life ('antecedents') and previous
> convictions. The magistrates then receive and read the social enquiry report.
> JONES's solicitor then addresses the court in mitigation and finally the magistrates
> proceed to sentence.

From this very straightforward example it should be noted that the court
has to decide what sentence to impose. It does this after receiving information
from both the prosecution and defence, and also from an independent
agency, the probation service.[1]

This chapter looks at the principles the court takes into account when
sentencing, and at factors which can affect the sentencing decision. It then
examines the various sentences available.

There are three crucial preliminary points which should be noted.

(i) The court almost always has a discretion over both the type of sentence to be imposed and the quantitative element of that sentence;
for example, how long it is to run or how much the defendant will
have to pay.

(ii) Sentences are conventionally divided into two groups, namely *punitive*
sentences and *individualised* sentences. A punitive sentence, may en-
compass elements of deterrence, retribution and protection of the
public. The sentences most commonly thought of as punitive are
imprisonment and fines. An individualised sentence is more likely to
be aimed at reformation or rehabilitation. The most obvious example
is a probation order.

(iii) The court will receive information about the offender from a variety
of sources. This may aggravate or mitigate the seriousness of the
matter. The defence solicitor's main task in the sentencing process is
concerned with the presentation of mitigating factors. These can help

1 See p 444, post.

determine the *type* of sentence—whether it is to be punitive or individualised—and also the *length* of sentence.

1 SENTENCING PRINCIPLES

(a) Discretion

With very few exceptions statutes which create offences give courts extremely wide discretion in dealing with offenders who are found guilty. There are, however, certain offences for which the sentence is fixed by law. Life imprisonment for murder is the obvious example. The court has no discretion.[2] More commonly, many motoring offences carry disqualification or endorsement as a mandatory penalty.[3] Magistrates are additionally subject to the important statutory restriction that they can never impose a fine of more than £2000 or imprisonment for more than 6 months per offence.[4]

(b) Judicial guidance[5]

As each sentence is a decision on the facts of an individual case, it is debatable to what extent courts are bound by previous sentencing decisions of higher courts, and in particular those of the Court of Appeal.[6] However, that court has recently pronounced 'guideline' judgments, such as in *Aramah*,[7] *Bibi*,[8] *Boswell*[9] and *Barrick*.[9a] In addition, it is generally recognised that the Court of Appeal has established a 'tariff' for certain offences to assist in determining the appropriate length for a term of imprisonment.

(c) The two types of sentence

(i) Punitive sentences

Imprisonment, and lesser custodial sentences, such as detention centre orders are often thought of as punitive in nature. Such sentences must obviously be both just and fair. The Court of Appeal has, as a deliberate policy in recent years, tried to establish appropriate 'bands' for lower courts to follow when imposing sentences of imprisonment. For example, an 'average' male in his thirties who commits burglary of a dwelling house and who has an 'average' list of previous convictions for the same or other offences of dishonesty should, if the court considers imprisonment is appropriate, receive a term of imprisonment within the prescribed band.

This process is known as 'tariff' sentencing. The operation of this 'tariff' has been identified from decisions of the Court of Appeal, Criminal Division, and comprehensively described by D.A. Thomas in his work *Principles of Sentencing*.[10] It is not the purpose of this book to go through the tariff and to

---

2 Murder (Abolition of Death Penalty) Act 1965, s 1.
3 Even here there is some discretion as to the length of the disqualification.
4 Magistrates' Courts Act 1980, ss 31 and 32. Frequently the statutory maximum will be less. Those situations in which the magistrates may impose *more* than 6 months are considered on p 395.
5 See 'Techniques of Guidance on Sentencing' by A. Ashworth [1984] Crim LR 519.
6 See eg *R v DeHavilland* [1983] Crim LR 489.
7 (1983) 76 Cr App Rep 190, CA: sentences for drug trafficking.
8 [1980] 1 WLR 1193, CA: prison sentences to be kept as short as possible.
9 [1984] 3 All ER 353, CA. Sentences for causing death by reckless driving.
9a (1985) Times, 4 May: immediate imprisonment in serious breach of trust cases.
10 2nd edn, 1978: Heinemann Library of Criminology and Penal Reform.

illustrate the categories. However, there are some important matters to consider.

It is very rare for a court to impose the maximum available sentence of imprisonment.[11] Because of this the 'tariff' is useful in order to establish the appropriate period for a custodial sentence. Save in extreme cases the sentence produced by the tariff may be reduced by mitigation which may be put forward on behalf of the defendant. For example, the fact that the offender has no previous convictions will normally provide a fairly strong element of mitigation and either lead to a reduction in a tariff sentence, or alternatively steer the court towards some form of individualised sentence such as probation. When, however, the first offence is a serious armed robbery, it is likely that a substantial sentence of imprisonment will be imposed because of the nature of the offence. 'Tariff' sentencing is far more important in the Crown Court, which has much wider sentencing powers, than magistrates' courts. It does not have any application to the other custodial sentences such as detention centre orders. As a principle the 'tariff' must also be considered in the light of *R v Bibi*, in which the Court of Appeal presided over by Lord Lane CJ stressed that custodial sentences must be kept as short as possible.

Fines are the obvious non-custodial form of punitive sentence. Fines are not specifically described as part of the tariff as such; they are however of considerable importance to the solicitor in practice. The Crown Court will, and the magistrates must, consider the means of the offender to pay when imposing fines. The court may not, however, impose a higher fine on a wealthy person than on a person who is not so well off merely because the former is better able to pay. The argument is that to do otherwise might imply that some people could 'buy' their way out of prison by submitting to a heavy fine instead.[12] The court may, however, increase fines to reflect the 'profit element' in an offence, and as will be shown, can impose a compensation order which requires the offender to repay a specified sum to the victim.

The nearest that fines come to having a tariff is in relation to motoring offences, when magistrates will be guided by a suggested series of penalties for motoring offences, prepared by the Magistrates Association. They are widely applied by magistrates' courts, in the absence of mitigation or aggravating factors. These suggested penalties have recently been updated and are available from the Association. The Crown Court is seldom concerned with motoring offences other than when it hears appeals from magistrates' courts.

(ii) Individualised sentences

An individualised sentence is one which is selected for the particular individual by the court. It is imposed with regard to the offender's needs rather than for the purposes of punishment, although there may be aspects of the order which appear to the offender to be unpleasant and equivalent to punishment. Furthermore, there is no strict dividing line between the two concepts. For example, a detention centre order is punitive in nature, but may be ordered specifically because the court believes that a 'short sharp shock' will do the offender good.

11 The rarely imposed extended sentence may achieve this: Powers of Criminal Courts Act 1973, s 28.
12 One solution to this is a 'day fine' whereby a court may impose a fine of say five times the offender's daily earning. The Home Secretary has indicated that such a scheme may be introduced in England and Wales in 1986.

A suspended sentence of imprisonment is a good example of a sentence which starts off as being a tariff penalty and is then individualised by the court. The term of imprisonment ordered must be appropriate for the offence and the offender's age, sex and criminal record, but the court then decides in the case of the particular individual that imprisonment ought to be suspended.[13]

If the court is considering an individualised sentence, it is particularly important that the court receives information about the offender. There are a variety of available sources. The court may ask the probation service to prepare a *social inquiry report* on the offender, who may have brought along friends to give evidence of his character, or a letter from his employer to the same effect. In addition, if the offender pleaded not guilty, the court which tried him assuming that it proceeds to sentence him[14] will already have formed a strong view of his character from what it has heard. The main role of the defence solicitor in the sentencing process is to mitigate on the basis of the information before the court. This may involve calling evidence or addressing the court on facts already before it.

(iii) Concurrent and consecutive imprisonment?

As will be seen throughout this chapter, a court may be faced with the prospect of sentencing an offender for more than one offence.

As a general rule, the types of sentence imposed should not be incompatible with one another, for example, it is not generally good sentencing practice to order probation for one offence and imprisonment for another. This section, however, is concerned with the principles governing those situations where a court is faced with imposing a term of *imprisonment* for more than one offence.

If sentences are expressed to run *consecutively* it means that when one sentence has finished the next one will start.

> EXAMPLE: An offender pleads guilty to burglary and theft. He receives three years' imprisonment for the burglary and six months' for the theft. They are ordered to run *consecutively*. His total sentence, ignoring remission, is *three years six months*.

If sentences are to run *concurrently*, then they all run at the same time.

> EXAMPLE: If on the same facts the sentences were to run concurrently his total term of imprisonment would be *three years*.

Sentences should be concurrent if they arise out of the same incident. They may be consecutive if they do not, but a court should not impose a sentence if the overall effect of it would be to make it too long.[15]

> EXAMPLE: *Duncan* McCARTHY (*case 1*). It will be recalled that McCARTHY is charged with burglary: on the facts he could easily have been charged with criminal damage as well. If that were the case and he were to be imprisoned, the court would treat the offences as being part of the same incident.

One would thus expect him to receive a sentence of, say, 18 months for the burglary, with 3 months for criminal damage, to run concurrently. Thus, the

---

13 It would thus be wrong to increase the length of the sentence to compensate for its being suspended: *R v Trowbridge* [1975] Crim LR 295, CA.
14 It is not essential that it is, see chapter 13, pp 438 et seq.
15 *R v Smith* [1975] Crim LR 468, CA.

sentences will reflect the relative seriousness of the offences in respect of which they were passed.

Supposing, however, that on being interviewed at home by DS Forsyth and DC Tarbuck, McCARTHY is alleged to have assaulted the officers. This would be a separate incident and one might imagine that any prison sentence for that would run consecutively to the others. He might therefore receive the following:

    (i)   burglary—18 months' imprisonment;

    (ii) criminal damage—3 months' concurrent to (i);

    (iii) assaulting a police officer—3 months' imprisonment consecutive to (i).

There are no absolute rules, however, and exceptions can always be made in appropriate circumstances. For example, in *R v Dillon*[16] the offender had taken a conveyance without authority, driven it whilst under the influence of drink and whilst he was disqualified from driving. He was, of course, also uninsured. The consecutive sentences for unlawful taking and driving whilst unfit were upheld by the Court of Appeal, largely on the basis of the offender's similar behaviour in the past, even though they arose out of essentially the same incident.

(d) Mitigation

What is mitigation?

Mitigation does not have a precise definition, but consists of attempting to reduce the severity of a punishment or the rigour of the law. The object of mitigation is thus to draw to the attention of the court the reason for committing the offence, the circumstances in which the offence was committed and the personal or other circumstances of the person committing them. The mitigator must emphasise to the court those matters which should reduce a tariff penalty to the minimum appropriate or replace a tariff penalty with an individualised penalty. The speech in mitigation has been described as a gentle, sophisticated and sadly neglected art.[17] You should be aware that it will be where you will gain your initial experience of advocacy.

It might be thought that in the English legal system, which has a number of agencies providing information to the court, mitigation is neither necessary nor desirable. This is, however, not so. There are many situations when factors may need to be drawn to the court's attention, even though a social inquiry report is ordered. Furthermore, in road traffic cases a social inquiry report will seldom if ever be ordered, even when the offender is in danger of losing his driving licence. The principal factors which are relevant to sentencing will now be considered. They may not always be in your client's favour. If they are, they must be stressed. If they are not, you must be able to deal with them if the court asks you to. Most of the factors which may be presented to the court as part of a speech in mitigation are, in a sense, statements of the obvious. This does not mean, however, that they will necessarily be obvious either to the court or to your client.

The preparation of mitigation: some factors

Age of the offender. There is no doubt that youth or advanced years are always material, and furthermore, that the younger the offender, the more

16 [1984] RTR 270, CA.
17 Per Eric Crowther: *Advocacy for the Advocate*, p 26 (Barry Rose, 1st edn 1984).

the court will be prepared to adopt an individualised approach rather than impose a tariff sentence. In any event, when the offender is under 21, he cannot be sent to prison at all, although other custodial penalties may be imposed. At the other end of the spectrum, advanced age will also be of itself a mitigating factor. The court is more inclined to extend mercy to persons at or beyond retirement age, merely because of their age.

The offender's record. The offender's past record, if any, has an important bearing on mitigation, in the sense that a person with no previous convictions can expect that in general this will be taken into account. On the other hand, previous convictions may well increase the likelihood of a punitive custodial sentence. The existence of previous convictions may exert a more specific influence. If the court has previously sentenced the offender to both probation and to heavy fines it may conclude that its range of options have been so narrowed as to render imprisonment inevitable. In other cases, it may be possible to suggest that as punitive measures have been attempted without any marked success it might be appropriate for the court to consider some other form of treatment which is not punitive.[18]

Must the previous conviction be revealed? The Rehabilitation of Offenders Act 1974 was passed to enable offenders to make a clean start, by enabling them to avoid disclosing their previous convictions, provided that they have not re-offended within the rehabilitation period. Each conviction has a rehabilitation period attached to it after which the conviction is 'spent'. If a person who has a previous conviction is convicted of an indictable offence whilst the rehabilitation period for the first offence is still running, then both offences are effectively amalgamated; neither offence will be rehabilitated until the period for the other offence has ceased to run.[19]

The Rehabilitation of Offenders Act does not, strictly speaking, apply to criminal proceedings at all.[20] The court is thus always entitled to know about an offender's previous convictions, although a *Practice Direction* protects details of convictions from being read out or referred to without the express leave of the court if they would otherwise be spent.[1] The prosecutor is responsible for supplying this information. If he fails to do so, the defence is not obliged to provide it.[2]

The court may, and usually will, take into account the fact that long gaps appear between convictions, giving credit for 'going straight' for a period. Similarly, when a person with a record commits an offence completely out of character with earlier offences, this may mitigate the effect that a further conviction might otherwise be expected to have. For example, a person with a number of previous convictions for burglary who is found guilty of careless driving would not be fined any differently from any other motorist. It does, of course, always depend on the nature of the new offence: one would not expect a person convicted of armed robbery for the first time to get any credit for the fact that he had changed his criminal activities from shoplifting, or a burglar for ringing the changes by switching to fraud.

Circumstances leading up to the offence. The circumstances in which offences were committed and the circumstances of the offender in committing

---

18 The 'last chance' gambit.
19 Rehabilitation of Offenders Act 1974, ss 1(4) and 4.
20 Ibid, s 7(1).
1 [1975] 2 All ER 172.
2 At the same time, the solicitor must not tell a court that his client has no previous convictions if he knows to the contrary, see p 170, ante.

them will always be relevant for the purpose of sentencing. There are four important areas where this applies.

Provocation. This will not normally provide a defence to criminal liability, but may well be relevant in mitigation. It is most likely to be relevant in cases when the accused is charged with an offence of violence or criminal damage. You should draw to the court's attention not only the nature of the provocation, but also the respective standing of the victim and the accused; whether, for example, the latter had been taunted about his stature or physical appearance.

The home background. A stressful home background will often provide important mitigation. Offences of violence or dishonesty may have been committed whilst the home background was in some way disturbed, or there may have been a pre-existing history of conflict between various members of the family. The victim may be another member of the family, particularly where the offence involves violence. These are factors which must be analysed and put forward as mitigation when appropriate. A lack of any home life or background, whether temporary or permanent can and should also be put forward in mitigation. Offences committed when an offender has been thrown out of his accommodation, particularly if committed shortly afterwards, will usually be regarded in a different light from, for example, wanton thefts by someone who in no sense could be said to 'need' the property stolen. Similarly the court will treat food or drink stolen for consumption in these circumstances in a different light from food or other items stolen with a view to realising profit.

Financial circumstances. Offences committed whilst the offender has no money will be treated on a different level from offences committed whilst the offender has a wallet stuffed full of bank notes, particularly if the offence is one of petty theft. However, you must always be in a position to explain how the financial embarrassment has arisen. Any offender over the age of 16 will, prima facie, be entitled to supplementary benefit.[3] A court will probably assume that supplementary benefit levels are adequate, in the absence of evidence to the contrary. When an offender is destitute you must be able to explain why your client had not applied for supplementary benefit. It may be that the offender was unaware of it, or could not face the bureaucratic nightmare that claiming sometimes involves. If the client has spent all his benefit, the court will probably want to know what it has been spent on.

In addition, the fact of financial embarrassment may be overridden by the nature of the offence itself. For example, an employee, who when short of money, steals from his employer will be regarded by most courts as having committed a very serious offence, particularly if he was in a position of trust. The reason for committing the offence will take second place to the breach of trust which it involves.

Drink or drugs. The extent to which alcohol or drugs constitute a defence to a criminal charge is outside the scope to this work. The effect of alcohol or drugs can be relevant to sentencing. An alcoholic may find himself made subject to an individualised sentence which in some way may assist him to be cured. This might involve a hospital order or probation. However, the mere fact that the offender was drunk when the offence was committed may or may not comprise mitigation. If it is coupled with other mitigating factors

3 Supplementary Benefits Act 1976, s 1:

such as youth or provocation, it may have more effect than otherwise. The court may well take the view that as the offender voluntarily induced the state of drunkenness, he cannot put forward his own voluntary acts in mitigation. This argument will also apply to an offender who has taken drugs. Of course, if his drink had been 'spiked', and he can provide some convincing evidence of that fact, he may well receive sympathetic consideration. In general, however, you should be prepared for the court to adopt an unsympathetic attitude.

Direct or indirect effects of convictions or sentence. The mere fact of conviction or of a particular type of sentence may have profound effects on the offender's future life or prospects. Both these matters can be put forward in mitigation. The court will consider the effect of conviction on the rest of the family, particularly the children, if the circumstances are exceptional. For example, if either the remaining parent is crippled and unable to cope alone, or if both parents have been involved in a crime, a court might well be persuaded to avoid a custodial sentence if it meant that the children would have to go into the care of the local authority.[4]

If conviction will result in dismissal from employment then the offender's family will inevitably suffer. The principal form of suffering will be financial hardship. This should mitigate against further financial penalties. For many, the loss of a driving licence will mean the loss of employment. This in itself will be hard on the family. If the family live in a rural area and no other members can drive, this will inevitably cause hardship in some form. If any members of the family are ill, then again this should comprise hardship which the court can be urged to take into account.

The behaviour of the offender subsequent to the offence. It may be possible to present matters which have arisen or occurred since the offence was committed so as to mitigate a penalty which might otherwise be imposed.

Remorse. It has been suggested[5] that a plea of guilty is the best evidence of remorse. It will certainly attract a 'discount' under the 'tariff' system. Conversely, a plea of 'not guilty', followed by conviction, is often treated as indicating a lack of remorse. When the court is imposing an individualised penalty, however, the nature of the offender's plea should not of itself, affect the order imposed.

Assistance to the police. The offender may have co-operated with the police in a variety of different ways, all of which may be factors which can be drawn to the court's attention in the process of mitigation. The most clear-cut example of this is when he not merely confesses to the offence of which he is accused, but in addition either tells the police of other crimes committed by him or informs against others. Another potent factor is where an offender has rendered assistance in the recovery of stolen property.

Reparation. If the offender has voluntarily made reparation in some way or other to the victim, this will constitute mitigation, which should be drawn to the court's attention. However, the court will not allow wealthy people to purchase their way out of prison by making reparation any more than it will allow them to purchase a non-custodial sentence by way of a heavy fine. In other words, if reparation is clearly seen as part of remorse and done gen-

---

4 For example, under the Child Care Act 1980 s 2.
5 Thomas (op cit) p 217.

uinely without prompting, it will be taken into account, but not if it appears to be part of a calculated 'sentence planning' operation.[6]

Mitigating factors arising from the criminal justice system. There may be a number of reasons why an offender has a legitimate cause for complaint about the way in which his case has been dealt with, notwithstanding the total lack of any impropriety in the proceedings themselves.[7] The most common problem concerns delay, particularly between committal for trial and trial on indictment.[8] The court may take account of the fact that the proceedings have been hanging over the defendant's head for a considerable time, especially where this combined with attempts at self-rehabilitation: for example, obtaining regular work if the offender has been on remand in custody prior to trial. Although such a period will go to reduce the amount of any custodial sentence that is actually served, [8,9] it may seem more just to the court to impose a non-custodial term.

Furthermore, a court may defer sentence on an offender.[10] It is not entitled to make promises as to the consequences of the offender obtaining a job or otherwise keeping out of trouble during the period of deferment, but evidence of such conduct[11] will be very important when the offender reappears for sentence.[12]

Future prospects

Work prospects. Many offenders come before the court without a job. There is no doubt that the prospects of obtaining work may operate as a potent factor in the offender's favour. There are, however, several important qualifications to be borne in mind. First, the court may be influenced where employment has been obtained prior to trial; it will not be impressed with vague hopes about obtaining a job in the near or not so near future. Secondly, the employment must be suitable to the offender's means and background. Thirdly, it must also be suitable in the light of the offence. To take an extreme example, the court will be unimpressed by an offer of employment in a wages department when the court is in the process of sentencing the offender for theft from an employer when in a similar position.

(e) Mitigating factors when the offender pleads not guilty

It has been assumed, so far, that the offender has pleaded 'guilty'. When he has pleaded not guilty mitigation may still be put forward but it is subject to certain constraints.

Since the offender has pleaded not guilty the court will have heard evi-

---

6 The Home Secretary has recently announced that he is considering the introduction of a sentence or order requiring an offender to make reparation to his victim.

7 Otherwise he would be able to apply for judicial review, or appeal to the Court of Appeal—considered in Chapter 14.

8 Regulations imposing time limits may alleviate delay: Prosecution of Offences Act 1985, s 22.

9 Criminal Justice Act 1967, s 67. Time spent in police custody also counts towards the term served: 1967 Act, s 1A, as inserted by Police and Criminal Evidence Act 1984, s 49. The same also applies to juveniles in remand homes but *not* to those remanded into care with a secure accommodation order.

10 Powers of Criminal Courts Act 1973, s 1.

11 *R v Skelton* (1983) Times, 18 May.

12 It would obviously be wrong for a court to renege on any promise wrongly made. *R v Marchant*, quoted in Thomas (op cit) p 221. However, a court must always explain why it is deferring sentence: *R v George* [1984] 3 All ER 13, CA.

dence called by the prosecution, together with any evidence called by the defence. It is not therefore generally appropriate to comment on the facts as part of mitigation: this may be seen as an attempt to contradict the findings of fact upon which the verdict was based. This is particularly important in the magistrates' court when the magistrates neither sum up nor give reasons for their decision so that it will be impossible to glean any idea of the court's own view of the evidence.

Furthermore, most defences are based on the assertion that the accused either was not present at all, or alternatively did not have the necessary intention to commit the offence. Accordingly, it will be well-nigh impossible to urge in mitigation that the accused has cooperated with the police or with the victim. If the accused has always contended that he is not an offender, and has also done so in the witness box, he cannot express regret for having committed the offence. Accordingly, in these types of cases mitigation must be confined in practical terms to the offender's circumstances.

(f) Taking offences into consideration (TICs)

The final area of mitigation is not of immediate concern to the defence solicitor in the sense that he is not concerned with presenting it to court. Asking for offences to be taken into consideration is, however, very important. In the course of an interview about a particular matter a suspect may volunteer information about other offences. Furthermore, he may be someone well known to the police and although he may have been arrested ostensibly on one matter there may be a number of recent offences in which they suspect he is implicated. It may well be in the suspect's interest that if he is to go before a court, all matters outstanding against him should be dealt with at the same time. Then for example, if a custodial sentence is imposed, the offender will at least not be liable to be interviewed on other charges whilst in prison. Furthermore, the police are obviously concerned that their detection rate shows some relationship with the rate of reported crime in their area. At some stage they may 'offer' an accused the opportunity of admitting other crimes that he has committed, on the basis that he will not be charged with them but on sentence he will ask the court to take those other offences 'into consideration'.

There are two ways in which this process is liable to abuse. The first is that the police could trick an offender into admitting offences which they could not otherwise prove and then charge the accused with those other offences.[13] The second potential abuse is that an accused may be pressured into asking for offences to be taken into consideration even though he has not in fact committed them. The police naturally tend to 'press' suspects when they see a similarity between the offence for which he was arrested and certain other unsolved crimes. For example, he may have been charged with one burglary, and may be asked whether or not he has committed two others. Let us suppose he has committed one of those, but not the other, and that, unknown to him, the police could not prove he committed either of them. They may ask him if he wishes to have both burglaries taken into consideration, and very clearly imply that if he declines they will charge him with the two other burglaries.

13 Subject, of course, to the confession not being ruled inadmissible under the Police and Criminal Evidence Act 1984, s 76.

In consequence of these potential abuses, a series of guidelines have been laid down over the years. The accused must be offered a form by the police which details the offences he is asking to be taken into consideration. The effect of agreeing to have them taken into consideration is explained on the form, which must be signed by him. Finally, the court must be satisfied that he is genuinely admitting the additional offences, during the sentencing process.

What offences can be taken into consideration?

In principle the accused can ask for any offence to be taken into consideration, but there are important constraints which are as follows.

(i)   He may not ask for an offence to be taken into consideration if it is more serious than the one with which he is charged. Seriousness in this context is judged by the maximum penalty available.

(ii) In the *magistrates' court* he cannot ask for an offence which is triable only on indictment to be taken into consideration on sentence.

(iii) He cannot ask for the court to take into consideration an offence when there is an obligation or discretion to disqualify from driving unless one of the principal offences with which he is charged is similarly disqualifiable.

(iv) He may not ask for the court to take into consideration an offence which was committed whilst he was on probation. Offences committed whilst a probation period is running must always be charged separately.[14]

The effect of asking for offences to be taken into consideration

The court, when sentencing an offender who asks for other matters to be taken into consideration, has the power to sentence only in respect of the offences with which he is *charged*. It cannot sentence in respect of the offences which are taken into consideration. The court is, however, entitled to impose a more severe sentence, for example, by way of a longer term of imprisonment, a heavier fine, or more hours to be served on a community service order, than it might otherwise have done. In practice, however, this may not be important when the offence charged is the most serious one.

Although the court may not impose separate sentences, certain of its ancillary powers are available; in particular it may impose a *compensation order* in respect of each offence taken into consideration. However, in such a case a further restriction exists in *magistrates'* courts. Compensation may only be awarded in respect of offences taken into consideration in so far as the aggregate amount of the orders do not exceed £2000 *for each offence charged*.

> EXAMPLE. A magistrates' court orders compensation of £200 in respect of the offence with which the offender is charged; it thus has a maximum of £1800 available in respect of all the offences taken into consideration. Had two offences been charged and £100 compensation ordered for each offence, £3800 would have been available for compensation in respect of the 'T.I.C.'s'.

Both the Crown Court and magistrates' courts can make *restitution* orders in

14 *R v Webb* [1953] 2 QB 390. See further Emmins, *A Practical Approach to Sentencing* (1985) (Financial Training) pp 73 et seq.

respect of offences taken into consideration in the same way and to the same extent that they can in respect of offences charged and proved.

The court has no power to make orders for costs or orders as to the disqualification or endorsement of driving licences in respect of offences taken into consideration.

2 TYPES OF SENTENCE AND OTHER ORDERS

In order to help his client at the sentencing stage a defence solicitor must know what the court has *power* to do, and he must appreciate what the court is *likely* to do. The powers themselves will now be examined.

Two crucial factors affect sentencing powers. The first is that for sentencing purposes there are three broad categories of offence and associated penalties. Set out below are the three categories and their main penalties.

Category	*Penalties*
(a) Non-imprisonable offences	fine; probation (adults only); absolute or conditional discharge; binding over; care and supervision orders (juveniles only).
(b) Imprisonable offences	prison (21 or over); suspended prison sentences; youth custody and detention centre orders (under 21); Mental Health Act orders; community service; attendance centres (under 21); *plus* all of (a) above.
(c) Most offences involving motor vehicles	disqualification from driving; endorsement of licence; *plus* all of (a) or (b) depending on age and whether the offence is imprisonable.

The second factor is the age of the offender. So far offenders have been divided into two broad categories, namely adults and juveniles. For the purposes of sentencing, however, a different classification must be adopted. The first group comprises offenders who are *21 or over*. The second group comprises offenders who are *17 and over but under 21* and the third group is those *under 17* (juveniles).[15] The differences between the first and second groups are mainly concerned with custodial sentences. The second and third groups share some features, but juveniles have for many years been sentenced primarily in the juvenile court.

There are two other matters relating to sentencing powers: the first is that the Crown Court has wider sentencing powers in respect of either way offences than a magistrates' court. Secondly, all courts have a wide range of ancillary powers for example to order compensation for victims of crime and to disqualify from driving and endorse the licences of motoring offenders. The various powers available to the court will now be examined by reference to the three age categories outlined above.

15 Juveniles are subdivided into 2 groups, *young persons* (14 or over) and *children* (under 14): see pp 305 and 319, ante.

(1) Sentences for offenders aged 21 and over

1 Immediate sentences of imprisonment

Most sentences of imprisonment are subject to maxima fixed by statute. Exceptions include offences punishable by imprisonment at common law, where the power to imprison is generally 'at large', in other words for a maximum of life.[16] Occasionally a maximum term of imprisonment of life is prescribed for grave statutory offences. These include rape, armed robbery and arson with intent to endanger life. The maximum period prescribed will usually be a period of years, or less commonly, of months. It should always be borne in mind, however, that the maximum term does not bear any relationship to the sentence actually imposed in an average case, because of the 'tariff' and the pressure on courts to impose as short a sentence as possible. It is only where statute provides not a maximum sentence, but a fixed sentence most notably in the case of murder, that a court has no discretion over length.[17]

Restrictions on the powers of courts to imprison. There are a number of important restrictions upon the powers of courts to impose terms of imprisonment, assuming that the offence is imprisonable in the first place, and the offender is 21 or over.[18] It is to be presumed that the relevant time for determining age is at the time of sentence.[19]

Persons under 21 are instead sentenced to youth custody, detention centre or to custody for life, all of which are considered later.

(a) Powers of Criminal Courts Act 1973, ss 20 and 20A. A court may not impose a term of imprisonment for the first time unless it is of the opinion that no other course is appropriate.[20] In deciding this it must take into account all the circumstances. Furthermore, a magistrates' court must state in open court that no other course of action is appropriate and this must be entered on the warrant committing the offender to prison.[1]

A person who has previously received a suspended sentence which was not activated and which has expired is treated as never having had a sentence of imprisonment imposed on him, as is a person who has only been imprisoned for defaulting on payment of fines or other breaches of court orders.[2] Where, however, the present offence was committed during the operational period of a suspended sentence,[3] then this restriction does not apply.

In order to see whether there is any method of dealing with the offender other than prison, a social inquiry report *must* be obtained unless the court does not consider it necessary.[4] It might be unnecessary when the offence is so serious that a custodial sentence is inevitable as for example, with armed

---

16 For example, manslaughter, conspiracy to defraud and affray. The most notable exceptions are common assault and assault occasioning actual bodily harm for the maxima are those prescribed by Offences against the Person Act 1861, s 47.

17 For an invaluable summary of maximum available terms see Cummins, op cit, pp 8, et seq.

18 Criminal Justice Act 1982, s 1. This includes a suspended sentence, but does not prevent such persons being remanded in custody (inter alia, a prison: s 18(2)).

19 It was, however, held in *R v Lowery* (1982) Times, 13 December, that age is taken at conviction. This was a decision on the similarly worded but now repealed s 1 of Criminal Justice Act 1967.

20 Powers of Criminal Courts Act 1973, s 20.

1 Ibid, s 20(2). Failure to observe this requirement does not, however, invalidate the sentence.

2 Ibid, ss 20(3) and 57(1).

3 Ie that the period for which imprisonment was suspended is still running.

4 Ibid, s 20A.

robbery. Alternatively, if a trial has been held the court may feel that it has enough information to sentence without a report, particularly if the offender gave evidence.

Again magistrates' courts, but not the Crown Court, must specify in open court and endorse on the warrant of commitment the reason why they did not consider it necessary to obtain a social inquiry report.[5]

(*b*) *Unrepresented defendants: 1973 Act, s 21.* Neither the Crown Court nor a magistrates' court may impose imprisonment including a suspended sentence for the first time unless the defendant is:

  (i) legally represented; or
 (ii) although unrepresented has applied for legal aid and been refused because his means were thought to be too great; or
(iii) although unrepresented and has been informed of his right to apply for legal aid and given the opportunity to do so, but has nevertheless failed to apply.[6]

There is no requirement that the accused is represented *prior* to conviction, only that he is represented by a solicitor or by counsel *after* he is found guilty but before sentence.[7] Legal aid can be granted purely for this purpose. Unlike social enquiry reports, the court cannot avoid this provision if it does not consider representation to be 'necessary'.[8] Some courts endeavour to comply with this rule by ordering a short adjournment and referring to the Duty Solicitor. A Duty Solicitor must be very careful not to be used as a 'rubber stamp' in order that a court may send the defendant to prison. He should ask for an adjournment if he has had insufficient time to obtain his client's instructions.

(*c*) *Magistrates' Courts Act 1980, s 31.* Magistrates' courts may not in general impose terms of imprisonment of more than six months in total.[9] Longer terms of imprisonment on summary conviction authorised in any enactment are reduced to this maximum, unless otherwise specifically provided for.[10] Statute may of course provide a lower maximum.[11]

This restriction is modified when justices are dealing with two or more *either way* offences. In such a case the court may impose *consecutive* terms of imprisonment, subject to a maximum of six months per offence and twelve months in aggregate.[12]

> EXAMPLES. (i) A magistrates' court finds a defendant guilty of taking a motor vehicle without consent and assaulting a police officer in the execution of his duty. The former is an either way offence but the latter a summary only offence. The overall maximum term of imprisonment is *six months.*
> (ii) Suppose the same defendant was found guilty of taking without consent and

---

5 Powers of Criminal Courts Act 1973, s 20A(3) and (4).
6 Ibid, s 21. By s 21(3)(a) a suspended sentence which has expired is not treated as a previous sentence of imprisonment.
7 Custodial sentences imposed in breach of this requirement will be void: see *McC v Mullan* [1984] 3 All ER 908, HL (a Northern Ireland case).
8 Although it can refuse legal aid on the basis of means—which can only be challenged by judicial review.
9 Magistrates' Courts Act 1980, s 31(1).
10 Ibid, s 31(2).
11 For example, the maximum term of imprisonment for criminal damage treated as a summary offence is three months: ibid, s 33. (See p 281, ante.)
12 Ibid, s 133(2). See p 277, ante.

assault occasioning actual bodily harm. These are both triable either way and thus the maximum term available to the court will be *twelve months* (six months per offence, consecutive).

(iii) A defendant is found guilty of three separate offences of burglary. The court can split up the sentence as it wishes by, for example, imposing *four months* consecutively in respect of each separate offence. The overall sentence must not, however, exceed *twelve months*.[13]

Finally, magistrates may, instead of imprisonment, impose short periods of detention, of up to four days. There is little research on how often this is done.[14]

What happens to the defendant after he is sentenced to imprisonment? When an offender receives a term of imprisonment he will be removed from the court and placed in a holding cell. In the magistrates' court he is looked after by the police and in the Crown Court by officers of HM Prison Service. Each court has a prison or prisons to which the offender is initially sent. For example, adult males sentenced to prison by Croydon Crown Court will be sent to Pentonville, Wormwood Scrubs or Wandsworth prisons, depending on the length of imprisonment imposed. The Prison Department of the Home Office will then decide where the sentence is to be spent. A short term of up to six months will usually to spent in a closed prison. Longer terms may result in the prisoner being transferred from one prison to another every so often. A minority of prisoners who are not considered a security risk and who are otherwise felt to be suitable may be sent to an 'open' prison where the security is less strict. The remainder will remain in a closed prison until release.

Release from prison

Most prisoners do not spend the entire period of their sentence in prison, because of the system of automatic *remission* which applies to all fixed term sentences. Prisoners may also be released *on licence*, known as 'parole', the effect of which is to further shorten the period of custody.

Remission. Any prisoner who is serving neither life imprisonment nor imprisonment for less than 35 days is entitled to remission of *one third* of his sentence.[15] The remission may be forfeited wholly or in part for breaches of prison discipline. A prisoner can, however, expect that he will be released after two thirds of the sentence has been served, after which he is treated as if he had served his sentence in full and cannot be recalled. The likelihood of remission is built into the 'tariff' and a sentence must not be increased because of it.[16]

Licence. Prisoners serving fixed term sentences who have served *six months*[16a] or *one third*[16b] of the term of the sentence, whichever is greater, are entitled to apply for release on licence, colloquially known as 'parole'.[17] In practical terms this means that the sentence imposed must have been for more than 9

---

13 Assuming that 12 months in total is not excessive.
14 See Magistrates' Courts Act 1980, s 134; also ss 135 and 136.
15 Prison Rules 1964, r 5.
16 *R v Maguire* (1956) 40 Cr App Rep 92, CCA.
16a Time spent on remand does *not* count.
16b Ie one third of the term *without* taking remission into account. Time spent on remand *does*, however, count: Criminal Justice Act 1967, s 60(2).
17 Criminal Justice Act 1967, s 60 (1A) and (1B). The Elegibility of Release on Licence Order 1983, SI 1983/1958.

months, as one third would normally be remitted automatically in any event. Parole is granted by the Home Secretary on the recommendation the Parole Board.[18] Prisoners released on parole will remain on licence until the time that they would have been released under remission. Note that if the Crown Court convicts a person released on licence of an imprisonable offence it may order the licence to be revoked. A magistrates' court convicting a person released on licence of any imprisonable offence may not revoke the licence but may commit him to the Crown Court.[19]

Do remands in custody prior to sentence affect the sentence imposed? Periods spent on remand in custody count as part of the sentence itself.[20] This applies to persons in custody either under the Police and Criminal Evidence Act or after they have been charged and brought before the court prior to trial or sentence. In the light of the length of time that some cases can take to get to trial this is very important.

> EXAMPLE. Suppose the Crown Court were to consider that three years' imprisonment was the appropriate period for a burglary charge, and that an offender had already been in custody for six months from the time of arrest until the Crown Court trial. He would still receive a sentence of three years but would only serve a maximum of a further 30 months. He would normally be entitled to remission after two years. In his case this would be 18 months after trial. Eligibility for parole would arise six months from the date of sentence.

The only exception is where the prisoner was already in custody serving a term of imprisonment for another offence.

2 Suspended sentences of imprisonment: 1973 Act, ss 22 to 27

Courts have a power to suspend sentences of imprisonment in appropriate circumstances. This power has been enlarged to enable a court to order that imprisonment should be partly suspended. Note that the prerequisites in respect of first time offenders contained in ss 20 to 21 of the 1973 Act are of equal application.[1]

The power to suspend. Any court may suspend a sentence of imprisonment provided that the sentence itself does not exceed *two years* and the period for which the sentence is suspended is for at least *one year* but not exceeding *two years*.[2] The period for which the sentence is suspended is known as 'the operational period' and must be specified when sentence is passed. Whilst these provisions apply both to the Crown Court and the magistrates' court, they do not increase the magistrates' restricted powers to impose a prison sentence. Thus magistrates may still generally only pass a sentence of up to six months but the sentence may be suspended for between one and two years.

The effect of a suspended sentence is that although a term of imprisonment is imposed on the offender, it does not take immediate effect. Unless the offender is convicted of an offence punishable by imprisonment committed within the period for which the sentence has been suspended, known as the

---

18 The Home Secretary has changed his parole policy so as to restrict parole to exclude certain categories of prisoner. See *Findlay v Secretary of State for the Home Department* [1984] 3 All ER 801, HL. He may also direct 'early release' for classes of offender.
19 Criminal Justice Act 1967, ss 60–62.
20 Ibid, s 67.
 1 1973 Act, ss 20, 20A and 21.
 2 Ibid, s 22.

'operational period', it will never be implemented. It is thus a 'Sword of Damocles' sentence.[3]

Before a suspended sentence is imposed the court must be satisfied that in the absence of a power to suspend, a sentence of immediate imprisonment would be the appropriate penalty,[4] and that the appropriate term is not one of more than two years' imprisonment. The court should first consider if a non-custodial penalty is appropriate. If not, it should decide what the term of imprisonment should be and only then should it consider if the sentence should be suspended. The court should not treat this power as a separate sentence and impose a longer term merely because it can be suspended.[5] The following would be a typical case for a suspended sentence.[6]

> EXAMPLE. An offender found guilty of burglary has many convictions for a variety of offences, but none recently. He has been working and his employer is prepared to have him back. If he goes to prison his wife and children will have to rely exclusively on state benefits.

All courts will, in addition, have in the back of their minds the dicta of Lord Lane CJ in *R v Bibi*,[7] reminding them that custodial sentences are a matter of last resort, particularly in the light of the present overcrowding in prisons. Thus custodial sentences should not be imposed unless absolutely necessary.

A court may consider that a suspended sentence is appropriate but that the offender also needs some form of supervision. Accordingly, a court which imposes more than six months as a suspended sentence of imprisonment for one offence may place the offender under the supervision of a probation officer.[8] The effect of this provision is that only the Crown Court may make such an order.[9] The magistrates' court for the area in which the offender resides may discharge or vary the order on the application of either the offender or the probation officer unless the Crown Court reserved the power to itself.

As has already been indicated, a suspended sentence gives the defendant the advantage of not losing his liberty, but has a built in 'Sword of Damocles'. You must always make sure that your client appreciates that the sentence may be implemented if he reoffends. The court is under a statutory obligation to explain this[10] but may not do so with sufficient clarity. Your client may be so pleased, elated or amazed not to receive a custodial sentence that he may well not take in what the court is saying.

What happens on breach of a suspended sentence? The basic principle is that if an offender who is subject to a suspended sentence of imprisonment is convicted of a further *imprisonable* offence which was committed within the *operational period*, the suspended sentence *must* normally be activated. Clearly this could cause injustice, and there are therefore other options. The original

---

3 After Damocles, a flatterer and courtier of Dionysius, who was made to sit at a banquet under his sword, which was suspended from the ceiling by a thread, to show how precarious his happiness actually was.

4 1973 Act, s 22(2).

5 *R v O'Keefe* [1969] 2 QB 29; *R v Trowbridge* [1975] Crim LR 295.

6 See generally Thomas (op cit) pp 244–246.

7 *R v Bibi* [1980] 1 WLR 1193.

8 1973 Act, s 26.

9 The Home Secretary is empowered to extend these periods so that they would be available to magistrates' courts.

10 1973 Act, s 22(4).

term may be substituted by a lesser immediate term, the court may resuspend the original sentence or make no order in respect of the suspended sentence at all. If, however, the court does not activate the suspended sentence in full because it considers it would be unjust to do so it must state its reasons.[11]

Alternatively, the court may consider that imprisonment should be imposed for the activating offence. In such circumstances, it may order that the activated sentence runs concurrently with the present term of imprisonment (so that the total time served will be based solely on whichever term is the longer) or that it runs consecutively to the current sentence (so that the two must be totalled up to find the aggregate term subject to remission). As a general principle, the suspended sentence should run consecutively with the sentence imposed for the current offence. This is because the offences cannot, *ipso facto*, be connected and terms of imprisonment should only be concurrent where they result from separate charges arising out of the same incident. However, the aggregate term must not be excessive; thus if imposing consecutive terms has this effect, the sentences should run concurrently. If the subsequent offence merits only a very short term of imprisonment this might constitute a ground for reducing the initial term as well.[12]

Certain orders do not count as convictions and thus do not activate a suspended sentence. These orders are:

(i) probation orders
(ii) absolute and conditional discharges.[13]

On the other hand, the making of such orders does not 'de-activate' a suspended sentence if the operational period has not yet expired.

EXAMPLE. An offender, presently subject to a sentence of 6 months' imprisonment suspended for two years, commits a very minor assault, and receives a conditional discharge. Later that year, whilst still subject to the suspended sentence, he commits and is convicted of burglary. The convicting court can still activate the suspended sentence.[14]

Procedure on breach of a suspended sentence: 1973 Act, s 24. It will become apparent that the offender is on a suspended sentence when the prosecution present details of his previous character. The court will require proof both that the defendant was previously given a suspended sentence and that he is in breach of it. The clerk will usually ask him if he admits these matters. Assuming that they are correct, he might as well do so. If he does not, then they must be proved by the prosecution. This will delay the proceedings, increase any costs that the offender may have to bear, and worst of all, aggravate the court.

Not all courts can activate suspended sentences. The Crown Court can activate a suspended sentence imposed by *any* court. A magistrates' court's powers are, however, more limited. It may activate any suspended sentence imposed either by *their own court* or by another *magistrates'* court (subject to the latter court's consent) but may not activate a sentence imposed by the Crown Court.[15] They must either commit the offender in custody or on bail to the Crown Court, or take no action in respect of the suspended sentence.

11 1973 Act, s 23.
12 *R v Smith* [1972] Crim LR 124, CA.
13 1973 Act, s 13.
14 It can also resentence for the breach of the conditional discharge: see p 406 post.
15 1973 Act, s 24—see chart on p 432.

They cannot ignore a Crown Court suspended sentence, however, and if they do not commit the offender[16] they must notify the Crown Court in writing of the action they have taken.[17] The matter will be referred to the presiding judge at the Crown Court. If he considers it appropriate he can order the issue of a summons or warrant requiring the offender to come before the court for it to decide whether to implement the suspended sentence.[18]

3 Part suspended sentences of imprisonment: Criminal Law Act 1977, s 47

Part suspended sentences have been available to courts since 29 March 1982.[19] The theory behind part suspended sentences is that offenders receive a term of imprisonment, the first part of which will be served, and the bulk of which will be suspended. The offender thus not only experiences prison and all that it entails, but is subject to the 'Sword of Damocles' of the suspended sentence on release.

If the court imposes at least *three months'* but not more than *2 years'* imprisonment on the offender, the sentence may be partly suspended.[20] This power is therefore equally available to the Crown Court and magistrates' courts. The court must specify the period of suspension. This is generally at the discretion of the court, save that the defendant must serve at least *28 days* in prison, and the part to be suspended must not be less than one quarter of the whole term imposed. Neither court can order supervision as part of these sentences.

When will a partly suspended sentence be imposed? In *R v Clarke*[1] Lord Lane CJ indicated that a court should first consider whether imprisonment is appropriate at all, and if it is not, impose a non-custodial penalty such as a Community Service Order. If imprisonment is appropriate, the court should first consider either imposing a very short term or fully suspended sentence. If an immediate custodial term is appropriate, and a short sentence is not enough, only then should a partially suspended sentence be imposed. An appropriate case would be one where at least six months' imprisonment would normally be merited as, for example, in the case of a serious but isolated act of violence or burglary, but with strong mitigating factors. Another example might include fraud, involving the use of credit cards to obtain medium range sums of money.[2]

Partly suspended sentences posses a feature which has already attracted comment from the judiciary. Judicial thinking has traditionally been opposed to combining certain types of sentence, in particular to combining an immediate term of imprisonment with a fully suspended sentence for another offence, so that the suspended sentence runs consecutively to the immediate term.[3] However, as was pointed out by the Divisional Court in *R v Ipswich*

---

16 Under Criminal Justice Act 1967, s 56.
17 A magistrates' court should not fetter this power of the Crown Court by ordering probation or a discharge for the current offence: *R v Tarry* [1970] 2 QB 560.
18 1973 Act s 25.
19 Criminal Law Act 1977, s 47, as amended by CJA 1982, s 30.
20 Ibid, s 47(2).
 1 [1982] 3 All ER 232 CA: decided on s 47 in its original form, when six months was the minimum. The principle ought to remain the same.
 2 As in *Clarke* itself. There is, however, no rule that the 'immediate' part should be the shorter: see *R v Lynn* (1982) 4 Cr App Rep (S) 343.
 3 Eg *R v Sapiano* (1968) 52 Cr App Rep 674, CA.

Crown Court ex p Williamson,[4] a partly suspended sentence achieves precisely this effect, albeit in respect of one offence rather than a number of offences.

The effect of re-offending whilst serving a partly suspended sentence. The same consequences as for fully suspended sentences will usually follow. However, it may be that the courts will take a different line, since the offender will actually have served a prison sentence of some length. Activation of the part that is suspended may thus depend on the proportion that it bears to the period served.

4 Fines

Introduction. A fine is a very common sentence, particularly in the magistrates' court, since the majority of summary only offences are non-imprisonable.[5]

Restrictions on fines in the Crown Court. Although the Crown Court itself is creature of statute it was left with its predecessors' common law power to fine 'at large' unless statute specifically provided a maximum. This means that not only is there no general maximum applicable to the Crown Court, but also that it may impose a fine after *any* conviction on indictment unless specifically prohibited.[6] This power is the same if the defendant has been committed to the Crown Court for sentence after summary conviction for an indictable offence.[7] In addition, a fine can be combined with any other sentence or order unless specifically precluded, although certain combinations, eg, fine and immediate imprisonment, are discouraged.[7a]

There are no other legal constraints on the Crown Court's power to fine. In particular, the Crown Court is not required to consider the offender's means to pay. However, the court will not impose a fine that the offender cannot pay, as this would be self defeating. Furthermore, it is not entitled to permit a fine to be used by a wealthy offender as a method of buying his way out of prison when a less wealthy offender would inevitably have faced a custodial sentence.[8] The level of fine will normally reflect the court's views of the seriousness of the offence and the capacity to pay will be considered subsequently as an element of mitigation.

Fines in the magistrates' court. The magistrates' court, unlike the Crown Court, has no power to fine unless given by statute, usually the statute creating the offence. The practical consequence is that there is a vast range of fines available to magistrates' courts. The scheme[9] is as follows.

    (i) 'Either way' offences carry a maximum fine of £2,000 per offence.[10] Statute may provide a different maximum for an either way offence, however, and where it does then the higher figure prevails. The

---

4 (1982) 4 Cr App Rep (S) 348.
5 The proportion of persons fined in the magistrates' courts in 1983 was: indictable, 53%; summary (non-motoring), 89% and summary (motoring), 98%.
6 1973 Act s 30(1).
7 Ibid, s 42.
7a Ibid, s 30(1); see further Emmins, op cit, pp 181 et seq.
8 *R v Reeves* (1972) 56 Cr App Rep 366.
9 In so far as the farrago of statutory provisions deserves such a description; a good summary of fines after the Criminal Justice Act 1982 was issued by Butterworths as part of Halsbury's Statutes of England.
10 Magistrates' Courts Act 1980, s 39(2): Criminal Penalties etc (Increase) Order 1984, Sch 1.

reason for this is that the either way offences to which the fine limit applies are specified in Schedule 1 to the Act of 1980. Any offence not thus specified but triable either way is not subject to the usual prescribed maximum.[11]

(ii) Most summary offences have been allocated to a 'standard' scale of fine. There are five scales. Offences were allocated to the scales by reference to the maximum fine they carried before the scale system was introduced in 1983.[12] They have now been updated as follows:

Scale	Amount of fine
1	£50
2	£100
3	£400
4	£1,000
5	£2,000

(iii) Other summary offences were not made subject to the 'standard scale' system. Certain summary fines, many of a minor or local nature, were kept at their pre-scale level. Other specified fines were made subject to considerable increases.[13]

(iv) Sometimes a statute enables a magistrates' court to imprison for an offence but does not give a power to fine. If the offence is triable either way the court may fine instead up to the usual maximum for such offences. If the offence is triable only summarily then a maximum is prescribed. This is presently £400.[14]

Almost all fines which can be imposed by magistrates' courts can be, and have been, increased by statutory instrument.[15] You cannot hope to advise your clients on the fine they might have to pay without consulting the current edition of *Stone's Justices' Manual*.

Magistrates are specifically required to take into account an offender's means when fixing a fine.[16] The court will be informed of this when it hears mitigation, and if legal aid has been granted the statement of means will contain further information. In many motoring offences, however, the offender may avail himself of the opportunity of pleading guilty by post, and the extent to which the court is aware of his means will depend on the information given there. Furthermore, in motoring offences the court may look to a 'recommended' fine as suggested by the Magistrates' Association Guidelines. The offender's means are still relevant in considering whether this penalty is appropriate.

Time for payment of fines and penalties in default

The Crown Court. When the Crown Court imposes a fine after a trial on indictment or committal for sentence, it may require immediate payment or give a later date for payment, or allow payment by instalments. In any

11 Eg Prevention of Oil Pollution Act 1974, s 14: maximum fine on summary conviction is £50,000; Customs and Excise Management Act 1979 s 64(4)—maximum fine on summary conviction is the prescribed sum for an either way offence or 3 times the value of the seized goods whichever is greater.
12 Criminal Justice Act 1982, s 37; Criminal Penalties etc Increase Order 1984.
13 1982 Act, Schs 2 and 3 respectively.
14 Magistrates' Courts Act 1980, s 34(3)(b).
15 Ibid, s 43; Criminal Penalties etc Increase Order 1984.
16 Ibid, s 35. Emmins, op cit, at p 179 suggests that there are 4 stages to be considered seriatim when fixing a fine: (i) gravity of offence; (ii) mitigating factors; (iii) means; (iv) time to pay.

event, it will specify when the payment or payments are to be made. Furthermore, the Crown Court must, when imposing a fine, specify a period of imprisonment which will be served in default of payment of that fine,[17] although in general the court cannot imprison if it does not first allow time to pay. The periods of imprisonment specified are maxima and vary depending on the amount of the fine which is outstanding. Thus for example, if the fine is of £50 or less, the maximum term which may be fixed in default is seven days' imprisonment. At the other end of the scale, if the fine exceeds £10,000 the maximum term that may be fixed is 12 months' imprisonment. Thus the court accordingly has no discretion as to imposing a period in default, but does have discretion over what that period shall be.

Magistrates' court Magistrates have similar powers to the Crown Court to allow payment by instalments or at a later date, rather than to insist on immediate payment.[18] Like the Crown Court, magistrates may not generally commit an offender to prison if the fine is not paid immediately. Unlike the Crown Court, a magistrates' court may not fix a term of imprisonment to be served in default of payment, although it may imprison up to the same period in the event of actual default.

Enforcement of fines.[19] Although you will not usually be appearing in connection with fine enforcement, you should be aware of the methods available, as your clients may be affected by them. Enforcement of all fines, whether imposed by the Crown Court or a magistrates' court, is carried out by the magistrates' court for the area in which the offender resides. A magistrates' court may issue a warrant committing the offender to prison for non-payment of fines, although this cannot be done unless there has been wilful default. In practice the enforcement court will first issue a summons against the defaulter, requiring him to attend a means inquiry. Here the defaulter will be examined on oath with the object of establishing whether he has deliberately failed to pay the fine. If the non-payment was not deliberate then the court will try to determine how payment can best be achieved in the future. Rather than imprisoning for default, the court may make an *attachment of earnings order* requiring the defaulter's employer to deduct a prescribed sum from his wages and pay it to the court. Alternatively it may make a Money Payment Supervision Order, whereby a probation officer attempts to supervise payment of the fine by regular instalments. The court can also order that the defaulter's goods be seized and sold by public auction. At the other end of the scale, magistrates' courts have power to remit entirely or in part money owed, including an unpaid fine if it considers it just to do so having regard to change in circumstances since the fine was imposed.[20]

5 Probation orders: 1973 Act, ss 2 to 6, and 8

Probation orders are designed to leave an offender in the community subject to assistance, supervision and advice from a probation officer. They are

---

17 1973 Act, s 31.
18 Magistrates' Courts Act 1980, s 75; default in payment of any one installment enables enforcement to proceedings to issue for the whole sum: ibid, s 75(3).
19 See generally 1980 Act, ss 75–91; 1973 Act, s 32.
20 1980 Act, s 85; in the case of Crown Court fines, consent is required: 1973 Act, s 32.

available in respect of *any* offence, but in practice are made in respect of imprisonable offences. They are aimed at re-habilitation rather than punishment, and certain conditions may be built into orders so as to increase their chances of success.[21]

Power to make orders. Both the Crown Court and magistrates' courts may make probation orders.[1] The minimum period of probation that may be imposed by either court is *six months,* and the maximum *three years.* The court ordering probation must stipulate the length of the order.

The offender must be *17 or over,* and give his *consent* to being placed on probation.[2] Before he does so, the court must warn him that in the event of committing any further offence during the probation period the court retains the power to re-sentence him for the original offence.

Curiously, a social inquiry report from a probation officer does not have to be available to the court before a probation order is made. In practical terms, however, no court will make such an order without a probation officer accepting the offender for probation.[3]

Conditions and restrictions which may be imposed. A court may wish to impose restrictions when making a probation order, rather than leave the treatment of the offender entirely up to the probation service. Although an offender must comply with any requirements that the court deems appropriate 'for securing the good conduct of the offender or preventing a repetition by him of the same offence or commission of other offences',[4] courts prefer to impose specific conditions under the provisions described below.

The court frequently requires that the probationer resides at a specified place. This may include residence at a probation hostel for a period of time, where the probationer will live, and be subject to the general guidance and supervision of the probation service or another approved agency. Probation hostels are not available in every petty sessions area and such a requirement may result in a move to a new locality.

The court may impose a requirement that the probationer attends a day centre, provided that it consults a probation officer and that satisfactory arrangements can be made at a centre. Such centres exist in various parts of the country, and are designed to assist the offender with acquiring social rehabilitative skills. The nature of individual centres varies, and the probationer will be required to attend one which is particularly suited to his needs, for up to a maximum of *60 days* in the currency of the order.[4]

As an *alternative* to day training, a court may, as part of probation, require a probationer to participate in schemes designed to improve self awareness and social skills, again up to a maximum of *60 days.* Many probation services have projects of this kind available. As before, the probation officer must be consulted before the order can be made.[4]

All the above requirements are positive in that they require the probationer to *do* something, but a court can also impose a 'negative' condition requiring him to refrain from doing something on specified days or for a specified period. As with the basic order, all these conditions can only be imposed with the probationer's consent. Of course, if he does not consent,

21 See further: 'The Sentence of the Court', Home Office, HMSO.
1 1973 Act, s 2.
2 This includes consent to any conditions the court imposes.
3 H/O Circular 30/1971.
4 1973 Act, s 2(3): permissible requirements and conditions are contained in ibid, ss 2, 4A and 4B.

the court may impose a different order altogether, which may be less to his liking.

Consequences of a probation order. A probation order does not strictly speaking count as a conviction other than for the purpose of the proceedings in which it was imposed.[5] As already mentioned, this is important because it means that it cannot activate a suspended or part-suspended sentence of imprisonment.[6] In addition it means that a probation order cannot be combined with any form of sentence for the *same offence*, such as a fine.[7] It can, however, be combined with any of the court's ancillary powers, including a compensation order, endorsement of driving licences or disqualification from driving, and another for costs, because they are not 'sentences'.

Future conduct and probation orders. An offender's future conduct can affect a probation order in one or both of two ways. A probationer may *break a condition* of the probation order itself, or may *commit a further offence* whilst the order is running. Only the first of these is, strictly speaking, breach of probation, but the second is commonly included in this term.

Breach of the order:1973 Act, s6

Irrespective of whether the probation order was made by the Crown Court or a magistrates' court, a probationer who is alleged to have broken a condition of probation or any requirements specified in the order may be brought by summons before the magistrates' court for the area in which he resides.[8] Alternatively, a warrant may be issued for his arrest. The court may, if the breach is proved:

- fine the probationer up to £400; or
- make an attendance centre order; or
- revoke the probation order and sentence the offender for the original offence (save in the case of Crown Court orders).[9]

In practice it is comparatively rare for probation officers to have to resort to these powers. The question of continuance or otherwise of the probation order arises more commonly when probationers are brought before the court charged with committing offences whilst still on probation.

Commission of further offences: 1973 Act, s8

When a probationer is convicted of any offence the convicting court may be able to sentence him for the *original offence as well*. The power to sentence de novo is broadly the same as for activating suspended sentences. As with suspended sentences, the existence of the probation order must be proved if the offender does not admit it.[9a]

---

5 1973 Act, s 13, op cit.
6 Nor a conditional discharge, see p 406 post.
7 1973 Act, s 2. It could be combined with a *fine* but not *imprisonment* for *another* offence dealt with at the same time; *R v Emmett* (1968) 53 Cr App Rep 203.
8 Alternatively, if the order was made by a different magistrates' court, then the informations can be tried there instead.
9 1973 Act, s 6. If the order was made by the Crown Court, the magistrates may either commit him in custody or on bail: ibid s 6(4). The 'right to bail' applies: see p 240, ante.
9a For the provisions relating to breach of suspended sentences see p 399, ante.

Will the court always sentence? Although a court has power to sentence the offender de novo for the original offence, this does not preclude the making of a further probation order both in relation to the original offence and the new offence. In practice, therefore, when a probationer is found guilty of committing further offences the view of the probation officer who has been supervising him is likely to be of crucial importance. If the probation officer is able to explain the circumstances behind and the reasons for the commission of the new offence, and otherwise confirm a positive response to the probation order it may be possible to persuade the court to make a further probation order. This particularly applies if it is a magistrates' court. If the new offence is dealt with by the Crown Court, a further probation order is much less likely as the new offence will normally be of a more serious nature. The Crown Court is quite likely to impose consecutive custodial terms for the present and previous offences.

(6) Absolute and conditional discharges: 1973 Act, s 7

Such an order may be imposed in respect of *any* offence if, having regard to the circumstances, including the nature of the offence and character of the offender, it is inexpedient to inflict punishment and probation is inappropriate.[10] The offender is discharged immediately in the case of an absolute discharge and after a period specified by the court in the case of a conditional discharge. The conviction and the discharge still appear on his record, and will be seen, the court is not precluded from making ancillary orders such as costs compensation disqualification or endorsement.[11] Absolute discharges tend to be reserved for those offenders who, although technically guilty, are virtually blameless, whereas conditional discharges are most common in non-motoring offences involving 'real' but minimal criminality.

(i) Absolute discharges. An absolute discharge cannot have supervision or any other conditions attached to it, and no other form of punishment can be imposed at the same time for the same offence other than ancillary orders. Unlike probation or a conditional discharge, there is no power to resentence in the event of reoffending.

(ii) Conditional discharges. These are analogous to suspended sentences and probation in that they constitute yet another 'Sword of Damocles' order. When making these orders the court must prescribe a period for which the conditional discharge will run. This can be for any period not exceeding three years. If the offender commits *any* other offence during the period of conditional discharge he is liable to be sentenced both for the fresh offence and for the offence for which the conditional discharge was imposed. The court must explain this to the offender at the time the conditional discharge is ordered.[12]

The chart set out on page 432 applies also to conditional discharges.

Practice on reoffending. Since conditional discharges tend to be imposed for relatively trivial offences most courts will resentence with reluctance, particularly if the period of conditional discharge has nearly finished, or if the new offence is of a different character. However, if the offences are

---

10 1973 Act, s 7. The only exception is where the sentence is fixed by law.
11 1973 Act, s 12; Road Traffic Act 1972, s 102.
12 Ibid, s 7(3).

exactly the same, the court may well allow the 'Sword of Damocles' to fall. Otherwise, the whole object of the discharge is lost.

7 Community service orders: 1973 Act, ss 14 to 17

Community service orders may be made by both the Crown Court and by magistrates' courts.[13] They require the offender to perform unpaid work, for a number of hours specified in the order, at the direction of an agency, normally the probation service appropriate to where the offender lives. The work prescribed will depend on the facilities of the scheme, but may consist of community projects such as clearing scrub land belonging to the National Trust, or heavy labouring work for a preserved steam railway. The work will normally be carried out in supervised teams. Subsequently offenders may be allowed to take over individual projects such as decorating or gardening for old people.

Community service orders can only be made when the offence is punishable by imprisonment. However, it is neither a requirement of the law, nor sentencing practice, that imprisonment would otherwise be the only appropriate sentence. The court must have obtained a social inquiry report[14] from the probation service, confirming that a scheme is available and that the offender is suitable for the project, and the offender must consent to the order. The order may run from a minimum of *40 hours* up to a maximum of *240 hours*. The actual number of hours will be specified by the court and must be completed within *12 months*.

Community service orders cannot be combined with any other sentence for the same offence but may be combined with ancillary orders. Furthermore, it is bad sentencing practice to impose a community service order for one offence and a suspended sentence for another offence dealt with at the same time.[15] A court can impose more than one community service order, but the aggregate number of hours ordered must not exceed 240 hours.

The effect of breaking a condition of a community service order. If the offender breaks a term of the order or fails to comply with his supervisor's requirements, for example, by being a disruptive influence or failing to attend as directed, the supervisor may apply to the magistrates' court specified in the order for a summons or warrant for arrest. The court may fine the offender up to a maximum of £400 or revoke the order and sentence de novo, provided that the order was made by a magistrates' court. A magistrates' court has no power to revoke a Crown Court order, but can commit the offender to the Crown Court on bail or in custody. The Crown Court may then either fine him and continue the order, or revoke the order and sentence de novo.[16]

The effect of reoffending. Reoffending does not necessarily bring the order to an end. Depending on the sentence imposed for the new offence, there is no reason why the order should not continue to run. Reoffending may, of course, result in the supervisor applying for the order to be revoked. Alternatively, if the convicting court is the one specified in the order, it may

13 The power to sentence de novo is contained in s 8 of the 1973 Act. Where dealing with a discharge imposed by a different court the rules are the same as for suspended sentences: see p 399, ante.
14 1973 Act, s 14(1): curiously, this is the only order where a social enquiry report is mandatory prerequisite.
15 *R v Starie* (1979) 69 Cr App Rep 239, CA; see generally Emmins, op cit, p 237.
16 1973 Act, s 16. Note that if the order has been substantially completed, credit must be given for that when resentencing: *R v Anderson* (1982) 4 Cr App Rep(s) 252.

revoke the order and sentence de novo or (in the case of a Crown Court order) commit the offender to the Crown Court in custody or on bail.[17] If the offender is convicted of an offence before any other magistrates' court, that court can only revoke the community service order or (in the case of a Crown Court order) commit him in custody or on bail.[18]

If a person serving any community service order is convicted at the Crown Court of another offence, or brought before the Crown Court for sentence, the Crown Court can revoke the order or revoke and sentence de novo, whether made by itself or by a magistrates' court if it seems in the interests of justice to do so.[19]

(2) Sentences for offenders over 17 but under 21 — 'Young adult offenders'

1 Custodial sentences on young adults

A new regime of custodial sentences for young adults was brought into being by the Criminal Justice Act 1982. This provided two main sentences for offenders in this age group, namely detention centre and youth custody orders, and at the same time removed the power to sentence persons under 21 years to imprisonment.[20] This does not mean, however, that they cannot find themselves in a prison on occasions if, for example, they are held there on remand.[21] In addition they may still be allocated to a prison if they prove to be unsuited to a youth custody centre.[1]

Statutory restrictions on custodial sentences. A young adult cannot receive a custodial sentence *at all* unless the court considers that there is *no alternative* on the ground that:

> he is unable or unwilling to respond to non-custodial penalties: or a custodial sentence is needed to protect the public: or a custodial sentence is necessary because of the nature of the offence.[2]

It appears that the courts' attention has not been sufficiently drawn to this provision: it should never be overlooked.

As with persons over 21, the offender must be represented, at least at the sentencing stage, before a custodial sentence can be imposed or have applied for legal aid and been refused on the basis of his means or have failed to apply for legal aid notwithstanding that he had been given the opportunity to do so. There is, however, one major difference between this provision in so far as it applies to young adults. In the case of young adult offenders it applies every time a court considers imposing a custodial sentence and not merely when considering imprisonment for the *first time*.[3]

---

17 1973 Act, s 17(2). The power only arises if the supervising officer applies.
18 Ibid, s 17(4A). The power only arises if the supervising officer applies.
19 Ibid, s 17(3), including under ss 16(3), 17(2) or 17(4A). If the original conviction was by a *magistrates' court*, the Crown Court can only impose a sentence which the magistrates could have imposed
20 Criminal Justice Act 1982, s 1(1).
21 Ibid, s 1(2).
 1 Ibid, s 12(1).
 2 Ibid, s 1(4). See also Burney, 'All things to all men' [1985] Crim LR 284.
 3 Ibid, s 3. Obviously it is less likely that someone in this age group will be refused legal aid on financial gounds. Contrast s 20 of the 1973 Act at p 395, ante.

Similarly, as with offenders aged 21 or over, a court must generally obtain a social inquiry report unless the circumstances render it unnecessary. In such a case a magistrates' court must state the reason why in its opinion it was unnecessary to obtain a report and this must be entered in the court record. It must also state in open court the reason why it considers that no penalty other than a custodial one is appropriate. Again, this provision applies *every* time the court is considering a custodial sentence, and not just to the first occasion.[4]

(a) Detention centre orders: 1982 Act, s 4. Orders for detention may be passed on any male offender aged between 14 and 20 inclusive and who has been convicted of an offence which is *punishable by imprisonment* in the case of a person aged 21 or over. The relevant date in determining age is presumably that of conviction.[5] In addition the court must be satisfied that a period of detention of no more than *four months* is appropriate. Detention cannot be ordered if the offender has previously served a sentence of youth custody, custody for life or, long term detention,[6] although there is nothing to prohibit a further period of detention if one has already been served. Before the 1982 Act it was comparatively rare for a second detention centre order to be made; it remains to be seen if the same will apply under the new regime.

The court must specify the length of detention, which cannot be for more than *four months* and must be for a minimum of *21 days*. In any event, if the offence carries a maximum term of imprisonment of less than four months, then that is also the limit for a detention centre order.[7]   If the offender is already serving a detention centre order when he comes before the court to be dealt with for a second offence, the court may make another detention centre order, but the aggregate term served must not be more than *four months*.[8]

Where will the detention centre order be served? There are a variety of detention centres in England and Wales to which the offender may be sent. All provide a 'short sharp shock' regime. The Home Office advises magistrates, courts of detention centre availability for offenders in this age group.[9]

Matters affecting the length of time served. Time spent on remand in custody counts towards the length of time that has to be served under the detention centre order. In addition, the detention centre system also allows for remission of up to a total of *one third* of the sentence passed or unless this is lost through breaches of discipline. Accordingly, the minimum length of time that can be served is *14 days*, namely the minimum sentence of *21 days* less one week for remission.

Supervision after release. The parole system does not apply to detention centres. However, when an offender is released from a detention centre he will be under supervision for *three months* from the date of release, irrespective of whether or not his release was as a result of receiving remission, and provided

4 Contrast s 20A of the 1973 Act at p 394, ante.
5 1982 Act s 1 and *R v Lowery*, op cit.
6 Also borstal or imprisonment, under the regime in existence prior to the 1982 Act.
7 Eg common assault, maximum penalty 2 months' imprisonment, Offences against the Person Act 1861 s 42.
8 1982 Act, s 5—although it can convert the order into one of youth custody if he is 15 or over.
9 H/O Circular 55/1983. See also Detention Centre Rules 1983.

that the supervision cannot extend beyond his 21st birthday. The supervising officer will be a probation officer or a social worker. This supervision is compulsory, but not analagous to release on parole or to a probation order, since if the offender breaks a term of the supervision or fails to cooperate with the supervisor he cannot be recalled to the detention centre as his sentence has finished. Failure to comply with any requirement specified in a notice from the Secretary of State constitutes an offence punishable on summary conviction with a fine not exceeding £400 or a further custodial sentence of up to 30 days.[10]

(b) Youth custody orders: 1982 Act, s 6. Whereas detention orders are mainly intended to be punitive, a youth custody order is intended as a longer-term measure, containing a substantial element of training.[11] Youth custody can be ordered against anyone aged *15 to 20 years* inclusive who has committed an offence punishable *by imprisonment* in the case of someone aged 21 or over. Unlike detention centre orders it is available for both males and females, although the powers in respect of females differ significantly. The court must state in open court the reasons why it has decided a custodial sentence is the only way of dealing with the offender.[12]

How long does an order last? One of the criticisms of the old borstal training orders was that the court neither knew nor had any control over the length of time for which the offender would be detained. An offender could be in a borstal for at least 6 months and for no more than two years. Other than · this, the length of time was in the discretion of the institution itself. Under the youth custody regime, a court will normally, when passing sentence, specify the length of time for which the order will run when it passes sentence. This is subject however to two important limitations.[13]

(i) *An order for youth custody cannot exceed the maximum term of imprisonment the court could impose on a person who is aged 21 or over.* Accordingly, although sentences of youth custody can be passed by both the Crown Court and magistrates' courts, the latter is subject to the usual 6 months maximum (*12 months* in aggregate if two or more indictable offences are tried summarily and consecutive terms are imposed).

(ii) *A youth custody order should normally be made for a term of more than four months.* It is only in certain circumstances, discussed below, that a shorter period can be imposed; even then, the period may not be less than 21 days.

Exceptions to the minimum period—male offenders. In respect of a male offender the court may impose less than four months if satisfied that less is merited *and provided* it is unable to pass a detention centre order either because the offender's mental or physical condition is such as to render him unsuitable to such an order, or because he has already served youth custody, long-term detention under s 53 of the Children and Young Person Act 1933 or custody for life under s 8 of the 1982 Act.[14]

Exceptions to the minimum period—female offenders. If a female offender has attained the age of *17 years*, four months or less youth custody can be imposed if merited.[15] Since there are no detention centres for females, this exception

10 1982 Act, s 15.
11 See eg 'Young Offenders' Cmnd 8045 at p 12 et seq.
12 See 1982 Act, s 6(1)(B).
13 Ibid, s 7.
14 Ibid, s 6(2) and in the absence of special circumstances rendering detention centre desirable.
15 Ibid, s 6(4).

enables an equivalent short sentence to be imposed. (However, this means that no short term custodial measure is available for females aged *15 or 16.*)

As with detention centre orders, the Prison Department will take into account any time spent in custody prior to conviction when calculating the release date, and one third remission also applies.[16] In addition to remission, release on licence is also possible.[17] Licence, or parole has the same meaning and the same general effect as in the case of a person aged 21 or over released from imprisonment on parole. Offenders released on licence from youth custody remain subject to recall until they reach the time when they would have been released as a result of remission, and until then they will be under the supervision of a probation officer. As with detention centre orders, even when the remission date is reached, an offender released from youth custody will be under supervision. As this work is mainly concerned with procedure up to and including sentencing, the rules as to the calculation of the various supervision periods will not be discussed in detail. In general, however, the offender will be under supervision for about three months, subject to the overall rule that supervision again cannot extend beyond the offender's 22nd birthday, or beyond 12 months from the date of release.[18]

Accommodation of young offenders serving youth custody orders. The White Paper on Young Offenders[19] indicated that those receiving short and medium youth custody sentences should be guaranteed places in youth custody centres, which would have training facilities. It recognised that, with the limited resources, there might not be room to accommodate offenders serving long terms of youth custody centres. Long sentences were considered to be orders for more than 18 months youth custody. All the borstal institutions and at least one of the young prisoner centres existing prior to the 1982 Act have been designated Youth Custody Centres. Accordingly, males sentenced to more than 4 but not more than 18 months youth custody must normally spend their sentence in a youth custody centre.[20] Any other offender may be kept in a youth custody centre, a remand centre or a prison, as directed by the Home Secretary. Females are not guaranteed places in youth custody centres, even if their sentence is between four and 18 months. However, the White Paper indicated that sufficient training places would be made available for them.

Finally, the Home Secretary has a variety of powers enabling him to direct that certain categories of offender be detained other than in youth custody centres for short periods, and also to alter the prescribed periods set out above if necessary. Furthermore, he may direct that offenders serving relatively long terms of youth custody who reach the age of 21 before they are due to be released may have their sentences converted into sentences of imprisonment. This will result in the offender being transferred to the nearest suitable prison appropriate for his age. Although it is too early to say whether or not such orders or directions will be made, it should be noted that already there is an overcrowding crisis in the new youth custody centres, as a result of which the Home Office was reported to be about to convert at least two detention centres into youth custody centres.[21] It would appear that magis-

16 CJA 1967, s 67; Youth Custody Centre Rules 1983, r 5.
17 CJA 1967, s 60.
18 1982 Act, s 15 contains the detailed rules. Breach of supervision constitutes an offence in the same way as breach of detention centre orders; see p 410, ante.
19 Cmnd 8045 (op cit).
20 Ibid, s 12; Prison Act 1952, s 43.
21 1983 The Guardian, 14 September.

trates' courts are exercising their power to make youth custody orders extensively, with the result that the youth custody centres are rapidly filling up. Thus it is likely that longer youth custody orders will be directed to be served in prison, and general overcrowding will make any useful training all the more difficult to achieve.

Custody for life: 1982 Act, s 8. If the Crown Court finds an offender *under 21* guilty of murder or other offences carrying life as a *fixed* penalty he *must* be sentenced to custody for life.[1] If the offender is found guilty of a crime which would carry imprisonment for life as a maximum in the case of someone of 21 or over, the court *may* sentence him to life custody if it considers this appropriate.[2] The usual qualifications as to requiring representation and reports apply to the second power, but not to the first, as in such a case the court has no discretion over the type or length of sentence and thus reports and representations on sentence are irrelevant.

2 Attendance centre orders, 1982 Act, s 17

An attendance centre order requires the offender to give up leisure time, often on a Saturday afternoon, when he will be supervised, usually by the police, in leisure activities, which may vary from physical training, to DIY or car maintenance classes. The order can be made by the Crown Court or a magistrates' court, but for young adult offenders it can only be passed on males as there are no attendance centres available for females in this age group. It is available in three situations only:[3]

   (i) If the offence is punishable by imprisonment in the case of someone aged 21 or over; or

  (ii) If the offender has failed to comply with any requirement of a probation order; or

 (iii) If the offender is in default of payment of a fine or a compensation order.

In the absence of special circumstances an order cannot be made[4] if the offender has previously received a custodial sentence. In any event there must be an attendance centre reasonably accessible to the offender where he can serve the order.[5]

The order is for a number of hours which must be specified by the court when it is made. The maximum available for young adult offenders is 36 hours, but the normal length is 12 hours unless there are reasons why this is too short. In any case, the maximum time that can be spent on the order in any one day is three hours. This means that most orders will occupy four sessions of three hours each, although it is for the centre supervisor to direct when and for what period of time the offender must attend.

Breach of the requirements of an attendance order. Bearing in mind the relatively short length of these orders, there are somewhat overcomplicated provisions concerned with variation, discharge and breach of them.[6]

---

1 1982 Act, s 8(1): save for persons under 18 who commit murder. They are detained 'during Her Majesty's pleasure': Children and Young Persons Act 1933, s 53(1).
2 1982 Act, s 8(2).
3 Ibid, s 17(1).
4 Ibid, s 17(3).
5 Courts are notified of the existence of centres by the Home Office: see H/O Circular 64/1983.
6 1982 Act, ss 18 and 19. Broadly the court may revoke the order and sentence him de novo.

3 Other sentences

All the other sentences considered in relation to offenders who are aged 21 or more apply equally to young adult offenders

(3) Sentences for persons under 17—Juveniles. It will be recalled that juveniles are split into two categories, namely *children* (aged under 14) and *young persons* (14 to 16 inclusive). The differences between these subgroups will be considered in relation to each sentence.[7] For the purposes of sentencing whether a person is a juvenile is determined by his age on the date he is dealt with.[8]

1 Detention centre orders. As with young adult offenders, these orders are only available for males, and the basic prerequisites as to reports and representation must again be complied with. They are not available for *children*, but only for *young persons*.

2 Youth Custody Orders. Youth custody orders are not available in respect of all juveniles but only in respect of those *young persons* who have attained the age of 15 years at the date of conviction.[9] The prerequisites as to report and representation must be observed. In addition, however, a young person of 15 or 16 cannot receive a term of youth custody exceeding *12 months*. This provision is absolute and cannot be avoided by a court imposing two terms of youth custody to run consecutively to each other, as any term in respect of such a person is treated as remitted in so far as it exceeds 12 months.[10] Furthermore, females can only receive youth custody if the court thinks that *more than four months* is necessary. This means that if they do not merit youth custody in excess of four months, then they cannot receive youth custody at all. They cannot, of course, be sent to detention centres because there are none available for them.

3 Detention 'during Her Majesty's Pleasure': CYPA 1933, s 53(1). A person who has not attained *18 years* who is found guilty of murder, must be detained 'during Her Majesty's Pleasure'.[11] If found guilty of any other offence punishable by life imprisonment, a juvenile will be sentenced under s 53(2), below. If the offender is released this will be on the instruction of the Home Secretary acting in conjunction with the parole board, the Lord Chief Justice, and the trial judge if still available.

4 Long term detention CYPA 1933, s 53(2). Long term detention is used for juveniles who are found to have committed offences carrying at least *14 years'* imprisonment in the case of a person aged 21 or over. It can only be ordered by the Crown Court and the juvenile will be committed for trial if the juvenile court feels that such a sentence appears likely in the event of a finding of guilt.[12] These orders are exceptional, and must only be made if there is no other suitable method of dealing with the offender.[13] Long term detention is used when the principle objective is not rehabilitation so much as the safety and protection of the public. The Crown Court will specify the

---

7 A chart showing sentences against juveniles is at the end of chapter 10.
8 *S (infant) v Manchester City Recorder* [1971] AC 481, HL, per Lord Guest.
9 1982 Act, s 6. Strictly speaking juveniles are not 'convicted' but are 'found guilty'.
10 Ibid, s 7(8) and (9).
11 Children and Young Persons Act 1933, s 53(1): thus including offenders in the last category as well.
12 1933 Act, s 53(2): see pp 306 et seq, ante.
13 Such sentences are extremely rare: see eg *R v Storey* [1984] Crim LR 438 and Emmins, op cit, pp 169 et seq.

period of long term detention which cannot exceed the sentence of imprisonment for the offence.

5 Attendance centres. Attendance centres are available in respect of any person aged 10 to 20 inclusive. The qualifications outlined earlier in the chapter apply equally here, save that junior attendance centres, for persons under 17, are available for both males and females. As for young adults, the order will normally be for 12 hours up to a maximum of 24 hours.[14]

6 Fines. Juveniles may be fined in the same circumstances in which an adult may be fined. In the Crown Court, there in theory is no limit placed on the fine, but it is comparatively rare for a juvenile to be sentenced there in any event.

In summary trials, whether in the adult court or as will be more usual, in the juvenile court, a young person cannot be fined more than £400, and a child more than £100.[15] Furthermore, fines against juveniles must be ordered to be paid by the parent or guardian unless 'it would be unreasonable to make an order for payment having regard to the circumstances of the case'.[16]

If necessary, enforcement can be carried out by any of the methods available against adults. In addition, however, a defaulting juvenile can receive an attendance centre order or the parent or guardian can be ordered to enter into a recognisance for payment, or to pay the fine (assuming he has not already been ordered to do so).[17]

7 Community service orders. The Crown Court or a juvenile court may sentence a young person who has attained the age of *16 years* to a term of community service, provided he consents. The order operates exactly as for an adult, save that while the minimum hours that can be ordered remain at 40, the maximum hours are limited to *120*.[18] An order cannot be made unless a scheme is available for the appropriate petty sessions area, and as with adults a report from the social services department or a probation officer is an essential prerequisite. The powers of rescission and revocation are the same as for adults.

8 Binding over of parents. Where a court finds a juvenile guilty of any offence other than murder his parents or guardians may be asked by the court to enter into a recognisance to take proper care and exercise proper control over him *irrespective of any other sentence or order that is made*.[19] The parent or guardian must consent to being bound over and the maximum amount of the recognisance which can be fixed by the court at that time is £1,000. The bind over can last for a maximum of three years. The parent does not, of course, pay any money over on entering into the recognisance; the amount may be ordered to be paid only if the juvenile offends again and the court thinks the parent should have been able to prevent it.

9 Discharges. These are available for use by courts when dealing with juveniles in the same way as for adults. Discharges, together with fines and bind overs of parents are the only orders that can be made against a juvenile by an adult magistrates' court, as opposed to a juvenile court or the Crown Court.

14 1982 Act, s 17(4), (5). An order of less than 12 hours may be imposed on a child if 12 hours is thought to be excessive.
15 Magistrates' Courts Act 1980, ss 24 and 36.
16 1933 Act, s 55, as substituted by 1982 Act, s 26.
17 MCA 1980, s 81.
18 1973 Act, s 14(1) and (1A).
19 Children and Young Persons Act 1969, s 7(7).

10 Care orders: CYPA 1969, s7. This is the first order of any significance mentioned so far that can only be made in respect of a juvenile. An order commits a juvenile into the care of the social services department of the local authority. The order can be made upon a finding of guilt of any offence punishable with *imprisonment* in the case of a person aged 21 or over[19]. A care order will last until the subject attains *18 years* when it will automatically terminate, unless the juvenile was aged 16 or more when the order was made, when it will run until he is 19.[20]

A care order may not be made *unless* it is appropriate because of the seriousness of the offence *and* the juvenile is otherwise unlikely to receive the care and control he needs. In addition, a care order may not be made unless the juvenile is either represented during the sentencing process or has had the opportunity of applying for legal aid but has neglected to do so, or has applied for and been refused legal aid on the ground of excessive disposable income and capital.[21] Although no Act specifically requires it, as a matter of practice a social inquiry report from the social services department will always be obtained.

The effect of a care order is to vest the local authority with practically all decisions which may be made about the juvenile, for example, these powers include the duty and the right to specify where the child will reside or be educated.[22] The child may thus find himself placed with foster parents or he may be placed in residential accommodation, known as a community home. The regime in the community home will depend on the local authority and the person in charge. The local authority also has the power to place the juvenile in *secure* accommodation, subject to the authorisation of a juvenile court;[23] on the other hand they may return the juvenile to his parents. This was a matter of considerable concern to the magistracy, particularly when they felt that a care order they had imposed was the only means of removing the child from the home and the undesirable influences there. Accordingly, if a juvenile who is *already in care as a result of having committed an offence* commits a further offence punishable by imprisonment in the case of a person aged 21 or over, the court may now add a *'residential condition'* to the existing care order.[24] The residential condition, which can only last for up to *six months*, prohibits the local authority from letting the juvenile live with a person or with persons specified in the order. The court must be satisfied that such a restriction is appropriate, although there is no specific requirement that they should obtain a social inquiry report for that purpose.

11 Supervision orders. A supervision order is the equivalent for a juvenile of a probation order for an adult.[25] It can only be made in respect of a person who is under the age of 17. In addition, a court may order that an existing care order made in criminal proceedings be substituted by a supervision order at a later date, usually on the application of the local authority. In the latter case an order cannot run beyond the juvenile's 18th birthday; otherwise a supervision order whenever made will last for three years unless the

20 Children and Young Persons Act 1969, s 20.
21 Ibid, s 7(7A)—a provision virtually identical to 1973 Act, s 20 and 1982 Act, s 3.
22 Child Care Act 1980, s 18; the local authority must take into account the child's wishes in so far as is practicable.
23 Ibid, s 21A. See also Secure Accommodation (No 2) Regs 1983.
24 Ibid, s 20A.
25 1969 Act, s 7(7).

court specifies a shorter period when the order is made.[1] If the juvenile is under 13 the supervisor will normally be the local authority, acting through a social worker, unless a probation officer has already had contact with another member of the family. If the juvenile is 13 or more the court may designate a probation officer or the local authority; it will usually be the former.

A wide variety of restrictions and conditions can be placed on supervision orders.[2] The following are the most important ones:

(i) *Residence.* The order may direct that the juvenile resides at a place specified in the order, although the individual with whom he is to live must agree.

(ii) *Intermediate treatment.* This is a collective term for a variety of different measures, comprising schemes run by local authorities to encourage juveniles to take part in a whole variety of activities so as to equip them with skills or enable them to play a proper role in society. The schemes vary depending on the policy and financial situation of the local authority concerned, but the court may order that the juvenile participates in such intermediate treatment as his superviser shall direct for a maximum period of *90 days* during the course of the supervision order, provided that an approved scheme or schemes exist in the area. This may involve the juvenile living in different places, including community homes or participating in day or evening activities or possibly becoming involved in 'outward bound' type activities.

(iii) *Directed intermediate treatment.* As an *alternative* to (ii), the court may impose intermediate treatment by specifically including in the order itself similar directions in relation to intermediate treatment as the supervisor might give under (ii). The effect of doing so is to take some of the discretion out of the supervisor's hands. Again, the maximum amount of treatment that can be ordered is *90 days.*

(iv) *Night restriction order.* The court may specify that the juvenile adheres to a curfew between the periods of 6.00 pm and 6.00 am. This may only be imposed for a total of *30 days.* It cannot be imposed if the intermediate treatment is left in the discretion of the supervisor. If the court orders both directed intermediate treatment and a curfew, the combined total of the two may not exceed 90 days.

(v) *Negative requirements.* These can be imposed as part of the order, again provided the court does not leave treatment in the discretion of the supervisor. The court has power to direct the supervised juvenile to refrain from an activity or activities for part or the whole of the supervision period. This might for example include a direction that he refrains from attending football matches at a particular ground.

Before the court imposes directed intermediate treatment, a night restriction order or negative restrictions the following must be satisfied: the supervisor must be consulted, the order must be both feasible and necessary for the good conduct of the offender, and either the offender or his parents must consent to the terms depending on whether he is a young person, or a child.

Subject to the above, the consent of the supervised offender is not required for a supervision order to be made. Furthermore, if a court subsequently

1   1969 Act, s 17.
2   Ibid, s 12. See further, Emmins, op cit, pp 221 et seq.

finds the offender guilty of a further offence then, in contrast to probation orders, it does not have the power to sentence de nova for the first offence, although the fact of re-offending may, of course, influence its decision as to the appropriate punishment for the new offence. The court may, on the application of the supervisor, discharge or vary the order if the offender fails to comply with any requirements in it. It may also impose a fine of up to £100, make an attendance centre order or substitute a care order for the supervision order.[3]

Which court will sentence a juvenile? Juveniles are of course normally tried in juvenile courts, but may occasionally be tried in adult courts.[4] Juvenile courts and the Crown Court have the full range of sentences open to them, save only that the former may have to commit to the Crown Court if it wishes to impose an order in excess of the magistrates' normal maximum.[5]

The Crown Court should always consider remitting a juvenile to the juvenile court for sentence, unless it is undesirable to do so.[6] In *R v Lewis*[7] Lord Lane CJ commented that with the changed sentencing regime introduced by the Criminal Justice Act 1982, the Crown Court and juvenile court's powers had largely been assimilated and the former should always be prepared to sentence rather than remit, if only to avoid the danger of disparity when two courts sentence different offenders both charged with the same offence. It may, however, be appropriate to remit if, for example, a report is needed and there can be no guarantee that the trial judge will be available on a subsequent occasion to sentence. It will, of course, be inappropriate to remit if the juvenile was committed for trial for murder or other grave crimes.

Magistrates' courts powers are very restricted. They must remit the juvenile to a juvenile court unless they intend to impose:

- a fine; or
- a discharge; or
- a bind over against the parent.

(4) Sentences for mentally disordered persons (all ages).

The court has three possibilities open to it when it appears that an offender suffers from a mental disorder,[7a] so that one of the normal sentences or orders is inappropriate. It may make a probation order or a supervision order, with a condition as to treatment. Alternatively it has the power to place the person in a hospital or under the guardianship of the local authority social services department.

1 Probation or supervision with a treatment requirement. Whenever the court makes a probation order or a supervision order it can include a 'treatment' condition subject to the consent of the offender if he is over 14.[8] The court must receive evidence from a medical practitioner, who must have special experience in the treatment of mental disorders. It may receive evidence in the form of a report a copy of which must be made available to the offender's advocate. The report must confirm that the offender both requires treatment

---

3 And provided he has not in the meantime attained 18 years: 1968 Act, ss 14 and 15.
4 See generally chapter 10.
5 Magistrates' Courts Act 1980, s 37, post.
6 1933 Act, s 56.
7 (1984) 79 Cr App Rep 94, CA.
7a Partly defined by Mental Health Act 1983, s 38.
8 1973 Act, s 3; 1969 Act, s 12(4).

and is likely to respond to it. Both the court and the defence can require the practitioner to attend to give oral evidence, and you are entitled to call rebutting evidence.

If the court is so satisfied, it may impose a requirement as to residential treatment in a hospital or nursing home, non-residential treatment as an outpatient or patient of a properly qualified doctor for all or part of the probation period. If the probationer fails to undergo the treatment[9] then this will be a breach of a condition of probation or supervision and can be dealt with as for any other breach of condition.

2 Guardianship and hospital orders after conviction: MHA 1983, s 37. A probation order with a treatment condition will not always be sufficient to cope with persons with mental disorders. These types of order[10] are appropriate for more serious problems. In both cases there are three basic requirements:

(i) the offence for which the offender is before the court must be impri- sonable in the case of a person of 21 or over; and

(ii) the court must receive evidence from two appropriately qualified medical practitioners that the offender is suffering from mental ill- ness, disorder or impairment; and

(iii) the court must consider that an order is the most suitable method of disposing of the case.

A guardianship order can be made in respect of an offender of any age, and usually places him under the guardianship of the social services department of the local authority. The proposed guardian must be willing to receive the person into guardianship.

A hospital order results in the offender being admitted to a specified hospital for treatment.[11] In this case evidence must be available to show that arrange- ments have been made for admission to hospital. Part II of the Mental Health Act 1983 contains detailed provisions concerned with the discharge of guardianship or hospital orders and the main points are summarised below:

(i) hospital orders only last initially for *one year*;

(ii) a patient of 16 or over can apply at frequent intervals to a mental health review tribunal for his case to be reviewed;

(iii) a hospital has an unfettered power to discharge a patient at any time;

(iv) a patient who has been discharged is not liable to re-call.

3 Hospital or guardianship orders without conviction. A magistrates' court may make one of these orders in respect of a person charged with an offence punishable by imprisonment as an alternative to conviction. It must be satisfied that the *actus reus* of the offence was performed by the accused, and that the three primary conditions set out under *2* above are met. This course of action will seldom be appropriate, and in practical terms is confined to persons who are too ill to be tried.[12]

4 Restriction orders: MHA 1983, s 41. When a court has to sentence a person

---

9 Other than for surgical, electrical or other treatment which he refuses on reasonable grounds, 1973 Act, s 6(6).

10 Mental Health Act 1983, s 37.

11 Both courts can also make interim hospital orders: ibid, s 38.

12 See eg *R v Lincolnshire (Kesteven) Justices, ex p O'Connor* [1983] 1 All ER 901; also *Stone's Justices' Manual* (1985) para 35.3. These orders are appealable as if they were convictions after a plea of not guilty—Mental Health Act 1983, s 45.

who is both ill and dangerous, hospital orders have disadvantages, mainly because of their lack of permanence. A *restriction order* is available if a hospital order is made *and* there is a danger of serious harm to the public if the offender were to be discharged. The order may be for a fixed period or without limit. The effect is that the hospital order continues whilst the restriction order is in force, and discharge, transfer or leave of absence can only be granted or effected with the consent of the Secretary of State.[13]

Restriction orders can only be made by the Crown Court, which must hear oral evidence from at least one doctor. A magistrates' court may commit any offender aged *14 years or more* to the Crown Court for sentence if the three primary conditions for making a hospital order are satisfied and the magistrates consider that in the light of the offence, the offender's past history, and the risk of reoffending, a restriction order ought to be made. The committal must be in custody, but may be to a hospital. The Crown Court is not bound to make a restriction order, but may make a hospital order or deal with the offender in any way in which the magistrates could have dealt with him.[14]

(5) Ancillary orders

In addition to a court's sentencing powers, other powers are available which, although not strictly speaking part of the 'sentence' as such may well contain a punitive element (eg disqualification from driving, criminal bankruptcy and forfeiture orders, and compensation orders). Conversely, the predominant purpose of other such orders is to compensate the victim (eg compensation and restitution orders. Although outside the scope of this work it is advisable, in addition, to be aware of the working of the Criminal Injuries Compensation Board[15] in case you are called upon to advise the victim rather than the perpetrator. If a magistrates' court commits an offender to the Crown Court for sentence under any of its powers, ancillary matters should be left for the Crown Court to deal with.[16]

1 Compensation orders: 1973 Act, s 35

Power to make orders. Any court may order compensation in respect of loss suffered by the victim of an offence. The court may make a compensation order as *well as or instead of* dealing with the offender in any other way.[17] Loss in this context includes both personal injury and physical loss of or damage to property, but is subject to a qualification in respect of loss suffered due to motor accidents. When there has been a motor accident, compensation cannot be ordered *unless* the offence was committed under the Theft Act *and* the property in respect of which compensation is sought was out of the owner's possession when the damage was done.[18] Thus, in *Quigley v Stokes*,[19] the defendant took a car without the owner's consent and in the course of driving it damaged not only that car but two other vehicles as well. Compensation

13 MHA 1983, ss 41 and 42.
14 Ibid, s 43.
15 Details available from the Board at 10–12 Russell Square, London, WC1.
16 See *R v Blackpool Justices, ex p Charlson and Gregory* [1972] 3 All ER 854 (restitution orders); Criminal Justice Act 1967, s 56(5) (deprivation and compensation orders).
17 1973 Act, s 35(1) as amended. It is therefore arguable that compensation should now be regarded as a sentence in its own right rather than as an ancillary order.
18 Ibid, s 35(2) and (3).
19 [1977] 2 All ER 317.

was awarded to the owner of the car taken by the defendant, but was not awarded to the owners of the other two vehicles. Although the offence was committed under the Theft Act, the second and third vehicles were still in their respective owners' possession. In most cases vehicles damaged because of road accidents will form part of the owner's claim in civil litigation against the tortfeasor. Damage to the vehicle will comprise part of the plaintiff's special damages. Motor vehicle accidents were excluded from compensation orders so as to avoid the criminal courts being inundated with what amounted to civil claims for damages arising out of careless driving prosecutions. *Quigley v Stokes* does, however, illustrate the unfortunate consequences of this. The offender may not be insured against liability so that the owner of the damaged car would have to claim against his own insurers, assuming he had comprehensive insurance. It is unlikely that any civil claim against the defendant would be worthwhile in such circumstances.

How much will be ordered? The basic principles that a court should take into account when considering an application was discussed in *R v Miller*:[20]

(i) the amount of compensation that should be awarded must be clear; if it is not, then this is a matter which should be decided by the civil court. This does not mean, however, that compensation can only be awarded if the prosecutor can prove that the defendant has a personal civil liability;
(ii) the court must consider the means of the defendant;
(iii) the order must set out the exact amount to be paid, by instalments if necessary;
(iv) the order must not be oppressive and must be an amount that the defendant can realistically pay. It is futile if it drives him back into crime.

Since *Miller* was decided the Powers of Criminal Courts Act has been amended, so that if the offender would be able to pay a fine or compensation, but not both, a court must order compensation in preference to a fine.[21]

Finally, magistrates' courts cannot order compensation exceeding £2,000 in respect of each offence upon which the defendant is found guilty. In addition they can make awards in respect of offences which the offender asks to have taken into consideration up to an aggregate maximum of £2,000 for each offence of which he is actually convicted.

Note that all the foregoing applies equally to adults and juveniles. The only difference is that just as with fines, the court will require the parents or guardian to pay unless there are reasons why they should not do so.

Procedure on applying for compensation. Although compensation can be ordered by a court of own motion, it will normally be applied for. The prosecution, who will normally be the police, will ascertain from the victim the value of any goods lost or damaged, and will include these particulars in their file. There is no reason why the prosecutor should not give particulars of the claims to the defence prior to the start of the case, but this is not always done. Some prosecutors wait until the magistrates or jury retires to consider its verdict. A solicitor should always take his client's instructions on the amount claimed and try to check if it is reasonable. If the defence objects to any of the claims, the prosecutor will have to call evidence in order to

20 [1976] Crim LR 694 and see *Archbold*, para 5–189.
21 1973 Act, s 35(4A), inserted by CJA 1982, s 67.

prove the loss. If the prosecutor cannot do this, he will either have to apply for an adjournment or may abandon the claim altogether. When there has been a trial, the court may be satisfied that the losses were sustained from the evidence it has heard. In any case, however, both the prosecutor and the defence are entitled to make representations as to amount.

If compensation is ordered, whether by a magistrates' court or the Crown Court, it will be collected through the magistrates' court for the area in which the offender resides who will remit it to the victim.

2 Restitution orders

A court may order an offender to return stolen goods to the person entitled to them or require the offender to pay the purchase price or the equivalent to the loser if in the meantime the goods have been disposed of. Both these orders can be made whether or not the loser actually applies for restitution.[1] In addition, the loser can also apply for the court to transfer substituted goods to him from the offender as when, for example, the latter has purchased other goods with the proceeds of sale of the stolen goods. As with compensation orders, criminal courts should not permit themselves to be used for litigating civil disputes, and these orders should only be made where legal title is certain.

3 Forfeiture and allied orders

Many statutes contain ancillary powers to order forfeiture of property as part of the court's adjudication, and some of the more important ones are set out below. In addition, the Powers of Criminal Courts Act 1973 gives a court a more general power to order the forfeiture of property.

(i) The Misuse of Drugs Act 1971. Any court convicting a person of an offence under the Act may order the forfeiture and destruction or other disposal of items which appear to the court to relate to the offence,[2] whether or not they[3] are owned by or in the possession of the offender.[3] Anyone who claims an interest in the property must be given the opportunity of making representation against forfeiture. For example, a drugs raid might reveal quantities of drugs, pipes or other material in the possession of a suspect, and as a result he is prosecuted. The court may order that this material be seized, even if it does not in fact really belong to the offender. A person wishing to object to forfeiture by claiming that the goods are in fact his may do so by applying at the trial. He does, however, run the risk of implicating himself.

(ii) Firearms. Whenever a person is sentenced to imprisonment, youth custody or detention, or is found guilty of a variety of offences under the Firearms Act 1968, the court may order the forfeiture and destruction of firearms in his possession.[4] This can include airguns, provided the offence is one where an air gun is treated as a type of firearm.

(iii) Obscene publications. A magistrates' court has power to order the forfeiture of obscene articles kept for publication for gain which have been seized pursuant to a warrant issued by a justice of the peace.[5] This power is not dependant upon conviction.

1 Theft Act 1968, s 28; Criminal Justice Act 1972, s 6.
2 Misuse of Drugs Act 1971, s 27.
3 *R v Ferguson* (1970) 54 Cr App Rep 415, CA.
4 Firearms Act 1968, s 52.
5 Obscene Publications Act 1959, s 3.

(iv) Forfeiture orders. Courts have wide powers over property under the offender's control at the time of his apprehension if the property has been used or was intended to be used for the purpose of committing or facilitating the commission of *any* offence.[6] The offence of which he is convicted must be punishable with not less than *two years'* imprisonment if tried on indictment. This means, of course, that the power is available to the magistrates' court, but only in respect of *either way* offences. For example, an offender who uses his van to transport stolen property may not only receive a sentence but also find that his van is made the subject of a forfeiture order.[7] You should therefore be prepared to present reasons why forfeiture should not be ordered as part of your mitigation.[8] There is an important limitation on this power: it may not be used where the property in question is the *proceeds* of crime rather than the means whereby it was committed.[8a] In cases involving the Theft Act 1968 it may be possible to deal with the proceeds by way of restitution orders, but this does assume that the victim can be found.

Note that under the Police (Property) Act 1897, either the accused or other persons may be entitled to apply to the police or to the court for an order for the return of property. This applies to both property which has been seized by the police, and property held by them under a forfeiture order.

4 *Criminal bankruptcy: 1973 Act, ss 39 and 40*

The Crown Court may make a criminal bankruptcy order against the offender if there are losses exceeding £15,000 to a known person or persons.[9] However, the loss must not be for personal injury, and the court must not have made a compensation order. If these qualifications are satisfied then the offender is treated as having committed an act of bankruptcy on the day that the order is made. The Director of Public Prosecutions or any creditor may thereafter present a bankruptcy petition and the affairs of the offender are investigated in broadly the same manner as in any other bankruptcy.

The object of such an order is to prevent large-scale professional criminals from reaping the rewards of their crimes when released from prison. It seems highly unlikely, however, that a sufficiently organised professional criminal will in practical terms be vulnerable to such an order.

5 *Recommendations for deportation: Immigration Act 1971*

Any court which convicts a person aged 17 or more of an imprisonable offence may recommend to the Home Secretary that the offender be deported, if the court thinks it is appropriate because of the nature of the offence, his past record and the possible effects of his remaining in the country. The offender must be given *seven clear days'* written notice of the court's intention to make a deportation recommendation.[10]

Deportation cannot be recommended against British citizens, including Commonwealth citizens with the right of abode or citizens of the Irish Republic who were permanently resident in the United Kingdom when the

---

6   1973 Act, s 43. See further Emmins, op cit, pp 189, et seq.
7   Note that the statutory power is applied narrowly: *R v Lucas* [1976] RTR 235, CA.
8   Eg *R v Brown* [1975] RTR 36, CA.
8a The Home Secretary has announced that legislation will shortly be introduced to remedy this anomaly.
9   1973 Act, ss 39 and 40. See further Emmins, op cit, pp 197 et seq.
10 Immigration Act 1971, ss 3(6) and 6.

Immigration Act 1971 came into force.[11] EEC nationals can be deported, subject to the Treaty of Rome and directives made under it.[12] The offender has the burden of proving that he is not within the categories of persons against whom a recommendation for deportation can be made. In any case, it is for the Home Secretary to order deportation and not the court, and he is not bound by the court's recommendation. A deportation order does not replace sentencing, and thus the court must normally sentence the offender in the usual way, and then add on a recommendation for deportation if appropriate. A court may release a person whom it recommends for deportation pending receipt of the Home Secretary's decision, subject to reporting conditions or other such conditions it considers appropriate. This would obviously not apply in a situation where the court recommends deportation but also passes an immediate custodial sentence.

6 Disqualification from driving and endorsement of driving licences

Many offences carry the punishment of disqualification from driving. Sometimes the court has an obligation to disqualify, but more usually it has a discretion. The relevant offences are mainly ones which are related to the driving of a motor vehicle, such as careless driving, or speeding, or allied matters such as driving whilst uninsured. In addition, there are certain Theft Act 1968 offences, such as theft of motor vehicles (s 1); and unlawful taking (s 12) which also carry disqualification. Schedule IV to the Road Traffic Act 1972, reprinted in *Stone* every year, sets out the offences which are disqualifiable whether under the Act of 1972 or otherwise.

Whenever a court finds a defendant guilty of a disqualifiable offence it must generally endorse the driving licence with particulars of the conviction. When it does *not disqualify* it must also endorse 'penalty points' on the licence. These can lead to disqualification if a sufficient number of points are 'scored' within the requisite time.[12a] The 'points table' is set out in Schedule 7 to the Transport Act 1981. A comprehensive survey of these matters is outside the scope of this work. What follows is merely a summary.

In order that endorsement and disqualification can be imposed a person charged with an endorsable offence must produce his licence to the court; it can either be sent to the court beforehand or produced at the hearing. This applies irrespective of plea, and also if he intends to plead guilty by post. Either the summons or charge sheet will contain a notice to this effect or it will be contained in a notice sent with the summons.[13] If the accused is convicted and his licence is not at court, not only does he commit a further offence, but his licence is suspended until it is produced. Furthermore, if the accused drives whilst it is suspended, he will commit a further endorsable offence. The solicitor should, therefore, always reinforce the warning on the summons with a letter to his client.

The Transport Act 1982 has extended the 'fixed penalty' system used initially against illegally parked cars, to certain endorsable offences, notably to speeding.[14] A slightly different procedure will occur when a person has committed an endorsable fixed penalty offence. He will have to surrender his licence to the police officer, who will send it to the clerk to the justices for

11 Immigration Act 1971, ss 2 and 7.
12 Directive 64(2).
12a Note that disqualification/endorsement is classically combined with a fine.
13 Road Traffic Act 1972, s 101(4). A specimen notice is shown on Mary ADAMS' summons (case 2)
14 It is not anticipated that the provisions will come into force until 1987.

endorsement. The fixed penalty systems will not be available if the licence reveals the possibility of disqualification under the 'points system', and in any event, the rules will enable the accused to demand a trial.

Note that both disqualification and endorsement are recorded at the Driver and Vehicle Licensing Centre even when the offender does not hold a licence at all, so that if he subsequently applies for one it will either be refused or a provisional licence when issued will already bearing endorsements. This is particularly important in relation to juvenile offenders. If they are convicted of taking a conveyance without consent they can be disqualified from driving even though they are not licence holders.

Disqualification

The power to disqualify. Disqualification may result from one or more of the following:

  (i) the offender is convicted of an offence which carries *mandatory* disqualification by virtue of the Road Traffic Act 1972 s 93. These offences include:—
    – causing death by reckless driving
    – reckless driving committed within three years of a previous conviction for reckless driving
    – driving with excess alcohol in the blood or whilst unfit through drink or drugs;
  (ii) the accused is convicted of an offence which carries *discretionary* disqualification but which is sufficiently serious to justify disqualification. All endorseable offences which do not carry mandatory disqualification carry discretionary disqualification. They include:—
    – reckless driving
    – careless or inconsiderate driving
    – speeding
    – theft or unlawful taking of a motor vehicle;
  (iii) the offender is convicted of an endorseable offence which carries a sufficient number of 'penalty points' to bring him up to 12 points. In such circumstances he must, subject as below, be disqualified;
  (iv) the offender is convicted by the Crown Court and the court has found that he used a vehicle for the purposes of the crime.[15] The offence must be punishable on indictment with at least two years' imprisonment. This is a rather odd provision because it does not give a power to endorse and is thus not relevant to totting up under the penalty points system.

The length of disqualification. When the offence carries *mandatory* disqualification, the offender must be disqualified for a minimum period, generally of *12 months*.[16] Other than this, the length of disqualification is at the discretion of the court and may be for much longer.

Where the disqualification is *discretionary* the court can impose any length of disqualification that it thinks appropriate.

When disqualification has to be ordered under the *'points' system,* it must generally be for at least *six months*. However, the Transport Act 1981 also provides for progressive disqualification: the minimum period escalates to *one year* if the offender has been disqualified once within three years of the

---

15 PCCA 1973, s 44: it also applies if the defendant has been committed for sentence under s 38 of the MCA 1980.
16 RTA 1972, s 93(1) but see s 93(4) (3 year minimum in certain drink/drive cases).

commission of the offence for which he is subsequently disqualified, and to *two years* if he has been disqualified more than once within the latter period.[17]

Although there is no maximum period of disqualification, the court should not disqualify for life, but fix a specific period. In particular, the court should consider if a long period will be self-defeating if all that happens is that the offender ignores the ban altogether.

The court may feel that the defendant's real problem is incompetence. It may then disqualify until he passes a driving test, irrespective of whether or not he has ever taken one previously. This particular order will be made when protection of the public appears to warrant it, and is most frequently, but not exclusively, used against elderly persons.[18]

Commencement of disqualification. The order will start as soon as it is made. If a solicitor thinks his client is in risk of disqualification he must warn him and advise him not to drive to court. Driving whilst disqualified is also an offence, but unlike most motoring offences, carries imprisonment.[19]

Disqualification can be suspended if the offender intends to appeal against it. Notice of appeal must first be given. The application for suspension is made orally to the magistrates. If refused, application may be made to the Crown Court, initially in writing and then orally if necessary.

Concurrent or consecutive disqualifications? Irrespective of the number of offences the accused faces, or whether they were committed on different occasions, and whether he is liable to disqualification under the 'points' system or for the offence itself, all disqualifications must run concurrently with any other disqualification imposed at the same time.

Removal of disqualification. The defendant may apply to the disqualifying court for an order removing the disqualification.[20] There will be a hearing at which the police will outline the circumstances of the original offence, and the applicant will try to establish why he needs to drive, calling evidence in support if desired. Not all disqualifications are subject to this procedure. No application can be made if the disqualification is for less than two years. Otherwise it can be made after two years or longer depending on the length of disqualification.

Endorsements

When a person is convicted of an endorseable offence his licence[1] must be endorsed with particulars of that offence, even if he is disqualified. The particulars are endorsed in code form, and include details of the court, any fine imposed and the period of disqualification if appropriate. In addition, 'penalty points' must be entered on his licence unless he is disqualified (under the 'points' system or for the offence itself). The number of points is set out by Transport Act 1981 Sch 7. The points generally reflect Parliament's view of the relative seriousness of the offences. Thus reckless driving carries 10 points and is seen as inherently more serious than speeding, which carries 3 points. However, some offences carry variable points and the court will have

17 Transport Act 1981, s 19(4).
18 RTA 1972, s 93(7).
19 Ibid, s 99(b). Other notable examples include reckless driving and drink/drive offences.
20 Ibid, s 95.
  1 This means a licence issued under the Road Traffic Act 1972, s 110. It does not include HGV licences, PSV licences or foreign licences.

to allocate points depending upon their view of the seriousness of the particular incident. The relevant offences are:

careless or inconsiderate driving:	2 to 5 points
failing to stop after an accident:	5 to 9 points
failing to give particulars or to report an accident:	4 to 9 points
insurance offences:	4 to 8 points.

An offender may commit more than one 'points' offence at one time, in which case the points noted on the licence will be those appropriate to the offence carrying the highest number. For this to apply the separate offences must be committed 'on the same occasion'. This will include all offences committed as part of the same incident.[2]

Successive endorsements and 'penalty points' disqualification

An offender who has previously been convicted of an endorseable offence will normally have had points endorsed on his licence unless he was disqualified. The effect of disqualification *for any reason* is to expunge from the licence any points shown on it for the future.[3] On conviction for the present offence, points which that offence carries must be added to any points on the licence which were endorsed prior to the date of conviction for the present offence, save that the following points are ignored:

(i) any points in respect of any offence *committed* more than three years before the *commission* of the most recent offence (which will normally, but not necessarily, be the present offence);

(ii) any points imposed prior to any disqualification *other than* for the present offence.

If the points attracted by the present offence, when added to the relevant earlier points, total *12* or more then the offender must be disqualified (subject as below) for a period of at least six months, concurrently with any other period of disqualification imposed on conviction.

Avoiding mandatory disqualification for offences and endorsement

Special reasons. When the offence itself carries mandatory disqualification, the normal consequences may be avoided if 'special reasons' are present. These comprise matters which are not capable of forming a defence but which are special to and directly connected with the *offence*, and which the court ought to take into account.[4] They must also comprise extenuating circumstances. *Wilkinson* discusses a number of cases on this topic, but a classic example is illustrated by *R v Lundt-Smith*.[5] An ambulance driver was found guilty of the offence of causing death by dangerous driving. However, because the purpose of his journey was taking a patient to hospital in an emergency, that was held to be a special reason for not disqualifying him. The effect on the *offender*, for example, the loss of employment as a driver, is not a special reason.

'Special reasons' may also be put forward so as to reduce a statutory minimum period of disqualification (usually 12 months). Furthermore, they

2 *Johnson v Finbow* [1983] 1 WLR 879; see further *Wilkinson* and generally 'Motoring Offences' College of Law 1985.
3 Transport Act 1981, s 19(3)(b).
4 *R v Wickins* (1958) 42 Cr App Rep 236.
5 [1964] 2 QB 167.

may also be presented so as to avoid endorsement, in which case no 'penalty points' will be noted on the licence either.

'Special reasons' must be proved by the defence calling evidence after conviction but prior to the speech in mitigation.[6] Evidence can only be dispensed with if the offender has pleaded not guilty and all the requisite facts necessary to show special reasons have been produced in evidence during the trial itself.

Note that offences which carry mandatory disqualification carry four points only. This is to reflect the fact that the offender will be disqualified for the offence itself in the absence of 'special reasons'.[7] However, if the reasons are sufficiently special to avoid mandatory disqualification, they may be sufficiently 'special' to avoid endorsement altogether.

Mitigation when disqualification is discretionary

Just as with any other type of sentencing procedure, mitigating circumstances can be urged on the court in an attempt to avoid the exercise of the discretion or reduce it to the minimum. Unlike 'special reasons', mitigating circumstances can relate both to the offender and to the offence. Evidence in support of mitigation is not strictly required but it is wise to ask the client to give evidence on oath of the effect of the loss of his licence. In addition the court may receive evidence from employers, either in person, or more usually by letter, if this is thought necessary in serious cases.

Mitigating the 'penalty points' disqualification

Where the instant offence(s) take the accused over the 12 point limit, disqualification may be avoided by showing '*mitigating circumstances*', even though the disqualification is mandatory.[8] However, the court may not take into account: (i) circumstances which are alleged to render the offence not serious; (ii) hardship unless it is '*exceptional*'; (iii) any circumstances which have in the three years immediately prior to the conviction been put forward so as to avoid or reduce the period of disqualification under the totting up rules.[9]

The first restriction is specific. It exists because the prime object of the 'points' system is to deal with persistent offenders. 'Exceptional hardship' still awaits judicial definition; it remains to be seen if it includes the loss of a job as a direct result of loss of licence, but this would normally be regarded as exceptional. The third restriction prevents an offender from avoiding disqualification under the points system time and time again by using the same excuse.

Reasons for not disqualifying, on whatever basis, must be given in open court and entered on the court record.[10] The offender will, as with 'special reasons' need to give evidence on oath of mitigating circumstances.

Construction and use offences. Most of the offences concerned with the condition of motor vehicles used on roads are not endorsable. However, the more serious do carry endorsement, particularly those involving defective brakes,

6 *Jones v English* [1951] 2 All ER 853, CCA.
7 Transport Act 1981, Sch 7, Pt I.
8 Ibid, s 19(3).
9 Ibid, s 19(6).
10 RTA 1972, s 105.

tyres and steering. As an exception, the offender's licence must not be endorsed if the motorist did not know of, or had no reasonable cause to know of, the defect, as for example, when the vehicle has recently been serviced by a garage but the steering fails. This is not a defence to the prosecution as such, but is a defence to the endorsement, akin to 'special reasons'.[11] This exemption must be specifically considered in all such offences and oral evidence from the offender is essential, preferably backed up by the service instruction to the garage and a receipt confirming the date of service and the work done.

3   MISCELLANEOUS POWERS

(1) Deferment of sentence

This is not an ancillary power in the same sense as the other powers and orders which have been considered in this part of the chapter. Sentence for any type of offence may be deferred once by either the Crown Court or a magistrates' court for a period which the court may specify, up to a maximum of *six months*.[12] The offender must consent to sentence being deferred. This power exists in addition to any other.

Effect of deferment. Deferment of sentence is not a sentence. The offender will accordingly have to return to court at the time specified, in order to be sentenced and if he fails to do so, may be brought to court by the issue of a summons or warrant. If in the meantime he is convicted of a further offence, then the convicting court may sentence for the original offence as well, save that a magistrates' court cannot deal with a Crown Court deferred sentence.

When is deferment appropriate? Deferment of sentence is available

'to enable the court that actually sentences the offender to have regard to his conduct after conviction (including, where appropriate, the making by him of reparation for his offence) or to any change in his circumstances'.[13]

This provision has recently been considered by the Court of Appeal in *R v George*.[14] In that case the defendant had received three months in a detention centre, after sentence had been deferred for six months for a social enquiry report. The latter was not available because the defendant had not sufficiently co-operated with the probation service, notwithstanding that he had apparently attended two out of the three appointments made for him. Furthermore, it appeared to the Court of Appeal that the Crown Court had never explained to him why it was so important for him to co-operate with the probation service. The Lord Chief Justice, in allowing the appeal against the detention centre order and substituting a conditional discharge for 12 months, made the following observations on the use of deferment:

(i)   it must not be used because the court cannot think of anything better to do;

(ii)   if a social inquiry report is required, it is preferable to adjourn for one to be prepared, rather than to defer sentence;

(iii)   the court must explain why it is deferring sentence and, in particular,

11   RTA 1972, s 40(5) and Sch 4.
12   1973 Act, s 1.
13   Ibid, s 1(1).
14   [1984] 3 All ER 13, CA.

indicate the sort of conduct or activity it is expecting from the defendant. This should be noted down by the judge and ideally a copy sent to the defendant;

(iv) if the court has very specific ideas of the sort of activity it expects from the defendant, a probation order might be more appropriate.

Sentencing after deferment. When an offender comes back to the court after sentence has been deferred, the court has available to it all those powers which were originally available. This would include, for example, in the case of a magistrates' court, the power to commit the defendant to the Crown Court for sentence if it had previously found him guilty of an either way offence. In *George*, the court indicated that if the defendant has substantially complied or attempted to comply with the objectives of the deferment, he can 'legitimately expect' not to receive a *custodial* sentence. If the court is not satisfied with his conduct, then it must explain where he has gone wrong. A solicitor must therefore warn his client that there is no guarantee that deferment will result in a sentence other than that which the court would have thought appropriate in the first place. However, it can be guaranteed that bad conduct during the period of deferment will be viewed very seriously. It should be noted that during the period of deferment the offender may not be remanded on bail, but that if he fails to appear, the court may issue a summons or warrant for his arrest.

(2) Committals for sentence

As has already been mentioned, there are a variety of powers under which magistrates may commit offenders to the Crown Court for sentence. They may also remit offenders to other magistrates' courts. We shall now look at these powers in greater detail.

Committal to the Crown Court for sentence for either way offences—Magistrates' Courts Act 1980, s 38

A magistrates' court which has convicted an adult may commit him to the Crown Court for sentence if, after obtaining information about his character and antecedents, it considers that greater punishment should be inflicted than it has power to impose.[15] It will be recalled that this must be explained to an accused by the court at the 'mode of trial' proceedings and before he may consent to summary trial.

This power is explicitly intended to cover situations where the defendant's previous character and convictions are such that the magistrates' power to punish is insufficient. If they consider their powers of punishment for the instant offence are inadequate they should decline jurisdiction at 'mode of trial' and hold committal proceedings.[16] If its seriousness emerges during the course of the trial, following a 'not guilty' plea, the court should switch to committal proceedings.[17] If the accused pleads 'guilty', the court cannot commit him under s 38 merely because the offence turns out to be more serious than it initially appeared. They may, however, commit if matters come to their knowledge which seriously impugn the defendant's character and which they could not have known about earlier. For example, this might

---

15 Magistrates' Courts Act 1980, s 38.
16 *R v Hartlepool Justices, ex p King* [1973] Crim LR 637.
17 See chapters 2 and 9.

apply if, after pleading guilty, the defendant asks for many offences to be taken into consideration on sentence.[18]

Consequences of committal under s 38. If the defendant is committed to the Crown Court for sentence, that court has all the powers that it would have had if it had tried the defendant on indictment, whether it be in respect of sentencing or the ancillary powers. Committal will be in custody or on bail; the 'right to bail' will not apply.

Committal of juveniles aged 15 or 16 to the Crown Court for sentence—Magistrates' Courts Act 1980, s 37

As has been seen, the maximum term of youth custody for a juvenile is *12 months*. As part of the magistrates' court system, juvenile courts cannot impose a custodial sentence of more than *6 months* for one offence. If the magistrates think that a longer sentence is appropriate they can commit a juvenile aged 15 or 16 to the Crown Court for sentence under this provision, which differs from s 38 in three important ways:

(i) s 38 applies to adults and s 37 to juveniles;
(ii) s 38 is almost invariably limited to committal for sentence in the light of the defendant's previous convictions. s 37 is not so limited.
(iii) under s 38 the Crown Court has the same sentencing powers *as if it had convicted the defendant on indictment*; under s 37 the Crown Court may either impose up to *12 months* youth custody or make any order which a *juvenile court* could have made.

Section 37 used to have considerable significance in the days of borstal, because magistrates had no power to sentence to borstal training. If they thought that this was the appropriate punishment they had to commit offenders to the Crown Court, which had exclusive jurisdiction to impose that sentence. Now that all magistrates' courts may impose youth custody of up to *six months* s 37 has probably ceased to have much significance.

Miscellaneous powers

A magistrates' court may also commit for sentence a person who is an incorrigible rogue[19] or who commits an indictable offence whilst on licence from prison.[20]

Powers of magistrates' courts to commit other offences to the Crown Court for sentence—Criminal Justice Act 1967, s 56

This provision enables a magistrates' court when exercising its powers to commit an offender to the Crown Court for sentence or to be dealt with under:—

(i) Magistrates' Courts Act 1980, s 38 (offenders guilty of either way offences)

18 *R v Vallett* [1951] 1 All ER 231: the argument here is that the other offences affect the court's view of character so much that committal for sentence is justified.
19 Vagrancy Act 1824 s 5.
20 CJA 1967, s 62(6).

    (ii) Magistrates' Courts Act 1980, s 37 (offenders of 15 or 16)
    (iii) Powers of Criminal Courts Act 1973, s 8(6) (offenders subject to Crown Court probation orders or conditional discharges)
    (iv) Powers of Criminal Courts Act 1973, s 24(2) (offenders subject to Crown Court suspended sentences)
    (v) Criminal Justice Act 1967, s 62(6) (offenders guilty of either way offences whilst subject to parole)
    (vi) Vagrancy Act 1824, s 5 (incorrigible rogues)

also to commit other offences not normally within the Crown Court's jurisdiction but to which the offender has pleaded or been found guilty, so that all outstanding matters can be dealt with at the same time. The offences that can be 'carried up' are:

In the case of (i), (ii) and (v)   —any offence
In the case of (iii), (iv) and (vi)—any offence carrying either punishment by imprisonment in the case of a person of 21 or over or disqualification from driving.

Where committal takes place under this provision, the Crown Court has the same sentencing powers as those of a magistrates' court.

> EXAMPLE 1. An offender has been found guilty of taking a conveyance without the consent of the lawful owner, contrary to s 12 of the Theft Act, and, as will inevitably be the case, has also been found guilty of driving whilst uninsured. He is committed to the Crown Court under s 38 of the 1980 Act, in the light of his previous convictions. The insurance conviction can be committed as well.

> EXAMPLE 2. A cyclist aged 25 out practising on his racing cycle for a cycle race is stopped for speeding and in the course of the subsequent interview assaults a police officer. He is prosecuted for exceeding the 30 mph limit on his cycle and for assaulting a police officer in the execution of his duty (both summary offences), and is found guilty. He is on a suspended sentence of imprisonment imposed by the Crown Court. The magistrates decide to commit him to the Crown Court for being in breach of a Crown Court suspended sentence by committing an imprisonable offence (the assault). They can commit the assault for sentence as it is imprisonable, but not the sentence for the offence of speeding on a bicycle as it is neither endorsable nor imprisonable. Sentencing in respect of that offence would accordingly be adjourned sine die until the Crown Court had sentenced in respect of assault and at the same time decided whether or not to activate its previous sentence of imprisonment. If the defendant had been a motorist, and was prosecuted for speeding in a motor vehicle, then of course both the assault and the speeding charge could be committed under s 56 for sentence, since speeding in a motor vehicle is a disqualifiable offence.

Note that this provision must not be confused with the power to commit for trial. The Crown Court can never *try* nor even accept a *plea of guilty* to, *summary* offences.

    Finally, when committing for any reason a magistrates' court may commit any suspended sentence with which they have power to deal. The Crown Court will then have to consider implementation.

(3) Transfers between magistrates' courts: Magistrates' Courts Act 1980, s 39

A common situation is for offenders to be facing numerous outstanding charges in a variety of magistrates' courts. It is obviously undesirable that different magistrates' courts should hand out different and perhaps conflicting sentences in respect of the same offender. Accordingly, a magistrates'

The courts' powers to sentence probationers, persons under conditional discharges and suspended and part suspended sentences

Court which imposed order	Court convicting on subsequent occasion	New Offence	Powers
X magistrates' court	X magistrates' court	Imprisonable	May implement suspended sentence or discharge and resentence for PO or CD
		other	cannot activate suspended sentence
Y magistrates' court	X magistrates' court	As above	As above save that cannot discharge PO without consent of Y court
Crown Court	X, magistrates' court	Any	may commit to Crown Court on bail or in custody or sentence for present offence and report to Crown Court
X magistrates' court	Crown Court	Any	may sentence for the original offence but limited to the powers of X magistrates' court
Crown Court	Crown Court	Any	has same power as if it had convicted on indictment

N.B. Similar powers are available for probationers or persons serving community service orders who fail to comply with the directions of their probation officers or supervisors.

court which has convicted an adult offender of an offence punishable by imprisonment or disqualification can transfer its sentencing powers to another magistrates' court.[1] The receiving magistrates' court must also have convicted him of an offence and must not have sentenced him, or dealt with him in any other way, or committed him to the Crown Court for sentence.[2]

Most applications for transfers are made by solicitors acting for offenders. It may be that a particular bench of magistrates is known to take a hard line on the type of offence with which the client is charged. The solicitor may therefore want sentence to be passed by another bench. If it orders the case transferred to another court, the original court will adjourn and deal with the question of remand if appropriate. Subsequent to this all matters will be dealt with by the court to which the matter is remitted.

1 MCA 1980, s 39.
2 Ibid, s 39(1).

SUMMARY OF SENTENCES BY COURT

Age Group	Non-custodial	Custodial	Other
		MAGISTRATES' COURTS	
10-16	Discharge Fine Bind Over of parents	–	Remit to juvenile court
17-20	Discharge Probation CSO Fine Attendance Centre	Detention Centre Youth Custody Hospital Order	Commit to Crown Court or another magistrates court for sentence
21+	as above, except Attendance Centre	Prison Hospital Order	As above
		JUVENILE COURTS	
10-13	Discharge Supervision Order Fine Bind Over of parents Attendance Centre	Care Order Hospital Order	Commit to Crown Court for trial (serious cases only)
14	as above	as above plus Detention Centre	as above
15-16	as above plus Community Service order if 16	as above plus Youth Custody	as above plus commit to Crown Court for sentence
		THE CROWN COURT	
10-16	as for juvenile court but no Fine limit	as for juvenile court but 12 months maximum Youth Custody	remit to juvenile court unless undesirable to do so
17-20	as for magistrates' court but no Fine limit	as for magistrates' court but no limit on Youth Custody	–
21+	as above	as for magistrates' court but no limit on term of Prison	–

PERMISSIBLE SENTENCING COMBINATIONS FOR ONE OFFENCE (OFFENDER AGED 17 YEARS OR OVER)

	Prison	YC	DC	PO	CSO	AC	Fine	AD	CD	HO	RO	Disq	Points
YC	N												
DC	N	N											
PO	N	N	N										
CSO	N	N	N	N									
AC	N	N	N	N	N								
Fine	Y	Y^1	Y^1	N	N	Y							
AD	N	N	N	N	N	N	N						
CD	N	N	N	N	N	N	N	N					
HO	N	N	N	N	N	N	N	N	N				
RO	N	N	N	N	N	N	N	N	N	N			
Disq	Y	Y	Y	Y	Y	Y	Y	Y	Y	Y	Y		
Points	Y	Y	Y	Y	Y	Y	Y	Y	Y	Y	Y	N	
Comp	Y	Y^1	Y^1	Y	Y	Y	Y	Y	Y	Y	Y	N^2	N^2

1. The fine or compensation order will be restricted because of age.

2. Unless the offence is under the Theft Act 1968.

Note: Y = Yes; N = No

TABLE OF PRINCIPAL SENTENCING POWERS BY REFERENCE TO AGE OF OFFENDER

Sentence or order	Type of offence	Age of offender
		10+ 11+ 12+ 13+ 14+ 15+ 16+ 17+ 18+ 19+ 20+ 21+
Imprisonment (actual or suspended)	Imprisonable	21+ →
Youth custody Males & females more than 4 months	Imprisonable	15+ — 20+
Males 4 months or less		15+ — 20+
Females 4 months or less		17+ — 20+
Detention centre Males only	Imprisonable	14+ — 20+
Probation order	Any	17+ — 20+
Supervision order	Any	10+ — 16+
Community service	Imprisonable	16+ — 20+
Attendance centre Males	Imprisonable	10+ — 20+
Females		10+ — 16+
Care order	Imprisonable	10+ — 16+
Parental bindover	Any	10+ — 16+
Fine[1]	Any	10+ →
AD or CD	Any	10+ →
Mental health	Imprisonable	

Hospital orders

Guardianship orders

Restriction order
(Hospital order)[2]

Restitution orders   Theft

Disqualification/
Endorsement   'Motoring'

Other Ancillary[1]

[1](Juveniles – Parent or Guardian to pay)

1. Juveniles – Parent or Guardian to pay.

2. Magistrates cannot make this order. They can only commit to the Crown Courts and then only if the defendant is 14 years or over

CHAPTER 13

Sentencing procedure

The last chapter was concerned with the principles behind sentencing practice and the powers available to courts. This chapter is concerned with the procedure on sentencing.

1 PROCEDURE ON SENTENCING IN THE MAGISTRATES' COURT

This part of the chapter follows the stages in the sentencing process, starting with the plea or finding of guilt. Throughout this chapter it is assumed that the defendant is present unless otherwise stated.[1]

Stage 1. Preliminaries to sentencing

The proceedings may have taken a number of courses. If the defendant pleads not guilty but is found guilty the court may proceed to sentence. As an alternative it might adjourn for reports on the offender. If it does adjourn for this purpose, it must be for a maximum of *four weeks* unless it remands the offender in custody, when the maximum is *three weeks*.[2] The position is exactly the same if he pleads guilty in the first place: the court may either proceed to sentence immediately or adjourn. The adjourned hearing should preferably be before the same bench of magistrates, although this is not mandatory.

Stage 2. The prosecution presents the facts of the offence to the court

(1) Offenders who plead guilty

When an offender pleads guilty the magistrates will, at this stage, know very little about the case. In respect of 'either way' offences some details of the offence will have been given to the court in order that it can decide whether or not the case is suitable for summary trial. In practical terms, however, when both prosecution and defence only make cursory representations because it has been agreed that summary trial is appropriate, having regard to the nature of the offence, for example, a shoplifting case, it is likely that very little in the way of detailed facts has been presented to the court. In any event, for the reasons outlined at **stage 1,** it is quite possible that sentencing is before a different bench. Accordingly, once the offender has pleaded guilty the prosecution will explain to the court what the case involves. This will usually be done in one of two ways, depending on the nature of the offence.

---

1 The court's powers where the defendant is absent are outlined in chapter 9.
2 Magistrates' Courts Act 1980, s 10(3).

In all cases except motoring offences, the prosecutor will usually summarise the evidence that the prosecution would have presented had the offender pleaded not guilty. For example, in a case of unlawful taking of a conveyance the prosecutor will normally summarise the prosecution evidence, starting with the circumstances of the taking and concluding with the offender's apprehension and charge. If the offender has made a written confession this will normally be read, if not in full, then at least in part so as to give the court a flavour of the admissions. If the confession also contains favourable material, the defence can and should insist that it is read out in full.

In motoring cases the accused is usually offered the opportunity of pleading guilty by post, the procedure for which is considered later.[3] If the prosecutor wishes to offer this procedure, he must send the defendant a statement of the facts which will be presented to the court if he pleads guilty, but does not wish to attend. As a matter of practice, most police forces will invariably send out motoring summonses offering this procedure. Even if the offender subsequently attends and pleads guilty in person rather than by post, the prosecutor will normally only read out the statement of facts which was served on him with the summons.

Can the defendant plead guilty but dispute some of the prosecution facts? Frequently you will find that your client is prepared to admit his guilt, but does not accept the prosecution's version of the facts. As the accused is pleading guilty there is no formal trial at which the facts can be challenged. The first and most obvious step is to contact the prosecution to see if they are prepared, on the basis of a guilty plea, to modify the facts which they propose to present to the court. There is nothing unethical in this, provided it is confined to explaining to the prosecution those aspects of their case which are challenged. The prosecution may, and usually will, be prepared to agree to omit those aspects of the matter which would be contentious.

If the prosecution are not prepared to take this step, and the dispute is material, you should indicate to them that you do not accept their version of the facts. In this case, either the magistrates can be addressed by prosecution and defence on how each perceives the facts of the case or, if this does not appear to the court to be an appropriate way of proceeding, both prosecution and defence can call witnesses, and cross-examine them in the usual way, so the court can make up its mind on the facts.[4] When facts are disputed, however, the court should not sentence until the issues are resolved by hearing submissions or evidence, or by one party agreeing to accept the version of the facts proffered by the other.[5]

These issues can be extremely important. For example, in cases of assault the prosecution's description of how the victim's injuries were caused and their view of the extent to which the victim was, in fact, a participator may be very different from those of the defendant.

Sample charges. The prosecution may, as part of their address to the court, describe the charge or charges which the defendant faces as 'samples'. The court will accept that the charges are 'samples' unless the defence makes it clear that this is not accepted. If the charges are genuinely sample ones,

---

3 This is also available in respect of any summary offence other than one punishable by more than 3 months' imprisonment in the case of a person over 21: ibid, s 21.

4 *R v Newton* (1982) 77 Cr App Rep 13, CA. If in doubt it should accept the version tendered by the defence.

5 See further [1983] Crim LR 199; 1983 LAG Bulletin 64.

there is no reason why the prosecution could not either offer the opportunity of having the other charges taken into consideration or charge them as such. Alternatively, if your client disputes the suggestion that the charges are samples you should notify the prosecutor and insist that he only presents the case on the basis of the charges to which pleas have been tendered.

(2) Defendants who plead not guilty

When an offender has pleaded not guilty, the court has usually received evidence on all the germane facts. Magistrates are not obliged to give reasons for their decisions, and usually do not do so. Accordingly the only facts that can be safely relied on are those which the prosecution and defence have both accepted, or which the magistrates have indicated that they accept.

In many cases the court will have adjourned after summary trial, and the sentencing court will be differently constituted. A defence solicitor must still, however, be very careful in his treatment of the facts since the clerk may have kept a record of the evidence, or the justices may be aware of their colleagues' views on the case.

Stage 3. The prosecution gives details of the offender

The prosecution will present to the court personal details of the age of the offender, his family background, education and work record, and other details such as his income and personal situation since arrest, including whether or not he was on bail or in custody, and details of his criminal record (called the 'antecedents'). This will be presented on a form which the prosecution must make available to the defence.[6] An officer will usually be called by the prosecutor to present these details. He may be the officer in charge of the case, or in a larger court 'an antecedents officer', who may well know little about the case other than what the form tells him.

Sources of the antecedents

After the accused has been charged the police will compile the antecedents form, mainly from information supplied by the accused either during interrogation or after the formal interrogation has been completed. In addition the police can include as part of the antecedents any information which they have about the history or background of the defendant obtained other than through interview with him. Antecedents are thus largely compiled from information requested at a time when the accused presumably wishes to be released from the police station, or at least to be left alone. In addition, he may already be regretting some of the things that he said to the police. The form itself is very sparse, and will not be presented to the court for some weeks or possibly for months after it has been prepared. It is thus usually out of date.

All in all, when the offender is represented, or a social inquiry report is obtained, or both, the antecedents are almost useless as a means of communicating to the court relevant information in respect of the offender's personal circumstances. The main task of the defence must therefore be to note any

---

6 *Practice Direction* [1966] 2 All ER 929. This contains full details of what the antecedents must contain. Although expressed as applying to the higher courts, it is treated as applying to magistrates' courts as well.

factors that are particularly useful, but more particularly to make sure that no unsubstantiated adverse comments are included.

Details of the previous convictions

Whenever a person has been convicted of virtually any offence, other than non-imprisonable motoring offences,[7] particulars of that conviction will be recorded against him in a file which will be entered on the Police National Computer and which is available to all British police forces if they so require. Fingerprint records and photographs will also be retained. It is from this computer record that the police will compile a list of the offender's previous convictions. Paradoxically, although when an offender is made subject to a probation order this does not count as a conviction for any purposes other than for the proceedings in which the order was made, the fact that the proceedings resulted in probation will be recorded. The same applies to conditional and absolute discharges. A further paradox is that findings of guilt against a juvenile are not normally referred to in proceedings once he has become an adult save with the leave of the court, but a separate file is not prepared and the juvenile record will appear immediately prior to the defendant's record as an adult.

Spent convictions

Although the Rehabilitation of Offenders Act 1974 does not apply to criminal proceedings, there are restrictions on referring in open court to offences which would otherwise be spent.[8] Police forces must mark on the note of previous convictions the ones which are spent, although you should always check as well. Of course, a number of clients will never have had the opportunity of convictions becoming spent because they have persistently re-offended. You must show your client the list of previous convictions and ask him to confirm that they are correct. He may be vague about this, but most defendants will recognise their own record. However, if there are offences which the defendant maintains he has not committed the police officer who presents the antecedents to the court must be cross-examined. The defendant does not need to give evidence that the convictions are not his, as the prosecution bears, if necessary, the burden of proving convictions. In the meantime there may have to be an adjournment and if necessary a fingerprint expert may have to be called to give evidence or an officer called to identify the defendant. The conviction itself would be proved by producing a certificate of conviction from the relevant court.[9] A considerable cost will be involved and this is likely to be borne by the defendant. However, when necessary the objection must be taken because of the considerable significance of previous convictions on the exercise of the sentencing powers.

Presentation of antecedent history and previous convictions

In many magistrates' courts the officer in charge of the case will be called to the witness stand and will take the 'voire dire' oath, which is a less formal oath than that used for evidence at trials. The witness swears that he 'will true answer make to all such questions as the court shall demand of me'. The

---

7 These will be recorded instead on the DVLC computer at Swansea.
8 Practice Direction (1975) 30 June 1975, unreported.
9 Police and Criminal Evidence Act 1984, s 73.

normal rules of evidence do not apply and the officer may be asked leading questions by the prosecutor. As indicated earlier, copies of the antecedent and previous conviction form must be made available for the court and also for the defence. Notwithstanding this, however, the prosecution will take the officer through the antecedents, and then through the list of previous convictions.

When there are a number of previous convictions the prosecutor will usually ask the bench which they require to be read out. There are three main reasons for this. First, findings of guilt against juveniles should not be read out in court without the court's permission.[10] Second, as mentioned above, a 'spent' conviction should not be referred to without the court's direction. Third, it may be that in any event the court does not consider that all the convictions are relevant to the present business in hand. This may be because of the length of time that has elapsed since they were incurred, or because of their different nature. The court, by indicating which ones it wishes to hear read out, is indicating those which it regards as being relevant to the present sentencing process.

Although the prosecutor may seek to elicit further information concerning the antecedents or the previous convictions it is unusual for this to be done. The sole function of the prosecution is to help the court with sentencing by providing information. It may not seek to influence the sentencing process in any way.

Previous suspended sentences and similar orders

The offender will be asked if he admits that he is in breach of certain types of sentence or orders revealed by the list of previous offences. The orders are:

(1) suspended sentences of imprisonment, if the present offence is punishable by imprisonment;
(2) conditional discharges;
(3) probation orders.

This is done in the officer's presence so that they can be formally proved if the offender does not admit them.

Defence cross examination of the antecedents officer

The officer may be cross examined by the defence and there are practical situations when it is desirable to do so. Suppose the defence want to suggest an order, such as probation, in circumstances when the offender has a long previous record. It may be helpful if the police will agree that, for example, the present offence is of different character, or that the client cooperated with them. Apart from any other considerations, however, the degree of helpfulness will depend on the officer's knowledge of the offender, as the list of previous convictions contains very little information.

A further problem, now mercifully becoming increasingly rare, may occur when antecedents are being given. Although the antecedent form is normally used, the police are not confined when giving antecedent details to the contents of that form. Accordingly you may be faced with damaging remarks about the defendant's character which are of a general nature and not

---

10 Once a person has attained 21 years, evidence of findings of guilt obtained when he was a child may not be given: Children and Young Persons Act 1963, s 16(2).

capable of substantiation as such, but which are clearly presented for the sole purpose of damning the defendant in the eyes of the court. Such phrases might include, for example, 'the defendant has been a lot of trouble to the police for a long time' or 'the defendant habitually resorts with known criminals' or even 'there has been an epidemic of this type of crime in the locality'. Such remarks can be seen as an attempt by certain police officers to influence the process of sentencing, particularly when they have been interested in the defendant for a considerable period of time, but have only now managed to charge him. As against that, it could be argued that it is the job of the prosecution and in particular the police to provide information for the court. The rule is, however, that a police officer in court should refer only to the form of antecedents, and any adverse comments should be included in this form;[11] however, such adverse evidence should not be given as part of the antecedents 'unless it is first hand information about which the officer giving the evidence can be questioned'. In addition, any evidence given by the officer must be sufficiently particularised for the defence to be able to cross-examine on it and specifically rebut it.[12] Thus, even if the officer has had 'dealings' with the defendant on a number of occasions in the past, any references must be specific and not general, even if they do come from the individual officer's knowledge. It goes without saying, therefore, that any officer presenting antecedents without previous specific knowledge of the defendant will be unable to present adverse evidence.

It has been so far assumed that evidence of character and previous convictions will be given by an officer under the 'voir dire' oath. However, evidence may be given in a variety of different ways depending on the local practice of the magistrates' court. In some areas an officer will give evidence of the antecedents and previous convictions, but without taking a 'voir dire' oath. In other areas the prosecuting solicitor or police officer presenting the case will simply read out the antecedent details and previous convictions. There is nothing objectionable in these practices so long as the defence solicitor does not wish to challenge or cross-examine on the antecedents. If this is necessary, then he must insist that the prosecution yield to the defendant's version of the events, particularly if the defendant is prepared to go to the witness box and give evidence, or an officer to give 'voir dire' evidence.

Information in motoring cases

There is no power to imprison for most of the common motoring offences, and although a wide range of sentences is theoretically available, the main issues are the size of the fine and, if the offence is endorsable, whether or not the court should exercise its discretion to disqualify. Endorsement will of course usually be mandatory. Accordingly, the police seldom prepare a note of the defendant's antecedent history, or of his previous convictions. They leave it to the defence to inform the court of personal factors affecting sentence. Previous offences which are likely to be relevant will be endorsed on his driving licence, which he must of course produce to the court.

---

11 *Practice Direction* [1966] 2 All ER 929 (op cit).
12 *R v Wilkins* (1977) 66 Cr App Rep 49, CA; *R v Robinson* (1969) 53 Cr App Rep 314, CA at 318.

Stage 4. The presentation of reports on the offender

All the reports mentioned in this section may be requested or ordered by the court. Reports or other evidence obtained by the defence solicitor will be considered later. Of course, these reports cannot be prepared overnight and an adjournment will invariably be required for this purpose, unless, for example, the defendant is already on probation and the probation service has prepared a report on its own initiative.

(a)   *The social inquiry report*

This is the most common report on an offender. The report is almost invariably prepared by the probation service, save in the case of juveniles when it is usually prepared by the local authority social services department. If the defendant has been in trouble previously, he may already be on probation, in which case the report will be prepared by his supervising officer. If not, an officer will be assigned to interview the defendant and make other appropriate inquiries from which he will prepare the report to be presented to the court. If the probation officer who prepared the report is not able to attend, it will be presented by the duty probation officer at court on the day in question. The defendant does not have a right to adjournment if 'his' probation officer is not present, and an application for an adjournment on that ground may be refused although it should be sought if necessary.

When will a social inquiry report be ordered?   There is only one situation where a report is a prerequisite, and that is prior to the making of a community service order.[13] However, certain types of sentence or order should not normally be made unless there is either a social inquiry report, or a good reason for not needing one.[14] Rather more obliquely, certain types of order cannot be made without consultation[15] which also in essence requires a social inquiry report. Although the Home Secretary has power to prescribe categories of offence for which a social inquiry report must be obtained on the offender,[16] reliance has been placed on a series of Ministerial circulars[17] and the good sense of courts. The effect of all this is that a social inquiry report should normally be ordered by magistrates' courts:

   (i)   before probation is ordered;
   (ii)   before a woman is sentenced to imprisonment;
   (iii)   before committal for sentence;
   (iv)   before first custodial sentence on an offender aged 21 or over;
   (v)   before detention centre or youth custody is ordered;
   (vi)   before community service is ordered (statutorily required);
   (vii)   before custody, supervision or care is ordered against a juvenile.

When you arrive at court the duty probation officer will give you a copy of the report to read. It is not made available to the prosecution. You should go through it with your client before the hearing is resumed. You should make sure that the client agrees with any material statements of fact and understands any recommendations, even if the report indicates that the pro-

13   See p 407 ante.
14   Eg PCCA 1973, s 20A.
15   Eg supervision orders with specified intermediate treatment.
16   PCCA 1973, s 45.
17   Eg HO Circulars 59/1971 and 118/1977.

bation officer has already discussed them with him. Check with the probation officer on any points of difficulty before the case is called.

The probation report will not be read out aloud to the court, and accordingly the defence solicitor must not, in his speech in mitigation do so either. This is because it is confidential to the court. The officer who presents the report may sometimes take a 'voir dire' oath but most magistrates' courts operate more informally and the report will not be presented on oath. In either case the solicitor for the defendant is entitled to ask the probation officer questions, but a rigorous cross-examination is unlikely to be productive either from the point of view of the individual client or with regard to future relations between the solicitor and the probation service.

Thus in difficult cases a defence solicitor should always contact the officer responsible for the social inquiry report at an early stage. Most, but by no means all, probation officers will be prepared to cooperate and exchange views before arriving at court. Such liaison can help to prevent difficulties arising in the event of the probation report being presented by another officer.[18] You should always work hard to establish a good relationship with your local probation service.

Finally, you must always be prepared for a social inquiry report with which the court is unable to concur. In the case of *R v James*[19] the appellant was found guilty of 'glassing'.[20] Lawton LJ described the offence as 'as bad a case of glassing as it was possible to imagine'. The probation officer in that case, both at the Crown Court and also in the Court of Appeal, recommended that the accused be placed on probation. Lawton LJ, in delivering the judgment in which leave to appeal against a sentence of five years' imprisonment was refused, indicated that unless a probation officer's recommendation is sensible, it will tend to do more harm than good.

This illustrates how important it is for a defendant's solicitor to preserve an independent sense of the appropriate sentence. You should not hesitate to adopt the recommendations of a probation officer when you think they are appropriate. However, if on taking instructions from the client, you believe the recommendations to be misconceived or based on incorrect information, you must be prepared to challenge it. Liaison with the probation service may in many cases be a way of avoiding this type of problem. If all else fails, however, and the report is clearly one which you consider is not in the client's interests, you should embark on a cross-examination of the probation officer; if necessary pressing for an adjournment first if the officer who prepared the report is not present.

(b) *Medical reports*

If the offence is punishable on summary conviction with *imprisonment* and the magistrates are satisfied that the accused committed the actus reus relevant to the offence, they may consider that they ought to have a report on his physical and/or mental condition before they decide how to deal with him. The court will obviously have to adjourn for this purpose, and must remand the *accused*. Its powers arise under s 30 of Magistrates' Courts Act 1980 and under s 35 of the Mental Health Act 1983. If the court adjourns under s 30, the right to bail applies, but the court must, if granting bail, impose a condition under s 3(6)(d) of the Bail Act 1976, that the accused makes himself

---

18 See further 'Social Enquiry Reports—a survey ' Home Office Research Study No 43. You may even be sent a copy of the report before a hearing.

19 (1981) Times, 22 July, CA.

20 Cutting the victim with the shaft of a broken bottle.

available for the purpose of enabling inquiries or a report to be made. One doctor will normally be required to examine the accused if some question has arisen as to his physical condition. If a question has arisen as to his mental condition two medical practitioners will normally examine him. This power (under s 30) exists quite independently of the power to adjourn for inquiries or a report after conviction but before sentence, under s 10(3) of the 1980 Act.[21] It is normally used if the court believes that the accused will not cooperate and therefore must either be remanded in custody, or on bail subject to specific conditions.

As an alternative, the magistrates may remand the accused to a hospital, which they must specify, for a report, under s 35 of the 1983 Act. The court must have at least written evidence from a doctor that there is mental disorder and must be satisfied that a report would be unobtainable if the accused was on bail. The accused can be remanded for a maximum of 28 days at a time, and further remands can be granted if necessary, up to a maximum of 12 weeks. If a further remand is needed, this can be done in the accused's absence, provided he is represented.

As with probation reports, medical reports obtained by the court will be made available to the defence on the day of sentence. They will not normally be presented by a medical practitioner but by the probation service which will have been liaising between the court and the doctors concerned.[22]

(c) *Prison department and community service reports*

Whenever the defendant has served a custodial sentence a report will be available to the court from the relevant institution; again this is normally presented through the probation officer. It will deal with the way in which the offender responded to the regime of training which was offered and will normally have been used by the probation officer to supplement his/her recommendations when preparing the social inquiry report. In addition, when a person has served a community service order there may well be a report from the probation service responsible for that particular scheme, particularly if the offender failed to respond, or if any problems arose. All these reports will be made available to the defence solicitor on the day of the hearing. You must go through the reports carefully with the accused, particularly if they are unfavourable, so as to get his reaction to them; some explanation must be presented to the court if possible.

(d) *Social services reports*

If the defendant, or his family, has been receiving support or assistance from a local authority social services department, a social worker may well either prepare a report or appear at the hearing. If the accused is a juvenile under the age of 13 the social services department rather than the probation service, will usually prepare the social inquiry report, and it will usually include a report from the school.

Stage 5. Mitigation

The defence advocate must now address the court by way of a speech in mitigation. If there is a probation report, you should not get on to the body

---

21 P 438, ante.
22 Remember that oral medical evidence is not essential for either a probation order with a treatment condition or a hospital order to be made: chapter 12, ante.

of mitigation until the report has been read. You may have been able to prepare your speech beforehand; for example in a motoring case when the defendant is pleading guilty and you have already seen the statement of facts served with the summons, or when a social inquiry report has been ordered, and you have obtained some idea of the recommendations from discussions with the probation officer. On other occasions, however, you may have to deliver the speech in mitigation almost immediately after the conclusion of the trial.

There are dangers in over-preparing a speech beforehand since it will take no account of the personalities of the magistrates or any of the other participants. This may not appear to be important, but in practice can be crucial, particularly in magistrates' courts staffed by lay justices. For example, experience in your local court will show that certain magistrates will react well or badly to particular phrases. To take a straightforward example, there is a tendency both by lawyers and others to describe acts of vandalism or shoplifting as 'cries for help'. Living in an age in which there is a variety of social work and other agencies available either on a statutory or voluntary basis, the use of this phrase in mitigation can produce an adverse reaction from magistrates particularly if the advocate is the eighth to have used it that morning!

Accordingly, when preparing to mitigate you should work from jottings, legibly written, which list out the mitigating factors relating to the offender. Try to be self-critical at all times. For example, it gives a poor impression if an advocate indicates that the accused has obtained, or has the prospect of a job if he cannot give precise details of it.

The mitigation speech should be presented in a logical sequence; starting with the offence. You should next proceed to the defendant's background when the crime was committed, and finally deal with future prospects. Throughout this process you should refer, where appropriate, to the social inquiry report.

What happens if the defence forgets to deal with a point?

If, after the magistrates have retired, you remember that you omitted a critical point, then you must tell the clerk that there is an important matter which you wish to put before them. It will be up to the justices whether or not they come out of retirement so as to hear the additional matters.

Some common errors in mitigation

Conflict over evidence. When the defendant has pleaded not guilty it is usually inappropriate to comment on the offence, save to draw to the court's attention to those facts on which both sides agree. For example, it might be agreed that the effect of a theft on the victim was very slight. Of course, when the defence is one of alibi the offence should not be commented on at all.

The problems that can arise when there is a conflict between the prosecution and the defence views, even when the defendant pleads guilty, were considered earlier. It is accordingly essential to check with the prosecution on their version of events.

Conflict within the mitigation. The mitigation must not contain any conflicts, nor any obvious weaknesses. The speech will sound better if it anticipates the magistrates' objections or questions. For example, it is common to hear advocates saying that a defendant committed an offence of dishonesty because he had no money. The instinctive reaction from many magistrates will be to ask why he did not receive supplementary benefit. The defence solicitor should, therefore, find out if he has applied for supplementary benefit, and if not, why not. This could be because he was not qualified to receive it, or because the office was shut when he went there. Alternatively, he may have applied, and the DHSS may have sent him a giro which was lost in the post. In any event it is a problem which must be anticipated.

Evidence in support of mitigation

The defence may present character evidence as part of mitigation. This should normally be done after the social inquiry report, if any, has been read, but before the speech in mitigation begins. However, it may be more convenient to call evidence in mitigation when the appropriate part of the speech has been reached. 'Character' witnesses may take the voir dire oath or, alternatively, be asked to step to the front of the court to give unsworn evidence, depending on the practice of the court in question. Character witnesses who can give evidence about the defendant's background, can be particularly useful if he has strong family or local ties and has not previously been in court. As with all witnesses you should contact them and arrange an interview to take a statement as soon as possible. Anyone can be called as a character witness, but obviously some will carry more weight than others; for example, the local minister, the leader of the youth club which the accused attends or helps to run, school teachers and employers, particularly one who is prepared to stand up in court and say that, notwithstanding the offence, he is still prepared to employ the defendant. Character witnesses may have difficulty getting to court, therefore it is normally acceptable to obtain a letter from them instead. This should make clear that the witness knows the details of the present conviction.[1]

Can the defence advocate suggest the appropriate sentence?

Traditionally advocates have been reluctant to suggest a sentence to the court, on the basis that sentencing is the function of the court and that whilst the advocate is there to assist the court, he is not there to usurp the court's function. However, magistrates have, for a number of years, received recommendations as part of the probation report, and there seems no reason why the advocate should not also suggest a particular type of sentence, provided that he has thought the matter out and can justify his suggestion. Indeed many magistrates are likely to be responsive to sensible, well thought out and argued suggestions especially if the case is a difficult one. Make sure, however, that you have discussed any possible permutations, and any suggestions you intend to put forward, with the client first. Making suggestions requires knowledge of the court's sentencing powers, experience of the circumstances in which this particular court is likely to exercise them, and an evaluation of the appropriateness of the suggested sentence to the client.

Deferment of sentence

The court can of course defer sentence, notwithstanding the speech in mitigation or any other evidence presented to it. In addition, the defence can

---

1 Remember that an oral witness will tend to carry more weight; a letter may have been written by a 'helpful' friend.

suggest a deferment. This would be appropriate in a case where, for example, the defendant is unemployed, but has definite prospects of a job, and the court is reluctant to impose a custodial sentence but cannot at present see any alternative, in the absence of some indication of reformation and the means to pay a fine. If sentence is deferred it is likely that the defence solicitor will be required in court when the defendant appears again. The magistrates may not be the same, but the clerk will have kept some form of record of the case. It is therefore vital that the mitigation which is then presented does not contradict the mitigation which was presented on the earlier occasion.

2 PLEADING GUILTY BY POST, MCA 1980, s 12

A person charged with certain offences before a magistrates' court may plead guilty without having to appear at all. The offence or offences must be triable *summarily only* and punishable by no more than *three months'* imprisonment. Most motoring offences come within this provision and it is uncommon for it to be used for anything other than typical road traffic cases, such as that of Mary ADAMS (case 3).

Initial procedure

The decision as to whether or not to use this procedure is taken by the prosecution which will at the same time as the information is laid indicate that it wishes to use s 12. The following procedure is more or less standard, but may vary slightly from one area to another. Assuming that the court is to serve the summons by post, the prosecutor will supply the court with a statement of the facts of the case when laying the information.[2] The court will attach to the summons the statement and a notice explaining that the defendant can plead guilty without attending and that the prosecution will be confined to reading out the statement of facts. The defendant will also be sent a form to complete and return. This enables him to confirm that he wishes to plead guilty without attending and set out any mitigating circumstances.

In theory, if the prosecutor wishes to draw the court's attention to any previous convictions for criminal offences he must serve a notice of any previous convictions on the defendant at the same time as the summons, or within seven days of the trial.[3] In practice, however, as the postal procedure is used almost exclusively for motoring offences the prosecution do not bother, since the only convictions of which the court are likely to take note are previous driving endorsements. If the present offence is endorsable, the defendant must produce his licence to the court anyway.

Procedure at the hearing

Providing that the defendant returns the form confirming his plea of guilty, (together with his driving licence if the offence is endorsable), the court will

2 Magistrates' Court Rules 1981, r 73.
3 MCA 1980, s 104.

IMPORTANT In connection with the summons, notice and statement of facts now served upon you, will you please acknowledge receipt by signing and returning this form as soon as possible. Postage must be prepaid.

ACKNOWLEDGMENT

To the Clerk of the Magistrates' Court Weyford

I hereby acknowledge receipt of the summons, notice, statement of facts * and notice of alleged previous convictions.

Signed *Mary Adams* ...... Date *25ᵗʰ January '98-*

(Present address   *45 Almas Road   Weyford* ....

PLEASE ALSO COMPLETE EITHER SECTION 'A' OR SECTION 'B' BELOW

but before you do so read the IMPORTANT NOTICE accompanying this summons

NOTE If you intend to consult a solicitor, you would be well advised to consult him before completing this form. If, having completed and returned the form, you change your mind, you should let the Clerk of the Court know immediately.

SECTION A If you propose to attend Court, considerable saving of time and expense may be effected if you will complete the following:—

Do you intend to plead guilty?........................

(*If you answer 'No' please read the next paragraph very carefully.*)

INTENTION The prosecution is NOT intending to bring any witnesses
TO PLEAD to Court on the hearing date set out on your summons.
NOT Accordingly, if you intend to plead 'Not Guilty', you need
GUILTY not then attend on the date stated on the summons. You will be notified in due course of the new date for the hearing when you should, of course, attend with any witnesses you wish to call. You must have your driving licence available on the date of hearing.

SECTION B If you desire a plea of guilty to be accepted without your attendance at Court, please complete the following:—

PLEA OF I have read the statement of facts relating to the charge
GUILTY against me shown on the summons

I plead guilty to the charge and I desire the Court to deal with the case in my absence and to take the following circumstances into account.

*I ENCLOSE MY DRIVING LICENCE

Male	
Female	✔

Please tick the appropriate box

Signed *Mary Adams*
Date of birth *25.8.195—*

MITIGATING CIRCUMSTANCES

(a) about the offence:—   (b)   about my financial circumstances:—

[*Omitted for reasons of space*]

A person giving information in writing that he pleads guilty to an offence involving endorsement of driving licence or disqualification is required by Section 104(2) of the Road Traffic Act, 1972 to furnish information about his or her date of birth and sex.

* Delete as necessary.

NOTICE TO THE DEFENDANT

PLEA OF GUILTY IN ABSENCE (Magistrates' Courts Act, 1980 Sec. 12)

Please read this carefully.
If you admit the offence(s) referred to in the summons served herewith and do not wish to appear before the Court, it is open to you under section 12 of the Magistrates' Courts Act, 1980, to inform the Clerk of the Court in writing that you wish to plead guilty to the charge(s) without appearing. If you decide to do this you should write to the Clerk *as soon as possible* and in any event at least three days before the date fixed for the hearing in order to avoid the unnecessary attendance of witnesses. In writing to the Clerk, you should mention any mitigating circumstances which you wish to put before the Court. If you write as mentioned, you are required to state your date of birth and sex. A Form A which you may use for this purpose is forwarded herewith.

If you send in a written plea of guilty, the Statement of Facts overleaf and your Statement in mitigation will be read out in open Court before the Court decides whether to accept your plea and hear and dispose of the case in your absence. Unless the Court adjourns the case after accepting your plea and before sentencing you, (in which case you will be informed of the time and place of the adjourned hearing so that you may attend), the prosecution will not be permitted to make any statement with respect to any facts relating to the offences other than the Statement of Facts.

If you send in a written plea of guilty, but the Court decides not to accept the plea, the hearing will be adjourned and you will be informed of the time and place of the adjourned hearing. The case will then be heard as if you had not sent in a written plea of guilty.

Vehicle Excise Offences.
A Notice from the vehicle licensing authority is also served herewith. This notice states that in the event of your being convicted it will be alleged that an order falls to be made requiring you to pay the amount specified in the notice (being the amount calculated to be the duty payable in respect of the period during which the vehicle was unlicensed). If you send in a written plea of guilty, you may nevertheless include in it a statement that the amount so specified is inappropriate (e.g. because you were not the keeper of the vehicle for the whole of the period during which the vehicle was unlicensed or because the vehicle was not kept or used on a public road during the whole of that period). If you do not include a statement that the amount is inappropriate, the Court will proceed on the assumption that the amount is correctly calculated. If you do include such a statement and you decide to appear in person and dispute the amount, you should arrange to have at Court any witnesses or documents which may help you to prove that the amount is inappropriate.

If you send in a written plea guilty you may, if you wish, withdraw it by informing the Clerk of the withdrawal at any time before the hearing.

Neither this notice nor any reply you may send limits your right to appear before the Court at the time fixed for the hearing, either in person or by counsel or a solicitor, and then to plead guilty or not guilty as you may desire, if after sending in a written plea of guilty you do so appear or if you inform the Clerk before the hearing of the withdrawal of your written plea, the case will be heard as if you had not sent it in. If after sending in a written plea of guilty you wish to appear and plead not guilty you will avoid delay and expense by informing the Clerk immediately of your change of intention; unless you do inform the Clerk in good time there will have to be an adjournment to allow the prosecution to bring their witnesses to Court.

NOTE:
1. If you want any more information you may get in touch with the Clerk of the Court.
2. If you intend to consult a Solicitor you would be well advised to do so before taking any action in response to this Notice.
3. Address any letter to the Clerk of the Court at Justices' Clerk's Office,

NOTICE TO PRODUCE DRIVING LICENCE [Road Traffic Act, 1972, Sec. 101(4)]

You must have your driving licence with you at the hearing of the case or else if you adopt the course described in the first paragraph above, cause it to be in the Clerk's hands, by then. If you do not produce the licence when you are required to do so, it will be suspended by the Court until it is produced and you yourself may be prosecuted and fined up to £100.

proceed with the case in his absence. The summons will be read out by the clerk, who will indicate that the defendant is pleading guilty by post. The prosecutor is usually present, and will then read out the statement of facts as served on the defendant. He is not allowed to make any other comment on the case or the facts.[4] The clerk will then read out to the magistrates any mitigation that the defendant has indicated on the form. The magistrates will then proceed to sentence the defendant provided that they do not wish to imprison or disqualify. 'Imprison' in this context appears to include any custodial sentence or suspended sentence. Furthermore, the court cannot impose any sentence or order which requires the offender's consent, such as probation or a community service order. The effect of these restrictions is that the only immediate sentence available is a fine. The defendant's driving licence will be forwarded to the DVLC and the defendant will be notified of the result and of the fine by post. He will normally have to pay the fine within 14 days unless the court orders otherwise.

Procedure when the court is considering disqualification

If the court proposes to disqualify it must adjourn the proceedings as it is not entitled to disqualify the defendant in his absence at this stage.[5] The clerk will notify the defendant of the adjourned date for the hearing and also the reason for the adjournment. The defendant thus has the opportunity of attending at the subsequent hearing if he wants. Provided that the notice of adjournment has been properly sent to and received by the defendant[6] the court may then disqualify irrespective of whether or not he attends.

As has already been seen, the usual method of securing the participation of an unwilling defendant is for the court to issue a warrant for arrest. However, the court may not do this unless and until the defendant fails to attend the adjourned hearing. Even then, the court must be satisfied that it is undesirable to continue in the defendant's absence in view of the gravity of the offence.[7]

Procedure when the court wishes to imprison

As no sentence of imprisonment can be imposed unless the defendant is present,[8] the court must adjourn if it feels that imprisonment is appropriate. Again the defendant must be notified and a warrant cannot be issued unless he fails to appear at the adjourned hearing. Because of this restriction a prosecutor is unlikely to use this procedure where imprisonment is even remotely possible.

Tactical considerations

From the point of view of the accused, one of the great attractions of pleading guilty by post is that he knows precisely what is being alleged against him and that no facts other than those contained in the prosecution 'statement of facts' will be read out to the court. Thus it might be that, having read the statement of facts served on her, Mary ADAMS (*case 3*) decides that she more

---

4 MCA 1980, s 12(5).
5 Ibid, s 13(4).
6 *R v Seisdon Justices ex p Dougan* (op cit).
7 MCA 1980, s 13(3)(b) and 13(5)(b).
8 Ibid s 11(3).

or less accepts them and therefore need not attend court. However, if she wishes to plead guilty but does not agree with the prosecution's version of the accident, she is perfectly entitled to attend and plead guilty in person. Furthermore, even if she does plead guilty by post, she may still change her mind at any time before the hearing either by notifying the clerk in writing or by attending court on the day of the hearing.[9] Even if the accused does exercise the option of pleading guilty by post, the court may still decline to deal with him in his absence,[10] for example, because the accused's statement in mitigation suggests that his plea of guilty may be equivocal or his plea is to a driving offence carrying compulsory endorsement with a variable number of 'penalty points'.

It is not always easy to advise the client as to whether he should plead guilty by post. To take the example of Mary ADAMS, much would depend on what her driving licence reveals. If this was her first offence, and on the basis of instructions received, you formed the view that a plea of 'not guilty' was unlikely to succeed, it might well be in her interests to plead guilty by post. If, on the other hand, she already had one or more endorsements, it might be in her interests to attend personally, possibly with representation. This would be especially desirable if there were a danger of a 'penalty points' disqualification.

Finally it should be noted that pleas of guilty by post may become less common in the future when the fixed penalty provisions contained in the Transport Act 1982 come into force.[11] These provisions extend the fixed penalty system to a large number of common road traffic offences, such as speeding and disobeying traffic signals, so that a road user can effectively be fined 'on the spot' and a summons will not be issued unless he wishes to contest the allegation. The provisions do not extend to offences of careless driving, failing to stop after an accident or failing to report, or driving whilst uninsured. The s 12 procedure is therefore likely to remain important in the context of the intermediate range of traffic offences.

3 SENTENCING PROCEDURE IN THE CROWN COURT

Preliminaries to sentencing

A defendant may be sentenced in the Crown Court either because he has been convicted by the Crown Court or because he has been committed to the Crown Court for sentence by a magistrates' court.[12] Finally, an appellant to the Crown Court from the magistrates' court either against conviction or sentence may be sentenced *de novo*.

Although solicitors have a general right of audience in appeals or committals for sentence[13] most defendants will be sentenced after trial and accordingly this section assumes that counsel will be instructed.

The mechanics of sentencing in the Crown Court

Defendants who have been tried by the Crown Court or who have unsuccessfully appealed against conviction may either be sentenced immediately

9 MCA 1980, s 12(3).
10 Ibid, s 127(b).
11 Probably in 1986.
12 This may involve committal of other offences as well under the Criminal Justice Act 1967, s 56.
13 See chapter 2 ante.

or as with summary trial, sentencing may be adjourned. The solicitor's brief to counsel for trial should include instructions to mitigate in the event of his client being found guilty. If the court is only concerned with sentence, the solicitor's brief to counsel will deal only with those matters relevant to sentence. This means that although it will normally be shorter than for a trial, all committal documents, papers and reports should be enclosed. The legal aid order must, of course, be sent with the brief, the backsheet of which should be marked 'Legal Aid' in the usual way.

The Crown Court may always adjourn after conviction for reports to be prepared,[14] and as with magistrates' courts, the most common and useful report will be that from the probation service. It is much less likely that an adjournment will be necessary, however. There are a number of reasons for this. First, in appeals against sentence it is likely that the magistrates will already have obtained reports in cases of difficulty. The Crown Court will therefore have a report available which will be updated by the probation service in time for the hearing of the appeal. Second, if the defendant is committed for sentence this will usually be after the court has adjourned for a report. Even if a report is not available, the justices may direct at committal that a report is prepared for the Crown Court.[15] Third, if the defendant is committed for trial the justices may also ask for a social enquiry report to be obtained. However, practice varies throughout the country as to the extent to which probation officers will prepare reports before trial on indictment if the defendant is intending to plead not guilty. If the probation service does prepare a report in such circumstances, it will not comment upon the offence for which the defendant is before the court. The Crown Court can also obtain reports under s 35 of the Mental Health Act 1983.[16]

As with trials, there ought to be a conference with counsel shortly before the hearing. Unlike a not guilty plea, it is not so necessary for a conference to take place at an early stage, but it is normally appropriate for counsel to look at the papers and to advise whether any further information should be obtained.

The procedure at the hearing will be largely the same as in the magistrates' court, save for the added solemnity of the Crown Court. For example, the antecedents officer will present details of the defendant's past history on oath. Similarly any probation officer will normally give evidence on oath.

4 AFTER SENTENCE

Obviously, after sentence has been concluded the case is normally at an end, in the sense that a legal aid bill can be prepared, counsel paid and the file closed. In the midst of this, however, the client must not be forgotten. If a custodial sentence has been imposed he will be taken from the court to holding cells. Access is available to legal representatives of defendants in custody. It is, of course, at this stage that initial instructions may be taken on further appeal. It should be remembered that any legal aid order covers such advice and also the lodging of a notice of appeal. In connection therewith it may be necessary to make an application for bail, the mechanics of which are considered in chapter 14.

14 A common law power preserved by the Supreme Court Act 1981, s 45.
15 *R v Lewis* (op cit): this case involved a juvenile committed for trial but presumably the same principle applies.
16 This power is also available to the Crown Court *before* trial.

You should always advise your client on the nature of the sentence imposed, particularly making sure that he understands the consequences of reoffending. This applies particularly to suspended sentences, conditional discharges, probation orders and fines where the court has specified a prison sentence to be served in default of payment. The court should explain this to the defendant, but it is as well for you to be satisfied that your client understands.

SENTENCING PROCEDURE IN A STRAIGHTFORWARD CASE

EXAMPLE: *Softsell Supermarket v Anthony JONES.* It will be recalled from Chapter 1 that on his first appearance JONES, on the advice of the Duty Solicitor, consented to summary trial. He also applied for Legal Aid, which was granted to the Duty Solicitor. Immediately afterwards the charge was read out to him and he pleaded 'guilty'. The prosecution solicitor gave the court brief details of the case and read out JONES's written confession, antecedent form and told the court that JONES was asking for 3 other offences to be taken into consideration, but that he had no previous convictions. Before JONES's solicitor started his speech in mitigation, the chairman of the bench announced that the court wanted a social inquiry report. The court then adjourned for 3 weeks and JONES was released until then on bail. In the intervening period JONES is interviewed by a probation officer. His solicitor also discusses the case with the latter and keeps his file up to date. The following occurs at the resumed hearing.

JONES meets his solicitor in the court ante-room. He has already received a copy of the probation officer's report on arrival at court and goes through it with JONES, checking that the details are correct and obtaining his views on the recommendation, which is a conditional discharge. Sometime later the case is called on.

Clerk: Softsell Supermarkets and JONES. Sir (to the chairman). On the 2nd of this month the defendant asked for summary trial in this case and pleaded guilty. The court adjourned the case until today for a social inquiry report. I understand that a report is available. Do you wish to hear the facts of the case?

Chairman: Yes please; I was present on that occasion, but my colleagues were not.

The prosecution solicitor then reads out the facts of the case, JONES's confession, and the antecedents, copies of which he hands up to the bench. Then he tells the court that JONES wishes for three other offences to be taken into consideration.

Chairman: Have you seen this form, Mr JONES? I assume that this is your signature?

JONES: Yes sir.

Chairman: and you want us to take these matters into account when sentencing you?

JONES: Yes sir.

The prosecution solicitor then tells the court that all of the losers are asking for compensation and gives details of the amounts. They are all small sums and JONES accepts that they are properly owing, so his solicitor does not challenge the claims. The probation officer on duty then hands up the social inquiry report to the bench and the magistrates retire to read the report. When they return they indicate that they do not wish to ask the probation officer any questions. As JONES's solicitor does not wish to do so either, he proceeds straightaway to give his speech in mitigation. He stresses the following:

- that the offence and those T.I.C.D. were committed just after JONES had been made redundant. He received no redundancy pay as he had not worked long enough at the job. He was very depressed.
- that he was already looking for work but had not yet found any.
- that he readily admitted the offence and cooperated with the police.
- the comments made by a probation officer that JONES has a settled home life and that these offences were very much out of character.

He ends by adopting the recommendation of the probation officer that JONES be given a conditional discharge, stressing that he has little money to pay a fine and that a custodial sentence is not appropriate. The court retires again, and on returning imposes a discharge, conditional for 2 years, and the chairman explains what this means. The court also orders compensation in the sums claimed, but does not order costs in the light of JONES's means.

Afterwards JONES's solicitor makes sure he understands the effect of the conditional discharge. On return to the office he completes and sends off his legal aid bill to the Area Secretary.

CHAPTER 14

Appeals and similar remedies

INTRODUCTION

A variety of appeals are available in criminal cases. The type and course of the appeal may depend upon whether the appeal is against a decision of a magistrates' court or of the Crown Court, and in the latter case whether or not it was hearing a trial or sitting as an appellate court. However, before considering appeals properly so called, other remedies that may be available will be discussed.

APPEALS AND OTHER REMEDIES AGAINST DECISIONS OF MAGISTRATES

(a) Powers of magistrates' courts to vary or correct decisions

Magistrates' Courts Act 1980, s 14

This provision was considered in chapter 9. It should be remembered that a defendant can make a statutory declaration if he did not know of the proceedings, the effect of which is that the summons and all subsequent proceedings are void, provided that such a declaration is served on the clerk to the justices within 21 days of the defendant acquiring knowledge. If available, the defence should always use this remedy rather than a full appeal as it is cheaper and quicker. Note however that it will not result in the *information* being dismissed, but in a retrial if the prosecution reissues the summons.

Magistrates' Courts Act 1980, s 142

Section 142 gives magistrates' courts wide powers to amend or vary decisions or orders. It should be noted that this section has a very strict time restriction. The powers can only be exercised within 28 days beginning with the date of the decision or order that is being challenged. 'Exercised' means not that the application must be made within that period, but that the application must be heard within that period. There is no power to extend the time.[1]

The powers are available in two different situations. Firstly, when the defendant has been found guilty, irrespective of plea, by a magistrates' court, the court may vary or rescind any sentence which it has imposed, or substitute any other sentence or order. This may include an increase in sentence, if, for example, the court learned that a part of the mitigation it had heard was untrue. The power may also be used when, for some reason, the original sentence was invalid.[2]

1 *Bradburn v Richards* [1976] RTR 275.
2 Magistrates' Courts Act 1980, s 142(1).

Secondly, if the defendant either pleaded not guilty or alternatively was tried in his absence[3] because he failed to appear when the case was called, the court may order that the finding of guilt and any sentence shall have no effect and the case is treated as if it had been adjourned immediately before the trial started.[4] This part of the section is most likely to be used when the court has proceeded in the defendant's absence and entered a not guilty plea on his behalf on proof of service of the summons. However, it can be used when the defendant is present.

> EXAMPLE. A motorist is prosecuted for driving whilst uninsured. He pleads not guilty but at trial fails to produce any evidence to show that he was insured. All he has available is an out of date certificate: he says he has lost his current one. He is convicted, but subsequently finds the certificate. As he is insured his conviction cannot be sustained. Production of the certificate to the court, and a request to the clerk to invoke this provision might be a more expeditious manner of dealing with the defendant than an appeal to the Crown Court, provided that the time limit of 28 days has not elapsed.

Neither the Act nor the Rules specify the procedure for activating s 142. The court may proceed of its own motion, or on the application of either the prosecutor or the defendant. In the absence of any procedure specified in the Rules, the solicitor could apply by letter on behalf of his client, perhaps checking first with the court office by telephone as to the procedure adopted by that court. Any application must be made to and heard by the original magistrates,[5] although if there were three or more justices sitting then it can be made to a majority of them. If on an application under s 142(2) the court decides that there should be a re-hearing, then the new trial should be before different magistrates.[6]

(b) Appeals to the Crown Court

Introduction

Magistrates' Courts Act 1980, s 108 gives a person convicted by a magistrates' court a right of appeal to the Crown Court. Leave is not required, provided that notice of appeal is given within *21 days* of the decision appealed against. This appeal is available only to the defendant and not to the prosecutor.[7] However aggrieved the latter may be he cannot appeal to the Crown Court against any magistrates' decision or order.[8]

The following preliminary matters will always require consideration.

(i) Bail. Your client may have received a custodial sentence. It should be remembered that both a magistrates' court and the Crown Court judge may grant bail, but that the right to bail under the Bail Act 1976 does *not* apply.[9] The magistrates will probably refuse bail, as to grant it implies that there

---

3 Under Magistrates' Court Act 1980, s 11(1).
4 Ibid, s 142(2).
5 *Morris v Grant* [1983] RTR 433; which produced the odd result that an attempt by magistrates to alter an invalid sentence was quashed, thus leaving the original invalid sentence intact.
6 Ibid, s 142(4).
7 Save in a few cases prescribed by statute.
8 With the rare exception that a prosecutor can appeal against an order for costs of more than £25 made against him on a magistrates' court dismissing committal proceedings—Costs in Criminal Cases Act 1973, s 1(5).
9 Magistrates' Courts Act 1980, s 113; Supreme Court Act 1981, s 81(1)(b).

may be some merit in the appeal. The Crown Court judge may be more inclined to grant bail, particularly if the appeal is against conviction, and the defendant has received a custodial sentence. Alternatively, the judge may refuse bail but ask the court administrator to bring the appeal on for hearing quickly, to avoid the risk of a defendant serving a short custodial sentence in full, prior to being acquitted on appeal. You must thus prepare the papers for the appeal, including the brief to counsel, quickly. The procedure on an application for bail is the same as an application to the Crown Court judge after committal for trial, save that the notice of appeal must have been lodged.

(ii) Legal aid. A legal aid order granted by a magistrates' court enables you to give advice on an appeal and to enter a notice of appeal, but not to conduct the appeal itself. When a person appeals to the Crown Court against conviction or sentence, legal aid for the appeal may be granted either by the magistrates' court against whose decision the appeal is made or by the Crown Court.[10]

The application forms to be used are the same as for the magistrates' court, including the statement of means. The latter will be necessary for the court to decide whether or not the person's disposable income and disposable capital are such that legal aid for the proceedings ought to be given. However, it should be remembered that a legal aid contribution order can only be made once, and this will normally be in respect of the *first* legal aid order granted. Any subsequent legal aid order, and in particular one covering appellate proceedings, cannot attract a *further* contribution order. Once a legal aid order has been granted, it will normally cover the use of solicitor and counsel. As with any earlier order, a legal aid order granted in these circumstances will include advice on and the preparation of an application for a further appeal.[11]

Finally, at the end of the appeal, the bill for work done on appeals to the Crown Court must be prepared and sent to the Crown Court Taxing Office in the same way as for trials on indictment.

(iii) Suspension of disqualification. Any court (whether a magistrates' court or another) which makes an order disqualifying a person, may, if it thinks fit, suspend the disqualification pending an appeal against the order.[11a] You should apply orally immediately after the decision has been made. If you have prepared a notice of appeal to hand in, your application is more likely to be successful. Unless the sentence is suspended your client will commit the offence of driving whilst disqualified if he drives a vehicle pending the appeal.

Nature of the appeal

The extent of the right of appeal will depend on the plea in the magistrates' court. If the appellant pleaded 'not guilty', but was convicted, he may appeal as of right against *conviction* or *sentence* or both. However, an appeal against conviction alone may be treated by the Crown Court as an appeal against conviction and sentence.

> EXAMPLE. Suppose that Mary ADAMS were to plead not guilty but was convicted. The magistrates take a lenient view, fine her £25, and endorse her driving licence with two penalty points, this being the minimum penalty for her offence.

---

10 Legal Aid Act 1974, s 28(5): see chapter 6, pp 207–208.
11 Ibid, s 30(6).
11a RTA 1972, s 94(2). As to fines and other orders see Harris, op cit, p 387.

If she appeals to the Crown Court against conviction and her conviction is upheld, she must then be prepared for the judge to take a more serious view than that taken by the magistrates on the sentence, quite apart from any increased costs she may be ordered to pay to the prosecution.

Conversely if the defendant pleaded 'guilty' in the magistrates' court, he may only appeal against *sentence*.

Appealable sentences

'Sentence' for the purposes of this right of appeal includes 'any order made on conviction by a magistrates' court.'[12] The only orders excluded are orders for costs, destruction orders in respect of animals and orders where the court has no discretion over sentence save that where a person is disqualified from driving in circumstances where such disqualification is mandatory, a right of appeal is provided by the Road Traffic Act 1972.[13] Probation orders and discharges do not count as convictions, but have been specifically made appealable.[14]

Appeals are also available against sentences imposed de novo on a person in breach of a conditional discharge or probation order,[15] or who is brought back before the court and resentenced as a result of breach, variation or revocation of a community service order.[16]

The most important exception to the right of appeal against orders made by magistrates' courts is in relation to legal aid contribution orders. These orders are not made 'on conviction' but when legal aid is granted. It should be remembered that there is no right of review against a contribution order, and no obligation to order repayment if the legally assisted person is acquitted. Similarly, there is no appeal against a refusal to order that the prosecution or defence costs be paid out of central funds, where applicable. It can be appreciated that this can operate as a penalty especially following an acquittal. The only way in which such action or inaction can be challenged is by way of application for judicial review, but it may be very difficult and expensive to prove that the order is perverse.

Finally, an order committing the defendant to the Crown Court for sentence is not appealable, as it does not constitute a sentence or order as such, but is more in the way of an interlocutory order.[17] Nevertheless an accused who pleaded not guilty could appeal against conviction. If unsuccessful, the Crown Court can presumably proceed to sentence on the basis of s 38 of the Act of 1980.

The notice of appeal

The procedural requirements on appeals to the Crown Court are set out in rule 7 of the Crown Court Rules 1982. Notice of appeal must be given in

---

12 Magistrates' Court Act 1980, s 108.
13 Ibid, s 94.
14 S 108(1A) inserted by Criminal Justice Act 1982, s 66. Similarly a statutory right of appeal is given in respect of bind overs which do not count as convictions.
15 Ibid, s 108(2).
16 Powers of Criminal Courts Act, ss 16(6) and 17(4).
17 *R v London Sessions Appeal Committee*, ex p Rogers [1951] 2 KB 74.

NOTICE OF APPEAL TO THE CROWN COURT

To the <u>Clerk of the Justices</u> of the Weyford Magistrates Court, The
Court House, Weyford

and to <u>Inspector Harold Keppel</u>, Blankshire Police, stationed at Weyford
Police Station

I, Mary Adams of 45, Alma Road, Weyford, do hereby give you notice
of my intention to appeal to the Crown Court sitting at Guildfleet
against my conviction and sentence of 5 penalty points and fine of
two hundred and fifty pounds passed on me by the said magistrates'
court on the 20th day of May 198- for having at Steephill Road, Weyford
on the 21st day of November 198- driven without due care and attention
contrary to s3 and schedule IV of the Road Traffic Act 1972.

The grounds of my appeal are:-

      1.   The conviction was contrary to the evidence

      2.   I am not guilty of the offence

      3.   The sentence was excessive

Dated 21st day of May 198-

Smith & Jones

Solicitors for the Appellant

writing within 21 days after the day 'on which the decision appealed against is given'. This is the date of conviction unless the offender is sentenced on a subsequent occasion, in which case it is that subsequent occasion. The 21 day period starts on the day after the final disposal. When, however, a court defers sentence, but the offender wishes to appeal against conviction, the 21 day period starts to run on the day after sentence is deferred and not from the day after the final disposal is made.[18]

If a solicitor has overlooked the 21 day period or his client has not instructed him until after it has elapsed, he may apply in writing for the period to be extended, even if it has expired. The application, usually by letter, must be sent to the Crown Court and will usually be referred to a senior officer or the presiding judge. The letter should specify the basis upon which the appeal is to be made. The judge may grant leave to lodge a notice of appeal against conviction or sentence out of time. There is no right to an oral hearing, although the judge may allow one.[19] An application made immediately after the expiry may well be successful. As the time lengthens, the chances will be greatly reduced. Accordingly you would be wise always to include in the letter the reason why the original time limit was not observed. If you forgot, then say so.

The notice of appeal itself in criminal cases does not otherwise need to set out the ground of appeal, as it is made as of right. It must, however, state whether or not the appeal is against conviction or sentence. It must be sent to the magistrates' court and the prosecution supplied with a copy. Curiously, you do not need to send a copy to the Crown Court itself. Accordingly, the only time the Crown Court will be directly involved in the initial stages of the appeal will be when, as indicated above, it is necessary to apply for an extension of time. There is no prescribed form, although pre-printed forms are available.

Preparation for the hearing

Rights of audience.   A general right of audience is given to solicitors in the Crown Court in any proceedings, comprising inter alia, a criminal appeal from a magistrates' court. The proviso, however, is that the magistrates' court hearing must have been conducted by the solicitor concerned or his partner, principal or employee.[20] This is an important right of audience particularly where the defendant appeals against conviction, as the appeal takes the form of a re-hearing. You are thus entitled to conduct what amounts to a Crown Court trial. It is up to you to decide whether you exercise this right. You may find it easier to start off by conducting appeals against sentence. As the proceedings are in open court you must be robed and wear a wing collar and tabs as if you were appearing in the county court. You may meet hostility from both bench and bar on occasions, but this should not stop you from appearing if you feel that you are the best person to represent your client. You should not, however, embark upon appearances in the Crown Court without a thorough study of *Archbold* and a familiarity with the court's usage.

18 Crown Court Rules 1982, r 7(3).
19 *R v Croydon Crown Court, ex p Smith* (1983) 77 Cr App Rep 277.
20 *Practice Direction* [1972] 1 All ER 608.

Appeals against conviction

Once notice of appeal has been given the clerk to the justices is responsible for transmitting the appropriate information to the Crown Court. The procedure from then on will be very similar to that of a trial on indictment.

Listing. The Crown Court Listing Officer will place the appeal into the Crown Court list for hearing and the solicitors instructed for the appellant will be notified in a similar way. The appeal will normally be brought into the list as soon as possible, particularly when the appellant has been sentenced to a custodial term and is presently in custody. Therefore, if you are intending to instruct counsel, you must send the brief to him as soon as possible.[1]

Constitution of the court. In appeals the Crown Court judge will sit with at least two and no more than four magistrates, rather than with a jury. The judge must decide matters of law, but the decision on the facts will be taken by a majority. The judge has a casting vote if necessary.

The course of an appeal against conviction

An appeal to the Crown Court against conviction takes the form of a re-hearing. This means that, notwithstanding that it is the defendant who is appealing, the case will be opened by the prosecution and will proceed in all practical respects as a Crown Court trial, save that there is no jury. In particular, because it is a re-hearing the parties are not confined to calling the evidence that was presented at the magistrates' court but may call additional evidence if they wish. The evidence given by a witness at the summary trial is not capable of corroborating the evidence that he gives on the appeal but may be used in cross-examination to show inconsistency.

Furthermore, the evidence presented at summary trial may not be available at all. The magistrates' clerk may not have taken any notes. If the clerk has taken notes, he cannot be compelled to make them available to the parties for use in an appeal to the Crown Court.[2] This presumably also applies to any notes taken by the magistrates themselves. The prosecutor will still have his witnesses' original statements, and you will normally have your own notes, assuming that you took them in a form which you can now read and understand!

The course of an appeal against sentence

The appeal will be listed in the same way as an appeal against conviction, and the same criteria as to whether or not the defendant is in custody or on bail will be instrumental in bringing the appeal before the Crown Court as soon as possible. It will be heard by the same format of judge and magistrates.

Otherwise, the proceedings will be similar to proceedings in the Crown Court after a finding of guilt. The court will receive any social inquiry report prepared by the probation service which was presented to the magistrates' court. It will make its decision as to confirmation or variation of sentence after the defence has presented mitigation.

---

1 See p 458, ante.
2 *R v Lancaster Justices ex p Hill* (1983) Times, 9 August.

Powers of the Crown Court—Supreme Court Act 1981, s 48

Powers in appeals against conviction. When the Crown Court hears an appeal it will effectively confirm or reverse the magistrates' decision as to guilt. If the appellant is successful in his appeal, then he is treated for all purposes as if he had been found not guilty by the magistrates' court in the first place and the criminal conviction recorded against him as a result of the original finding is null and void and must be deleted from his record.

Equivocal pleas. The nature of an equivocal plea has already been considered.[3] Where a solicitor has represented the defendant in the magistrates' court, he should have ensured that the defendant fully understood the plea that he was tendering. It may be, however, that you are not instructed by the client until after he has been convicted. In this case the basis of the appeal will normally be that an equivocal plea should not have been accepted. Alternatively the Crown Court may of its own motion raise the question of whether or not the plea in the magistrates' court was equivocal. Irrespective of how the issue is raised, the Crown Court will normally remit the case to the convicting court with the opinion that the case should be retried before different magistrates.[4]

This type of appeal will be equally appropriate when the plea itself was unequivocal but the magistrates subsequently heard matters which should have led them to consider whether the defendant ought to change his plea.[5]

> EXAMPLE. A defendant has entered a plea of guilty. After the police officer in the case has given details of the defendant's character, but before sentence has been pronounced, the defendant explains that he is sorry for having committed the offence and that he accepts he must be punished, even though he did not intend to steal.

This is not an equivocal plea, but rather a situation when the magistrates should allow the defendant to change his plea.[6]

In both of these cases the appeal is in essence against conviction, whereas the records of the magistrates' court will show that 'guilty' pleas were entered. Therefore, the notice of appeal should set out what was wrong with the plea tendered, otherwise the Crown Court may refuse to treat it as an appeal against conviction.

Sentencing powers

In hearing both appeals against conviction and against sentence, the Crown Court has virtually all the powers available to the magistrates' court save that it cannot commit the offender to itself for sentence under s 38 of the Act of 1980. Whatever sentence it does impose cannot exceed one which the magistrates could have imposed. Accordingly even if the offence is one triable 'either way' the maximum term of imprisonment that can be imposed by the Crown Court on hearing an appeal against sentence will remain at six months.

The Crown Court does, however, have power to *increase* the severity of the

---

3 See p 295, ante.
4 *R v Tottenham Justices, ex p Rubens* [1970] 1 All ER 879: the Crown Court should enquire what took place in the magistrates' court, preferably by taking an affidavit from the justices' clerk or the chairman of the bench: *R v Rochdale Justices ex p Allwork* [1981] 3 All ER 434.
5 *S (infant) v Manchester City Recorder* [1971] AC 481, HL; *R v Durham Quarter Sessions, ex p Virgo* [1952] 2 QB 1.
6 Supreme Court Act 1981, s 48(4).

sentence up to the maximum that the magistrates could have imposed. This can include changing the type of sentence imposed. Although this sanction is rarely exercised, it does exist to discourage offenders from making spurious or trivial appeals. Even if the court does not increase sentence, it can as part of its decision change the date of commencement of sentence. This could include changing the date of commencement from the date of the original hearing to the date of the appeal.

The Crown Court will normally consider any social inquiry report already available to the magistrates, although there is nothing to stop it adjourning for a social inquiry report to be obtained. This is unlikely to happen frequently, however, and you should anticipate that in the event of the appeal being dismissed the court will proceed immediately to disposition.

Powers in respect of ancillary orders

The Crown Court may confirm or vary ancilliary orders made on conviction, such as orders for compensation or forfeiture. It may also make such orders for costs inter partes as the magistrates could have made.[7] Thus it may order the defendant to pay all or part of the prosecutor's costs both of the appeal and in the magistrates' court. In addition, the Court may order that the prosecution expenses be met out of central funds if the appeal relates to an indictable offence irrespective of the outcome, but those of the defendant may only be ordered if the appeal is successful.[8]

(c) Appeals by way of case stated to the Divisional Court of the Queen's Bench Division

Introduction

The Magistrates' Courts Act 1980 gives a right of appeal to the Divisional Court of the Queen's Bench Division. There are two grounds of appeal, namely that the proceedings in the magistrates' court were either wrong in law, or that the magistrates were acting in excess of their jurisdiction.[9] The proceedings must have been concluded by conviction, acquittal or the discharge of the accused at committal proceedings. There is no appeal against a decision of magistrates to commit for trial as this does not conclude the proceedings.[10]

Appeals on matters of law tend to arise if, for example, it is alleged that a magistrates' court has construed a statute incorrectly, wrongly admitted inadmissible evidence, or that a conviction was wrong because there was no evidence to support an essential element of the offence(s) charged. Appeals on the ground of lack of jurisdiction are much less common, but might arise if a magistrates' court purported to try an offence which was triable only on indictment, or purported to sentence an offender to seven months imprisonment when the statutory maximum was six months.

---

7 Supreme Court Act 1981, s 48; Crown Court Rules 1982, r 13.
8 Costs in Criminal Cases Act 1973, s 3; see pp 203–204, ante.
9 Magistrates' Courts Act 1980, s 111(1).
10 *Atkinson v United States of America Government* [1971] AC 197, HL.

Who may apply?

'Case stated' is available to any party to the proceedings or anyone aggrieved at the result.[11] Therefore not only is it available to both prosecution and defence, irrespective of whether or not the defendant was convicted or acquitted, but also to an applicant for a compensation order who is thwarted by the defendant's acquittal. It thus differs from an appeal to the Crown Court which is, of course, only available to the defendant. From the point of view of the defence, however, the most significant point is that an appeal by way of case stated automatically bars the right of appeal to the Crown Court.[12] Given that the defendant may apply to the Crown Court to state a case, having first appealed to that court from the magistrates' court, an appeal to the Crown Court always appears more attractive. It is essential to appeal to the Crown Court first if, notwithstanding any argument over matters of law, the *real* complaint on the appellant's part is that he was not believed; in other words, there is a contested issue of *fact* rather than on a matter of *law*.

Method of application

The essence of the case stated procedure is that the magistrates set out the findings that they made, and address a question to the Divisional Court as to whether or not they proceeded correctly. Any person wishing to apply must ask the magistrates' court to 'state a case' and this must be done by written notice within 21 days, starting with the day after the conclusion of the proceedings. This will normally be the day of conviction, unless the magistrates adjourned after conviction and sentenced subsequently, in which case it will be 21 days after the day of sentence.[13] Neither the High Court nor the magistrates' court have power to extend this period. The notice must be in writing and signed on behalf of the applicant, and must identify the question or questions of law or jurisdiction with which the appeal is concerned. The notice must be sent to the clerk of the appropriate magistrates court.

On receipt of the notice the clerk to the justices must prepare a draft case and send it to the parties and the justices concerned, usually within 21 days. They may all make representations to the clerk, as a result of which a final case to be stated is settled by him and sent to the appellant's solicitors, after it has been signed by at least two of the magistrates concerned, or by the stipendiary magistrate, as appropriate. The clerk to the justices may consult with the parties at any stage over problems or issues that arise on stating the case.

Magistrates may refuse to 'state a case' if they consider the application to be frivolous.[14] The only way to challenge that decision is by an application for judicial review to compel them to do so. This is considered in the next part of this chapter.

---

11 Magistrates' Courts Act 1980, s 111(1).
12 Ibid, s 111(4).
13 Ibid, s 111(2) and (3).
14 They can also take a surety from the appellant to prosecute the appeal properly, but this appears little used in criminal cases.

From filing to hearing

The case must be lodged at the Crown Office at the Royal Courts of Justice[15] within ten days of receipt, and the appellant must give notice to the clerk to the justices and all other parties within four days of lodgment. The Divisional Court of the Queen's Bench Division is, of course, a civil court. At this point the matter ceases to be regulated by the Magistrates' Courts Act and the Magistrates' Courts Rules, and becomes regulated instead by the Rules of the Supreme Court.[16] The case will be listed for hearing in the usual High Court system involving weekly and daily lists.

The hearing will usually be before two judges of the High Court or the Court of Appeal, and if the parties wish to appear they must do so either by counsel or in person. Argument is confined to matters of law arising out of the case as stated by the magistrates, and no additional evidence may be presented. The magistrates do not usually appear.

At the end of the hearing, the Divisional Court may remit the matter to the magistrates' court with its opinion. The magistrates are obliged to follow the decision of the Divisional Court. Alternatively in appropriate circumstances the court may exercise its wide powers to reverse, vary or amend the decision.[17] The normal order for costs is that the loser pays the winner's costs; no order can be made against magistrates unless they appeared at the hearing.[18] The court can also order either party's costs to be paid out of central funds.[19] The costs awarded may include those incurred in the magistrates' court.

Legal aid

Initial advice on the stating of a case, including the lodging of an application, is covered by the legal aid order granted for the proceedings before the magistrates.[20] Case stated proceedings are essentially civil in nature, and thus criminal legal aid is not available thereafter. However, a civil legal aid certificate is available for proceedings in the Divisional Court.[1] The civil legal aid application form A1, and an emergency application form A3 should be completed, signed by your client, and sent to the relevant Area office.[2] If a certificate is granted, it must as usual be filed at the High Court on the issue of the certificate or on the lodging of the case stated, whichever is later. The usual notice is served on the other parties to the appeal. At the end of the proceedings the legal aid bill will have to be taxed on a common fund basis, as usual in civil legal aid cases, unless it comes to less than £500, when it can be assessed by the Legal Aid Area Committee.[3]

---

15 See Magistrates Courts Rules 1981, rr 76–81.
16 RSC Ord 56.
17 Summary Jurisdiction Act 1857, s 6.
18 Ibid, s 6.
19 Costs in Criminal Cases Act 1973, s 5.
20 Legal Aid Act 1974, s 30(5).
 1 Legal Aid Act 1974, s 7 and Sch I, Part I.
 2 An emergency application is suggested because of the short timescale that can be involved. Note also that the client may have to pay a contribution towards civil legal aid, even if he has already paid a legal aid contribution order.
 3 Legal Aid (General) Regulations 1980, reg 100(2)(a)

Bail

When a person applies for a case to be stated he may, if he is in custody, apply to the magistrates court for bail.[4] As usual, the procedure for applying for bail in the magistrates' court is oral. If he is refused, he can apply to a High Court judge. The bail provisions as provided in the Magistrates' Courts Act 1980 are, however, rather peculiar.[5] If bail is granted, the defendant must appear back at the magistrates' court within *10 days* of the judgment of the Divisional Court on the case stated, at a time which will be specified when bail is granted, unless the decision of the magistrates' court is reversed. The bail provision is thus much more open ended than is normally the case in the magistrates' court and is more akin to the granting of bail on committal to the Crown Court for trial which is also, of course, a grant of bail to an unspecified date.

Application to the Divisional Court for judicial review

Introduction

A detailed consideration of judicial review is clearly outside the scope of this work. This section will therefore be confined to a brief description of the nature of these remedies and the situations in which they are available.

The Divisional Court exercises supervisory and controlling functions over inter alia inferior courts. It is principally concerned to see that decisions are made and discretions exercised in the proper manner and after consideration of the appropriate factors. It is not so concerned with the decision itself. Supervisory jurisdiction exists over magistrates' courts and the Crown Court other than when the issue arises out of a trial on indictment.[6] It is thus available against the Crown Court sitting to hear appeals, or to deal with offenders who have been committed for sentence. Anyone can apply for judicial review, provided they can show that they have *locus standi*, namely sufficient interest in the proceedings. Both the prosecutor and the defendant clearly come within this definition.

The orders that can be made

There are three principal orders that can be made. These are as follows.

(i) Certiorari.   This order enables the Divisional Court to quash the decision of an inferior court because of irregularity in the proceedings, excess of jurisdiction, errors of law on the face of the court's record, bias, or breach of the rules of natural justice.[7] This type of order partially overlaps with case stated, which may also be used to challenge jurisdiction.[8]

(ii) Mandamus.   This order compels an inferior court to perform a duty. It might be used, for example, against a magistrates' court which refused to state a case. Until recently mandamus was the only effective way of challenging a magistrates' court's refusal to grant a legal aid order. It is available

---

4 Presumably a conviction will count as a change in circumstances enabling a further 'full' application to be made.
5 Magistrates' Courts Act 1980, s 113(1). Rules of the Supreme Court, Ord 79.
6 Supreme Court Act 1981, s 29.
7 Even if it is the prosecutor, not the court, that has broken the rules. *R v Leyland Justices, ex p Hawthorn* [1979] 1 All ER 209.
8 See Magistrates' Courts Act 1980, s 111, p 465 ante.

if the appellant contends that the court did not consider the application properly or take into account the correct principles. Thus the order does not and cannot compel the magistrates to grant legal aid, but it can compel them to reconsider the matter, taking into account the correct factors. It may be that the right to apply for review to the C.A.C. now provided in the Legal Aid Act 1982 will make applications even less common than they were previously.[9] It remains, however, the only way to challenge a refusal to grant legal aid for summary offences.[10]

Certiorari and mandamus are frequently combined so as to quash a decision and compel a magistrates' court to take other action.

(iii) Prohibition. This order may be considered as the converse of mandamus, and is available as an order to prevent a magistrates' court from proceeding with a matter, irrespective of whether or not the proceedings have actually been commenced. It could be used to challenge an excess of jurisdiction, for example, if a magistrates' court was purporting to commit an offence for trial which was triable only summarily.[11] It is also available to cover the same ground as certiorari, but at an earlier stage. In practical terms, however, it has little significance in criminal matters, as a defendant will normally wait until a decision has been taken before he decides whether or not to challenge it.

There are other orders also available as part of judicial review. An injunction can be granted, including one ordering a person not to act in an office or position which they do not hold. The court can also grant a declaration. In practical terms, however, these are not so important in criminal procedure, as usually the complainant is asking that a decision be quashed.

Method of application

The procedure for applying for judicial review is set out in Order 53 of the Rules of Supreme Court. It includes reference to standard forms on which the application must be made. In brief, judicial review is obtained by a two stage process. The first stage is to seek leave to apply, by lodging a notice[12] giving particulars of the applicant and of the issue on which review is sought. This must be supported by an affidavit. The application for leave must be made within three months of the decision complained of. It is considered, usually without a hearing, by a High Court judge of the Queen's Bench Division who may grant or refuse leave. In the latter case the application may be renewed to the full Divisional Court. If leave is granted then the next stage is to apply for judicial review itself by originating motion to the Divisional Court. The applicant must be represented by counsel, unless he applies in person. The notice of motion must have been served by the applicant or his solicitors on all parties affected so as to give ten days' notice. This will include not only the prosecutor but also the magistrates.

As with case stated, the application is not normally supported by evidence, but the court will be addressed by counsel and read the affidavit in support of the application, together with any affidavits that may have been filed by any other interested party.

---

9 See further chapter 6, pp 215–216.
10 See eg *R v Highgate Justices, ex p Lewis* [1977] Crim LR 611.
11 As in *R v Hatfield Justices, ex p Castle* [1980] 3 All ER 509.
12 In form 86A.

Legal aid

Civil legal aid is available and again an emergency certificate may be necessary. The solicitor should discuss this with the Area Secretary before or at the time of applying for legal aid. Note, however, that unlike case stated, a criminal legal aid order neither includes advice on whether judicial review should be sought, nor covers lodging an application.

Bail

When a person applies for judicial review they may be in the process of serving a custodial sentence. Their solicitor may apply for bail on their behalf but only to a High Court judge.[13] The magistrates do not, apparently, have jurisdiction to grant bail to a convicted person if he applies for judicial review by way of certiorari[14] and presumably this applies to mandamus as well. Prohibition is unlikely to be appropriate at this stage. When the applicant is represented, the application will normally be made orally.

The effect of judicial review

If certiorari is ordered then the decision of the magistrates' court is transferred into the Divisional Court in order that it may be quashed. This generally means that the court will order a re-trial. If, however, the magistrates have imposed an incorrect sentence outside their jurisdiction the Court can substitute any sentence which the magistrates would have had power to pass.[15] If mandamus is ordered, the person or court to whom that order is directed must comply with it. If as a result of judicial review the Court makes an order of prohibition, then the proceedings against which review was sought cannot be continued. Note, however, that were prohibition to be ordered to a magistrates' court which purported to commit a summary only offence to the Crown Court for trial, that would not invalidate the summons or the information.

Unlike case stated there is no statutory provision which extinguishes the right of appeal to the Crown Court when judicial review is sought. Presumably were the applicant to apply for both, the Crown Court would not proceed pending the decision of the Divisional Court.

Judicial review and double jeopardy

If the Divisional Court quashes the decision of a lower court, it is arguable that the defendant stands in risk of double jeopardy, the rule being that a person should not have to risk conviction more than once for the same offence. The House of Lords has recently drawn a distinction between an order that, in essence, declares the proceedings to have been a nullity, and an order that might put the defendant in risk of double jeopardy.

In *Re Harrington*[16] the House of Lords granted an order of certiorari where magistrates had summarily dismissed an information on a prosecutor's application for an adjournment, before giving the prosecutor the opportunity of presenting evidence.[17] Their lordships observed that the accused did not

13 RSC Ord 79, r 9.
14 *Ex p Blyth* [1944] KB 532.
15 Supreme Court Act 1981, s 43.
16 [1984] AC 743, HL.
17 See Magistrates' Courts Act 1980, ss 9(2) and 10(1).

stand in risk of double jeopardy because he had not been lawfully convicted or lawfully acquitted. As the proceedings had been invalid, he was in the same position as if the case had been adjourned prior to trial. The House did, however, observe that had the accused been acquitted after, for example, breaches of the rules of natural justice but within the framework of the correct procedure, judicial review might not then lie to quash the decision. The House conceded that such a case would be unusual, and it is difficult to imagine a situation occurring that would achieve this result.

A problem similar to that in *Ex p Harrington* arose in *Weight v Mackay*[18] where an appeal against conviction was wrongly stopped by the judge. As the court had not proceeded properly, its proceedings were a nullity, and thus the defendant was restored to the position he was in after conviction but before appeal.

A comparison of appeal to the Crown Court, case stated, and judicial review

Firstly, it should be remembered that the right of appeal to the Crown Court exists both on matters of law and of fact. Both case stated and judicial review are concerned with matters of law rather than of fact. Thus if the appellant wishes to raise not only matters of *law*, but also *factual issues* as well, his appeal should initially be to the Crown Court. If the appellant appeals by way of case stated, he will forfeit his right to appeal to the Crown Court, whatever the *factual* merits of his appeal would have been.

If the issue is solely one of jurisdiction, both case stated and judicial review are available. Judicial review may be preferable in that the procedure is simpler and quicker. If the issue is one of bias, partiality or improper behaviour, judicial review by way of certiorari is the remedy that should be pursued in any event. If the issue in the appeal is solely a matter of law, for example, an argument over the wrongful admission of evidence, then judicial review will not be available but case stated will be.[19] If, however, the magistrates refused to state a case, the remedy would be an order of mandamus to compel them to do so. Note that an apparent point of law may, however, conceal a more fundamental defect. For example, in *R v Bromley Justices, ex p Haymill (Contractors) Ltd*,[20] justices had adjourned a case involving a defective motor vehicle for hearing by another bench, as they could not decide between the prosecution and the defence evidence. Judicial review quashed this decision and compelled them to bring in a verdict. They had no power to adjourn, but the main point emphasised by the Divisional Court was that in the event of doubt they should not adjourn, but acquit.

In terms of the cost, judicial review or case stated may, in fact, be cheaper than a full blown Crown Court retrial on appeal. However, legal aid may well be granted more readily for a Crown Court appeal than for the Divisional Court proceedings, and for most aggrieved defendants it may well be the availability or otherwise of legal aid which determines the form of appeal to be pursued.

---

18 [1984] 2 All ER 673, HL.
19 *R v Wells St Stipendiary Magistrate, ex p Seillon* [1978] 3 All ER 257; *R v Horsham Justices, ex p Bulkhari* (1981) 74 Cr App Rep 291.
20 (1984) Times, 7 February.

APPEALS AND OTHER REMEDIES AGAINST THE CROWN COURT

(a) Recourse back to the Crown Court

The Crown Court may within *28 days* beginning with the day of sentence vary or rescind any sentence it has imposed whether after trial or committal for sentence. This power is similar to that of magistrates,[21] but additionally includes the power, rarely exercised, to increase sentence. The variation is limited to the *28-day* period after which there is no power to vary any sentence. There is no power to order a retrial as there is in the magistrates' court, presumably because of the sanctity of the jury's verdict.

(b) Applications from the Crown Court to the Divisional Court of the Queen's Bench Division

Whenever a Crown Court is sitting *other* than in relation to *a trial on indictment* parties or persons aggrieved may apply to the Divisional Court of the Queen's Bench Division for judicial review[22] or to the Crown Court for a case to be stated.[23] This covers situations where the Crown Court is sitting as an appellate court, or where it is resentencing an offender who is in breach of a community service order imposed by a magistrates' court on an earlier occasion,[24] but not where the Crown Court judge refuses to grant legal aid for a trial on indictment.[25] The procedure in respect of judicial review is exactly the same as in summary cases. As far as case stated is concerned, the procedure is broadly similar,[1] and in particular the application must still be made within *21 days* starting with the day after the decision is made; like the magistrates' court the Crown Court can refuse to state a case if it is frivolous.

(c) The Court of Appeal

Appeals from the Crown Court to the Criminal Division of the Court of Appeal

The jurisdiction, powers and duties of the Criminal Division of the Court of Appeal are contained in the Criminal Appeal Act 1968 and regulations made thereunder. The function of this court and the working of the Act is outside the scope of this work. If a solicitor encounters a problem in this area he should consult *Archbold*, or the excellent Guide to Proceedings in the Criminal Division of the Court of Appeal, available from the Court of Appeal Office and all branches of the Crown Court.[2]

As will be seen, the Court of Appeal is almost exclusively concerned with appeals from *trials on indictment*. Note, however, that whenever counsel is briefed to appear in the Crown Court the brief should always be accompanied by a short set of Instructions to Counsel. These should ask counsel, in the event of conviction or sentence, to advise on whether or not there should be an appeal, and to settle grounds of appeal if appropriate in the event of conviction or sentence.

---

21 Magistrates' Courts Act 1980, s 142(1), ante.
22 Supreme Court Act 1981, s 29(3).
23 Ibid, s 28.
24 *R v Crown Court at Newcastle upon Tyne, ex p Bradley* (1984) 149 JP 154.
25 *R v Crown Court at Chichester, ex p Abodunrin and Sogbanmu* (1984) 149 JP 54.
 1 It is set out in full in Crown Court Rules 1982, r 26.
 2 It is also reproduced at [1983] Crim LR 415.

Appeals against conviction

If the defendant appeals against conviction on a ground which comprises pure law, then he does not need leave. If, however, the appeal is based on fact, or matters of mixed law and fact, then either the Court of Appeal must grant leave or a Crown Court judge must certify that the case is fit for appeal. Most appeals are likely to involve some issues of fact as well as an issue of law. For example, any appeal on the question of the admissibility of evidence must involve an evaluation of the evidence itself as well as the question of admissibility.

There are only three bases upon which the appeal can be upheld, namely:

the conviction is *unsafe or unsatisfactory* in all the circumstances of the case; or

the conviction should be set aside because of a *wrong decision* on a matter of *law;* or

a *material irregularity* occurred in the course of the trial.

It should be clear that the second and third grounds are likely to arise only on matters of law rather than of fact. The first ground is wider than this, but does not enable an appeal to succeed merely because the Court of Appeal would not have convicted. Furthermore, an appeal may be turned down even if a ground is made out if the Court is satisfied that no miscarriage of justice has occurred.[3]

As with appeals to the Crown Court, an appeal against conviction is normally appropriate only when the defendant pleaded 'not guilty'. An appeal is possible, however, on the basis of a guilty plea which is alleged to be equivocal.

The parties are, of course, under a general duty to present all their evidence at the trial on indictment. New evidence can only be presented to the Court of Appeal if it would have been admissible at the trial and there is a reasonable explanation for it not having been presented.[4] This is of course completely different to the rule on appeals in the Crown Court, where new evidence can be adduced as of right.

Appeals against sentence

Whenever the defendant wishes to appeal against sentence, leave of the Court of Appeal or a certificate granted by the sentencing judge is required.[5] An appeal may be made against any sentence passed after trial on indictment. An appeal may also be made against certain sentences or orders imposed by the Crown Court after conviction by a magistrates' court, provided they consist of:

(i) a sentence of imprisonment or youth custody of *six months* or more; or
(ii) an order of *disqualification* from driving; or
(iii) a recommendation for *deportation;* or
(iv) a sentence the magistrates could not have imposed.

---

3 Criminal Appeal Act 1968, s 2 and proviso thereto.
4 Ibid, s 23.
5 It is only in exceptional circumstances that it will be appropriate to approach the trial judge; otherwise one is asking the judge to certify that he may have made a mistake. *R v Dawson* (1984) Times, 28 June.

Application and hearing

The person who wishes to appeal must normally complete an application within *28 days* of the decision or order against which the appeal is made. This should contain the grounds of the appeal and must be sent to the Registrar of Criminal Appeals. If leave is required, a single judge will normally consider whether or not it should be granted on the basis of the written application, together with the relevant parts of the transcript of the judge's summing up and/or evidence given at the trial which may be obtained through the Registrar of Criminal Appeals.

If the judge decides to grant leave, the case will be listed for appeal. If he refuses leave to appeal, the applicant has *14 days* in which to serve notice on the Registrar that he wants to renew his application before the Court.

Once leave has been granted, or the Registrar of Criminal Appeals is satisfied that it is not required, the case will be listed for hearing before the Court of Appeal. The appellant will normally be represented, as will the prosecution.

Bail

Bail may be granted by the Court of Appeal, or by a judge at the Crown Court if he certifies that the case is fit for appeal. An application to the Crown Court judge should be made first, which means that he must be asked for a certificate.[6] The judge will be very wary of granting bail, and in essence it is only appropriate for him to do so where the circumstances are sufficiently unusual for him to grant a certificate anyway.

Application to the Court of Appeal is made initially by written application in the prescribed form, but counsel may be instructed to appear. The application is normally considered by a single judge. The defence solicitor should note, however, that a legal aid order for the Crown Court does not cover a bail application to the Court of Appeal. Bail is not often granted. The Court of Appeal prefers to expedite the appeal.

Legal aid

The Court of Appeal alone may grant legal aid for proceedings before it, and as an exception to the general rule, legal aid so granted may be retrospective.[7] In addition, it will be remembered that a Crown Court legal aid, order covers the cost of advising on whether or not appeal should be made, and also the lodging of the notice of appeal or a notice of application for leave as appropriate. Legal aid will in most cases be for counsel only, who will be instructed by the Registrar of Criminal Appeals.

Attorney General's references

As mentioned earlier,[7a] the Attorney General can refer to the Criminal Division of the Court of Appeal a point of law upon which he requires guidance, arising out of an acquittal at a trial on indictment.[8] The hearing

---

6 Prescribed forms C and BC which are set out in the Guide are the orders granting the certificate and granting bail respectively
7 Legal Aid Act 1974, s 28(8).
7a See p 13, ante.
8 Criminal Justice Act 1972, s 36.

will consist of argument by counsel for the Attorney General. The defendant may also appear by counsel if he wishes, but whether or not he does so the defendant is protected by anonymity and the result of the trial is not impugned. This provision is, of course, not necessary for magistrates' courts trials because both the prosecution and the defence can proceed to the Divisional Court by way of case stated. The same applies to the Crown Court when it hears an appeal from magistrates.

Home Secretary's references

Any case where a defendant has been found guilty after trial on indictment may be referred by the Home Secretary to the Court of Appeal.[9] He may refer the entire case, or ask the Court to consider a specific point. This power is primarily used where fresh evidence has materialised after an unsuccessful appeal. If an entire case is referred the reference is treated as if the defendant had obtained full leave to appeal. He is not confined to arguing those matters which led to the reference being made.[10] The power to refer is not exercised frequently.

OTHER APPEALS AND REMEDIES

(a) Appeals to the House of Lords

Appeals lie from the Divisional Court or the Court of Appeal to the House of Lords. Legal aid is available. In appeals from the Divisional Court it is granted by the Area Legal Aid Offices. The Court of Appeal grants legal aid for proceedings against its decisions in the House of Lords. In both cases leave is needed, and this text does not consider either procedure further. *Archbold* and the *Supreme Court Practice* should be consulted for this. Furthermore, the Judicial Office of the House of Lords produces a booklet entitled 'Form of Appeal and Directions as to Procedure applicable to Criminal Appeals from England and Wales' which explains the procedure.

(b) European Commission of Human Rights

It may also be possible to petition the European Commission of Human Rights if a person considers himself to have been the victim of a violation of the European Convention on Human Rights.[11] A civil legal aid certificate is available.

(c) Application for writ of habeas corpus

The last type of appeal or quasi-appeal which will be considered is an application for a writ of habeas corpus.[12] There are, in fact, five different types of writ of habeas corpus but this text is only concerned with the challenge to the detention of a person and securing his release if the detention is not lawful.

It is not an alternative method of applying for bail. It goes only to the lawfulness or otherwise of the detention and is not concerned with the results

---

9 Criminal Appeal Act 1968, s 17.
10 *R v Chard* [1984] AC 279, HL.
11 Details are available from the Commission in Strasbourg, France.
12 Rules of the Supreme Court, Ord 54.

of a lawful detention. Traditionally it has most commonly been used in criminal proceedings to challenge detention by the police after arrest when the arrested person has been neither released, nor produced before the magistrates.[13]

Application and hearing

The writ is issued by order of the High Court and an oral application must be made *ex parte* to a judge in chambers, supported by an affidavit made either by the person restrained or, as is more likely, by someone acting on his behalf. If there is no judge sitting the application can be made to a judge otherwise than at court, and arrangements exist at the Royal Courts of Justice for you to be put in touch with a duty judge when the court is not sitting. A High Court judge is always available if needed.

The judge in chambers is not entitled in a criminal case to refuse an application for a writ and accordingly, if he does not grant the application, he will normally direct that the application must be renewed before a Divisional Court by originating motion. He will then adjourn for notice to be given of the application to the respondent. *Eight clear days' notice* is specified in the Rules, although the judge may, and usually will, direct a lesser period.

In practice, the judge will not normally grant an application for a writ of habeas corpus *ex parte*. He is much more likely to direct that an application should be made on notice to the Divisional Court, whilst at the same time shortening the period of notice required to be given.

At the hearing the court will hear argument for the applicant, and for the respondent, assuming that he appears. If the Divisional Court is satisfied that the detention is unlawful it may direct that a writ of habeas corpus be issued, which means that the recipient of the writ must produce the named person to the court on the day and at the time specified in the writ. It is therefore only at this stage that the person must be actually produced to the court.

In practice, however, it is seldom necessary for a writ of habeas corpus actually to be issued. The single judge will not order a writ to be issued against the police, who will almost invariably be respondents, unless the circumstances clearly show the detention to be illegal.[14] Instead he will normally direct that a notice of motion is served on the police. This does not require them to release the suspect or to produce him before the court unless it says so. Whether or not it does will depend on the direction given at the ex parte hearing. The police have usually therefore at least the period between service of the notice of motion and the return date to decide what to do with the suspect. They will normally either release him on bail, or bring him before a magistrates' court asking for a remand in custody. Either of these courses will defeat the application for a writ of habeas corpus, which will not be issued if the detention has ceased, or has clearly become lawful.

Finally, as in other civil courts a civil legal aid certificate and an emergency certificate are available. At the conclusion of the habeas corpus application, the assisted person's bill will have to be taxed on a Common Fund basis in the usual way.

13 See eg *Re Sherman and Apps* [1981] Crim LR 335, a case on s 43(4) of Magistrates' Courts Act 1980 prior to amendment by Police and Criminal Evidence Act 1984.
14 If the circumstances are clearly illegal, he can direct the person to be released immediately pending a hearing. The governor of the prison, or as the case may be, must obey that direction: Ord 54, r 4.

Appendix

THE PROSECUTION OF OFFENCES ACT

Orders for costs

The Act makes significant changes to the powers available to criminal courts to make orders for costs. Sections 16–21 will replace the Costs in Criminal Cases Act 1973 with a new code.

Section 16 creates the 'Defendants Costs Order'. This is an order for defendant's expenses out of central funds, and can be made by any court in respect of *any* offences. So far as orders made by magistrates' courts or the Crown Court are concerned, the order will only be available if the defendant is acquitted. The court may order all or part of the expenses; the latter may be more appropriate if, for example, the defendant has been acquitted on some but not all charges. Defendants costs orders will not be very common in legal aid cases because the cost of legal aid is not an expense for the purposes of the bill. Legally aided defendants will thus, in practical terms, not be entitled to orders from central funds. The main significance is thus that magistrates will be able to award the defendant costs from central funds after acquittal of a summary offence.

Section 17 enables a prosecutor's expenses to be paid from central funds, win or lose, provided the offence is indictable. Furthermore, it will not be available to a public authority, the definition of which includes the new Crown Prosecutors and the police. They will thus only be available in a minority of cases, for example, when a shop prosecutes for theft.

Orders *against* the defendant and in favour of the prosecution can, however, be made on conviction by either court for any offence, and also on appeal, by virtue of section 18. The opportunity has been taken to undo the effect of the line of cases culminating with *R v Maher* ([1983] 2 WLR 764— see chapter 6), so that the costs can be those that are just and reasonable, and are not limited to those expenses that could have been ordered out of central funds. Sections 19 and 20 contain very wide enabling powers exercisable by way of regulations to be made by the Lord Chancellor. In particular, regulations may provide for the payment of witnesses' expenses, in the same way as at present under the Act of 1973. They may also provide for inter partes costs, either during or at the end of the proceedings, if a party has incurred costs as a result of an unnecessary or improper act by the other.

The Crown Prosecution Service

Sections 1 to 15 of the Act create the Crown Prosecuting Service, which will take over all prosecutions from the police, save for categories to be prescribed by the Attorney General. In addition, the service will be able to take over prosecutions brought by anyone else, although the common law right to prosecute will be preserved. The head of the service will be the Director of Public Prosecutions, responsible as at present to the Attorney General.

Prosecutions will be conducted by Crown Prosecutors, who must be either solicitors or barristers, and who will have the same right of audience as solicitors presently have. The powers under s 83 of the Supreme Court Act 1981 to extend the rights of audience of solicitors, will also apply to Crown Prosecutors.

Index